MW01690842

CAMBRIDGE
EDUCATIONAL SERVICES

AMERICA'S PREMIERE TESTING READINESS PROGRAM

Victory for the ACT® Test

STUDENT TEXT

Our Mission: Progress Through Partnership

Cambridge Educational Services partners with educators who share the significant mission of educational advancement for all students. By partnering together, we can best achieve our common goals: to build skills, raise test scores, enhance curriculum, and support instruction. A leading innovator in education for over twenty-nine years, Cambridge is the nation's premiere provider of school-based test preparation and supplemental curriculum services.

Cambridge Publishing, Inc.
www.CambridgeEd.com

 First edition 1994
Fifteenth edition 2019

Printed in the United States of America
25 24 23 22 5 6 7 8

ISBN-13: 978-1-58894-324-8

TABLE OF CONTENTS

Course Overview v

ESTABLISH A BASELINE WITH A FULL-LENGTH TEST 1

Pre-Assessment Administration 2
How to Use the Pre-Assessment Reports 3
Setting a Test Score Target 6
Planning a Schedule for the Course 8

MASTER TEST MECHANICS AND STRATEGIES 9

English 11

Course Concept Outline 11
Test Mechanics 15
Lessons 23
Quizzes 51
Review 69
Strategy Summary 79

Reading 83

Course Concept Outline 83
Test Mechanics 85
Lessons 95
Quizzes 135
Review 149
Strategy Summary 163

Writing 165

Course Concept Outline 165
Test Mechanics 167
Lessons 173
Quizzes 177
Strategy Summary 185

Math 187

Course Concept Outline 187
Test Mechanics 191
Lessons 201
Quizzes 257
Review 271
Strategy Summary 279

Science 281

Course Concept Outline 281
Test Mechanics 283
Lesson 293
Quizzes 329
Review 341
Strategy Summary 359

Perfect Your Pacing with Practice 361

Section 1: English Test 363
Section 2: Mathematics Test 378
Section 3: Reading Test 394
Section 4: Science Test 404
Section 5: Writing Test 418

Take a Final Look with a Full-Length Test 419

Post-Assessment Administration 420
How to Use the Post-Assessment Reports 422
Planning for Further Study 424

Appendix A: Answers and Explanations 426

Item Index 479

Error Correction and Suggestion Form 497

COURSE OVERVIEW

CAMBRIDGE'S *VICTORY* PROGRAM

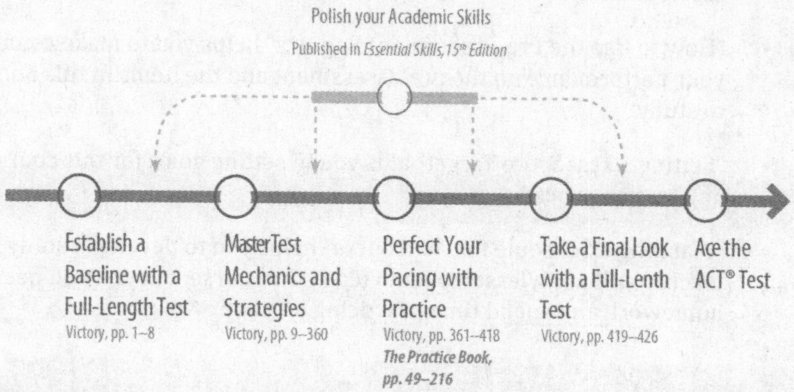

Your Cambridge *Victory* course has been scientifically designed to give you maximum score improvement through complete coverage of the ACT test. The program is organized into six parts, as shown above. The six parts are:

- **Establish a Baseline with a Full-Length Test.** You want to see your score improve, and to do that you need a baseline. The best way of determining your baseline is to take a full-length, retired ACT test under the same conditions that you'll experience on the big day. This is as close as you can get to taking the real ACT test without actually reporting to a testing center with your ID and several No. 2 pencils. Your teacher will send your answer sheet to Cambridge's Data Processing Center, and you'll receive score reports that will tell you your score and show you where you made mistakes. Then you and your teacher will develop a plan to reach your ACT goal.

- **Polish Your Academic Skills.** The ACT exam asks you to show what you know. *Essential Skills*, which is available both in print and online, serves as a refresher for the critical skills that you'll need on the ACT test. The beauty of *Essential Skills* is that the review is presented in multiple-choice format, just like the test. Plus, the skills are divided into three difficulty levels. So you will work at your present level and then move to higher levels.

- **Master Test Mechanics and Strategies.** Test Mechanics and Strategies are the "magic" of test preparation. You're going to learn how to manage the testing environment, what to do when you draw a blank, and how to answer algebra and geometry questions without using algebra or geometry. Mechanics and Strategies alone can raise your ACT score 4 or 5 points.

- **Perfect Your Pacing with Practice.** Pacing on the ACT Test is absolutely essential. You'll never get a top score unless you utilize every single second. So you're going to learn how long to spend on each item, when to skip items, when and how to guess, and how to get the most value from every minute. Of course, practice makes perfect. You have three full-length practice tests in *The Practice Book*.

- **Take a Final Look with a Full-Length Test.** After you've completed the steps above, you'll look back to see how far you have come and whether or not there is some clean-up work left to do. You will take a second full-length, retired ACT test. And again your answer sheet will be scored at our Data Processing Center, and you'll get your score and several reports to help with your self-evaluation. Self-evaluation is important because even though you may have prepared conscientiously, there may be some areas where you need to do a little more work.

- **Ace the ACT® Test.** On test day, other test-takers simply won't have the training that you've gotten. They won't have reviewed important skills, learned almost "magical" techniques for answering questions, and mastered the intricacies of the testing environment. Your training will give you an amazing advantage.

ESTABLISH A BASELINE WITH A FULL-LENGTH TEST

To begin your course, you will establish a baseline using a pre-assessment. You will take a full-length, retired ACT, Inc. ACT practice exam as the pre-assessment under conditions that closely reflect the real test. Then, with the help of your instructor, you will examine your Student Summary and Student Item Analysis reports and determine your strengths and weaknesses. Your instructor will also receive reports that help her determine exactly which topics to cover in class, for how long, and in what order. There are four sections in the Pre-Assessment/Course Planning chapter of this book that will help get you started:

- "Pre-Assessment Administration" explains the logistics of taking the full-length pre-assessment. You will be taking a retired ACT, Inc. ACT practice exam.
- "How to Use the Pre-Assessment Reports" helps you to make connections between your performance on the pre-assessment and the items in this book that you most need to study.
- "Setting a Test Score Target" aids you in setting goals for this course and for the college application process.
- "Planning a Schedule for the Course" helps you to develop a study schedule. Your teacher will use a lesson plan to teach the course, but you will need to keep up with any homework and spend time practicing on your own.

POLISH YOUR ACADEMIC SKILLS

The Cambridge Edge

The *Essential Skills* material is available both in print and online. If your program purchased the online version of the material, your teacher will give you a username and password. Go to www.CambridgeVictory.com to log in.

Essential Skills, 15th Edition serves as a companion to this *Victory* book. It provides targeted skill building material to help you fill any skill gaps as you prepare for test day. Your instructor may cover this material in class or assign it as homework.

There are four chapters in *Essential Skills*:

- English and Writing
- Reading
- Mathematics
- Science

The English and Writing (except the Writing an Essay section), Reading, Mathematics, and Science chapters are organized into three sections: basic, intermediate, and advanced. Each section addresses a group of skills essential for college and career success.

MASTER TEST MECHANICS AND STRATEGIES

Test Mechanics and Strategies make up the heart of this course. This part of the book contains items that look like those found on the real test. When compared with items on the real test, the items in this part of the book have similar content, represent the same difficulty levels, and can be solved by using the same problem-solving skills and alternative test-taking strategies.

There are five chapters in Test Mechanics and Strategies, each chapter representing a core component of the exam:

- English
- Reading
- Writing
- Mathematics
- Science

Each of the above chapters begins with a Course Concept Outline, which acts as a syllabus, listing the concepts that are tested for each item-type. The items in each chapter are organized to correspond with the respective outline. For each concept in the outline, there is a group of items. The group contains a greater number of items if the item-type appears with great frequency on the real test, and it contains a lesser number of items if the item-type appears with less frequency. Although the concepts are not grouped in this way on the real test, we organize the lessons in this manner so that the concepts are emphasized and reinforced. After you learn the concepts, you will be able to practice applying this conceptual knowledge on the practice tests.

PERFECT YOUR PACING WITH PRACTICE

You will perfect your pacing with four practice tests in the Cambridge Practice Test Reinforcement portion of this course. The tests are located in two volumes:

- *Victory* (*Victory* Practice Test)
- *The Practice Book* (Practice Tests I–III)

In these tests, the items not only mimic the real test in content and difficulty level, but they are also arranged in an order and with a frequency that simulates the real test.

You will complete each test with time restrictions. You may complete these tests in class or your instructor may assign them as homework. Either way, adhering to the time restrictions forces you to pace yourself as you would on the real test. If you complete all four of the practice tests, any test anxiety you may have will be greatly reduced. Answers and explanations to the tests are located in Appendix A of the book in which each test appears.

TAKE A FINAL LOOK WITH A FULL-LENGTH TEST

In order to know how far you've come since the pre-assessment, you will take a second full-length, retired ACT, Inc. ACT practice exam. You will take this post-assessment under actual testing conditions. You will then receive a second set of Student Summary and Student Item Analysis reports to help you determine final areas for review. The Post-Assessment contains three sections to help you see how far you've come:

- "Post-Assessment Administration" explains the logistics of taking the full-length post-assessment. You will be taking a retired ACT, Inc. ACT practice exam.

- "How to Use the Post-Assessment Reports" shows you how to use the Student Summary and Student Item Analysis reports you will receive to identify areas of study, as well as particular items in your textbook, upon which to focus as you continue to prepare for the real test.

- "Planning for Further Study" includes advice on how to make the most of an effective and concrete action plan. You will learn how to maximize your remaining course time and prioritize material to be reviewed before you take the actual test.

A NOTE ABOUT THE NOTES

Throughout this book you will see marginal notes with tips and further insights. The types of notes you will encounter are listed below. Use the margins to make your own notes, emphasizing any strategies or tips you find especially helpful.

Ace the Pace
Need to work on your pacing? These notes will help you do that.

Closer Look
Test terms can be confusing. These tips give examples and further explanation.

Debrief
Look for Debrief notes summarizing what you've already learned.

Ditch the Directions
Don't waste test time reading directions. Learn them beforehand.

Goldilocks Rule
Look for the answer that's "just right," not too big or too small.

Master Moves
Ready for some advanced strategies? These tips will help you with that.

Passage Perfect
Learn to use test passages to your advantage.

Plug & Chug
Some math items can be solved by plugging in values you choose.

Read Twice Answer Once
These tips point out examples where careful reading is key.

Test Specs
Learn more about the test design and how it can help you.

Test-the-Test
Some math items can be solved by testing the answer choices.

The Cambridge Edge
Cambridge offers strategies we've developed to help you on test day.

Throwback to English
Don't forget what your English teacher taught you.

Throwback to Math
Don't forget what your math teacher taught you.

Throwback to Science
Don't forget what your science teacher taught you.

Use POE
Use the process of elimination to find the correct answer.

Use Your Test Booklet
You're given a tool on test day—your test booklet. You just need to learn to use it.

Establish a Baseline with a Full-Length Test

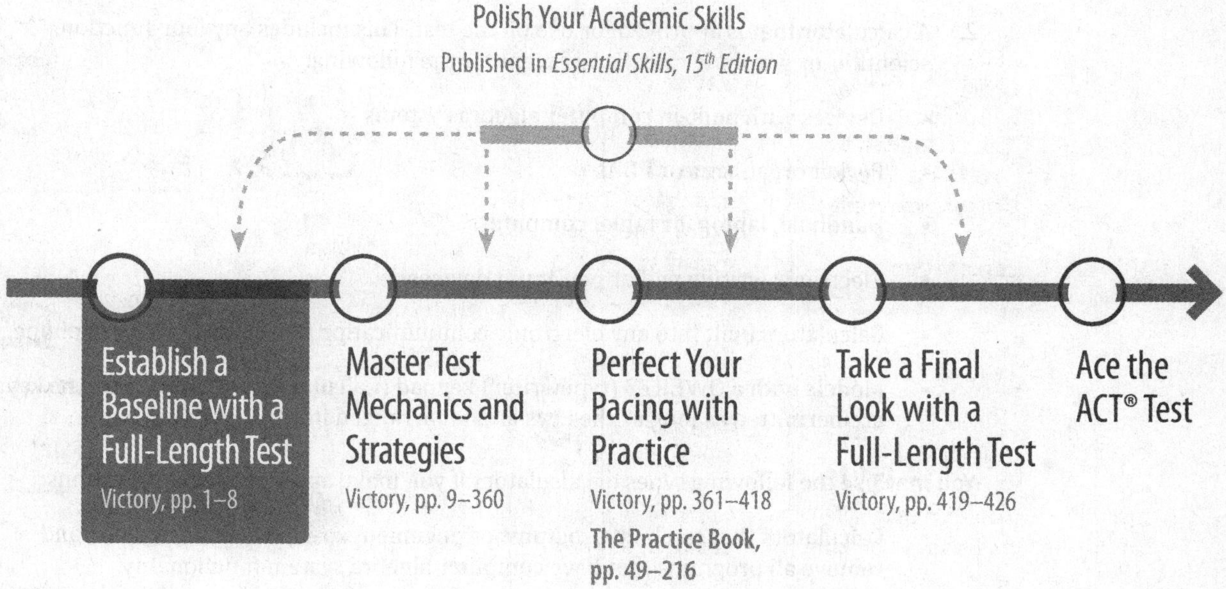

CAMBRIDGE
VICTORY FOR THE
ACT® TEST

PRE-ASSESSMENT ADMINISTRATION

At the beginning of the course, you will take a pre-assessment. This pre-assessment is an ACT, Inc. ACT practice exam. When you take the pre-assessment, you should bring the following items to the classroom, in addition to anything else your teacher instructs you to bring:

1. Sharpened, soft-lead No. 2 pencils
2. A calculator that is approved for use on the test. This includes any four-function, scientific, or graphing calculator, except for the following:
    - Devices with built-in computer algebra systems
    - Pocket organizers or PDAs
    - Handheld, laptop, or tablet computers
    - Electronic writing pad or pen-input devices
    - Calculators built into any electronic communication device, such as a cell phone
    - Models with a QWERTY (typewriter) keypad (Calculators with letters on the keys are permitted as long as the keys are not arranged in a QWERTY keypad.)

    You may use the following types of calculators if you make appropriate modifications:

    - Calculators that can hold programs or documents: remove all documents and remove all programs that have computer algebra system functionality.
    - Models with paper tape: the paper must be removed.
    - Models that make noise: the sound feature must be turned off.
    - Models that have an infrared data port: the port must be covered with duct tape, electrician's tape, or another heavy, opaque material.
    - Models that have a power cord: the power cord must be removed.

      (For more detailed information on calculator usage, go to http://www.act.org/content/dam/act/unsecured/documents/ACT-calculator-policy.pdf.)
3. A watch (to pace yourself as you work through each test section)

If your program has ordered pre-assessment Student Summary reports, you will receive one of these reports with your pre-assessment results. This report will help you determine the areas in which you need the most study and enable you to target the skills that are necessary to lay a foundation for success in the course. You can then utilize the course time to prepare in those areas so that when you take the real test, you are ready to do your best. You will learn more about how to read and use the Student Summary report in the "How to Use the Pre-Assessment Reports" section on the next page.

HOW TO USE THE PRE-ASSESSMENT REPORTS

In the transition from Pre-Assessment/Course Planning to Test Mechanics, Concepts, and Strategies, you and your teacher will use the results of your pre-assessment to recognize your individual strengths and weaknesses. Having this valuable information will allow you to create a realistic study plan for the course so that you can effectively manage your time.

You will receive the results of your pre-assessment in the form of a Student Summary and a Student Item Analysis. These reports provide details about your performance and will help you to determine where to focus your efforts during the course by strategically targeting those skills that will help you to improve in your areas of weakness. Review the details of the sample Student Summary and Student Item Analysis reports on the next two pages so that you are familiar with their contents.

SAMPLE STUDENT REPORTS

On the following pages are a sample Student Summary report and Student Item Analysis report.

STUDENT SUMMARY

The Student Summary report summarizes all your scaled scores based on your test performance. In addition, you are able to see how you performed within specific categories for each of the four subject tests (English, Mathematics, Reading, and Science). For example, English includes the categories Conventions of Standard English (CE), Knowledge of Language (KL), and Production of Writing (PW).

Colleges typically base about 45% of their admissions decision on the composite score. Other factors they consider include GPA, extracurricular involvement, and social service activities.

There is no penalty for incorrect answers, so be sure not to leave any questions blank—even if you need to guess!

Cambridge TestPrep PLUS™
(800) 444-4373
data@cambridgeed.com
www.cambridgeed.com

CAMBRIDGE Educational Services

Site: SAMPLE SCHOOL
Student: SAMPLE STUDENT (20170207)
Grade: 11
ACT® Test: 16MC1

Student Summary

TEST	SCORE	PERCENTILE
English	26	84
Mathematics	23	68
Reading	19	41
Science	21	57
Composite	22	63
STEM	23	
Writing	9	
ELA	22	

ENGLISH

	RIGHT	WRONG	OMIT
Conventions of Standard English (SE)	32	8	0
Production of Writing (PW)	20	3	0
Knowledge of Language (KL)	8	4	0
TOTAL English	60	15	0

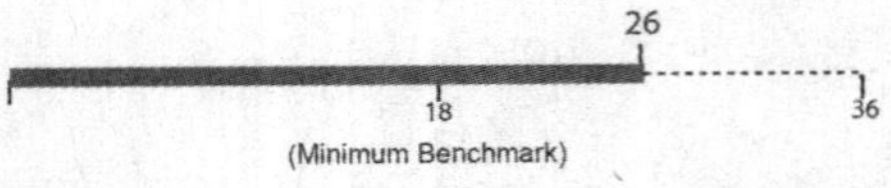

MATHEMATICS

	RIGHT	WRONG	OMIT
Integrating Essential Skills (IE)	13	10	2
Preparing for Higher Math	22	10	3
Number and Quantity (NQ)	4	1	0
Algebra (AL)	5	2	0
Functions (FN)	6	2	1
Geometry (GE)	5	3	1
Statistics and Probability (SP)	2	2	1
Modeling	18	7	0
TOTAL Mathematics	35	20	5

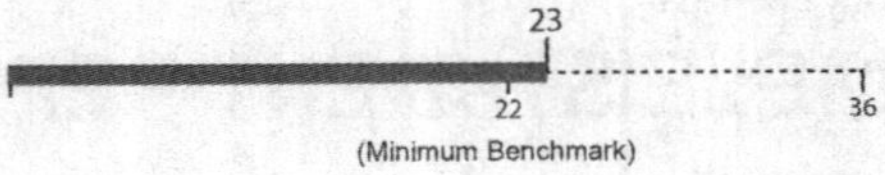

READING

	RIGHT	WRONG	OMIT
Key Ideas and Details (KD)	12	11	0
Craft and Structure (CS)	7	4	3
Integration of Knowledge and Ideas (IK)	1	2	0
TOTAL Reading	20	17	3

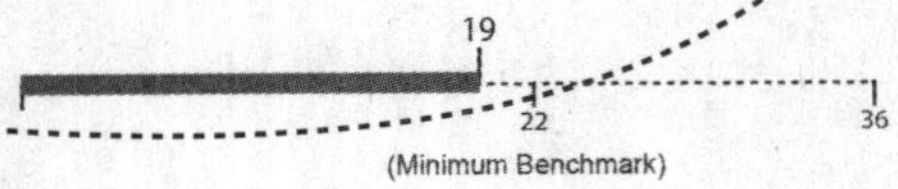

SCIENCE

	RIGHT	WRONG	OMIT
Interpretation of Data (ID)	10	5	3
Scientific Investigation (SI)	6	7	0
Evaluation of Models (EM)	5	4	0
TOTAL Science	21	16	3

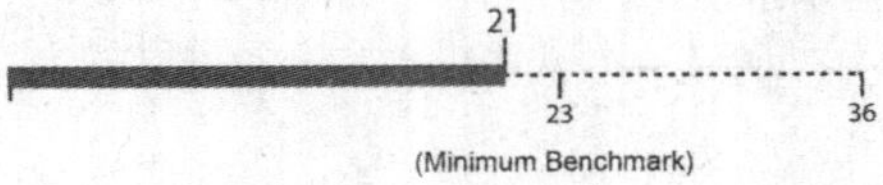

English: The English test measures your ability to find and correct errors in a piece of writing. Items are divided into three categories: Conventions of Standard English (Punctuation, Grammar and Usage, and Sentence Structure), Production of Writing (Strategy and Organization), and Knowledge of Language (Style).

Mathematics: The Mathematics test measures your ability to apply the knowledge and skills taught in high school mathematics courses. Items are divided into two main categories: Preparing for Higher Math (concepts you have learned recently), and Integrating Essential Skills (concepts such as perimeter and percents that you learned before eighth grade). Some mathematics items also measure your ability to work with models. These items are also included in one of the two main categories.

Reading: The Reading test measures your ability to read and think carefully about passages typically encountered in a first-year college course. You are asked to comprehend and respond to the passages through a variety of item-types, including Key Ideas and Details (main ideas, explicit and implied details), Craft and Structure (passage development and word choice), and Integration of Knowledge and Ideas (items asking you to compare or contrast two passages).

Science: The Science test measures your ability to apply scientific concepts and reasoning. You will read six or seven passages and answer the questions that follow. The questions are grouped into three item types: Interpretation of Data, Scientific Investigation, and Evaluation of Models, Inferences, and Experimental Results.

Writing: The optional Writing test measures your ability to develop a perspective on a given issue and evaluate other perspectives with a well organized and clearly written essay. You will have 40 minutes to write a response. The Writing test does not affect the composite score or scores on the individual subject tests.

STUDENT ITEM ANALYSIS

The Student Item Analysis provides a comprehensive breakdown of each item: its category (corresponding to the categories listed on the Student Summary), the correct answer, and how you answered each item.

When you see the correct answer to an item that was missed, ask yourself why it was missed:

1. The concept was never learned.
2. It was a careless mistake.
3. It would have been answered correctly if the concept had been reviewed before the test.

On the math test section, the last few items were left blank. Consider whether this was due to the student running out of time or to the increase in difficulty at the end of the math test.

Cambridge TestPrep PLUS™
(800) 444-4373
data@cambridgeed.com
www.cambridgeed.com

CAMBRIDGE
EDUCATIONAL SERVICES

Site: SAMPLE SCHOOL
Student: SAMPLE STUDENT
Test Date: 02/07/17
ACT® Test: 16MC1

Student Item Analysis

ENGLISH

Problem Number:	1	2	3	4	5	6	7	8	9	10	11	12	13	14	15	16	17	18	19	20	21	22	23	24
Category:	SE	PW	SE	KL	SE	SE	PW	SE	KL	PW	SE	PW	SE	SE	SE	SE	SE	PW	KL	PW	PW	SE	PW	SE
Correct Answer:	B	G	D	J	C	H	A	J	C	J	A	H	D	G	D	F	B	G	A	J	B	J	C	H
Your Answer*:	+	H	+	+	+	+	D	+	+	+	D	+	+	+	+	+	+	+	+	+	+	+	+	+

Problem Number:	25	26	27	28	29	30	31	32	33	34	35	36	37	38	39	40	41	42	43	44	45	46	47	48
Category:	SE	KL	SE	KL	SE	SE	PW	SE	PW	PW	SE	KL	SE	SE	SE	SE	SE	PW	KL	PW	PW	SE	PW	SE
Correct Answer:	B	G	D	J	C	H	A	J	C	J	A	H	D	G	D	F	B	G	A	J	B	J	C	H
Your Answer*:	+	H	+	+	+	+	+	+	+	+	D	G	+	+	+	+	A	+	+	+	+	+	+	+

Problem Number:	49	50	51	52	53	54	55	56	57	58	59	60	61	62	63	64	65	66	67	68	69	70	71	72
Category:	SE	PW	SE	KL	SE	SE	PW	SE	PW	KL	SE	PW	SE	SE	SE	SE	SE	KL	KL	PW	PW	SE	PW	PW
Correct Answer:	B	G	D	J	C	H	A	J	C	J	A	H	D	G	D	F	B	G	A	J	B	J	C	H
Your Answer*:	+	+	+	+	+	+	D	+	+	+	D	+	+	+	+	+	A	F	+	+	+	H	+	+

Problem Number:	73	74	75
Category:	SE	KL	SE
Correct Answer:	B	J	A
Your Answer*:	C	H	D

MATHEMATICS

Problem Number:	1	2	3	4	5	6	7	8	9	10	11	12	13	14	15	16	17	18	19	20	21	22	23	24
Category:	NQ*	AL	IE	FN	IE*	IE	GE*	NQ*	AL	IE	SP	IE*	IE*	IE	AL*	NQ*	GE	IE	FN*	AL	SP	IE*	GE	IE
Correct Answer:	B	G	D	J	C	H	A	J	C	J	A	H	D	G	D	F	B	G	A	J	B	J	C	H
Your Answer*:	+	H	+	+	+	F	D	+	+	+	D	G	+	+	+	H	C	F	+	+	D	+	A	+

Problem Number:	25	26	27	28	29	30	31	32	33	34	35	36	37	38	39	40	41	42	43	44	45	46	47	48
Category:	IE	GE*	AL*	AL	IE*	NQ	FN	SP*	GE	IE	IE*	AL	IE*	IE	FN	GE	FN*	IE	IE*	SP	FN*	NQ	IE*	IE*
Correct Answer:	B	G	D	J	C	H	A	J	C	J	A	H	D	G	D	F	B	G	A	J	B	J	C	H
Your Answer*:	+	+	+	+	D	+	D	+	+	+	D	G	+	+	+	+	+	K	+	+	+	+	A	+

Problem Number:	49	50	51	52	53	54	55	56	57	58	59	60
Category:	IE	FN*	FN*	IE	GE*	IE	GE*	IE	IE	SP	GE	FN
Correct Answer:	B	G	D	J	C	H	A	J	C	J	A	H
Your Answer*:	D	H	+	G	+	J	+	•	•	•	•	•

"•" = omitted   + = correct response   ? = scan error

ENGLISH:

SE = Conventions of Standard English
PW = Production of Writing
KL = Knowledge of Language

MATHEMATICS:

NQ = Number and Quantity
AL = Algebra
FN = Functions
GE = Geometry
SP = Statistics and Probability
IE = Integration of Essential Skills
* = Modeling

SETTING A TEST SCORE TARGET

Your test score target is unique to you and depends on your future educational and career goals. Setting your test score target involves several steps, outlined below: test, research, and action.

Test

Your first step is to take the pre-assessment that is part of your Cambridge course. After you take this test, you will receive a score report that gives you a very accurate measure of where you stand. To begin the process of setting a test score target, fill in your pre-test scores below:

TEST SECTION	SCORE
English	
Mathematics	
Reading	
Science	
Composite	
Writing	

As you use these scores to make a plan for improvement throughout this course, remember that if you had a bad test day (for example, if you were ill or distracted by personal problems), your scores may not be reflective of your true abilities. Be sure to take this into account as you set a goal for your post-test and your real ACT test.

Research

Now, make a list of schools that you are interested in attending and research the average scores and GPAs of admitted students so that you can get an idea of how you stack up. Fill in the score that you estimate you need for each school. If you are interested in applying for scholarships, make sure you also research the scores each school requires for scholarship eligibility.

School: ______________	Average ACT Test Score of Admitted Students: ____ Average GPA of Admitted Students: ____ Scholarship Score Requirement: ____ Estimated ACT Test Score Needed: ____ Additional Points Needed: ____
School: ______________	Average ACT Test Score of Admitted Students: ____ Average GPA of Admitted Students: ____ Scholarship Score Requirement: ____ Estimated ACT Test Score Needed: ____ Additional Points Needed: ____
School: ______________	Average ACT Test Score of Admitted Students: ____ Average GPA of Admitted Students: ____ Scholarship Score Requirement: ____ Estimated ACT Test Score Needed: ____ Additional Points Needed: ____
School: ______________	Average ACT Test Score of Admitted Students: ____ Average GPA of Admitted Students: ____ Scholarship Score Requirement: ____ Estimated ACT Test Score Needed: ____ Additional Points Needed: ____

Once you have this chart filled in for several schools, you should have a good idea of the difference between your pre-test score and the score you will need to get into your schools of interest. Fill in this information below:

Pre-Test Date: ______	Score: ______

Action

How do you translate these numbers into an action plan? See your Student Item Analysis report. This report gives you valuable information for every question on the pre-test. You'll see your answer, the correct answer, and the type of question that was asked. With a little analysis, you can see exactly where your weaknesses are and make a plan to address them. Also, make sure to review the "Planning a Schedule for the Course" section on the next page.

PLANNING A SCHEDULE FOR THE COURSE

The most significant aspect of an effective study plan is that it is a written plan. A written study plan is more concrete than one that you simply draw on from memory. So, when creating your plan, write out a day-by-day schedule for reviewing all of the materials that are necessary for success in the course. This written format will provide a clear and dependable guide for study. The schedule should be prioritized according to the time that you need to devote to each of the different subjects, based on the amount of time that you have.

Consider how you can plan your study time so that it corresponds with the course topics. In addition to assignments given in class, you may wish to devote extra study time to your particular areas of weakness. The "to do" list you created based on your Student Summary report is a good place to start. Use the calendar template that follows to develop a plan of action with your teacher, determining what topics you will study each day and allotting time to study those sections of the book and complete the relevant exercises. Remember that it is not necessary for you to do everything all at once. Instead, picking a few things to focus on each week will help you to better manage your time.

Use the following empty calendar as a template, filling in your assignments and study plan for each day. Your teacher can help you set goals for each subject.

MONTH: ____________________

Sunday	Monday	Tuesday	Wednesday	Thursday	Friday	Saturday

Master Test Mechanics and Strategies

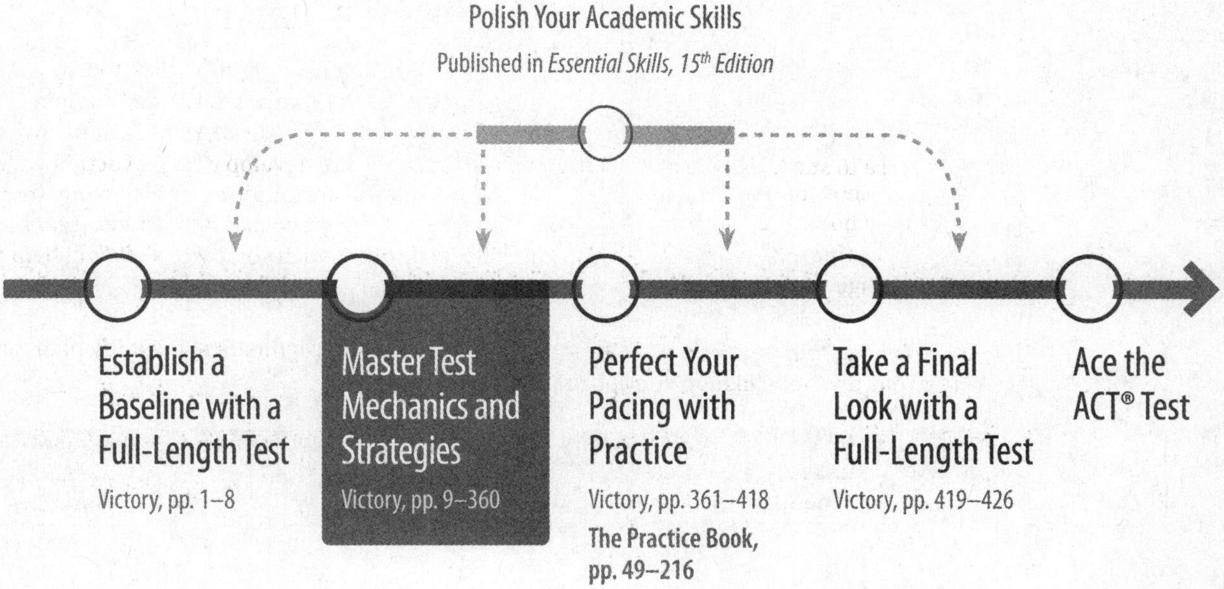

CAMBRIDGE
VICTORY FOR THE
ACT® TEST

ENGLISH

Course Concept Outline

I. TEST MECHANICS **15**

- **A. Overview** **16**
- **B. Anatomy** *(Items #1–4)* **17–18**
- **C. Pacing** **19**
- **D. Time Trial** *(Items #1–8)* **20–21**
- **E. Game Plan** **21**
  1. Don't Read the Directions 21
  2. Do the Passages in Order 21
  3. Read as You Go 22
  4. Read Any Items with Underlined Parts, Looking for Errors 22
  5. Work Backward from the Answer Choices 22
  6. Don't Look for Spelling or Capitalization Errors 22
  7. Make Educated Guesses 22
  8. Don't Be Afraid to Pick "No Change" 22

II. LESSON | PRELIMINARIES[1]

- **A. Item Profiles**
- **B. Notational Information**
  1. Underlined Words or Phrases
  2. Boxed Numbers
  3. Bracketed Numbers
  4. Boxed Information
- **C. Item Types**
  1. Grammar and Usage
  2. Sentence Structure
  3. Punctuation
  4. Strategy
  5. Organization
  6. Style

1 Some concepts in this Course Concept Outline are not illustrated through examples in your student text but may be covered by your instructor in class. They are included here to provide a complete outline of your course.

III. LESSON 1 | GRAMMAR AND USAGE 23

A. **Subject-Verb Agreement** *(Item #1)* 24
   1. Material Inserted Between Subject and Verb *(Items #2–7)* 24–25
   2. Inverted Sentence Structure *(Items #8–9)* 25
   3. Compound Subjects *(Items #10–12)* 25

B. **Pronoun Usage** 26
   1. Pronouns Must Have Antecedents *(Items #13–14)* 26
   2. Antecedents Must Be Clear *(Item #15)* 26
   3. Pronoun-Antecedent Agreement *(Items #16–19)* 26
   4. Pronouns Must Have Proper Case *(Items #20–21)* 27

C. **Adjectives versus Adverbs** 27
   1. Adjectives Modify Nouns; Adverbs Modify Verbs, Adjectives, and Other Adverb *(Items #22– 23)* 27
   2. Linking Verbs *(Items #24–25)* 27
   3. Watch for Adjectives Posing as Adverbs *(Items #26–28)* 27–28

D. **Double Negatives** *(Items #29–30)* 28
E. **Nouns and Noun Clauses** *(Items #31–33)* 28
F. **Faulty or Illogical Comparisons** *(Items #34–38)* 29
G. **Verb Tense** 29
   1. Principal Parts of Verbs *(Items #39–41)* 29–30
   2. When to Use the Perfect Tenses *(Items #42–44)* 30
   3. The Subjunctive Mood *(Items #45–46)* 30
   4. Sequence and Verb Tense *(Items #47–50)* 30–31

H. **Diction** 31
   1. Wrong Preposition *(Items #51–52)* 31
   2. Wrong Word Choice *(Items #53–54)* 31
   3. Gerund versus Infinitive *(Items #55–56)* 31

IV. LESSON 2 | SENTENCE STRUCTURE 32

A. **Run-On Sentences** *(Items #1–2)* 32
B. **Comma Splices** *(Items #3–4)* 32
C. **Fragments** *(Items #5–6)* 33
D. **Problems of Coordination and Subordination** *(Items #7–14)* 33–34
E. **Faulty Parallelism** *(Items #15–17)* 34
F. **Incomplete Split Constructions** *(Items #18–19)* 34
G. **Misplaced Modifiers** *(Items #20–22)* 35
H. **Unintended Meanings** *(Items #23–24)* 35

V. LESSON 3 | PUNCTUATION 36

A. **Commas** *(Items #1–20)* 36–39
B. **Semicolons** *(Items #21–25)* 39
C. **Colons** *(Items #26–27)* 40

D. **End-Stop Punctuation** *(Item #28)* 40
E. **Dashes** *(Items #29–30)* 40
F. **Quotation Marks** *(Item #31)* 41
G. **Apostrophes** *(Items #32–34)* 41
H. **Punctuating for Clarity Exercise** *(Item #35)* 41

VI. LESSON 4 | PRODUCTION OF WRITING AND KNOWLEDGE OF LANGUAGE **42**

A. **Production of Writing** *(Items #1–12)* 42

1. Strategy 43
   a) Appropriate Supporting Material *(Item #1, #10)* 43, 45
   b) Effective Opening, Transitional, and Concluding Sentences *(Item #2, #7, #11)* 43, 45
   c) Main Idea *(Item #3, #12)* 43, 45
   d) Audience *(Item #4)* 43
2. Organization 43
   a) Sentence-Level Structure *(Item #9)* 45
   b) Paragraph-Level Structure *(Item #5)* 43
   c) Passage-Level Structure *(Item #6, #8)* 44–45

B. **Knowledge of Language** 45

1. Conciseness *(Items #13–18)* 46
2. Clarity of Meaning *(Item #19)* 46
3. Idiomatic Expression *(Item #20)* 46

VII. LESSON 5 | GENERAL STRATEGIES **47**

VIII. QUIZZES **51**

A. **Directed Study Quiz** *(Items #1–32)* 52–63
B. **Timed Quiz** *(Items #1–29)* 64–68

IX. REVIEW **69**

X. STRATEGY SUMMARY **79**

ENGLISH

TEST MECHANICS

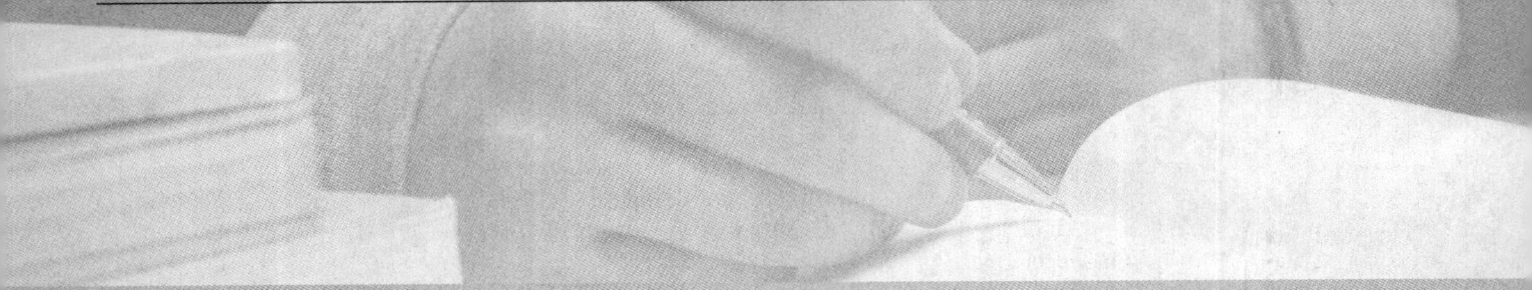

OVERVIEW

> *The Cambridge Edge*
>
> What's the difference between *using* a grammar rule correctly and *stating* a grammar rule?
>
> Well, in this example, you need to be able to fix the subject-verb agreement error by choosing (B) as the correct answer, but you don't need to write a sentence describing the error. That's not so bad, right?

The English Test consists of 75 questions. You'll have 45 minutes to read the passages and answer the questions. It doesn't seem like a lot of time, but you are being tested on what you should already know so you won't have to spend a lot of time on each question. You are not being tested on spelling or vocabulary or even the exact rules of grammar. Rather, you are being tested on your understanding of the rules of grammar and your ability to apply those rules.

For example, you might be asked to correct an error.

Example:

The recently created wildlife refuge, which includes nearly 30 small ponds for migrating geese and ducks, <u>were</u> made possible by substantial gifts from an anonymous donor to the Wildlife Protection Fund.

A. NO CHANGE
B. was
C. have been
D. being

The correct answer is (B) because the sentence should read "refuge . . . was," not "refuge . . . were." *A verb must agree in both number and person with its subject.* You must be aware of this grammatical rule in order to answer the question correctly, but you would not be asked to state the rule that explains why your choice is correct.

The items used by the English Test fall into one of three categories:

Category	What Is Tested	Number of Questions
Conventions of Standard English	Grammar Usage Sentence Structure Punctuation	38–42
Production of Writing	Organization Strategy	21–24
Knowledge of Language	Conciseness Clear Meaning Idiomatic Usage	9–14

You'll see specific examples of these types in the "Anatomy" section that follows.

ANATOMY

Ditch the Directions

The directions for the English Test are fairly long, and it would take you a while to read them during the test. You'd be wasting valuable time that could be used to answer questions. By the time you get to the test, you'll know what to do in the English Test, so skip the directions altogether.

DIRECTIONS: In the passage below, certain parts of the sentences have been underlined and numbered. In the right-hand column, you will find different ways of writing each underlined part; the original version is indicated by the "NO CHANGE" option. For each item, select the choice that best expresses the intended idea, is most acceptable in standard written English, or is most consistent with the overall tone and style of the passage.

There are also items that ask about a section of the passage or the passage as a whole. These items do not refer to an underlined portion of the passage; these items are preceded by statements that are enclosed in boxes.

Read the passage through once before you begin to answer the accompanying items. Finding the answers to certain items may depend on looking at material that appears several sentences beyond the item. So, be sure that you have read far enough ahead before you select your answer choice.

Coastal Polynyas in Antarctica

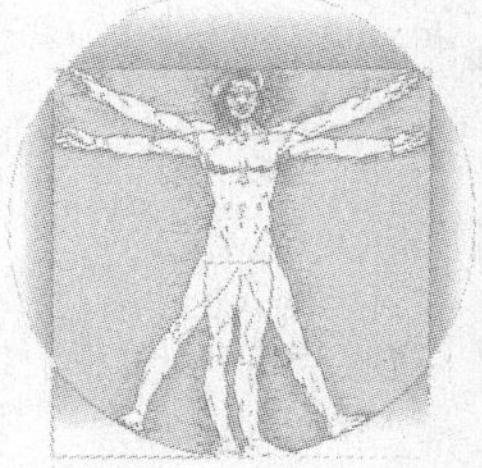

Although you might not think it, the Antarctic waters are rich in nutrients. The lack of <u>ice, combined</u> [1] with shallow coastal waters, provides the top layers of the ocean with

1. A. NO CHANGE
B. ice combined
C. ice combined,
D. ice—combined

1. **(A)** *This item tests punctuation. When you insert an aside or clarifying remark, you need to set off that material from the main part of the sentence, usually with commas—one at the start and one at the end of the material. The original sentence is correctly punctuated.*

added sunlight, so polynyas <u>(large open areas of waters surrounded by sea ice)</u> [2] offer ideal conditions for phytoplankton blooms. Because the ice around polynyas is thin in the early spring when the long days begin, they are the first areas to get strong sunlight. The open waters retain more heat, further thinning ice cover and leading to early, intense, and short-lived plankton blooms. These blooms

2. The writer is considering deleting the information in parentheses. If the writer removed this material, the essay would primarily lose:

F. a transition from the first paragraph to the second paragraph.
G. further examples of the animals that depend upon krill for food.
H. a definition of a term that might be unfamiliar to the reader.
J. additional information about the climate of Antarctica.

2. **(H)** *Why does the writer include the parenthetical material? The writer includes the parenthetical material to define a key term that might otherwise be unfamiliar to the reader.*

feed krill, <u>a tiny, shrimp-like animal</u>, which
3
in turn are eaten by Adelie penguins, seals, whales, and other seabirds and animals.

3. A. NO CHANGE
B. tiny, shrimp-like animals
C. a tiny animal like a shrimp
D. an animal like a tiny shrimp

3. **(B)** *The original sentence lacks parallelism. In the main part of the sentence, the writer is talking about krill in the plural: "krill . . . which in turn are eaten." But in the appositive phrase, the writer uses the singular "animal." In order to be parallel to the plural noun "krill," "animal" must be changed to "animals."*

<u>Because</u> relatively small in area, coastal
4
polynyas play an important role. In eastern Antarctica, more than 90 percent of all Adelie

4. F. NO CHANGE
G. Although
H. Therefore
J. Furthermore

4. **(G)** *"Because" is a word used to introduce an explanation, so the reader expects the information in the independent clause to be the outcome of the information provided in the dependent ("because") clause. The writer, instead, intends to contrast the two ideas in the sentence: even though polynyas are small in area, they are very important to Adelie penguins.*

penguin colonies <u>live next to coastal polynyas</u>
5
<u>right beside their natural habitats</u>. Polynya
5
productivity explains, to a great extent, the increase and decrease in penguin population.

5. A. NO CHANGE
B. live next to costal polynyas right beside their habitats
C. live right next to costal polynyas
D. live next to costal polynyas

5. **(D)** *The original is needlessly wordy. (D), by far the shortest of the choices, solves the needless repetition problems and illustrates that in a question testing conciseness, the shortest choice (in word count) is often the best.*

PACING

> **Ace the Pace**
>
> At the end of each passage, check your time. If you are taking longer than 9 minutes to answer all the questions with a passage, try guessing on the Production of Writing questions because those take the most time.

> **Ace the Pace**
>
> Synchronize your watch to test time. Set the minute hand or use a stopwatch to time each section and stay on track.

The English Test consists of five passages, each approximately 300 words in length and with 15 corresponding items, for a total of 75 items. The time limit is 45 minutes. So, a fairly simple and easy-to-follow plan is to allocate nine minutes to each of the five passages:

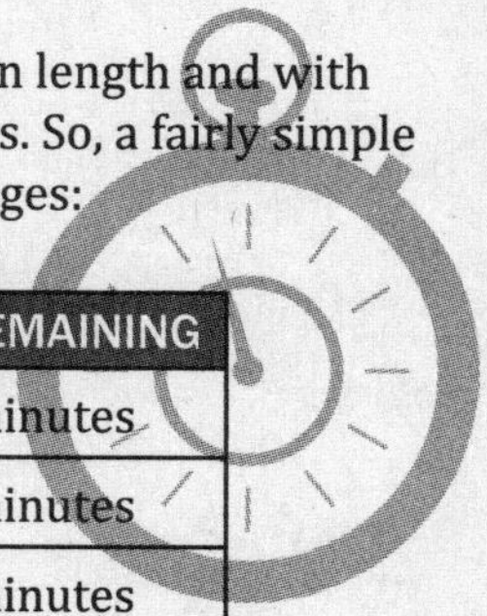

TASK	ALLOTTED TIME	TIME REMAINING
First passage and questions	9 minutes*	36 minutes
Second passage and questions	9 minutes*	27 minutes
Third passage and questions	9 minutes*	18 minutes
Fourth passage and questions	9 minutes*	9 minutes
Fifth passage and questions	9 minutes*	0 minutes

*Approximately 36 seconds per question

This schedule describes what would happen in a perfect world; but, of course, the ACT test does not take place in a perfect world. Some items are going to take longer than others, particularly those that ask about the overall development of the passage. This means that you'll need to spend less time on the simple grammar items, building up a time reserve for those more difficult items that are coming. And the more difficult items are usually placed at the end of a passage because that's where it makes sense to ask, "What is the main idea?" and "How could the passage be improved?" The schedule actually gives you a feedback loop that lets you know whether you need to skip some items. For example, if you are nearing the nine-minute mark and still have two or three items to do on the first passage, then skip any Production of Writing items and go straight away to the next passage. The Production of Writing items take longer, and there will be some simple grammar items waiting to be cherry-picked in the next passage. Remember, every item is worth one point.

TIME TRIAL *(8 items; 5 minutes)*

DIRECTIONS: In the passage below, certain parts of the sentences have been underlined and numbered. In the right-hand column, you will find different ways of writing each underlined part; the original version is indicated by the "NO CHANGE" option. For each item, select the choice that best expresses the intended idea, is most acceptable in standard written English, or is most consistent with the overall tone and style of the passage.

There are also items that ask about a section of the passage or the passage as a whole. These items do not refer to an underlined portion of the passage; these items are preceded by statements that are enclosed in boxes.

Read the passage through once before you begin to answer the accompanying items. Finding the answers to certain items may depend on looking at material that appears several sentences beyond the item. So, be sure that you have read far enough ahead before you select your answer choice.

PASSAGE I

The Orchid Family

The orchids are the most diverse plant family with 20,000 to 30,000 species in over 800 genera. This represents about 10 percent of all flowering plant species. DNA research suggesting [1] that the orchids are among the most ancient flowering plant families, as old as 90,000,000 years. They are still evolving rapidly into new species. For example, many endemic species in the genus *Telipogon* are found in the Andes Mountains in areas that were buried under glaciers as recent as [2] 10,000 years ago. Orchids are found on all continents except Antarctica.

Like all monocots, including lilies orchids [3] are flowering plants that have only one seed

1. A. NO CHANGE
   B. suggest
   C. suggests
   D. to suggest

2. F. NO CHANGE
   G. as recently as
   H. so recently as
   J. recently

3. A. NO CHANGE
   B. lilies orchids,
   C. lilies, orchids,
   D. lilies, orchids

Ace the Pace

These items are all basic grammar and punctuation items. If you took less than the 5 minutes allotted to finish this time trial, you should have no problem answering all 75 questions on the test. If you didn't quite get to all the questions, practice your pacing to see if you can improve. And remember to guess on any questions you don't have time to read through carefully.

leaf and typically lacks [4] woody tissue. All orchids have a single reproductive structure, called the column, which is forming [5] by the fusion of the male stamens and female style. These structures are separate in the flowers of most other families. Orchids also have a modified third petal called a lip, and produce [6] enormous numbers of very tiny seeds.

The vast majority of orchid species are native to the tropics, and its [7] numbers increase with proximity to the equator. The most richest [8] diversity of orchid species is found in the lush tropical forests of equatorial South America, Southeast Asia, and New Guinea. New species are constantly being discovered in these areas.

4. F. NO CHANGE
G. lacking
H. lack
J. lacked

5. A. NO CHANGE
B. forming
C. are formed
D. is formed

6. F. NO CHANGE
G. lip and produce
H. lip and produce,
J. lip, and produces

7. A. NO CHANGE
B. their
C. one's
D. your

8. F. NO CHANGE
G. more richer
H. richest
J. richly

GAME PLAN

Don't Read the Directions

By the time you get to the test, you'll know what to do when you see the English Test just by the way it looks. Let the appearance of the items on the page be all the direction you need, and get started on reading the first passage immediately.

Do the Passages in Order

Unlike the Reading Test with passages that fall into categories such as Humanities and Natural Science, the passages on the English Test are not really about any particular subject area. Of course, the passages do have a topic and some items do ask Reading-type questions, but the English items mainly test usage, not reading comprehension. In Reading, there is an advantage to predetermining an order for the passages; in English, however, you should just do them in the order presented.

Read as You Go

You don't have much time on test day, so read the passage and answer questions as you go. As you read, pay attention to the overall development. At the end there may be questions asking about the logic in the author's presentation or how the passage is organized. If you've paid attention as you read, you will know where to return in the passage to look for answers to these big-picture questions.

The Cambridge Edge

Circle key words as you go to help you pay attention to the development of the passage.

Read Any Items with Underlined Parts, Looking for Errors

When an item asks about rewriting an underlined part, begin by reading the sentence, looking for an error. If you can spot an error, then you're more than halfway home. Later in the English Lessons, you'll cover the important principles of writing and grammar that are tested, and there is a list of these principles provided in the English "Course Concept Outline" (p. 3). You can treat this outline as a checklist of important things to look for in English items.

Work Backward from the Answer Choices

If you are having difficulty locating the right answer, use the answer choices to help you. Compare each answer choice with the original, and explain to yourself what the important difference is between the two of them. This can help you see an error that you may have overlooked. Additionally, you can compare choices to each other, asking yourself in what way one choice is better or worse than another one. Again, this technique can help you uncover a hidden error and make the right choice.

Don't Look for Spelling or Capitalization Errors

These topics are not tested, so don't waste your time looking for errors of this sort. Even if you think you've found a spelling mistake (and you're almost certain to be wrong anyway), there is nothing you can do with the information. The correct response is correct because it "follows the requirements of standard written English."

Make Educated Guesses

You should be able to eliminate some answer choices on most items because they introduce new errors that are not found in the original. Or, a choice may fail to correct an error that you know to be in the underlined part of the sentence. You should always guess, even if you are unable to eliminate any answer choices, because there is no penalty for guessing on the ACT test. However, your chances improve if you are able to eliminate even one answer choice.

Don't Be Afraid to Pick "No Change"

Choose "NO CHANGE" if you think that the original is correct as written. Many students automatically refuse to pick "NO CHANGE" because they figure that there must be something wrong with the original—even if they are unable to say what. But this reasoning is faulty. "NO CHANGE," when it is an option, is statistically as likely to be correct as is one of the other three choices.

ENGLISH

LESSONS

LESSON 1

Grammar and Usage

The items in this section accompany the in-class review of the grammar and usage skills and concepts tested by the ACT English Test. You will work through the items with your instructor in class. Answers are on page 428.

DIRECTIONS: For items #1–56, identify the phrasing that best expresses the meaning of the underlined material. The answer choice "NO CHANGE" indicates that the underlined material is correct as written.

SUBJECT-VERB AGREEMENT

Material Inserted Between Subject and Verb
Items #2–7

Use Your Test Booklet

Remember, you can write in your test booklet. Some students find it helpful to circle key parts of the sentence. For example, if the underlined phrase includes a subject or verb, circle both the subject and verb in the sentence (only one might be part of the underlined phrase) in order to quickly check for subject-verb agreement.

1. The professor were traveling in Europe when she received notice of her promotion.

A. NO CHANGE
B. was traveling
C. travels
D. is traveling

2. The professor voted Teacher of the Year by the students were traveling in Europe when she received notice of her promotion.

F. NO CHANGE
G. was traveling
H. travels
J. is traveling

3. Most teachers, unless they have an appointment to a prestigious university, earns relatively less as teachers than they might in business.

A. NO CHANGE
B. earned
C. earn
D. will be earning

4. Many nutritionists now believe that a balanced diet and not large doses of vitamins are the best guarantee of health.

F. NO CHANGE
G. is
H. was
J. will be

Inverted Sentence Structure
Items #8–9

Compound Subjects
Items #10–12

5. Television comedies in which there is at least one really detestable character captures the interest of viewers.

A. NO CHANGE
B. did capture
C. captured
D. capture

6. The opposition to smoking in public places are prompting many state legislatures to consider banning smoking in such locations.

F. NO CHANGE
G. is prompting many state legislatures to consider
H. are prompting many state legislatures considering
J. is prompting many state legislatures considering

Read Twice Answer Once

Some questions include more than one error in the original or the answer choices. Be alert for all errors.

7. Diplomats sent to an unstable region or a genuinely hostile territory usually is assigned an aide or chauffeur who function also as a bodyguard.

A. NO CHANGE
B. are assigned an aide or chauffeur who function
C. are assigned an aide or chauffeur who functions
D. is assigned an aide or chauffeur that function

Debrief

Watch for inverted sentence structures. Regardless of the order of the sentence—subject-verb or verb-subject—the verb must always agree with its subject. If a sentence has a complex structure, it often helps to circle the subject and verb and look at each element in isolation.

8. Though this is the wealthiest country in the world, within a few blocks of the White House, there is scores of homeless people who live on the streets.

F. NO CHANGE
G. there could be
H. there are
J. are there

9. Just a few miles from the factories and skyscrapers stand a medieval castle that looks exactly as it did in the twelfth century.

A. NO CHANGE
B. stood
C. is standing
D. stands

10. John, his wife, and the rest of his family plans to attend the award dinner hosted by the company to honor the employees with the most seniority.

F. NO CHANGE
G. plan
H. having planned
J. they plan

11. Either the governor or one of his close aides prefer not to have the senator seated at the head table where he would be conspicuous.

A. NO CHANGE
B. was preferring
C. does prefer
D. prefers

12. Surrounded by layers of excelsior, none of the crystal goblets were broken when the workers dropped the crate.

F. NO CHANGE
G. got broke
H. had broken
J. broken

PRONOUN USAGE

Pronouns Must Have Antecedents
Items #13–14

Debrief

Except for a few idiomatic expressions ("It" is getting late, "It" will be sunny today), every pronoun must have an antecedent. An antecedent must be a noun, not a thought or phrase. Identify a pronoun's antecedent and then check that it is correct by substituting it for the pronoun in the sentence.

13. During her rise to fame, she betrayed many of her friends, <u>and because of it</u>, very few people trust her.

A. NO CHANGE
B. and in spite of it
C. and even though
D. and because of her behavior

14. In New York City, <u>they are</u> brusque and even rude but quick to come to one another's assistance in a time of crisis.

F. NO CHANGE
G. the people there are
H. people are
J. some are

Antecedents Must Be Clear
Item #15

15. Ten years ago, the United States imported ten times as much French wine as Italian wine, but today Americans are drinking more <u>of it</u>.

A. NO CHANGE
B. of them
C. French wine
D. Italian wine

Pronoun-Antecedent Agreement
Items #16–19

16. Although a police officer used to be a symbol of authority, today <u>they receive</u> little respect from most people.

F. NO CHANGE
G. they received
H. he or she receives
J. police officers can receive

Use POE

Trust your ear. One of the best ways to determine whether an ACT English item needs revising is to see if *you* understand it. Are you able to comprehend exactly what the sentence is saying and what it is referring to at different points? If not, what parts are ambiguous? This thought process can point you straight to the error.

17. Mrs. Martinez was an effective administrator who attempted to assign each volunteer a task particularly suited to <u>their</u> talents and training.

A. NO CHANGE
B. his or her
C. your
D. there

18. After three years of college education, one should be allowed to apply to graduate school, because by that time <u>you are ready to choose a profession</u>.

F. NO CHANGE
G. a profession can be chosen
H. your profession is ready to be chosen
J. one is ready to choose a profession

19. If one wishes to apply for a scholarship, <u>you must submit a completed application</u> by March 1.

A. NO CHANGE
B. one must have submitted the application already
C. a completed application must be submitted
D. your application must be submitted

Debrief

Watch for shifting subject errors. These errors occur if different forms of the same pronoun are used to refer to the antecedent.

Pronouns Must Have Proper Case
Items #20–21

20. The judges were unable to make a final decision on a single winner, so they divided the first prize between John and he.

F. NO CHANGE
G. he and John
H. John and himself
J. John and him

21. Although Peter had been looking forward to the debate for weeks, a sore throat prevented him taking part.

A. NO CHANGE
B. taking his
C. his taking
D. he from taking

Debrief

Pronoun Usage Rules

1. A pronoun must have an antecedent (referent) to which it refers.
2. The pronoun must refer clearly to the antecedent.
3. The pronoun and antecedent must agree in number.
4. The pronoun must have the proper case.

ADJECTIVES VERSUS ADVERBS

Adjectives Modify Nouns; Adverbs Modify Verbs, Adjectives, and Other Adverbs
Items #22–23

22. The company's mission statement took into consideration the significant changes that were made in the field of technology.

F. NO CHANGE
G. significantly changes
H. significant changed
J. significantly changed

23. When asked about the chance that the defenders might concentrate their forces at the beachhead, the general responded tart that he was fully aware of all the possibilities.

A. NO CHANGE
B. tartly that he was full
C. tart that he was full
D. tartly that he was fully

Linking Verbs
Items #24–25

24. When the door burst open, Kevin looked up angry from his desk.

F. NO CHANGE
G. was looking up angry
H. looked up angrily
J. looks up angrily

25. The director explained that the scene required Edmund to look distraughtly on hearing the news of his sister's death.

A. NO CHANGE
B. looking distraughtly
C. to have looked distraughtly
D. to look distraught

Watch for Adjectives Posing as Adverbs
Items #26–28

26. Some psychologists maintain that a child who has seen violence on television is more likely to react violent in situations of stress.

F. NO CHANGE
G. to react violently
H. to react with violent
J. reacting violently

27. The recent created commission has done nothing to address the problem except to approve the color of its stationery.

A. NO CHANGE
B. recent creation
C. recently created
D. created recently

28. The track meet begins at 10:00 a.m., so the team needs to depart from the school at a reasonable early hour.

F NO CHANGE
G. at a reasonably early hour
H. during a reasonable early hour
J. at a reasonably hour that is early

DOUBLE NEGATIVES

29. Not hardly a sound could be heard in the auditorium when the speaker approached the dais to announce the result of the contest.

A. NO CHANGE
B. No sounds could not be heard
C. Hardly a sound could be heard
D. Sounds couldn't not be heard

30. Although she had been hired by the magazine to write book reviews, she knew scarcely nothing about current fiction.

F. NO CHANGE
G. as if she knew anything
H. she didn't know nothing
J. she knew scarcely anything

Ace the Pace

Remember that there is no penalty for wrong answers on the ACT test, so make sure to answer every question, even if you must guess. Revisit your guesses later if you have time. If you struggle with double negatives, which Questions 29 and 30 test, for example, guess on them and revisit them later if you have time.

NOUNS AND NOUN CLAUSES

The Cambridge Edge

Always be concise. For example, in item #31 three answers consist of only one word, while one answer is four words. This doesn't mean (D) is wrong, but you should be suspicious of a choice that is longer than all the rest. Do the extra words add anything essential?

31. The reason Harriet fired her secretary is because he was frequently late and spent too much time on personal phone calls.

A. NO CHANGE
B. although
C. that
D. because of the fact

32. The reason the manager changed pitchers was because he knew that the opposing side had a left-handed batter.

F. NO CHANGE
G. The reason that pitchers were changed by the manager was because
H. The reason the manager changed pitchers which
J. The manager changed pitchers because

33. I read in a magazine where scientists believe they have discovered a new subatomic particle.

A. NO CHANGE
B. in which
C. that
D. about

FAULTY OR ILLOGICAL COMPARISONS

Debrief

Be alert for sentences that attempt to make an illogical comparison between two dissimilar concepts.

34. The company offers plastic key cards so that employees can carry them in their wallet.

F. NO CHANGE
G. can carry them in their wallets
H. can carry it in their wallet
J. can carry it in their wallets

35. The great pianist Vladimir Horowitz played the music of the Romantic Era better than any pianist in history.

A. NO CHANGE
B. the best of any pianist in history
C. better than any other pianist in history
D. better compared to any other pianist in history

36. Like Neil Simon, many of Tennessee Williams' plays reflect a culture familiar to the playwright.

F. NO CHANGE
G. Many of Tennessee Williams' plays, like Neil Simon's,
H. Many of Tennessee Williams' plays, like Neil Simon,
J. As with the plays of Neil Simon, many of Tennessee Williams' plays

37. Educators are now expressing their concern that American school children prefer watching television to books.

A. NO CHANGE
B. prefer television to reading books
C. prefers television to books
D. prefer watching television to reading books

38. The novels of Nathaniel Hawthorne contain characters who are every bit as sinister and frightening as the master of cinematic suspense, Alfred Hitchcock.

F. NO CHANGE
G. as those of the master
H. like the master
J. like those of the master

VERB TENSE

Principal Parts of Verbs
Items #39–41

39. After the broken glass and other debris were cleaned up, we realized that the thief had took not only the necklace but a valuable ring as well.

A. NO CHANGE
B. had taken
C. was took
D. was taken

40. Everyone was very surprised when Sylvia brought her grandfather to music class and asked him to perform several Spanish songs on the guitar.

F. NO CHANGE
G. because Sylvia bringing
H. that Sylvia brang
J. for Sylvia to bring

When to Use the Perfect Tenses
Items #42–44

The Subjunctive Mood
Items #45–46

Throwback to English Class

The subjunctive mood is used:

1. To express a wish not likely to be fulfilled or impossible to realize
2. In a subordinate clause after a verb that expresses a command, a request, or a suggestion
3. To express a condition known or supposed to be contrary to fact
4. After "as if" or "as though"

41. The sheriff called off the search for the escaped convict because he doubted that the convict can successfully cross the river because the current was so swift.

A. NO CHANGE
B. the convict successfully crossed the river because the current was so swift
C. the convict would have been successful in crossing the river, the current being so swift
D. a successful attempt to cross the river was made by the convict because the current was so swift

42. Elaine is the favorite to win the final event because she had always run well at the 100-meter distance.

F. NO CHANGE
G. has always run
H. always ran
J. will always run

43. My computer crashed several times before I finally figured out that I had loaded a corrupted copy of the program.

A. NO CHANGE
B. had finally figured out that I loaded
C. had finally figured out that I had loaded
D. finally had figured out that I loaded

44. At the current rate of consumption, we have exhausted our supply of firewood before the weather turns warm.

F. NO CHANGE
G. had exhausted
H. will exhaust
J. will have exhausted

45. The will is going to be read at 3:00 p.m., so the lawyer has asked that all family members are present in the office at that time.

A. NO CHANGE
B. are presently
C. are going to be present
D. be present

46. A dangerous situation could arise if the override switch were left open and the water drops below 50 percent of capacity.

F. NO CHANGE
G. dropped
H. allowed to drop
J. allows to drop

Use POE

In questions like #46, try filling in the answer choices one at a time to see if the sentence still makes sense. Eliminate the ones you're sure are wrong. If you're uncertain about the correct answer, guess from the remaining choices and move on.

SEQUENCE AND VERB TENSE

Debrief

Watch for shifting verb tenses. Make sure that verb tenses properly reflect the sequence, as well as the duration, of any action described in the sentence.

47. The teacher began to discuss the homework assignment when he will be interrupted by the sound of the fire alarm.

A. NO CHANGE
B. had been interrupted by
C. was interrupted by
D. interrupted

48. The conductor announced that the concert would resume as soon as the soloist replaces the broken string on her violin.

F. NO CHANGE
G. replaced
H. will replace
J. would replace

49. Many patients begin to show symptoms again after they stopped taking the drug.

A. NO CHANGE
B. will stop taking
C. stop to take
D. stop taking

50. The winter was so severe that several of Hillary's prize rose bushes had sustained serious damage from the frost.

F. NO CHANGE
G. are in danger of sustaining
H. will sustain
J. sustained

DICTION

Wrong Preposition
Items #51–52

51. In contrast of the prevailing opinion, the editorial lays the blame for the strike on the workers and their representatives.

A. NO CHANGE
B. Contrasting
C. In contrast to
D. In contrast with

52. Although ballet and modern dance are both concerned in movement in space to musical accompaniment, the training for ballet is more rigorous than that for modern dance.

F. NO CHANGE
G. concerned with
H. concerning
J. concerned to

Wrong Word Choice
Items #53–54

53. By midnight the guests still had not been served anything to eat, so they were ravishing.

A. NO CHANGE
B. they are ravenous
C. they had been ravishing
D. they were ravenous

54. The raise in the number of accidents attributable to drunk drivers has prompted a call for stiffer penalties for driving while intoxicated.

F. CHANGE
G. raising
H. rise
J. rising

Gerund versus Infinitive
Items #55–56

55. The idea of trying completing the term paper by Friday caused Ken to cancel his plans for the weekend.

A. NO CHANGE
B. complete
C. to complete
D. to completing

56. Psychologists think that many people eat satisfying a need for affection that is not otherwise fulfilled.

F. NO CHANGE
G. to satisfy
H. to have satisfied
J. satisfy

Debrief

Watch for gerund/infinitive switching. Sometimes an infinitive is used instead of a gerund (or vice versa) and the result is non-standard written English.

LESSON 2

Sentence Structure

The items in this section accompany the in-class review of the sentence structure skills and concepts tested by the ACT English Test. You will work through the items with your instructor in class. Answers are on page 428.

DIRECTIONS: Identify the re-phrasing that best expresses the meaning of the underlined material. The answer choice "NO CHANGE" indicates that the underlined material is correct as written.

RUN-ON SENTENCES

Use Your Test Booklet

Remember our advice in Lesson 1 about circling subjects and verbs? That practice will help you with sentence structure, too. For example, if you can't find a verb to go with your subject, you know you're dealing with a fragment.

1. The armor plating on the new tank protects more vulnerable areas than the armor on the old tank it costs about three times as much to manufacture and install.

A. NO CHANGE
B. areas than the armor on the old tank, because it costs
C. areas than the armor on the old tank, and it costs
D. areas than the armor on the old tank, which costs

2. The filibuster continued late into the night some senators slept sitting upright in the chairs while others slumped over their desks.

F. NO CHANGE
G. As the filibuster continued late into the night, some
H. The filibuster continued late into the night with some
J. The filibuster, which continued late into the night, some

COMMA SPLICES

3. The weather forecast predicted heavy rain, the baseball game was postponed until the following day.

A. NO CHANGE
B. rain while the
C. rain, so the
D. rain the

4. The devastation caused by the flood was so complete, it was impossible to tell that the pile of debris had once been a house.

F. NO CHANGE
G. so complete, and it
H. so complete that it
J. so completely, it

FRAGMENTS

5. The audience, dazzled by the sequined costumes and brilliant lights and applauded wildly.

A. NO CHANGE
B. brilliant lights, applauded
C. brilliant lights applauding
D. brilliant lights had applauded

6. Most of the delegates, who were from smaller villages and rural areas and so opposed any plans to improve conditions in the large cities.

F. NO CHANGE
G. rural areas and so opposed to
H. rural areas, they opposed
J. rural areas, opposed

PROBLEMS OF COORDINATION AND SUBORDINATION

Debrief

Coordinating conjunctions join independent clauses to form a compound sentence.

Examples:
and, but, for, so, yet

Subordinating conjunctions turn independent clauses into dependent clauses that join with another independent clause to form a complex sentence.

Examples:
although, because, whether, which

7. Carlos telephoned to say that weather had delayed his plane, but he will not be able to attend the meeting.

A. NO CHANGE
B. plane, so he will
C. plane, but he would
D. plane because he will

8. By the fifth inning, Cindy was showing signs of fatigue and walked three consecutive batters, so the coach refused to take her out of the game.

F. NO CHANGE
G. batters, when
H. batters, moreover
J. batters, but

9. Because the wetlands were protected by federal law, the owners were not able to build the shopping center that they had planned.

A. NO CHANGE
B. However
C. Moreover
D. So that

10. Victoria was nominated to the office of club president, or it is doubtful that she would serve even if elected.

F. NO CHANGE
G. president so
H. president, though
J. president, in that

11. The driving snow made the roadway slippery and reduced visibility to no more than a few feet, and fortunately there were no accidents despite the heavy volume of traffic.

A. NO CHANGE
B. but fortunately there were no
C. if fortunately there were no
D. so fortunately there were no

12. The land surrounding Las Vegas is characterized by parched red dunes and flats with dry ravines, but it is almost entirely lacking in vegetation.

F. NO CHANGE
G. or it is
H. and it is
J. whereas it is

13. Kari stopped applying to schools and she learned of her acceptance at her first choice.

A. NO CHANGE
B. so she learned
C. but she learned
D. when she learned

14. Although the American relay team did not qualify for the finals, the anchor runner dropped the baton shortly after the hand-off.

F. NO CHANGE
G. When the American relay team did not qualify for the finals, the
H. The American relay team did not qualify for the finals because the
J. Not qualifying for the finals, the American relay team's

FAULTY PARALLELISM

The Cambridge Edge

Lists show up often on the ACT test, and they are usually tied to an item that is testing either parallelism or comma usage. When you see part of a list in an underlined phrase, always check for these two potential errors.

15. To abandon their homes, leave behind their families, and traveling across the ocean required great courage on the part of the immigrants who moved to America.

A. NO CHANGE
B. travel across the ocean
C. to travel across the ocean
D. while traveling across the ocean

16. The review praised the wit, charm, and interpreting of the recitalist but never once mentioned her voice.

F. NO CHANGE
G. interpretation of the recitalist
H. interpreted the recitalist
J. interpretive of the recitalist

17. To acknowledge that one has something to learn is taking the first step on the road to true wisdom.

A. NO CHANGE
B. taken the first step
C. to taking the first step
D. to take the first step

INCOMPLETE SPLIT CONSTRUCTIONS

18. The students are critical of the dean because he is either unfamiliar or doesn't care about the urgent need for new student housing on campus.

F. NO CHANGE
G. more unfamiliar than or
H. unfamiliar with or
J. unfamiliar about or

19. Baseball has and probably always will be the sport that symbolizes for people in other countries the American way of life.

A. NO CHANGE
B. has been
C. has been and
D. have been and

The Cambridge Edge

Phrases that are interrupted by intervening material are difficult to check for errors of split construction. Therefore, when checking split constructions, read the sentence and skip the intervening material—it should make sense and be grammatically correct.

MISPLACED MODIFIERS

Debrief

Watch for misplaced modifiers. A modifier should be as close as possible to what it's supposed to modify.

20. Letters were received by the editor of the newspaper that complained of its editorial policy.

F. NO CHANGE
G. Letters were received by the editor of the newspaper having complained of its editorial policy.
H. The editor of the newspaper received letters complaining of the newspaper's editorial policy.
J. Letters were received by the editor complaining of the newspaper's editorial policy by the editor.

21. Riding in a coach and wearing the crown jewels, the crowd cheered the royal couple.

A. NO CHANGE
B. cheering for the royal couple was done by the crowd
C. the royal couple was cheered by the crowd
D. the royal couple's cheering was done by the crowd

22. Wrapped in several layers of newspaper, packed carefully in a strong cardboard carton, and bound securely with tape, the worker made sure that the fragile figurines would not be broken.

F. NO CHANGE
G. Wrapped in several layers of newspaper, packed carefully in a strong cardboard carton, and then binding the carton securely with tape, the worker made sure that the fragile figurines would not be broken.
H. The worker, wrapping the figurines in several layers of newspaper, packing them carefully in a strong cardboard carton, and securely binding the carton with tape, made sure that they would not be broken.
J. To make sure that the figurines would not be broken, the worker wrapped them in several layers of newspaper, packed them carefully in a strong cardboard carton, and securely bound the carton with tape.

UNINTENDED MEANINGS

23. Mary Lou was awarded the gold medal because she scored more points than any child participating in the field day.

A. NO CHANGE
B. more points than any other child participating
C. the most points than any child participating
D. more points than all of the children participating

24. Appearing in his first American tour, the British singer's album rose to the top of the charts.

F. NO CHANGE
G. While appearing
H. While he was appearing
J. While it appeared

LESSON 3

Punctuation

The items in this section accompany the in-class review of the punctuation skills and concepts tested by the ACT English Test. You will work through the items with your instructor in class. Answers are on page 429.

DIRECTIONS: For items #1–34, identify the re-phrasing that best expresses the meaning of the underlined material. The answer choice "NO CHANGE" indicates that the underlined material is correct as written.

COMMAS

Debrief

Use a comma before coordinating conjunctions joining two independent clauses, unless the two clauses are very short.

1. I think that Doré's illustrations of Dante's *Divine Comedy* are excellent: but my favorite drawing is "Don Quixote in His Library."

   A. NO CHANGE
   B. are excellent, but my favorite drawing is "Don Quixote in His Library."
   C. are excellent in that my favorite drawing is "Don Quixote in His Library."
   D. are excellent even though "Don Quixote in His Library" is my favorite drawing.

2. Practically all nitrates are crystalline and readily soluble, and they are characterized by marked decrepitation when heated on charcoals by a blowpipe.

   F. NO CHANGE
   G. crystalline and readily soluble and
   H. crystalline, and readily soluble, and
   J. crystalline and readily soluble and,

3. The door was ajar and the house had been ransacked, but it did not seem as though any of his possessions were missing.

   A. NO CHANGE
   B. was ajar and the house, had been ransacked, but
   C. was ajar, and the house had been ransacked but
   D. was ajar, the house had been ransacked but

4. Since many diseases and insects cause serious damage to crops, special national legislation has been passed to provide for the quarantine of imported plants.

   F. NO CHANGE
   G. crops; special
   H. crops. Special
   J. crops special

Debrief

Use Commas for Clarity

1. Use a comma if the sentence might be subject to different interpretations without it.
2. Use a comma if a pause would make the sentence clearer and easier to read.

The Cambridge Edge

Use the breath test to figure out whether you need a comma. If you read a sentence aloud, you will hear how a natural pause suggests where a comma should be inserted. Although the practice of listening for a pause isn't fail-safe, it is a good last resort when all other comma rules seem to fail.

5. <u>A full train crew consists of a motorman, a brakeman, a conductor, and two ticket takers.</u>

A. NO CHANGE
B. A full train crew consists of a motorman, a brakeman, a conductor and, two ticket takers.
C. A full train crew consists of a motorman, a brakeman a conductor and two ticket takers.
D. A full train crew consists of a motorman a brakeman a conductor, and two ticket takers.

6. The procedure requires that you open the outer cover <u>plate, remove the thermostat, replace the broken switch, and</u> then replace the thermostat.

F. NO CHANGE
G. plate remove the thermostat, replace the broken switch; and
H. plate remove, the thermostat replace the broken switch, and
J. plate remove the thermostat replace the broken switch and

7. After Peter finished painting <u>the bird feeder he and Jack hung it</u> from a limb of the oak tree.

A. NO CHANGE
B. the bird feeder, he and Jack hung it
C. the bird feeder; he and Jack hung it
D. the bird feeder, he and Jack, hung it

8. When Pat explained to his <u>mother that ten was the highest mark given on the entrance test</u> she breathed a sigh of relief.

F. NO CHANGE
G. mother, that ten was the highest mark given on the entrance test,
H. mother that ten was the highest mark given on the entrance test,
J. mother that ten was the highest mark given on the entrance test;

9. <u>Tim hopes to score well on the exam because he plans to go to an Ivy League school.</u>

A. NO CHANGE
B. Tim hopes to score well on the exam: he plans to go to an Ivy League school.
C. Tim hopes to score well on the exam, because he plans to go to an Ivy League school.
D. Tim hopes to score well on the exam he plans to go to an Ivy League school.

10. <u>In this impoverished region with its arid soil a typical diet may contain only 800 calories per day.</u>

F. NO CHANGE
G. In this impoverished region with its arid soil; a typical diet may contain only 800 calories per day.
H. In this impoverished region, with its arid soil, a typical diet may contain only 800 calories per day.
J. In this impoverished region with its arid soil, a typical diet may contain only 800 calories per day.

11. <u>Begun in 1981 and completed in 1985 the bridge</u> provided the first link between the island and the mainland.

A. NO CHANGE
B. Begun in 1981 and completed in 1985, the bridge
C. The bridge begun in 1981 and completed in 1985
D. Begun—in 1981 and completed in 1985—the bridge

12. <u>To slow the bleeding Van tied a pressure bandage around the lower portion of the leg.</u>

F. NO CHANGE
G. To slow the bleeding—Van tied a pressure bandage around the lower portion of the leg.
H. To slow the bleeding, Van tied a pressure bandage around the lower portion of the leg.
J. To slow the bleeding, Van tied a pressure bandage, around the lower portion of the leg.

13. Niagara Falls, which forms part of the border between the United States and Canada, was the site of a saw mill built by the French in 1725.

A. NO CHANGE
B. Niagara Falls forms part of the border between the United States and Canada
C. Niagara Falls, which forms part of the border between the United States and Canada—
D. Niagara Falls, which forms part of the border between the United States and Canada; it

14. Dean Acheson, the Secretary of State, made a reasoned defense of the treaty.

F. NO CHANGE
G. Dean Acheson, the Secretary of State, he made a reasoned defense of the treaty.
H. Dean Acheson; the Secretary of State, made a reasoned defense of the treaty.
J. Dean Acheson the Secretary of State made a reasoned defense of the treaty.

15. Until the end of the eighteenth century, the only musicians in Norway, were simple peasants who traveled about the countryside.

A. NO CHANGE
B. the eighteenth century, the only musicians in Norway were simple peasants
C. the eighteenth century, the only musicians in Norway were simple peasants,
D. the eighteenth century the only musicians in Norway were simple peasants—

The Cambridge Edge

When in doubt, leave it out. If you are not sure whether a sentence requires a comma or you do not see a clear reason to insert one (such as ambiguous sentence meaning), the sentence probably does not require a comma.

16. Prizes will be awarded in each event, and the participant, who compiles the greatest overall total, will receive a special prize.

F. NO CHANGE
G. event; and the participant, who compiles the greatest overall total, will receive
H. event, and the participant who compiles the greatest overall total will receive
J. event, and the participant who compiles the greatest, overall, total will receive

17. Since learning of the dangers of caffeine, neither my wife nor I have consumed any beverage, containing caffeine.

A. NO CHANGE
B. caffeine neither my wife nor I have consumed any beverage,
C. caffeine—neither my wife nor I have consumed any beverage—
D. caffeine, neither my wife nor I have consumed any beverage

18. After months of separation, Gauguin finally joined Van Gogh in Arles in October of 1888, Gauguin left a few weeks later.

F. NO CHANGE
G. in Arles in October of 1888; Gauguin, however, leaving a few weeks later
H. in Arles in October of 1888, it was three weeks later when Gauguin was gone
J. in Arles in October of 1888, but a few weeks later Gauguin left

19. By the middle of June, the foliage on the trees and the underbrush was lush and green and so thick that it was impossible to see very far, into the woods.

A. NO CHANGE
B. By the middle of June the foliage on the trees and the underbrush was lush and green; and it was so thick that it was impossible to see, very far, into the woods.
C. By the middle of June the foliage, on the trees and the underbrush, was lush and green and so thick that it was impossible to see very far, into the woods.
D. By the middle of June, the foliage on the trees and the underbrush was lush and green and so thick that it was impossible to see very far into the woods.

20. Students who plan to graduate with joint majors, must declare their intention and identify the two areas of study by the end of their junior years.

F. NO CHANGE
G. Students who plan to graduate with joint majors must declare
H. Students, who plan to graduate with joint majors, must declare
J. Students—who plan to graduate with joint majors—must declare

SEMICOLONS

Master Moves

The following options are all correct ways to separate independent clauses:

1. a comma followed by a conjunction
2. a semicolon
3. end-stop punctuation

If you see at least two answer choices with these features (and no other differences), you can eliminate those choices, since there can't be more than one correct answer and those choices would essentially be equal.

21. He grew up on a farm in Nebraska; he is now the captain of a navy ship.

A. NO CHANGE
B. He grew up on a farm in Nebraska, he is now the captain of a navy ship.
C. He grew up on a farm in Nebraska he is now the captain of a navy ship.
D. He grew up on a farm in Nebraska; while he is now the captain of a navy ship.

22. The Smithtown players cheered the referee's decision; the Stonybrook players booed it.

F. NO CHANGE
G. The Smithtown players cheered the referee's decision the Stonybrook players booed it.
H. The Smithtown players cheered the referee's decision, the Stonybrook players booed it.
J. The Smithtown players cheered the referee's decision: the Stonybrook players booed it.

23. When John entered the room; everyone stood up.

A. NO CHANGE
B. room, everyone
C. room, everyone,
D. room everyone

24. Clem announced that the prize would be donated to Harbus House; a well-known charity.

F. NO CHANGE
G. would be donated to Harbus House a well-known
H. would be donated to, Harbus House, a well-known
J. would be donated to Harbus House, a well-known

25. The nineteenth-century composers Wagner and Mahler did more than just write music, they conducted their own works.

A. NO CHANGE
B. music, in that they conducted
C. music; they conducted
D. music, with their conducting of

COLONS

Master Moves

Remember that colons replace phrases that introduce a list, including "such as," "like," "that is," etc. Use one or the other, but not both.

26. The seemingly tranquil lane has been the scene of many crimes <u>including: two assaults, three robberies, and one murder</u>.

F. NO CHANGE
G. including two assaults, three robberies, and one murder
H. including two assaults three robberies and one murder
J. including: two assaults three robberies and one murder

27. In addition to test scores, college admissions officers take into consideration many other <u>factors such as: grades, extracurricular activities, and letters of recommendation</u>.

A. NO CHANGE
B. factors such as grades, extracurricular activities, and letters of recommendation
C. factors: such as grades, extracurricular activities, and letters of recommendation
D. factors such as grades extracurricular activities and letters of recommendation

END-STOP PUNCTUATION

28. <u>Peter notified Elaine. The guidance counselor, that he had been accepted.</u>

F. NO CHANGE
G. Peter notified Elaine the guidance counselor, that he had been accepted.
H. Peter notified Elaine, the guidance counselor that he had been accepted.
J. Peter notified Elaine, the guidance counselor, that he had been accepted.

DASHES

29. <u>Peanuts—blanched or lightly roasted, add an interesting texture and taste to garden salads.</u>

A. NO CHANGE
B. Peanuts—blanched or lightly roasted—add an interesting texture and taste to garden salads.
C. Peanuts blanched or lightly roasted—add an interesting texture and taste to garden salads.
D. Peanuts, blanched or lightly roasted—add an interesting texture and taste to garden salads.

30. The rug gets its striking colors from the weaver's skilled use of <u>dyes—both natural and synthetic to create</u> shades in subtle variations.

F. NO CHANGE
G. dyes both natural and synthetic to create
H. dyes—both natural—and synthetic to create
J. dyes—both natural and synthetic—to create

QUOTATION MARKS

31. The first chapter of *The Scarlet Letter* is "The Custom House."

A. NO CHANGE
B. The first chapter of *The Scarlet Letter* is The Custom House.
C. The first chapter of *The Scarlet Letter* is *The Custom House.*
D. The first chapter of "*The Scarlet Letter*" is "The Custom House."

APOSTROPHES

The Cambridge Edge

As a general rule of thumb, singular nouns and indefinite pronouns add the apostrophe and "-s." Plural nouns ending in "-s" add only the apostrophe.

32. According to legend, King Arthurs court consisted of twenty-four knights, each of whom was chosen by Arthur for a special talent or virtue.

F. NO CHANGE
G. King Arthurs' court
H. King Arthur's court
J. Kings Arthurs's court

33. In the turmoil of our modern times, it is important to try to keep in mind the fundamental moral values that structure our society.

A. NO CHANGE
B. modern times'
C. modern time's
D. modern times's

34. While she addressed the barbell, the weightlifters face had an expression of deep concentration.

F. NO CHANGE
G. the weightlifters' face
H. the weightlifters's face
J. the weightlifter's face

PUNCTUATING FOR CLARITY EXERCISE

Master Moves

Put everything you've learned about punctuation to the test in item #35. Remember to read with the eye of an editor and to focus more on the architecture of the paragraph than on the story being told. Mark it up, underline components, and cross out parts as you need to in order to make sure the punctuation is perfect.

DIRECTIONS: Item #35 requires punctuation of the paragraph.

35. On Monday Mark received a letter of acceptance from State College He immediately called his mother herself a graduate of State College to tell her about his acceptance When he told her he had also been awarded a scholarship she was very excited After hanging up Mark's mother decided to throw a surprise party for Mark She telephoned his brother his sister and several of his friends Because the party was supposed to be a surprise she made them all promise not to say anything to Mark Mark however had a similar idea a party for his mother to celebrate his acceptance at her alma mater He telephoned his brother his sister and several of his parents' friends to invite them to a party at his house on Saturday night and he made them all promise to say nothing to his mother On Saturday night both Mark and his mother were surprised.

LESSON 4

Production of Writing and Knowledge of Language

The items in this section accompany the in-class review of the sentence structure skills and concepts tested by the ACT English Test. You will work through the items with your instructor in class. Answers are on page 429.

PRODUCTION OF WRITING

Passage Perfect

Remember that you are free to mark up your test booklet however you please. We recommend underlining what you believe to be:

1. The Thesis
2. Each Paragraph's Main Idea
3. Conclusion

We also encourage you to underline terms that indicate the tone of the passage, or the author's attitude toward the topic. Look for words that attribute value to or question the value of certain things ("important," "better," "should," etc.).

DIRECTIONS: The following passages are early drafts of essays. Some parts of the passages need to be rewritten. Read each passage and answer the items that follow. Some items are about particular sentences or parts of sentences and ask you to improve sentence structure and word choice. Other items refer to parts of the passage or the entire passage and ask you to consider organization and development. In making your decisions, follow the conventions of standard written English.

Items #1–5 are based on the following essay, which is a response to an assignment to write about an issue that is facing America and what might be done to resolve it.

[1] In my mind, one of the most pressing issues facing America today is healthcare. [2] One aspect of the problem is lack of access to a doctor. [3] Many people just cannot afford to pay for a visit to a doctor. [4] They avoid going to the doctor until they are really sick. [5] If they were treated in the first place, they wouldn't get so sick. [6] This practice not only causes human suffering but is wasteful. [7] Health insurance for surgery is also an issue. [8] Many people do not get adequate health insurance with their jobs and cannot afford to pay for it. [9] The inability to pay for health insurance also creates an unfair distribution of healthcare in America.

[10] An even more important aspect of the healthcare problem in America is the choices that people make for themselves. [11] Take smoking for example. [12] Scientific evidence proves that smoking causes lung cancer and other diseases. [13] Yet, many people continue to smoke, and young people continue to start smoking. [14] There are other health problems such as being overweight and using drugs that may also come from private choices.

[15] Some government assistance is needed for those who cannot afford medical care or health insurance. [16] The most important thing is for people to be concerned with their own health. [17] If we take care of ourselves by eating better, exercising more, and avoiding destructive choices, we will all live longer, healthier, and happier lives.

Strategy
Items #1–4

Debrief

Writers support their ideas in four main ways:

1. Interpreting a statement
2. Clarifying a general statement with examples
3. Furthering an argument with information and reasoning
4. Quoting an expert

The Cambridge Edge

Questions about the passage as a whole, such as #3 and #4, are likely to appear at the end of a passage. If you are paying attention to the development of the passage as you read, you should only need to skim back through the passage or look for keywords to answer these questions.

Organization
Items #5–6

1. The author considers inserting the following factual statement between sentences 13 and 14:

Nicotine, which is found in tobacco, is one of the most addictive chemicals known to science.

Would this statement add to the development of the paragraph?

A. Yes, because the paragraph identifies smoking as a serious problem.
B. Yes, because the sentence explains why young people start to smoke.
C. No, because scientific evidence is irrelevant to the author's point.
D. No, because the addictive mechanism behind smoking is not relevant.

2. Which of the following revisions to Sentences 15 and 16 best clarifies the author's position?

F. NO CHANGE
G. Some government assistance is needed for those who cannot afford medical care or health insurance and people need to be concerned with their own health.
H. The most important thing is for people to be concerned with their own health and for them to ask for government assistance.
J. Even though some government assistance is needed for those who cannot afford medical care or health insurance, the most important thing is for people to be concerned with their own health.

3. In context, which of the following best describes the main purpose of the essay?

A. To expose faulty reasoning
B. To evaluate a theory set forth earlier
C. To provide specific illustrations
D. To propose a solution to a problem

4. In writing this passage, the author was most probably addressing:

F. a convention of surgeons.
G. a group of concerned citizens.
H. a meeting of insurance executives.
J. a conference of tobacco executives.

5. What should be done to Sentence 7 to strengthen the organization of the essay?

A. NO CHANGE
B. Begin a new paragraph
C. Switch Sentence 6 with Sentence 7
D. OMIT Sentence 7

Item #6 is based on the following essay, which is a response to an assignment to write about a chore for which you are responsible and why you like or dislike doing the chore.

[1]

Each year, my family plants a vegetable garden. Both my parents work, and with this, it is the job of the children to tend the garden.

[2]

Work starts several weeks before the growing season actually begins. We put little pots of soil containing seeds that must sprout before they are planted outdoors on the sun porch. Then, my father prepares the ground with a rototiller. When the danger of frost is past, it is time to plant.

[3]

For the first few weeks, we water the seed beds regularly and pull weeds by hand. Once the plants are established, the leaves of the good plants block the sunlight so weeds can't grow. However, there are other jobs such as staking tomatoes and tending to running vines.

[4]

Then the blossoms appear and are pollinated by bees and other insects. As small vegetables appear, the blossoms drop off. They continue to grow and later in the summer begin to ripen. Up to this point, tending the garden has been a chore, but now it becomes a pleasure. Each afternoon, we pick the ripe ones and wash them so that they are ready for cooking. I suppose that I feel proud that I have helped to feed my family. I have to admit that my greatest enjoyment is the taste of the freshly picked vegetables.

6. The overall organization of the passage can best be described as:

F. chronological development.
G. explanation of two sides of an issue.
H. generalization of a statement with illustrations.
J. posing a question and then answering it.

Use POE

In questions like #6, read each answer choice, check whether it is accurate, and cross off incorrect answers as you go. Remember also to focus on the passage as a whole, not individual paragraphs or techniques.

Items #7–12 are based on the following essay, which is a response to an assignment to write about a significant activity or experience from the summer vacation.

[1]

On my vacation to Alaska, I took a trip to Porcupine. In 1905, Porcupine was a thriving town of 2,000 people, retail stores, and a post office. Hardly any of the town remains today, but there is still gold there, and our guide showed us how to pan for gold. It's easy to learn how, and anyone **7** can do it.

[2]

The technique of panning depends on the weight of gold. It's about 20 times heavier than water, so the gold stays at the bottom of a stream and gets caught in the sand in slow-flowing water around bends and along the edge of the stream. It can also get stuck in small crevices of rock and even wedged into pieces of wood. **9**

[3]

You need to find where the gold is. There's no sense in panning for gold in a stream where there isn't any, so go to a stream where people have found gold before. Then concentrate on those areas that are most likely to trap the little bits of gold.

[4]

Keep moving the pan until about half the original material has been carried away. Lift the pan out of the water, tilt it toward the side with the riffles (the small ridges), **10** and swirl until the water is gone. Repeat this process until nearly all the material is gone.

[5]

To start panning, put a few handfuls of material into your gold pan. Then submerge the pan in the water of the stream. Hold the pan under the surface and move it in a circular motion so that the lighter material sloshes over the edge. You have to be careful not to be too aggressive or you'll send your gold downstream along with the silt and other debris.

[6]

Use a small stream of water suction pipette (or even a spray bottle with a concentrated setting on the nozzle) to sort the gold from the remaining debris. Pick up the flecks with a tweezers or your fingers and place them in a small glass container such as a test tube or a medicine bottle.

[7]

Panning takes practice, patience, and luck, but even a little bit of gold is a big thrill. [11] You're probably not going to find a lot of gold.

Additional Practice
Items #7–12

7. Which of the following sentences inserted at [7] would best introduce the remaining paragraphs of the essay?

A. Gold is one of the most valuable substances on earth.
B. Just follow these simple instructions.
C. I try to do a lot of different things on my vacations.
D. Did you even know that there was a gold rush in Alaska?

8. Which of the following sequences of paragraphs is most logical?

F. NO CHANGE
G. 6, 4, 5
H. 4, 6, 5
J. 5, 4, 6

9. The best placement for the final sentence in Paragraph 2 would be:

A. where it is now.
B. as the first sentence of Paragraph 2.
C. in Paragraph 2, following the sentence ending "... weight of gold."
D. as the first sentence of Paragraph 3.

10. Is the parenthetical note following the word "riffles" in Paragraph 4 appropriate?

F. Yes, because it clarifies a technical term for the reader.
G. Yes, because it presents an idea that is essential to the passage.
H. No, because it distracts the reader from the directions for panning.
J. No, because the author does not cite a source for the definition.

11. The best placement for the sentence: "Panning takes practice, patience, and luck, but even a little bit of gold is a big thrill" would be:

A. where it is now.
B. at the end of the passage.
C. at the beginning of Paragraph 2.
D. at the beginning of Paragraph 6.

12. Suppose the author had been assigned to write a brief essay on an interesting travel destination. Assuming that all of the following statements are true, would this essay successfully fulfill the assignment?

F. Yes, because many gold-seekers came to Porcupine during the nineteenth century.
G. Yes, because panning for gold would be a fun activity on a trip.
H. No, because very little remains today of the town of Porcupine.
J. No, because most people have never before heard of Porcupine.

Test Specs

Notice that in #12, you are instructed to assume that all of the following statements are true. Do not spend your time confirming these statements by referring back to the essay. You might even be able to eliminate some answers without reading the passage.

KNOWLEDGE OF LANGUAGE

DIRECTIONS: Items #13–20 consist of questions in which either a single part of a sentence is underlined or the entire sentence is underlined. Identify the re-phrasing that best expresses the meaning of the underlined material. The answer choice "NO CHANGE" indicates that the underlined material is correct as written.

Conciseness
Items #13–18

The Cambridge Edge

When it comes to items testing conciseness, shorter is better. As a general rule of thumb, you can expect the shortest answer to be the best. If you're running out of time and need to guess and go on an item testing conciseness, pick the shortest answer.

13. Angela is hoping to save enough for a trip to Europe, during which the small village where her grandparents were born will be visited.

A. NO CHANGE
B. the small village where her grandparents had been born will be visited
C. she will visit the small village where her grandparents were born
D. there will be a visit to the small village where her grandparents were born

14. Finally and at long last the old dog opened his eyes and noticed the intruder.

F. NO CHANGE
G. Finally
H. So finally
J. Yet at long last

15. The speaker declared that alternative ways of utilizing waterfront land ought to be explored.

A. NO CHANGE
B. alternatives of use for
C. alternative utilizations of
D. alternative uses of

16. Since only the ruling party is allowed to vote, its members are able to maintain the existing status quo.

F. NO CHANGE
G. remaining status quo
H. existed status quo
J. status quo

17. Each year, the geese make their annual migration from Northern Canada to their winter habitats in the United States.

A. NO CHANGE
B. migration
C. annually migration
D. annual

18. Although the committee met for over two weeks and issued a 50-page report, its findings were of little importance or consequence.

F. NO CHANGE
G. importance or significance
H. importance and consequence
J. consequence

Clarity of Meaning
Item #19

Debrief

Watch for errors in clarity of meaning by being alert for sentences that run two or more ideas together. Usually the error can be corrected by adding words to clarify the two ideas as distinct and to separate them from one another.

19. Along with an end to featherbedding and no-show jobs, the new head of the Transit Authority has eliminated many other inefficient employment practices.

A. NO CHANGE
B. In addition to eliminating featherbedding and no-show jobs
C. Not only did he end featherbedding and no-show jobs
D. Besides featherbedding and no-show jobs coming to an end

Idiomatic Expression
Item #20

20. Being that the hour was late, we agreed to adjourn the meeting and reconvene at nine o'clock the following morning.

F. NO CHANGE
G. Since
H. Because that
J. During

Debrief

Here are a few other examples of non-idiomatic expressions:

Instead of:	Say:
bunch (of people)	group (of people)
kind of	somewhat; rather
theirselves	themselves
would of	would have

LESSON 5

General Strategies

The Cambridge Edge

Basic Method for Solving English Items

1. Read the passage, stopping at each underlined word or phrase.
2. Decide what, if anything, is wrong with each underlined portion.
3. Without looking at the answer choices, imagine appropriate corrections.
4. Look for the correction among the answer choices.
5. Plug the selected answer choice back into the passage.
6. If you are unable to determine the correct answer, eliminate any obviously wrong choices and make an educated guess.

The items in this section accompany the in-class review of the general strategies tested by the ACT English Test. You will work through the items with your instructor in class. Answers are on page 429.

DIRECTIONS: Items #1–10 are based on the passage below. In the passage, certain parts of the sentences have been underlined and numbered. In the right-hand column, you will find different ways of writing each underlined part; the original version is indicated by the "NO CHANGE" option. For each item, select the choice that best expresses the intended idea, is most acceptable in standard written English, or is most consistent with the overall tone and style of the passage.

There are also items that ask about a section of the passage or the passage as a whole. These items do not refer to an underlined portion of the passage; these items are preceded by statements that are enclosed in boxes.

Read the passage through once before you begin to answer the accompanying items. Finding the answers to certain items may depend on looking at material that appears several sentences beyond the item. So, be sure that you have read far enough ahead before you select your answer choice.

Appalachia's European Settlers

The first Europeans who adopted Appalachia as <u>home, followed</u> (1) the trails pounded out by those earliest mountain <u>engineers: the</u> (2) buffalo, elk, deer, and other wild

1. A. NO CHANGE
   B. home followed
   C. home: followed
   D. home; followed

2. F. NO CHANGE
   G. engineers, the
   H. engineers the
   J. engineers. The

The Cambridge Edge

Try to apply the Basic Method above to answer the questions in this passage. Try covering up the answer choices with a piece of paper until you get to step 4.

Master Moves

If you can't remember a grammar rule, be on the lookout for any similar uses in the rest of the passage. For example, #2 includes a colon. If you can't figure out whether the use of the colon is correct, take a guess and move on. But when you reach the sentence that includes #5, notice that it also uses a colon. And you know this use must be correct because it's not underlined. Jump back up to #2. Does this give you any additional clues about the right answer?

game. (Later, they found the great traces forged by the Indian tribes on their trading and fighting forays.) [3] Gradually, these first Europeans hewed out passages that become part of [4] America's history, portions of which may still be discovered along today's interstates and back roads. Their very names connect us to [5] the past in the region: The Great Warrior's Trail, Boone's Trace (which became the Wilderness Road), and the Cumberland Gap.

Geographic isolation [6] greatly influenced the region's culture. From the beginning, numerous ethnic groups contributed to Appalachian settlement. During the late 1600s and into the next century, Germans from the Rhineland settled in the Great Appalachian Valley. Building [7] fat barns and tight houses on the fertile fields of Pennsylvania, Maryland, Virginia, and North Carolina. They were the "Pennsylvania Dutch."

The German settlers made important contributions. [8] One of the important contributions made by German settlers to frontier life was the Pennsylvania rifle—also called the Kentucky rifle or the Long rifle.

3. A. NO CHANGE
B. Great traces forged by the Indian tribes, however, were later found on their trading and fighting forays.
C. (Finding later, great traces forged by the Indian tribes, on their trading and fighting forays.)
D. Later, they found the great traces forged by the Indian tribes on their trading and fighting forays.

4. F. NO CHANGE
G. will become a part of
H. became part of
J. became part

5. A. NO CHANGE
B. connecting us to
C. connected us to
D. connect us

6. F. NO CHANGE
G. Geographically isolated
H. Isolated geographically
J. Isolated geography

7. A. NO CHANGE
B. Valley, building
C. Valley: building
D. Valley,

8. F. NO CHANGE
G. (The German settlers made important contributions.)
H. "The German settlers made important contributions."
J. OMIT the underlined portion.

A weapon born of necessity and economy, its extended barrel assured greater <u>accuracy and precision</u> **9** than could be achieved with the old muskets, and its smaller bore required less powder and lead for each shot <u>(precious commodities)</u> **10**. Such rifles were highly prized possessions, and their manufacture was one of the central industries of pioneer Appalachia.

9. A. NO CHANGE
B. accuracy as well as precision
C. accuracy plus precision
D. accuracy

10. The most appropriate placement of the underlined phrase in this sentence would be:

F. where it is now.
G. after the word *powder.*
H. after the word *lead.*
J. after the word *each.*

ENGLISH
QUIZZES

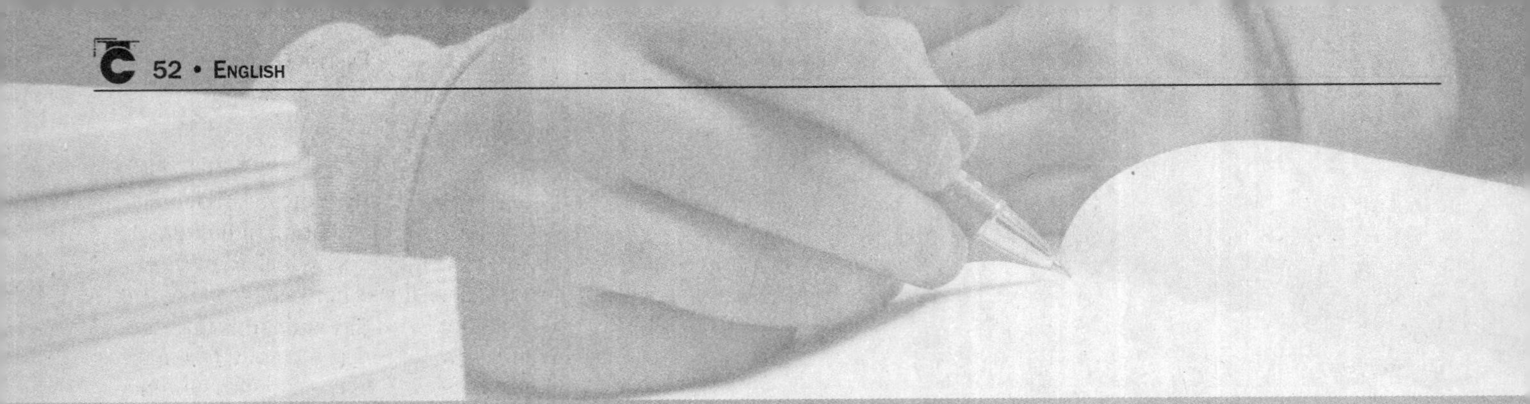

This section contains two English quizzes. The first quiz is a directed study quiz. The directed study quiz is not timed. Answer each question and check your work as you go. The second quiz is a timed quiz. Take the second quiz under the indicated timed conditions to practice your pacing as you apply what you learned in the English Lessons.

DIRECTED STUDY QUIZ *(32 items)*

> **The Cambridge Edge**
>
> This Directed Study Quiz is designed to help you practice applying what you've learned so far without worrying about pacing (we'll get to that soon). Use a piece of paper to cover up the answers. Check your work after you answer each question.

DIRECTIONS: In the passages below, certain parts of the sentences have been underlined and numbered. In the right-hand column, you will find different ways of writing each underlined part; the original version is indicated by the "NO CHANGE" option. For each item, select the choice that best expresses the intended idea, is most acceptable in standard written English, or is most consistent with the overall tone and style of the passage.

There are also items that ask about a section of the passage or the passage as a whole. These items do not refer to an underlined portion of the passage; these items are preceded by statements that are enclosed in boxes.

Read the passage through once before you begin to answer the accompanying items. Finding the answers to certain items may depend on looking at material that appears several sentences beyond the item. So, be sure that you have read far enough ahead before you select your answer choice.

Passage I

Shakespeare's Mirror of Life

No writer can please many readers and please them for a long time excepting by **1** accurately representing human nature.

1. A. NO CHANGE
   B. except by
   C. except for
   D. excepting

EXPLANATIONS

1. (B) ***English/Conventions of Standard English/Sentence Structure/Unintended Meanings***
   The original sentence contains a diction error. The verb "excepting" means "excluding," but that meaning is not appropriate in the original sentence. (B) provides the correct preposition.

EXPLANATIONS

"Except by" correctly indicates that the accurate representation of human nature is the means by which the writer accomplishes his or her task. (C) is wrong because "for" also has an inappropriate meaning in this context. Finally, (D) makes the same mistake as the original sentence.

Shakespeare, <u>however</u>, is above all writers, the poet of human nature, the writer who holds [2]

2. F. NO CHANGE
   G. moreover
   H. therefore
   J. furthermore

2. **(F)** ***English/Production of Writing/No Change***
"However" correctly sets up a contrast between Shakespeare and all other writers. As for (G) and (J), "moreover" and "furthermore" are used to join together two similar ideas—the second adding force to the first. In (H), "therefore" signals a logical transition, but what follows the underlined word is not a conclusion drawn from earlier reasoning.

up to his readers a <u>faithful and true</u> mirror of manners and life. [3]

3. A. NO CHANGE
   B. faithful
   C. faithfully true
   D. true and real

3. **(B)** ***English/Knowledge of Language/Style/Conciseness***
The original sentence is incorrect because "faithful" and "true" mean more or less the same thing, so the underlined portion is redundant; (B) corrects the error. (C) and (D) are also needlessly wordy.

Shakespeare's characters are not modified by the customs of particular places unknown to the rest of the world, by peculiarities of study or professions known <u>to just a few, or</u> by the latest fashions or popular opinions. Shakespeare's characters [4]

4. F. NO CHANGE
   G. about by only a few, and
   H. to just a few, but
   J. to only a few, since

4. **(F)** ***English/Conventions of Standard English/No Change***
The original sentence is correct. (G) is wrong because it is wordy. (H) is wrong because "but" creates an opposition that is not intended. Finally, (J) creates a meaningless sentence.

are each genuine representations of common humanity. Hamlet and Othello act and speak according to the general passions and principles that affect all of us. In the writings of other poets, whoever they may be, a character is too often an individual; in that of Shakespeare, it is commonly a species.

Other dramatists can gain attention only by using exaggerated characters. Shakespeare

EXPLANATIONS

5. A. NO CHANGE
   B. every
   C. all
   D. each one a

5. (C) *English/Conventions of Standard English/Grammar and Usage/Pronoun Usage*
The referent of "each" is "characters," but "each" is singular, while "characters" is plural. (B) and (D) are also incorrect for this reason. (C) corrects the problem by using a plural pronoun.

6. F. NO CHANGE
   G. acting and speaking
   H. acted and spoke
   J. acted and spoken

6. (F) *English/Conventions of Standard English/No Change*
The original sentence is correct. (G) reduces the sentence to a sentence fragment by eliminating the only conjugated verbs. (H) and (J) both create conflicts of verb tenses between this sentence and the other sentences of the paragraph, which use present tense verbs.

7. A. NO CHANGE
   B. whoever they may be
   C. whomever they may be,
   D. OMIT the underlined portion.

7. (D) *English/Knowledge of Language/Style/Conciseness*
The underlined material is needlessly repetitious and should be deleted.

8. F. NO CHANGE
   G. the one of Shakespeare
   H. those of Shakespeare's
   J. those of Shakespeare

8. (J) *English/Conventions of Standard English/Grammar and Usage/Pronoun Usage*
The original sentence is incorrect because the pronoun "that" does not agree with its plural antecedent "writings." (G) fails for the same reason. (H) uses the correct pronoun, but the use of "Shakespeare's" is incorrect. Possession is already indicated by "of." (J) is correct because the pronoun

has no heroes; his scenes only are occupied
9 10

by persons who act and speak as the reader

Passage Perfect

Notice all the space between lines here. This is a feature of the ACT test too, but it's more pronounced here because we've included the explanations. The advantage is that the questions are always lined up with the corresponding line in the passage. Just make sure you look back to the previous page to read or reread the beginning of a sentence.

thinks he or she would of spoken or acted on
11

EXPLANATIONS

"those" agrees with "writings," and the possessive is correctly formed.

9. A. NO CHANGE
B. has no heroes: his
C. has no heroes his
D. has no heroes, his

9. (A) ***English/Conventions of Standard English/No Change***
The original sentence is correct because the semicolon correctly separates two independent clauses.

10. The most appropriate placement of the underlined phrase in this sentence would be:

F. where it is now.
G. after the word *act.*
H. before the word *act.*
J. after the word *occupied.*

10. (J) ***English/Production of Writing/ Organization/Sentence-Level Structure***
The placement of "only" in the original sentence is incorrect. The original sentence intends to say that all of Shakespeare's characters act and speak as ordinary people would. (J) makes this clear by placing "only" after the word "occupied."

11. A. NO CHANGE
B. would have speaked
C. would have spoken
D. would speak

11. (C) ***English/Conventions of Standard English/Grammar and Usage/Diction***
The original sentence commits a diction error. "Would of" does not exist in standard written English. The correct expression is "would have." (C) is correct because "would have spoken" is the correct form of the verb.

EXPLANATIONS

the same occasion. This, therefore, is the praise of <u>Shakespeare that</u> (12) his drama is the mirror of life. [13]

12. F. NO CHANGE
G. Shakespeare,
H. Shakespeare. That
J. Shakespeare: that

12. (J) ***English/Conventions of Standard English/Sentence Structure/Run-On Sentences***
The original sentence is incorrect because it is a run-on sentence. (J) corrects the error; the colon serves to introduce an explanation or a restatement. (G) results in a comma splice. (H) creates a sentence fragment.

13. Is the final sentence an appropriate ending?

A. Yes, because it makes a final point about Shakespeare that was not previously mentioned and will leave the reader with something to think about.
B. Yes, because it is a summary of what was said in the introductory paragraph and will give the reader a sense of closure.
C. No, because it is irrelevant to the essay and will leave the reader confused.
D. No, because it is so repetitious that it will make the reader impatient.

13. (B) ***English/Production of Writing/ Strategy/Effective Concluding Sentence***
In the passage, the author praises Shakespeare. The final sentence appropriately summarizes the development of the passage.

Items #14–17 ask about the preceding passage as a whole.

14. What assumption is the essay's author making?

F. Everyone believes Shakespeare is a good writer.
G. No one has ever heard of Shakespeare.
H. An accurate representation of human nature is important for great art.
J. We could not understand Shakespeare's characters in the twentieth century.

Passage Perfect

Were you paying attention to the content of the passage as you read? That's what these last few questions are measuring. Don't be afraid to go back and skim through the passage again, but remember not to get bogged down answering a single question.

15. Where might you find this essay published?

A. In a book of literary criticism
B. In a journal for Renaissance scholars
C. In a Shakespeare biography
D. In a sociology textbook

16. Which of the following is NOT a strategy the author uses to make his/her point?

F. Comparison
G. Argument
H. Examples
J. Personal anecdote

17. Which of the following would most strengthen the author's argument that Shakespeare is the poet of human nature?

A. A discussion of Shakespeare's poetry
B. An analysis of the characters Hamlet and Othello
C. Biographical background on Shakespeare
D. A description of Shakespeare's Globe Theater

EXPLANATIONS

14. (H) ***English/Production of Writing/Organization/Passage-Level Structure***
In the first paragraph, the author commends Shakespeare for accurately representing human nature.

15. (A) ***English/Production of Writing/Strategy/Audience***
The topic of the passage is a favorable analysis of Shakespeare's plays. The passage is a form of literary criticism.

16. (J) ***English/Production of Writing/Organization/Passage-Level Structure***
The author compares Shakespeare to other playwrights and argues that his work is superior. Additionally, the author specifically mentions the examples of Hamlet and Othello.

17. (B) ***English/Production of Writing/Strategy/Appropriate Supporting Material***
The author mentions Hamlet and Othello as Shakespearean characters who reflect human nature. An analysis of those characters with an eye toward demonstrating the ways in which they reflect human nature would strengthen the argument of the passage.

Passage II

Diary of a Black Hole

[1]

In the course of billions of years, millions of stars may sometimes occasionally [18] become concentrated in a region, or regions, only a few light years across, and in these crowded conditions colliding [19] with one another. Some of these collisions would occur [20] at high speeds, in which case the stars are partially

18. F. NO CHANGE
G. sometimes, occasionally
H. occasionally
J. off and on

18. (H) ***English/Knowledge of Language/Style/Conciseness***
The original sentence is incorrect because it is redundant—"sometimes" and "occasionally" have the same meaning. (G) fails for the same reason. (J) is wrong because the phrase "off and on" does not have an appropriate meaning in this sentence.

19. A. NO CHANGE
B. colliding
C. and in these crowded conditions, they collide
D. which causes them to collide

19. (C) ***English/Conventions of Standard English/Grammar and Usage/Nouns and Noun Clauses***
The original sentence is incorrect because the material following the comma lacks a conjugated verb. A conjugated verb is needed because the material after the comma has no logical connection to anything that comes before the comma; this material must therefore stand on its own in an independent clause. (C) solves the problem by providing a subject and a verb, thereby creating an independent clause. (B) is wrong because the material following the comma still has no logical relationship to the rest of the sentence. "Colliding" is the participle of "to collide" and seems to be an adjective. However, there is no noun in the first part of the sentence for "colliding" to modify. (D) suffers from a similar problem. "Which" is a relative pronoun and needs an antecedent.

20. F. NO CHANGE
G. will occur
H. to occur
J. occur

EXPLANATIONS

20. (J) ***English/Conventions of Standard English/Sentence Structure/Unintended Meanings***
The incorrect use of the subjunctive "would occur" suggests that the event is contingent upon some other event, but that is not the intended meaning. (G) is wrong because the use of the future tense in this sentence is inconsistent with the use of the present tense in the rest of the paragraph. (H) is wrong because the use of the infinitive creates a meaningless sentence. (J) is the correct choice because the present tense is consistent with the rest of the paragraph.

or completely torn apart. Other collisions are gentle <u>bumps, but the stars coalesce</u>[21]. The

21. A. NO CHANGE
B. bumps, since the stars
C. bumps, and the stars coalesce
D. bumps, with the stars coalescing

21. (C) ***English/Conventions of Standard English/Sentence Structure/Problems of Coordination and Subordination***
The original sentence is incorrect because "but" signals an opposition that is not intended. "Coalescing" is the result of the "bumping," so the best choice is (C).

bigger the star <u>becomes, the more likely</u>[22] it is to be hit again and the faster it grows until

22. F. NO CHANGE
G. becomes the more
H. becomes the more,
J. becomes; the more

22. (F) ***English/Conventions of Standard English/No Change***
The original sentence is correct. A comma is needed following "becomes" to make the comparison clear. The best way to prove this is to read the sentence without the comma: "The bigger the star becomes the more...." (G) is wrong because without the comma, the sentence is subject to misreading. Finally, the comma in (H) and the semicolon in (J) actually encourage a misreading of the sentence.

it reaches instability, collapses on itself, <u>and forms a black hole</u>[23].

23. A. NO CHANGE
B. and a black hole is formed
C. and when this happens a black hole is formed
D. and thus a black hole is formed at this very moment

[2]

When most of the stars and gas in the core of a galaxy has been swallowed up by the black hole, the nucleus of the galaxy settles down to a relative quiet existence. This is probably the state of the nucleus of our own galaxy, but every hundred million years or so it may flare for a brightness 100 times its present level when a globular cluster or

EXPLANATIONS

23. (A) ***English/Conventions of Standard English/No Change***
The original sentence is correct because the present tense is consistent with the other tenses in the sentence and the verb form maintains the parallel structure "reaches," "collapses," and "forms."

24. F. NO CHANGE
G. have been
H. will have been
J. would have been

24. (G) ***English/Conventions of Standard English/Grammar and Usage/Subject-Verb Agreement***
The problem with the original sentence is subject-verb agreement. Since the subject "most of the stars and gas" is plural, the verb must be plural. However, the verb "has been" is singular. (G) is correct because the plural verb "have been" agrees with the subject. (H) is wrong because the future tense is inconsistent with the other verb tenses in the paragraph. (J) is wrong because the use of the subjunctive implies contingency, but the idea of the sentence is that the "swallowing" does occur, not that it might occur if something else happens.

25. A. NO CHANGE
B. to a relatively
C. for a relative and
D. relatively

25. (B) ***English/Conventions of Standard English/Grammar and Usage/Adjectives versus Adverbs***
The original sentence is incorrect because an adverb is required to modify the adjective "quiet." (B) is correct because the adverb "relatively" modifies "quiet." (C) is wrong because it is not idiomatic; the correct expression is "settles down to," not "settles down for." Additionally, the sentence would say the "nucleus...settles down for a relative...existence," a phrase that is meaningless. Finally, (D) destroys the logic of the sentence.

26. F. NO CHANGE
G. by
H. up to
J. OMIT the underlined portion.

EXPLANATIONS

26. (H) ***English/Conventions of Standard English/Grammar and Usage/Diction***
The original sentence is incorrect because "for" does not have the meaning required by the sentence. (H) solves this problem. (G) is wrong because it is not idiomatic. (J) is wrong because the omission of the phrase creates a meaningless sentence.

especially large gas cloud <u>of enormous size</u> **27** spirals into the nucleus.

27. A. NO CHANGE
B. of great enormity
C. which is huge
D. OMIT the underlined portion.

27. (D) ***English/Production of Writing/Style/Conciseness***
The underlined phrase "of enormous size" is needlessly repetitious of "large," so it should be deleted.

[3]

Once formed, a central "seed" black hole grows mainly through the accretion of gas accumulated in the <u>nucleus; gas</u> **28** obtained from disrupted stars, from supernova explosions, or from stars torn apart by the gravitational field of the black hole. Perhaps an entire galaxy

28. F. NO CHANGE
G. nucleus and gas
H. nucleus. Gas
J. nucleus gas

28. (G) ***English/Conventions of Standard English/Sentence Structure/Problems of Coordination and Subordination and Punctuation/Semicolons***
The material that follows the semicolon is not an independent clause because it lacks a conjugated verb; therefore, the semicolon is incorrect. The material following the semicolon must be incorporated into the main body of the sentence, so the semicolon should be changed to "and," (G). (H) is wrong because everything following the period would be a sentence fragment. As for (J), no punctuation at all creates a run-on sentence.

can collide with another galaxy, and the result would be the transfer of large amounts of gas [29]

from one galaxy to each other. [30]

EXPLANATIONS

29. A. NO CHANGE
B. galaxy to result in
C. galaxy. Such a collision could result in
D. galaxy with the results that

29. (C) *English/Knowledge of Language/Style/Clarity of Meaning*
The original sentence is incorrect because it is awkward and ambiguous. It is not clear whether or not "perhaps" is intended to govern both clauses of the sentence. (C) solves the problem by starting a new sentence. The period clearly limits the scope of "perhaps." (B) is wrong because it is also ambiguous. The sentence resulting from the substitution of (B) seems to imply that the galaxies collide in order to transfer gas, but that is not the intended meaning of the original sentence. As for (D), "that" seems to introduce a clause, but there is no verb in the remaining part of the sentence.

30. F. NO CHANGE
G. to the other
H. an other
J. and another

30. (G) *English/Conventions of Standard English/Sentence Structure/Unintended Meanings*
The original sentence has a logical expression error. The sentence means to say that one galaxy transfers its gas to the other galaxy involved in the collision; for this, the expression in (G) is necessary.

Items #31–32 ask about the preceding passage as a whole.

31. Which of the following represents the most logical sequence for the paragraphs?

A. 1, 2, 3
B. 1, 3, 2
C. 2, 3, 1
D. 3, 1, 2

32. The author's intended audience is most likely:

F. astronomers.
G. young children.
H. high school students.
J. physicists.

EXPLANATIONS

31. (B) ***English/Production of Writing/Organization/Passage-Level Structure***
This item tests understanding of the overall logic and organization of the selection. The selection should be organized chronologically. (1) describes the formation of a black hole. (3) describes its growth. (2) describes its mature stage. Thus, the best order for the selection is (1), (3), and (2).

32. (H) ***English/Production of Writing/Strategy/Audience***
The exposition is interesting and advanced, so eliminate (G). However, it is not overly technical, so eliminate both (F) and (J). Therefore, (H) is the correct choice.

TIMED QUIZ *(29 items; 20 minutes)*

DIRECTIONS: In the passages below, certain parts of the sentences have been underlined and numbered. In the right-hand column, you will find different ways of writing each underlined part; the original version is indicated by the "NO CHANGE" option. For each item, select the choice that best expresses the intended idea, is most acceptable in standard written English, or is most consistent with the overall tone and style of the passage.

There are also items that ask about a section of the passage or the passage as a whole. These items do not refer to an underlined portion of the passage; these items are preceded by statements that are enclosed in boxes.

Read the passage through once before you begin to answer the accompanying items. Finding the answers to certain items may depend on looking at material that appears several sentences beyond the item. So, be sure that you have read far enough ahead before you select your answer choice. Answers are on p. 430.

Ditch the Directions

Remember, skip the directions. You should already know from the English lessons what you're supposed to do, so don't waste time reading them again.

Passage I

The Influence of the Southwest on Artists

Georgia O'Keeffe, who's (1) death at age ninety-eight (2) closed one of the most fertile chapters of American creativity and flourished (3) as a maverick in her life and work. Since other (4) painters spent a season or two in the country trying to come to terms with the scenes and settings of the Southwest—O'Keeffe stayed a lifetime. When the canvases of other artists, working in the region (5) faded from view and

1. A. NO CHANGE
   B. which
   C. that
   D. whose

2. F. NO CHANGE
   G. at the old age of ninety-eight
   H. at the age of ninety-eight years
   J. when she was ninety-eight years old

3. A. NO CHANGE
   B. creativity, and flourished
   C. creativity—flourished
   D. creativity, flourished

4. F. NO CHANGE
   G. Because other
   H. In that other
   J. Other

5. A. NO CHANGE
   B. artists working in the region,
   C. artists working in the region
   D. artists, who worked in the region

then were neglected in the chronicle of American visual history,[6] her stylized images made an indelible and permanent[7] impression on countless eyes.

6. F. NO CHANGE
   G. got neglected then in the chronicle of American visual history
   H. were also then neglected in the American visual history chronicle
   J. then they were also totally neglected in the chronicle of American visual history

7. A. NO CHANGE
   B. indelible
   C. indelible—and permanent—
   D. indelible but permanent

Between 1900 and 1945, the region now called New Mexico both fascinated and also it perplexed[8] two generations of American artists. Despite their successes,[9] many of those artists wearied of the industrial world of the East. The vast expanse of the West offered a promise for inspiration.[10] For these artists, life and art, so separate in New York and Paris, seemed inextricably bounded[11] in Southwestern cultures. Painters of every persuasion were convinced[12] that sampling this mysterious phenomenon will strengthen[13] and enrich their own work. Most were touched by what D. H. Lawrence called the "spirit of the place." Besides the scenic beauty bathed in

8. F. NO CHANGE
   G. and perplexed
   H. while perplexing
   J. but perplexed

9. A. NO CHANGE
   B. Despite their having many successes
   C. In spite of their having their successes
   D. Ensuring successes,

10. F. NO CHANGE
    G. America's West, with its vast expanse, offered an inspiring promise.
    H. America's vast expanse of the West offered a promise for inspiration.
    J. Offering a promise of inspiration to the artists was the vast expanse of the American West.

11. A. NO CHANGE
    B. inextricably bound
    C. inextricable bounding
    D. inextricably bounding

12. F. NO CHANGE
    G. could be convinced
    H. will be convinced
    J. are convincing

13. A. NO CHANGE
    B. would strengthen
    C. strengthens
    D. strengthening

clear golden <u>light. The</u> [14] rich traditions of New Mexico's Indian and Hispanic people <u>who were living there</u> [15] became frequent subjects of the artists who traveled to Taos and Santa Fe.

Use POE

Remember, don't get stuck on tough questions. If you're having trouble with a question, guess and move on. You can always come back to the question later if you have time.

14. F. NO CHANGE
G. light, the
H. light the
J. light: the

15. A. NO CHANGE
B. who lived there
C. living there
D. OMIT the underlined portion.

Items #16–17 ask about the preceding passage as a whole.

16. Is the author's quote of D. H. Lawrence in the last paragraph appropriate?

F. Yes, because the author is talking about how this spirit inspired artists, and the quote strengthens his argument.
G. No, because the author has already made his point about the spirit, and the quote is redundant.
H. No, because the author does not make it clear that Lawrence is an authority on the subject.
J. Yes, because it is always a good idea to end an article with a quotation.

17. How might the author have developed the essay so that it was more interesting?

A. The author could have told an anecdote about D. H. Lawrence.
B. The author could have eliminated all mention of Georgia O'Keeffe.
C. The author could have discussed the settling of New Mexico.
D. The author could have been more specific about the other artists who went to the Southwest.

Passage II

Chippewa Chief Demands Timber Payment

In early November 1850, the work of a logging detail from Fort Gaines in the Minnesota Territory was interrupted by a party of Chippewa warriors who demanded payment for the timber. The loggers refused, so [18] the Indians, acting at the direction of Chief Hole-in-the-Day [19] confiscated the government's oxen. The loggers had established their camp on Chippewa lands without his authorizing it [20]. Therefore [21], in a move designed to force reimbursements for the timber, Hole-in-the-Day was ordering [22] his braves to seize the oxen.

Captain John Todd, the commanding officer at Fort Gaines, demanded that the cattle had to be returned to them [23]. The chief's reply was firm, and at the same time, it was friendly [24]. In his message to Captain Todd, Hole-in-the-Day

Ace the Pace

When you start working on a new passage, check your pace. At this point you should have about 8 or 9 minutes left. If you don't have that much time left, pick up your pace a little bit.

18. F. NO CHANGE
G. The loggers refused—
H. The loggers refused:
J. The loggers refused so

19. A. NO CHANGE
B. that acted at the direction of Chief Hole-in-the-Day,
C. acting at the direction of Chief Hole-in-the-Day,
D. (acting at the direction of Chief Hole-in-the-Day),

20. F. NO CHANGE
G. without his authorization
H. without their authorizing it
J. without his authorization of it

21. A. NO CHANGE
B. Henceforth
C. Since
D. On the contrary

22. F. NO CHANGE
G. gave orders that
H. orders
J. ordered

23. A. NO CHANGE
B. the return of the cattle
C. the cattle's returning
D. that they return the cattle

24. F. NO CHANGE
G. but, at the same time, it was friendly
H. yet friendly
J. at the same time—friendly

explained that he had <u>delayed to seize</u> [25] the cattle until he could meet Todd in council and had sent a messenger to the officer requesting a conference at Crow Wing. When Todd did not come, he <u>acted, additionally</u> [26] he later decided that since the army had not paid for timber cut the previous winter, he intended to keep the oxen until the tribe <u>was reimbursed by</u> [27] all the timber taken for the fort. Hole-in-the-Day concluded by saying, "Do not think hard of me, but I do as others would—the timber is mine." [28]

25. A. NO CHANGE
B. delayed to have seized
C. delayed to seized
D. delayed seizing

26. F. NO CHANGE
G. acted but additionally
H. acted. Additionally,
J. acted additionally,

27. A. NO CHANGE
B. reimbursed for
C. reimbursed
D. was reimbursed for

28. Is the author's use of the quote in the final paragraph appropriate?

F. Yes, because it neatly summarizes the main point of the essay.
G. No, because the chief's thoughts were irrelevant to the events.
H. Yes, but the author should have included a quotation from Captain Todd.
J. No, because quotations have no place in expository writing.

Item #29 asks about the preceding passage as a whole.

29. Which of the following best describes the overall character of the essay?

A. Description of a scene
B. Narration of events
C. Comparison of two theories
D. Argument for a change

ENGLISH
REVIEW

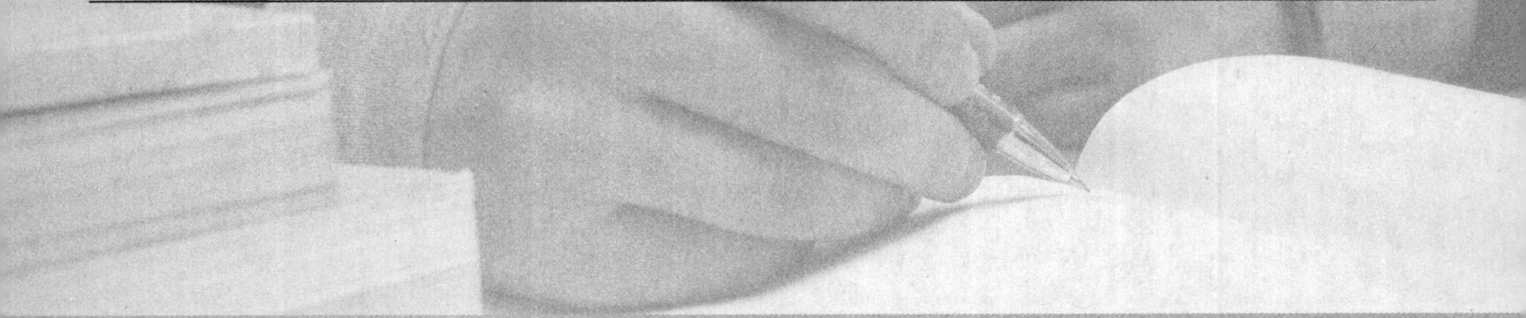

This section contains additional English items for further practice. Answers are on page 430.

DIRECTIONS: In the passages below, certain parts of the sentences have been underlined and numbered. In the right-hand column, you will find different ways of writing each underlined part; the original version is indicated by the "NO CHANGE" option. For each item, select the choice that best expresses the intended idea, is most acceptable in standard written English, or is most consistent with the overall tone and style of the passage.

There are also items that ask about a section of the passage or the passage as a whole. These items do not refer to an underlined portion of the passage; these items are preceded by statements that are enclosed in boxes.

Read the passage through once before you begin to answer the accompanying items. Finding the answers to certain items may depend on looking at material that appears several sentences beyond the item. So, be sure that you have read far enough ahead before you select your answer choice.

Passage I

Significance of Symbolism in Medieval Art

Art of the Middle Ages is first and foremost a sacred script, the symbols and meanings of which are well settled 1. A circular halo placed vertically behind the head of a figure signifies sainthood, meanwhile 2 the halo impressed with a cross signifies divinity.

1. A. NO CHANGE
   B. is well settled
   C. are settled well
   D. would be settled

2. F. NO CHANGE
   G. sainthood, because
   H. sainthood because
   J. sainthood, while

A tower with a window indicates a village, and should an angel be watching from the battlements, that city is thereby identified as Jerusalem.

Mathematics is also an important element of this iconography. "The Divine Wisdom," wrote Saint Augustine, "reveals itself everywhere in numbers." A doctrine derived from the Neoplatonists who revived the teachings of Pythagoras. Furthermore, numbers require symmetry. At Chartres, a stained-glass window shows the four prophets Isaac, Ezekiel, Daniel, and Jeremiah carrying on their shoulders the four evangelists Matthew, Mark, Luke, and John.

Every painting is also an allegory, showing us one thing and inviting us to see another. In this respect, the artist was asked to imitate God, who had hidden a profound meaning behind the literal and who wished nature to be a moral lesson to man. In a painting of the final judgment, the foolish virgins can be seen by us at the left hand of Jesus and the wise can be seen on the right, and we understand that this symbolizes those

3. A. NO CHANGE
B. (Do NOT begin a new paragraph) A tower
C. Towers
D. Having a tower

4. F. NO CHANGE
G. numbers," which
H. numbers." This doctrine was
J. numbers" which

5. A. NO CHANGE
B. Neoplatonists that
C. Neoplatonist's that
D. Neoplatonist's who

6. F. NO CHANGE
G. (Do NOT begin a new paragraph) Every painting
H. However, every painting
J. (Do NOT begin a new paragraph) However, every painting

7. A. NO CHANGE
B. Furthermore, the artist was
C. The artist, however, was
D. Generally, artists are

8. F. NO CHANGE
G. meaning which was behind
H. meaning being behind
J. meaning behind and in back of

9. A. NO CHANGE
B. by all of us
C. by each of us
D. OMIT the underlined portion.

who are lost and those that have been saved.
10

Within such a system, even the most
11
mediocre talent was elevated by the genius of centuries, and the first artist of the
12
Renaissance broke with the tradition at great risk. Even when they are great, medieval artists are no more than the equals of the old masters who passively followed the sacred rules. When they are not outstanding, they scarcely avoid banality and insignificance in
13
their religious works.

10. F. NO CHANGE
G. those who have been saved
H. those who are saved
J. the saved

11. A. NO CHANGE
B. (Do NOT begin a new paragraph) Within such a system
C. (Do NOT begin a new paragraph) Inside of such a system
D. (Do NOT begin a new paragraph) To be inside such a system

12. F. NO CHANGE
G. with
H. however
J. since

13. A. NO CHANGE
B. always
C. ever
D. OMIT the underlined portion.

Items #14–16 ask about the preceding passage as a whole.

14. The author most likely wrote this essay for which of the following?

F. A scholarly art journal
G. A book tracing the history of mathematics
H. A history of the Catholic Church
J. A book surveying the history of Western art

15. The author relies on which of the following to develop the passage?

A. Examples
B. Extensive quotations from other authorities
C. Statistics
D. Personal experience

16. The author probably quotes Saint Augustine in order to:

F. ridicule his position.
G. emphasize the importance of numbers and symmetry.
H. prove the importance of Church teaching.
J. illustrate Augustine's knowledge of art.

Passage II

Pursuit of the Bottomless Pit

A persistent and universal symbol in the mythology of virtually every <u>culture, is</u> [17] that of a bottomless pit or an engulfing whirlpool.

17. A. NO CHANGE
B. culture is
C. culture are
D. cultures are

The whirlpool is the maw of the <u>abyss: and those</u> [18] venturing too close are dragged inward toward chaos by an irresistible force. Socrates <u>(a Greek philosopher who committed suicide)</u> [19] talked of a chasm that pierced the world straight through from side to side. Ulysses <u>also encountering it</u> [20], as did a mythical Cherokee who escaped, but not before he was drawn down to the narrowest circle of the maelstrom where he could peer into the netherworld of the dead. <u>Many primitive cultures bury their dead with tools in the belief that the tools will be useful to them in the afterlife.</u> [21]

18. F. NO CHANGE
G. abyss, and those
H. abyss meanwhile those
J. abyss due to the fact that

19. A. NO CHANGE
B. (a philosopher from Greece who committed suicide)
C. (a Greek philosopher who had committed suicide)
D. OMIT the underlined portion.

20. F. NO CHANGE
G. also encountered it
H. also encountered them
J. encountered them also

21. For the sake of the logic and coherence of this paragraph, the underlined sentence should be:

A. left as it is now.
B. placed before the word *Ulysses.*
C. placed at the end of the passage.
D. omitted.

On the other hand, the search for a solution [22] to one of astronomys' most persistent and [23] perplexing riddles, black holes, could be viewed by one [24] as a continuation of the search for [25] the whirlpool that is the maw of the abyss, a depth our telescopes cannot reach and from which nothing will have returned [26]. What is incredible to contemplate, and what sets us [27] apart from the ancients, is that we think we have a fair idea not only as to [28] how they are formed, but also how large they are and so forth. A combination of theory and observation have led to [29] the growing suspicion among astrophysicists that the nucleus of virtually every galaxy harbors a massive black hole.

22. F. NO CHANGE
G. The search
H. (Do NOT begin a new paragraph) The search
J. Also, the search

23. A. NO CHANGE
B. astronomy's
C. astronomy
D. astronomys

24. F. NO CHANGE
G. by one astronomer
H. by those
J. OMIT the underlined portion.

25. A. NO CHANGE
B. continuing the search of
C. continuation to the search for
D. continuation for the search for

26. F. NO CHANGE
G. will return
H. returns
J. returning

27. A. NO CHANGE
B. setting us
C. and that sets us
D. and we are set

28. F. NO CHANGE
G. about
H. not about
J. OMIT the underlined portion.

29. A. NO CHANGE
B. has led to
C. has led
D. led

Passage III

Tradition Preservation During Meiji Restoration

Instead of casting aside traditional values during the Meiji Restoration of 1888, those who strove to dismantle feudalism and to modernize the country chose to preserve three traditions as the foundations <u>on which they could build a modern Japan upon</u>.[30]

The <u>older</u>[31] tradition and basis of the entire Japanese value system was <u>respect for and even worshipping</u>[32] the Emperor. During the early centuries of Japanese history, the Shinto cult, in which <u>the Imperial family traced its ancestry to the Sun Goddess</u>,[33] became the people's sustaining faith. <u>Being later subordinated</u>[34] to imported Buddhism and Confucianism, Shintoism was perpetuated in Ise and Izumo, the great shrines of the Imperial family, until the Meiji modernizers established it as a quasi state religion to unify

30. F. NO CHANGE
G. on which they could be building a modern Japan upon
H. upon which they could build a modern Japan
J. upon which they someday could probably build a modern Japan

31. A. NO CHANGE
B. oldest
C. old
D. OMIT the underlined portion.

32. F. NO CHANGE
G. respecting and even worshipping
H. respect for and even worship of
J. respect and even worship

33. A. NO CHANGE
B. the Imperial family got its ancestry traced back to the Sun Goddess
C. the Imperial family's ancestry was traced back to the Sun Goddess
D. the Sun Goddess was considered to be the ancestor of the Imperial family

34. F. NO CHANGE
G. Later subordinated
H. Later subordinated,
J. Subordinated later,

the people and restore the Emperor as the symbol of national unity and the object of loyalty <u>to the Japanese</u>. **35**

<u>Another tradition that was enduring</u> **36** was the hierarchical system of social relations based on feudalism. Confucianism prescribed <u>a pattern by</u> **37** ethical conduct between groups of people within a fixed hierarchy. Four of the five Confucian relationships <u>(those between ruler and subject, husband and wife, father and son, and elder brother and younger brother)</u> **38** <u>were</u> **39** <u>vertical since they</u> **40** required loyalty and obedience from the inferior toward the superior <u>and benevolence and protection from the superior to the inferior</u>. **41** Only the

35. A. NO CHANGE
B. the Japanese had
C. by the Japanese
D. for the Japanese

36. F. NO CHANGE
G. Another tradition
H. (Do NOT begin a new paragraph) Another tradition
J. The other tradition

37. A. NO CHANGE
B. patterns by
C. a pattern for
D. patterns with

38. Is the author's use of parentheses appropriate?

F. Yes, because the examples are irrelevant to the passage.
G. Yes, because although the information is relevant, the material is not part of the main development of the passage.
H. No, because the examples are relevant to the meaning of the sentence.
J. No, because the material is essential to the reader's understanding of the passage.

39. A. NO CHANGE
B. was
C. are
D. could be

40. F. NO CHANGE
G. vertical, they
H. vertical, since it
J. vertical, being they

41. A. NO CHANGE
B. and also benevolence and protection from the superior to the inferior
C. with the benevolence and protection being from the superior to the inferior
D. and from the superior to the inferior, the benevolence and protection

fifth relationship, that between friend and friend—was horizontal. A third tradition was respect for learning, another basic idea of Confucius. In traditional Japan, study was the absolute duty of man. It was a religious mandate as well as a social duty and was a means of promoting a harmonious and stable society. The individual's behavior was strictly prescribed by law and custom. Only the Samurai had the right to retaliate with force if they were displeased. But his primary duty was to the lord.

(42: relationship, that; 43: A; 44: idea of Confucius; 45: mandate as well; 46: The individual's behavior; 47: But his)

42. F. NO CHANGE
G. relationship that
H. relationship—that
J. relationship

43. A. NO CHANGE
B. Furthermore, a
C. (Begin a new paragraph) A
D. (Begin a new paragraph) Also a

44. F. NO CHANGE
G. Confucius idea
H. idea of Confucianism
J. Confucianism idea

45. A. NO CHANGE
B. mandate as well as being
C. mandate as well,
D. mandate,

46. F. NO CHANGE
G. An individual behavior
H. Behavior by individual's
J. The individuals behavior

47. A. NO CHANGE
B. But their
C. Being that their
D. Because their

Item #48 asks about the preceding passage as a whole.

48. The best description of the development of this essay would be:

F. argument and rebuttal.
G. a personal narrative.
H. a three-part exposition.
J. question and answer.

STRATEGY SUMMARY

ENGLISH STRATEGIES

1. After you have memorized the directions, they can be safely ignored; therefore, do not waste valuable test time by re-reading instructions.

2. Read the entire selection for comprehension of the overall meaning. Look for possible errors. Mentally note how to correct possible errors.

3. Study the answer choices, looking for one that matches your anticipated answer.

4. Compare the answer choices. What makes them different from one another?

5. Do not choose answer choices that introduce new errors or change the meaning of the selection.

6. Use the additional strategies presented below when searching for errors.

STRATEGIES FOR CONVENTIONS OF STANDARD ENGLISH CONTENT AREA

Check for Grammatical Errors

a) Look for obvious subject-verb agreement problems. The test-writers may try to obscure agreement by inserting material between the subject and the verb, inverting the sentence structure so that the verb precedes the subject, or introducing compound subjects.

b) Check for proper pronoun usage. Remember that all pronouns must have antecedents. The pronoun must clearly refer to the antecedent and must agree in case, number, and person.

c) Be alert to the proper usage of adjectives and adverbs. Note that adjectives modify nouns, while adverbs modify verbs. Also, adjectives, not adverbs, follow linking verbs. Lastly, watch out for adjectives posing as adverbs. Sometimes, adjectives can be transformed into adverbs by adding "-ly," so it is important to identify whether the modifier is an adjective or an adverb.

d) Watch for double negatives. Even though double negatives are sometimes used colloquially, they are not grammatically correct.

e) Check for proper noun clause introductions. A noun clause is a group of words that functions as the subject of a sentence and must be introduced with "that." Note that "because" and "why" should not be used to introduce noun clauses.

f) Watch for illogical comparisons. Comparisons can only be made between similar objects. Be alert to the use of the comparative form of an adjective (for comparing two objects) and the superlative form of an adjective (for comparing three or more objects). Remember that some adjectives and adverbs express the highest degree of quality; therefore, they cannot be improved upon.

g) Check for improper verb and mood shifts. The same verb tense and mood should be used within a sentence or paragraph unless there is a valid reason for a change. Also, be alert to the improper usage of verb tenses in general. Make sure that the verb tense within a sentence or a paragraph is logical.

h) Make sure that the choice of verb tense in a sentence reflects the sequence and the duration of the events described.

i) Check for diction errors such as wrong prepositions, improper word choice, and gerund-infinitive switching.

Check for Sentence Structure Errors

a) Check to see if the sentence is a run-on.

b) Be aware of comma splice errors in sentences.

c) Check to see if the sentence is a fragment.

d) Make sure the sentence contains logical coordinating conjunctions.

e) Watch for faulty parallelism in a sentence. Note that whenever elements of a sentence perform similar or equal functions, they should have the same form.

f) Be alert for sentence structures in which a thought that is interrupted by intervening material is completed later in the sentence. Check that the interrupted thought is correctly completed. A simple way to check for this type of error is to read the sentence without the intervening material—the sentence should make sense, be grammatically correct, and represent a complete thought.

g) Look for misplaced modifiers. Modifiers should be placed as close as possible to what they modify. Errors in placement of modifiers create ambiguous and illogical constructions.

h) Be alert to misplacements or omissions of certain elements of a sentence. These errors lead to unintended meanings. Make sure the intended meaning of the sentence follows from its logical structure.

Check for Punctuation Errors

a) Check to see if commas are used correctly in the sentence. The following list summarizes the most important uses and misuses of commas:

(1) Use a comma before a coordinating conjunction joining two clauses.

(2) Use commas for clarity.

(3) Use commas to separate words in a series.

(4) Use commas to mark the end of an introductory phrase.

(5) Use pairs of commas to set off appositive, parenthetical, and nonrestrictive elements.

(6) A comma should not be used to separate a subject from its verb.

(7) Commas should not be used to set off restrictive or necessary clauses or phrases.

(8) A comma should not be used in place of a conjunction.

b) Check for correct semicolon usage. The following list summarizes the appropriate uses of semicolons:

(1) Use a semicolon to separate two complete ideas.

(2) Use a semicolon to separate a series of phrases with commas.

(3) Use a semicolon to separate independent clauses.

(4) Do not use semicolons to separate dependent clauses.

c) Check for correct end-stop punctuation. Make sure that any material that has a period is a complete sentence.

d) Check for correct usage of dashes. The following are the rules for situations requiring the use of a dash:

(1) Use a dash for emphasis or to set off an explanatory group of words.

(2) Use a dash before a word or group of words that indicates a summation or reversal of what preceded it.

(3) Use a dash to mark a sudden break in thought that leaves a sentence unfinished.

e) Check for correct apostrophe usage. Apostrophes are most commonly used to show possession. They are also used when a noun is used to modify another noun or a gerund.

f) Check to see if a punctuation mark is needed to clarify the selection.

STRATEGIES FOR PRODUCTION OF WRITING CONTENT AREA

Check to See if the Strategy Used by the Writer Is Appropriate

a) Make sure that all supporting material is appropriate to the selection.

b) Be alert to opening, transitional, and concluding sentences. Check to see if they are effective or if they need improvement.

c) Read the selection for the main ideas and identify the main purpose of the entire passage.

d) Look for diction, purpose, and tone clues that identify the writer's audience.

Check for Organization Errors

a) Check the sentence-level structure. Sentences should be in logical and appropriate order within the paragraph.

b) Check the paragraph-level structure. Paragraphs should be divided logically and unified around a central theme.

c) Check the passage-level structure. Passages should follow an identifiable pattern of development, with paragraphs appearing in a logical order.

STRATEGIES FOR KNOWLEDGE OF LANGUAGE CONTENT AREA

Check for Stylistic Problems

a) Make sure that the sentences are concise and to the point.

(1) Look for awkward sentences or weak passive verbs.

(2) Look for needlessly wordy sentences.

b) Check for ambiguous sentences. Such sentences run two or more ideas together and require further clarification to separate and connect the disparate ideas.

c) Check for idiomatic usage.

READING

Course Concept Outline

I. TEST MECHANICS 86

- **A. Overview** 86
- **B. Anatomy** *(Items #1–4)* 86–88
- **C. Pacing** 88
- **D. Time Trial** *(Items #1–3)* 89–90
- **E. Game Plan** 90
  1. Quickly Preview the Test Section, but Skip the Directions 90
  2. Personalize the Passage Order 90
  3. Read Any Introductory Notes 90
  4. Preview the Passage 90–91
  5. Preview the Item Stems 91–92
  6. Read the Passage 92
  7. Answer the Items 92–93
  8. Remember to Review 93
  9. Don't Be Distracted by the Clock 93

II. LESSON | PRELIMINARIES[1]

- **A. Passage Profiles**
- **B. Item Profiles**
- **C. Facts about Passages**
  1. Four Passage Topics, Unfamiliar Subjects
  2. Passages Test Comprehension, Not "Speed-Reading"

III. LESSON 1 | ITEM-TYPES AND STRATEGIES 96

- **A. Item-Types** 97
  1. Main Idea *(Items #1–2)* 97
  2. Explicit Detail *(Items #3–5)* 97
  3. Vocabulary *(Item #6)* 97
  4. Development *(Items #7–8)* 98

1 Some concepts in this Course Concept Outline are not illustrated through examples in your student text but may be covered by your instructor in class. They are included here to provide a complete outline of your course.

5. Implied Idea *(Items #9–11)* 98
6. Application *(Items #12–13)* 98
7. Voice *(Items #14–15)* 99

B. Strategies **99**

1. Three Reading Comprehension Levels
   a) General Theme
   b) Specific Points
   c) Evaluation
2. Using the Three Comprehension Levels
3. Five Steps to Approaching Passages *(Items #16–24)* 99–101
   a) Label Passages as "Easy" or "Hard"
   b) Preview First and Last Sentences of Selection
   c) Preview Item Stems
   d) Read the Passage
   e) Answer the Items
4. Item-Type Strategies 102
   a) Main Idea Clues *(Items #25–27)* 102–103
   b) Explicit Detail Clues *(Item #28)* 103
   c) Vocabulary Clues *(Items #29–33)* 103
   d) Development Clues *(Items #34–35)* 103
   e) Implied Idea Clues *(Items #36–37)* 103–104
   f) Application Clues *(Item #38)* 104
   g) Voice Clues *(Item #39)* 104

IV. LESSON 2 | PAIRED PASSAGES **105**

A. Questions that Compare and Contrast *(Items #1–9)* **105–108**
B. Further Practice *(Items #10–33)* **109–114**

V. LESSON 3 | FURTHER USE OF READING STRATEGIES, PART 1 .... **115**

VI. LESSON 4 | FURTHER USE OF READING STRATEGIES, PART 2 .... **125**

VII. QUIZZES **135**

A. Directed Study Quiz *(Items #1–18)* **136–144**
B. Timed Quiz *(Items #1–17)* **145–148**

VIII. REVIEW **149**

IX. STRATEGY SUMMARY **163**

READING

TEST MECHANICS

TEST MECHANICS

Reading

OVERVIEW

> The Cambridge Edge
>
> Remember, you don't need any prior knowledge of the reading passage topics to do well on the test. Reading passages test *comprehension*, not subject knowledge.

The Reading Test consists of four sections, with either one passage or two shorter paired passages (approximately 700 words total), each followed by 10 items. You will read a passage and answer the items based upon what is stated or implied in the reading selection.

You will be given one passage or set of paired passages from each of the following four categories: Prose Fiction, Social Science, Humanities, and Natural Science. In most cases, the passage will be about a topic with which you are not familiar. The test-writers choose unusual topics so that the Reading Test will assess your reading skill and not your prior knowledge.

The time limit for the 40 items on the Reading Test is 35 minutes. Given the time limit, you obviously need to work quickly. The exam, however, is not a test of "speed-reading." Instead, the exam is a test of reading *comprehension*.

ANATOMY

> **DIRECTIONS:** The passage below is followed by a set of items. Read the passage and choose the best answer for each item. You may refer to the passage as often as necessary to answer the items.

The directions make Reading items sound easy: read this and answer the items. As a result, the directions aren't very helpful, and you can ignore them from now on.

(**NOTE:** *Given space restrictions, this passage is much shorter than those used on the ACT test.)*

PASSAGE I

SOCIAL SCIENCE: This passage is adapted from a government report about the history of alcohol abuse.

Most of the passages include an introductory note telling you where the passage comes from. A note may provide some useful information, so you should read it.

The movement to prohibit alcohol began in the early years of the nineteenth century. Local societies formed in New York and Massachusetts to promote temperance in the use of alcohol. Many of these societies were affiliated with Protestant evangelical denominations and met in local churches. As time passed, most temperance societies changed their goal to call for complete abstinence from all alcohol.

Typically, reading passages discuss an unfamiliar topic. Even if you know something about Prohibition, that information may or may not be helpful since you'll only be asked about this particular passage.

This passage is organized chronologically. The first paragraph talks about the "early years of the nineteenth century," in other words, the early 1800s.

In 1919, largely in response to these efforts, the Eighteenth Amendment to the Constitution was passed. This Amendment banned the production, transportation, and sale of all alcoholic beverages. The Amendment, also known as the Prohibition Amendment, provided for concurrent enforcement by both federal and state law. By 1920, in addition to the federal Volstead Act, the nation had laws in thirty-three states prohibiting alcohol entirely.

The second paragraph starts with 1919. Then, the passage briefly traces the events leading up to Prohibition.

Prohibition, however, proved unworkable. Bootleggers and speakeasies quickly organized to satisfy the public's thirst for alcohol. Thirteen years later, the "Noble Experiment," doomed by the difficulty of enforcement, ended with the repeal of the Prohibition Amendment.

The third paragraph explains why Prohibition failed: people wanted to drink, so bootleggers and illegal clubs satisfied that demand. Eventually, Prohibition was repealed.

The Cambridge Edge

The Reading Test is an open-book test—you can refer back to the passage at any time.

1. The passage is primarily concerned with the:

A. social problems caused by alcohol abuse.
B. founding of anti-alcohol temperance societies.
C. origins of Prohibition and its subsequent failure.
D. efforts to enforce Prohibition legislation.

1. (C) *This is a common type of Reading item: the item asks you to identify the main idea of the passage. The passage discusses the origins and failure of Prohibition.*

2. According to the passage, in the early nineteenth century, temperance societies originally:

F. encouraged moderation in alcohol use.
G. demanded the repeal of the Eighteenth Amendment.
H. supported efforts to enforce the Volstead Act.
J. refused to align with religious groups.

2. (F) *This item asks about something that is specifically stated in the passage. The author clearly states that the temperance societies were originally founded to "promote temperance" (line 4) as opposed to complete prohibition.*

3. The passage implies that Prohibition failed because:

A. religious organizations withdrew their support for the program.
B. the repeal of the Eighteenth Amendment was only experimental.
C. too many states passed laws prohibiting the sale of alcohol.
D. widespread demand for alcohol made enforcement impossible.

3. (D) *This item requires that you "read between the lines" of the passage. In the third paragraph, the author does not specifically say why Prohibition failed, but you can figure it out from what's said: people simply refused to quit consuming alcohol, even if it was illegal.*

4. In line 17, the word *concurrent* means:

F. unsuccessful.
G. shared.
H. practicable.
J. intermittent.

4. **(G)** *This item asks you for the definition of a term in the context of the passage. The passage states that the federal government and the states were given "concurrent" authority and that the states, as well as the federal government, passed laws against alcohol. So, "concurrent" must mean something like "joint" or "shared."*

PACING

Ace the Pace

Here's our list of four top tips to ace the pace on the Reading Test:

- Don't "speed-read." The reading test rewards *comprehension*, not raw speed.
- Stay on task. Though "speed-reading" is a bad idea, it is important to cover as many items as possible.
- Don't get bogged down. If no answer is obvious after spending a reasonable amount of time on an item (60 seconds maximum), then eliminate all the wrong answers, guess, and move on.
- Don't become obsessed with time. Pacing guidelines are just that—guidelines. Encourage students to work quickly but accurately and not to dwell on the exact timing.

The Reading Test has 40 items and a 35-minute time limit. The fact that there are four sections (with either one passage or two shorter paired passages in each section) of approximately equal length, each with the same number of items, and a 35-minute time limit leads naturally to the conclusion that you should spend eight minutes and 45 seconds on each passage—and that's a pretty good plan. The following table summarizes the timing for this approach.

TASK	ALLOTTED TIME	TOTAL TIME SPENT
Read the first selected passage	2.5 minutes	2.5 minutes
Answer the accompanying items	6.25 minutes*	8.75 minutes
Read the second selected passage	2.5 minutes	11.25 minutes
Answer the accompanying items	6.25 minutes*	17.5 minutes
Read the third selected passage	2.5 minutes	20 minutes
Answer the accompanying items	6.25 minutes*	26.25 minutes
Read the fourth selected passage	2.5 minutes	28.75 minutes
Answer the accompanying items	6.25 minutes*	35 minutes

*Approximately 37 seconds per item

Note that the table refers to "first selected passage," "second selected passage," and so on. These references are to the order in which you decide to do the passages, not to the order in which they are presented in your test booklet. For reasons discussed in the "Game Plan" feature, you might choose to start with the passage that appears last. It's up to you.

TIME TRIAL *(3 items; 3 minutes)*

DIRECTIONS: The passage below is followed by a set of items. Read the passage and choose the best answer for each item. You may refer to the passage as often as necessary to answer the items.

PASSAGE I

NATURAL SCIENCE: This passage is excerpted from an essay about the possible reasons for the extinction of salmon runs in New England rivers.

Folklore holds that Atlantic salmon were once so abundant in New England rivers that early colonists walked across the backs of the fish as they ran up the rivers in spring. Then, according to the received wisdom, at the turn of the nineteenth century, increasing pollution in the rivers and the construction of large dams across rivers caused salmon to become severely depleted. If this theory were accurate, then there should be ample archaeological evidence that salmon played a major role in the diets of the aboriginal peoples of New England. But in site after site, although bones of many other fish species have been recovered, no salmon bones have been found. It's more likely that the accounts of salmon were embellished by early writers.

In fact, salmon did not begin to colonize New England streams until a period of climatic cooling known as the Little Ice Age (C.E. 1550–1800). At the end of this period, the climatic warming created less favorable environmental conditions for salmon. Thus, their range retracted. The idea that initial colonization did not occur until this time, and then only as a temporary range expansion, explains the lack of salmon in prehistoric sites and the depletion of the fish at the end of the eighteenth century.

While authorities such as D. W. Lufkin have stated that "the circumstances leading to the demise of *Salmo salar* are relatively simple to identify" and have cited dams, pollution, logging practices, and over-fishing, causes behind its demise are more complex, with ecological and climatological bases. If pollution and dams were the major cause of the extinctions, then why were the runs not made extinct on the Penobscot, a heavily dammed and polluted river in Maine? Why did salmon runs become extinct downstream of the dams on the Connecticut River? The general lack of success in salmon restoration programs over the last two centuries suggests a fundamental ecological cause for impoverished salmon runs in New England rather than an anthropogenic one.

1. The primary purpose of the passage is to:

A. propose a long term plan for restoring salmon runs to the rivers of New England.
B. undermine the theory that human activity caused the extinction of salmon runs in New England rivers.
C. demonstrate that anthropogenic factors are often more powerful than natural ones in shaping the environment.
D. provide evidence that the disappearance of *Salmo salar* was caused by the damming and pollution of the rivers.

2. The author cites the lack of salmon bones in archaeological digs as evidence that:

F. the salmon population in New England rivers declined sharply after the end of the Little Ice Age.
G. aboriginal Americans, who consumed other fish species, refused to eat the abundant salmon.
H. salmon were not available to aboriginal Americans before the time of the arrival of the first colonists.
J. anthropogenic factors were largely responsible for the extinction of the salmon runs.

3. It can be inferred that D. W. Lufkin would most likely:

   A. agree with the author that the primary causes of the depletion of salmon stocks are climatological.
   B. accept the author's contention that early reports about the abundance of salmon were greatly exaggerated.
   C. reject the author's thesis and insist that the causes of salmon extinction are anthropogenic.
   D. disagree with the author that salmon stocks have declined precipitously since the end of the eighteenth century.

GAME PLAN

Quickly Preview the Test Section, but Skip the Directions

Last-minute adjustments to the test format are theoretically possible (though not common), so check the test section before you start to work, especially the number of passages, the number of items, and the time limit. And yes, the test-writers always tell you to "read the directions carefully." But they don't tell you that you have to read them during the test. Instead, become familiar with them *before* test day. That way, you won't waste 30 seconds or more (enough time to answer an item) re-reading directions with which you are already familiar.

Personalize the Passage Order

Remember that you don't have to do the items in the order in which they are presented in the booklet. For some sections, like the math section, doing problems in order (more or less) makes good sense because the difficulty of the questions increases as you move through the test. However, on the Reading Test it is a sound strategy to make a choice about the order in which you're going to work through the section. You may decide to do the reading passages in the order presented, or you may want to change the order.

What factors should you consider? Start by reading the introductory sentence to see how easy it is to understand. Then skim over the passage to see how challenging the vocabulary is. Label two passages as EASY in the margin of your test booklet, based on this quick preview. And label one passage HARD. That leaves you with one passage of middle-level difficulty.

Next, start working on the two easy passages. Begin with whichever passage has a topic that interests you more. Then work on the other easy passage, then the middle-level passage, and finally the hard passage.

Read Any Introductory Notes

Many passages, particularly longer ones, will include an introductory note telling you where the passage comes from and maybe some other information. Sometimes, this information is useful for getting a better understanding of the passage. Therefore, before starting on a passage and items, always read any introductory notes.

Preview the Passage

Before you begin reading a particular passage, take 15 to 30 seconds to preview key sentences. Key sentences are the first and last sentences of the passage and the first sentence of each paragraph. Why preview? First sentences are often topic sentences, so reading a series of topic sentences will tell you what the author is trying to say, and it can give you an outline of the development of the passage. Sometimes, though not always, the last sentence is a conclusion.

To see how this can work, preview the following passage about solar energy, in which only the key sentences are visible.

At the present time, 98 percent of world energy consumption comes from sources such as fossil fuels. [redacted]

Our energy consumption amounts to about one-ten thousandth of the energy we receive from the sun. [redacted]

It is often stated that the growth rate will decline or that energy conservation measures will preclude any long-range problem. [redacted]

The only practical means of avoiding the problem of thermal pollution is the use of solar energy. [redacted]

To see what you can learn from just a few sentences, think about these questions:

What's the passage about?

- Gas mileage.
- Space exploration.
- Solar energy.

What is a common attitude about energy conservation?

- That it doesn't work.
- That it might work.
- That it will probably work.

What's the author's view on solar energy?

- It doesn't work.
- It's unnecessary.
- It's absolutely essential.

The answers can be determined from the few sentences you have previewed: the passage is about solar energy. A lot of people think conservation will probably solve all our problems. The author believes solar energy is necessary.

Preview the Item Stems

Additionally, before reading a particular passage, you may find it helpful to preview the item stems, which are presented either as questions or incomplete statements. If a stem mentions a key word or phrase, make a mental note and look for it as you read the selection. See what you would learn from the following items, in which only the item stems are visible.

1. According to the passage, the most important disadvantage of nuclear energy is:

A. [redacted]
B.
C.
D.

Previewing would tell you to look for certain information in your reading. The first stem uses the phrase "most important disadvantage of nuclear energy." So, you know that the passage will discuss disadvantages of nuclear energy. When you find the "most important" one, mark that reference so that you can answer this item.

2. According to the author, shifting climate patterns will have all of the following effects EXCEPT:

F.
G.
H.
J.

The second stem tells you that the author discusses "shifting climate patterns," probably in some detail since the passage mentions multiple effects. Each time you find one of the effects, mark it so that when you answer this item you can eliminate those choices that mention such effects. ("EXCEPT" means to look for the one NOT mentioned in the passage.)

3. The author's attitude toward scientists who deny that average temperatures are rising can best be described as:

A.
B.
C.
D.

The third stem lets you know that the passage discusses average temperatures and a theory advanced by some scientists. If you find that reference in your reading, you'll be able to figure out the author's attitude and then you'll have the answer to this item.

4. Which of the following best describes the main point of the passage?

F.
G.
H.
J.

Finally, the last stem tells you to look for the main idea. That, in and of itself, is not particularly helpful because you're always reading for the main idea—even if you don't get a question that asks about it. So, some stems are general while others are more specific.

Note that some students may not find this technique useful. Try it, and use it if you like it.

Read the Passage

Keep the following points in mind when reading a passage:

- Read the passage(s) quickly but carefully. You'll probably need about two to three minutes to read a passage or set of paired passages. This is about 300 to 350 words a minute.
- Read the passage(s) for important themes. Many of the items will ask about important themes of the passage, such as the main point, the purpose of a particular paragraph, or the author's intention.
- Do not try to memorize details. If you need detailed information, you can always go back to the passage(s) to find it. This is an "open-book" test.
- Pause at the end to summarize your reading. One of the most helpful reading techniques is to summarize in your own words what you have just read. What is the main point? What did the author do in the first paragraph? In the second paragraph? What did the author prove?

Answer the Items

Keep the following points in mind when answering the accompanying items:

- Identify the question being asked. Reading items fall into one of seven categories (such as "Main Idea," "Explicit Detail," and "Vocabulary"). Specific item-types have characteristic kinds of answers. If you identify the category first, it will be easier to find the right answer. You'll learn more about the seven item-types later in the Reading Lesson.

- Answer the question being asked. One of the most common mistakes made by examinees is to read the item stem carelessly and then answer the "wrong" question. That is, they *respond* to what they think they read rather than what is actually on the page. Since wrong answers often sound plausible, if you make this mistake, you're probably going to find a pretty good answer—to the wrong question.

- Read the answer choices carefully. You'll learn how to recognize the seven Reading item-types and what the correct answer to each should look like. Do this experiment: estimate how many words are in the passage and then how many are in the answer choices. The answer choices are just about as long as the passage itself. That means reading comprehension doesn't stop at the end of the last sentence of the passage. It continues all the way through to the last word of the last answer choice to the last item.

- Pay attention to thought-reversers. Thought-reversers are words in the item stem like "NOT," "BUT," and "EXCEPT." These words turn the question upside down. What is normally the right answer is now a wrong answer, and what is normally a wrong answer is the right answer.

- Do not spend too much time on any one item. Remember that you get +1 for the hardest question and +1 for the easiest. With Reading items, the easiest ones can theoretically be the last in the group and the hardest ones can be the first. So, if you sense that you're spinning your wheels, make a guess and then move along. You should always guess, even if you are unable to eliminate any answer choices, because there is no penalty for guessing on the ACT test. However, your chances improve if you are able to eliminate even one answer choice.

Remember to Review

If you are taking the test on a computer, you will be able to flag questions you may want to review. Use the flag to your advantage, but watch out for three potential pitfalls. First, make sure to at least guess before moving on to the next question in case time runs out and you aren't able to review as you had planned. Second, don't flag too many items, or you won't have time to review all the items you flagged. Save the flags for items on which you guess or about which you are very unsure. And use the answer eliminator tool to eliminate answers you are sure are wrong, to save you time when you review. Third, time your review just right. Wait until you have answered every item before clicking the review button to return to the items you flagged.

Don't Be Distracted by the Clock

If you are taking the test on a computer, you will see a clock onscreen while you are testing. Don't let it distract or worry you. Look at it periodically to make sure you are staying on track, but don't try to time your responses to every item. Try to check the clock every 15 minutes, and in the last 15 minutes of the exam try to check the clock every 5 minutes to help you prioritize any review time.

READING LESSONS

LESSON 1
Item-Types and Strategies

The passages and items in this section accompany the in-class review of the skills and concepts tested by the ACT Reading Test. You will work through the items with your instructor in class. Answers are on page 431.

DIRECTIONS: Each passage below is followed by a set of items. Read the passage and choose the best answer for each item. You may refer to the passage as often as necessary to answer the items.

Passage Perfect

As you read, underline the main idea, the topic sentence of each paragraph, the conclusion, and important words that convey tone which reveal the author's perspective.

PASSAGE I

SOCIAL SCIENCE: This passage is excerpted from an essay in a history book about the presidential election of 1796.

To broaden their appeal in the presidential election of 1796, the Federalists selected Thomas Pinckney, a South Carolinian, as running mate for the New Englander John Adams. But Pinckney's Southern friends chose to ignore their party's intentions and regarded Pinckney as a presidential candidate, creating a political situation that Alexander Hamilton was determined to exploit. Hamilton had long been wary of Adams' stubbornly independent brand of politics. He preferred to see Pinckney, who was more pliant and over whom Hamilton could exert more control, in the president's chair.

The election was held under the system originally established by the Constitution. At that time, there was but a single tally, with the candidate receiving the largest number of electoral votes declared president. The candidate with the second largest number was declared vice president. Hamilton anticipated that all the Federalists in the North would vote for Adams and Pinckney equally in an attempt to ensure that Jefferson would not be either first or second in the voting. Pinckney would be solidly supported in the South while Adams would not. Hamilton concluded if it were possible to divert a few electoral votes from Adams to Pinckney, Pinckney would receive more than Adams, yet both Federalists would outpoll Jefferson.

Various methods were used to persuade the electors to vote as Hamilton wished. In the press, anonymous articles were published attacking Adams for his monarchical tendencies and Jefferson for being overly democratic, while pushing Pinckney as the only suitable candidate. In private correspondence with state party leaders, the Hamiltonians encouraged the idea that Adams' popularity was slipping, that he could not win the election, and that the Federalists could defeat Jefferson only by supporting Pinckney.

Had sectional pride and loyalty not run as high in New England as in the deep South, Pinckney might well have become Washington's successor. New Englanders, however, realized that equal votes for Adams and Pinckney in their states would defeat Adams; therefore, eighteen electors scratched Pinckney's name from their ballots and deliberately threw away their second votes to men who were not even running. It was fortunate for Adams that they did, for the electors from South Carolina completely abandoned him, giving eight votes to Pinckney and eight to Jefferson.

In the end, Hamilton's interference in Pinckney's candidacy lost him even the vice presidency. Without New England's support,

Pinckney received only 59 electoral votes, finishing third to Adams and Jefferson. He might have been president in 1797, or as vice president a serious contender for the presidency in 1800; instead, stigmatized by a plot he had not devised, he served a brief term in the United States Senate and then dropped from sight as a national influence.

ITEM-TYPES

Main Idea
Items #1–2

Closer Look

Examples of Main Idea Items:

1. Which of the following is the main point of the passage?
2. The primary purpose of the passage is to….
3. The author is primarily concerned with….
4. Which of the following titles best describes the content of the passage?

1. The main purpose of the passage is to:

A. propose reforms to the procedures for electing the president and vice president.
B. condemn Alexander Hamilton for interfering in the election of 1796.
C. describe the political events that led to John Adams' victory in the 1796 presidential election.
D. contrast the political philosophy of the Federalists to that of Thomas Jefferson.

2. Which of the following titles best describes the content of the passage?

F. The Failure of Alexander Hamilton's Plan for Thomas Pinckney to Win the 1796 Presidential Election
G. The Roots of Alexander Hamilton's Distrust of John Adams and New England's Politics
H. Important Issues in the 1796 Presidential Campaign as Presented by the Federalist Candidates
J. The Political Careers of Alexander Hamilton, John Adams, and Thomas Pinckney

Explicit Detail
Items #3–5

Closer Look

Examples of Explicit Detail Items:

1. The author mentions which of the following?
2. According to the passage, …?
3. The author provides information that would answer which of the following questions?

3. According to the passage, which of the following was true of the presidential election of 1796?

A. Thomas Jefferson received more electoral votes than did Thomas Pinckney.
B. John Adams received strong support from the electors of South Carolina.
C. Alexander Hamilton received most of New England's electoral votes.
D. Thomas Pinckney was selected by Federalist party leaders to be the party's presidential candidate.

4. According to the passage, Hamilton's plan included all of the following EXCEPT:

F. articles published in newspapers to create opposition to John Adams.
G. South Carolina's loyalty to Thomas Pinckney.
H. private contact with state officials urging them to support Thomas Pinckney.
J. John Adams' reputation as a stubborn and independent New Englander.

5. The passage supplies information that answers which of the following questions?

A. How many electoral votes were cast for John Adams in the 1796 presidential election?
B. Under the voting system originally set up by the Constitution, how many votes did each elector cast?
C. Who was Jefferson's running mate in the 1796 presidential election?
D. What became of Alexander Hamilton after his plan to have Thomas Pinckney elected president failed?

Vocabulary
Item #6

6. In line 13, the word *pliant* most nearly means:

F. assertive.
G. public.
H. national.
J. yielding.

Closer Look

Examples of Vocabulary Items:

1. The word ------- in line ## means....
2. In line ##, what is the best definition of the word -------?

Development
Items #7–8

Closer Look

Examples of Development Items:

1. The author develops the passage primarily by….
2. The author proceeds primarily by….
3. The author mentions…in order to….
4. Which of the following best explains why the author introduces…?

Implied Idea
Items #9–11

Application
Items #12–13

Closer Look

Examples of Application Items:

1. With which of the following statements would the author most likely agree?
2. The author would probably consider which of the following a good example of his/her theory?
3. The passage is most likely taken from which of the following sources?

7. Why does the author refer to the election procedure established by the original Constitution?

A. To prove to the reader that New England as a whole had more electoral votes than the state of South Carolina.
B. To persuade the reader that Thomas Pinckney's defeat could have been avoided.
C. To alert the reader that the procedure used in 1796 was unlike the procedure in use today.
D. To encourage the reader to study Constitutional history.

8. The overall development of the passage can best be described as:

F. refuting possible explanations for certain phenomena.
G. documenting a thesis with specific examples.
H. offering an explanation of a series of events.
J. making particular proposals to solve a problem.

9. The passage implies that some electors voted for John Adams because they were:

A. in favor of a monarchy.
B. persuaded to do so by Hamilton.
C. afraid South Carolina would not vote for Pinckney.
D. eager to have a president from their geographical region.

10. Which of the following can be inferred from the passage?

F. Thomas Pinckney had a personal dislike for Jefferson's politics.
G. The Federalists regarded themselves as more democratic than Jefferson.
H. The Hamiltonians contacted key Southern leaders to persuade them to vote for Adams.
J. Electors were likely to vote for candidates from their own geographical region.

11. It can be inferred that had South Carolina not cast any electoral votes for Jefferson, the outcome of the 1796 election would have been a:

A. larger margin of victory for John Adams.
B. victory for Thomas Jefferson.
C. Federalist defeat in the Senate.
D. victory for Thomas Pinckney.

Closer Look

Examples of Implied Idea Items:

1. The passage implies that….
2. The author uses the phrase "…" to mean….
3. It can be inferred from the passage that…

12. The electors who scratched Pinckney's name from their ballots behaved most like which of the following people?

F. A newspaper publisher who adds a special section to the Sunday edition to review the week's political events.
G. A member of the clergy who encourages members of other faiths to meet to discuss solutions to the community's problems.
H. An artist who saves preliminary sketches of an important work even after the work is finally completed.
J. A general who orders his retreating troops to destroy supplies they must leave behind so the enemy cannot use the supplies.

13. Hamilton's strategy can best be summarized as:

A. divide and conquer.
B. retreat and regroup.
C. feint and counterattack.
D. hit and run.

Voice
Items #14–15

14. The tone of the passage can best be described as:

F. witty.
G. comical.
H. scholarly.
J. frivolous.

15. The author's attitude toward Hamilton's plan can best be described as:

A. angry.
B. approving.
C. analytical.
D. regretful.

Closer Look

Examples of Voice Items:

1. The tone of the passage can best be described as....
2. The author regards...as....
3. Which of the following best describes the author's attitude toward...?

STRATEGIES

PASSAGE II

HUMANITIES: This passage is adapted from an essay in a philosophy textbook about citizenship.

The liberal view of democratic citizenship that developed in the seventeenth and eighteenth centuries was different from that of the classical Greeks. The pursuit of private interests with little interference from government was seen as the road to happiness and progress rather than the public obligations and involvement that were emphasized by the Greeks. Freedom was to be found by limiting governmental activity, not through immersion in the life of the *polis.* The role of the citizen was to select leaders and keep public authority in check. The rights of citizens against the state were the focus.

Over time, the liberal notion of citizenship developed in two directions. First, there was a movement to increase the proportion of people who were eligible to participate as citizens. Second, there was a broadening of legitimate governmental activities and a use of governmental power to redress economic and social imbalances. Political citizenship became an instrument through which groups with sufficient numbers of votes could use the state's power to enhance their social and economic well-being.

Within the liberal view of democratic citizenship, tensions have developed over the degree to which the government can and should be used to promote happiness and well-being. Political philosopher Martin Diamond has categorized two views of democracy. On the one hand, there is the "libertarian" perspective that stresses the private pursuit of happiness. It emphasizes restraint on government and protection of individual liberties. On the other hand, there is the "majoritarian" view that emphasizes the "task of the government to uplift and aid the common man." The tensions between these two views are evident today. Taxpayer revolts and calls for smaller government clash with demands for greater government involvement in the economy and social sphere.

Five Steps to Approaching Passages
Items #16–24

16. The author's primary purpose is to:

F. study ancient concepts of citizenship.
G. contrast different notions of citizenship.
H. criticize modern libertarian democracy.
J. describe the importance of universal suffrage.

17. It can be inferred from the passage that the Greek word *polis* (line 12) means:

A. family life.
B. military service.
C. marriage.
D. political community.

The Cambridge Edge

Take Five Steps to Success in Approaching Passages:

1. Label passages as "aasy" or "hard"
2. Preview the first and last sentences of each paragraph
3. Preview the item stems
4. Read the passage
5. Answer the items

Master Moves

When answering vocabulary questions within the ACT Reading section, remember:

1. Always check a word's meaning in context in the passage. It may have a different meaning or connotation within the text than the one you bring to the table.
2. Draw on Greek and Latin roots you already know. Or consider related words if you are stuck. In item #17, for example, does "polis" sound like other terms you know?

18. The author cites Martin Diamond in the last paragraph because the author:

F. regards Martin Diamond as an authority on political philosophy.
G. wishes to refute Martin Diamond's views on citizenship.
H. needs a definition of the term "citizenship."
J. is unfamiliar with the distinction between libertarian and majoritarian concepts of democracy.

19. According to the passage, all of the following are characteristics that would distinguish the liberal idea of government from the Greek idea of government EXCEPT:

A. the emphasis on the rights of private citizens.
B. the activities that government may legitimately pursue.
C. the obligation of citizens to participate in government.
D. the size of the geographical area controlled by a government.

20. A majoritarian would be most likely to favor legislation that would:

F. eliminate all restrictions on individual liberty.
G. cut spending for social welfare programs.
H. provide greater protection for consumers.
J. lower taxes on the wealthy and raise taxes on the average worker.

Passage Perfect

The short description that precedes every Reading passage offers a quick preview of the passage. Use this description to help you preview the passage.

PASSAGE III

HUMANITIES: This passage is adapted from an article about John Dewey.

The place of public education within a democratic society has been widely discussed and debated. Perhaps no one has written more widely on the subject in the United States than John Dewey. Sometimes called "the father of public education," his theories of education have a large social component; that is, he places an emphasis on education as a social act and the classroom as a replica of society.

Dewey defined various aspects of education. First, it was a necessity of life. Just as humans needed sleep, food, water, and shelter for physiological renewal, they also needed education to renew their minds.

A second aspect of education was its social component. It provided the young with a nurturing environment that encouraged the growth of their social customs.

A third aspect of public education was the provision of direction to youngsters who needed the steadying influences of school. Direction was not overt, but rather indirect through the school situations in which the youngster participated.

Finally, Dewey saw public education as a catalyst for growth. Since the young came to school capable of growth, it was the role of education to provide opportunities for that growth to occur. The successful school environment is one in which a desire for continued growth is created. In Dewey's model, the role of education is not seen as a preparation for some later stage in life. Rather, education is seen as a process of growth that never ends, with human beings continuously expanding their capacity for growth. Neither did Dewey's model see education as a means by which the past was repeated. Instead, education was a continuous reconstruction of experiences, grounded very much in the present environment.

21. Which of the following best states the main idea of this passage?

A. The role of education is extremely complex.
B. Dewey's notion of education contains a significant social component.
C. Dewey's model of education is not relevant today.
D. Direction provided in education must not be overt.

22. The phrase "a continuous reconstruction of experiences" (line 42) used in reference to education means that education is:

F. based in life experiences.
G. a never-ending process.
H. a meaning-based endeavor.
J. an individual pursuit.

23. The passage implies that:

A. true education fosters the desire for lifelong learning.
B. a truly educated person understands physics.
C. Dewey was a radical philosopher.
D. education must cease at some point.

24. The tone of this passage can best be described as:

F. humorous.
G. serious.
H. dramatic.
J. informal.

PASSAGE IV

SOCIAL SCIENCE: This passage is adapted from an article on Aleut language and culture.

The Aleuts reside on several islands of the Aleutian Chain, the Pribilof Islands, and the Alaskan Peninsula. They have possessed a written language since 1825, when the Russian missionary Ivan Veniaminov selected characters of the Cyrillic alphabet to represent Aleut speech sounds, recorded the main body of Aleut vocabulary, and formulated grammatical rules. The Czarist Russian conquest of the proud, independent sea hunters was so devastatingly thorough that tribal traditions, and even tribal memories were almost obliterated. The slaughter of most adults was enough to destroy the continuity of tribal knowledge, which was dependent upon oral transmission. Consequently, the Aleuts developed a fanatical devotion to their language as their only cultural heritage.

The Russian occupation placed a heavy linguistic burden on the Aleuts. They were compelled to learn Russian to converse with their overseers and governors. They also had to learn Old Slavonic in order to take an active part in church services as well as to master the skill of reading and writing in their own tongue. In 1867, when the United States purchased Alaska, the Aleuts were unable to break sharply with their immediate past and substitute English for any one of their three languages.

To members of the Russian Orthodox Church, knowledge of Slavonic remained vital, as did Russian, the language in which one conversed with the clergy. The Aleuts came to regard English education as a device to wean them from their religious faith. The introduction of compulsory English schooling caused a minor renaissance of Russian culture as the Aleut parents sought to counteract the influence of the schoolroom. The harsh life of the Russian colonial rule began to appear more happy and beautiful in retrospect.

Regulations forbidding instruction in any language other than English increased its unpopularity. The superficial alphabetical resemblance of Russian and Aleut linked the two tongues so closely that every restriction against teaching Russian was interpreted as an attempt to eradicate the Aleut tongue. From the wording of many regulations, it appears that American administrators often had not the slightest idea that the Aleuts were clandestinely reading and writing in their own tongue or that they even had a written language of their own. To many officials, anything in Cyrillic letters was Russian and something to be stamped out. Bitterness bred by abuses and the exploitations that the Aleuts suffered from predatory American traders and adventurers kept alive the Aleut resentment against the English language.

Gradually, despite the failure to emancipate the Aleuts from a sterile past by relating the Aleut and English languages more closely, the passage of years has assuaged the bitter misunderstandings and caused an orientation away from Russian toward English as their second language. However, Aleut continues to be the language that molds their thought and expression.

Item-Type Strategies

Main Idea Clues
Items #25–27

The Goldilocks Principle

In a Main Idea question, not every true answer choice is the correct answer choice. Why? Some answers may be true statements but too limited (too small). Others maybe be true statements but beyond the author's scope (too big). The right answer will describe exactly what the author is concerned about, no more or less (it will be just right).

25. The author is primarily concerned with describing:

A. the Aleuts' loyalty to their language and American failure to understand the language.
B. Russian and American treatment of Alaskan inhabitants both before and after 1867.
C. how the Czarist Russian occupation of Alaska created a written language for the Aleuts.
D. American government attempts to persuade the Aleuts to use English as a second language.

26. The author is primarily concerned with:

F. describing the Aleuts' loyalty to their language and American failure to understand the language.
G. criticizing Russia and the United States for their mistreatment of the Aleuts.
H. praising the Russians for creating a written language for the Aleuts.
J. condemning Russia for its mistreatment of the Aleuts during the Czarist Russian occupation.

27. Which of the following titles best fits the passage?

A. Aleut Loyalty to Their Language: An American Misunderstanding
B. Failure of Russian and American Policies in Alaska
C. Russia's Gift to the Aleuts: A Written Language
D. Mistreatment of Aleuts During Russian Occupation

Explicit Detail Clues
Item #28

28. According to the passage, the most important reason for the Aleuts' devotion to their language was:

F. the invention of a written version of their language.
G. the introduction of Old Slavonic for worship.
H. the disruption of oral transmission of tribal knowledge.
J. the institution of compulsory English education.

Vocabulary Clues
Items #29–33

29. In line 21, the word *linguistic* relates to:

A. orthodoxy.
B. commerce.
C. language.
D. laws.

30. In line 39, the word *renaissance* most nearly means:

F. resurgence.
G. rejection.
H. repeal.
J. reassessment.

31. In line 55, the word *clandestinely* most nearly means:

A. secretly.
B. reliably.
C. openly.
D. casually.

32. In line 66, the word *sterile* most nearly means:

F. germ-free.
G. unproductive.
H. fortunate.
J. ill-timed.

33. In line 69, the word *assuaged* most nearly means:

A. failed.
B. created.
C. intensified.
D. eased.

Development Clues
Items #34–35

34. The passage is developed primarily by:

F. testing the evidence supporting a theory.
G. describing causes and effects of events.
H. weighing the pros and cons of a plan.
J. projecting the future consequences of a decision.

35. The author mentions that the Russians killed the majority of adult Aleuts to:

A. call attention to the immorality of foreign conquest.
B. urge Russia to make restitution to the children of those killed.
C. stir up outrage against the Russians for committing such atrocities.
D. explain the extreme loyalty that Aleuts feel to their language.

Implied Idea Clues
Items #36–37

36. Which of the following statements about the religious beliefs of the Aleuts can be inferred from the passage?

F. Prior to the Russian occupation, they had no religious beliefs.
G. American traders and adventurers forced them to abandon all religious beliefs.
H. At no time in their history have the Aleuts had an organized religion.
J. The Russians forced Aleuts to become members of the Russian Orthodox Church.

Application Clues
Item #38

Use POE

If you struggle with this item, use the process of elimination. Do any of the choices seem wrong in the extreme? Eliminate them and select an answer from the remaining choices.

Voice Clues
Item #39

37. The passage implies that:

A. the Cyrillic alphabet was invented for the Aleut language.
B. all of the Cyrillic characters were used in writing the Aleut language.
C. Russian and the Aleut language have some similar speech sounds.
D. English is also written using the Cyrillic alphabet.

38. Distributing which of the following publications would be most likely to encourage Aleuts to make more use of English?

F. Russian translations of English novels
G. English translations of Russian novels
H. An English-Russian bilingual text devoted to important aspects of Aleutian culture
J. An Aleut-English bilingual text devoted to important aspects of Aleutian culture

39. The author's attitude toward the Aleuts can best be described as one of:

A. understanding and sympathy.
B. callousness and indifference.
C. condemnation and reproof.
D. ridicule and disparagement.

LESSON 2

Paired Passages

QUESTIONS THAT COMPARE AND CONTRAST

Test Specs

A double passage includes questions, usually three or four, that ask about similarities or differences between the two passages, either in content or style.

The Cambridge Edge

This first passage is challenging simply because it is taken from a speech given in 1796. When working with a passage written before 1900, don't get bogged down in foreign style or rhetoric. Focus on the main ideas.

PASSAGE I

SOCIAL SCIENCE: Passage A is adapted from the Farewell Address to the Nation in 1796 by George Washington, the first president of the United States. Passage B is adapted from the Farewell Address to the Nation in 1961 by Dwight D. Eisenhower, the 34th president of the United States.

Passage A

Europe has a set of primary interests which to us have none, or a very remote relation. Hence she must be engaged in frequent controversies, the causes of which are essentially foreign to our concerns. Hence, therefore, it must be unwise in us to implicate ourselves by artificial ties in the ordinary vicissitudes of her politics, or the ordinary combinations and collisions of her friendships or enmities.

Why forego the advantages of so peculiar a situation? Why quit our own to stand upon foreign ground? Why, by interweaving our destiny with that of any part of Europe, entangle our peace and prosperity in the toils of European ambition, rivalship, interest, humor, or caprice?

It is our true policy to steer clear of permanent alliances with any portion of the foreign world; so far, I mean, as we are now at liberty to do it; for let me not be understood as capable of patronizing infidelity to existing engagements. I hold the maxim no less applicable to public than to private affairs, that honesty is always the best policy. I repeat it, therefore, let those engagements be observed in their genuine sense. But, in my opinion, it is unnecessary and would be unwise to extend them.

Taking care always to keep ourselves by suitable establishments on a respectable defensive posture, we may safely trust to temporary alliances for extraordinary emergencies.

Passage B

America is today the strongest, the most influential, and most productive nation in the world. Understandably proud of this pre-eminence, we yet realize that America's leadership and prestige depend, not merely upon our unmatched material progress, riches and military strength, but on how we use our power in the interests of world peace and human betterment.

Throughout America's adventure in free government, such basic purposes have been to keep the peace; to foster progress in human achievement, and to enhance liberty, dignity, and integrity among peoples and among nations.

To strive for less would be unworthy of a free and religious people.

Any failure traceable to arrogance or our lack of comprehension or readiness to sacrifice would inflict upon us a grievous hurt, both at home and abroad.

Progress toward these noble goals is persistently threatened by the conflict now engulfing the world. It commands our whole attention, absorbs our very beings. We face a hostile ideology global in scope, atheistic in character, ruthless in purpose, and insidious in method. Unhappily the danger it poses promises to be of indefinite duration. To meet it successfully, there is called for, not so much the emotional and transitory sacrifices of crisis, but rather those which enable us to carry forward steadily, surely, and without complaint the burdens of a prolonged and complex struggle—with liberty the stake. Only thus shall we remain, despite every provocation, on our charted course toward permanent peace and human betterment.

Questions 1–3 ask about both passages.

1. Both Washington and Eisenhower address the issue of:

A. United States foreign policy.
B. American prestige in the world.
C. European treaties and alliances.
D. world domination by hostile enemies.

2. Which of the following replies to Washington might Eisenhower make to justify his view of the role of the United States in world affairs?

F. United States involvement in world politics and military affairs is a short-term necessity that will fade away when the country is no longer threatened.
G. Conditions have changed since Washington's presidency, and the United States is facing a global threat that it cannot avoid by isolating itself.
H. Since Washington's time, foreign nations have settled the differences among them and now see themselves as aligned toward common goals.
J. The United States is sufficiently strong both politically and militarily that it no longer needs to worry about what European nations might think.

3. The two addresses are alike in that both Washington and Eisenhower:

A. warn against the military threat posed by the European nations.
B. advise that the United States should retreat in the face of danger.
C. argue that the United States is the most powerful nation on earth.
D. offer advice on how the United States should act in world affairs.

PASSAGE II

HUMANITIES: These passages are adapted from articles discussing two baroque artists.

Passage A

St. Andrew on the Cross by Caravaggio is a ruthlessly compelling masterpiece. The painting is dark, and the time is night. The body of a half-naked old man has been tied roughly to a cross. The murderers surround him in an unruly pack, jostling one another, like a pack of hyenas on a fresh kill. The figures are starkly visible against a dark and ill-defined background, illuminated as though by a spotlight. The action is at the front of the canvas, so close to the viewer that one feels as though it would be possible to reach out and touch the figures. These are not canvas stereotypes from central casting. These are flesh-and-blood heavies, glistening and howling in the dark: real faces twisted in agony, bodies with visible bones experiencing pain. Caravaggio gives us brutal reality.

Caravaggio's style of painting was much more radical than the style of other talented baroque artists such as Rembrandt, and for that reason he was a great master. He taught the entire baroque age that the human imagination sees more in the dark. And to do that, he invented a new set of rules for art.

Passage B

It is well known that Rembrandt was influenced by Caravaggio. Indeed, every significant artist of the times was influenced by Caravaggio. But Rembrandt not only never met Caravaggio, he also never saw a Caravaggio painting. And Rembrandt was not a radical.

Both painters were masters of *chiaroscuro*, the use of dramatic contrasts of light and shadow to describe form, but Rembrandt's technique produces an altogether warmer result, a friendlier presence than that of Caravaggio. He doesn't want to invade your reality so much as to tell you a story. Rembrandt made things look real in order to speak your language; Caravaggio does it to scare you out of your wits. Both of them prefer the dark, but whereas Rembrandt's gloom is homely and comforting, Caravaggio's is sinister and nightmarish.

Rembrandt lived almost twice as long as Caravaggio, and his later works scream with a passion for paint that you never sense in the uptight handiwork of Caravaggio. Rembrandt dared to do what Caravaggio never wanted.

Questions 4–6 ask about both passages.

4. The two commentators would probably agree that:

F. Rembrandt was a better painter than Caravaggio.
G. Caravaggio was more influential than Rembrandt.
H. Rembrandt and Caravaggio were both great artists.
J. Rembrandt is a more realistic painter than Caravaggio.

5. The two commentators would probably agree that Caravaggio and Rembrandt differ significantly in the:

A. choice of subject matter.
B. effect of darkness in painting.
C. size of their canvasses.
D. value of their masterpieces.

6. Which of the following best describes the relationship between the two passages?

F. Passage A describes the influence of Caravaggio on Rembrandt while Passage B explains the influence of Rembrandt on Caravaggio.
G. The author of Passage A praises Caravaggio for his willingness to break with tradition while the author of Passage B praises Rembrandt for his conventional approach.
H. The author of Passage A criticizes Rembrandt for his lack of radicalism while the author of Passage B criticizes Caravaggio for his aggressive style.
J. The author of Passage A prefers Caravaggio while the author of Passage B prefers Rembrandt.

PASSAGE III

NATURAL SCIENCE: These passages are adapted from articles about alcohol abuse and dependence and opioid use disorder.

Passage A

Alcohol abuse and dependence are serious problems affecting 10 percent of adult Americans. Three out of 100 deaths in the United States can be linked directly to alcohol. In addition to traffic crashes, injuries in the home and on the job, and serious long-term medical consequences, alcohol abuse has been implicated in aggression and crime. The cost of alcohol abuse and alcohol dependence is estimated to be as high as $1 trillion annually.

Alcohol abuse and alcohol dependence are related but are separate problems. "Alcohol abuse" refers to problems accomplishing basic living activities due to alcohol use. Alcohol abuse manifests as repetitive patterns of heavy drinking impairing functioning and/or health.

"Alcohol dependence" describes a severe disability in which the individual loses the ability to control the drinking behavior. Alcohol dependence is associated with additional symptoms such as craving, tolerance, and physical dependence that elevate the importance of drinking in the individual's life and impair the individual's ability to exercise behavioral restraint.

Knowledge of the differences is important because research shows that alcoholism treatment methods are more effective when they take differences in patient characteristics into account.

The Cambridge Edge

When you preview double passages, pay attention to how the two passages relate. Do the authors agree or disagree about the topic they are discussing? This will help you anticipate the questions you might need to answer.

Passage B

Opioids include substances such as morphine, heroin, codeine, and oxycodone. "Opioid use disorder" is a medical condition characterized by a problematic pattern of opioid use that causes clinically significant impairment or distress. It often includes a strong desire to use opioids, increased tolerance to opioids, and withdrawal syndrome when opioids are abruptly discontinued. Dependence and addiction are components of a substance use disorder, and addiction represents the most severe form of the disorder.

Opioid use disorders affect about 0.4% of people in a given year. About 16 million people have been affected at one point in time. In the United States in 2015 there were 33,000 deaths due to drug overdose involving opioids. Of those 33,000 deaths, about 15,000 were from prescribed opioids and 13,000 from heroin.

No single treatment works for everyone, so several strategies have been developed including therapy and drugs. Opioid use disorder can be treated with opioid replacement therapy. Additionally, individuals with opioid use disorder may benefit from twelve-step programs and support from mental health professionals through individual or group therapy. Opioid use disorders require long-term treatment and care; most strategies aim ultimately to reduce drug use and lead to abstinence.

Questions 7–9 ask about both passages.

7. Which of the following distinctions made in Passage B is parallel to a similar distinction made in Passage A?

A. Opioid use disorder differs according to whether the substance used is morphine, heroin, codeine, or oxycodone.
B. Many of the deaths from opioid overdose were caused by opioids prescribed by doctors and not illegal drugs such as heroin.
C. People with opioid use disorder need long-term treatment and care, beginning with a reduction in drug usage and leading to abstinence.
D. Addiction to and dependence upon opioids are characteristics of substance use disorder, but addiction is the more severe.

8. With which of the following statements would the authors of the two passages be most likely to agree?

F. Opioid use disorder, including both addiction and dependence, is a more serious problem than alcohol abuse.
G. Patients require different treatments for their addictions, whether to alcohol or opioids.
H. Opioid addiction and dependence are conditions more difficult to treat than alcohol abuse and dependence.
J. Treatment of alcohol abuse and dependence is hampered by the unavailability of a substance for replacement therapy.

9. The main purpose of both passages is to:

A. caution against the use of a dangerous substance.
B. define the terms of a serious public health problem.
C. call for public action against a tragic situation.
D. show the extent of the damage caused by addiction.

FURTHER PRACTICE

The Cambridge Edge

The remaining passages in this lesson feature a mix of question types, including the ones you learned in Lesson 1 and the compare/contrast questions we just introduced in this lesson.

The Cambridge Edge

Always make sure you are looking at the correct passage when answering questions about double passages. The test includes headings that will tell you which passage each question refers to.

PASSAGE IV

HUMANITIES: These passages are adapted from essays on the nature of comedy.

Passage A

Comedy appeals only to the intelligence, for laughter is incompatible with emotion. Depict some fault, however trifling, in such a way as to arouse sympathy, fear, or pity, and it is impossible to laugh. On the other hand, a vice—even one that is, generally speaking, of an odious nature—can be made ludicrous by a suitable contrivance. So long as it leaves our emotions unaffected, it is funny. This is not to say that the vice itself is ludicrous but only that the vice, as embodied in a particular character, is ludicrous. The only requirement is that it must not engage our feelings.

Passage B

Absentmindedness is always comical. Indeed, the deeper the absentmindedness the higher the comedy. Systematic absentmindedness, like that of Don Quixote, is the most comical thing imaginable; it is the comic itself, drawn as nearly as possible from its very source. Take any other comic character, however unconscious he may be of what he says or does: he cannot be comical unless there is some aspect of his person of which he is unaware, one side of his nature which he overlooks. On that account alone does he make us laugh.

Questions 10–11 ask about Passage A.

10. The author of Passage A implies that laughter:

F. is not an emotional reaction.
G. counteracts feelings of dread.
H. can correct a vice.
J. is triggered only by a vice.

11. The author of Passage A discusses vice primarily in order to:

A. advise the reader on how to avoid certain behavior.
B. make it clear that comedy does not engage the emotions.
C. provide an example that the reader will find amusing.
D. demonstrate that emotions are more powerful than intelligence.

Question 12 asks about Passage B.

12. As used in line 17, *deeper* means:

F. complete.
G. complex.
H. courageous.
J. futile.

Question 13 asks about both passages.

13. Which of the following best describes the logical connection between the views expressed in the two passages?

A. Passage B provides examples that show that the views of Passage A are incorrect.
B. Passage B redefines a key term that is used by the author of Passage A.
C. The two passages reach the same conclusion based on different evidence.
D. The two passages discuss different aspects of the topic.

PASSAGE V

NATURAL SCIENCE: The following passages suggest two plausible scenarios for an *E. coli* outbreak.

Passage A

An *E. coli* outbreak at a county fair sickened hundreds of people. Epidemiologists concluded that individuals with culture-confirmed cases of *E. coli* infection were exposed on August 28 by consuming beverages sold by vendors supplied with water from Well 6. A dye study performed in late September showed a hydraulic connection between the septic system of a nearby 4-H dormitory and Well 6. Tests of a cattle manure storage area suspected as a possible contamination source did not show a hydraulic connection with Well 6 nor with the presence of the relevant strain of *E. coli.* Therefore, the outbreak was caused by leakage from the dormitory septic system.

Passage B

Manure runoff from the nearby cattle barn cannot be ruled out as a cause of the outbreak because exact environmental conditions, including drought followed by heavy rain, could not be replicated during the later study. Additionally, manure in the storage area was removed daily. Thus, it can never be known if manure-contaminated water percolated from the manure storage area to Well 6.

Question 14 asks about Passage B.

14. In line 26, the word *percolated* most nearly means:

F. boiled.
G. infected.
H. tested.
J. seeped.

Question 15 asks about both passages.

15. Which of the following best describes the relationship between the two passages?

A. The two speakers agree that *E. coli* caused the illnesses but believe that two different strains were involved.
B. The two speakers agree that *E. coli* caused the illnesses but disagree about the source of the contamination.
C. The two speakers agree that the same strain of *E. coli* caused the outbreak and agree that the dormitory septic system was the source.
D. Speaker 1 maintains that *E. coli* was the cause of the outbreak of illness, but Speaker 2 thinks that some other agent might have been involved.

PASSAGE VI

HUMANITIES: Passage A and Passage B are excerpts from two different sources, both published in 1989, discussing the habits of two nineteenth-century authors.

Passage A

Many readers, faced with Thoreau's enigmatic Yankee persona, have resorted to a kind of pop-culture shorthand for describing his life: Thoreau was an oddball loner who lived by a lake and wrote *Walden* (published in 1854) in praise of nature and against modern progress. But the full story of Thoreau's life involves subtleties that call this popular image into question.

Thoreau's retreat into the backwoods was more like a child pitching a tent in the backyard. His cabin was only a half-mile from his nearest neighbor and just two miles from the village, so he could easily obtain any needed supplies. The so-called New England Hermit circulated petitions for neighbors in need; he was involved in the Underground Railroad; his essay "Civil Disobedience" was a tract against both slavery and imperialism, two vital social and political issues.

Passage B

In 1861, the *Atlantic Monthly* magazine asked the poet Emily Dickinson for a photograph of her that it might publish. Her response was: "I don't have one." This polite, but emphatic, refusal was one of the strategies that allowed Dickinson to turn her back on America's burgeoning mass audience and to imagine herself as an artist governed solely by inspiration.

Suspicious of the techniques by which publishing houses transformed authors into marketable commodities for the masses, she considered herself a romantic poet writing from her garret for art alone. She wanted to publish in ways that preserved her control and ownership of her work. Except for a few poems published either without her permission or in order to benefit the Union army, Dickinson never published in the sense we understand it.

Questions 16–17 ask about Passage A.

16. The primary purpose of Passage A is to:

F. demonstrate that a writer can praise nature without himself living as a hermit.
G. show that the popular view of Thoreau as an oddball loner is an oversimplification.
H. illustrate some ways in which Thoreau misrepresented his commitment to an alternative lifestyle.
J. show that active involvement with social issues is inconsistent with a hermit's lifestyle.

17. The author includes all of the following in Passage A to disprove the suggestion that Thoreau was a simple hermit EXCEPT:

A. that he was involved in the Underground Railroad.
B. that he wrote about social and political issues of the day.
C. that his cabin stood close to a village and neighbors.
D. that he wrote a book on the virtue of living with nature.

Question 18 asks about Passage B.

18. As used in line 34, *romantic* means:

F. concerned with love between two individuals.
G. motivated by artistic considerations.
H. eager to profit from one's writings.
J. anxious to earn the approval of readers.

Question 19 asks about both passages.

19. Which of the following provides the most accurate comparison of the personalities of the authors discussed in the two passages?

A. Thoreau was a hermit in reputation only while Dickinson was a genuine recluse.
B. Dickinson wished for anonymity while Thoreau sought a remote, rustic lifestyle.
C. Dickinson lived in an attic room while Thoreau resided permanently in a tent.
D. Thoreau championed popular causes while Dickinson ignored political issues.

PASSAGE VII

PROSE FICTION: Passage A is an excerpt from the article "The New Sequoia Forests of California" in *Harper's New Monthly Magazine.* Passage B is an excerpt from *Old Indian Days* by Charles Eastman.

Passage A

Shortly after sunrise, just as the light was beginning to come streaming through the trees, I caught the big bright eyes of a deer gazing at me through the garden hedge. The expressive eyes, the slim black-tipped muzzle, and the large ears were perfectly visible, as if placed there at just the right distance to be seen. She continued to gaze while I gazed back with equal steadiness, motionless as a rock. In a few minutes she ventured forward a step, exposing her fine arching neck and forelegs, then snorted and withdrew.

Trembling sprays indicated her return, and her head came into view; several steps later, she stood wholly exposed inside the garden hedge, gazed eagerly around, and again withdrew, but returned a moment afterward, this time advancing into the middle of the garden. Behind her I noticed other pairs of eyes.

It then occurred to me that I might possibly steal up to one of them and catch it, not with any intention of killing it, but only to run my hand along its beautiful curving limbs. They seemed, however, to penetrate my conceit and bounded off with loud, shrill snorts, vanishing into the forest.

I have often tried to understand how so many deer, wild sheep, bears, and grouse—nature's cattle and poultry—could be allowed to run at large through the mountain gardens without in any way marring the beauty of their surroundings. I was, therefore, all the more watchful of this feeding flock, and carefully examined the garden after they left, to see what flowers had suffered; I could not, however, detect the slightest disorder, much less destruction. It seemed rather that, like gardeners, they had been keeping it in order. I could not see one crushed flower, nor a single blade of grass that was bent or broken down. Nor among the daisy, gentian, or bryanthus gardens of the Alps, where the wild sheep roam at will, have I ever noticed the effects of destructive feeding or trampling. Even the burly, shuffling bears beautify the ground on which they walk, decorating it with their awe-inspiring tracks, and writing poetry on the soft sequoia bark in boldly drawn hieroglyphics. But, strange to say, man, the crown, the sequoia of nature, brings confusion with all his best gifts and with the overabundant, misbegotten animals that he breeds, sweeps away the beauty of the wilderness like a fire.

Passage B

The night was intolerable for Antoine. The buffalo were about him in countless numbers, regarding him with vicious glances. It was only due to the natural offensiveness of man that they gave him any space. The bellowing of the bulls became louder, and there was a marked uneasiness on the part of the herd. This was a sign of an approaching storm.

Upon the western horizon were seen flashes of lightning. The cloud that had been a mere speck had now become an ominous thunderhead. Suddenly the wind came, and lightning flashes became more frequent, showing the ungainly forms of the animals like strange monsters in the white light. The colossal herd was again in violent motion. It was a blind rush for shelter, and no heed was paid to buffalo wallows or even deep gulches. All was in the deepest of darkness. There seemed to be groaning in heaven and earth—millions of hoofs and throats roaring in unison.

As a shipwrecked sailor clings to a mere fragment of wood, so Antoine, although almost exhausted with fatigue, stuck to the saddle of his pony. As the mad rush continued, every flash displayed heaps of bison in death's struggle under the hoofs of their companions.

When he awoke and looked around him again, it was morning. The herd had entered the strip of timber which lay on both sides of the river, and it was here that Antoine conceived his first distinct hope of saving himself.

"Waw, waw, waw!" was the hoarse cry that came to his ears, apparently from a human being in distress. Antoine strained his eyes and craned his neck to see who it could be. Through an opening in the branches ahead he perceived a large grizzly bear lying along an inclined limb and hugging it desperately to maintain his position. The herd had now thoroughly pervaded the timber, and the bear was likewise hemmed in. He had taken his unaccustomed refuge after making a brave stand against several bulls, one of which lay dead nearby, while he himself was bleeding from several wounds.

Antoine had been assiduously looking for a friendly tree, by means of which he hoped to escape from captivity. His horse, by chance, made his way directly under the very box-elder that was sustaining the bear and there was a convenient branch just within his reach. He saw at a glance that the occupant of the tree would not interfere with him. They were, in fact, companions in distress. Antoine sprang desperately from the pony's back and seized the cross-limb with both his hands.

By the middle of the afternoon the main body of the herd had passed, and Antoine was sure that his captivity had at last come to an end. Then he swung himself from his limb to the ground, and walked stiffly to the carcass of the nearest cow, which he dressed, and prepared himself a meal. But first he took a piece of liver on a long pole to the bear!

Questions 20–26 ask about Passage A.

20. As used in line 14, *sprays* refers to:

F. minute droplets.
G. light mist.
H. thin legs.
J. small branches.

21. As used in line 23, *steal up* means:

A. acquire unlawfully.
B. prepare for action.
C. promise faithfully.
D. approach undetected.

22. In the first two paragraphs, the author of Passage A is primarily concerned with:

F. recounting an experience.
G. exploring a theory.
H. teaching a lesson.
J. offering an opinion.

23. As used in line 27, *conceit* means:

A. arrogance.
B. selfishness.
C. fanciful notion.
D. dissatisfaction.

24. According to the passage, the deer and the sheep are alike in that they both:

F. are wary of human beings.
G. inhabit remote Alpine gardens.
H. feed without causing destruction.
J. live untamed in wilderness regions.

25. The "boldly drawn hieroglyphics" (lines 51–52) are probably:

A. claw marks.
B. park signs.
C. rare flowers.
D. hoofprints.

26. The author compares the deer to gardeners (lines 40–43) in order to:

F. encourage the reader to learn more about deer.
G. refute the idea that deer are aggressive.
H. illustrate the similarity between deer and humans.
J. emphasize that deer are not destructive.

Questions 27–33 ask about Passage B.

27. As used in line 76, *wallows* means:

A. deep cave.
B. shallow depression.
C. rugged cliff.
D. low hill.

28. By "the natural offensiveness of man" (line 61–62), the author of Passage B probably refers to man's:

F. frequent rudeness.
G. disagreeable odor.
H. uncontrolled aggression.
J. distasteful behavior.

29. All of the following are true of the comparison drawn in the third paragraph of Passage B EXCEPT:

A. Antoine, like a shipwrecked sailor, is in a desperate situation.
B. The herd of buffalo are like the storm-driven sea.
C. The environment is filled with dangerous creatures that threaten a sailor the way Antoine fears the buffalo.
D. Antoine's pony supports him the way that debris might support a shipwrecked sailor.

30. The tone of the first two paragraphs of Passage B is:

F. frivolous.
G. suspenseful.
H. animated.
J. reserved.

31. The phrase "unaccustomed refuge" (line 105) suggests that the bear:

A. preferred open areas to confined spaces.
B. rarely climbed a tree for safety.
C. did not often encounter buffalo.
D. was fearful of the presence of a human.

32. As used in line 127, *dressed* means:

F. adorned.
G. clothed.
H. prepared.
J. bound.

33. The mood of Passage B moves from:

A. joy to despair.
B. hopelessness to hope.
C. happiness to gloom.
D. apprehension to courageousness.

LESSON 3

Further Use of Reading Strategies, Part 1

The passages and items in this section accompany the in-class review of the skills and concepts tested by the ACT Reading Test. You will work through the items with your instructor in class. Answers are on page 431.

DIRECTIONS: Each passage below is followed by a set of items. Read the passage and choose the best answer for each item. You may refer to the passage as often as necessary to answer the items.

The Cambridge Edge

Use the Five-Step Approach to complete these passages:

1. Label passages as "easy" or "hard"
2. Preview the first and last sentences of each paragraph
3. Preview the item stems
4. Read the passage
5. Answer the items

PASSAGE I

PROSE FICTION: This passage is adapted from the short story "Mrs. Gay's Prescription" by Louisa May Alcott.

The poor little woman looked as if she needed rest but was not likely to get it; for the room was in a chaotic state. The breakfast table presented the appearance of having been devastated by a swarm of locusts, the baby began to fret, little Polly set up her usual whine of "I want sumpin to do," and a pile of work loomed in the corner waiting to be done.

"I don't see how I ever shall get through it all," sighed the despondent matron as she hastily drank a last cup of tea. Two great tears rolled down her cheeks as she looked from one puny child to the other, and felt the weariness of her own tired soul and body more oppressive than ever.

"A good cry" was impending, when there came a brisk ring at the door and a step in the hall. A large, rosy woman came bustling in, saying in a cheery voice as she set a flower-pot down upon the table, "Good morning! Nice day, isn't it? Came in early on business and brought you one of my Lady Washingtons. You are so fond of flowers."

"Oh, it's lovely! How kind you are. Do sit down if you can find a chair; we are all behind hand today, for I was up half the night with poor baby, and haven't energy enough to go to work yet," answered Mrs. Bennet, with a sudden smile that changed her whole face. Baby stopped fretting to stare at the rosy clusters, and Polly found employment in exploring the pocket of the newcomer, as if she knew her way there.

"Let me put the pot on your stand first. Girls are so careless, and I'm proud of this. It will be an ornament to your parlor for a week." Opening a door, Mrs. Gay carried the plant to a sunny bay window where many others were blooming beautifully.

Mrs. Bennet and the children followed to talk and admire, while the servant leisurely cleared the table.

"Now give me that baby, put yourself in the easy chair, and tell me all about your worries," said Mrs. Gay, in the brisk, commanding way which few people could resist.

"I'm sure I don't know where to begin," sighed Mrs. Bennet, dropping into the comfortable seat while baby changed bearers with great composure.

"I met your husband and he said the doctor had ordered you and these chicks off to Florida for the winter. John said he didn't know how he should manage it, but he meant to try."

"Isn't it dreadful? He can't leave his business to go with me, and we shall have to get Aunt Miranda to come and see to him and the boys while I'm gone, and the boys can't bear her strict, old-fashioned ways, and I've got to go that long journey all alone and stay among strangers, and these heaps of fall work to do first, and it will cost an immense sum to send us, and I don't know what is to become of me."

Here Mrs. Bennet stopped for breath. Mrs. Gay asked briskly, "What is the matter with you and the children?"

"Well, baby is having a hard time with his teeth and is croupy. Polly doesn't get over scarlet fever well, and I'm used up; no strength or appetite, pain in my side and low spirits. Entire change of scene, milder climate, and less work for me, is what we want, the doctor says. John is very anxious about us, and I feel regularly discouraged."

"I'll spend the day and cheer you up a bit. You just rest and get ready for a new start tomorrow; it is a saving of time to stop short now and then and see where to begin next. Bring me the most pressing job of work. I can sew and see to this little rascal at the same time."

1. As used in line 1, *little woman* refers to:

A. Lady Washington.
B. a servant.
C. Mrs. Bennet.
D. Mrs. Gay.

2. When Alcott compares the breakfast table to something "devastated by a swarm of locusts" (lines 5–6), she means:

F. that it is a mess left by an uncaring mob.
G. that children are no more meaningful than insects to Mrs. Bennet.
H. to illustrate the chaos of Mrs. Bennet's life.
J. that the Bennets are pests.

3. Had Mrs. Gay not arrived when she did, the author leads us to suspect that:

A. Mrs. Bennet would have gone back to bed.
B. the children would have continued to cry.
C. Mrs. Bennet would have accomplished little all day.
D. sickness would have overtaken the entire family.

4. As used in line 32, *rosy clusters* refers to:

F. Mrs. Gay's cheeks.
G. Mrs. Bennet's cheeks.
H. candies from Mrs. Gay's pockets.
J. flowers.

5. In lines 36–41, the author:

A. reveals Mrs. Bennet's only talent.
B. uses the sunny parlor as a symbol of hope.
C. contrasts Mrs. Gay's sunniness with Mrs. Bennet's dullness.
D. contrasts Mrs. Bennet's plants with her children.

6. When Mrs. Bennet says that she's "used up" (line 74), she means that she:

F. has no energy.
G. is abused.
H. is exploited.
J. has spent all her money.

7. As used in line 84, *pressing* means:

A. heavy.
B. ardent.
C. forceful.
D. important.

Use POE

In questions like item #8 with several numbered descriptions, it is in your best interest to use the process of elimination on the Roman numeral choices (not the answer choices).

8. The disposition of Mrs. Bennet's friend is indicated by:

I. her name.
II. her speech.
III. her clothing.

F. I only
G. III only
H. I and II only
J. I and III only

9. The author implies that Mrs. Bennet's real problem is:

A. her inability to cope.
B. a touch of fever.
C. the cold winter weather.
D. a lack of common sense.

10. Mrs. Gay's primary quality seems to be her:

F. lethargy.
G. anxiety.
H. dignity.
J. practical nature.

PASSAGE II

PROSE FICTION: This passage is adapted from the memoir series "Old Times on the Mississippi" by Mark Twain that appeared in *Atlantic Monthly*.

Passage Perfect

As you preview the item stems, if you see a reference to a specific line in the passage, add a star by that line or circle the word in that line that is being referenced. This way you can pay attention to the context as you read and easily find these words later.

At the end of what seemed a tedious while, I had managed to pack my head full of islands, towns, bars, "points," and bends; and a curiously inanimate mass of lumber it was, too. However, inasmuch as I could shut my eyes and reel off a good long string of these names without leaving out more than ten miles of river in every fifty, I began to feel that I could make her skip those little gaps. But of course my complacency could hardly get started enough to lift my nose a trifle into the air, before Mr. Bixby would think of something to fetch it down again. One day he turned on me suddenly with this settler:

"What is the shape of Walnut Bend?"

He might as well have asked me my grandmother's opinion of protoplasm. I reflected respectfully, and then said I didn't know it had any particular shape. My gunpowdery chief went off with a bang, of course, and then went on loading and firing until he was out of adjectives.

I had learned long ago that he only carried just so many rounds of ammunition, and was sure to subside into a very placable and even remorseful old smoothbore as soon as they were all gone. That word "old" is merely affectionate; he was not more than thirty-four. I waited. By and by he said:

"My boy, you've got to know the *shape* of the river perfectly. It is all there is left to steer by on a very dark night. Everything else is blotted out and gone. But mind you, it hasn't the same shape in the night that it has in the daytime."

"How on earth am I ever going to learn it, then?"

"How do you follow a hall at home in the dark? Because you know the shape of it. You can't see it."

"Do you mean to say that I've got to know all the million trifling variations of shape in the banks of this interminable river as well as I know the shape of the front hall at home?"

"On my honor, you've got to know them *better* than any man ever did know the shapes of the halls in his own house."

"I wish I was dead!"

"Now I don't want to discourage you, but..."

"Well, pile it on me; I might as well have it now as another time."

"You see, this has got to be learned; there isn't any getting around it. A clear starlight night throws such heavy shadows that, if you didn't know the shape of a shore perfectly, you would claw away from every bunch of timber, because you would take the black shadow of it for a solid cape; and you see you would be getting scared to death every fifteen minutes by the watch. You would be fifty yards from shore all the time when you ought to be within fifty feet of it. You can't see a snag in one of those shadows, but you know exactly where it is, and the shape of the river tells you when you are coming to it. Then there's your pitch-dark night; the river is a very different shape on a pitch-dark night from what it is on a starlit night. All shores seem to be straight lines, then, and mighty dim ones, too; and you'd *run* them for straight lines, only you know better. You boldly drive your boat right into what seems to be a solid straight wall (you knowing very well that in reality there is a curve there), and that wall falls back and makes way for you. Then there's your gray mist. You take a night when there's one of these grisly, drizzly, gray mists, and then there isn't any particular shape to a shore. A gray mist would tangle the head of the oldest man that ever lived. Well, then different kinds of *moonlight* change the shape of the river in different ways."

The Cambridge Edge

When you review the item stems, take note of any inference and tone questions and then watch for clues as you read. For example, when you preview item #18 consider circling Mr. Bixby's name in the passage and write "character?" in the margin as a reminder to pay attention to how he is described.

The Cambridge Edge

Remember to answer all the items for this passage before you move on. On test day, make a guess if you're not sure of an answer and revisit the problem at the end of the test if you have time.

11. In line 15, the word *settler* is used to mean:

A. a pioneer.
B. a perch on the railing.
C. a remark that decides the issue.
D. a humbling problem.

12. When the narrator compares Bixby's question to asking his "grandmother's opinion of protoplasm" (lines 17–18), he means that:

F. the question is inane.
G. the speaker is very old.
H. he does not know the answer.
J. his grandmother would be able to respond.

13. Comparing the chief to a gun (lines 21–23) points out the chief's:

A. accuracy.
B. peppery temper.
C. love of hunting.
D. violent past.

14. When Twain writes that Mr. Bixby "carried just so many rounds of ammunition," (line 25) he means that:

F. Bixby used a pistol to settle arguments.
G. Bixby loaded and fired his gun at random.
H. Bixby was an impossible employer.
J. Bixby's hot temper would soon subside.

15. The narrator's reaction to Mr. Bixby's insistence on the need to know the river at night is:

A. despair.
B. elation.
C. puzzlement.
D. anger.

16. In the phrase "pile it on me" (line 53), "it" refers to:

F. clothing.
G. information.
H. the river.
J. the shoreline.

17. The word *cape* (line 61) means:

A. cloak.
B. robe.
C. peninsula.
D. waterway.

18. Mr. Bixby is shown to be extremely:

F. knowledgeable.
G. rude.
H. condescending.
J. fearful.

19. What is the purpose of including the lengthy explanation provided in the last paragraph of the selection?

I. To show how well Bixby speaks
II. To show how much a riverboat captain must know
III. To show the many modes of the river

A. I only
B. II only
C. I and III only
D. II and III only

20. According to the passage, which of the following is true?

F. A riverboat should always be within 100 feet of the shore.
G. On a clear, starlit night, the shoreline is easy to see.
H. On a pitch-dark night, the pilot cannot discern the curve of the shoreline.
J. The river's shape gives no hint of underwater snags.

Passage Perfect

Here we have a thought-reverser question (indicated by the EXCEPT). Look for the answer choice that does NOT describe Miss Hepzibah. To avoid confusion, cross off the answer choices that do describe her, so you are left with the one that does not.

PASSAGE III

PROSE FICTION: This passage is adapted from Nathaniel Hawthorne's *The House of the Seven Gables.*

It still lacked a half hour of sunrise when Miss Hepzibah—we will say awoke, it being doubtful whether the poor old lady had so much as closed her eyes during the brief night of midsummer—but, at all events, arose from her solitary pillow, and began the adornment of her person. She was alone in the old house—quite a house by itself, indeed—with locks, bolts, and oaken bars on all the intervening doors. Inaudible, consequently, were poor Miss Hepzibah's gusty sighs. Inaudible were the creaking joints of her stiffened knees, as she knelt down by the bedside. And inaudible too, by mortal ear, that almost agony of prayer—now whispered, now a groan, now a struggling silence—wherewith she sought the Divine assistance through the day! Evidently this is to be the day of more than ordinary trial to Miss Hepzibah. For above a quarter of a century gone by, she has dwelt in strict seclusion, taking no part in the business of life, and just as little in its intercourse and pleasures.

Here comes Miss Hepzibah. Forth she steps into the dusky, time-darkened passage. A tall figure, clad in black silk, with a long and shrunken waist, she feels her way towards the stair like a nearsighted person, which in truth she is.

Her scowl—as the world persisted in calling it—had done Miss Hepzibah every ill office, in establishing her character as an ill-tempered old maid; nor does it appear improbable that, by often gazing at herself in a dim looking glass, and perpetually encountering her own frown within its ghostly sphere, she had been led to interpret the expression almost as unjustly as the world did. But her heart never frowned.

21. According to the passage, Miss Hepzibah is all of the following EXCEPT:

A. elderly.
B. reclusive.
C. religious.
D. vain.

22. The author's portrait of Miss Hepzibah is:

F. critical and disparaging.
G. loving and intimate.
H. sarcastic and mocking.
J. interested and sympathetic.

23. It can be inferred that Miss Hepzibah views the day's coming events with:

A. apprehension.
B. confidence.
C. eagerness.
D. boredom.

24. Which of the following correctly describes the scene as set by the passage?

I. The season is summer.
II. The weather is threatening.
III. The time is morning.

F. I only
G. III only
H. I and II only
J. I and III only

The Goldilocks Principle

For Item 26, remember to choose the title that is just right. It should not be too specific (such as describing only one of the paragraphs), but it should also not be too broad (such as suggesting that the passage covers additional or more general material than it actually does).

25. In the last paragraph, the author implies that Miss Hepzibah is:

A. old and wicked.
B. affable and outgoing.
C. good-hearted but misunderstood.
D. sincere but blasphemous.

PASSAGE IV

SOCIAL SCIENCE: This passage discusses the contest over the vice presidency in the 1792 election.

In 1792, there was no contest for the presidency. George Washington received the unanimous vote of the electors, Federalist and Republican alike. But the struggle over the vice presidency hinted at the rekindling of old divisions sparked by Alexander Hamilton's system. Southern planters who in 1789 had been ready, in fact eager, to cooperate with the monied men of the North, parted with them when they realized that the policies designed to benefit Northern merchants and bankers brought no profit to them. Even more, they saw themselves paying for a system that contributed to another section's prosperity. Although in 1792 they were willing to continue with Washington, they were not as willing to go along with Vice President John Adams, who represented the commerce, shipbuilding, fisheries, and banking institutions of New England and the North. If the Federalists were to have the first office, then the followers of Jefferson—who had already come to call themselves Republicans instead of the unpopular term anti-Federalist—insisted that they were to command the second office.

Appealing to the shopkeepers, artisans, laboring men, and farmers of the North based on their sympathy with the French Revolution, and to the Southern planters with their agrarian bias, the Republicans waged a gallant but losing campaign for the second office. However, the campaign served notice to the overconfident Federalists that when the Republicans became better organized nationally, they would have to be more seriously considered. This did not take long. In 1793, England declared war with republican France over the murder of Louis XVI. And in 1794, John Jay's treaty ending the United States' difficulties with Britain seemed to suggest a sympathetic policy toward monarchical and conservative England, instead of republican, liberty-loving France. The treaty intensified party spirit and gave the Republicans a sense of mission that legitimized their existence. The contest was now between the Republican "lovers of liberty" and the Monocrats.

26. Which of the following titles best describes the content of the passage?

F. The Origins of Jefferson's Republican Party
G. Jefferson's Defeat in the 1792 Election
H. The Legacy of Hamilton's Political System
J. Political Differences Between the Rich and the Poor

27. According to the passage, all of the following are true of the Republicans EXCEPT:

A. they opposed the monied interests of the North.
B. they were led by Thomas Jefferson.
C. they disapproved of the French Revolution.
D. they and the Federalists supported the same candidate for president in 1792.

28. It can be inferred from the passage that the term *Monocrats* (line 50) was:

F. used by John Jay in his treaty to refer to France's King Louis XVI.
G. invented by the Federalists to refer to the aristocratic landowners of the South.
H. coined by the Republicans to disparage the Federalists' support of England.
J. employed by Republicans to describe their leader, Thomas Jefferson.

29. The passage implies that Thomas Jefferson was unsuccessful in his 1792 bid for the vice presidency because the Republican Party:

A. did not have a presidential candidate.
B. was not as well organized as the Federalists.
C. refused to support John Adams.
D. appealed to workers in the North.

30. The tone of the passage can best be described as:

F. enthusiastic and impassioned.
G. scholarly and neutral.
H. opinionated and dogmatic.
J. argumentative and categorical.

PASSAGE V

SOCIAL SCIENCE: This passage is adapted from an article about attempts to change the healthcare system.

Considerable advances have been made in healthcare services since World War II. These include better access to healthcare (particularly for the poor and minorities), improvements in physical plants and facilities, and increased numbers of physicians and other health personnel. All have played a part in the recent improvement in life expectancy. But there is mounting criticism of the large remaining gaps in access, unbridled cost inflation, the further fragmentation of service, excessive indulgence in wasteful high-technology "gadgeteering," and breakdowns in doctor-patient relationships. In recent years, proposed panaceas and new programs, small and large, have proliferated at a feverish pace, and disappointments have multiplied at almost the same rate. This has led to an increased pessimism—"everything has been tried and nothing works"—that sometimes borders on cynicism or even nihilism.

It is true that the automatic "pass through" of rapidly spiraling costs to government and insurance carriers produced for a time a sense of unlimited resources. It allowed a mood to develop whereby every practitioner and institution could "do his own thing" without undue concern for the "Medical Commons." The practice of full-cost reimbursement encouraged capital investment, and now the industry is overcapitalized. Many cities have hundreds of excess hospital beds; hospitals have proliferated a superabundance of high-technology equipment; and structural ostentation and luxury were the order of the day. In any given day, one-fourth of all community beds are vacant; expensive equipment is underused or, worse, used unnecessarily. Capital investment brings rapidly rising operating costs.

Yet, in part, this pessimism derives from expecting too much of healthcare. Care is often a painful experience accompanied by fear and unwelcome results; although there is room for improvement, it will always retain some unpleasantness and frustration. Moreover, the capacities of medical science are limited. Humpty Dumpty cannot always be put back together again. Too many physicians are reluctant to admit their limitations to patients; too many patients and families are unwilling to accept such realities. Nor is it true that everything has been tried and nothing works, as shown by the prepaid group practice plans at the Kaiser Foundation and Puget Sound. However, typically such undertakings have been drowned by a veritable flood of public and private funds that have supported the continuation of conventional practices and subsidized their shortcomings on a massive, almost unrestricted scale. Except for the most idealistic and dedicated, there were no incentives to seek change or to practice self-restraint or frugality. In this atmosphere, it is not fair to condemn as failures all attempted experiments; it may be more accurate to say that many never had a fair trial.

> Closer Look
>
> Vocabulary questions, particularly those like item #31, ask for the meaning in the context of the stated line in the passage. Expect to encounter multiple answer choices that can describe the meaning of the vocabulary word in different contexts. Do not panic; remember to check the context.

31. In line 18, the word *feverish* most nearly means:

A. diseased.
B. rapid.
C. controlled.
D. timed.

32. According to the author, the pessimism mentioned in line 44 is partly attributable to the fact that:

F. there has been little real improvement in healthcare services.
G. expectations about healthcare services are sometimes unrealistic.
H. large segments of the population find it impossible to get access to healthcare services.
J. advances in technology have made healthcare service unaffordable.

33. The author cites the prepaid plans (lines 58–59) as:

A. counterexamples to the claim that nothing has worked.
B. examples of healthcare plans that were overfunded.
C. evidence that healthcare services are fragmented.
D. proof of the theory that no plan has been successful.

34. It can be inferred that the sentence "Humpty Dumpty cannot always be put back together again" (lines 51–53) means that:

F. the cost of healthcare services will not decline.
G. some people should not become doctors.
H. medical care is not really essential to good health.
J. medical science cannot cure every ill.

35. With which of the following descriptions of the system for the delivery of healthcare services would the author most likely agree?

A. It is biased in favor of doctors and against patients.
B. It is highly fragmented and completely ineffective.
C. It has not embraced new technology rapidly enough.
D. It is generally effective but can be improved.

Map It Out

Questions like item #36 are big-picture questions that require you to look at passage-level structure. Circle or underline the topic sentences of each paragraph as you read so that you can quickly find the answer to this item.

36. Which of the following best describes the logical structure of the selection?

F. The third paragraph is intended as a refutation of the first and second paragraphs.
G. The second and third paragraphs are intended as a refutation of the first paragraph.
H. The second and third paragraphs explain and put into perspective the points made in the first paragraph.
J. The first paragraph describes a problem, and the second and third paragraphs present two sides of the dilemma.

37. The author's primary concern is to:

A. criticize physicians and healthcare administrators for investing in technologically advanced equipment.
B. examine some problems affecting the delivery of healthcare services and assess the severity of those problems.
C. defend the medical community from charges that healthcare has not improved since World War II.
D. analyze the reasons for the healthcare industry's inability to provide quality care to all segments of the population.

PASSAGE VI

HUMANITIES: This passage is adapted from an article about literary genres.

When we speak casually, we call *Nineteen Eighty-Four* a novel, but to be more exact we should call it a political fable. This requirement is not refuted by the fact that the book is about a man, Winston Smith, who suffers from a varicose ulcer, or by the fact that it takes account of other individuals, including Julia, Mrs. Parsons, Syme, and O'Brien. The figures claim our attention, but they exist mainly in their relation to the political system that determines them. It would indeed be possible to think of them as figures in a novel, though in that case they would have to be imagined in a far more diverse set of relations. They would no longer sustain a fable, because a fable is a story relieved of much contingent detail so that it may stand forth in an unusual degree of clarity and simplicity. A fable is a structure of types, each of them deliberately simplified lest a sense of difference reduce the force of the typical. Let us say, then, that *Nineteen Eighty-Four* is a political fable, projected into a near future and including historical references.

Since a fable requires a typology, it must be written from a certain distance. The author cannot afford the sense of familiarity that is induced by detail. A fable, in this respect, asks to be compared to a caricature, not to a photograph. It follows that in a political fable there is bound to be some tension between a political sense dealing with the diversity of social and personal life, and a fable sense committed to simplicity of form and feature. If the political sense were to prevail, the narrative would be drawn away from fable into the novel. If the sense of fable were to prevail, the narrative would appear unmediated, free or bereft of conditions. The risk would be considerable: a reader might feel that the fabulist has lost interest in the variety of human life. The risk is greater still if the fabulist projects his narrative into the future: the reader cannot question by appealing to life conditions already known. He is asked to believe that the future is another country and that "they just do things differently there."

In a powerful fable, the reader's feeling is likely to be mostly fear: he is afraid that the fabulist's vision of life may be true. The fabulist's feeling may be more various. A fable such as *Nineteen Eighty-Four* might arise from disgust, despair, or world-weariness caused by evidence that nothing, despite one's best efforts, has changed; it is too late now to hope for the change one wants.

38. In line 18, the word *contingent* most nearly means:

F. dependent.
G. essential.
H. boring.
J. unnecessary.

39. In drawing an analogy between a fable and a caricature (lines 31–32), the author would most likely regard which of the following pairs of ideas as also analogous?

A. The subject of a caricature and the topic of a fable
B. The subject of a caricature and the main character in *Nineteen Eighty-Four*
C. The subject of a fable and the artist who draws the caricature
D. The artist who draws the caricature and a novelist

Use POE

If item #39 seems daunting, use the process of elimination. For example, (C) is comparing two different things—a subject and an artist—so it is unlikely to be correct.

40. Which of the following would be the most appropriate title for the passage?

F. A Critical Study of the Use of Characters in *Nineteen Eighty-Four*
G. *Nineteen Eighty-Four*: Political Fable Rather Than Novel
H. *Nineteen Eighty-Four*: Reflections on the Relationship of the Individual to Society
J. The Use of Typology in the Literature of Political Fables

41. According to the passage, which of the following is characteristic of a political fable?

A. It is widely popular at its time of development.
B. The reader is unlikely to experience fear as his reaction to the political situation described.
C. Its time frame must treat events that occur at some point in the future.
D. Its characters are defined primarily by their relationship to the social order.

42. The author mentions that Winston Smith suffers from a varicose ulcer to:

F. demonstrate that a political fable must emphasize type over detail.
G. show that Winston Smith has some characteristics that distinguish him as an individual.
H. argue that Winston Smith is no more important than any other character in *Nineteen Eighty-Four.*
J. illustrate one of the features of the political situation described in *Nineteen Eighty-Four.*

The Goldilocks Principle

"Primary" is the key word in item #46. The primary concern should describe the passage as a whole, not a small part of it and nothing beyond it.

43. The tension that the author mentions in line 34 refers to the:

A. necessity of striking a balance between the need to describe a political situation in simple terms and the need to make the description realistic.
B. reaction the reader feels because he is drawn to the characters of the fable as individuals but repulsed by the political situation.
C. delicate task faced by a literary critic who must interpret the text of a work while attempting to accurately describe the intentions of the author.
D. danger that too realistic a description of a key character will make the reader feel that the fable is actually a description of his own situation.

44. The author's attitude toward *Nineteen Eighty-Four* can best be described as:

F. condescending.
G. laudatory.
H. disparaging.
J. scholarly.

45. The author uses the phrase "another country" (line 49) to describe a political fable in which:

A. political events described in a fable occur in a place other than the author's country of origin.
B. a lack of detail makes it difficult for a reader to see the connection between his own situation and the one described in the book.
C. too many minor characters create the impression of complete disorganization, leading the reader to believe he is in a foreign country.
D. the author has allowed his personal political convictions to infect his description of the political situation.

46. The author's primary concern is to:

F. define and clarify a concept.
G. point out a logical inconsistency.
H. trace the connection between a cause and an effect.
J. illustrate a general statement with examples.

LESSON 4

Further Use of Reading Strategies, Part 2

The passages and items in this section accompany the in-class review of the skills and concepts tested by the ACT Reading Test. You will work through the items with your instructor in class. Answers are on page 432.

DIRECTIONS: Each passage below is followed by a set of items. Read the passage and choose the best answer for each item. You may refer to the passage as often as necessary to answer the items.

PASSAGE I

HUMANITIES: This passage is adapted from the speech "Is it a Crime for a Citizen of the United States to Vote?" by Susan B. Anthony.

Friends and fellow citizens: I stand before you tonight under indictment for the alleged crime of having voted at the last presidential election without having a lawful right to vote. It shall be my work this evening to prove to you that in thus voting, I not only committed no crime, but, instead, simply exercised *my citizen's rights*, guaranteed to me and all United States citizens by the National Constitution, beyond the power of any State to deny. The preamble of the Federal Constitution says: "We, the people of the United States, in order to form a more perfect union, establish justice, insure *domestic* tranquility, provide for the common defense, promote the general welfare, and secure the blessings of liberty to ourselves and our posterity."

It was we, the people, not we, the white male citizens; but we, the whole people, who formed the Union. And we formed it, not to give the blessings of liberty, but to secure them; not to the half of ourselves and the half of our posterity but to the whole people—women as well as men. And it is a downright mockery to talk to women of their enjoyment of the blessings of liberty while they are denied the use of the only means of securing them provided by this government—the ballot.

For any State to make sex a qualification that results in the disfranchisement of one entire half of the people is a violation of the supreme law of the land. By it the blessings of liberty are forever withheld from women and their female posterity. To them this government has no just powers derived from the consent of the governed. To them this government is not a democracy. It is not a republic. It is a hateful oligarchy of sex. An oligarchy of learning, where the educated govern the ignorant, might be endured; but this oligarchy of sex, which makes father, brothers, husband, sons, the oligarchs or rulers over the mother and sisters, the wife and daughters of every household—which ordains all men sovereigns, all women subjects, carries dissension, discord and rebellion into every home of the nation.

Webster's Dictionary defines a citizen as a person in the United States, entitled to vote and hold office.

The only question left to be settled now is: Are women persons? And I hardly believe any of our opponents will have the hardihood to say we are not. Being persons, then, women are citizens; and no State has a right to make any law, or to enforce any old law, that shall abridge their privileges or immunities. Hence, every discrimination against women in the laws of the States is today null and void.

> *Passage Perfect*
>
> To answer questions like item #1, pay attention to the relationships within, not so much to the details of, the analogies. What similarities does the relationship between Susan B. Anthony and her fight for women's right to vote share with the relationships of each figure in the answer choices to his or her situation? For example, consider the power balances operating in each scenario.

1. The nineteenth-century feminist leader Susan B. Anthony fought long and hard to guarantee women the right to vote. In this speech, based on her situation at the time, she talks as if she were a:

   A. defendant on trial.
   B. chairperson of a committee.
   C. legislator arguing for a new law.
   D. judge ruling at a trial.

2. Anthony broadens her appeal to her audience by showing how her case could affect all:

   F. existing laws.
   G. United States citizens.
   H. women.
   J. uneducated persons.

3. Anthony quotes the preamble to the Constitution (lines 13–18) in order to:

   A. impress the audience with her intelligence.
   B. utilize a common legalistic trick.
   C. point out which part of the preamble needs to be changed.
   D. add force to her argument.

> *Passage Perfect*
>
> For a moment, suspend what you know about what qualifies a democracy and refer to the passage to understand what Anthony qualifies as a democracy. Pay attention to details in the proximity of the argument and locate key words from the answer choices, but do not blindly choose an answer choice that regurgitates certain words and phrases from the passage without also making sure they answer the question.

4. According to Anthony, who formed the Union?

   F. Only one-half of the people
   G. The whole people
   H. White male citizens only
   J. White female citizens

5. When Anthony says that the blessings of liberty are forever withheld from women and their female posterity, she means that:

   A. all classes of women are discriminated against.
   B. women of the past have been victimized.
   C. female children of the poor will be the only ones affected.
   D. women of the present and the future will suffer.

6. Anthony argues that a government that denies women the right to vote is not a democracy because its powers do not come from:

   F. the Constitution of the United States.
   G. the rights of the states.
   H. the consent of the governed.
   J. the vote of the majority.

7. According to this speech, an "oligarchy of sex" would cause:

   A. women to rebel against the government.
   B. men to desert their families.
   C. problems to develop in every home.
   D. the educated to rule the ignorant.

8. In this speech, a citizen is defined as a person who has the right to vote and also the right to:

   F. acquire wealth.
   G. speak publicly.
   H. hold office.
   J. pay taxes.

9. Anthony argues that state laws that discriminate against women are:

   A. being changed.
   B. null and void.
   C. helpful to the rich.
   D. supported by the Constitution.

PASSAGE II

HUMANITIES: This passage is adapted from an essay by Oliver Goldsmith that appeared in 1762 in *The Citizen of the World.*

Were we to estimate the learning of the English by the number of books that are every day published among them, perhaps no country, not even China itself, could equal them in this particular. I have reckoned not less than twenty-three new books published in one day, which makes eight thousand three hundred and ninety-five in one year. Most of these are not confined to one single science, but embrace the whole circle. History, politics, poetry, mathematics, metaphysics, and the philosophy of nature are all comprised in a manual not larger than that in which our children are taught the letters. If then, we suppose the learned of England to read but an eighth part of the works which daily come from the press (and surely none can pretend to learning upon less easy terms), at this rate every scholar will read a thousand books in one year. From such a calculation, you may conjecture what an amazing fund of literature a man must be possessed of, who thus reads three new books every day, not one of which but contains all the good things that ever were said or written.

And yet I know not how it happens, but the English are not, in reality, so learned as would seem from this calculation. We meet but few who know all arts and sciences to perfection; whether it is that the generality are incapable of such extensive knowledge, or that the authors of those books are not adequate instructors. In China, the Emperor himself takes cognizance of all the doctors in the kingdom who profess authorship. In England, every man may be an author that can write; for they have by law a liberty, not only of saying what they please, but also of being as dull as they please.

Yesterday, I testified my surprise to the man in black, where writers could be found in sufficient number to throw off the books I daily saw crowding from the press. I at first imagined that their learned seminaries might take this method of instructing the world. But, to obviate this objection, my companion assured me that the doctors of colleges never wrote, and that some of them had actually forgotten their reading. "But if you desire," continued he, "to see a collection of authors, I can introduce you to a club, which assembles every Saturday at seven...." I accepted his invitation; we walked together, and entered the house some time before the usual hour for the company assembling.

My friend took this opportunity of letting me into the characters of the principal members of the club....

"The first person," said he, "of our society is Doctor Nonentity, a metaphysician. Most people think him a profound scholar, but, as he seldom speaks, I cannot be positive in that; he generally spreads himself before the fire, sucks his pipe, talks little, drinks much, and is reckoned very good company. I'm told he writes indexes to perfection: he makes essays on the origin of evil, philosophical inquiries upon any subject, and draws up an answer to any book upon 24 hours' warning...."

Map It Out

To organize your thoughts while answering item #10, underline the passage sections indicated by the line numbers in each answer choice, and then refer to the underlined portions to determine which one reflects the description in the question ("Goldsmith's disdainful attitude toward English authors"). If multiple sections fit the bill, pick the one that does it most effectively.

10. Goldsmith's disdainful attitude toward English authors is best explicated in:

F. lines 1–5.
G. lines 15–20.
H. lines 36–40.
J. lines 44–50.

11. Goldsmith believes that:

A. we can tell how knowledgeable English authors are by counting the number of books they publish.
B. the number of books published in England is not up to standards set in China.
C. the number of books published in England says nothing about English scholarship.
D. every English scholar reads a thousand books a year.

12. Goldsmith calculates the number of books published in England to:

F. impress his readers with English erudition.
G. make the point that anyone can be an author.
H. make a defense for his argument that England is better than China.
J. make a comparison with publication quotas in other lands.

Use POE

Remember to cross off Roman numeral choices in questions like item #16. Eliminating these will enable you to more quickly match the remaining ones to an answer choice, as opposed to having to check the Roman numeral options in each answer choice one at a time.

13. The tone of the second paragraph may best be described as:

A. self-satisfied.
B. awestruck.
C. affectionate.
D. sardonic.

14. Goldsmith first assumes that English writers come from:

F. foreign lands.
G. seminaries.
H. China.
J. clubs.

15. As used in line 47, *obviate* means:

A. clarify.
B. obscure.
C. turn.
D. negate.

16. Goldsmith's opinion of the first member of the club is illuminated by which of the following?

I. His conversation with the character
II. The given name for the character
III. His friend's description of the character

F. I only
G. II only
H. I and III only
J. II and III only

17. One of Goldsmith's major objections to English authors is their:

A. deficiency in language skills.
B. inclination to drink.
C. tendency to write about everything at once.
D. inability to retain information.

PASSAGE III

HUMANITIES: This passage discusses the impact of the Southwest's environment and culture on twentieth-century artists.

The Goldilocks Principle

While the passage may address various themes and ideas at different points, pay attention to the over-arching theme when answering questions such as item #18. Do not pick a theme that is far more broad than what the passage describes, but also refrain from picking a theme that is actually only a subtheme of the passage.

Georgia O'Keeffe, whose death at age 98 closed one of the most fertile chapters of American artistic creativity, flourished as a maverick in her life and work. While other painters spent a season or two in the country trying to come to terms with the scenes and settings of the Southwest, O'Keeffe stayed a lifetime. When the canvases of other artists working in the region faded from view, her stylized images and motifs made an indelible impression on countless eyes.

Between 1900 and 1945, the region now called New Mexico both fascinated and perplexed two generations of American artists. Luminaries such as Stuart Davis, Marsden Hartley, and John Sloan built their reputations on depictions of modern life in Eastern cities. Despite successes, these artists wearied of the industrial world of the East. The vast expanse of the American West offered a promise for inspiration. It was a new world to their eyes—an enchanted land far removed from urban conventions.

For these artists, life and art, so separate in New York and Paris, seemed inextricably bound in Southwestern cultures. Painters were convinced that sampling this phenomenon would strengthen and enrich their own work. Most were touched by what D.H. Lawrence called the "spirit of the place." Besides the scenic possibilities bathed in clear golden light, the rich traditions of New Mexico's Native American and Latino people—their dress, crafts, pueblos, plaza life, rituals, and simple dignity—became frequent subjects of the artists who came to Taos and Santa Fe.

Some of the artists were traditionalists—local color realists; some were modernists—like O'Keeffe, painters of the abstract. Their talents coupled with the appeal of the land gave New Mexico's art centers a status unrivaled among other summer colonies.

18. This passage deals primarily with:

F. the life of Georgia O'Keeffe.
G. the major trends of American modern art.
H. the mystery and spirit of the Southwest.
J. artists in the American Southwest.

19. The author implies that the Southwest attracted artists for all of the following reasons EXCEPT:

A. the quality of life was different from that of large urban centers.
B. the inhabitants and culture provided interesting subject matter.
C. New Mexico was the only state to support young, avant-garde painters.
D. the region offered unusual geological features and landscapes.

20. The author implies that most of the artists who painted in the Southwest:

F. originally studied in Paris.
G. lived there only temporarily.
H. painted only landscapes.
J. received considerable recognition.

21. The author mentions which of the following facts about Georgia O'Keeffe?

I. She resided permanently in the Southwest.
II. She enjoyed considerable and lasting fame.
III. She created modern, abstract paintings.

A. I only
B. II only
C. I and III only
D. I, II, and III

22. Stuart Davis, Marsden Hartley, and John Sloan were painters who painted mainly in:

F. Paris.
G. New Mexico.
H. cities in the Eastern United States.
J. Rome.

PASSAGE IV

NATURAL SCIENCE: This passage discusses the development of basic inheritance theories and the role of DNA in genetic mutation processes.

Master Moves

Students tend to get nervous about Natural Science passages in the Reading section—after all, why are they there? This is the Reading section, isn't it? Luckily, you know that you do not need to bring any science content knowledge to the ACT test (not in the Reading section and not in the Science). All of the information you will need to answer questions is in the provided text, so you and a science whiz will be on a level playing field in attacking this passage.

In 1866, Gregor Mendel published the results of his studies on the breeding of different races of pea plants. Through his experiments, Mendel discovered a pattern of inheritance and subsequently developed the concept of a "unit of inheritance."

Mendel started with a pure stock of pea plants that had recognizably different characteristics. He artificially cross-pollinated the different races of plants and noted the characteristics of the different offspring over several generations. Mendel concluded that a pair of discrete "factors" governed each trait and that they segregated upon the formation of the gametes. This pair of factors is now known as the maternally and paternally derived alleles on homologous chromosomes that first come together at fertilization and later segregate during meiosis.

Subsequent studies have shown that new genes could appear as mutations of existing genes and that crossing over and recombination could redistribute maternal and paternal characteristics. Genes can occur in a linear sequence, and groups of genes that segregate together are called "linkage groups." The chromosome is the carrier of the linear array of genes and the physical basis of the linkage groups.

It was originally thought that proteins were the genetic carrier. In contrast to nucleic acids, proteins were known to mediate complex reactions and to be composed of a variety of different building blocks. There are approximately 20 different amino acids in a protein, but only 4 different nucleotides in a nucleic acid molecule. It was not until 1944 that Avery et al. noted that deoxyribonucleic acid (DNA) was the genetic carrier, not protein. Avery and his co-workers conducted experiments on the transformation in pneumococcus. Two strains of the bacteria had been isolated: one produced colonies having a smooth (S) appearance and was able to cause pneumonia in a suitable host; the other grew into rough (R) colonies because of a defect in its capsule and was non-virulent. When a cell-free extract of the S bacteria was added to the medium in which the R strain was growing, a few of the R bacteria grew into smooth colonies and were virulent. They had become transformed. From the time of transformation, the progeny of that cell continued to have the properties of the S strain. The

Map It Out

If you are a visual learner, mapping out or diagramming the relationships or things described in a Natural Science passage can help you organize your thoughts and clarify your understanding of the passage. These diagrams will become especially helpful for explicit detail or simple inference questions which may refer back to the relationships or things described.

Passage Perfect

In questions like item #28, you must pay attention to all of the qualifications listed in the question. The correct answer choice will both 1) reflect a departure in paragraph five from the paragraphs preceding it and 2) describe the primary intention of paragraph five. DO NOT select an answer choice that only meets one of these qualifications.

transformation was a stable genetic change. Avery and his co-workers purified the contents of cells in detergent after their disruption and found that among the contents of the cells, only the purified DNA was capable of causing the transformation. As a result of these and future experiments, it was determined that in order for transformation to occur, DNA fragments entered the recipient cell intact and substituted in the bacterial chromosome for the original DNA, which was eliminated. This process resulted in the creation of a genetically different microorganism.

DNA is a very long, fibrous molecule with a backbone composed of alternate sugar and phosphate groups joined by 3'-5'-phosphodiester linkages. Attached to each sugar is one of four possible nitrogenous bases. There are two types of bases: the pyrimidines, cytosine (C) and thymine (T); and the purines, adenine (A) and guanine (G). The amount of purine equals the amount of pyrimidine, and, more specifically, the amount of adenine equals the amount of thymine, and the amount of guanine equals the amount of cytosine.

In 1953, Franklin, Watson, and Crick proposed that DNA was made of two chains of nucleotides coiled around a common axis, with the sugar-phosphate backbone on the outside and the bases pointing in toward the axis, and that the two chains were held together by hydrogen bonds. The hydrogen bonds occur between each base of one chain and an associated base on the other chain. Based on the 20-angstrom width of the fiber, a pyrimidine from one chain is always paired with a purine from the other chain. Adenine is the only purine capable of bonding to thymine and guanine is the only purine capable of bonding to cytosine.

Franklin, Watson, and Crick proposed that the information in DNA was coded for by the linear sequence of the base pairs. They theorized that a mutation could be accounted for by a chance mistake in the formation of the sequence during duplication. Another major aspect of the Watson and Crick model was the proposed complementarity between hydrogen-bonded nucleotides. For example, adenine is complementary to thymine, AGC is complementary to TCG, and one chain is complementary to the other. If the base sequence of one chain is known, then the base sequence of the complementary chain can be derived. The concept of complementarity of nucleic acids in DNA and RNA chains is the basis of most research in which these classes of molecules are involved.

23. Mendel conducted his studies using the method known as:

A. cloning.
B. genetic mapping.
C. cross-pollination.
D. transformation.

24. Mendel's findings were important because they indicated which of the following?

I. DNA fragments can replace original DNA.
II. Specific units, handed down from one generation to the next, govern traits in organisms.
III. Proteins are composed of approximately 20 different amino acids.

F. I only
G. II only
H. I and III only
J. I, II, and III

25. Contrary to earlier beliefs, Avery et al. discovered that:

A. there are only four nucleotides in DNA.
B. pneumonia can be passed from host to host.
C. genes can mutate.
D. DNA, not protein, carries genetic information.

26. If you infected R strain pneumococcus with S extract and saw a few R strain pneumococcus transformed to S strain, you would expect:

F. the remaining R strain pneumococcus to transform later.
G. only the new S strain cells to survive.
H. offspring of those transformed cells to be S strain as well.
J. a few S strain pneumococcus to transform to R strain.

27. The author uses the word *non-virulent* (line 49) to mean:

A. harmless.
B. toxic.
C. bacterial.
D. sweet.

28. In contrast to the paragraphs before, the fifth paragraph is intended primarily to:

F. give historical genetic research information.
G. describe the results of Mendel's experiments.
H. speculate on the future of genetic research.
J. provide a definition for an essential element in genetic research.

Passage Perfect

Notice that item #32 does not ask for your opinion on why the concept of complementarity in DNA is important. The word "apparently" in the question indicates that the passage advances a view on this issue, and it is your job to discover what the justification for this view is. Underline relevant support in the text for your answer to this question.

29. A chain of DNA with the pattern CAG would bond with a chain with the pattern:

A. GAC.
B. TGA.
C. GTC.
D. Cannot be determined from the given information

30. Which of the following is (are) classified as (a) purine(s)?

I. Cytosine
II. Guanine
III. Thymine

F. I only
G. II only
H. III only
J. I and II only

31. Which of the following was Watson and Crick's contribution to the study of genetics?

I. Information about the transfer of genes across membranes
II. The notion that pairs of genes could work together
III. A suggestion about the structure of DNA

A. I only
B. II only
C. III only
D. I, II, and III

32. The concept of complementarity in DNA is apparently important because:

F. it contradicts the notion that proteins are the basis for genetic transformation.
G. hydrogen bonds connect the nucleotides.
H. if maternally and paternally derived alleles were not complementary, life could not exist.
J. if you know one chain's sequence, you can determine that of the other.

PASSAGE V

NATURAL SCIENCE: This passage is adapted from a science magazine article about galaxies.

Galaxies come in a variety of sizes and shapes: majestic spirals, ruddy disks, elliptically shaped dwarfs and giants, and a menagerie of other, more bizarre forms. Most currently, popular theories suggest that conditions prior to birth—mass of the protogalactic cloud, its size, its rotation—determine whether a galaxy will be large or small, spiral or elliptical; but about 10 percent of all galaxies are members of rich clusters of thousands of galaxies. The gravitational forces of fields of nearby galaxies constantly distort galaxies in the crowded central region of rich clusters. In addition, rich clusters of galaxies are pervaded by a tenuous gas with a temperature of up to 100 million degrees. Galaxies are blasted and scoured by a hot wind created by their motion through the gas. In crowded conditions such as these, environment becomes a more important determinant of the size and shape of a galaxy than heredity. In fact, if our galaxy had happened to form well within the core of a cluster such as Virgo, the Sun would probably never have formed, because the Sun, a second- or third-generation star located in the disk of the galaxy, was formed from leftover gas five billion years or so after the initial period of star formation. By that time, in a rich cluster, the galaxy may well have already been stripped of its gas.

As a galaxy moves through the core of a rich cluster, it is not only scoured by hot gas; it encounters other galaxies as well. If the collision is one-on-one at moderate to high speeds of galaxies of approximately the same size, both galaxies will emerge relatively intact, if a little distorted and ragged about the edges. If, however, a galaxy coasts by a much larger one in a slow, grazing collision, the smaller one can be completely disrupted and assimilated by the larger.

Under the right conditions, these cosmic cannibals can consume 50 to 100 galaxies. The accumulative effect of these collisions is to produce a dynamic friction on the large galaxy, slowing it down. As a result, it gradually spirals in toward the center of the cluster. Eventually, the gravitational forces that bind the stars to the infalling galaxy are overwhelmed by the combined gravity of the galaxies in the core of the cluster—just as the ocean is pulled away from the shore at ebb tide by the Moon, the stars are pulled away from their infalling parent galaxy. If there is a large galaxy at the center of the cluster, it may ultimately capture these stars. With the passage of time, many galaxies will be torn asunder in the depths of this gravitational maelstrom and be swallowed up in the ever-expanding envelope of the central cannibal galaxy.

Galactic cannibalism also explains why there are few if any bright galaxies in these clusters other than the central supergiant galaxy. That is because the bright galaxies, which are the most massive, experience the greatest dynamical friction. They are the first to go down to the gravitational well and be swallowed up by the central galaxies.

Over the course of several billion years, 50 or so galaxies may be swallowed up, leaving only the central supergiant and the 51st, the 52nd, etc., brightest galaxies. Given time, all the massive galaxies in the cluster will be absorbed, leaving a sparse cluster of a supergiant galaxy surrounded by clouds of small, dim galaxies.

The Cambridge Edge

Here's a handy rule of thumb to remember for inference questions: answer choices that use superlatives or sweeping generalizations are almost always incorrect because they can be so vulnerable to exceptions. Be wary of inference claims that use words such as "always," "never," or "totally."

33. In line 4, the word *menagerie* most nearly means:

A. odd mixture.
B. open environment.
C. uniform collection.
D. flat area.

34. It can be inferred from the passage that the physical features of a galaxy that does not belong to a rich cluster are determined primarily by the:

F. size and rotation of the protogalactic cloud.
G. intensity of light emanating from the galaxy.
H. temperature of the interstellar gas.
J. age of the protogalactic cloud.

Master Moves

Questions that begin "According to the passage" may, at first glance, appear simple and straightforward: find the answer in the passage. However, note that the answer will not be glaringly obvious in the text; in fact, the answer choices will often recycle buzz words or even entire phrases from the passage, sometimes in ways that vary only slightly from the correct answer choice, so be on your toes and make sure all answer choices line up with evidence from the passage—not just parts.

Map It Out

Questions like item #36 are big-picture questions that require you to look at passage-level structure. Circle or underline the topic sentences of each paragraph as you read so that you can quickly find the answer to this item.

35. The author implies that the currently accepted theories on galaxy formation are:

A. completely incorrect and misguided.
B. naive and out-of-date.
C. speculative and unsupported by observation.
D. substantially correct but in need of modification.

36. According to the passage, a cluster with a central, supergiant galaxy will:

F. contain no intermediately bright galaxies.
G. have 50–100 galaxies of all sizes and intensities.
H. consist solely of third- and fourth-generation stars.
J. produce only spiral and disk-shaped galaxies.

37. According to the passage, the outcome of a collision between galaxies depends on:

A. the relative velocities of the galaxies.
B. the relative ages of the galaxies.
C. the relative sizes of the galaxies.
D. the relative velocities and sizes of the galaxies.

38. According to the passage, as a galaxy falls inward toward the center of a cluster, it:

F. collides with the central core and emerges relatively intact.
G. absorbs superheated gases from the interstellar medium.
H. is broken apart by the gravitational forces of the core.
J. is transformed by collisions into a large, spiral galaxy.

39. The passage provides information that will answer which of the following questions?

A. What is the age of our sun?
B. What proportion of all galaxies are found in clusters?
C. Approximately how many galaxies would be found in a rich cluster?
D. What type of galaxy is ours?

40. The tone of the passage can best be described as:

F. light-hearted and amused.
G. objective but engaged.
H. detached and unconcerned.
J. cautious but sincere.

PASSAGE VI

Natural Science: This passage reviews the basic physical chemistry of atoms and radioactive decay.

An atom consists of a nucleus (containing protons and neutrons) surrounded by electrons. Each proton has a positive charge of +1, and each electron has a negative charge of −1. A neutron has no charge. The number of protons in their nuclei determines the identities of the different elements. For example, hydrogen atoms have only one proton, while oxygen atoms have eight protons. The total number of protons in the nucleus is the "atomic number" of that element. The total number of protons and neutrons in the nucleus is the "atomic mass" of the atom. Different atoms of the same element may contain a different number of neutrons, and so have different atomic masses. (But they will have the same number of protons and the same atomic number.) Atoms of the same element with different atomic masses are called isotopes of that element.

Certain elements are radioactive—they emit various types of radiation from their atomic nuclei. Two common types of radiation are alpha particles and beta particles. An alpha particle, which is the equivalent of a helium nucleus, consists of two protons and two neutrons. It is written ${}^{4}_{2}\text{He}$ (the superscript 4 is the mass number of the particle, and the subscript 2 is its atomic number). A beta particle is an electron traveling at high speed. It is written ${}^{0}_{-1}\text{e}$. Both types of radiation are emitted at a very high speed and can easily penetrate other substances.

When atoms of a substance emit radiation, they are said to undergo radioactive decay. The result is a different element with a different atomic number and a different mass number. For example, when a radium atom emits an alpha particle, it decays into an atom of radon. This reaction is shown in the following equation:

$$ {}^{226}_{88}\text{Ra} \rightarrow {}^{4}_{2}\text{He} + {}^{222}_{86}\text{Rn} $$

Note that the equation is balanced. That is, the atomic number of the original atom on the left side of the equation equals the sum of the atomic numbers of the products on the right side of the equation. Similarly, the mass number of the original atom equals the sum of the mass numbers of the products. Every nuclear reaction balances in this same manner.

Some types of nuclear radiation take place very slowly; other types are very rapid. The rate of radiation is measured in half-lives. A half-life is the time required for one-half the amount of a given radioactive substance to decay.

Map It Out

This passage has a lot of different things going on—different elements, atoms, charges, and definitions. Do not let these overwhelm you—remember that everything you need to get these questions right can be found in the text. If you find yourself losing track of all the information, diagram the atoms, jot down important information (such as the properties of each atom), and legibly organize your thoughts so you can synthesize the information while reading and refer back to it to answer the questions.

41. As radium emits alpha particles, the mass of radium will:

A. increase.
B. decrease.
C. stay the same.
D. either increase or decrease, depending on the conditions.

42. In nuclear chemistry notation, two isotopes, or forms, of cobalt are written ${}^{59}_{27}\text{Co}$ and ${}^{60}_{27}\text{Co}$. The difference between the two isotopes is:

F. an alpha particle.
G. a beta particle.
H. a proton.
J. a neutron.

43. An alpha particle has:

A. no electric charge.
B. a positive electric charge.
C. a negative electric charge.
D. a variable electric charge.

44. A beta particle has:

F. no electric charge.
G. a positive electric charge.
H. a negative electric charge.
J. a variable electric charge.

45. When an atom emits a beta particle, the atomic mass number will:

A. increase.
B. decrease.
C. stay the same.
D. either increase or decrease, depending on the conditions.

READING QUIZZES

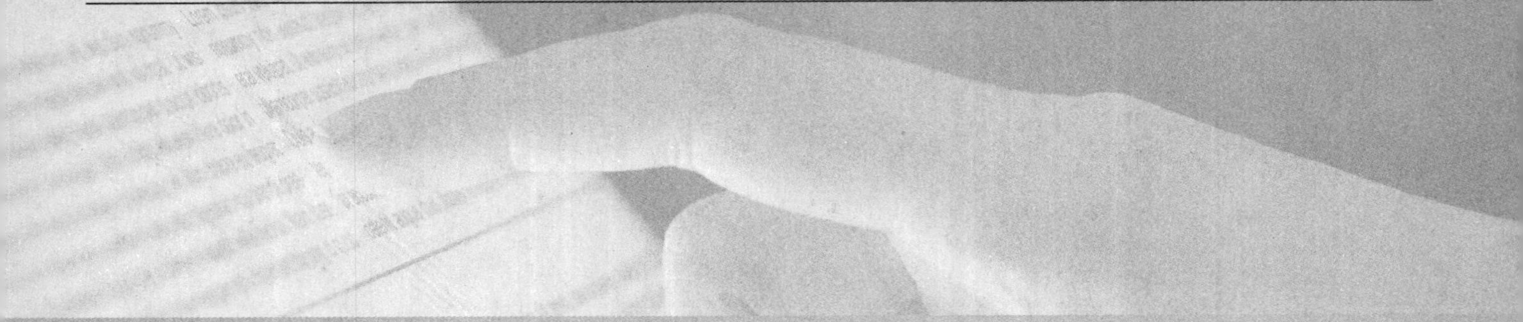

This section contains two Reading quizzes. The first quiz is a directed study quiz. The directed study quiz is not timed. Answer each question and check your work as you go. The second quiz is a timed quiz. Take the second quiz under the indicated timed conditions to practice your pacing as you apply what you learned in the Reading Lessons.

DIRECTED STUDY QUIZ *(18 items; 15 minutes)*

DIRECTIONS: Each passage below is followed by a set of items. Read the passage and choose the best answer for each item. You may refer to the passage as often as necessary to answer the items.

Passage I

SOCIAL SCIENCE: This passage discusses the economic structure of current healthcare policy.

The healthcare economy is replete with unusual and even unique economic relationships. One of the least understood involves the peculiar roles of producer or "provider" and purchaser or "consumer" in the typical doctor-patient relationship. In most sectors of the economy, the seller attempts to attract a potential buyer with various incentives of price, quality, and utility, and the buyer makes the decision. When the buyer has no choice because there is effectively only one seller and the product is essential, the government usually asserts a monopoly and places the industry under price and other regulations. Neither of these conditions prevails in most of the healthcare industry.

In the healthcare industry, the doctor-patient relationship is the mirror image of the ordinary relationship between producer and consumer. Once an individual has chosen to see a physician—and even then there may be no real choice—it is the physician who usually makes all significant purchasing decisions: whether the patient should return "next Wednesday," whether X-rays are needed, whether drugs should be prescribed, etc. It is a rare and sophisticated patient who will challenge such professional decisions or raise in advance questions about price, especially when the ailment is regarded as serious.

This is particularly significant in relation to hospital care. The physician must certify the need for hospitalization, determine what procedures will be performed, and announce when the patient may be discharged. The patient may be consulted about some of these decisions, but ultimately it is the doctor's judgments that are final. Little wonder, then, that in the eyes of the hospital, the physician is the real "consumer." Consequently, the medical staff represents the "power center" in hospital policy and decision-making, not the administration.

Although usually there are in this situation four identifiable participants—the physician, the hospital, the patient, and the payer (generally an insurance carrier or government)—the physician makes the key decisions for all of them. The hospital becomes an extension of the physician; the payer generally meets most of the bona fide bills generated by the doctor/hospital; and, for the most part, the patient plays a passive role. In routine or minor illnesses, or just plain worries, the patient's options are, of course, much greater with respect to use and price. In illnesses that are more serious, however, such choices tend to evaporate, and it is for these illnesses that the bulk of the healthcare dollar is spent. Seventy-five to eighty percent of healthcare expenditures are determined by physicians, not patients. For this reason, economy measures directed at patients or the public are relatively ineffective.

1. In lines 1–2, the phrase *replete with* most nearly means:

A. filled with.
B. restricted by.
C. enriched by.
D. damaged by.

2. The author's primary purpose is to:

F. speculate about the relationship between a patient's ability to pay and the treatment received.
G. criticize doctors for exercising too much control over patients.
H. analyze some important economic factors in healthcare.
J. urge hospitals to reclaim their decision-making authority.

3. It can be inferred that doctors are able to determine hospital policies because:

A. it is doctors who generate income for the hospital.
B. most of a patient's bills are paid by health insurance.
C. hospital administrators lack the expertise to question medical decisions.
D. a doctor is ultimately responsible for a patient's health.

EXPLANATIONS

1. (A) ***Reading/Craft and Structure/ Vocabulary***
The passage discusses the variety of economic relationships in the healthcare sector that turn ordinary relationships upside down. For example, the decisions are primarily made not by the consumer (patient) or payer (government or insurance) but by the provider, namely, the doctor. According to the passage, these strange relationships are the norm in healthcare. So, to be "replete with" such relationships means to be "filled with" them.

2. (H) ***Reading/Key Ideas and Details/Main Idea***
Surveying the opening words of each choice, we can eliminate (J), and probably (F) and (G) as well. As for (J), although a reader might use the information supplied in the passage to support some action, the primary purpose of the passage itself is not to "urge" or persuade. Similarly, although someone might use the information supplied to criticize doctors, criticism is not the author's primary goal. Eliminate (F) because the author may be said to investigate or analyze an issue, but he does not ever speculate.

3. (A) ***Reading/Key Ideas and Details/Implied Idea***
In the second paragraph, the author states that it is the physician who is the real "consumer." It is not surprising that physicians would make key decisions. Although the author does not specifically say so, we may infer that physicians control power because they control the money, (A). (B) mentions a related issue, but the author states that carriers are generally rubber stamps, paying whatever the physician approves. Thus, it is the

EXPLANATIONS

physician, not the carrier, who has the real power. As for (C), the passage never mentions anything about the expertise of hospital administrators nor anything related to that topic. Finally, (D) is arguably an explanation to the question, but it is not the one given by the author. The author cites economic factors, not professional ones; though this may be a true statement, it is not a response to the question that is being asked.

4. According to the author, when a doctor tells a patient to "return next Wednesday," the doctor is in effect:

F. taking advantage of the patient's concern for his health.
G. instructing the patient to buy more medical services.
H. warning the patient that a hospital stay might be necessary.
J. advising the patient to seek a second opinion.

4. **(G)** ***Reading/Key Ideas and Details/Explicit Detail***
The reference you need is in the second paragraph. The author states that it is the physician who makes the purchasing decisions on behalf of the patient. One example is whether to schedule a return visit. Thus, when the doctor tells a patient to make another appointment, the doctor is effectively telling the patient to buy more of his services. As for (F), the author does not indict the motives of the doctor. A doctor may believe that a patient badly needs another visit, but this does not mean that the doctor is taking advantage of the patient's concern for his or her own health. As for (H), there is no hidden meaning in the doctor's statement. Finally, (J) is certainly not the meaning of the statement. The doctor is requesting that the patient return to him or her, not that the patient see another doctor.

5. The author is most probably leading up to:

A. a proposal to control medical costs.
B. a discussion of a new medical treatment.
C. an analysis of the causes of inflation in the United States.
D. a study of lawsuits against doctors for malpractice.

5. **(A)** ***Reading/Key Ideas and Details/Application***
The author concludes the passage with the statement that, because of the factors cited, cost control measures aimed at patients are ineffective. Patients do not decide what medical services to buy. Logically, the author could be leading up to a discussion of a plan to solve this problem. (B) would not be a logical extension of the argument. Though the passage discusses medicine, it analyzes the economics of healthcare, not medical knowledge. (C) goes beyond the scope of the passage. The passage focuses specifically on the problem of cost control in the healthcare industry. Finally, as for (D), although in the real world medical malpractice suits may be tied to

EXPLANATIONS

problems of cost control, there is nothing in the passage to suggest that this is the direction in which the author is moving.

6. The tone of the passage can best be described as:

F. whimsical.
G. cautious.
H. analytical.
J. inquisitive.

6. (H) ***Reading/Craft and Structure/Voice*** The statements in the passage—though critical in their content—are made in an analytical tone. So, (H) is the best description of the tone of the passage. (F) can easily be eliminated because there is no sense of whimsy in the passage. As for (J), though the author does answer some questions, the tone of the passage is more assertive than inquisitive. The author confidently makes some bold claims. For this reason, (G), too, must be wrong.

7. With which of the following statements would the author be most likely to agree?

A. Few patients are reluctant to object to the course of treatment prescribed by a doctor or to question the cost of the services.
B. The payer, whether an insurance carrier or the government, is less likely to acquiesce to demands for payment when the illness of the patient is regarded as serious.
C. Today's patients are more informed as to what services and procedures they will need from their healthcare providers.
D. The more serious the illness of a patient, the less likely it is that the patient will object to the course of treatment prescribed or question the cost of services.

7. (D) ***Reading/Key Ideas and Details/Application*** (D) is something that the author would accept. In the last paragraph, he notes that this problem is particularly pronounced when the ailment is a serious one. (A) is something with which the author is unlikely to agree. Had it said "Most patients" rather than "Few patients," the author would have agreed: the author states that it is a "rare and sophisticated" patient who challenges a doctor's decision regarding treatment (lines 27–29). (B) is not something that the author would likely accept. In the fourth paragraph, the author states that the payer generally meets most of the bona fide bills of a patient. Here, the author does not draw a distinction between serious and not-so-serious illnesses. (C) is incorrect, as the author begins the narrative discussing the reversed role of the consumer/provider relationship between patient and doctor in which the patient must rely completely on the doctor for information regarding what services and procedures to "purchase."

8. The author's primary concern is to:

F. define a term.
G. clarify a misunderstanding.
H. refute a theory.
J. discuss a problem.

EXPLANATIONS

8. (J) ***Reading/Key Ideas and Details/Main Idea***

(J) is the best description of the passage since the author discusses the problem of the cost structure of the healthcare industry. Even if we allow that the author does define a term (for example, "payer"), (F), providing a definition is not the main point of the passage. As for (G), it is true that the author argues that the ordinary economic relationships are reversed in the healthcare sector, but the fact that the relationships are unusual does not mean that they are misunderstood. Finally, (H) is incorrect for the same reason. The author does not attack the economic theory that applies to most sectors of the economy. Indeed, the author is implicitly committed to the assumption that the general theory of economic relations is correct.

Passage II

HUMANITIES: This passage discusses Leif Ericsson's and Biarni's voyages to North America.

In the summer of 999, Leif Ericsson voyaged to Norway and spent the following winter with King Olaf Tryggvason. Substantially the same account is given by both the *Saga of Eric the Red* and the *Flat Island Book*. Of Leif's return voyage to Greenland, the latter says nothing. But according to the former, it was during this return voyage that Leif discovered America. The *Flat Island Book*, however, tells of another and earlier landfall by Biarni, the son of a prominent man named Heriulf. It makes this trip Leif's inspiration for the voyage to the new land. In short, like Leif, Biarni and his companions discovered three countries in succession before reaching Greenland. To come upon each new land takes one "doegr" more than the last until Biarni comes to land directly in front of his father's house in the last-mentioned country.

Most later writers have rejected this narrative, and they may be justified. Possibly, Biarni was a companion of Leif when he voyaged from Norway to Greenland via America. Or it may be that the entire tale is but a garbled account of that voyage and Biarni is another name for Leif. It should be noted, however, that the stories of Leif's visit to King Olaf and Biarni's to that king's predecessor are in the same narrative in the *Flat Island Book*. So there is less likelihood of duplication than if they were from different sources. Also, Biarni landed on none of the lands he passed, but Leif apparently landed on one, for he brought back specimens of wheat, vines, and timber. Nor is there any good reason to believe that the first land visited by Biarni was Wineland. The first land was "level and covered with woods," and "there were small hillocks upon it." Later writers do not emphasize forests particularly in connection with Wineland, though they are often noted incidentally; and of hills, the *Saga* says of Wineland only "wherever there was hilly ground, there were vines."

Additionally, if the two narratives were from the same source, we should expect a closer resemblance of Helluland. The *Saga* says of it: "They found there hellus" (large flat stones). According to the Biarni narrative, however, "this land was high and mountainous." The intervals of one, two, three, and four "doegr" in both narratives are suggestive. But mythic formulas of this kind may be introduced into narratives without altogether destroying their validity. It is also held against the Biarni narrative that its hero is made to come upon the coast of Greenland exactly in front of his father's home. But it should be recalled that Heriulfsness lay below two high mountains that served as landmarks for navigators.

Biarni could be given up more readily were it not that the story of Leif's voyage, contained in the supposedly more reliable *Saga*, is almost as amazing. But Leif's voyage across the entire width of the North Atlantic is said to be "probable" because it is documented in the narrative of a preferred authority. Biarni's is "improbable," or even "impossible," because the document containing it has been condemned.

EXPLANATIONS

9. The author's primary concern is to demonstrate that:

A. Leif Ericsson did not visit America.
B. Biarni might have visited America before Leif Ericsson.
C. Biarni did not visit Wineland.
D. Leif Ericsson visited Wineland first.

10. The passage provides information that defines which of the following terms?

I. Doegr
II. Hellus
III. Heriulfsness

F. I only
G. II only
H. I and II only
J. II and III only

11. It can be inferred from the passage that scholars who doubt the authenticity of the Biarni narrative make all of the following objections EXCEPT:

A. Biarni might have accompanied Leif Ericsson on the voyage to America, and that is why a separate, erroneous narrative was invented.
B. the similarity of the voyages described in the *Saga* and in the *Flat Island Book* indicates that there was but one voyage, not two voyages.
C. it seems very improbable that a ship, having sailed from America to Greenland, could have found its way to a precise point on the coast of Greenland.
D. both the *Saga of Eric the Red* and the *Flat Island Book* make use of mythic formulas, so it is probable that the same person wrote them both.

9. (B) *Reading/Key Ideas and Details/Main Idea*

The author offers several reasons why the Biarni narrative does not describe the same series of events as those in the *Saga* in order to prove that Biarni visited America before Leif Ericsson did, (B). (A) misinterprets the author's strategy: the author need not prove that Leif Ericsson did not visit America, only that Biarni did so before him. (C) is too narrow to be the author's main point. It is true that the author wants to show that the two voyages are to some extent dissimilar, and that is why he tries to prove that Biarni did not visit Wineland. However, this is only a small part of the overall development. As for (D), again, the author needs only to argue that Biarni did not visit the same three lands later visited by Leif Ericsson.

10. (J) *Reading/Key Ideas and Details/Explicit Detail*

In line 47–48, the author defines "hellus," (II), as "large flat stones;" therefore, eliminate (F) and (H). "Heriulfsness," (III), is implicitly defined in lines 58–59 as the home of Biarni's father. Although it is clear that a "doegr," (I), is a unit of time, the amount of time it spans could be a day, two days, a week, a fortnight, or a month. Therefore, the correct answer includes (II) and (III) only, (J).

11. (D) *Reading/Key Ideas and Details/Implied Idea*

In the second paragraph, the author acknowledges that Biarni may have been Leif Ericsson's companion and that the Biarni narrative might be a garbled tale of that adventure. This suggests that objectors might try to explain away the "other voyage" in this way, (A). Since the author spends so much effort attempting to prove that the two voyages did not include exactly the same countries, it is inferable that objectors use the similarity between the two voyages as proof that there was only one, (B). In the third paragraph, the author argues that it is reasonable to believe that Biarni could sail directly to his father's house since the house was situated by known navigational landmarks, suggesting that objectors

EXPLANATIONS

of the Biarni narrative must argue that the event was improbable, (C). (D) is the only choice that would not undermine the authenticity of the Biarni narrative. The similarity of the two sequences of "doegr" might suggest that two accounts were based on the same events, causing objections to the authenticity of the Biarni narrative. Yet, this does not prove that the same author wrote the two narratives. Furthermore, someone who rejects the authenticity of the Biarni narrative would argue that it is actually from the same source as the authentic *Saga* story.

12. The author mentions the two high mountains (lines 59–60) in order to show that it is:

F. reasonable for Biarni to land precisely at his father's home.
G. possible to sail from Norway to Greenland without modern navigational equipment.
H. likely that Biarni landed on America at least 100 years before Leif Ericsson.
J. probable that Leif Ericsson followed the same course as Biarni.

12. (F) ***Reading/Key Ideas and Details/Implied Idea***
One objection to the Biarni narrative is that it would have been difficult for Biarni to navigate so accurately. The author points out that the location of Heriulf's house was clearly indicated by mountains to provide an explanation for how Biarni could have landed at that precise location, (F).

13. All of the following are mentioned as similarities between Leif Ericsson's voyage and Biarni's voyage EXCEPT:

A. both visited Norway.
B. on the return voyage, both visited three different lands.
C. both returned to Greenland.
D. both sighted Wineland.

13. (D) ***Reading/Key Ideas and Details/Explicit Detail***
(A), (B), and (C) are all mentioned in the first paragraph. In lines 34–36, the author says that there is no good reason to believe that the first land sighted by Biarni was Wineland. Since the author is comparing the similarities between Leif and Biarni, this implies that Leif did see Wineland first. However, there is nothing to suggest that Biarni actually saw Wineland. Therefore, (D) is the false statement and the correct answer.

14. It can be inferred that the author regards the historicity of the Biarni narrative as:

F. conclusively proved.
G. almost conclusively proved.
H. possibly true.
J. highly unlikely.

14. (H) ***Reading/Craft and Structure/Voice***
The author gives several arguments for the historicity, or historical accuracy, of the narrative, so eliminate (J). On the other hand, the author does not claim to have proven his case conclusively—he admits in line 21 that the objectors to the Biarni narrative "may be justified," so eliminate (F). In lines 61–64, the author states, "Biarni could be given up more

EXPLANATIONS

readily were it not that the story of Leif's voyage, contained in the supposedly more reliable *Saga*, is almost as amazing," which strongly suggests that the author does not regard the issue as settled. Therefore, eliminate (G). (H) is the best answer: the author considers the Biarni narrative to be possibly true.

15. In the final paragraph, the author suggests that some authorities who regard the *Saga* as authentic are guilty of which of the following errors in reasoning?

A. Oversimplification
B. Logical contradiction
C. False analogy
D. Circular reasoning

15. (D) *Reading/Key Ideas and Details/Implied Idea*
In the final paragraph, the author states that the *Saga* attributes to Leif feats that are similar to those attributed to Biarni in the *Flat Island Book*. Nonetheless, most authorities regard Leif's voyage as authentic and thus probable, while they consider Biarni's voyage to be inauthentic and thus improbable. The passage does not qualify the condition of authenticity as being "that which is believable." Therefore, since circular reasoning, (D), makes assumptions, it is not a valid method of reasoning. The other choices describe logical errors that might make an argument fallacious, but they are not descriptive of the author's argument in the last paragraph.

16. According to the passage, Heriulf is:

F. Leif Ericsson's son.
G. one of Leif Ericsson's sailors.
H. Biarni's father.
J. King Olaf Tryggvason's son.

16. (H) *Reading/Key Ideas and Details/Explicit Detail*
In lines 10–11, the author states that Biarni is the son of a prominent man named Heriulf, (H).

17. According to the author, most authorities regard the Biarni narrative as:

A. conclusively demonstrated.
B. probably true.
C. probably untrue.
D. an attempted fraud.

17. (C) *Reading/Key Ideas and Details/Explicit Detail*
In lines 20–21, the author notes that most writers have rejected the Biarni narrative, (C).

18. Biarni's home was in:

F. Norway.
G. Greenland.
H. Wineland.
J. Flat Island.

18. (G) *Reading/Key Ideas and Details/Explicit Detail*
In lines 15–19, the author notes that Biarni returned to his father's house in Greenland, (G).

TIMED QUIZ *(17 items; 15 minutes)*

DIRECTIONS: Each passage below is followed by a set of items. Read the passage and choose the best answer for each item. You may refer to the passage as often as necessary to answer the items. Answers are on p. 432.

Passage I

SOCIAL SCIENCE: This passage discusses the 1796 presidential election between Thomas Jefferson and John Adams.

"Heartily tired" from the brutal, almost daily, conflicts that erupted between himself and Alexander Hamilton, Thomas Jefferson resigned his position as Secretary of State in 1793. His Federalist opponents were convinced that this was merely a strategic withdrawal to allow him an opportunity to plan and promote his candidacy for the presidency should Washington step down in 1796. Jefferson, however, insisted that this retirement from public life was to be final.

But even in retirement, the world of politics pursued him. As the election grew nearer and it became apparent that Washington would not seek a third term, rumors of Jefferson's presidential ambitions grew in intensity. He reacted to these continuous insinuations in a letter to James Madison. Jefferson admitted that while his enemies had originated the idea that he coveted the office of chief executive, he had been forced to examine his true feelings on the subject for his own peace of mind. In so doing, he concluded that his reasons for retirement—the desire for privacy and the delight of family life—coupled with his now failing health were insuperable barriers to public service. The "little spice of ambition" he had in his younger days had long since evaporated and the question of his presidency was forever closed.

Jefferson did not actively engage in the campaign on his own behalf. The Republican Party, presaging modern campaign tactics, created a grass roots sentiment for their candidate by directing their efforts toward the general populace. In newspapers, Jefferson was presented as "the uniform advocate of equal rights among the citizens" while Adams was portrayed as the "champion of rank, titles, heredity, and distinctions."

Jefferson was not certain of the outcome of the election until the end of December. Under the original electoral system established by the Constitution, each presidential elector cast his ballot for two men without designating between them as to office. The candidate who received the greater number of votes became the president; the second highest, the vice president. Based on his own calculations, Jefferson foresaw that the electoral vote would be close. He wrote to Madison that in the event of a tie, he wished for the choice to be in favor of Adams. The New Englander had always been his senior in public office, he explained, and the expression of public will being equal, he should be preferred for the higher honor. Jefferson, a shrewd politician, realized that the transition of power from the nearly mythical Washington to a lesser luminary in the midst of the deep and bitter political divisions facing the nation could be perilous. He had no desire to be caught in the storm that had been brewing for four years and was about to break. "This is certainly not a moment to covet the helm," he wrote to Edward Rutledge. When the electoral vote was tallied, Adams emerged as the victor. Rejoicing at his "escape," Jefferson was completely satisfied with the decision. Despite their obvious and basic political differences, Jefferson genuinely respected John Adams as a friend and compatriot. Although he believed that Adams had deviated from the course set in 1776, Jefferson never felt a diminution of confidence in Adams' integrity and was confident he would not steer the nation too far off its Republican tack. Within two years, Jefferson's views would be drastically altered as measures such as the Alien and Sedition Acts of 1798 convinced him of the need to wrest control of the government from the Federalists.

1. The phrase *heartily tired* (line 1) is most probably a quotation from:

A. Alexander Hamilton.
B. Thomas Jefferson.
C. George Washington.
D. John Adams.

2. The "escape" mentioned in line 66 refers to the fact that Jefferson:

F. was no longer Secretary of State.
G. would not be burdened with the problems of the presidency.
H. fled the country following the election.
J. was hoping that the votes would be recounted.

3. According to the passage, the Republican Party appealed primarily to:

A. wealthy landowners.
B. ordinary people.
C. prosperous merchants.
D. high society.

4. The author states that all of the following were reasons Jefferson resigned as Secretary of State EXCEPT:

F. Jefferson disliked Madison.
G. Jefferson wanted to spend time with his family.
H. Jefferson was weary of the demands of public service.
J. Jefferson wished for greater privacy.

5. The author is primarily concerned with revealing:

A. the feud between Alexander Hamilton and Thomas Jefferson.
B. the difference between the Federalists and the Republicans.
C. the strategies used by early American political parties.
D. Thomas Jefferson's character and personality.

6. The author relies on which of the following in developing the selection?

I. Personal correspondence
II. Newspapers
III. Voter registration rolls

F. I only
G. II only
H. I and II only
J. I and III only

7. One reason for Jefferson's retirement was his disagreement with:

A. Alexander Hamilton.
B. George Washington.
C. James Madison.
D. Edward Rutledge.

8. As used in lines 63–64, *covet the helm* means:

F. to aspire to be President.
G. to desire to purchase a boat.
H. to wish to be left in peace.
J. to hope to become wealthy.

9. The passage suggests that two years after the 1796 election, Jefferson would:

A. ally himself with Alexander Hamilton.
B. ally himself with John Adams.
C. disagree with John Adams.
D. disagree with Edward Rutledge.

10. The newspaper depicted Jefferson and Adams as:

F. conservative and liberal, respectively.
G. liberal and conservative, respectively.
H. conservatives.
J. liberals.

Passage II

NATURAL SCIENCE: This passage discusses human social evolution and adaptation.

Man, so the truism goes, lives increasingly,in a man-made environment. This puts a special burden on human immaturity, for it is plain that adapting to such variable conditions must depend on opportunities for learning, or whatever the processes are that are operative during immaturity. It must also mean that during immaturity, man must master knowledge and skills that are neither stored in the gene pool nor learned by direct encounter. Rather, they are contained in the culture pool—knowledge about values and history, skills as varied as an obligatory natural language or an optional mathematical one, as mute as levers or as articulate as myth telling.

Yet, it would be a mistake to leap to the conclusion that because human immaturity makes possible high flexibility, anything is possible for the species. Human traits were selected for their survival value over a four- to five-million-year period with a great acceleration of the selection process during the last half of that period. There were crucial, irreversible changes during that final man-making period: the recession of formidable dentition, a 50-percent increase in brain volume, the obstetrical paradox—bipedalism and strong pelvic girdle, larger brain through a smaller birth canal—an immature brain at birth, and creation of what Washburn has called a "technical-social way of life," involving tool and symbol use.

Note, however, that hominidization consisted mainly of adaptations to conditions in the Pleistocene. These preadaptations, shaped in response to earlier habitat demands, are part of man's evolutionary inheritance. This is not to say that close beneath the skin of man is a naked ape, that civilization is only a veneer. The technical-social way of life is a deep feature of the species adaptation. But we would err if we assumed that man's inheritance placed no constraint on his power to adapt. Some of the preadaptations can be shown to be presently maladaptive. Man's inordinate fondness for fats and sweets no longer serves his individual survival well. Furthermore, the human obsession with sexuality is plainly not fitted for survival of the species now, however well it might have served to populate the upper Pliocene and the Pleistocene. Nevertheless, note that the species typically responds to these challenges by technical innovation rather than by morphological or behavioral change. Contraception dissociates sexuality from reproduction. Of course, we do not know what kinds and what range of stresses are produced by successive rounds of such technical innovation. Dissociating sexuality and reproduction, for example, surely produces changes in the structure of the family, which in turn redefines the role of women, which in turn alters the authority pattern affecting the child, etc. Continuing and possibly accelerating change seems inherent in such adaptation. This, of course, places an enormous pressure on man's uses of immaturity, preparing the young for unforeseeable change—more so if there are severe restraints imposed by human preadaptations to earlier conditions of life.

11. The primary purpose of the passage is to:

A. refute some misconceptions about the importance of human immaturity.
B. introduce a new theory of the origins of the human species.
C. describe the evolutionary forces that formed the physical appearance of modern humans.
D. discuss the importance of human immaturity as an adaptive mechanism.

12. It can be inferred that the obstetrical paradox is puzzling because:

F. it occurred very late during the evolution of the species.
G. evolutionary forces seemed to work at cross purposes to each other.
H. technological innovations have made the process of birth easier.
J. an increase in brain size is not an ordinary evolutionary event.

13. Which of the following statements can be inferred from the passage?

A. Human beings are today less sexually active than were our ancestors during the Pleistocene era.
B. During the Pleistocene era, a fondness for fats and sweets was a trait that contributed to human survival.
C. Mathematics was invented by human beings during the latter half of the Pleistocene era.
D. The use of language and tools is a trait that is genetically transmitted from one generation to the next.

14. As it is used in line 35, the word *preadaptations* refers to traits that:

F. were useful to earlier human beings but have since lost their utility.
G. appeared in response to the need to learn a natural language and the use of tools.
H. humans currently exhibit but that developed in response to conditions of an earlier age.
J. are disadvantageous to creatures whose way of life is primarily technical and social.

15. The author mentions contraception to demonstrate that:

A. human beings may adapt to new conditions by technological invention rather than by changing their behavior.
B. sexual promiscuity is no longer an aid to the survival of the human species.
C. technological innovation is a more important adaptive mechanism than either heredity or direct encounter.
D. conditions during the upper Pliocene and Pleistocene eras no longer affect the course of human evolution.

16. With which of the following statements would the author LEAST likely agree?

F. The technical-social way of human life is an adaptive mechanism that arose in response to environmental pressures.
G. The possibility of technical innovation makes it unlikely that the physical appearance of humans will change radically in a short time.
H. Technological innovations can result in changes in the social structures in which humans live.
J. The fact that humans have a technical-social way of life makes the species immune from evolutionary pressures.

17. The author is most probably addressing which of the following audiences?

A. Medical students in a course on human anatomy
B. College students in an introductory course on archaeology
C. Psychologists investigating the uses of human immaturity
D. Biologists trying to trace the course of human evolution

READING

REVIEW

This section contains additional Reading items for further practice. Answers are on page 432.

DIRECTIONS: Each passage below is followed by a set of items. Read the passage and choose the best answer for each item. You may refer to the passage as often as necessary to answer the items.

Passage I

NATURAL SCIENCE: This passage discusses systems for reporting and investigating adverse drug effects.

A key principle of pharmacology is that all drugs have multiple actions. Actions that are desirable in the treatment of disease are considered therapeutic. Those that are undesirable or pose risks to the patient are called "effects." Adverse drug effects range from the trivial, for example, nausea or dry mouth, to the serious, such as massive gastrointestinal bleeding; some drugs can even be lethal. Therefore, an effective system for the detection of adverse drug effects is an important component of the healthcare system of any nation. Much of the research conducted on new drugs aims to identify the conditions of use that maximize beneficial effects and minimize the risk of adverse effects. The intent of drug labeling is to reflect this body of knowledge accurately so that physicians can properly prescribe the drug or, if it is to be sold without prescription, so that consumers can properly use the drug.

The current system of drug investigation in the United States has proven very useful in identifying the side effects associated with new prescription drugs. By the time a new drug is approved by the Food and Drug Administration, its side effects are usually well described in the package insert for physicians. The investigational process, however, cannot be counted on to detect all adverse effects because of the relatively small number of patients involved in pre-marketing studies and the relatively short duration of the studies. Animal studies are, of course, done before marketing in an attempt to identify any potential for toxicity, but negative results do not guarantee the safety of a drug in humans, as evidenced by such well-known examples as the birth deformities due to thalidomide.

In many countries, this recognition prompted the establishment of programs to which physicians report adverse drug effects. The United States and other countries also send reports to an international program operated by the World Health Organization. These programs, however, are voluntary reporting programs and are intended to serve a limited goal: alerting a government or private agency to adverse drug effects detected by physicians in the course of practice. Other approaches must be used to confirm suspected drug reactions and to estimate incidence rates. These other approaches include conducting retrospective control studies, for example, the studies associating endometrial cancer with estrogen use, and monitoring hospitalized patients to determine the incidence of acute common side effects. This approach was typified by the Boston Collaborative Drug Surveillance Program.

Thus, the drug surveillance system of the United States is composed of a set of information bases, special studies, and monitoring programs, each contributing in its own way to our knowledge about marketed drugs. The system is decentralized among a number of governmental units and is not administered as a coordinated function. Still, it would be unwise at this time to attempt to unite all of the disparate elements into a comprehensive surveillance program. Instead, the challenge is to improve each part of the system and to take advantage of new online strategies to improve coordination and communication.

1. In line 70, the word *disparate* most nearly means:

A. useless.
B. expensive.
C. temporary.
D. unconnected.

2. The author's primary concern is to discuss:

F. methods for testing the effects of new drugs on humans.
G. the importance of having accurate information about the effects of drugs.
H. procedures for determining the long-term effects of new drugs.
J. attempts to curb the abuse of prescription drugs.

3. The author implies that a drug with adverse side effects:

A. will not be approved for use by consumers without a doctor's prescription.
B. must wait for approval until lengthy studies prove the effects are not permanent.
C. should be used only if its therapeutic value outweighs its adverse effects.
D. should be withdrawn from the marketplace pending a government investigation.

4. Which of the following can be inferred from the passage?

F. The decentralization of the overall drug surveillance system results in it being completely ineffective in any attempts to provide information about adverse drug effects.
G. Drugs with serious adverse side effects are never approved for distribution.
H. Some adverse drug effects are discovered during testing because they are very rare.
J. Some adverse drug effects cannot be detected prior to approval because they take a long time to develop.

5. The author introduces the example of thalidomide in the last sentence of the second paragraph to show that some:

A. drugs do not have the same reactions in humans that they do in animals.
B. drug testing procedures are ignored by careless laboratory workers.
C. drugs have no therapeutic value for humans.
D. drugs have adverse side effects as well as beneficial actions.

6. It can be inferred that the estrogen study mentioned at the end of the third paragraph:

F. uncovered long-term side effects of a drug that had already been approved for sale by the Food and Drug Administration.
G. discovered potential side effects of a drug that was still awaiting approval for sale by the Food and Drug Administration.
H. revealed possible new applications of a drug that had previously been approved for a different treatment.
J. is an example of a study that could be more efficiently conducted by a centralized authority than by volunteer reporting.

7. The author is most probably leading up to a discussion of some suggestions about how to:

A. centralize authority for drug surveillance in the United States.
B. centralize authority for drug surveillance among international agencies.
C. coordinate better sharing of information among the drug surveillance agencies.
D. eliminate the availability and sale of certain drugs now on the market.

8. The author makes use of which of the following devices in the passage?

F. Definition of terms
G. Examples
H. Analogy
J. Definition of terms and examples

Passage II

NATURAL SCIENCE: This passage is adapted from a science magazine article that discusses lightning.

Lightning is an electrical discharge of immense proportions. Some 80 percent of lightning occurs within clouds; about 20 percent is cloud-to-ground lightning; and an extremely small percentage is cloud-to-sky lightning.

Cloud-to-ground lightning begins when complex meteorological processes cause a tremendous electrostatic charge to build up within a cloud. Typically, the bottom of the cloud is negatively charged. When the charge reaches 50 to 100 million volts, air is no longer an effective insulator, and lightning occurs within the cloud itself. Ten to 30 minutes after the onset of intracloud lightning, negative charges called stepped leaders emerge from the bottom of the cloud, moving toward the earth in 50-meter intervals at speeds of 100 to 200 kilometers per second and creating an ionized channel. As the leaders near the Earth, their strong electric field causes streamers of positively charged ions to develop at the tips of pointed objects that are connected directly or indirectly to the ground. These positively charged streamers flow upward.

When the distance, known as the striking distance, between a stepped leader and one of the streamers reaches 30 to 100 meters, the intervening air breaks down completely, and the leader is joined to the Earth via the streamer. Now a pulse of current known as a return stroke ranging from thousands to hundreds of thousands of amperes moves at one tenth to one third the speed of light from the Earth through the object from which the streamer emanated and up the ionized channel to the charge center within the cloud. An ionized channel remains in the air and additional negative charges called dart leaders will quickly move down this path resulting in further return strokes. This multiplicity causes the flash to flicker. The entire event typically lasts about one second.

The return stroke's extremely high temperature creates the visible lightning and produces thunder by instantly turning moisture into steam. Most direct damage results from the heavy return stroke current because it produces high temperatures in the channel, or from arcing at the point of ground contact. If the lightning current is carried by an enclosed conductor (e.g., within a jacketed cable, through a concrete wall, or beneath a painted surface), entrapped moisture is turned into high-pressure steam that can cause a cable, wall, or painted object to explode. Arcing frequently ignites combustibles.

Lightning causes hundreds of millions of dollars in property losses annually and the majority of forest fires. Lightning is also the leading weather-related killer in the United States, causing 100 to 200 deaths each year.

The Cambridge Edge

Pay attention to the context when answering Vocabulary items such as #9. Sometimes the context will give you clues as to the correct answer, but you may still need to guess. And sometimes simply reading the context gives you the correct answer.

9. In line 15, the word *intracloud* most nearly means:

A. between clouds.
B. within a cloud.
C. from cloud to sky.
D. from ground to cloud.

10. The selection defines the striking distance as the distance between:

F. the ground and the cloud.
G. a stepped leader and a dart leader.
H. a dart leader and a return stroke.
J. a streamer and a stepped leader.

11. According to the selection, the flickering appearance of a lightning strike is created by:

A. the stepped movement of leaders.
B. multiple return strokes.
C. water being vaporized.
D. arcing at ground contact.

12. What topic might the author logically address in a continuation of the passage?

F. Precautions to minimize lightning damage
G. Other weather phenomena that cause injury
H. Basic principles governing electricity
J. Identifying different types of clouds

13. According to the passage, which of the following is NOT true of stepped leaders?

A. They develop 10 to 30 minutes after intracloud lightning.
B. As they traverse the distance from cloud to ground, they create an ionized channel.
C. Their powerful positive charge causes streamers to develop in grounded objects.
D. They emerge from the bottom of the cloud and move downward in intervals of 50 meters.

The Cambridge Edge

Watch out for thought-reversers, such as the word "NOT" in item #13. In this case, three out of the four answers will explicitly appear in the text; the one that is NOT included in the text is the correct answer.

14. The passage answers which of the following questions?

F. How does lightning produce the associated thunder?
G. How far above the ground is the bottom of the typical lightning-producing cloud?
H. How frequently will lightning strike a given object?
J. How long does it take a cloud to build up an electrostatic charge?

15. The author's primary concern is to:

A. warn about the dangers posed by lightning strikes.
B. describe the sequence of events that make up a lightning strike.
C. discuss fundamental scientific laws pertaining to electricity.
D. support the commonly held view that lightning strikes the ground.

Passage III

SOCIAL SCIENCE: This passage discusses the history of hospitals.

Public general hospitals originated in almshouse infirmaries. Established as early as colonial times, these infirmaries were created by local governments to care for the poor. Later, in the late eighteenth and early nineteenth centuries, the infirmary separated from the almshouse and became an independent institution supported by local tax money. At the same time, private charity hospitals began to develop. Both private and public hospitals mainly provided food and shelter for the impoverished sick. There was little that medicine could actually do to cure illness, and the middle class was treated at home by private physicians.

Late in the nineteenth century, private charity hospitals began trying to attract middle-class patients. Although the depression of 1890 stimulated the growth of charitable institutions and an expanding urban population became dependent on assistance, there was a decline in private contributions to these organizations. This decline forced them to look to local government for financial support. Since private institutions had also lost benefactors, they began to charge patients. In order to attract middle-class patients, private institutions provided services and amenities that distinguished between paying and nonpaying patients, making the hospital a desirable place for private physicians to treat their own patients. As paying patients became more necessary to the survival of the private hospital, the public hospitals slowly became the only place for the poor to get treatment. By the end of the nineteenth century, cities were reimbursing private hospitals for their care of indigent patients. The public hospitals remained dependent on tax dollars.

The advent of private hospital health insurance gave middle-class patients the power to pay for private hospital services and guaranteed the private hospital a regular source of income. Private hospitals could restrict themselves to revenue-generating patients while the public hospitals were left to care for the poor. Although public hospitals continued to provide outpatient services, emergency services, and services for patients with contagious diseases, the Blue Cross plans developed around the needs of the private hospitals and the inpatients they served. Thus, reimbursement for ambulatory care has been minimal under most Blue Cross plans. Provision of outpatient care has not been a major function of the private hospital, in part because private patients can afford to pay for the services of private physicians. Also, since World War II, there has been a huge influx of federal money into private medical schools and their hospitals. Further, large private medical centers with expensive research equipment and programs have attracted the best administrators, physicians, and researchers. Because of the greater resources available to the private medical centers, it is harder for public hospitals to attract highly qualified research and medical personnel. With the mainstream of healthcare firmly established in the private medical sector, the public hospital has become a "dumping ground."

16. In line 38, the word *indigent* most nearly means:

F. without the means to pay.
G. having emergency medical needs.
H. lacking health insurance.
J. reimbursed by the government.

17. According to the passage, the very first private hospitals:

A. developed from almshouse infirmaries.
B. provided better care than public infirmaries.
C. were established mainly to service the poor.
D. were supported by government revenues.

18. It can be inferred that the author believes the differences that currently exist between public and private hospitals are primarily the result of:

F. political considerations.
G. economic factors.
H. ethical concerns.
J. legislative requirements.

19. It can be inferred that the growth of private health insurance:

A. relieved local governments of the need to fund public hospitals.
B. guaranteed that the poor would have access to medical care.
C. forced middle-class patients to use public hospitals.
D. reinforced the distinction between public and private hospitals.

20. Which of the following would be the most logical topic for the author to introduce in the next paragraph?

F. A plan to improve the quality of public hospitals
G. An analysis of the profit structure of health insurance companies
H. A proposal to raise taxes on the middle class
J. A discussion of recent developments in medical technology

21. The author's primary concern is to:

A. describe the financial structure of the healthcare industry.
B. demonstrate the importance of government support for healthcare institutions.
C. criticize wealthy institutions for refusing to provide services to the poor.
D. identify the historical causes of the division between private and public hospitals.

22. The author cites all of the following as factors contributing to the decline of public hospitals EXCEPT:

F. government money was used to subsidize private medical schools and hospitals to the detriment of public hospitals.
G. public hospitals are not able to compete with private institutions for top-flight managers and doctors.
H. large private medical centers have better research facilities and more extensive research programs than public hospitals.
J. Blue Cross insurance coverage does not reimburse subscribers for medical expenses incurred in a public hospital.

23. The author's attitude toward public hospitals can best be described as:

A. contemptuous and prejudiced.
B. apprehensive and distrustful.
C. concerned and understanding.
D. enthusiastic and supportive.

24. The author implies that any outpatient care provided by a hospital is:

F. paid for by private insurance.
G. provided in lieu of treatment by a private physician.
H. supplied primarily by private hospitals.
J. a source of revenue for public hospitals.

The Cambridge Edge

The short description at the beginning of a passage can help you preview the passage, and may even help you answer a Main Idea item, such as #21.

Passage IV

SOCIAL SCIENCE: This passage discusses a conflict that emerged following US military unification.

The National Security Act of 1947 created a national military establishment headed by a single Secretary of Defense. The legislation had been a year-and-a-half in the making. It began when President Truman first recommended that the armed services be reorganized into a single department. During that period, the President's concept of a unified armed service was torn apart and put back together several times; the final measure to emerge from Congress was a compromise. Most of the opposition to the bill came from the Navy and its spokesmen, including Secretary of the Navy James Forrestal. In support of unification (and a separate air force that was part of the plan) were the Army air forces, the Army, and, most importantly, the President of the United States.

Passage of the bill did not end the disputes. Rather than unify, the act served only to federate the military services. It neither halted the rapid demobilization of the armed forces that followed World War II nor brought to the new national military establishment the loyalties of officers steeped in the traditions of the separate services. At a time when the balance of power in Europe and Asia was rapidly shifting, the services lacked any precise statement of United States foreign policy from the National Security Council on which to base future programs. The services bickered over their roles and missions, already complicated by the Soviet nuclear capability that, for the first time, made the United States subject to devastating attack. Not even the appointment of Forrestal as first Secretary of Defense allayed the suspicions of naval officers and their supporters that the role of the US Navy was threatened with permanent eclipse. Before the war of words died down, Forrestal himself was driven to resignation and then suicide.

By 1948, the United States military establishment was forced to make do with a budget approximately 10 percent of what it had been at its wartime peak. Meanwhile, the cost of weapons was rising exponentially as the nation came to put more and more reliance on the atomic bomb. These two factors inevitably made adversaries of the Navy and the Air Force, as the battle between advocates of the B-36 and the supercarrier so amply demonstrates. Given severe fiscal restraints on the one hand, and on the other the nation's increasing focus on nuclear deterrence, the conflict between these two services over roles and missions was essentially a contest over slices of an ever-diminishing pie.

Yet if in the end neither service was the clear victor, the principle of civilian dominance over the military clearly was. If there had ever been any danger that the US military establishment might exploit, to the detriment of civilian control, the goodwill it earned as a result of its victories in World War II, that danger disappeared in the interservice animosities formed by the battle over unification.

25. In line 21, the word *demobilization* most nearly means:

A. shift to a unified military.
B. realignment of allies.
C. change from war to peace.
D. adoption of new technology.

26. According to the passage, the interservice strife that followed unification occurred primarily between the:

F. Army and Army air forces.
G. Army and Navy.
H. Army air forces and Air Force.
J. Air Force and Navy.

27. It can be inferred from the passage that Forrestal's appointment as Secretary of Defense was expected to:

A. placate members of the Navy.
B. result in decreased levels of defense spending.
C. outrage advocates of the Army air forces.
D. win Congressional approval of the unification plan.

28. According to the passage, President Truman supported:

F. elimination of the Navy.
G. a unified military service.
H. establishment of a separate air force.
J. a unified military service and establishment of a separate air force.

29. With which of the following statements about defense unification would the author most likely agree?

A. Unification ultimately undermined United States military capability by inciting interservice rivalry.
B. The unification legislation was necessitated by the drastic decline in appropriations for the military services.
C. Although the unification was not entirely successful, it had the unexpected result of ensuring civilian control of the military.
D. In spite of the attempted unification, each service was still able to pursue its own objectives without interference from the other branches.

30. According to the selection, the political situation following the passage of the National Security Act of 1947 was characterized by all of the following EXCEPT:

F. a shifting balance of power in Europe and in Asia.
G. fierce interservice rivalries.
H. lack of strong leadership by the National Security Council.
J. a lame-duck President who was unable to unify the legislature.

31. The author cites the resignation and suicide of Forrestal in order to:

A. underscore the bitterness of the interservice rivalry surrounding the passage of the National Security Act of 1947.
B. demonstrate that the Navy eventually emerged as the dominant branch of service after the passage of the National Security Act of 1947.
C. suggest that the nation would be better served by a unified armed service under a single command.
D. provide an example of a military leader who preferred to serve his country in war rather than in peace.

32. The author is primarily concerned with:

F. discussing the influence of personalities on political events.
G. describing the administration of a powerful leader.
H. criticizing a piece of legislation.
J. analyzing a political development.

Passage V

HUMANITIES: This passage is adapted from an article about early American education.

The founders of the American Republic viewed their revolution mostly in political rather than economic or social terms. Furthermore, they talked about education as essential to the public good. This goal took precedence over knowledge as job training or as a means to self-improvement. Over and over again, the Revolutionary generation, both liberal and conservative in outlook, asserted its belief that the welfare of the Republic rested upon an educated citizenry. Schools, especially free public schools, would be the best means of educating the people in civic values and the obligations required of everyone in a democratic society. All agreed that the key ingredients of a civic education were literacy and instruction in patriotic and moral virtues. Some added to these the study of history and of principles of government itself.

The founders, as was the case with almost all their successors, were long on rhetoric regarding the value of civic education. But they left it to the textbook writers to distill the essence of those values for schoolchildren. Texts in American history and government appeared as early as the 1790s. The textbook writers turned out to be largely conservative, more likely Federalist in outlook than Jeffersonian. They almost all agreed that political virtue must rest upon moral and religious precepts. Since most textbook writers were from New England, this meant that the texts were infused with a Protestant, and above all Puritan, view.

In the first half of the Republic, education emphasized civic values. It made little attempt to develop participatory political skills. That was a task left to political parties, town meetings, churches, and the coffee or ale houses where men gathered for conversation. Also, as a reading of certain Federalist papers of the time would show, the press probably did more to provide realistic, partisan knowledge of government than the schools. The goal of education, however, was to achieve a higher form of *unum* for the new Republic. In the middle half of the nineteenth century, the political values taught in the public and private schools did not change much from those of the first fifty years of the Republic. In the textbooks of the day, their rosy hues, if anything, became golden. To the strong values of liberty, equality, and a Christian morality were now added the middle-class virtues of hard work, honesty, the rewards of individual effort, and obedience to parents and authority. But of all the political values taught in school, patriotism was at the top; and whenever teachers explained to children why they should love their country above all else, the idea of liberty assumed pride of place.

33. In lines 5–6, the phrase *took precedence over* most nearly means:

A. set an example for.
B. formulated a policy of.
C. enlightened someone on.
D. had greater importance than.

34. The passage deals primarily with the:

F. content of textbooks used in early American schools.
G. role of education in late eighteenth- and early to mid-nineteenth-century America.
H. influence of New England Puritanism on early American values.
J. origin and development of the Protestant work ethic in modern America.

35. According to the passage, the founders of the Republic regarded education primarily as:

A. a religious obligation.
B. a private matter.
C. an unnecessary luxury.
D. a political necessity.

36. The author states that textbooks written in the middle part of the nineteenth century:

F. departed radically in tone and style from earlier textbooks.
G. mentioned for the first time the value of liberty.
H. treated traditional civic virtues with even greater reverence.
J. were commissioned by government agencies.

37. Which of the following would LEAST likely have been the subject of an early American textbook?

A. Basic rules of English grammar
B. The American Revolution
C. Patriotism and other civic virtues
D. Effective farming methods

38. The author's attitude toward the educational system discussed in the passage can best be described as:

F. cynical and unpatriotic.
G. realistic and analytical.
H. pragmatic and frustrated.
J. disenchanted and bitter.

39. The passage provides information that would be helpful in answering which of the following questions?

A. Why was a disproportionate share of early American textbooks written by New England authors?
B. Was the Federalist Party primarily a liberal or conservative force in early American politics?
C. How many years of education did the founders believe were sufficient to instruct young citizens in civic virtue?
D. What were the names of some of the Puritan authors who wrote early American textbooks?

40. The author implies that an early American Puritan would likely insist that:

F. moral and religious values are the foundation of civic virtue.
G. textbooks should instruct students in political issues of vital concern to the community.
H. textbooks should give greater emphasis to the value of individual liberty than to the duties of patriotism.
J. private schools with a particular religious focus are preferable to public schools with no religious instruction.

Passage VI

SOCIAL SCIENCE: This passage discusses the relationship between the US economy and international commerce.

International commerce is woven thoroughly into the fabric of the American economy. Exports and imports amounted to more than 11 percent of the US gross domestic product (GDP) in 1991. This was up dramatically from 7.5 percent just five years before. More than 7 million American jobs are related to exports. Millions more depend on the overall economic activity generated by export trade. Export-related jobs pay more—almost 17 percent more—than the average American job.

Exports are vital to the economic health of many key sectors of the manufacturing economy. For instance, makers of computers, heavy earthmoving equipment, and farm implements are increasingly dependent on export markets. For these exports, slow growth abroad translates to declining vitality at home. The same picture is true of agriculture. Roughly one in four farm acres is now harvested for the export market. International sales of business-related services—construction, finance, insurance, and engineering, among others—amount to tens of billions of dollars each year.

In the early years of the post-World War II era, the United States stood virtually alone as the industrial and technological leader of the world. At that time, the US produced almost half of the world's GDP. This included much of the world's manufactured goods. The US also had roughly 80 percent of the world's hard currency reserves. Today, while the US remains the world's leading economy, its share of world GDP has shrunk to about 24 percent. Its share of world manufacturers is even lower. Experts agree that, relative to the size of the economy and the diversity of its industrial and technological base, the US has lagged far behind its export potential.

Meanwhile, the potential for growth in US exports is enormous. Markets in Europe and Japan are huge and stable. There is growing promise in Asia's $5.7 trillion economy and Latin America's $1 trillion economy. These markets are generating a rapidly growing demand for infrastructure investment, aircraft, and high-technology capital goods—all areas in which the United States has real or potential strengths. In addition, new entrants into the world economy, such as Central and Eastern Europe and the countries of the former Soviet Union, show real promise as potential markets for US exports.

Growing world markets, however, do not automatically translate into US export sales. The fierce competition for international markets comes primarily from the more innovative firms in Europe and Japan. In particular, Japanese companies have set the pace with a mix of aggressive business practices and an economy-wide commitment to quality, rapid time to market, ongoing innovation, and customer satisfaction. American companies are beginning to try to meet the competition abroad, as well as to view their success as a benchmark for improvement, whether that best is in Chicago, Frankfurt, or Osaka.

The new realities of international competition yield lessons for the US government as well. Economic diplomacy and high-level advocacy, competitive and focused export financing, and improved efforts at information-gathering have become necessary components of an export promotion policy. Many foreign governments have been more aggressive and more focused than the US government in working with their firms to secure export sales. Senior government officials, up to and including the President or Prime Minister, often will travel to support the sale of their home country's goods and services. The US government needs to begin to measure its export strategy against the flexibility and effectiveness of the competition. Exports are central to growth, jobs, and a rising standard of living for all Americans. Our role in building a better America at home and acting as an economic leader abroad is dependent on our ability to develop a coherent, aggressive, and effective national export strategy.

41. Which of the following US economic sectors has declined most seriously since World War II?

A. Agriculture
B. Manufacturing
C. High-technology products
D. Business-related services

42. Which of the following best expresses the central point of the passage?

F. Exports drive the US economy.
G. US exports have declined since shortly after World War II.
H. Exports are so important to the US economy that steps should be taken to increase US exports worldwide.
J. The US government should encourage US corporations to expand into markets in Asia and Latin America.

43. Which of the following areas is NOT mentioned in the passage as a potential market for US goods abroad?

A. Asia
B. Latin America
C. Central Europe
D. Northern Africa

44. The passage suggests that both US corporations and the US government should:

F. discourage imports in favor of exports.
G. focus on improving the quality of American products.
H. try to meet the competition abroad.
J. take steps to reduce the economy's dependence on exports.

45. With which of the following explanations for the decline in the United States' share of world GDP would the author be most likely to agree?

I. Other countries are relatively uninterested in purchasing the goods and services the United States has to offer.
II. Other governments have done more to encourage their countries' exports than has the US government.
III. Companies in some other countries have been more enterprising in producing high-quality goods and services.

A. II only
B. I and II only
C. I and III only
D. II and III only

46. According to the passage, an increase in US exports abroad would generate:

F. more high-paying jobs for American workers.
G. increased profits for American farmers.
H. greater diversity in American industry.
J. resentment among foreign competitors.

STRATEGY SUMMARY

READING STRATEGIES

Understanding the three levels of reading comprehension and how they relate to the seven Reading item-types will help you to quickly identify the question that is being asked by a particular item.

Level 1—General Theme

The first level of reading, appreciation of the general theme, is the most basic. Main Idea items test whether you understand the passage at the most general level. The first sentence of a paragraph—often the topic sentence—may provide a summary of the content of that paragraph. Also, the last sentence of a paragraph usually provides concluding material that may also be helpful in understanding the general theme of the passage.

Main Idea items ask about the central theme that unifies the passage(s):

- *Which of the following is the main point of the passage?*
- *The primary purpose of the passage is to....*

Level 2—Specific Points

The second level of reading, understanding specific points, takes you deeper into the selection. Explicit Detail, Vocabulary, and Development items all test your ability to read carefully. Since this is an "open-book" test, you can always return to the selection. Therefore, if something is highly technical or difficult to understand, do not dwell on it for too long— you can always come back to it later if necessary.

Explicit Detail items ask about details that are specifically mentioned in the passage. This type of item differs from a Main Idea item in that explicit details are points provided by the author in the passage. Explicit Detail items provide "locator words" that identify the required information in the passage.

- *The author mentions which of the following?*
- *According to the passage,...?*

Vocabulary items test your understanding of a word or phrase in context. The nature of the Vocabulary items indicates two points. First, the correct answer choice will make sense when it is substituted for the referenced word. Second, the correct answer choice may not be the most commonly used meaning of the word; in fact, if it were, then what would be the point of including the item on the test? Thus, the general strategy for this type of item is to favor the less commonly used meaning.

- *The word ------- in line ## means....*
- *In line ##, what is the best definition of the word -------?*

Development items ask about the overall structure of the passage or about the logical role played by a specific part of the passage.

- *The author develops the passage primarily by....*
- *The author mentions...in order to....*

Level 3—Evaluation

The third level of reading, evaluation of the text, takes you even deeper into the selection. Implied Idea, Application, and Voice items ask not just for understanding, but also require a judgment or an evaluation of what you have read. This is why these items are usually the most difficult.

Implied Idea items don't ask about what is specifically stated in the passage; rather, Implied Idea items ask about what can be logically inferred from what is stated in the passage. For example, the passage might explain that a certain organism (X) is found only in the presence of another organism (Y). An accompanying Implied Idea item might ask the following question: "If organism Y is not present, what can be inferred?" Since the passage implies that in the absence of Y, X cannot be present, the answer would be "X is not present." Since this type of item generally builds on a specific detail, "locator words" for identifying information in the passage are often provided in the item stem.

- *The passage implies that....*
- *The author uses the phrase "..." to mean....*

Application items are similar to Implied Idea items, but they go one step further: examinees must apply what they have learned from the passage to a new situation.

- *With which of the following statements would the author most likely agree?*
- *The passage is most probably taken from which of the following sources?*

Voice items ask about the author's attitude toward a specific detail or the overall tone of the passage.

- *The tone of the passage can best be described as....*
- *The author regards...as....*

GENERAL STRATEGIES

Reading strategies are not an exact science. Practice is essential to mastering the following techniques:

Preview the Passage

Read the first sentence of each passage in the Reading Test. After reading the first sentence of each passage, label each passage as either "Easy" or "Hard" based on your initial understanding of the material and your level of interest. Analyze the easier passages first.

Preview Each Paragraph

Preview the first and last sentences of each paragraph. There is usually an introductory paragraph for excerpted passages that identifies the author and provides a brief description of the selection. First, read this introductory material to gain clues about the author's point of view. Then, preview the first and last sentences of each paragraph, as they often provide paragraph summaries.

Read the Passage

After previewing each paragraph, ask what the author is attempting to describe, especially in the case of Evaluation items. Bracket difficult material, either mentally or with some sort of a mark, and then simply revisit it if necessary or if time permits. Instead of wasting time re-reading, attempt to understand the context in which the author introduces a particular concept.

Code in Groups

Circle the answers to the items in the test booklet, and transcribe the answers to all the items for a passage to the answer sheet after finishing each passage. This approach helps increase accuracy and makes checking your work easier and more efficient. Only when the time limit approaches should you transcribe each answer individually.

WRITING

Course Concept Outline

I. TEST MECHANICS ... 167

A. Overview ... 168
B. Anatomy ... 169
C. Pacing ... 170
D. Time Trial ... 171
E. Game Plan ... 172

1. Use a Pencil ... 172
2. Respond to the Specific Prompt ... 172
3. Write Legibly ... 172
4. Don't Copy the Prompt ... 172
5. Don't Skip Lines ... 172
6. Be Specific ... 172

II. LESSON | PRELIMINARIES ... 173

A. What Is Tested[1]
B. Directions
C. Item Format
D. Scoring

1. Essay Scoring Guide
2. Test Scores

III. LESSON 1 | COMPOSING THE ESSAY ... 173

A. Pre-Writing
B. Beginning the Writing Process
C. The Introduction
D. The Body
E. The Conclusion
F. Revising

1 Some concepts in this Course Concept Outline are not illustrated through examples in your student text but may be covered by your instructor in class. They are included here to provide a complete outline of your course.

IV. LESSON 2 | ESSAY WRITING STRATEGIES 173

A. Begin with the Prompt
B. Write Only on the Assigned Topic
C. Do Not Try to Do Too Much
D. Outline the Essay
E. Organize Ideas into Paragraphs
F. Write Using Correct Grammar
G. Punctuate and Spell Correctly
H. Write Clearly, Concisely, and Legibly
I. Proofread the Essay

V. QUIZZES 177

A. Directed Study Quiz 178
B. Timed Quiz 183

VI. STRATEGY SUMMARY 185

WRITING

TEST MECHANICS

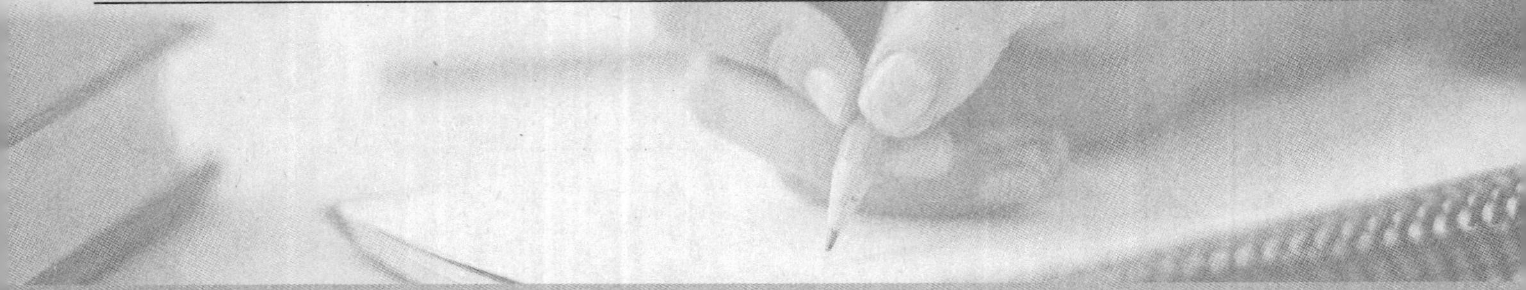

OVERVIEW

The Writing Test will assess, in broad terms, your ability to develop and express your ideas in writing. It is not intended to evaluate whether you'd be a good novelist or how well you'd write if given time to do research and write several drafts. In short, you will produce an on-demand piece of writing that will likely be of rough draft quality.

The Writing Test is also not intended to test your mastery of any body of knowledge. The topic will be sufficiently broad so that arguments and explanations can be drawn from personal experience. For example, the topic might ask you to express your opinions about sports, music, psychology, current events, or even modern technology such as video games.

The essay topic will be described as a "prompt." The word "prompt" was chosen because it indicates that the topic is really just an *excuse* or *opportunity* for you to write something. The test could just as easily say, "During the next forty minutes, write an essay on anything of interest to you." However, the readers would then have to deal with essays on an unwieldy number of topics; the prompt keeps everyone more or less on the same page.

Essays are scored *holistically*, which means they are given a grade based on the overall impression created. Bonus points are not awarded for a well-turned phrase, and points are not deducted for specific grammatical mistakes. However, consistently poor grammar that interferes with meaning will affect the essay score. You will receive three types of scores for your essay. First, the overall Writing Test score is reported on a scale of 2–12. Second, additional scores are reported within four domains: Ideas and Analysis, Development and Support, Organization, and Language Use and Conventions. These domains will also be scored on a scale of 2–12 for each domain (the two readers' scores are combined to determine each domain score). Third, the Writing Test score is combined with your English Test and Reading Test scores to produce an English Language Arts (ELA) score on a scale of 1–36. The Writing Test score is NOT included in your composite score.

Test Specs

The prompt won't require any specialized knowledge.

Here are a few prompts you definitely WON'T see:

Why is *Hamlet* a great play? (You would need to have read *Hamlet* to respond to this.)
What was the defining moment of the Civil Rights Movement? (You would need to have studied the movement enough to know how to answer, and you would need to reference historical details of the movement to support your answer.)

Compare those examples to prompts that don't require specialized knowledge:

Should teenagers have a curfew?
Should students have the right to *not* attend high school?

ANATOMY

DIRECTIONS: You have 40 minutes to plan and write an essay. Read the prompt carefully and make sure you understand the instructions.

The Electoral College

In light of the results of the 2000 and 2016 presidential elections, our indirect method of selecting our president through the Electoral College (all Electoral College votes are declared to the winning candidate in each of the 50 states) has come into question. Direct popular election is presented most often as the fairest way to choose a president. Adoption of this process would simply mean that the candidate who received the most general population votes would become president. Some argue that the Electoral College could be kept and votes in the states could be designated to a candidate in a proportional method, so that a person who received 60% of a state's votes would receive 60% of its electoral votes. Those who favor this method argue this is the fairest way to choose the country's leader, but would changing the constitution to address a situation that was problematic in only two elections in the last 100 years be an extreme and unwise change? No matter which side you choose, this conversation is an important one for our nation's future.

Perspective 1

Direct election of the president by popular vote is the fairest way to choose our chief executive. Such a change in our process of selecting the president would reinforce our view that America is a government of the people, by the people, and for the people.

Perspective 2

The Electoral College has served the United States for over 250 years. Radical change is not always the best course. A tweaking of the selection process would provide candidates a percentage of the votes earned in each state.

Perspective 3

Changing the constitution is never to be done lightly. The founding fathers thought long and hard about this step. We should think long and hard about such a change to our constitution and its possible negative consequences.

Essay Task

Write a unified, coherent essay in which you evaluate multiple perspectives on the impact of direct popular election of the President of the United States. In your essay be sure to:

- Analyze and evaluate perspectives given
- State and develop your own perspective
- Explain the relationship between your perspective and those given

Your perspective may be in full agreement with any of the others, in partial agreement or wholly different. Whatever the case, support your ideas with logical reasoning and detailed, persuasive examples.

Master Moves

Typically, the three perspectives offered in the ACT Writing Test will represent three types of views: 1) one strongly in favor of one view, 2) another strongly in favor of the opposite view, and 3) one that advocates for a middle path between the two views, or a moderate view. Keep these differences in mind so that you can quickly decide which view you feel you can best support.

Notice that the prompt does not test a specific body of knowledge. For example, it does not ask, "What were the causes of World War II?" or "What is the best recipe for chocolate cake?" Also, notice that the prompt is constructed so you can provide a successful response based simply on the perspectives listed and your personal experiences. Finally, notice that the prompt points you in the right direction. It asks you a question, and all you need to do is respond to the question and meet the requirements outlined above. These requirements will be discussed in more detail later in the Writing Lesson.

PACING

> **Ace the Pace**
>
> You may be concerned about the time limit and want to just read the prompt and start writing. Don't do it! Give yourself some time to make a plan and write an outline before you write. That way you won't get stuck halfway through, unsure about what to say or how to finish your essay.

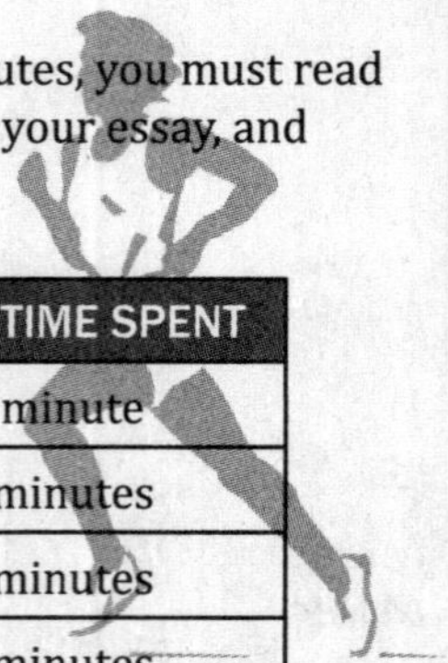

There is one essay prompt with a 40-minute time limit. During the 40 minutes, you must read the prompt, formulate a position, outline your argument or analysis, write your essay, and proofread your essay. Here is a suggested breakdown for those tasks:

TASK	TIME TO EXECUTE	TOTAL TIME SPENT
Read the prompt.	1 minute	1 minute
Evaluate the given perspectives.	2 minutes	3 minutes
Formulate your perspective.	2 minutes	5 minutes
Outline your essay.	2 minutes	7 minutes
Write the introduction.	4 minutes	11 minutes
Write the first paragraph.	7–8 minutes	18–19 minutes
Write the second paragraph.	7–8 minutes	25–27 minutes
Write the third paragraph.	7–8 minutes	32–35 minutes
Write the conclusion.	3 minutes	35–38 minutes
Proofread your essay.	2–5 minutes	40 minutes

If you follow this approximate schedule, it is likely your essay will score at least an 8. After all, your essay will include an introduction that evaluates the given perspectives and states your perspective, three supporting paragraphs (each of which will provide specific support for your perspective), and a brief conclusion that clearly expresses your point of view. If your essay also exemplifies clear and precise language, and if it does not include any major grammatical errors, you will likely receive an even higher score.

TIME TRIAL *(1 prompt; 11 minutes)*

DIRECTIONS: Write an outline for your essay. Then write an introductory paragraph.

Planned Obsolescence

Many technology manufacturers follow a policy of planned obsolescence. Obsolescence describes the condition of no longer being used or useful. Planned obsolescence means that manufacturers make products that are designed to wear out and be replaced quickly. New smartphone applications only function on the latest version of a phone. High repair costs encourage consumers to buy a new laptop instead of fixing a broken one. Spare parts for a computer are no longer available after a few years. Planned obsolescence cuts costs for the manufacturer and the consumer, but what are the risks for both parties when the consumer must frequently replace a product? With technology's prevalent role in our society, planned obsolescence has a strong financial impact on our lives.

Perspective 1

Planned obsolescence can be unfair to consumers, forcing them to spend more money than necessary on products that do not offer significant improvements to the older ones. Manufacturers should deliver high quality, long-lasting products.

Perspective 2

Some industries, such as the automotive industry, are focusing on creating new products that are more environmentally friendly than what is currently available. Planned obsolescence could encourage consumers to buy these newer products and ultimately have a positive impact on the environment.

Perspective 3

Planned obsolescence cuts manufacturing costs and encourages companies to design better products in a shorter period of time. This allows for greater innovation and ultimately gives the consumer a superior product.

Essay Task

Write a unified, coherent essay in which you evaluate multiple perspectives on the impact of planned obsolescence. In your essay be sure to:

- Analyze and evaluate perspectives given
- State and develop your own perspective
- Explain the relationship between your perspective and those given

Your perspective may be in full agreement with any of the others, in partial agreement or wholly different. Whatever the case, support your ideas with logical reasoning and detailed, persuasive examples.

GAME PLAN

Use a Pencil

Write your essay in pencil. Do not use a pen. Any essay written in pen will automatically receive a "0."

Respond to the Specific Prompt

Write on the topic that is presented. If you write an essay that is off-topic, your essay will automatically receive a "0" because it will be considered "not responsive." Also, remember to evaluate each of the given perspectives, present your own perspective, and describe how your perspective relates to each of the given perspectives. Following all the required steps outlined in the prompt is an easy—and essential—way to earn points.

Write Legibly

Write clearly and legibly. If you write an essay that is illegible, your essay will automatically receive a "0." Readers cannot give a grade to what they cannot read. So, if your handwriting is hard to read, take a little extra time and try printing.

Don't Copy the Prompt

Do not copy the prompt onto the lined paper. The readers know the topic, and it is already written on the page. If you copy the prompt onto the lined paper, it looks like you're simply trying to fill up space.

Don't Skip Lines

Do not skip lines when writing your essay on the lined paper. You should be able to make your essay legible without skipping lines. If you skip lines, it looks like you're trying to "pad" your essay to make it look longer.

Be Specific

When writing your essay, be specific. Avoid vague generalizations. For example, here are a few sentences that are weak because they are too vague:

> *"Perfection in house painting is very time-consuming and requires a lot of hard work. You just can't do it in a short time; you've got to invest a lot of effort."*

If you include specific details, the same point can be made much more persuasively. For example, here is the same argument about house painting, backed up with specific details:

> *"House painting requires attention to details. You have to prepare the surface by scraping away all old and loose paint and carefully washing it. You have to put down hundreds of strips of masking tape to protect those areas that should not receive paint, such as glass panes, trim to be painted a second color, and fixtures. You have to apply a primer, then a base coat, and then the finish coat. Finally, you have to apply the second color and clean up all the mistakes. A perfect paint job would take 6 months or longer, and the cost would be prohibitive. That is why when you look closely, you will always see imperfections."*

As you can see, this response is much more compelling because the point of view is supported by specific details. Use of specific details is frequently the difference between an essay that receives a Development and Support score of 4 or 6 and an essay that receives a Development and Support score of 8 or 10.

WRITING

LESSON

LESSON

The following essay topic will be used during the Writing Lesson to illustrate proper essay development and good writing skills. Follow along with your instructor to outline and develop sample responses to the prompts. Sample essay responses begin on page 433.

Don't Ditch the Directions

Up until now, we have encouraged you to ditch the directions when approaching each test section. If you can memorize the Writing section directions, great! However, many students find it nelpful to refer back to the Writing test directions to structure and remember what to address in their essays. The directions for this section contain crucial information about what your Writing test graders will be looking for when evaluating your essay.

DIRECTIONS: You have 40 minutes to plan and write an essay. Read the prompt carefully and make sure you understand the instructions. A successful essay will have the following features: it will evaluate each of the perspectives given in the prompt; it will state and develop a personal perspective; it will explain the relationship between the given perspectives and your personal perspective; it will present ideas with logical reasoning and clear, persuasive examples; and, finally, it will include clear and effective language in accordance with the conventions of standard written English.

Technological Advances

Technological advances have enhanced our capacity to communicate. Email, Twitter, Instagram, and other social media platforms have made sharing information and networking with others exponentially more efficient. Whether the 'other' is our next-door neighbor or someone halfway around the planet, our ability to connect with one another has been almost infinitely improved. However, critics claim that while we now communicate more quickly, we also interact more superficially, and the ease of interaction has rendered us more isolated. Although technology has made communication easier, are we actually lonelier with more digital and less face-to-face interaction? As more and more communication happens online, it is important to assess the psychological effects of this changed interaction.

Read and consider the perspectives below. Each perspective suggests a particular way of thinking about the impact of technology on human interaction.

Perspective 1

Despite technology improving information sharing, so much of what is shared is facile and shallow. We are now in a "fast food" age of information: quick turnaround with only "empty calories" of communication.

Perspective 2

Though we connect more easily with one another, there is a feeling that we are becoming ever more isolated from each other. We have a need for closer contact with the people we know.

Perspective 3

Technological advances have made it far easier to communicate in today's world. We can connect to individuals, groups, and societies in an instant.

Use Your Test Booklet

This is not a textbook from your school or library; you are free to mark it up however it helps you to write your essay. We recommend that you underline:
1) the description of the issue or situation,
2) the main criticism of the issue or situation, and
3) the stakes or concerns regarding the issue.
Refer to these notes to develop your argument in a way that thoroughly addresses each of these points.

Essay Task

Write a unified, coherent essay in which you evaluate multiple perspectives on the impact of technology on human interaction. In your essay be sure to:

- Analyze and evaluate the perspectives given
- State and develop your own perspective
- Explain the relationship between your perspective and those given

Your perspective may be in full agreement with any of the others, in partial agreement, or wholly different. Whatever the case, support your ideas with logical reasoning and detailed, persuasive examples.

WRITING QUIZZES

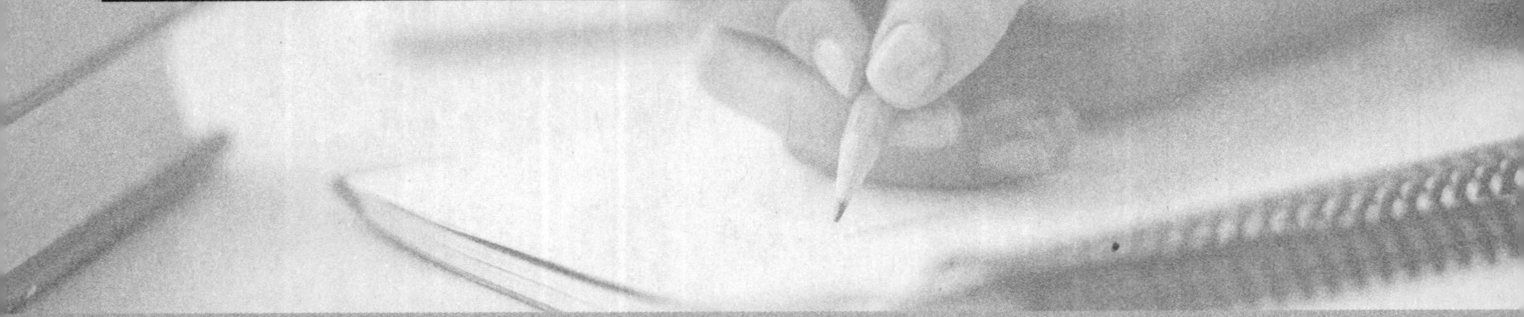

This section contains two Writing quizzes. The first quiz is a directed study quiz and is not timed. Write your essay and then review the provided sample responses. The second quiz is a timed quiz. Take the second quiz under the indicated timed conditions to practice your pacing as you apply what you learned in the Writing Lessons.

DIRECTED STUDY QUIZ *(1 Essay Prompt)*

DIRECTIONS: You have 40 minutes to plan and write an essay. Read the prompt carefully and make sure you understand the instructions.

Fracking

The quest for finding additional sources of energy is never-ending, and our demand for fossil fuels has dominated our energy consumption. Fracking (hydraulic fracturing), which "pries" fossil fuel resources from the earth's crust, is one recent development at the forefront of innovations to provide our country with sufficient energy. While fracking offers great promise in delivering fuel to the world, some critics point to the environmental damage it can cause, including pollution and destabilization of the earth's crust. Also, critics say that the success of fracking will bring a halt to the development of renewable energy sources as alternatives to fossil fuel. Although fracking would greatly increase our access to fossil fuels, is it a sustainable solution, given the environmental risks? As other fossil fuel sources diminish, policymakers must address the benefits and risks of fracking.

Perspective 1

Dependence on fossil fuels must stop. We need to find alternative energy sources that are reliable, renewable, and safe. Human ingenuity must be put to the test to find such sources as quickly as possible for our survival.

Perspective 2

Fracking holds promise for greater energy sufficiency in the US. However, the process also has environmental risks that pose tremendous dangers to human, plant, and animal life.

Perspective 3

Fossil fuels are necessary for our societies to function. Methods of extracting fossil fuels from the earth's crust, including fracking, are crucial because there are still great quantities of fossil fuel beneath the earth's surface.

Essay Task

Write a unified, coherent essay in which you evaluate multiple perspectives on the impact of fracking. In your essay, be sure to:

- Analyze and evaluate perspectives given
- State and develop your own perspective
- Explain the relationship between your perspective and those given

Your perspective may be in full agreement with any of the others, in partial agreement or wholly different. Whatever the case, support your ideas with logical reasoning and detailed, persuasive examples.

Above Average Response

With fuel to heat our homes and run our cars, our need for fossil fuels will not disappear any time soon. However, because of the environmental risks involved, fracking should be undertaken with caution, and the long-term focus should be on renewable energy sources. The methods used through fracking to extract natural gas could cause environmental problems, such as pollution or even earthquakes. Companies, therefore, should be required to follow strict environmental and safety regulations and to cooperate with nearby communities. Furthermore, fracking should not detract from long-term goals of developing renewable energy sources.

Although the debate is controversial, critics of fracking argue that it causes serious environmental problems, such as air and water pollution and instability of the earth's crust. The process of fracking involves drilling at least a few thousand feet below the earth's surface, as well as drilling horizontally. A combination of water and chemicals is poured down the drill at an extremely high pressure, which fractures shale rocks and releases natural gas. Studies in communities near fracking sites reported higher amounts of methane in well water, which could endanger the local population. Critics also argue that because fracking wells run thousands of feet deeper than wells for more traditional methods of natural gas extraction, fracking could destabilize the earth's crust and cause earthquakes.

However, because renewable energy sources are not sufficiently developed to replace fossil fuel consumption, it is important to find additional sources of fossil fuels. Fracking, therefore, should be undertaken with caution. Governmental agencies should regulate which chemicals can be used during fracking and should require companies to construct wells in ways that would minimize the risk of natural gas leakage. Additionally, companies should be required to drill at a safe distance from surrounding communities, to eliminate health risks involved with fracking. Although fracking could bring many economic benefits, especially greater energy independence for the US, the process should not jeopardize local ecosystems and the health of surrounding communities.

Furthermore, fracking is not a permanent solution because it extracts a nonrenewable resource. It should not compromise efforts to develop renewable sources of energy. Although developing equipment and researching safe methods for fracking will be an extremely expensive endeavor, it should not cripple government and private funding for development of other sources of energy, such as wind or solar energy. Renewable energy sources will have a greater long-term impact on energy independence and will be safer for the environment than fracking.

Despite the environmental problems that it can cause, fracking is currently a necessary risk, until renewable energy resources are more developed and widely available. However, companies should be required to follow strict regulations to minimize risks for the surrounding communities. Economic gains from fracking should not come at the expense of environmental and health disasters.

Ideas and Analysis: The writer considers arguments for and against fracking and clearly states his or her thesis in the introduction: fracking should be undertaken with caution and should not detract from research on renewable energy. The body paragraphs incorporate all three perspectives. The first paragraph addresses the environmental concerns of Perspective 2, and the second paragraph acknowledges the current need for more fossil fuel sources (Perspective 3). Finally, the third paragraph focuses on Perspective 1: the need to end dependence on fossil fuels. Although the writer engages with multiple viewpoints, the thesis is still clear.

Development and Support:

- The introduction states the thesis in its second sentence and previews the arguments that will support it.
- The body paragraphs begin with topic sentences that clearly state the main point or argument to be made in the paragraph.
- The body paragraphs include details that consider scientific, economic, and social perspectives. The writer does not merely express his or her opinion on the subject.
- The writer develops a "compromise" position on the subject by incorporating information from all three perspectives. However, the writer still takes a clear position on the issue, and all body paragraphs support a cautious approach towards fracking:
    - Body paragraph 1: The writer supports the argument that fracking is environmentally risky by describing the process of fracking and mentioning a scientific study.
    - Body paragraph 2: The writer acknowledges the current necessity of fossil fuels and supports a compromise position: allowing fracking with regulations.
    - Body paragraph 3: The writer presents two arguments for renewable energy sources: they are safer for the environment and more sustainable in the long run.
- The conclusion is rhetorically effective because it both restates the thesis and ends with a moral appeal: the need to avoid environmental and health-related problems.

Organization:

- The writer introduces each paragraph with a topic sentence.
- The writer uses transitions to connect ideas between and within paragraphs. For example, the second body paragraph begins with the transition "however" because it argues that fracking may be necessary, despite the economic risks.
- The writer could improve the essay by including a greater variety of transitions. (The essay repeatedly uses "although," "however," and "furthermore").

Language Use and Conventions:

The essay contains at least three principal strengths in this area:

- The essay does not have any mechanics/usage errors. As a result, the reader's attention is not distracted from the substance of the essay.
- The essay does not have any informal language.

- Stylistically, the writer varies sentence structures.

- The writer uses vivid verbs and avoids vague language. The verb choice shows a sophisticated vocabulary.

Summary and Conclusions: This essay demonstrates writing skills that are very well developed and analyzes multiple viewpoints on the issue. The writer incorporates all three perspectives in his or her argument. This essay would likely receive a score of 10.

Below Average Response

Fracking can be a dangerous process, causing pollution and other environmental problems. It can even cause health issues for people who live nearby. However, we use fossil fuels for so many things, like heating and driving, so we have no choice but to do it.

People who argue against fracking argue that it causes environmental problems. For example, if the well used for drilling isn't built correctly, gas and chemicals could leak out and pollute the surrounding community. I even heard that it could cause earthquakes because you have to dig so deeply underground.

These environmental problems can be harmful for the surrounding communities. Water pollution can kill animals that live nearby and can also cause health problems for humans. Wouldn't want to live in a community that was harmed by fracking. Just look at past oil spills to see how much damage drilling can do. For example, the Gulf of Mexico oil spill in 2010 killed workers, destroyed local ecosystems, and is still contaminating the water.

However, the reality is that we still need fossil fuels, so fracking might be a good thing. Communities might need to move away from fracking cites if they're unsafe, and unfortunately, our energy needs make us cause environmental problems.

Ideas and Analysis: The thesis of the essay is not well supported. The writer devotes most of the essay to arguing why fracking is dangerous, but the final paragraph abruptly changes positions and argues that fracking is necessary. Unlike the above average essay, this essay does not attempt to find a compromise to reconcile these two positions. The writer addresses Perspective 2 (environmental risks) and mentions Perspective 3 (dependence on fossil fuels) but does not engage with Perspective 1 (alternative energy sources).

Development and Support:

- The essay's argument is not strong because it brings up two opposing points without reconciling them. There is no clear thesis in the introduction.

- The first body paragraph has a clear focus but should use concrete evidence instead of hearsay.

- The second body paragraph uses an example that could support the writer's argument: the Gulf of Mexico oil spill. However, the writer needs to acknowledge that this spill was not related to fracking, but is nevertheless an example of what can happen if energy companies do not follow regulations.

- The final paragraph does not relate to the rest of the essay. The writer needs to either eliminate this paragraph or reconcile the argument with the environmental dangers of fracking.

Organization:

- The writer brings up three separate arguments in the introduction but fails to combine them into a cohesive thesis.

- Although the fourth paragraph begins with a transition (however), this transition is not enough to link it to the two previous body paragraphs. An effective transition must acknowledge the preceding idea and connect it to the idea that follows.

- It is not clear whether the final paragraph of the essay is a conclusion or a third body paragraph. The writer needs a conclusion that summarizes the thesis and recalls all main points of the essay.

Language Use and Conventions:

- The essay contains some usage and mechanics errors:
  - Body paragraph 2: "Wouldn't want to live in a community that was harmed by fracking" is a sentence fragment.
  - The final paragraph uses the verb "cites" instead of the noun "sites."
- The essay uses vague language:
  - Introduction: In the second sentence, it is unclear what "we" and "thing" refer to.
  - Body paragraph 1 uses a vague pronoun. Instead of saying "I even heard that it could cause earthquakes," the writer should say, "I even heard that fracking could cause earthquakes." (In the previous sentence, the writer does not mention fracking.)
- The writer should avoid repetitive language. (Example from body paragraph 1: People who argue against fracking argue that it causes environmental problems.)

Summary and Conclusions: The essay lacks a clear thesis and presents contradicting arguments. The body paragraphs also do not have enough evidence to support their arguments. This essay would likely receive a score of 5.

TIMED QUIZ *(1 Essay Prompt; 40 minutes)*

DIRECTIONS: You have 40 minutes to plan and write an essay. Read the prompt carefully and make sure you understand the instructions. Sample essays are on p. 436.

Introducing Technology in Pre-Kindergarten Programs

Children are often introduced to technology at a young age, sometimes through their pre-kindergarten programs. Students play educational games on tablets with interactive touch screens. Technology can also help children gain social skills if they play computer games with a partner. Teachers can use digital cameras to document students' progress and share it with their parents. Technology can provide activities that are fun for students and convenient for teachers, but should technology play a central role in pre-kindergarten classrooms? Since children use technological devices at an increasingly young age, it is important to consider how technology could enhance or inhibit early childhood development.

Perspective 1

Technological devices are impractical for the pre-K classroom because they are expensive, are easy for children to break, and quickly become outdated. Furthermore, children should not become too reliant on computers for entertainment.

Perspective 2

Games on computers or tablets can make learning basic skills, such as counting or memorizing the alphabet, more entertaining and interactive. Children will see the task as a form of play rather than of work.

Perspective 3

It is important to make the use of technology a natural and integral part of children's lives. They will be required to use it in the classroom, and eventually in the workforce, and they will adapt to it more quickly if they start using technological devices at a young age.

Essay Task

Write a unified, coherent essay in which you evaluate multiple perspectives on the impact of introducing technology in pre-kindergarten programs. In your essay be sure to:

- Analyze and evaluate perspectives given
- State and develop your own perspective
- Explain the relationship between your perspective and those given

Your perspective may be in full agreement with any of the others, in partial agreement or wholly different. Whatever the case, support your ideas with logical reasoning and detailed, persuasive examples.

STRATEGY SUMMARY

WRITING STRATEGIES

1. Begin with the prompt.
2. Write only on the assigned topic. Writing on any other topic will result in a score of "0."
3. Remember to evaluate the given perspectives, develop your own perspective, and describe how your perspective relates to the given perspectives.
4. Do not try to do too much. Try to limit the scope of your topic to a reasonable effort.
5. Organize your thoughts and write an outline before beginning the essay. Do not spend more than two minutes writing the outline.
   a) Familiarize yourself with the essay prompt and the given perspectives.
   b) Develop your own perspective.
   c) Develop a thesis.
   d) Identify three to four important points.
   e) Decide on the order of presentation of the major points.
6. Organize ideas into paragraphs.
   a) Begin with an introduction.
   b) Create three to four body paragraphs.
   c) End with a conclusion.
7. Write using correct grammar.
8. Write clearly, concisely, and legibly.
9. Punctuate and spell correctly.
10. Spend a few minutes proofreading your essay.

MATH

Course Concept Outline

I. TEST MECHANICS **191**

- **A. Overview** **192**
- **B. Anatomy** *(Items #1–4)* **193–194**
- **C. Pacing** **194**
- **D. Time Trial** *(Items #1–5)* **195**
- **E. Game Plan** **196**
  1. Quickly Preview the Test Section, but Skip the Directions 196
  2. Answer the Question That Is Being Asked 196
     - a) Read the Question Carefully 196
     - b) Pay Attention to Units 196
     - c) Pay Attention to Thought-Reversers 197
  3. Use the Answer Choices 197
     - a) Eliminate Answer Choices That Cannot Be Correct 197
     - b) Use the Answer Choices to Check Your Math 198
  4. Don't Go Calculator Crazy 198
- **F. Calculator Exercise** *(Items #1–10)* **198–199**
- **G. Calculator Race** *(Items #1–10)*[1]

II. LESSON | PRELIMINARIES AND STRATEGIES **201**

- **A. Item Profiles**
- **B. Item-Types** **202**
  1. Number and Quantity *(Item #1)* 202
  2. Algebra and Functions *(Items #2–6)* 202–203
  3. Coordinate Geometry *(Item #7)* 203
  4. Geometry *(Items #8–9)* 203
  5. Trigonometry *(Item #10)* 203
  6. Statistics, Probability, and Data Representation *(Items #11–12)* 204

1 Some concepts in this Course Concept Outline are not illustrated through examples in your student text but may be covered by your instructor in class. They are included here to provide a complete outline of your course.

C. **General Strategies** 204

1. Use the Figures *(Items #13–16)* 204–205
2. Use the Answer Choices *(Item #17)* 205
    a) Answer Choices Are Arranged in Order
    b) Wrong Choices Correspond to Conceptual Errors
3. Pay Special Attention to "Signal" Words *(Items #18–21)* 205
4. Answer the Question Being Asked *(Items #22–26)* 206
5. Carefully Consider "Cannot Be Determined" *(Item #27)* 206

D. **Time-Saving Shortcuts and Power Strategies** 207

1. Time-Saving Test Prep Shortcuts
2. Test-the-Test *(Items #28–29)* 207
3. Plug-and-Chug *(Item #30)* 207
4. Eliminate-and-Guess *(Item #31)* 207

III. **LESSON 1 | NUMBER AND QUANTITY** 208

A. **Basic Arithmetic Strategies** 208

1. Just Do It *(Items #1–2)* 208
2. Look for Shortcuts *(Items #3–11)* 208–209
3. Bridge the Gap *(Items #12–13)* 209

B. **Properties of Numbers** *(Items #14–19)* 210
C. **Scientific Notation** *(Items #20–21)* 211
D. **Complex Numbers** *(Items #22–23)* 211
E. **Matrices and Vectors** *(Items #24–26)* 212
F. **Rates and Proportions** *(Items #27–34)* 212–213
G. **Percentages** *(Items #35–41)* 214
H. **Arithmetic Strategy: "Test-the-Test"** *(Items #42–46)* 215

IV. **LESSON 2 | ALGEBRA AND FUNCTIONS** 216

A. **Manipulating Algebraic Expressions** 216

1. Basic Algebraic Manipulations *(Items #1–2)* 216
2. Evaluating Expressions *(Items #3–7)* 216
3. Manipulating Expressions Involving Exponents *(Items #8–9)* 217
4. Factoring Expressions *(Items #10–12)* 217
5. Logarithmic Expressions *(Items #13–14)* 217

B. **Evaluating Sequences** *(Items #15–18)* 218
C. **Solving Algebraic Equations or Inequalities with One Variable** 219

1. Simple Equations *(Item #19)* 219
2. Simple Inequalities *(Item #20)* 219
3. Equations Involving Rational Expressions *(Items #21–23)* 219
4. Inequalities Involving Rational Expressions *(Item #24)* 219

5. Equations Involving Radical Expressions *(Items #25–28)* 220
6. Equations Involving Integer and Rational Exponents *(Items #29–32)* 220
7. Equations Involving Logarithms *(Items #33–34)* 220
8. Equations Involving Absolute Value *(Items #35–36)* 221
9. Inequalities Involving Absolute Value *(Items #37–39)* 221

D. Evaluating, Interpreting, and Creating Algebraic Functions **221**

1. Function Notation *(Items #40–47)* 221–222
2. Concepts of Domain and Range *(Items #48–51)* 222
3. Functions as Models *(Items #52–54)* 222–223

E. Solving Simultaneous Equations *(Items #55–60)* **223–224**
F. Solving Quadratic Equations and Relations *(Items #61–65)* **224**
G. Algebra Strategies: "Test-the-Test" and "Plug-and-Chug" *(Items #66–77)* **225–226**

V. LESSON 3 | COORDINATE GEOMETRY 227

A. The Coordinate System *(Items #1–6)* **227–228**
B. Slope of a Line *(Items #7–10)* **229**
C. Slope-Intercept Form of a Linear Equation *(Items #11–15)* **230**
D. Distance and Midpoint Formulas *(Items #16–19)* **231**
E. Graphs of Linear Equations *(Items #20–21)* **232**
F. Graphs of First-Degree Inequalities *(Item #22)* **233**
G. Graphs of Quadratic Equations and Relations *(Items #23–24)* **233–234**
H. Qualitative Behavior of Graphs of Functions *(Items #25–26)* **234**
I. Transformations and Their Effects on Graphs of Functions *(Items #27–28)* **235**

VI. LESSON 4 | GEOMETRY 236

A. Geometric Notation
B. Lines and Angles *(Items #1–5)* **236–237**
C. Triangles **237**

1. Pythagorean Theorem *(Item #6)* 237
2. 45°-45°-90° Triangles *(Items #7–8)* 237
3. 30°-60°-90° Triangles *(Item #9)* 237
4. Properties of Triangles *(Items #10–11)* 238

D. Rectangles and Squares *(Items #12–14)* **238–239**
E. Circles *(Item #15)* **239**
F. Properties of Tangent Lines *(Items #16–19)* **239–240**
G. Complex Figures *(Items #20–25)* **240–241**
H. Solids *(Items #26–29)* **242**
I. Geometry Strategies **243**

1. "Guesstimating" *(Items #30–32)* 243
2. Measuring *(Items #33–34)* 243
3. "Meastimating" *(Items #35–36)* 244

VII. LESSON 5 | TRIGONOMETRY **245**

A. **Definitions of the Six Trigonometric Functions** *(Items #1–5)* **245–246**
B. **Trigonometric Relationships** *(Item #6)* **246**
C. **Trigonometry as an Alternative Method of Solution** *(Items #7–10)* **247**
D. **Graphs of Trigonometric Functions** *(Items #11–12)* **248**

VIII. LESSON 6 | STATISTICS, PROBABILITY, AND DATA REPRESENTATION **249**

A. **Measures of Center** *(Items #1–7)* **249–250**
B. **Counting Methods** *(Items #8–9)* **250**
C. **Sets** *(Items #10–15)* **251**
D. **Probability** *(Items #16–20)* **252–253**
E. **Data Representation** **253**

1. Bar, Cumulative, and Line Graphs *(Items #21–25)* 253–254
2. Pie Charts *(Items #26–27)* 254–255
3. Tables *(Item #28)* 255
4. Scatterplots *(Item #29)* 255

IX. QUIZZES **257**

A. **Directed Study Quiz** *(Items #1–20)* **258–267**
B. **Timed Quiz** *(Items #1–20)* **268–270**

X. REVIEW **271**

XI. STRATEGY SUMMARY **279**

MATH

TEST MECHANICS

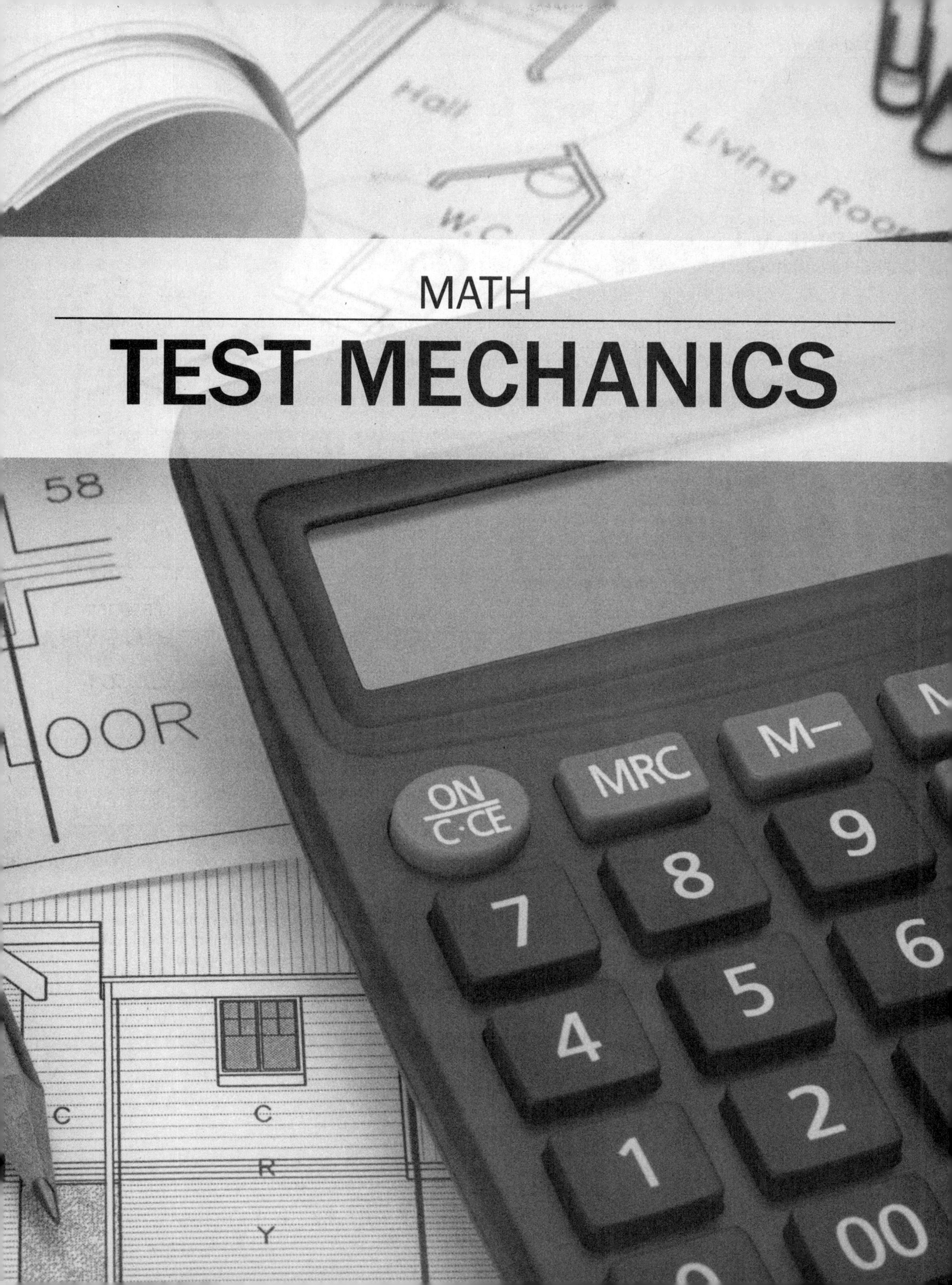

OVERVIEW

The ACT Mathematics Test, according to the test-writers, presupposes a knowledge of basic math formulas and computational skills. The ACT Mathematics Test items are pretty much the same kind of questions you'd see on a regular test—except they are multiple-choice questions.

Here is the distribution of items by topic on the ACT Mathematics Test:

ACT MATHEMATICS TEST TOPICS (60 items; 60 minutes)		
Content	Approximate Number	Approximate Percentage
Integration of Essential Skills (rates, percentages, proportions, area, volume, averages)	25	42%
Number and Quantity (properties of numbers, complex numbers, vectors, matrices)	5	8%
Algebra and Functions (evaluating sequences, solving equations and inequalities, solving quadratic equations, slope of a line, graphs of equations)	16	27%
Geometry (triangles, rectangles and squares, circles, trigonometry)	8	13%
Statistics and Probability (average, median, mean, probability, data representation)	6	10%

You do not have to know all of the tested topics to do well on the exam. For example, you could choose to skip all of the geometry and statistics and probability items, miss another eight questions, and still get a 24 on the ACT Mathematics Test, which is a good score. For a very respectable score of 21 (above the national average), you need a raw score of about 33, which you can get if you choose to skip all the geometry and statistics and probability items plus the eight hardest algebra and functions items and keep your wrong answers down to five.

This is not a recommended strategy. You want to make sure that you answer any questions you know how to answer and guess on the rest. But these calculations show that you can do quite well on the math portion of the ACT test even if you're not exactly a math whiz.

ANATOMY

The Cambridge Edge

For most Mathematics items, answer choices are arranged in order from least to greatest or vice versa.

This answer choice arrangement makes it easier for you to find your choice in the list. It also sets up an important test-taking strategy of starting with the middle choice when applying the "test-the-test" strategy, which you'll learn about later.

DIRECTIONS: Solve each item and choose the correct answer choice. Calculator use is permitted; however, some items are best solved without the use of a calculator.

You really do not need the directions at all. You can use a calculator, and there will be further discussion of this in class.

Also, figures are not necessarily drawn to scale. However, in practice, the figures are almost always drawn to scale. Again, this issue will be discussed in detail later during the Math Lesson.

NOTE: All of the following should be assumed, unless otherwise stated.

1. Illustrative figures are NOT necessarily drawn to scale.
2. The word *average* indicates arithmetic mean.
3. The word *line* indicates a straight line.
4. Geometric figures lie in a plane.

1. Paulo bicycled $6\frac{1}{3}$ miles on Wednesday and $8\frac{2}{5}$ miles on Thursday. How many miles did he bicycle during those two days?

A. $14\frac{2}{15}$
B. $14\frac{1}{4}$
C. $14\frac{3}{8}$
D. $14\frac{11}{15}$
E. $14\frac{13}{15}$

1. (D) *This item is solved by addition:*

$$6\frac{1}{3}+8\frac{2}{5}=\frac{19}{3}+\frac{42}{5}$$
$$=\frac{95}{15}+\frac{126}{15}$$
$$=\frac{221}{15}$$
$$=14\frac{11}{15}$$

The Cambridge Edge

Answer choices are carefully constructed. The choices on the ACT test usually correspond to errors in thinking—not errors in arithmetic. You are not likely to find a problem with answer choices like the following:

A. $183.27
B. $183.28
C. $183.29
D. $183.30
E. $183.31

This feature is important because it is the basis for a couple of time-saving strategies that you'll learn shortly.

2. The average weight of 5 packages in a shipment is 8.7 pounds. The weights of 4 of the packages are 6.3 pounds, 7.5 pounds, 8.9 pounds, and 9.6 pounds. What is the weight of the fifth package?

F. 8.5
G. 8.8
H. 9.4
J. 11.2
K. 12.3

2. (J) *This item is a bit more difficult. First, set up an equation for the average:*

$$\frac{6.3+7.5+8.9+9.6+x}{5}=8.7$$

Then, solve for the missing weight:

$$(6.3+7.5+8.9+9.6)+x=(8.7)(5)$$
$$x=43.5-32.3=11.2$$

3. If $3x+4=7x-2$, $x=?$

A. $-\frac{1}{4}$
B. $\frac{1}{2}$
C. $\frac{3}{5}$
D. $\frac{2}{3}$
E. $1\frac{1}{2}$

3. **(E)** *For this item, you need to solve for x:*

$$3x+4=7x-2$$
$$3x-7x=-2-4$$
$$-4x=-6$$
$$4x=6$$
$$x=\frac{6}{4}=\frac{3}{2}=1\frac{1}{2}$$

4. The ratio of the radii of two circles is $3:4$. What is the ratio of their areas?

F. $7:1$
G. $3:4$
H. $9:16$
J. $3:4\pi$
K. $9:16\pi$

4. **(H)** *With this item, since the ratio of the radii of the two circles is* $3:4$, *the ratio of their areas is* $\frac{\pi(3)^2}{\pi(4)^2}=\frac{9\pi}{16\pi}=\frac{9}{16}=9:16$.

PACING

The Mathematics Test consists of 60 items. The time limit is 60 minutes. The items are arranged on a ladder of difficulty, so you'll need a pacing plan that helps you move more quickly through the easier items at the beginning of the test and allows you to build up a time reserve for the harder items that are located toward the end. The following table summarizes the timing for this approach:

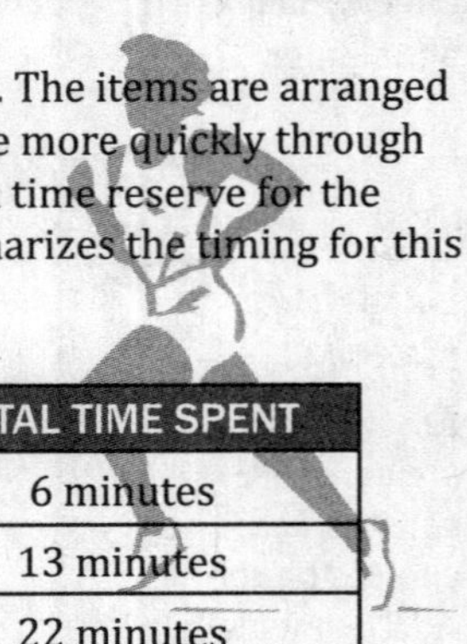

ITEM NUMBERS	TIME TO SPEND PER ITEM	TOTAL TIME SPENT
#1–10	36 seconds	6 minutes
#11–20	42 seconds	13 minutes
#21–30	54 seconds	22 minutes
#31–40	66 seconds	33 minutes
#41–50	72 seconds	45 minutes
#51–60	90 seconds	60 minutes

The Cambridge Edge

Items are arranged on a ladder of difficulty. Of course, you can't tell this from the four examples provided in the Anatomy section, but the ladder of difficulty is an important feature of the math test. Given that the problems become more difficult as you proceed, you're obviously going to have to make some important decisions about speed and possibly randomly guessing on some items. You'll get more advice on this later.

This table is a schedule for the best of all possible math worlds. It's intended to be a guideline, not a rule. Try to stay on schedule, but be prepared to adjust your timing according to how many items you can realistically complete. Trying to stay on a schedule during the test will help you avoid the two biggest time wasters for timed tests.

First, staying on schedule will ensure that you are not plodding through the easy items at the beginning of the test. At first, with a 60-minute time limit, it will seem like you've got all the time in the world. But you don't. From the moment the test begins, you're behind schedule and playing catch-up. So, keep a sense of urgency.

Second, the schedule will serve as a constant reminder that you cannot afford to spend too much time on any one problem. If you make a mistake and spend three minutes on item #22, you'll find that you're falling behind schedule. Leave that problem, hoping you'll have time at the end of the test to come back and finish it. But spending three minutes to get +1 when three minutes could get you +5 is an inefficient use of time.

TIME TRIAL *(5 items; 5 minutes)*

DIRECTIONS: Solve each item and choose the correct answer choice. Calculator use is permitted; however, some items are best solved without the use of a calculator.

NOTE: All of the following should be assumed, unless otherwise stated.

1. Illustrative figures are NOT necessarily drawn to scale.
2. The word *average* indicates arithmetic mean.
3. The word *line* indicates a straight line.
4. Geometric figures lie in a plane.

1. $\frac{1}{10^{25}} - \frac{1}{10^{26}} = ?$

A. $\frac{9}{10^{25}}$
B. $\frac{1}{10^{25}}$
C. $\frac{9}{10^{26}}$
D. $-\frac{9}{10^{25}}$
E. $-\frac{1}{10}$

2. The table below shows readings of water levels for the Red River at various times. If readings of the rise of the water level followed a geometric progression, how many inches above normal was the water level at 3:00 p.m.?

RED RIVER WATER LEVEL READINGS				
Time (p.m.)	1:00	2:00	3:00	4:00
Inches above Normal	0.5	1.5	?	13.5

F. 4
G. 4.5
H. 4.75
J. 5
K. 5.25

3. If s, t, and u are different positive integers and $\frac{s}{t}$ and $\frac{t}{u}$ are positive integers, which of the following CANNOT be a positive integer?

A. $\frac{s}{u}$
B. $s(t)$
C. $\frac{u}{s}$
D. $(s+t)u$
E. $(s-u)t$

4. In the figure below, $\overline{AD} = \overline{DC}$. What is the value of $\overline{AD} + \overline{DC}$?

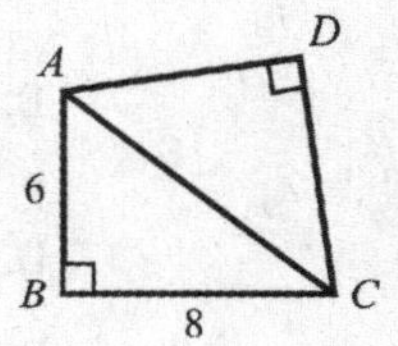

F. $18\sqrt{2}$
G. 18
H. $10\sqrt{2}$
J. 10
K. $6\sqrt{2}$

5. In the figure below, the length of $\overline{AC}$ is 5 units. Which of the following is the best approximation for the number of units in the length of $\overline{BC}$? ($\tan 22° \approx 0.4$)

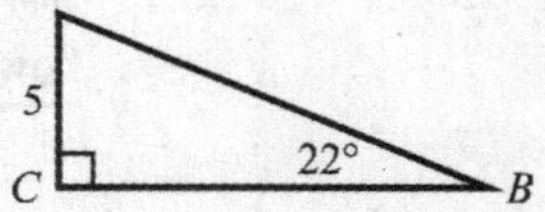

A. 2.0
B. 3.0
C. 7.5
D. 12.5
E. 16

GAME PLAN

Quickly Preview the Test Section, but Skip the Directions

As you get started on test day, take a few seconds to preview the Mathematics Test. It's 99.99% certain that you're going to find everything in place and just as you expect. But a quick overview will guarantee against any unanticipated changes. Do NOT, however, read the directions. Remind yourself of your pacing plan and then get to work.

Answer the Question That Is Being Asked

Some problems are fairly simple, but others are more complex, particularly practical word problems and more difficult geometry problems. The more complex the question, the easier it is to misread and set off down the wrong track. If the question is very long, underline key parts of the question.

Read the Question Carefully

Example:

If Mark traveled 20 miles in 3 hours and Lester traveled twice as far in half the time, what was Lester's average speed?

A. $3\frac{1}{3}$ miles per hour
B. $6\frac{2}{3}$ miles per hour
C. 12 miles per hour
D. 26 miles per hour
E. $26\frac{2}{3}$ miles per hour

The stem states that Lester traveled twice as far as Mark in half the time, or 40 miles in 1.5 hours. Therefore, Lester's average speed was $\frac{40 \text{ miles}}{1.5 \text{ hours}} = 26.66\overline{6} = 26\frac{2}{3}$ miles per hour.

Pay Attention to Units

Some items require you to convert units (e.g., feet to inches or hours to minutes). The item stem will tell you what units to use. When you see an item stem that includes units, circle the unit and put a star beside it.

Example:

A certain copy machine produces 13 copies every 10 seconds. If the machine operates without interruption, how many copies will it produce in an hour?

F. 780
G. 4,200
H. 4,680
J. 4,800
K. 5,160

Create an expression that, after cancellation of like units, gives the number of copies produced in an hour: $\frac{13 \text{ copies}}{10 \text{ seconds}}\left(\frac{60 \text{ seconds}}{1 \text{ minute}}\right)\left(\frac{60 \text{ minutes}}{1 \text{ hour}}\right) = 4,680 \text{ copies/hour}$.

Therefore, the copy machine produces 4,680 copies in an hour.

Pay Attention to Thought-Reversers

A thought-reverser is any word, such as "not," "except," or "but," that turns a question inside out. As shown, below, make sure you mark the thought-reverser so that you do not forget it as you work the problem.

Example:

How many integers in the set of integers from 1 to 144, inclusive, are NOT a square of an integer?

A. 0
B. 2
C. 12
D. 132
E. 144

Since 1 is the square of 1, and 144 is the square of 12, there are a total of 12 integers in the set of integers from 1 to 144, inclusive, that are a square of an integer (1^2, 2^2, 3^2, 4^2, 5^2, 6^2, 7^2, 8^2, 9^2, 10^2, 11^2, 12^2). Therefore, there are a total of $144 - 12 = 132$ integers in the set that are NOT a square of an integer.

Use the Answer Choices

In the Math Lessons, you will learn some very powerful test-taking strategies that use the multiple-choice answers to test items to help solve the items. For now, there are two simple suggestions to keep in mind.

Eliminate Answer Choices That Cannot Be Correct

Sometimes, the array of answers will include choices that, taken at face value, seem to be plausible, but when examined more carefully, must be incorrect.

Example:

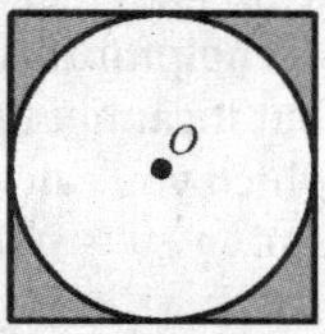

In the figure above, a circle with center O and a radius of 2 is inscribed in a square. What is the area of the shaded portion of the figure?

F. $2 - \pi$
G. $4 - 2\pi$
H. $16 - 2\pi$
J. $16 - 4\pi$
K. $16 - 6\pi$

The shaded area is equal to the area of the square minus the area of the circle. Since the radius of the circle is 2, the side of the square is 4 and its area is $4(4) = 16$. The area of the circle is $\pi(2)^2 = 4\pi$. Therefore, the shaded area is $16 - 4\pi$.

Notice that without even solving the item, you can eliminate answer choices. Take a closer look at (F), (G), and (K). Since π is approximately 3.14, (F), (G), and (K) are negative. Area, however, cannot be a negative number, so (F), (G), and (K) must be wrong, and you can eliminate them without doing any other work. Now, if you had to, you can make an educated guess from the remaining choices and the odds of guessing correctly are 50/50. (Note that even if you are unable to eliminate answer choices, you still should guess, since the ACT test does not penalize for wrong answers.)

Use the Answer Choices to Check Your Math

While the ACT test does not test repetitive number crunching, most items do require a calculation or two. One of the fundamental rules of math is to "check your work." On the ACT test, however, this is a real time waster. Let's say you do a calculation (with or without your calculator) and the result is \$23.10. If one of the choices is \$23.10, pick it, mark your answer sheet, and move on to the next item. Do NOT check your arithmetic. The possibility that you did the arithmetic, made a mistake, and still got a number like 23.10 is just too unlikely to consider. On the other hand, if you do not find a choice that matches your calculation, then you'd better check both your set-up of the problem and your arithmetic to find the error. In this way, the answer choices function as a feedback loop on the accuracy of your calculations.

Don't Go Calculator Crazy

Just because you are allowed to use a calculator on the test does not mean that you should try to solve every problem with your calculator. In fact, for most problems, using the calculator is a less efficient method of arriving at a solution. Assume, for example, that you have to do the following arithmetic to get your answer: $\left(\frac{2}{3}\right)\left(\frac{7}{4}\right)\left(\frac{1}{6}\right)$. Since this problem involves single digit multiplication, it's going to be easier to do the arithmetic with a pencil than with a calculator: $\left(\frac{2}{3}\right)\left(\frac{7}{4}\right)\left(\frac{1}{6}\right)=\frac{2(7)(1)}{3(4)(6)}=\frac{14}{72}=\frac{7}{36}$. Use the calculator when it will be a definite advantage, but don't automatically assume that every problem is easier to solve with a calculator.

CALCULATOR EXERCISE

This exercise is designed to illustrate when and when not to use your calculator. Make sure that the calculator you bring to the ACT test is one with which you are thoroughly familiar. (For more detailed information on calculator usage, including specific models that are prohibited on the test, go to http://www.actstudent.org.) Although no item requires the use of a calculator, a calculator may be helpful at times. It may be useful for any item that involves complex arithmetic computations, but it cannot take the place of understanding how to set up a mathematical item. The degree to which you can use your calculator will depend on its features. Answers are on page 438.

DIRECTIONS: Label each of the items that follow according to one of the following categories. Then solve each item.

Category 1: A calculator would be very useful (it would save valuable test time).
Category 2: A calculator might or might not be useful.
Category 3: A calculator would be counterproductive (it would waste valuable test time).

1. What is the average of 8.5, 7.8, and 7.7?

A. 8.3
B. 8.2
C. 8.1
D. 8.0
E. 7.9

2. If $0 < x < 1$, which of the following has the greatest value?

F. x
G. $2x$
H. x^2
J. x^3
K. $x+1$

3. If 4.5 pounds of chocolate cost \$10, how many pounds of chocolate can be purchased for \$12?

A. $4\frac{3}{4}$

B. $5\frac{2}{5}$

C. $5\frac{1}{2}$

D. $5\frac{3}{4}$

E. 6

4. What is the value of $\frac{8}{9}-\frac{7}{8}$?

F. $\frac{1}{72}$

G. $\frac{1}{8}$

H. $\frac{1}{7}$

J. $\frac{15}{72}$

K. $\frac{15}{7}$

5. Which of the following fractions has the greatest value?

A. $\frac{111}{221}$

B. $\frac{75}{151}$

C. $\frac{333}{998}$

D. $\frac{113}{225}$

E. $\frac{101}{301}$

6. Dr. Leo's new office is 2.8 yards by 4 yards. She plans to run a decorative border around the perimeter of the office. How many yards of wallpaper border should she purchase?

F. 8.0
G. 13.2
H. 13.6
J. 14.2
K. 16.7

7. What is the value of $\frac{2}{3}-\frac{5}{8}$?

A. 1

B. $\frac{15}{16}$

C. $\frac{3}{24}$

D. $\frac{1}{24}$

E. $\frac{1}{100}$

8. If $3x+y=33$ and $x+y=17$, then what is the value of x?

F. 8
G. 12
H. 16
J. 24
K. 33

9. If the perimeter of the rectangle below is 40, what is its area?

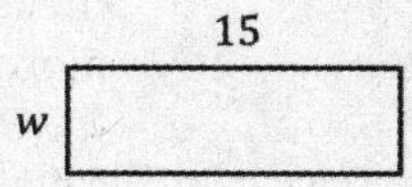

A. 5
B. 15
C. 25
D. 45
E. 75

10. If the price of a book increases from \$10.00 to \$12.50, what is the percent increase in price?

F. 2.5%
G. 12.5%
H. 25%
J. 33%
K. 50%

MATH LESSONS

LESSON

PRELIMINARIES AND STRATEGIES

ITEM-TYPES

Number and Quantity
Item #1

Algebra and Functions
Items #2–6

DIRECTIONS: Solve each item and choose the correct answer choice. Calculator use is permitted; however, some items are best solved without the use of a calculator. Answers are on page 438.

NOTE: All of the following should be assumed, unless otherwise stated.

1. Illustrative figures are NOT necessarily drawn to scale.
2. The word *average* indicates arithmetic mean.
3. The word *line* indicates a straight line.
4. Geometric figures lie in a plane.

1. If the price of fertilizer has been decreased from 3 pounds for \$2 to 5 pounds for \$2, how many more pounds of fertilizer can be purchased for \$10 than could have been purchased before?

A. 2
B. 8
C. 10
D. 12
E. 15

2. Five students formed a political club to support a candidate for local office. They project that club membership will double every three weeks. Which of the following can be used to find the number of members that the club projects to have after twelve weeks?

F. $5\left(2^{\frac{1}{4}}\right)$
G. $5\left(2^{\frac{2}{3}}\right)$
H. $5\left(2^{\frac{3}{2}}\right)$
J. $5(2^4)$
K. $5+5(2^4)$

3. If $\frac{2x-5}{3}=-4x$, then $x=?$

A. -1
B. $-\frac{5}{14}$
C. 0
D. $\frac{5}{14}$
E. 1

4. The oil-fired boiler in the basement of a school building consumes fuel at a rate of g gallons every h hours. Which of the following expressions can be used to calculate the amount of fuel consumed during m minutes of uninterrupted operation?

F. ghm
G. $\frac{g}{hm}$
H. $\frac{60g}{hm}$
J. $\frac{gm}{60h}$
K. $\frac{g}{60hm}$

5. If $f(x) = 2x - 3$ and $g(x) = x^2 - 2$, then what does $f(g(2))$ equal?

A. -1
B. 0
C. 1
D. 4
E. 7

6. If $|x+3| = 5$, then $x = ?$

F. −8 or 2
G. −2 or 8
H. −8
J. −2
K. 2 or 8

Coordinate Geometry *Item #7*

7. In the figure below, the line has a slope of 1. What is the y-intercept of the line?

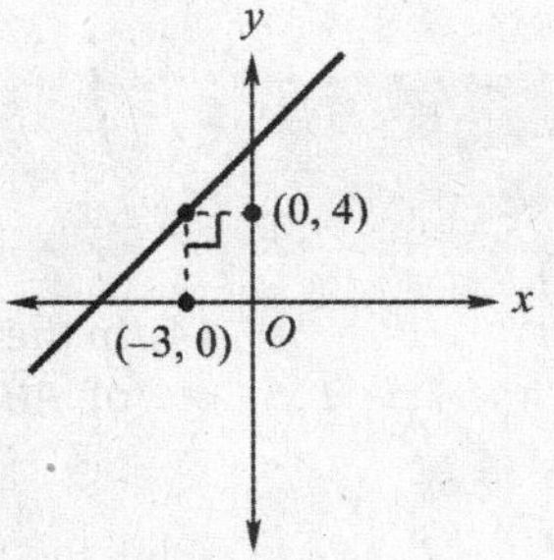

A. −5
B. −3
C. 0
D. 3
E. 7

Geometry *Items #8–9*

8. In the figure below, ΔPQR is inscribed in a circle with center O. What is the area of the circle?

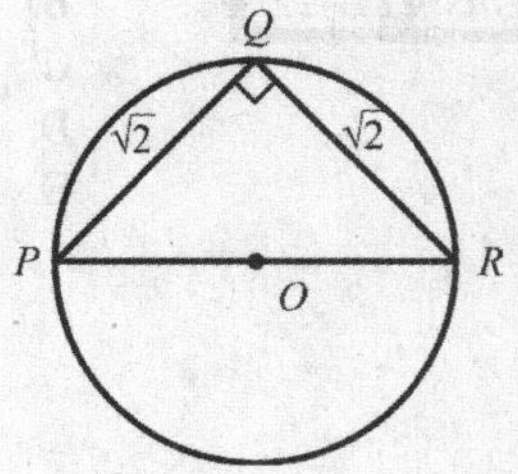

F. $\frac{\pi}{2}$
G. $\frac{\pi}{\sqrt{2}}$
H. π
J. $\pi\sqrt{2}$
K. 2π

9. In the figure below, $\overline{QP}$ is tangent to circle O at point P, and $\overline{QR}$ is tangent to circle O at point R. What is the degree measure of the minor arc PSR?

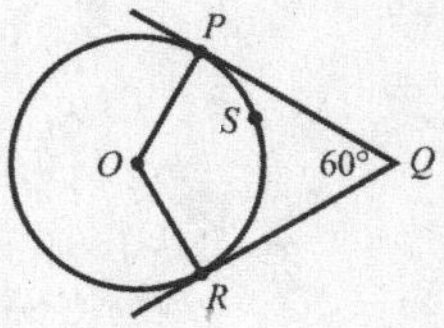

A. 30
B. 60
C. 90
D. 120
E. 180

Trigonometry *Item #10*

10. In the figure below, $\sin A = ?$

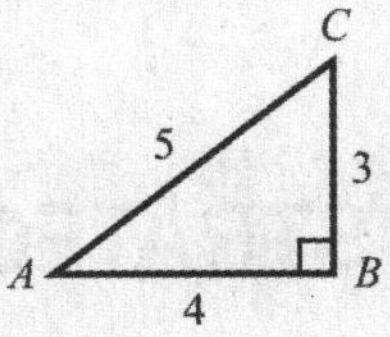

F. $\frac{3}{5}$
G. $\frac{3}{4}$
H. $\frac{4}{5}$
J. $\frac{5}{4}$
K. $\frac{5}{3}$

Statistics, Probability, and Data Representation
Items #11–12

11. What is the average of 8.5, 7.8, and 7.7?

A. 8.3
B. 8.2
C. 8.1
D. 8.0
E. 7.9

12. The following graph shows the data for domestic and foreign sales for Company X over five years.

Sales of Company X (in millions)

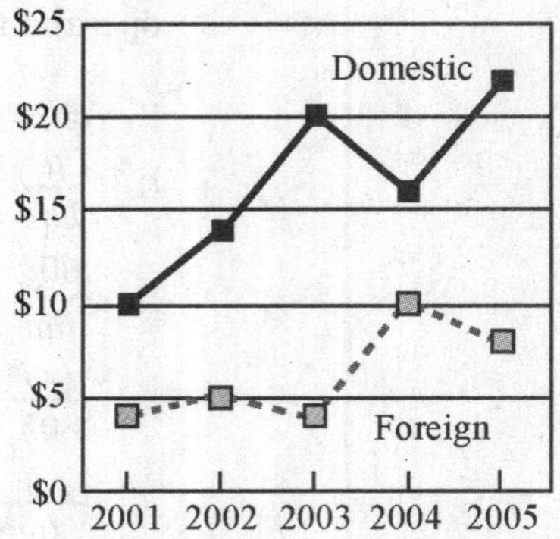

Which of the following pie graphs best represents the division of total sales between foreign and domestic sales for 2004?

F.
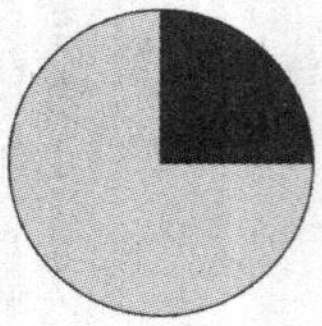

J.
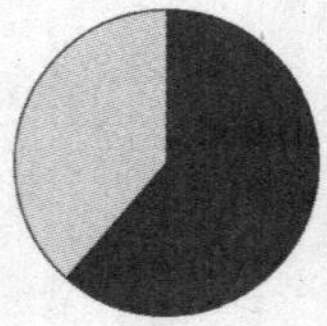

G.
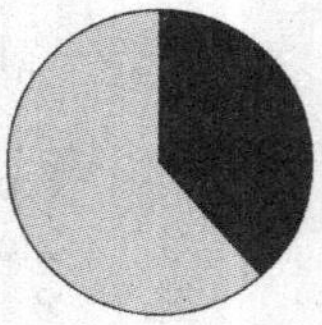

K.
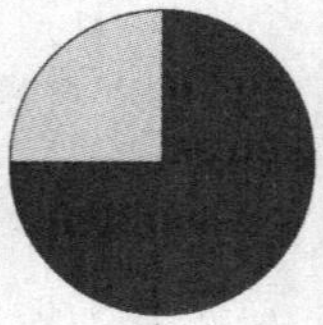

H.
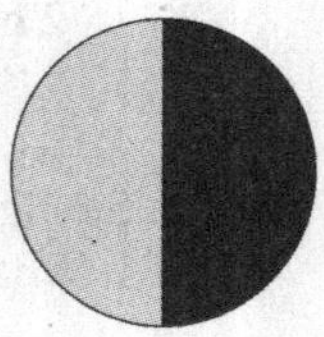

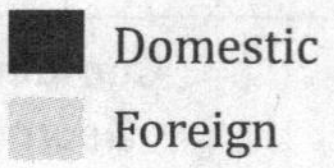

GENERAL STRATEGIES

Use the Figures
Items #13–16

13. In the figure below, x =?

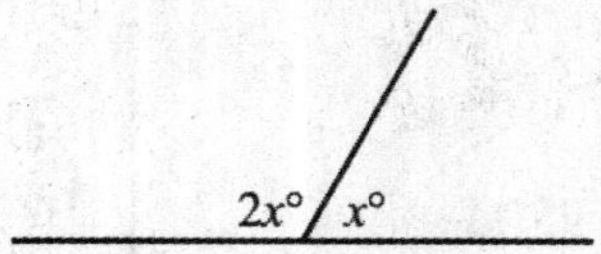

A. 15
B. 30
C. 45
D. 60
E. 120

14. In the figure below, what is the length of $\overline{AB}+\overline{CD}$?

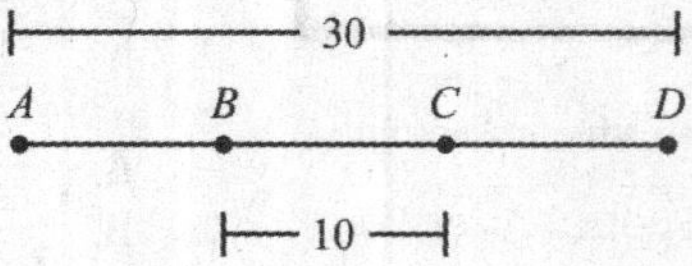

F. 5
G. 10
H. 15
J. 20
K. 40

The Cambridge Edge

Reference these strategies as you work through the math lessons with your teacher. These strategies can be used as alternatives to "traditional" solutions and can save you valuable test time.

The Cambridge Edge

Use the figures you are given. Even though the directions say the figures aren't necessarily drawn to scale, 9 times out of 10 they are drawn correctly, so you can rely on them in a pinch.

The Cambridge Edge

Items #15 and 16 are designed to help you see the difference between valid and invalid conclusions based on figures that are not drawn to scale. In this case, knowing the actual values of the angles is irrelevant to answering the questions.

Use the Answer Choices
Item #17

Pay Special Attention to "Signal" Words
Items #18–21

Items #15–16 refer to the following figure.

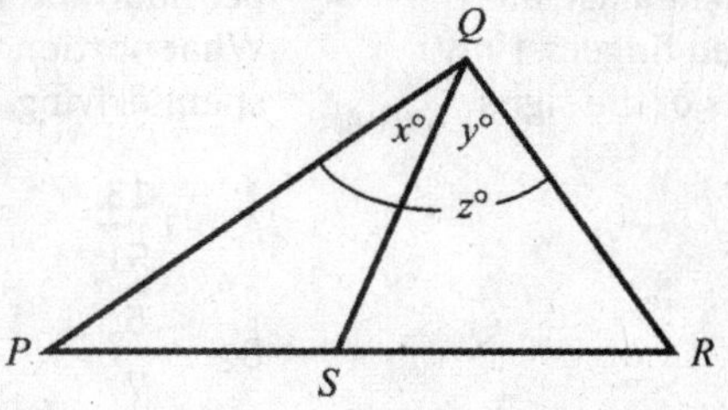

15. Which of the following must be true?

I. $\overline{PS} < \overline{SR}$
II. $z = 90$
III. $x > y$

A. I only
B. I and II only
C. I and III only
D. I, II, and III
E. Neither I, II, nor III

16. Which of the following must be true?

I. $\overline{PR} > \overline{PS}$
II. $z > x$
III. $x + y = z$

F. I only
G. I and II only
H. I and III only
J. I, II, and III
K. Neither I, II, nor III

17. In a certain year, the number of girls who graduated from City High School was twice the number of boys who graduated. If $\frac{3}{4}$ of the girls and $\frac{5}{6}$ of the boys went to college immediately after graduation, what fraction of the graduates that year went to college immediately after graduation?

A. $\frac{5}{36}$
B. $\frac{16}{27}$
C. $\frac{7}{9}$
D. $\frac{29}{36}$
E. $\frac{31}{36}$

The Cambridge Edge

Item #17 illustrates how the wrong answers correspond to errors in thinking or a misreading of the question.

The Cambridge Edge

Signal words include required units or other terms underlined, capitalized, or italicized for clarity. They also include thought-reversers such as NOT, CANNOT, and EXCEPT.

18. A jar contains black and white marbles. If there are 10 marbles in the jar, then which of the following could NOT be the ratio of black to white marbles?

F. 9:1
G. 7:3
H. 1:1
J. 1:4
K. 1:10

19. If n is a negative number, which of the following is the ***least*** in value?

A. $-n$
B. $n-n$
C. $n+n$
D. n^2
E. n^4

20. If a machine produces 240 thingamabobs per hour, how many minutes are needed for the machine to produce 30 thingamabobs?

F. 6
G. 7.5
H. 8
J. 12
K. 12.5

21. Of the 120 people in a room, $\frac{3}{5}$ are women. If $\frac{2}{3}$ of the people are married, what is the maximum number of women in the room who could be unmarried?

A. 80
B. 72
C. 48
D. 40
E. 32

Answer the Question Being Asked
Items #22–26

The Cambridge Edge

Practice reading math questions carefully to make sure you are answering the question being asked.

22. Three friends are playing a game in which each person simultaneously displays one of three hand signs: a clenched fist, an open palm, or two extended fingers. How many *unique* combinations of the signs are possible?

F. 3
G. 9
H. 10
J. 12
K. 27

23. If $\frac{1}{3}$ of the number of girls in a school equals $\frac{1}{5}$ of the total number of students, what is the ratio of girls to boys in the school?

A. 5:3
B. 3:2
C. 2:5
D. 1:3
E. 1:5

24. Peter walked from point P to point Q and back along the same route, a total distance of 2 miles. If he averaged 4 miles per hour on the trip from P to Q and 5 miles per hour on the return trip, what was his average walking speed in miles per hour for the entire trip?

F. $2\frac{2}{9}$
G. 4
H. $4\frac{4}{9}$
J. $4\frac{1}{2}$
K. 5

25. On a certain trip, a motorist drove 10 miles at 30 miles per hour, 10 miles at 40 miles per hour, and 10 miles at 50 miles per hour. What portion of her total driving time was spent driving 50 miles per hour?

A. $1\frac{13}{51}$
B. $\frac{5}{7}$
C. $\frac{5}{12}$
D. $\frac{1}{3}$
E. $\frac{12}{47}$

26. At Glenridge High School, 20% of the students are seniors. If all of the seniors attended the school play, and 60% of all the students attended the play, what percentage of the <u>non-seniors</u> attended the play?

F. 20%
G. 40%
H. 50%
J. 60%
K. 100%

Carefully Consider "Cannot Be Determined"
Item #27

The Cambridge Edge

Only choose the answer "Cannot Be Determined" if you have a mathematical reason to do so. In other words, if you chose "Cannot Be Determined" as your answer simply because you thought the test writers didn't provide enough information in the question, then you're probably wrong.

27. In the figure below, $m+n+o+p+q+r=?$

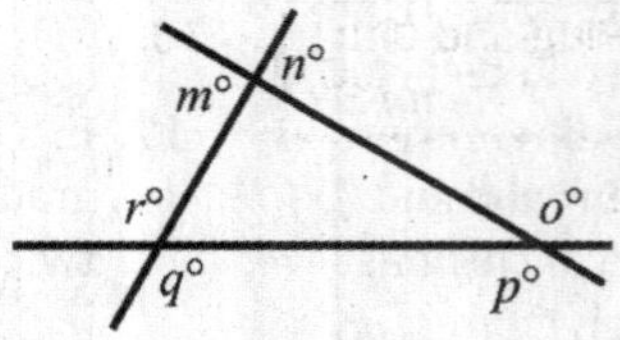

A. 360
B. 540
C. 720
D. 900
E. Cannot be determined from the given information

TIME-SAVING SHORTCUTS AND POWER STRATEGIES

Test-the-Test
Items #28–29

Test-the-Test

When you test-the-test, you plug the answer choices back into the item and see which one works.

28. A telephone call from City X to City Y costs \$1.00 for the first three minutes and \$0.25 for each additional minute thereafter. What is the maximum duration of a phone call, in minutes, for \$3.00?

F. 8
G. 11
H. 12
J. 13
K. 15

29. The water meter at a factory displays the reading below. What is the minimum number of cubic feet of water that the factory must use before four of the five digits on the meter are again the same?

Water Usage in Cubic Feet

7 1 , 1 1 1

A. 10,000
B. 1,000
C. 999
D. 666
E. 9

Plug-and-Chug
Item #30

30. After a 20% decrease in price, the cost of an item is *D* dollars. What was the price of the item before the decrease?

F. 0.75*D*
G. 0.80*D*
H. 1.20*D*
J. 1.25*D*
K. 1.5*D*

Plug & Chug

When you plug-and-chug, you make a hypothetical scenario concrete. In item #30, decide what original price was decreased by 20%. Now you can find *D* and then plug *D* into the answer choices to see which of them returns the correct original price.

Eliminate-and-Guess
Item #31

31. What is the maximum number of non-overlapping sections that can be created when a circle is crossed by three straight lines?

A. three
B. four
C. five
D. six
E. seven

The Cambridge Edge

Your worst-case scenario strategy will be to guess. There is no guessing penalty, so really, that's not a bad worst-case scenario. And you can improve your odds by eliminating a few answers before you guess.

LESSON 1

Number and Quantity

BASIC ARITHMETIC STRATEGIES

Just Do It
Items #1–2

The Cambridge Edge

Calculators are permitted on the ACT Mathematics Test. So you have three options: do mental or longhand math, estimate values, or use your calculator. Use whichever method will get you the correct answer to a problem the quickest!

1. If 30% of some number is 480, what is 125% of the number?

A. 2,000
B. 1,800
C. 1,600
D. 200
E. 180

2. If Gerard played soccer for $2\frac{1}{6}$ hours on Friday and $1\frac{3}{4}$ hours on Sunday, what is the total time, in hours, Gerard played soccer during those 2 days?

F. $3\frac{1}{12}$
G. $3\frac{5}{6}$
H. $3\frac{11}{12}$
J. 4
K. $4\frac{1}{12}$

Look for Shortcuts
Items #3–11

The Cambridge Edge

Which time-saving test prep shortcut can you use in each item, #3–11?

1. Simplifying
2. Factoring
3. Approximation
4. The "Flying-X" Method
5. Decimal-Fraction Equivalents

3. $\frac{1}{2}\left(\frac{2}{3}\right)\left(\frac{3}{4}\right)\left(\frac{4}{5}\right)\left(\frac{5}{6}\right)\left(\frac{6}{7}\right)\left(\frac{7}{8}\right) = ?$

A. $\frac{1}{56}$
B. $\frac{1}{8}$
C. $\frac{28}{37}$
D. $\frac{41}{43}$
E. $\frac{55}{56}$

4. $86(37) - 37(85) = ?$

F. 0
G. 1
H. 37
J. 85
K. 86

5. Which of the following is a prime factorization of 120?

A. (2)(2)(15)
B. (2)(3)(4)(5)
C. (2)(2)(3)(10)
D. (2)(2)(2)(3)(5)
E. (2)(2)(3)(3)(5)

Throwback to Math Class

The *prime factorization* of a number is a product of prime numbers that equals the number. A number is prime if it is divisible only by 1 and itself.

6. $-4.01(3.2) + 0.2(0.4) = ?$

F. −12.752
G. −4.536
H. 0.432
J. 1.251
K. 12.783

7. $\frac{0.2521(8.012)}{1.014}$ is approximately equal to which of the following?

A. 0.25
B. 0.5
C. 1.0
D. 1.5
E. 2.0

Bridge the Gap
Items #12–13

Throwback to Math Class

The "flying-x" method is used to add and subtract fractions:

$$\frac{a}{b}+\frac{c}{d}=\frac{a}{b}\overset{\nwarrow\nearrow}{+}\frac{c}{d}=\frac{ad+bc}{bd}$$

Step 1: Find the new denominator by multiplying the original denominators.
Step 2: Multiply the first fraction's numerator by the second fraction's denominator.
Step 3: Multiply the second fraction's numerator by the first fraction's denominator.
Step 4: Add (or subtract) the results of Step 2 and Step 3.

This method is particularly useful when a common denominator is not obvious.

The Cambridge Edge

Don't panic when you see a story problem! Practice using the steps above to organize your approach and you'll master story problems in no time.

8. Which of the following fractions is the largest?

F. $\frac{111}{221}$
G. $\frac{75}{151}$
H. $\frac{333}{998}$
J. $\frac{113}{225}$
K. $\frac{101}{301}$

9. If $z=\frac{x+y}{x}$, $1-z=?$

A. $\frac{1-x+y}{x}$
B. $\frac{x+y-1}{x}$
C. $\frac{1-x-y}{x}$
D. $-\frac{y}{x}$
E. $1-x-y$

10. $0.125(0.125)(64)=?$

F. 0.125
G. 0.5
H. 0.625
J. 1
K. 8

11. $\frac{0.111(0.666)}{0.166(0.125)}$ is approximately equal to which of the following?

A. 6.8
B. 4.3
C. 3.6
D. 1.6
E. 0.9

The Cambridge Edge

Perform the following steps when solving a story problem:

Step 1: Identify what is being asked.
Step 2: Identify the information that is given in the item.
Step 3: Determine how to bridge the gap between Step 1 and Step 2, including any units both indicated and implied.
Step 4: Execute the needed operations.
Step 5: Double-check remaining units.

12. If the senior class has 360 students, of whom $\frac{5}{12}$ are women, and the junior class has 350 students, of whom $\frac{4}{7}$ are women, how many more women are there in the junior class than in the senior class?

F. $(360-350)\left(\frac{4}{7}-\frac{5}{12}\right)$
G. $\frac{(360-350)\left(\frac{4}{7}-\frac{5}{12}\right)}{2}$
H. $\left(\frac{4}{7}\right)\left(\frac{5}{12}\right)(360-350)$
J. $\left(\frac{4}{7}\right)(350)-\left(\frac{5}{12}\right)(360)$
K. $\left(\frac{5}{12}\right)(360)-\left(\frac{4}{7}\right)(350)$

13. If the price of candy increases from 5 pounds for \$7 to 3 pounds for \$7, how much less candy (in pounds) can be purchased for \$3.50 at the new price than at the old price?

A. $\frac{2}{7}$
B. 1
C. $1\frac{17}{35}$
D. 2
E. $3\frac{34}{35}$

PROPERTIES OF NUMBERS

Throwback to Math Class

Recall the following definitions of the different types of numbers:

Natural: all positive whole numbers plus zero
Integers: all negative and positive whole numbers, plus zero
Rational: all numbers that can be written as a ratio (fraction)
Real numbers: all rational and irrational numbers
Complex numbers: all real and imaginary numbers
Consecutive numbers: numbers in counting order

14. If n is the first number in a series of three consecutive even numbers, which of the following expressions represents the sum of the three numbers?

F. $n+2$
G. $n+4$
H. $n+6$
J. $3n+6$
K. $6(3n)$

15. If n is an odd number, which of the following expressions represents the third odd number following n?

A. $n+3$
B. $n+4$
C. $n+6$
D. $3n+3$
E. $4n+4$

16. If $0 < x < 1$, which of the following expressions is the largest?

F. x
G. $2x$
H. x^2
J. x^3
K. $x+1$

17. Two cables with lengths 360 inches and 420 inches are to be cut into pieces of all the same length without any waste. If the pieces are to be the greatest possible length, how many pieces can be cut?

A. 6
B. 7
C. 13
D. 20
E. 60

18. $|-2|+3-|-4|=?$

F. -5
G. -4
H. -1
J. 1
K. 9

19. For all nonzero values of a and b, the value of which of the following expressions is *always* positive?

A. $|-a|+b$
B. $a+|b|$
C. $-|a|+|b|$
D. $-|a|-|b|$
E. $|-a|+|-b|$

Throwback to Math Class

Memorize the following principles of positive and negative numbers:

$(+)(+)=(+)$
$(-)(-)=(+)$
$(+)(-)$ or $(-)(+)=(-)$
$(+)\div(+)=(+)$
$(-)\div(-)=(+)$
$(+)\div(-)$ or $(-)\div(+)=(-)$

Plug & Chug

Be careful when using the plug-and-chug strategy for items such as #16. In some of the previous problems, you could plug in any value for x, but item #16 states that x must be between 0 and 1. Thus, choose a simple fraction between 0 and 1 to test. If you pick a value outside of this range, you will arrive at an incorrect answer.

SCIENTIFIC NOTATION

The Cambridge Edge

Know how to use your calculator to do scientific notation problems. Some calculators allow you to input the numbers in scientific notation and return the product in scientific notation as well. If you don't have a calculator that takes scientific notation inputs, then use the calculator to multiply the coefficients.

20. Which of the following is equivalent to $120(10^5)$?

F. 1.2×10^{-7}
G. 1.2×10^{-6}
H. 1.2×10^{6}
J. 1.2×10^{7}
K. 1.2×10^{8}

21. A sound wave travels at approximately 1,125 feet/second. If a person hears a sound $2\frac{1}{2}$ minutes after it happens, how far away, in feet, is the person from the source of the sound?

A. 1.6875×10^{1}
B. 2.8125×10^{3}
C. 2.8125×10^{4}
D. 1.6875×10^{5}
E. 1.6875×10^{6}

Throwback to Math Class

To multiply a number in scientific notation by 10 to a power, multiply the tens together by adding the exponents.

To multiply two numbers in scientific notation, multiply the coefficients and add the exponents.

To divide a number in scientific notation by 10 to a power, subtract the exponents.

To divide two numbers in scientific notation, divide the coefficients and subtract the exponents.

COMPLEX NUMBERS

Throwback to Math Class

Memorize these imaginary number values:

$i=\sqrt{-1}$
$i^2=-1$
$i^3=-\sqrt{-1}$
$i^4=1$

22. Which of the following expressions is equivalent to $(3+i)(4-3i)$, where $i^2=-1$?

F. $12+3i^2$
G. $12-3i^2$
H. $9-5i^2$
J. $9-5i$
K. $15-5i$

23. Which of the following expressions is equivalent to $\frac{1}{2-i}$, where $i=\sqrt{-1}$?

A. -2
B. -1
C. $\frac{2+i}{5}$
D. $\frac{2-i}{5}$
E. $\frac{2+i}{3}$

MATRICES AND VECTORS

Throwback to Math Class

To *add or subtract two vectors*, add or subtract the corresponding components.

To *multiply a vector by a scalar*, simply multiply the similar components, that is, the vector's magnitude by the scalar's magnitude.

24. What is the matrix product $a\begin{bmatrix}1\\2\end{bmatrix}\begin{bmatrix}-1 & 1 & 0\end{bmatrix}$?

F. $\begin{bmatrix}-a & a & 0\\-2a & 2a & 0\end{bmatrix}$

G. $\begin{bmatrix}-3a & 3a & 0\\-2a & 2a & 0\end{bmatrix}$

H. $\begin{bmatrix}a\\3a\\0\end{bmatrix}$

J. $\begin{bmatrix}a & 3a & 0\end{bmatrix}$

K. The matrix product is undefined.

25. If $a=\langle -3,2\rangle$, $b=\langle 2,0\rangle$, and $c=\langle 1,1\rangle$ what is the vector form of $a-b+2c$?

A. $\langle -5,2\rangle$
B. $\langle -4,1\rangle$
C. $\langle -3,4\rangle$
D. $\langle 4,-3\rangle$
E. $\langle 3,4\rangle$

26. Vector **u** has initial point $(3,2)$ and terminal point $(4,2)$. Vector **v** has initial point $(-2,3)$ and terminal point $(-1,4)$. Given that $-4\mathbf{u}+2(\mathbf{v}+\mathbf{w})=0$, what is the form of **w** in unit vector notation?

F. $\mathbf{i}-\mathbf{j}$
G. $-\mathbf{i}+\mathbf{j}$
H. $\mathbf{i}-2\mathbf{j}$
J. $\mathbf{i}+\mathbf{j}$
K. $2\mathbf{i}-\mathbf{j}$

The Cambridge Edge

When multiplying matrices, don't do more work than is necessary to answer the item. Eliminate any choices that don't contain the correct number of rows and columns. Then, determine only as many elements in the product matrix necessary to choose between the remaining choices.

RATES AND PROPORTIONS

Test Specs

You will be expected to know basic conversions like 12 inches = 1 foot, 3 feet = 1 yard, and 60 minutes = 1 hour. If a problem requires any conversion factors beyond the basics, the conversion factor will be included in the item stem.

27. A clown is filling helium balloons from tanks that contains 80 cubic feet of helium each. At most, how many 11-inch helium balloons can be filled from 2 tanks? (1 balloon = 480 cubic inches)

A. 40
B. 288
C. 480
D. 576
E. 3,456

28. Doreen can wash her car in 15 minutes, while her younger brother Dave takes twice as long to do the same job. If they work together, how many minutes will the job take them?

F. 5
G. $7\frac{1}{2}$
H. 10
J. $22\frac{1}{2}$
K. 30

The Cambridge Edge

To solve rate problems, create expressions of rates in which the units cancel leaving a quantity in the desired units. This is true for any problem involving rates, measurements, and unit conversions.

The Cambridge Edge

Notice the thought-reverser NOT in item #30. Remember to keep the thought-reverser in mind when selecting your final answer.

Throwback to Math Class

When setting up proportions, a common technique for solving for an unknown is *cross-multiplying*. Cross-multiplying is when you multiply the numerator of the first fraction with the denominator of the second and the denominator of the first fraction with the numerator of the second and set both products equal to each other. Cross-multiplying eliminates the fractions and returns an equation that is easy to solve algebraically.

29. Clyde drove at a constant rate of speed for 4 hours and covered a distance of 200 miles. If he had driven at the same rate for 5 hours, how many miles would he have driven?

A. 160
B. 180
C. 200
D. 220
E. 250

30. At Star Lake Middle School, 45% of the students bought a yearbook. If 540 students bought yearbooks, how many students did NOT buy a yearbook?

F. 243
G. 540
H. 575
J. 660
K. 957

31. A train traveling at a constant speed, k, takes 90 minutes to go from point P to point Q, a distance of 45 miles. What is the value of k, in miles per hour?

A. 20
B. 30
C. 45
D. 60
E. 75

32. The cost of picture framing depends on the outer perimeter of the frame. If a 15-inch-by-15-inch picture frame costs $35 more than a 10-inch-by-10-inch picture frame, what is the cost of framing, in dollars per inch?

F. $3.50
G. $2.75
H. $2.25
J. $1.75
K. $1.50

33. Walking at a constant speed of 4 miles per hour, it took Jill exactly 1 hour to walk home from school. If she walked at a constant speed of 5 miles per hour, how many *minutes* would the trip take?

A. 48
B. 54
C. 56
D. 72
E. 112

34. Ms. Peters drove from her home to the park at an average speed of 30 miles per hour and returned home along the same route at an average speed of 40 miles per hour. If her driving time from home to the park was 20 minutes, how many minutes did it take Ms. Peters to drive from the park to her home?

F. 7.5
G. 12
H. 15
J. 24
K. 30

PERCENTAGES

The Cambridge Edge

Percentage problems can be summarized as "*a* is *x* percent of *b*," or, less formally, "this is some percentage of that." To solve these problems, create a fraction with *b* or "of that" as the denominator and *a* or "this is" as the numerator. Set this fraction equal to the percentage over 100. Cross-multiply to solve for the unknown.

$$\frac{\text{is}}{\text{of}} = \frac{\%}{100}$$

Throwback to Math Class

What about percentages greater than 100? Let's consider an example. If the number of students on Thursday is 150% of the number of students on Wednesday, then the number of students on Thursday is equal to the number of students on Wednesday *plus* 50% of the number of students on Wednesday. In other words, 150% is the same as multiplying by 1.5.

Throwback to Math Class

To find percentage change, put the change in the quantity over the original amount. Multiply this fraction by 100 to change the fraction to a percentage.

$$\frac{|\text{New Amount} - \text{Original Amount}|}{\text{Original Amount}}(100) = \%\ \text{Change}$$

35. A jar contains 24 white marbles and 48 black marbles. What percentage of the marbles in the jar are black?

A. 10%
B. 25%
C. $33\frac{1}{3}\%$
D. 60%
E. $66\frac{2}{3}\%$

36. A group of three friends shared the cost of a tape recorder. If Andy, Barbara, and Donna each paid \$12, \$30, and \$18, respectively, then Donna paid what percentage of the cost of the tape recorder?

F. 10%
G. 30%
H. $33\frac{1}{3}\%$
J. 50%
K. $66\frac{2}{3}\%$

37. Twenty students attended Professor Rodriguez's class on Monday and 25 students attended on Tuesday. The number of students who attended on Tuesday was what percentage of the number of students who attended on Monday?

A. 5%
B. 20%
C. 25%
D. 80%
E. 125%

38. If the population of a town was 20,000 in 1997 and 16,000 in 2007, what was the percent decline in the town's population?

F. 50%
G. 25%
H. 20%
J. 10%
K. 5%

Items #39–41 refer to the following table.

CAPITOL CITY FIRES	
Year	Number of Fires
2002	100
2003	125
2004	140
2005	150
2006	135

39. The number of fires in 2002 was what percentage of the number of fires in 2003?

A. 25%
B. $66\frac{2}{3}\%$
C. 80%
D. 100%
E. 125%

40. The number of fires in 2006 was what percentage of the number of fires in 2005?

F. 90%
G. 82%
H. 50%
J. 25%
K. 10%

41. What was the percent decrease in the number of fires from 2005 to 2006?

A. 10%
B. 25%
C. 50%
D. 82%
E. 90%

ARITHMETIC STRATEGY: "TEST-THE-TEST"

The Cambridge Edge

Always use number sense to eliminate answer choices. You should be able to eliminate three of the five answer choices in item #42 immediately using number sense.

42. Which of the following is the larger of 2 numbers, the product of which is 600 and the sum of which is 5 times the difference between the 2 numbers?

F. 10
G. 15
H. 20
J. 30
K. 50

43. If $\frac{1}{3}$ of a number is 3 more than $\frac{1}{4}$ of the number, then what is the number?

A. 18
B. 24
C. 30
D. 36
E. 48

44. If both 16 and 9 are divided by *n*, the remainder is 2. What is *n*?

F. 3
G. 4
H. 5
J. 6
K. 7

45. The sum of the digits of a 3-digit number is 16. If the tens digit of the number is 3 times the units digit, and the units digit is $\frac{1}{4}$ of the hundreds digit, then what is the number?

A. 446
B. 561
C. 682
D. 862
E. 914

46. If the sum of 5 consecutive integers is 40, what is the smallest of the 5 integers?

F. 4
G. 5
H. 6
J. 7
K. 8

LESSON 2

ALGEBRA AND FUNCTIONS

MANIPULATING ALGEBRAIC EXPRESSIONS

Basic Algebraic Manipulations
Items #1–2

Throwback to Math Class

In item #2, remember to distribute the minus sign to both monomials in the expression in parentheses.

Evaluating Expressions
Items #3–7

The Cambridge Edge

The best strategy for evaluating expressions problems is to Just Do It—just make the required substitution and simplify.

1. If $a^3 + b = 3 + a^3$, then $b = ?$

A. 3^3
B. $3\sqrt{3}$
C. 3
D. $\sqrt[3]{3}$
E. $-\sqrt{3}$

2. Which of the following expressions is equivalent to $4a + 3b - (-2a - 3b)$?

F. $2a$
G. $12ab$
H. $2a + 6b$
J. $6a + 6b$
K. $8a + 9b$

3. If $x = 3$, what is the value of $x^2 + 2x - 2$?

A. 0
B. 4
C. 6
D. 10
E. 13

4. If $x = 2$, then $\frac{1}{x^2} + \frac{1}{x} - \frac{x}{2} = ?$

F. $-\frac{3}{4}$
G. $-\frac{1}{4}$
H. 0
J. $\frac{1}{4}$
K. $\frac{1}{2}$

5. If $p = 1$, $q = 2$, and $r = 3$, what is the value of $\frac{(q \cdot r)(r - q)}{(q - p)(p \cdot q)}$?

A. −3
B. −1
C. 0
D. 3
E. 6

6. If $\frac{1}{3}x = 10$, then $\frac{1}{6}x = ?$

F. $\frac{1}{15}$
G. $\frac{2}{3}$
H. 2
J. 5
K. 30

7. If $x + y = 3$, then $2x + 2y = ?$

A. $-\frac{2}{3}$
B. $\frac{1}{2}$
C. $\frac{3}{2}$
D. 6
E. Cannot be determined from the given information

Manipulating Expressions Involving Exponents
Items #8–9

Factoring Expressions
Items #10–12

Throwback to Math Class

In general, the difference of two squares $x^2 - y^2$ factors into $(x - y)(x + y)$. Item #10 demonstrates that knowing the difference of two squares can save time on the exam.

Logarithmic Expressions
Items #13–14

Throwback to Math Class

A logarithm is the inverse of an exponential function. In the exponential function $y = b^x$, the inverse is $\log_b y = x$. This can be read as "*b* needs to be raised to what power *x* in order to get *y*?"

Make sure you know these logarithm basics:

$\log_b b^x = x$

$\log_b 1 = 0$

$\log_b 0 = \text{undefined}$

8. $\dfrac{9(x^2y^3)^6}{(3x^6y^9)^2} = ?$

F. 1
G. 3
H. x^2y^3
J. $3x^2y^3$
K. $x^{12}y^{12}$

Throwback to Math Class

Remember to apply the distributive property to terms in parentheses. In item #8, be sure to distribute the exponent of 6 and 2 to all elements contained in the parentheses, including coefficients.

9. $2\left(4^{-\frac{1}{2}}\right) - 2^0 + 2^{\frac{3}{2}} + 2^{-2} = ?$

A. $-2\sqrt{2} - \dfrac{1}{4}$
B. $2\sqrt{2} - \dfrac{1}{4}$
C. $2\sqrt{2}$
D. $2\sqrt{2} + \dfrac{1}{4}$
E. $2\sqrt{2} + \dfrac{5}{4}$

10. Which of the following expressions is equivalent to $\dfrac{x^2 - y^2}{x + y}$?

F. $x^2 - y^2$
G. $x^2 + y^2$
H. $x^2 + y$
J. $x + y^2$
K. $x - y$

Throwback to Math Class

Let's review the rules for exponents:

1. $x^m(x^n) = x^{m+n}$
2. $\dfrac{x^m}{x^n} = x^{m-n}$
3. $(x^m)^n = x^{m(n)}$
4. $(x^m[y^m])^n = x^{mn}(y^{mn})$
5. $\left(\dfrac{x^m}{y^m}\right)^n = \dfrac{x^{mn}}{y^{mn}}$

11. Which of the following expressions is equivalent to $\dfrac{x^2 - x - 6}{x + 2}$?

A. $x^2 - \dfrac{x}{2} - 3$
B. $x^2 - 2$
C. $x - 2$
D. $x - 3$
E. x

12. Which of the following is the factorization of $6x^2 + 4x - 2$?

F. $(6x + 1)(x - 3)$
G. $(6x + 3)(x - 1)$
H. $(3x - 1)(2x - 2)$
J. $(2x + 2)(3x - 1)$
K. $(2x + 4)(3x - 2)$

13. Evaluate $\log_5 125 + \log_2\left(\dfrac{1}{2}\right)$.

A. -1
B. 0
C. 1
D. 2
E. 3

14. If $\log_b x = m$ and $\log_b y = n$, then $\log_b xy = ?$

F. $m + n$
G. bmn
H. bxy
J. $m - n$
K. mn

Throwback to Math Class

Memorize these properties:

Product Property of Logs:
$\log_b(xy) = \log_b x + \log_b y$

Quotient Property of Logs:
$\log_b\left(\dfrac{x}{y}\right) = \log_b x - \log_b y$

Power Property of Logs:
$\log_b(x^y) = y\log_b x$

Be careful: a common mistake students make is assuming that $\log(x + y) = \log(x) + \log(y)$. This is incorrect! We cannot split apart the $(x + y)$ expression.

EVALUATING SEQUENCES

Throwback to Math Class

In exponential growth sequences, each term is a constant multiple of the preceding term. For example, consider the geometric sequence 3, 9, 27, 81,.... Each consecutive term is equal to 3 times the preceding term, so the common ratio between terms is 3. Here's a more formal definition:

Any term (a_n) is related to the preceding term (a_{n-1}) by the common ratio (r):

$$a_n = a_{n-1}r$$

The relationship between the nth term (a_n) and the first term (a_1) is as follows:

$$a_n = a_1 r^{n-1}$$

15. In a geometric sequence of positive numbers, the fourth term is 125 and the sixth term is 3,125. What is the second term of the sequence?

A. 1
B. 5
C. 10
D. 25
E. 50

16. City University projects that a planned expansion will increase the number of enrolled students every year for the next five years by 50%. If 400 students enroll in the first year of the plan, how many students are expected to enroll in the fifth year of the plan?

F. 25
G. 600
H. 675
J. 1,350
K. 2,025

17. Jimmy's uncle deposited $1,000 into a college fund account and promised that at the start of each year, he would deposit an amount equal to 10% of the account balance. If no other deposits or withdrawals were made and no additional interest accrued, what was the account balance after three additional annual deposits were made by Jimmy's uncle?

A. $1,030
B. $1,300
C. $1,331
D. $1,500
E. $1,830

18. A tank with a capacity of 2,400 liters is filled to capacity with water. If a valve is opened that drains 25% of the contents of the tank every minute, what is the volume of water (in liters) that remains in the tank after 3 minutes?

F. 1,800
G. 1,350
H. 1,012.5
J. 600
K. 325.75

Throwback to Math Class

Exponential growth and decay are special cases of geometric sequences, with the formula $a_t = a_0 r^{\frac{t}{T}}$.

In the above equation, a_t is the amount after time t, a_0 is the initial amount ($t = 0$), r is the proportionality constant, t is the total period of growth (decay), and T is the time per cycle of constant growth (decay). Note that for exponential growth, $r > 1$; for exponential decay, $0 < r < 1$; and if $r = 1$, there is no change in amount.

SOLVING ALGEBRAIC EQUATIONS OR INEQUALITIES WITH ONE VARIABLE

Simple Equations
Item #19

19. If $(2+3)(1+x)=25$, then $x=?$

A. $\frac{1}{5}$
B. $\frac{1}{4}$
C. 1
D. 4
E. 5

Throwback to Math Class

Remember to solve for a variable means to isolate that variable. The general technique is to get the variable alone on one side with all other terms on the other side of the equation.

Simple Inequalities
Item #20

20. If $2x+3>9$, which of the following can be the value of x?

F. −4
G. −3
H. 0
J. 3
K. 4

Throwback to Math Class

Manipulating inequalities is the same as manipulating equations except you have an inequality symbol, and whenever you multiply or divide by a negative number you must flip the sign.

Equations Involving Rational Expressions
Items #21–23

21. If $\frac{12}{x+1}-1=2$, and $x \neq -1$, then $x=?$

A. 1
B. 2
C. 3
D. 11
E. 12

22. If $\frac{x}{x+2}=\frac{3}{4}$, and $x \neq -2$, then $x=?$

F. 6
G. 4
H. 3
J. 2
K. 1

23. If $\frac{x}{x-2}-\frac{x+2}{2(x-2)}=8$, and $x \neq 2$, which of the following is the complete solution set for x?

A. {}
B. {−2}
C. {2}
D. {4}
E. {8}

Inequalities Involving Rational Expressions
Item #24

24. If $\frac{3}{x-2}>\frac{1}{6}$, which of the following defines the possible values for x?

F. $x<20$
G. $x>0$
H. $x>2$
J. $0<x<20$
K. $2<x<20$

Throwback to Math Class

Steps for solving inequalities involving rational expressions:

Step 1: Rewrite the terms using a common denominator and factor it out of the equation. Do not transpose multiplicative factors involving x. Solving for x gives a range of values with an upper or lower limit.

Step 2: Check this range for values of x that make the denominator zero or that change the sign of the rational expression. If necessary, further limit the possible range to exclude these values.

Equations Involving Radical Expressions
Items #25–28

Test-the-Test

The test-the-test strategy is quick to use with item #25 because the answer choices are exactly one value. In item #26, the test-the-test strategy is also quick to use, but you need to recognize the overlap between some of the answer choices.

25. If $\sqrt{2x+1}-1=4$, then $x=$?

A. -5
B. -1
C. 1
D. 12
E. 24

26. Which of the following is the complete solution set for $\sqrt{3x-2}-3=-4$?

F. {}
G. {− 1}
H. {1}
J. {− 1, 1}
K. {1, 2}

27. If $\sqrt{2x-5}=2\sqrt{5-2x}$, then $x=$?

A. 1
B. 2
C. $\frac{5}{2}$
D. 10
E. 15

28. Which of the following is the complete solution set for $\sqrt{x^2+9}=5$?

F. {− 4, 4}
G. {− 4}
H. {0}
J. {4}
K. {}

Equations Involving Integer and Rational Exponents
Items #29–32

Throwback to Math Class

Memorize the following fact for zero, integer, and rational exponents:

1. $a^0=1$ if $a\neq 0$
2. $a^{-n}=\frac{1}{a^n}$
3. $a^{\frac{1}{n}}=\sqrt[n]{a}$

29. If $4^{x+2}=64$, then $x=$?

A. 1
B. 2
C. 3
D. 4
E. 5

30. If $8^x=2^{x+3}$, then $x=$?

F. 0
G. 1
H. $\frac{2}{3}$
J. 3
K. $\frac{3}{2}$

31. If $3^{2x}=\frac{1}{81}$, then $x=$?

A. −2
B. $-\frac{3}{2}$
C. $-\frac{2}{3}$
D. $\frac{2}{3}$
E. $\frac{3}{2}$

32. If $5^3=(\sqrt{5})^{-2x}$, then $5^x=$?

F. $\frac{1}{125}$
G. $\frac{1}{25}$
H. $\frac{1}{5}$
J. 5
K. 25

Equations Involving Logarithms
Items # 33–34

33. Which of the following is a value of x that satisfies the equation $\log_4 x=4$?

A. 1
B. 16
C. 160
D. 256
E. 512

34. Which of the following is a value of x that satisfies the equation $2\log_x 16+\log_x 16=6$?

F. 2
G. 4
H. 16
J. 32
K. 64

Throwback to Math Class

Steps for solving radical equations:

Step 1: Isolate the radical expression.
Step 2: Eliminate the radical sign by squaring (if a square root) or cubing (if a cube root) both sides of the equation.
Step 3: Solve for the unknown variable.
Step 4: Check the solution(s) in the original equation.

It is extremely important that you check your answers when dealing with radical equations. Squaring both sides of an equation while solving for x can generate extraneous solutions.

Equations Involving Absolute Value
Items #35–36

Throwback to Math Class

To solve equations involving absolute values, construct two derived equations and solve for x in each equation. Test the values for x in the original equation to verify that each is a valid solution.

35. Which of the following is the complete solution set for $\left|\frac{2x+1}{3}\right|=5$?

A. {−8, −7}
B. {−8, 7}
C. {−7, 7}
D. {7}
E. {8}

36. Which of the following is the complete solution set for $|x+6|=3x$?

F. $\left\{-3, \frac{3}{2}\right\}$
G. $\left\{-\frac{3}{2}, 3\right\}$
H. $\left\{\frac{3}{2}, 3\right\}$
J. {3}
K. {}

Inequalities Involving Absolute Value
Items #37–39

37. Which of the following is the complete solution set for $|2x-1|>3$?

A. All real numbers
B. The null set
C. All real numbers less than −1 or greater than 2
D. All real numbers less than −2 or greater than 1
E. All real numbers less than −3

38. If $|3x-6|>9$, then which of the following must be true?

F. $-3<x<2$
G. $-2<x<3$
H. $x<-3$ or $x>2$
J. $x<-1$ or $x>5$
K. $x<-1$ or $x>9$

39. Which of the following identifies exactly those values of x that satisfy $|-2x+4|<4$?

A. $x>-4$
B. $x<4$
C. $x>0$
D. $0<x<4$
E. $-4<x<0$

Throwback to Math Class

The key to solving inequalities involving absolute value is to recall the following properties of absolute value:

If $|x|\geq a$ $(a>0)$, then $x\leq -a$ or $x\geq a$.

If $|x|\leq a$ $(a>0)$, then $x\leq a$ or $x\geq -a \Rightarrow -a\leq x\leq a$.

EVALUATING, INTERPRETING, AND CREATING ALGEBRAIC FUNCTIONS

Function Notation
Items #40–47

Throwback to Math Class

Function notation is $f(x)$, which means the output is a function of x.

40. If $f(x)=x^2+x$, what is the value of $f(-2)$?

F. −8
G. −2
H. 2
J. 8
K. 12

41. If $y=f(x)=\left(\frac{6x^2-2^{-x}}{|x|}\right)^{-\frac{1}{2}}$ for all integers and $x=-1$, what is the value of y?

A. 2
B. $\frac{1}{2}$
C. $\frac{1}{4}$
D. $-\frac{1}{2}$
E. −2

The Cambridge Edge

Item #42 requires you to evaluate one function for a given value and to use that result to evaluate a second function. This is also known as composing one function with another.

42. If $f(x) = x + 3$ and $g(x) = 2x - 5$, what is the value of $f(g(2))$?

F. −2
G. 0
H. 2
J. 4
K. 10

43. If $f(x) = 3x + 2$ and $g(x) = x^2 + x$, what is the value of $g(f(-2))$?

A. 15
B. 12
C. 6
D. 3
E. −2

Concepts of Domain and Range
Items #48–51

44. If $f(x) = 2x^2 + x$ and $g(x) = f(f(x))$, what is the value of $g(1)$?

F. 3
G. 18
H. 21
J. 39
K. 55

Throwback to Math Class

A function is an equation where each input has exactly one output. For example, $x = y^2$ is NOT a function because the input $x = 1$ corresponds to both $y = 1$ and $y = -1$. Graphically, a function will always pass the vertical line test (any vertical line will intersect a function at no more than one point).

45. If $f(x) = 3x + 4$ and $g(x) = 2x - 1$, for what value of x does $f(x) = g(x)$?

A. −5
B. −2
C. 0
D. 3
E. 7

46. If $\boxed{x} = x^2 - x$ for all integers, then $\boxed{-2} = ?$

F. −6
G. −2
H. 0
J. 4
K. 6

Functions as Models
Items #52–54

47. If $\boxed{x} = x^2 - x$ for all integers, then $\boxed{3} = ?$

A. 27
B. 30
C. 58
D. 72
E. 121

48. If $f(x) = 3x - 2$ and $-5 < x < 5$, which of the following defines the range of $f(x)$?

F. $-17 < f(x) < 13$
G. $-13 < f(x) < 17$
H. $-5 < f(x) < 12$
J. $0 < f(x) < 17$
K. $3 < f(x) < 13$

49. If $f(x) = \dfrac{x+2}{x-1}$, for which of the following values of x is $f(x)$ undefined?

A. −2
B. −1
C. $\frac{1}{2}$
D. 1
J. 2

50. If $f(x) = \dfrac{2-2x}{x}$, which of the following defines the range of $f(x)$?

F. All real numbers
G. All real numbers except −2
H. All real numbers except 0
J. All real numbers except 2
K. All real numbers greater than 2

51. If $|4x - 8| < 12$, which of the following defines the possible values of x?

A. $-8 < x < -4$
B. $-4 < x < 8$
C. $-1 < x < 5$
D. $1 < x < 5$
E. $4 < x < 8$

52. In a certain game, a player picks an integer between 1 and 10, adds 3 to it, multiplies the sum by 2, and subtracts 5. If x is the number picked by a player, which of the following correctly expresses the final result of the game?

F. $x + (3)(2) - 5$
G. $3x + 2 - 5$
H. $2(x + 3 - 5)$
J. $2(x + 3) - 5$
K. $(2)(3)(x) - 5$

Throwback to Math Class

Expressions and functions can be used to formally describe relationships between real world factors like price and sales or number of students and number of required texts. Functions as Models items will challenge you to create an expression or equation that expresses these relationships. Note that a function is the same as any equation representing one variable as a function of another.

53. At 9:00 a.m., when the heat is turned on, the temperature of a room is 55°F. If the room temperature increases by n°F each hour, which of the following expressions can be used to determine the number of hours needed to bring the temperature of the room to 70°F?

A. $(55+70)(n)$
B. $(55-70)(n)$
C. $\frac{(70-55)}{n}$
D. $\frac{n}{(70-55)}$
E. $\frac{n}{(55+70)}$

54. The cost of making a call using a phone card is \$0.15 for dialing and \$0.04 per minute of connection time. Which of the following equations could be used to find the cost, y, of a call x minutes long?

F. $y=x(0.04+0.15)$
G. $y=0.04x+0.15$
H. $y=0.04+0.15x$
J. $y=0.15-0.04x$
K. $y=0.04-0.15x$

Throwback to Math Class

The domain, or input of a function, is the set of all values for which the function is defined. The range is the set of all values that are the result, or output, of the function for the values in the domain.

Remember that the domain can be tricky when you're dealing with rational or radical equations. Recall that for rational equations, values that make the denominator zero are not in the domain. For radical equations, values that make the radicand negative are not in the domain.

SOLVING SIMULTANEOUS EQUATIONS

55. If $x+y=4$ and $y-x=2$, then $x=?$

A. 0
B. 1
C. 2
D. 3
E. 4

56. If $2x+y=8$ and $x-y=1$, then $x=?$

F. -2
G. -1
H. 0
J. 1
K. 3

57. If $7x=2$ and $3y-7x=10$, then $y=?$

A. 2
B. 3
C. 4
D. 5
E. 6

58. If $2x+y=8$ and $x-y=1$, what is the value of $x+y$?

F. -1
G. 1
H. 2
J. 3
K. 5

59. If $4x+5y=12$ and $3x+4y=5$, what is the value of $7(x+y)$?

A. 7
B. 14
C. 49
D. 77
E. 91

60. Which of the equations that follow correctly describes the relationship between the values shown for x and y in the table below?

x	-2	-1	0	1	2
y	$\frac{10}{3}$	$\frac{8}{3}$	2	$\frac{4}{3}$	$\frac{2}{3}$

F. $3x + 2y = 6$
G. $3x - 2y = 3$
H. $3x + 3y = -6$
J. $6x + 4y = 7$
K. $2x + 3y = 6$

SOLVING QUADRATIC EQUATIONS AND RELATIONS

Throwback to Math Class

Follow these steps to solve quadratic equations.

Step 1: Move all the terms to one side of the equation. The sum of the terms is then equal to zero: $ax^2 + bx + c = 0$.

Step 2: If the expression side of the equation is factorable, factor.

Step 3: Set each of the factors equal to zero. Solve these equations for x, which has no more than two values.

61. Which of the following is the solution set for $2x^2 - 2x = 12$?

A. $\{-2, -3\}$
B. $\left\{\frac{2}{3}, 3\right\}$
C. $\{-2, 3\}$
D. $\left\{\frac{3}{2}, 2\right\}$
E. $\{2, 3\}$

62. If $x^2 - 3x = 4$, then which of the following shows all possible values of x?

F. $\{4, 1\}$
G. $\{4, -1\}$
H. $\{-4, 1\}$
J. $\{-4, -1\}$
K. $\{-4, 4\}$

Throwback to Math Class

Remember the quadratic formula:

if $ax^2 + bx + c = 0$,

then

$$x = \frac{-b \pm \sqrt{b^2 - 4ac}}{2a}.$$

63. If $x^2 + 30 = 11x$, then which of the following shows all possible values of x?

A. $\{-5, 6\}$
B. $\{5, 6\}$
C. $\{5, -6\}$
D. $\{-3, -10\}$
E. $\{3, 10\}$

64. Which of the following is the solution set for $3x^2 + 3x = 6$?

F. $\{1, -2\}$
G. $\{1, 2\}$
H. $\left\{\frac{1}{2}, 1\right\}$
J. $\left\{\frac{1}{2}, \frac{1}{3}\right\}$
K. $\{-1, -2\}$

65. Which of the following is the solution set for $2x^2 - 3x = 2$?

A. $\left\{\frac{1}{2}, 2\right\}$
B. $\left\{-\frac{1}{2}, 2\right\}$
C. $\left\{-\frac{1}{2}, -2\right\}$
D. $\{2, -2\}$
E. $\{2, 4\}$

Test-the-Test

Test-the-test is a great strategy if the factors of a quadratic equation aren't easy to identify and you have trouble with the quadratic formula. Simply plug the given answer choices into the quadratic equation in the item stem until you find an answer that works.

ALGEBRA STRATEGIES: "TEST-THE-TEST" AND "PLUG-AND-CHUG"

66. Diana spent $\frac{1}{2}$ of her weekly allowance on a new book and another $3 on lunch. If she still had $\frac{1}{6}$ of her original allowance left, how much is Diana's allowance?

F. $24
G. $18
H. $15
J. $12
K. $9

67. In a certain game, a player had five successful turns in a row, and after each one, the number of points added to his total score was double what was added the preceding turn. If the player scored a total of 465 points, how many points did he score on the first play?

A. 15
B. 30
C. 95
D. 155
E. 270

68. At a certain firm, *d* gallons of fuel are needed per day for each truck. At this rate, *g* gallons of fuel will supply *t* trucks for how many days?

F. $\frac{d}{gt}$
G. $\frac{gt}{d}$
H. dgt
J. $\frac{dg}{t}$
K. $\frac{g}{dt}$

69. *Y* years ago, Paul was twice as old as Bob. If Bob is now 18 years old, how old is Paul today in terms of *Y*?

A. $36+Y$
B. $18+Y$
C. $18-Y$
D. $36-Y$
E. $36-2Y$

70. After filling the car's fuel tank, a driver drove from point *P* to point *Q* and then to point *R*. She used $\frac{2}{5}$ of the fuel driving from *P* to *Q*. If she used another 7 gallons to drive from *Q* to *R* and still had $\frac{1}{4}$ of a tank left, how many gallons does the tank hold?

F. 12
G. 18
H. 20
J. 21
K. 35

71. If pencils cost *x* cents each, how many pencils can be purchased for *y* dollars?

A. $\frac{100}{xy}$
B. $\frac{xy}{100}$
C. $\frac{100y}{x}$
D. $\frac{y}{100x}$
E. $100xy$

72. A merchant increased the original price of an item by 10%. If she then reduces the new price by 10%, the final price, in terms of the original price, is equal to which of the following?

F. a decrease of 11%
G. a decrease of 1%
H. no net change
J. an increase of 1%
K. an increase of 11%

73. Harold is twice as old as Jack, who is 3 years older than Dan. If Harold's age is 5 times Dan's age, how old (in years) is Jack?

A. 2
B. 4
C. 5
D. 8
E. 10

74. A tank with capacity T gallons is empty. If water flows into the tank from pipe X at the rate of X gallons per minute, and water is pumped out by pipe Y at the rate of Y gallons per minute, and X is greater than Y, in how many *minutes* will the tank be filled?

F. $\frac{T}{Y-X}$
G. $\frac{T}{X-Y}$
H. $\frac{T-X}{Y}$
J. $\frac{X-Y}{60T}$
K. $\frac{60T}{XY}$

75. Machine X produces w widgets in five minutes. Machine X and Machine Y, working at the same time, produce w widgets in two minutes. How long will it take Machine Y working alone to produce w widgets?

A. 2 minutes, 30 seconds
B. 2 minutes, 40 seconds
C. 3 minutes, 20 seconds
D. 3 minutes, 30 seconds
E. 3 minutes, 40 seconds

76. If a train travels m miles in h hours and 45 minutes, what is its average speed in miles per hour?

F. $\frac{m}{h+\frac{3}{4}}$
G. $\frac{m}{1\frac{3}{4}h}$
H. $m\left(h+\frac{3}{4}\right)$
J. $\frac{m+45}{h}$
K. $\frac{h}{m+45}$

77. On a playground, there are x seesaws. If 50 children are all riding on seesaws, 2 to a seesaw, and 5 seesaws are NOT in use, what is the value of x?

A. 15
B. 20
C. 25
D. 30
E. 35

LESSON 3

COORDINATE GEOMETRY

THE COORDINATE SYSTEM

Throwback to Math Class

A coordinate plane is described with reference to an *x*-axis (horizontal line) and a *y*-axis (vertical line), which are perpendicular to each other. The intersection of the axes is called the origin (0,0). Coordinate pairs are used to locate points on the plane—the general form is (x,y). The first element gives location with reference to the *x*-axis; the second element gives location with reference to the *y*-axis.

1. Point *A* and point *B* lie in the standard (x,y) coordinate plane. The coordinates of point *A* are (x,y). Point *B* is located 12 units to the right of point *A*. What is the *x*-coordinate of point *B*?

A. $x - 12$
B. $x + 12$
C. $y + 12$
D. $y - 12$
E. Cannot be determined from the given information

2. In the figure below, what is the length of $\overline{PQ}$?

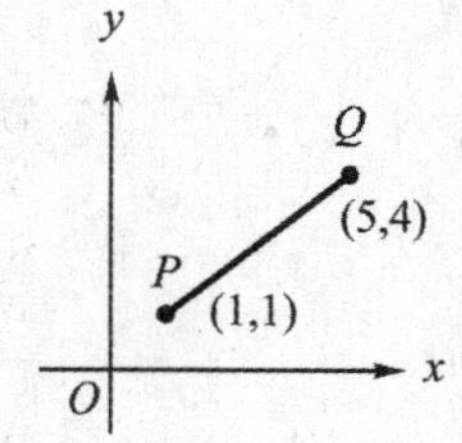

F. $\sqrt{2}$
G. $\sqrt{3}$
H. 3
J. 4
K. 5

3. In the figure below, the line segment joining points (3,3) and (7, 3) forms one side of a square. Which of the following CANNOT be the coordinates of another vertex of the square?

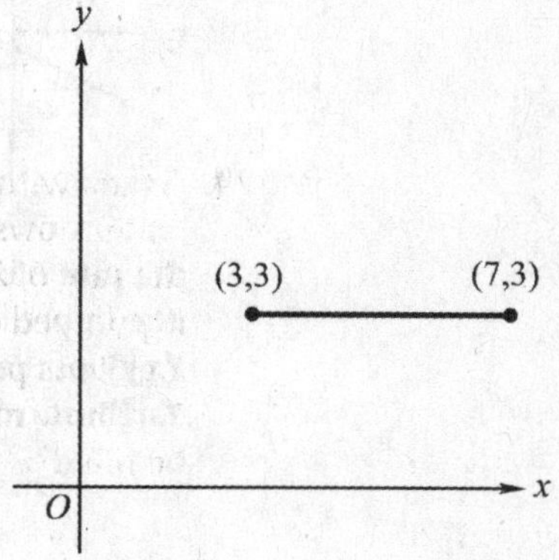

A. $(3,-1)$
B. $(3,7)$
C. $(7,-3)$
D. $(7,-1)$
E. $(7,7)$

4. Which of the following is a graph of the line that passes through the points $(-5,3)$, $(-1,1)$, and $(3,-1)$?

F. 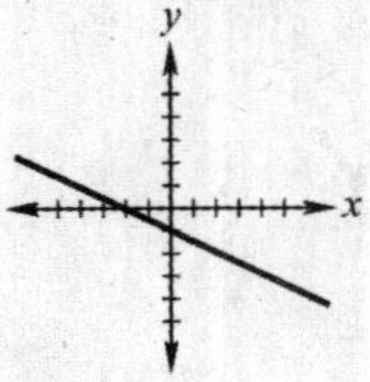

J. 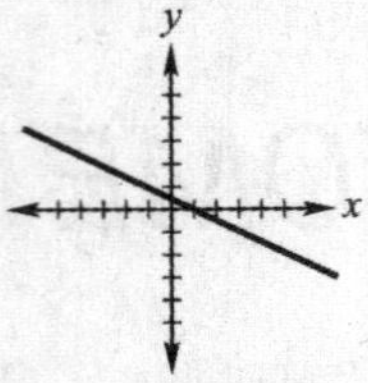

G. 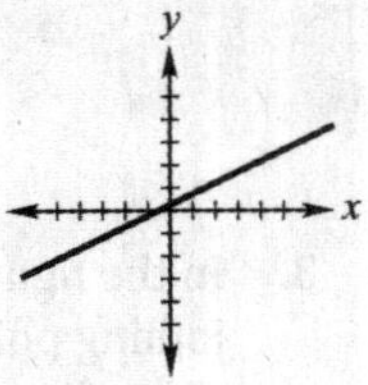

K. 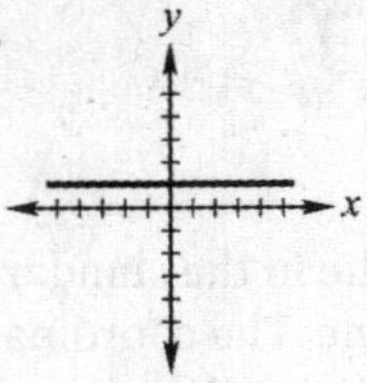

H. 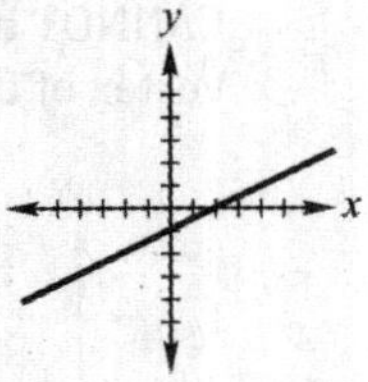

5. If point A is the center of the semicircle in the figure below, what are the coordinates, (x,y), of the point on the semicircle that is farthest from the y-axis?

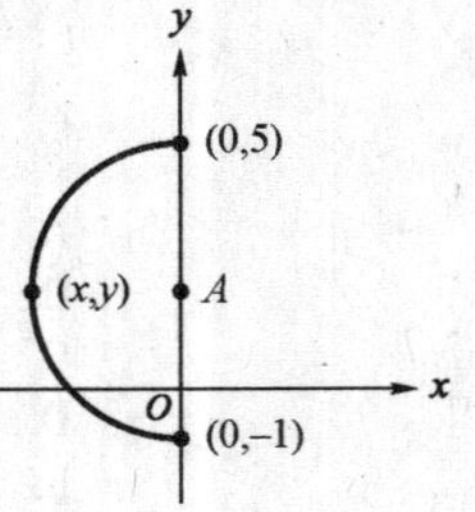

A. $(-4,4)$
B. $(-3,3)$
C. $(-2,3)$
D. $(-3,2)$
E. $(3,2)$

6. In the figure below, the area of ΔABC is 8. What is the value of k?

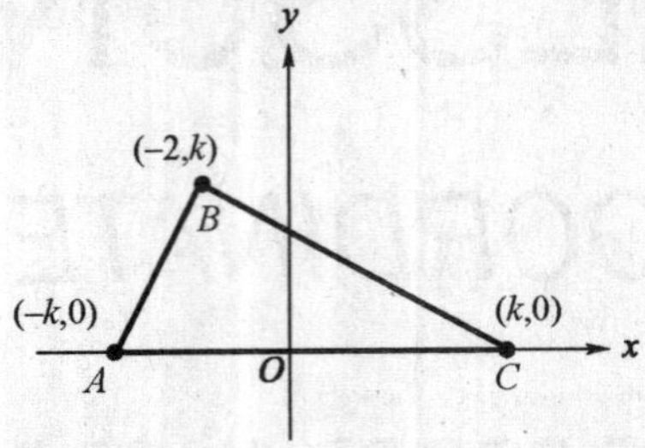

F. 2
G. $2\sqrt{2}$
H. 4
J. $4\sqrt{2}$
K. 8

SLOPE OF A LINE

Throwback to Math Class

A line that runs between (x_1, y_1) and (x_2, y_2) on the coordinate plane has the following slope:

$$m = \frac{y_2 - y_1}{x_2 - x_1} = \frac{\Delta y}{\Delta x}$$

If the slope is *positive*, then as x increases, y increases. If the slope is *negative*, then as x increases, y decreases.

If the slope is 0, then the line is horizontal. If the slope is undefined, then the line is vertical.

Use POE

In item #7 the graph shows that as x increases, y decreases. Use this fact to eliminate a few answer choices.

Throwback to Math Class

If two lines are *parallel*, they have the same slope. If two lines are *perpendicular*, they have negative reciprocal slopes.

7. In the figure below, what is the slope of the line?

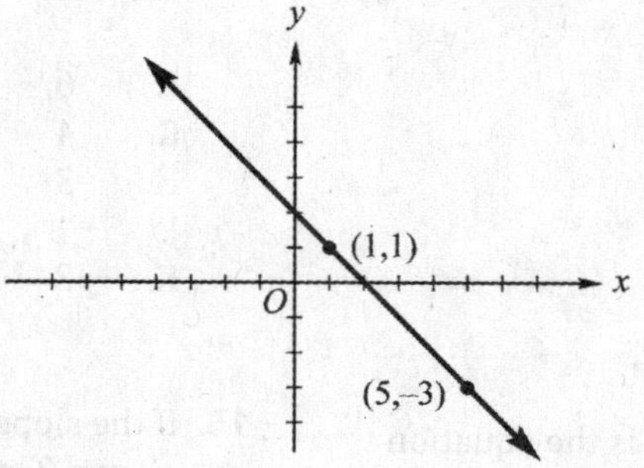

A. −3
B. −2
C. −1
D. 1
E. 2

8. In the figure below, which two sides of polygon *PQRST* have the same slope?

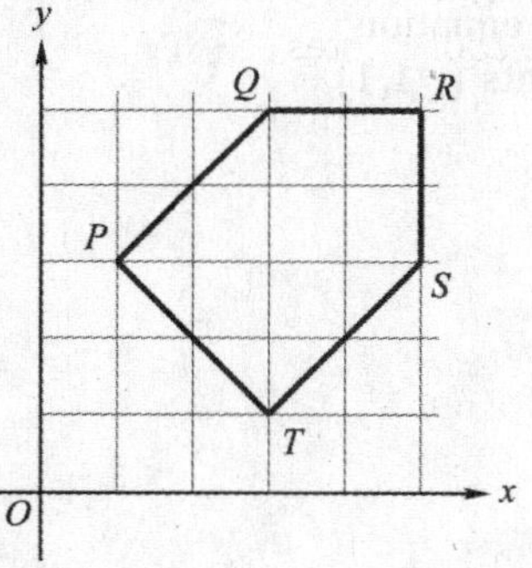

F. $\overline{PQ}$ and $\overline{QR}$
G. $\overline{QR}$ and $\overline{RS}$
H. $\overline{PQ}$ and $\overline{ST}$
J. $\overline{QR}$ and $\overline{ST}$
K. $\overline{RS}$ and $\overline{ST}$

9. Line l is the graph of the equation $y = \frac{3x}{2} + 2$. The graph of which of the following equations is perpendicular to line l at $(0, 2)$?

A. $y = \frac{3x}{2} - 2$
B. $y = \frac{2x}{3} - 2$
C. $y = -\frac{2x}{3} + 2$
D. $y = -\frac{3x}{2} + 3$
E. $y = -3x + 4$

10. If set $A = \{(-2,3), (-1,1), (-4,-5)\}$, and set $B = \{(3,4), (4,3), (2,-1)\}$, how many lines can be drawn with a positive slope that include exactly one point from set A and one point from set B?

F. Two
G. Three
H. Four
J. Five
K. Six

SLOPE-INTERCEPT FORM OF A LINEAR EQUATION

Throwback to Math Class

The slope-intercept form of a linear equation is $y = mx + b$, where m is the slope of the line and b is the y-intercept of the line.

Test the Test

As a last resort, you can use test-the-test by plugging both points into every answer choice. The correct answer choice is the one where both points satisfy the equation. This should be a last resort because it will require more computation than finding the equation directly.

11. A line includes the points (2,3) and (3,6). What is the equation of the line?

A. $y = 2x - 3$
B. $y = 3x - 3$
C. $y = \frac{3x - 3}{2}$
D. $y = 3x + 3$
E. $y = x - 3$

12. Which of the following is the equation for the line with slope of 2 that includes point (0,2)?

F. $y = x - 1$
G. $y = 2x - 1$
H. $y = 2x - 2$
J. $y = 2x + 2$
K. $y = x + 1$

13. Which of the following is the equation for the line that includes points $(-1,1)$ and (7,5)?

A. $y = \frac{x}{2} + 2$
B. $y = \frac{x}{2} + \frac{3}{2}$
C. $y = \frac{x}{2} + \frac{2}{3}$
D. $y = 2x + \frac{3}{2}$
E. $y = 2x + 2$

14. If the graph of a line includes the points (2,4) and (8,7), what is the y-intercept of the line?

F. 6
G. 4
H. 3
J. -1
K. -3

15. If the slope and y-intercept of a line are -2 and 3, respectively, then the line passes through which of the following points?

A. $(-5, -10)$
B. $(-5, 10)$
C. $(-2, 3)$
D. $(3, 4)$
E. $(4, -5)$

DISTANCE AND MIDPOINT FORMULAS

Throwback to Math Class

The distance formula is derived from the Pythagorean theorem for a right triangle, in which the distance length corresponds to the hypotenuse: $d = \sqrt{(x_2-x_1)^2+(y_2-y_1)^2}$.

Throwback to Math Class

The midpoint between a point with coordinates (x_1,y_1) and a point with coordinates (x_2,y_2) has coordinates $\left(\frac{x_1+x_2}{2},\frac{y_1+y_2}{2}\right)$.

16. What is the distance between the points $(-3,-2)$ and $(3,3)$?

F. $\sqrt{3}$
G. $2\sqrt{3}$
H. 5
J. $\sqrt{29}$
K. $\sqrt{61}$

17. In the coordinate plane below, $\overline{MO} \cong \overline{MN}$ and $\overline{MO} \perp \overline{MN}$. What is the value of y?

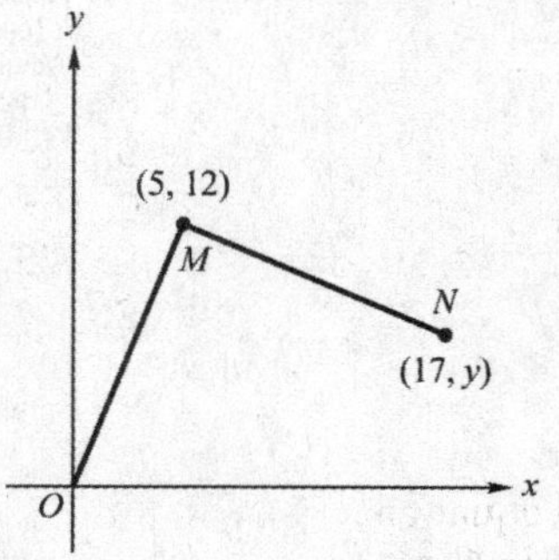

A. 5
B. 7
C. 12
D. 13
E. 17

18. In the figure below, what is the area of the square region?

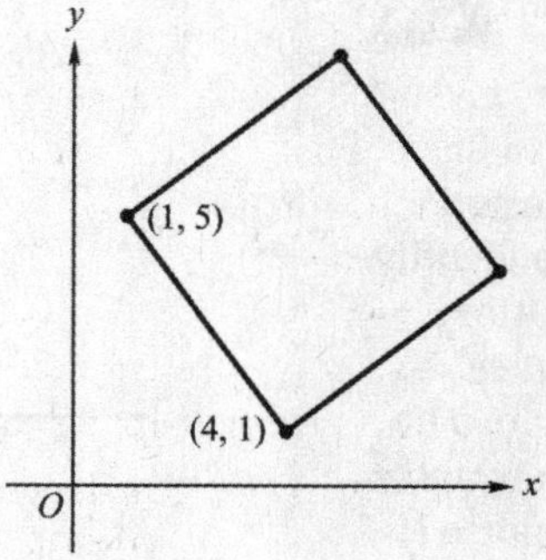

F. 4
G. 8
H. $8\sqrt{2}$
J. 16
K. 25

19. In the coordinate plane, what is the midpoint of the line segment with endpoints (–3,–5) and (5,7)?

A. (1,1)
B. (1,6)
C. $\left(3,\frac{7}{2}\right)$
D. (4,6)
E. (8,12)

GRAPHS OF LINEAR EQUATIONS

> **Test the Test**
>
> If you are given the graph of a linear equation and asked to identify the equation, substitute a coordinate pair from the graph into the answer choices.

20. The figure below is the graph of which of the following equations?

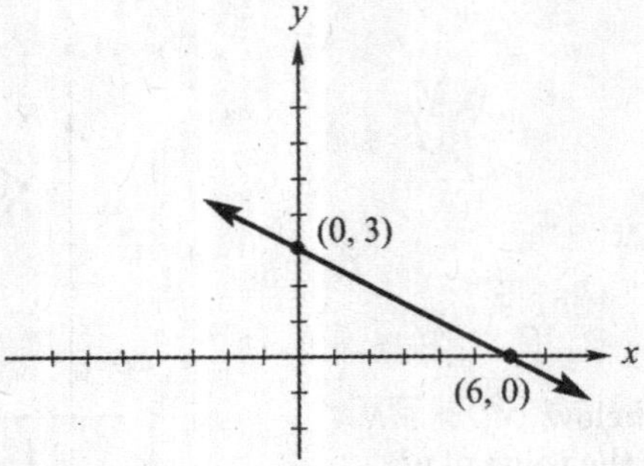

F. $x + 2y = 6$

G. $2x + y = 6$

H. $x + \frac{y}{2} = 6$

J. $\frac{x}{2} + y = 2$

K. $x - 3y = 2$

21. A school rented a hotel ballroom for a dance. The cost of the rental is $1500 plus $5.00 per person who attends. Each person who attends will pay an admission charge of $12.50. If *x* represents the number of people who attend, which of the graphs can be used to determine how many people must attend for the admission charges to cover exactly the cost of renting the ballroom?

A.

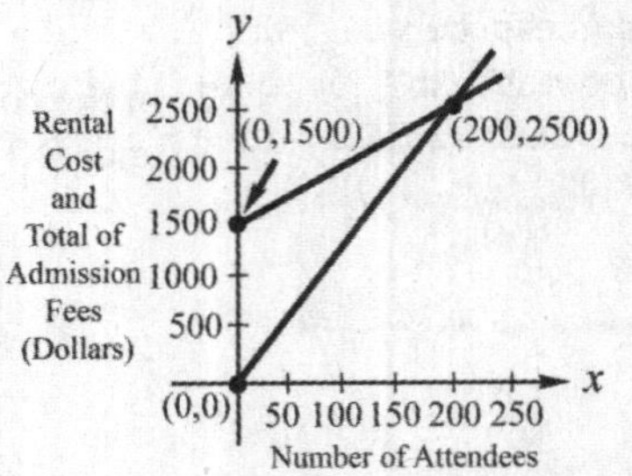

B.

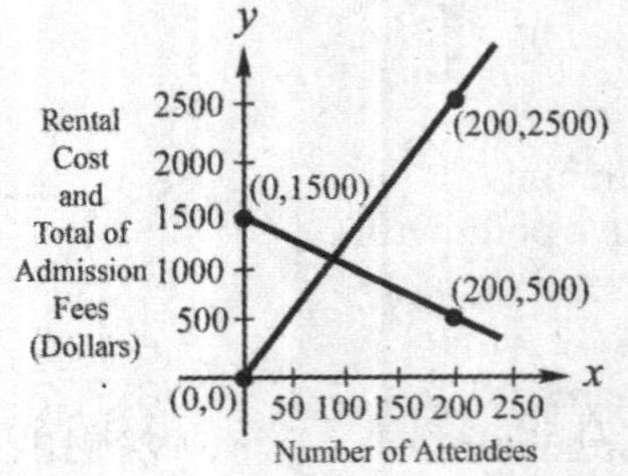

C.

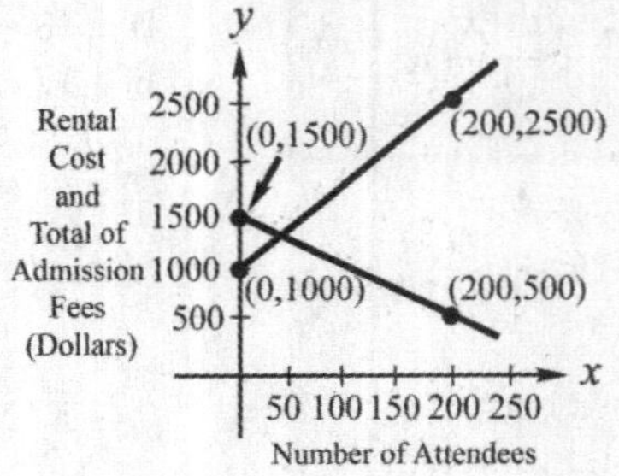

D.

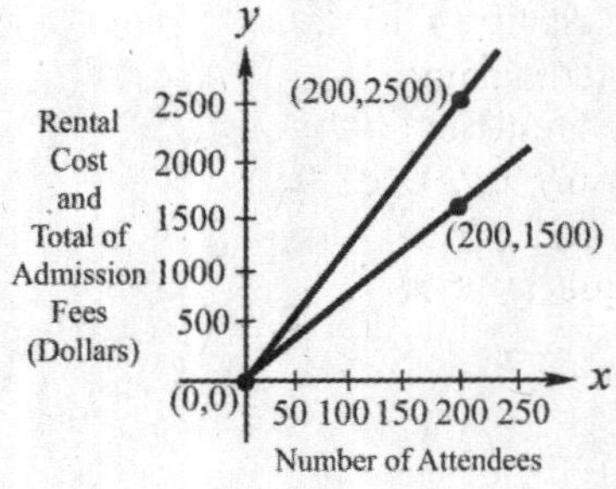

E.

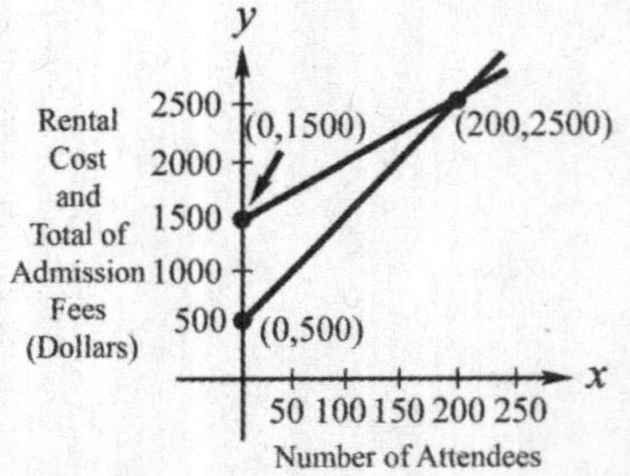

GRAPHS OF FIRST-DEGREE INEQUALITIES

Throwback to Math Class

To graph an inequality:

1. Replace the inequality symbol with an equal sign and graph that line.
2. Shade the side that satisfies the inequality.
3. If the inequality is greater than or equal to, or less than or equal to, then the line should be solid. If the inequality is less than or greater than (not equal to), then the line should be dashed to show that the line does NOT satisfy the inequality.

22. Which of the following is the graph of the inequality $y \geq 2x$?

F.
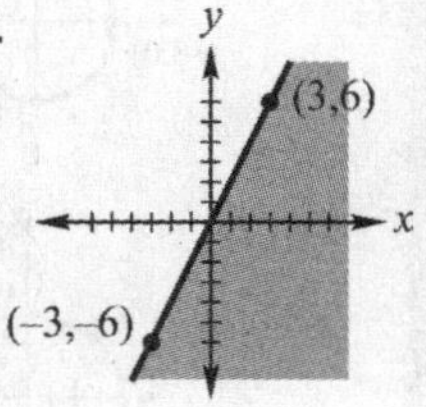

J.
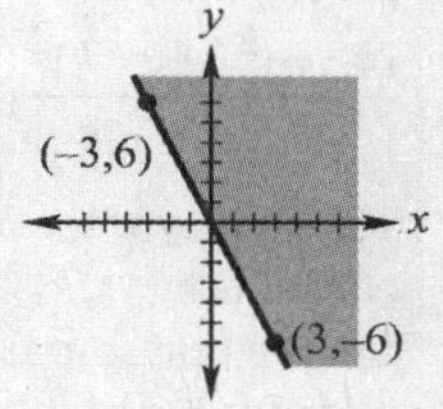

G.
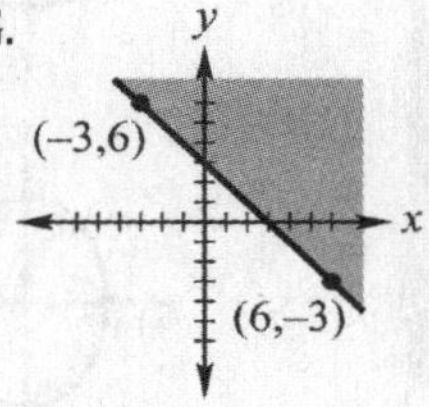

K.
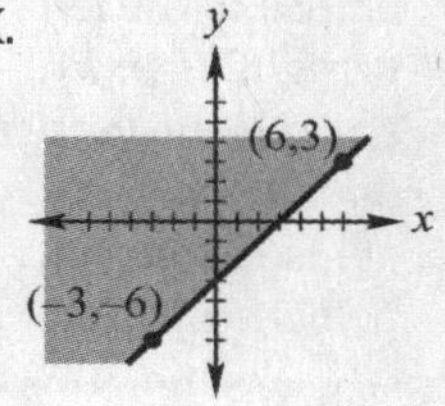

H.
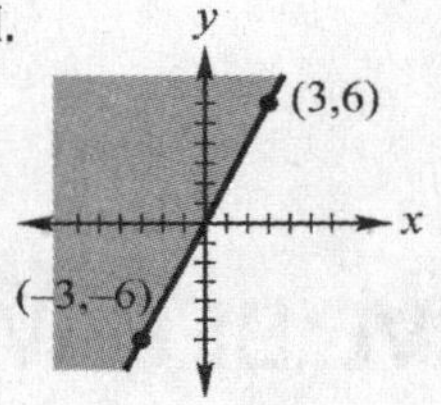

GRAPHS OF QUADRATIC EQUATIONS AND RELATIONS

Throwback to Math Class

Circles and ellipses are not functions because they fail the vertical line test: a function can only have one output, *y*, for each unique input, *x*.

23. Which of the following is the graph of the equation $(x-1)^2 + y^2 = 4$?

A.
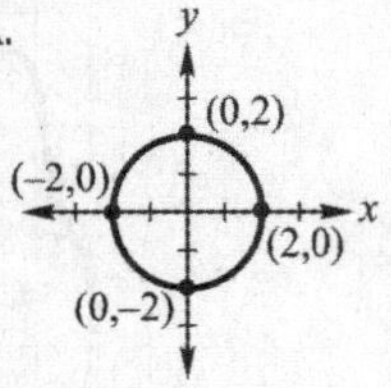

D.
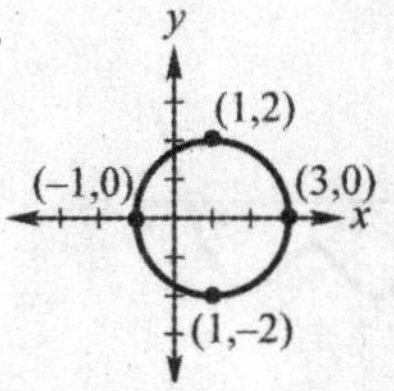

B.
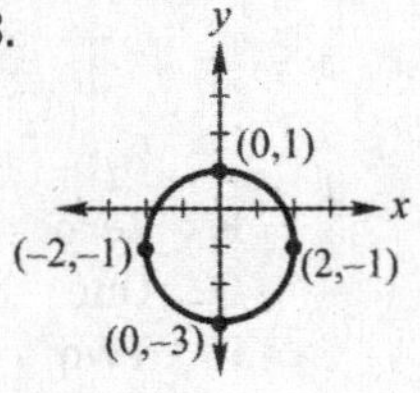

E.
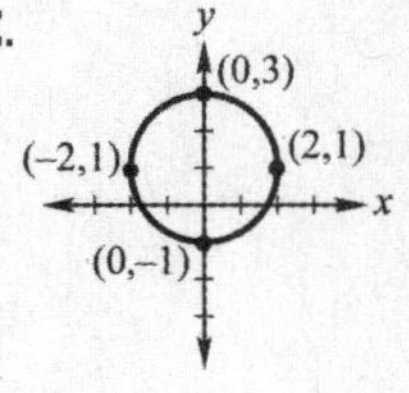

C.
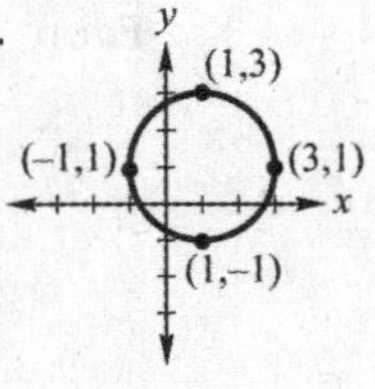

Throwback to Math Class

The vertex is the lowest point or minimum for a parabola going upward and the vertex is the highest point or maximum for a parabola going downward.

Throwback to Math Class

The equation of a circle is $r^2 = (x-h)^2 + (y-k)^2$, where *r* is the radius of the circle, and (*h*,*k*) is the center of the circle on the coordinate plane.

Throwback to Math Class

The equation of an ellipse is $\frac{(x-h)^2}{p^2}+\frac{(y-k)^2}{q^2}=1$. The center of the ellipse is at (h,k), p is the horizontal distance to the ellipse to the left or right of (h,k), and q is the vertical distance to the ellipse above or below (h,k).

24. Which of the following is the graph of the equation $\frac{x^2}{9}+\frac{y^2}{16}=1$?

F. 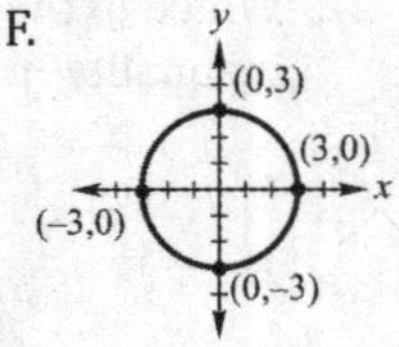

G. 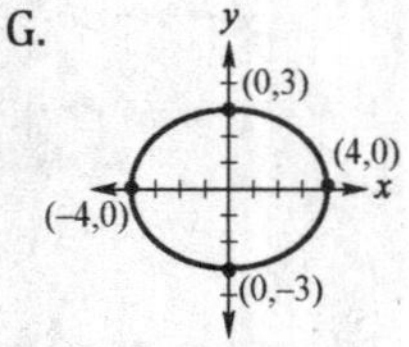

H. 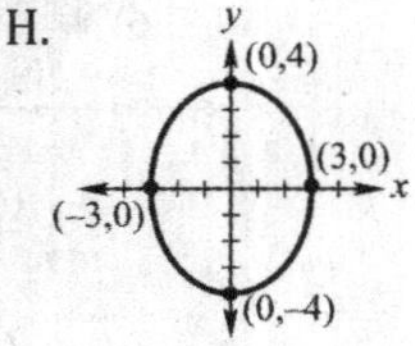

J. 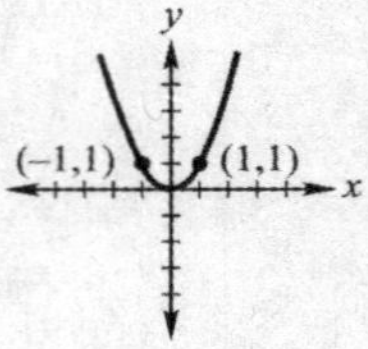

K. 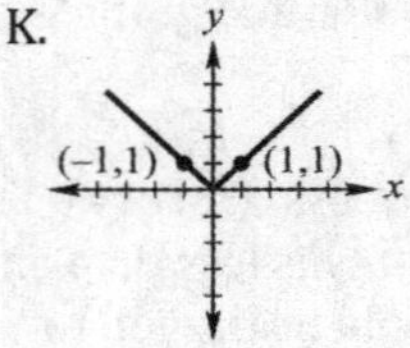

Use POE

In item #24, since you know the equation represents an ellipse, we can eliminate (F), (J), and (K) immediately. Now you would have a 50/50 chance of guessing correctly.

QUALITATIVE BEHAVIOR OF GRAPHS OF FUNCTIONS

Throwback to Math Class

The degree of $g(x)$ is the highest exponent in the equation of $g(x)$.

25. The figure below shows the graph of a function $g(x)$. What is the minimum degree of $g(x)$?

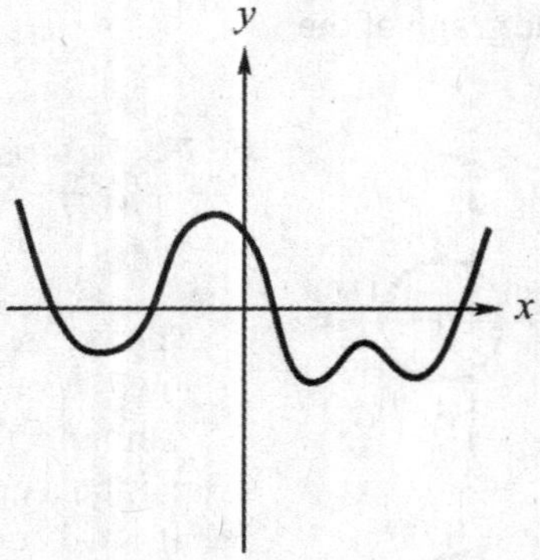

A. One
B. Two
C. Three
D. Four
E. Five

26. The figure below shows the graph of $f(x)$ in the standard (x,y) coordinate plane. For the portion of the graph shown, for how many values of x is $f(x) = 3$?

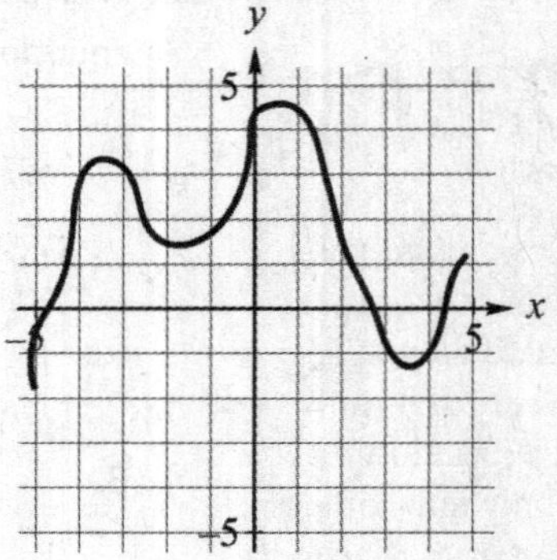

F. Zero
G. One
H. Two
J. Three
K. Four

TRANSFORMATIONS AND THEIR EFFECTS ON GRAPHS OF FUNCTIONS

> **Throwback to Math Class**
>
> *Vertical Translations*: $f(x) + b = f(x)$ moved up b units, and $f(x) - b = f(x)$ moved down b units.
>
> *Horizontal Translations*: $f(x + b) = f(x)$ shifted b units to the left, and $f(x - b) = f(x)$ shifted b units to the right.

27. The figure below represents the graph of $y = f(x)$ in the coordinate plane.

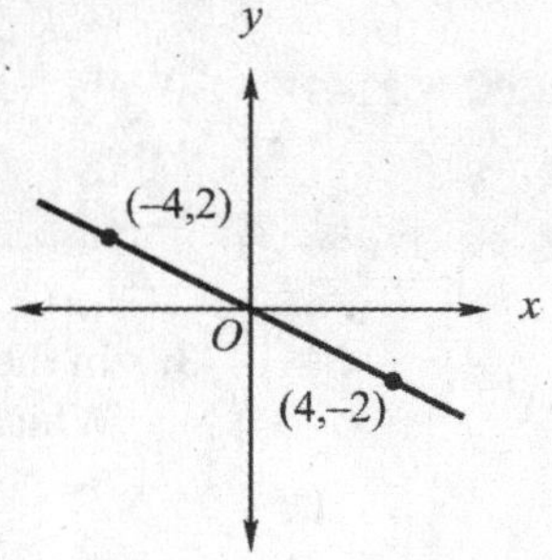

Which of the following is the graph of $y' = f(x - 1)$?

A.
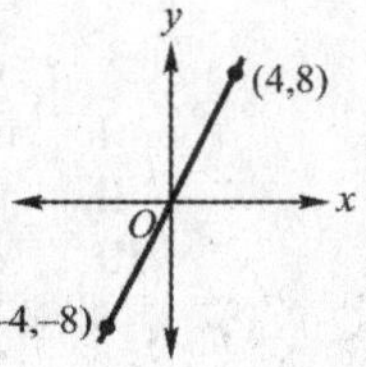

B.
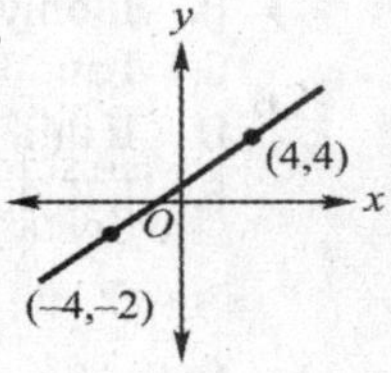

C.
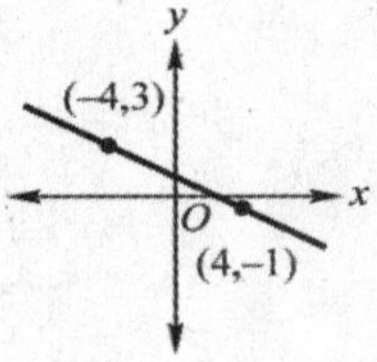

D.
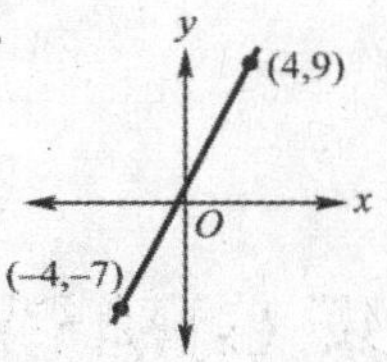

E.
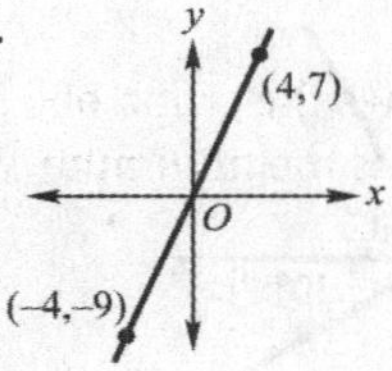

28. If the triangle in the figure below is reflected across the y-axis and then reflected across the x-axis, which of the graphs that follow shows the resulting position of the triangle?

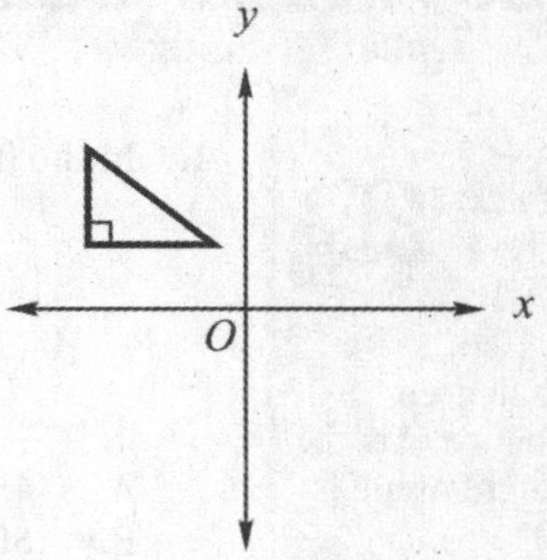

F.
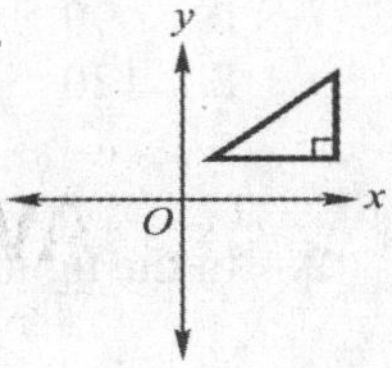

G.
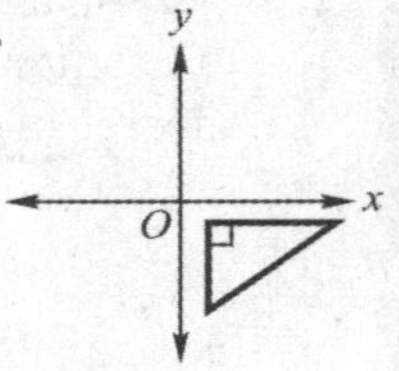

H.
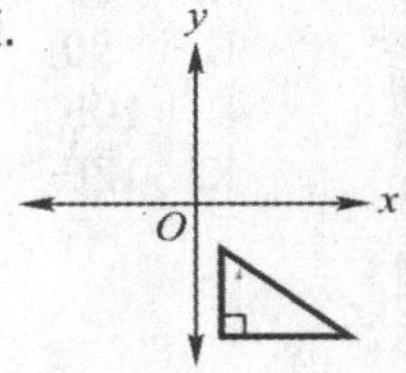

J.
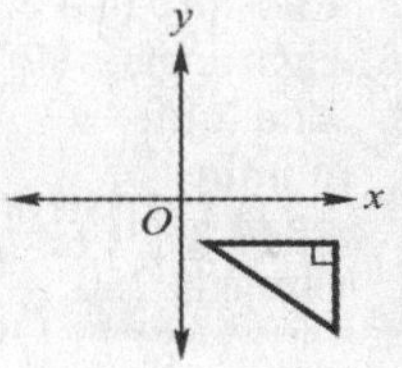

K.
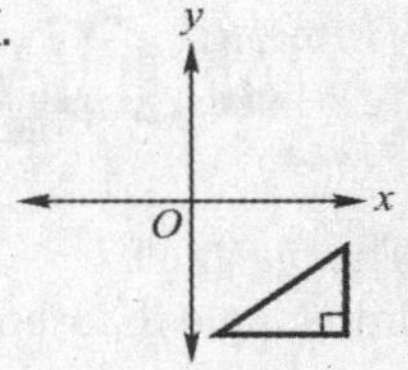

LESSON 4

Geometry

LINES AND ANGLES

Throwback to Math Class

1. The degree measure of a straight angle is 180°.
2. The degree measure of a right angle is 90°.
3. The total number of degrees in a circle is 360°.

Throwback to Math Class

The big angle/little angle theorem comes in handy:

When two parallel lines are intersected by a third line, the following are true: (1) all of the big angles are equal; (2) all of the little angles are equal; and (3) the degree measure of any big angle plus any little angle equals 180°.

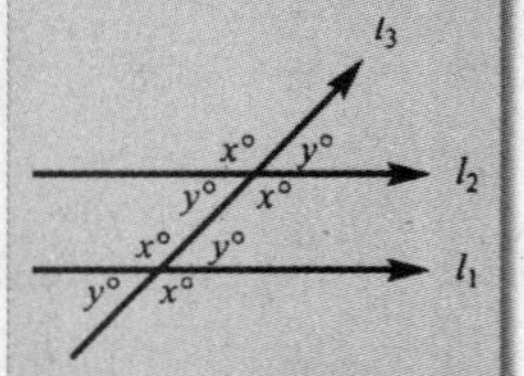

$x + y = 180$

1. In the figure below, $x = ?$

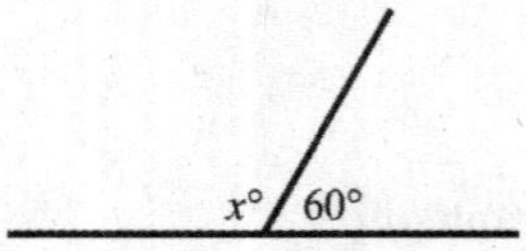

A. 45
B. 60
C. 75
D. 90
E. 120

2. In the figure below, $x = ?$

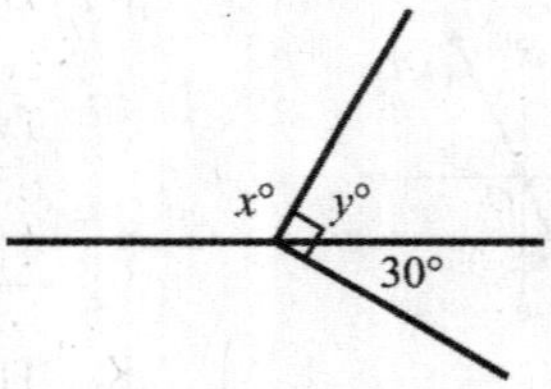

F. 45
G. 60
H. 90
J. 105
K. 120

3. In the figure below, l_1 is parallel to l_2. Which of the following *must* be true?

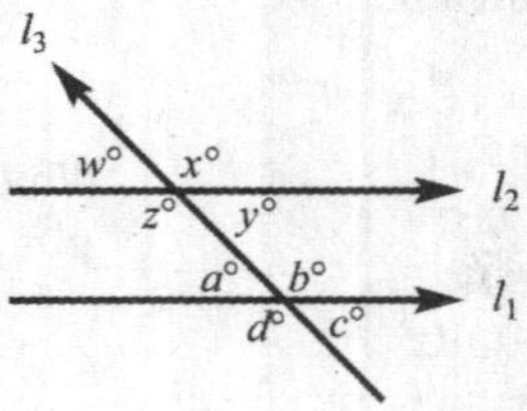

I. $w = a$
II. $y + b = 180$
III. $x + d = 180$

A. I only
B. II only
C. I and II only
D. II and III only
E. I, II, and III

4. In the figure below, $x = ?$

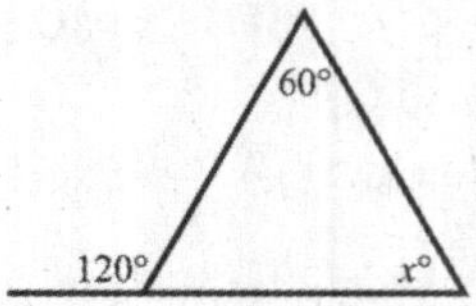

F. 30
G. 45
H. 60
J. 75
K. 90

Throwback to Math Class

Remember the following facts about triangles:

1. The sum of the interior angles of a triangle is 180°.
2. An equilateral triangle (three equal sides) has three 60° angles. Therefore, any triangle with three equal angles has three equal sides.
3. If a triangle has two equal angles, the sides opposite the two equal angles are equal in length, forming an isosceles triangle.

Throwback to Math Class

The sum of the interior angles of an n-sided polygon is $180(n-2)°$.

5. In the figure below, what is the sum, in degrees, of the indicated angles?

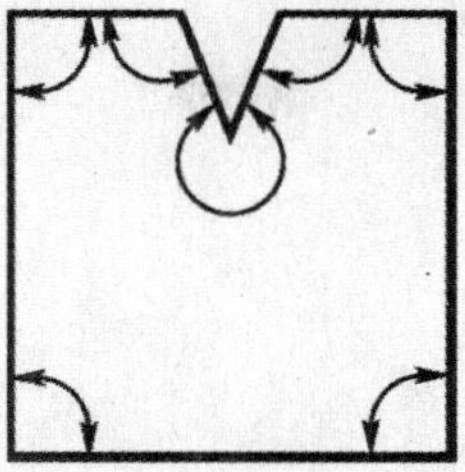

A. 540
B. 720
C. 900
D. 1,080
E. 1,260

TRIANGLES

Pythagorean Theorem
Item #6

Throwback to Math Class

The Pythagorean theorem states the following:

In a right triangle, the square of the longest side (the hypotenuse) is equal to the sum of the squares of the other two sides (the legs):

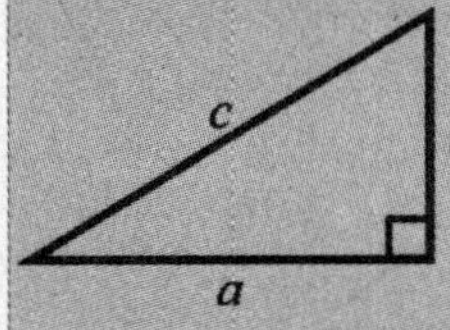

$a^2+b^2=c^2$

45°–45°–90° Triangles
Items #7–8

30°–60°–90° Triangles
Item #9

6. In the figure below, what is the length of $\overline{AB}$?

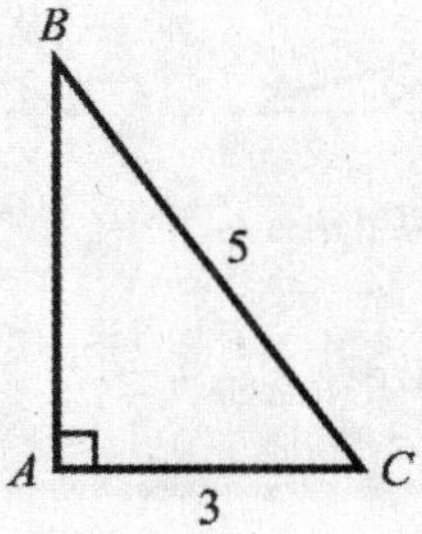

F. 2
G. $2\sqrt{3}$
H. 4
J. $4\sqrt{2}$
K. 8

7. In the figure below, what is the length of $\overline{PQ}$?

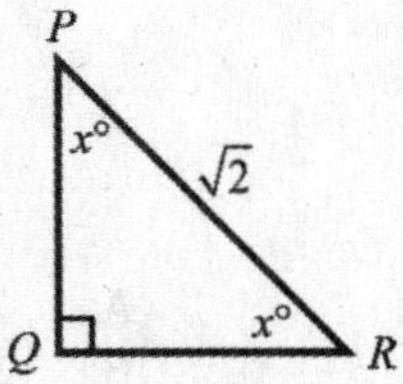

A. 1
B. $\sqrt{2}$
C. $2\sqrt{2}$
D. 4
E. 5

8. In a right isosceles triangle, the hypotenuse is equal to which of the following?

F. Half the length of either of the other sides
G. The length of either of the other sides multiplied by $\sqrt{2}$
H. Twice the length of either of the other sides
J. The sum of the lengths of the other two sides
K. The sum of the lengths of the other two sides multiplied by $\sqrt{2}$

9. In the triangle below, what is the length of $\overline{AC}$?

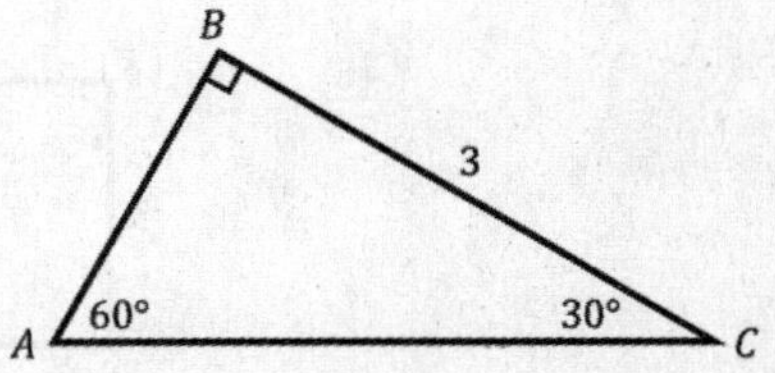

A. $\sqrt{3}$
B. 2
C. $2\sqrt{3}$
D. $3\sqrt{3}$
E. 6

Properties of Triangles
Items #10–11

10. In the figure below, the perimeter of $\Delta PQR = ?$

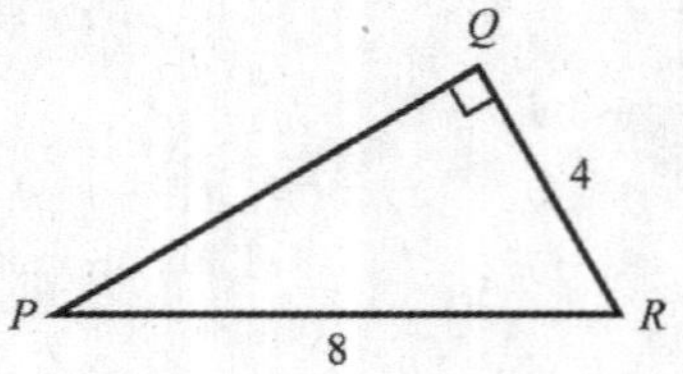

F. $12+\sqrt{3}$
G. $12+2\sqrt{3}$
H. $12+4\sqrt{3}$
J. 28
K. 56

11. In the figure below, what is the area of ΔMNO?

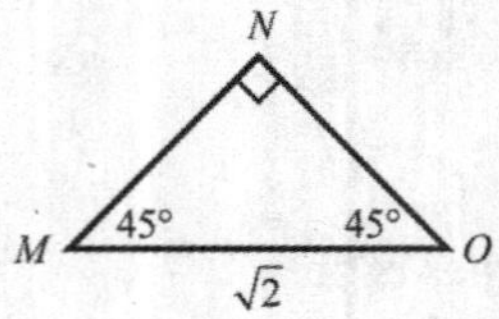

A. $\frac{1}{2}$
B. $\frac{\sqrt{2}}{2}$
C. 1
D. $\sqrt{2}$
E. 2

Throwback to Math Class

Triangles with angles measuring 45°, 45°, and 90° are right isosceles triangles with a hypotenuse equal to the length of either side multiplied by $\sqrt{2}$.

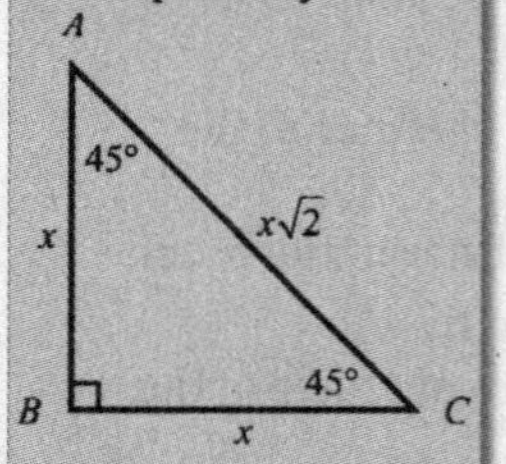

Throwback to Math Class

Remember that a triangle's height is perpendicular to its base. Often, you won't be given a line perpendicular to the base so you will have to sketch it in and determine the length using the Pythagorean theorem.

Throwback to Math Class

The perimeter of a triangle is the sum of the lengths of its sides. The area of a triangle is equal to one-half of the base, b, multiplied by the height (altitude), h. The base and height are always perpendicular to each other:

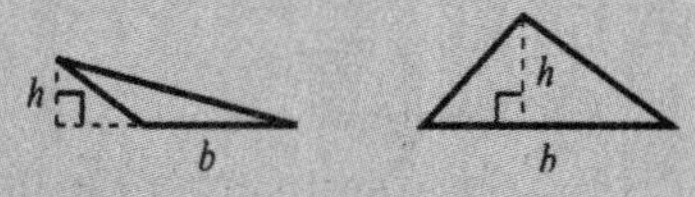

$$\text{Perimeter}_{\text{triangle}} = s_1 + s_2 + s_3$$

$$\text{Area}_{\text{triangle}} = \frac{1}{2}bh$$

Throwback to Math Class

In a 30°–60°–90° triangle, the leg opposite the 30° angle equals the hypotenuse length multiplied by $\frac{1}{2}$; the leg opposite the 60° angle equals the hypotenuse length multiplied by $\frac{\sqrt{3}}{2}$.

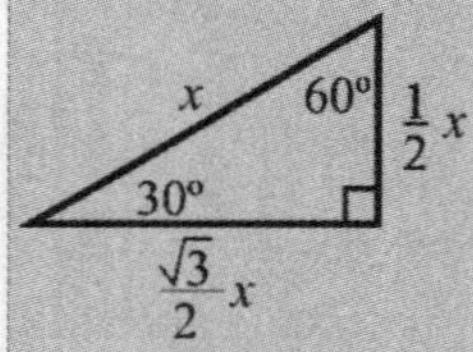

RECTANGLES AND SQUARES

12. If the area of the rectangle below is 18, what is the perimeter?

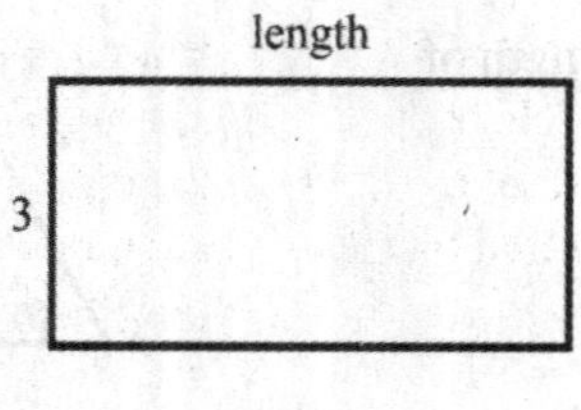

F. 9
G. 12
H. 18
J. 24
K. 30

13. In the figure below, $PQRS$ is a rectangle. If $\overline{PR} = 5$ centimeters, what is the area, in square centimeters, of the rectangle?

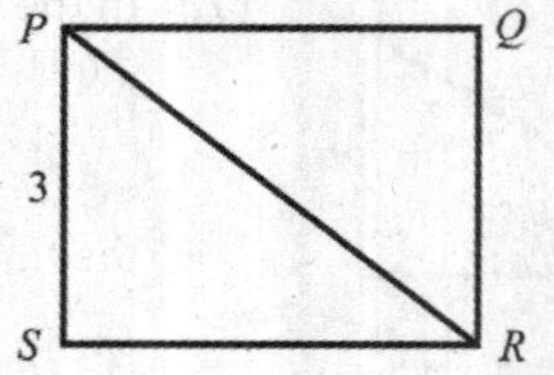

A. 2
B. 3
C. 4
D. 8
E. 12

14. If the width of a rectangle is increased by 10% and the length of the rectangle is increased by 20%, by what percentage does the area of the rectangle *increase*?

F. 2%
G. 10%
H. 15%
J. 32%
K. 36%

> Throwback to Math Class
>
> 1. The *diagonal* of a rectangle is the hypotenuse of a right triangle with legs that are the length and width of the rectangle.
> 2. The *perimeter* of a rectangle is equal to the sum of the lengths of the four sides: $\text{perimeter}_{\text{rectangle}} = s_1 + s_2 + s_3 + s_4 = 2w + 2l$.
> 3. The *area* of a rectangle is equal to the length multiplied by the width: $\text{area}_{\text{rectangle}} = lw$.

CIRCLES

15. If the area of a circle is equal to 9π, which of the following is (are) true?

I. The radius is 3.
II. The diameter is 6.
III. The circumference is 6π.

A. I only
B. II only
C. III only
D. I and II only
E. I, II, and III

> Throwback to Math Class
>
> 1. The *radius* of a circle is equal to one-half of the *diameter*: $r = \frac{d}{2}$.
> 2. The *circumference* of a circle is equal to the diameter multiplied by π: $\text{circumference} = \pi d = 2\pi r$.
> 3. The *area* of a circle is equal to the radius squared multiplied by π: $\text{area}_{\text{circle}} = \pi r^2$.

PROPERTIES OF TANGENT LINES

16. In the figure below, O is the center of the circle, and $\overline{PQ}$ is tangent to the circle at P. If the radius of circle O has a length of 6, what is the area of the shaded portion of the figure?

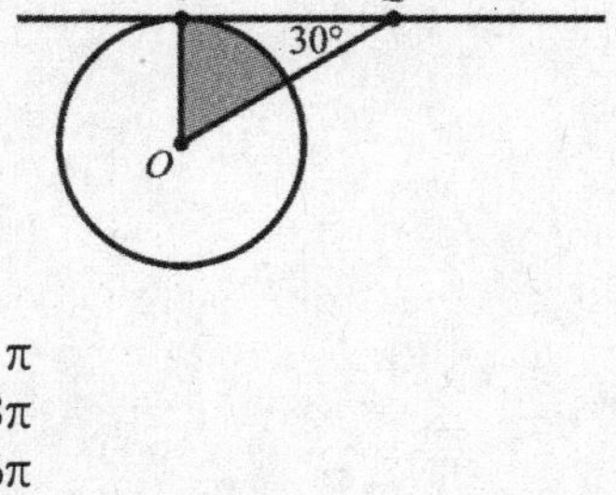

F. π
G. 3π
H. 6π
J. 9π
K. 12π

17. The figure below shows two pulleys connected by a belt. If the centers of the pulleys are 8 feet apart and the pulleys each have a radius of 1 foot, what is the length, in feet, of the belt?

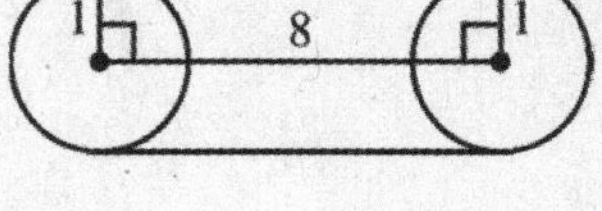

A. 4π
B. 8π
C. $8 + \pi$
D. $16 + \pi$
E. $16 + 2\pi$

18. In the figure below, a circle is inscribed in an equilateral triangle. If the radius of the circle is 1, what is the perimeter of the triangle?

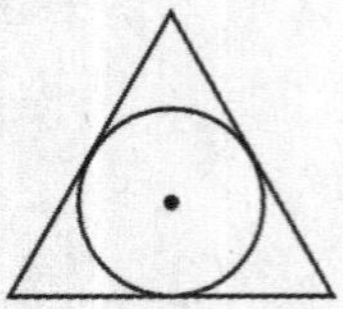

F. $\sqrt{3}$
G. $2\sqrt{3}$
H. $3\sqrt{3}$
J. 6
K. $6\sqrt{3}$

19. The figure below shows two circles of diameter 2 that are tangent to each other at point *P*. The line segments form a rectangle and are tangent to the circles at the points shown. What is the area of the shaded portion of the figure?

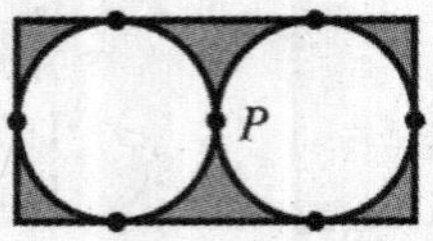

A. $4 - 2\pi$
B. $4 - \pi$
C. $8 - 2\pi$
D. $8 - \pi$
E. 2π

COMPLEX FIGURES

20. If a circle with a radius of 1 foot is inscribed in a square, what is the area, in square feet, of the square?

F. $\frac{\sqrt{2}}{2}$
G. 1
H. $\sqrt{2}$
J. 2
K. 4

21. An isosceles right triangle is inscribed in a circle with a radius of 1 inch such that all three vertices of the triangle are points on the circle. What is the area, in square inches, of the triangle?

A. $\frac{\sqrt{2}}{3}$
B. $\frac{1}{2}$
C. 1
D. $\sqrt{2}$
E. $2\sqrt{2}$

22. In the figure below, *BCDE* is a square with an area of 4. What is the perimeter of ΔABE?

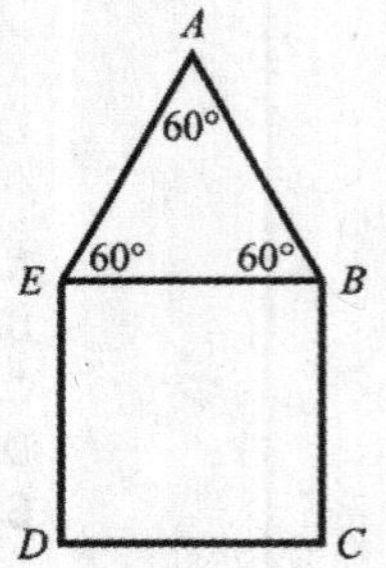

F. 3
G. 4
H. 6
J. 8
K. 12

23. In the figure below, if *QRST* is a square and the length of $\overline{PQ}$ is $\sqrt{2}$, what is the length of $\overline{RU}$?

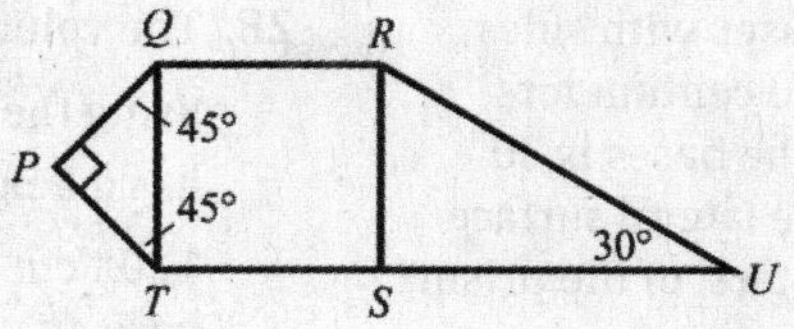

A. $\sqrt{2}$
B. $\sqrt{6}$
C. $2\sqrt{2}$
D. 4
E. $4\sqrt{3}$

24. In the figure below, *PQRS* is a square, and $\overline{PS}$ is the diameter of a semicircle. If the length of $\overline{PQ}$ is 2, what is the area of the shaded portion of the diagram?

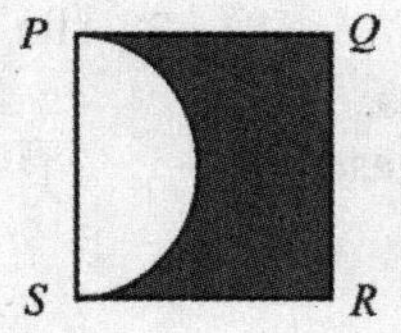

F. $4-2\pi$
G. $4-\pi$
H. $4-\frac{\pi}{2}$
J. $8-\pi$
K. $8-\frac{\pi}{2}$

25. If the lengths of the sides, in inches, are as marked on the figure below, what is the area, in square inches, of the quadrilateral?

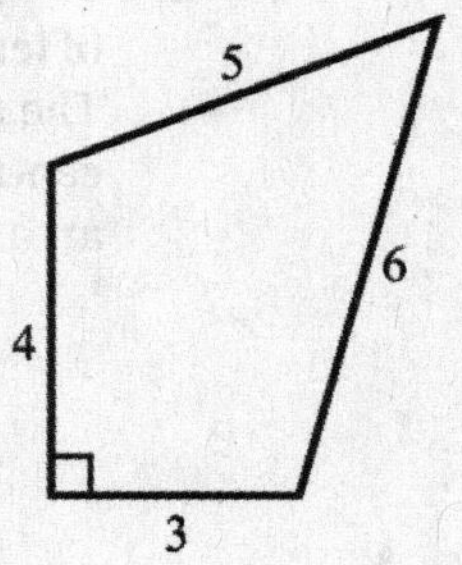

A. 6
B. $6+\sqrt{3}$
C. 12
D. 18
E. 24

SOLIDS

26. The prism below has bases with sides of lengths 12, 16, and 20 centimeters. The distance between the bases is 30 centimeters. What is the lateral surface area, in square centimeters, of the prism?

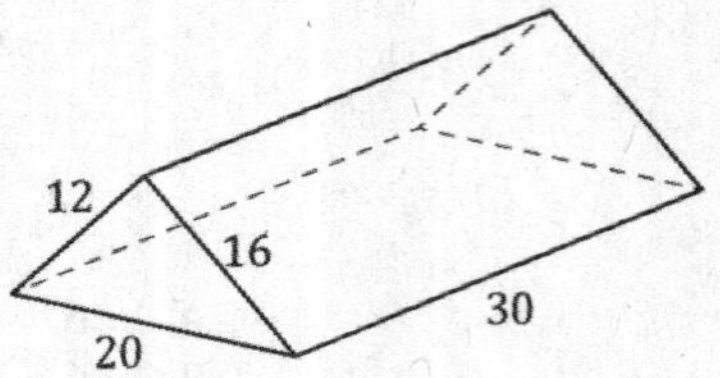

F. 1,632
G. 1,440
H. 600
J. 480
K. 360

27. What is the approximate surface area, in square inches, of a ball with a largest circumference of 12π inches?
($SA_{\text{Sphere}} = 4\pi r^2$)

A. 12π
B. 36π
C. 144π
D. 576π
E. $2,304\pi$

28. The volume of a cone can be found using the formula $V = \frac{1}{3}\pi r^2 h$. If a cone has a height of 10 cm and a volume of 120π cm^3, what is the diameter of its base, in centimeters?

F. 6
G. 12
H. 36
J. 72
K. 144

29. A construction company is building a silo. The silo is a cylinder with a hemisphere on top. The diameter of the cylinder is 42 feet and the height of the cylinder is 40 feet. How much hay can be stored in the silo, in cubic feet?

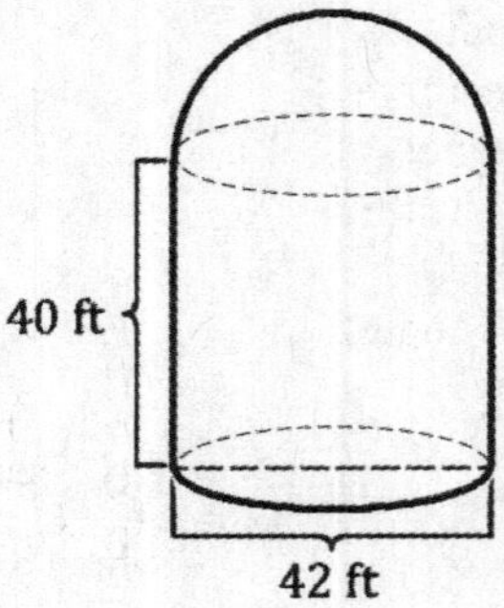

A. $23,814\pi$
B. $29,988\pi$
C. $711,774\pi$
D. $717,948\pi$
E. $70,560 + 6,174\pi$

Throwback to Math Class

Cube volume: $V = x^3$
Cube surface area: $SA = 6x^2$
Prism volume: $V = bwh$
Prism surface area: $SA = 2bw + 2wh + 2bh$
Cylinder volume: $V = \pi r^2 h$
Cylinder lateral surface area: $LSA = 2\pi rh$
Cylinder total surface area: $TSA = 2\pi rh + 2\pi r^2$
Sphere volume: $V = \frac{4}{3}\pi r^3$
Sphere surface area: $SA = 4\pi r^2$

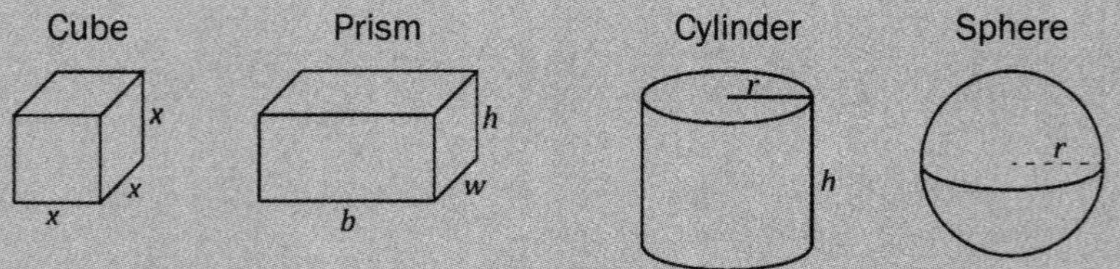

Cube	Prism	Cylinder	Sphere
$V = x^3$	$V = bwh$	$V = \pi r^2 h$	$V = \frac{4}{3}\pi r^3$
$SA = 6x^2$	$SA = 2bw + 2wh + 2bh$	$LSA = 2\pi rh$	$SA = 4\pi r^2$
		$TSA = 2\pi rh + 2\pi r^2$	

GEOMETRY STRATEGIES

"Guesstimating"
Items #30–32

Measuring
Items #33–34

Use Your Test Booklet

The answer sheet has four right angles—one at each corner. If you have trouble visualizing angles, the answer sheet will help; use any corner of the answer sheet to measure angles. This will indicate immediately whether an angle is larger than, smaller than, or exactly 90°.

30. In the figure below, $x = ?$

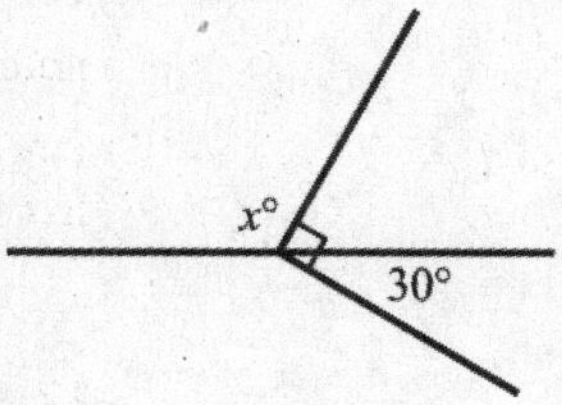

F. 30
G. 65
H. 120
J. 150
K. 170

31. What is the perimeter of the triangle shown below?

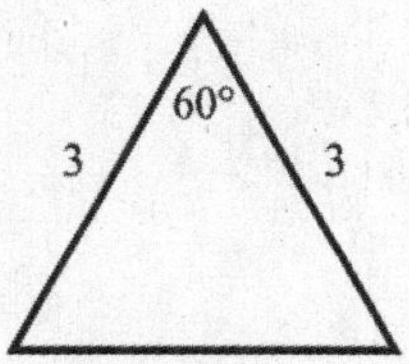

A. $3\sqrt{2}$
B. 6
C. 7.5
D. 9
E. 15

32. In the figure below, $x = ?$

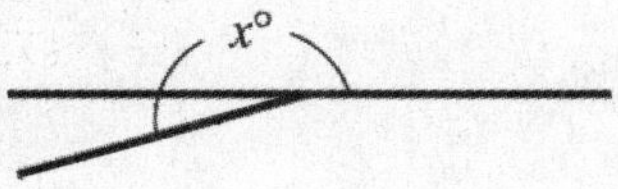

F. 120
G. 150
H. 180
J. 210
K. 240

33. In the figure below, $x = ?$

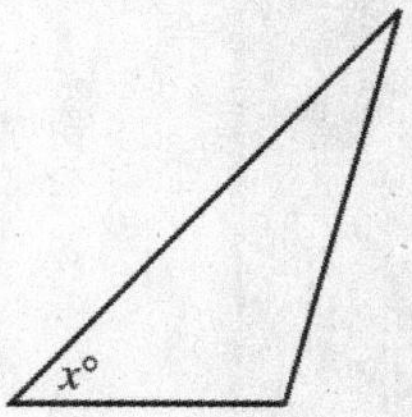

A. 30
B. 45
C. 60
D. 75
E. 90

34. In the figure below, what is the length of $\overline{AC}$?

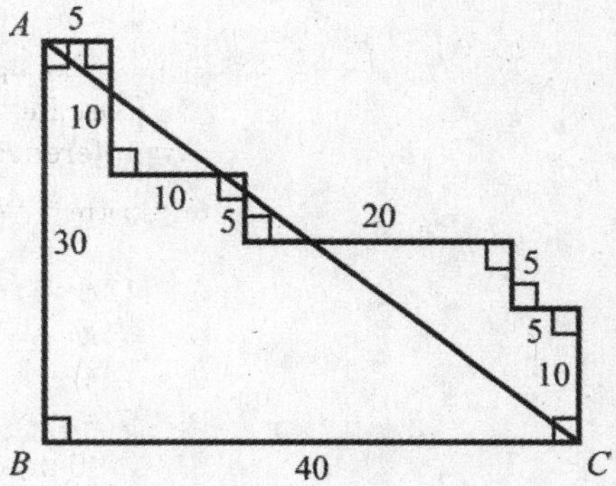

F. $30\sqrt{2}$
G. 50
H. 75
J. $60\sqrt{2}$
K. 100

"Meastimating"
Items #35–36

The Cambridge Edge

"Meastimating" is a combination of "guesstimating" and measuring. The idea is to approximate measurements based on the information that is provided in the figure.

35. In the figure below, what is the area of square $ABCD$?

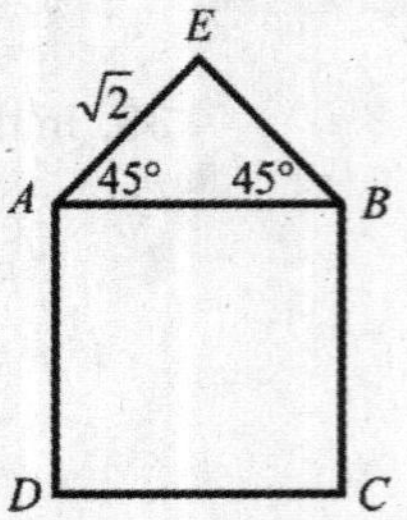

A. 2
B. $2\sqrt{2}$
C. 4
D. $4\sqrt{2}$
E. 8

36. In the triangle below, the measure of $\angle BAC$ is 30° and the length of $\overline{AB}$ is 2. Which of the following best approximates the length of $\overline{AC}$?

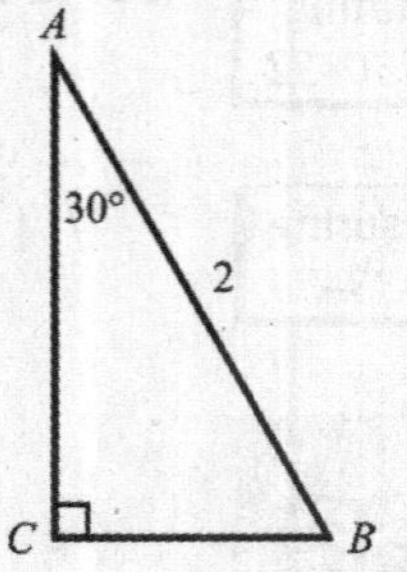

F. 0.8
G. 1.0
H. 1.7
J. 1.9
K. 2.3

LESSON 5

Trigonometry

DEFINITIONS OF THE SIX TRIGONOMETRIC FUNCTIONS

The Cambridge Edge

The mnemonic SOH-CAH-TOA can be used to remember the definitions of sine, cosine, and tangent.

SOH:
$\text{Sin } \theta = \dfrac{\text{side Opposite } \theta}{\text{Hypotenuse}}$

CAH:
$\text{Cos } \theta = \dfrac{\text{side Adjacent } \theta}{\text{Hypotenuse}}$

TOA:
$\text{Tan } \theta = \dfrac{\sin \theta}{\cos \theta} = \dfrac{\dfrac{\text{side opposite } \theta}{\text{hypotenuse}}}{\dfrac{\text{side adjacent } \theta}{\text{hypotenuse}}} = \dfrac{\text{side Opposite } \theta}{\text{side Adjacent } \theta}$

1. For the figure below, $\sin \theta = \dfrac{12}{13}$. Which of the following is INCORRECT?

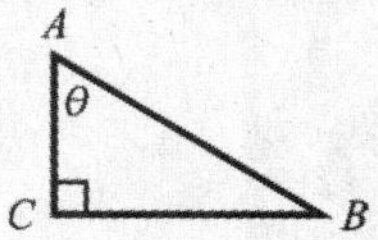

A. $\cos \theta = \dfrac{5}{13}$

B. $\tan \theta = \dfrac{12}{5}$

C. $\cot \theta = \dfrac{5}{12}$

D. $\sec \theta = \dfrac{13}{5}$

E. $\csc \theta = \dfrac{12}{13}$

2. In the right triangle below, the length of $\overline{AB}$ is 5 centimeters and $\angle A$ measures 30°. What is the length, in centimeters, of $\overline{BC}$? ($\sin 30° = \dfrac{1}{2}$)

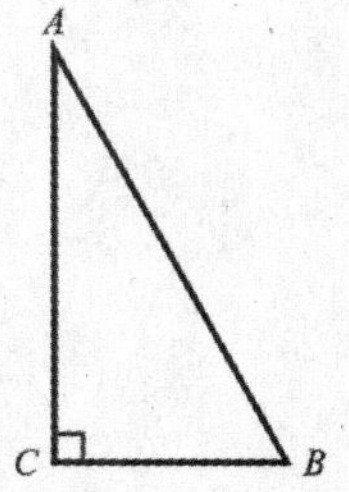

F. 4

G. $3\dfrac{1}{2}$

H. $2\dfrac{3}{4}$

J. $2\dfrac{1}{2}$

K. 2

3. Which of the following is equivalent to $\dfrac{\sin A}{\cos A}$?

A. $\tan A$

B. $\cot A$

C. $\sec A$

D. $\csc A$

E. $\dfrac{1}{\tan A}$

4. A six-foot-tall surveyor is standing on the ground 207 feet from the base of a building 1,776 feet tall. Which of the following expressions gives the angle of elevation from the top of the surveyor's head to the top of the building?

F. $\cot\left(\dfrac{1{,}770}{207}\right)$

G. $\tan\left(\dfrac{1{,}776}{207}\right)$

H. $\sin^{-1}\left(\dfrac{207}{1{,}770}\right)$

J. $\cos^{-1}\left(\dfrac{207}{1{,}776}\right)$

K. $\tan^{-1}\left(\dfrac{1{,}770}{207}\right)$

The Cambridge Edge

Determine whether a trig function is positive or negative using the mnemonic "All Students Take Cambridge."

1. *All* trig functions are positive in the first quadrant.
2. Only the *sine* and its reciprocal are positive in the second quadrant.
3. Only the *tangent* and its reciprocal are is positive in the third quadrant,.
4. Only the *cosine* and its reciprocal are positive in the fourth quadrant.

Use POE

If you are running out of time on the exam, you may have to make an educated guess on item #5. Knowing $\frac{\pi}{2} < \theta < \pi$ means the angle is in Quadrant II and the ASTC mnemonic is enough to immediately eliminate (A), (B), and (C), since these are all negative. That leaves a 50/50 chance of guessing correctly!

5. Assume an angle with radian measure θ exists such that $\cos\theta = -\frac{3}{5}$ and $\frac{\pi}{2} < \theta < \pi$. What is the value of $\sin\theta$?

A. $-\frac{5}{3}$
B. $-\frac{4}{5}$
C. $-\frac{3}{5}$
D. $\frac{4}{5}$
E. $\frac{5}{4}$

TRIGONOMETRIC RELATIONSHIPS

The Cambridge Edge

Memorize these trig relationships:

$\sin x = \frac{1}{\csc x}$

$\csc x = \frac{1}{\sin x}$

$\cos x = \frac{1}{\sec x}$

$\sec x = \frac{1}{\cos x}$

$\tan x = \frac{\sin x}{\cos x}$

$\cot x = \frac{\cos x}{\sin x}$

$\tan x = \frac{1}{\cot x}$

$\cot x = \frac{1}{\tan x}$

$\sin^2 x + \cos^2 x = 1$

$1 + \cot^2 x = \csc^2 x$

$\tan^2 x + 1 = \sec^2 x$

6. If $\sin 60°$ is equal to $\frac{\sqrt{3}}{2}$, what is the value of $\sin^2 30° + \cos^2 30°$?

F. $\sqrt{5}$
G. $\frac{\sqrt{3}+1}{2}$
H. $\frac{\sqrt{5}}{2}$
J. 1
K. $\frac{3}{4}$

TRIGONOMETRY AS AN ALTERNATIVE METHOD OF SOLUTION

7. In the figure below, ΔPQR and ΔQRS are isosceles right triangles. If $\overline{QP} = 3$, what is the length of $\overline{QS}$? $\left(\sin 45^\circ = \dfrac{\sqrt{2}}{2}\right)$

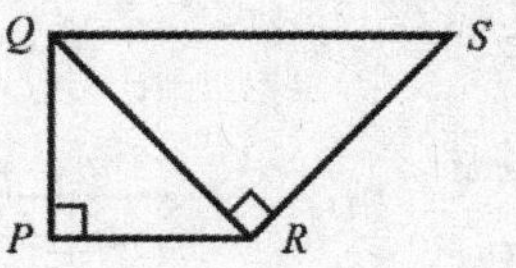

A. $\sqrt{2}$
B. $2\sqrt{2}$
C. 4
D. 6
E. 8

8. If the area of the square $JKLM$ in the figure below is 4, what is the sum of the lengths of the diagonals $\overline{JL}$ and $\overline{KM}$? $\left(\sin 45^\circ = \dfrac{\sqrt{2}}{2}\right)$

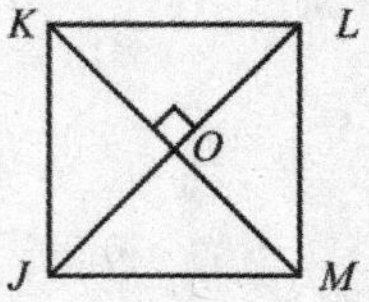

F. $\dfrac{\sqrt{2}}{2}$
G. $2 + \dfrac{\sqrt{2}}{2}$
H. $4\sqrt{2}$
J. $4 + 4\sqrt{2}$
K. $8\sqrt{2}$

9. In the figure below, O is the center of the circle with radius 10. What is the area of ΔAOB? $\left(\sin 30^\circ = \dfrac{1}{2};\ \sin 60^\circ = \dfrac{\sqrt{3}}{2}\right)$

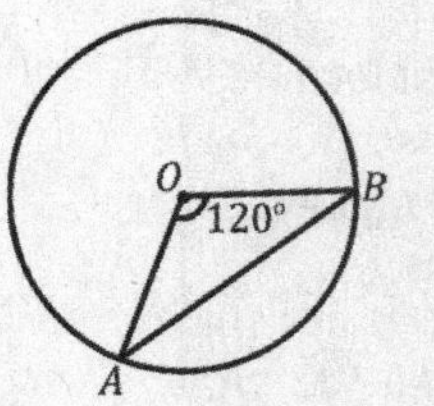

A. 10
B. $10\sqrt{3}$
C. 25
D. $25\sqrt{3}$
E. 50

10. The triangle in the figure below has an area of 434 square centimeters and $\overline{BC}$ is 50 cm. What is the value of $\cos A$?

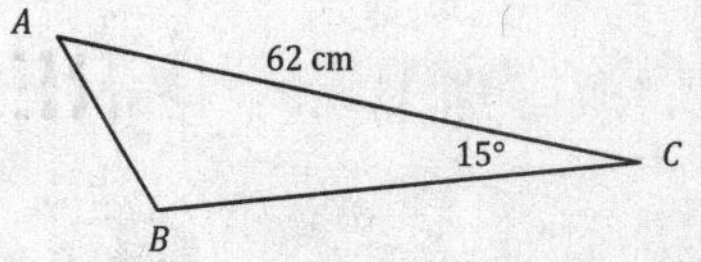

F. $\dfrac{1}{2}$
G. $\dfrac{\sqrt{2}}{2}$
H. 1
J. 2
K. $2\sqrt{2}$

GRAPHS OF TRIGONOMETRIC FUNCTIONS

Throwback to Math

The general form for the equation of a trigonometry function is:

$y = Af[B(x + C)] + D$

where *f* is the trigonometry function, *A* is the amplitude, *B* helps determine the period, *C* is the shift left (+) or right (–), and *D* is the shift up (+) or down (–).

11. Which of the following does NOT correctly describe the graph of $f(x) = \frac{1}{2}\sin(x + \pi)$ in the standard (*x*,*y*) coordinate plane?

A. $f(x)$ has half the amplitude of $g(x) = \sin x$

B. $f(x)$ has half the amplitude of $g(x) = \sin(x + \pi)$

C. $f(x)$ is shifted to the left of $g(x) = \frac{1}{2}\sin x$ by π

D. $f(x)$ is identical to $g(x) = \frac{1}{2}\sin(x - \pi)$

E. $f(x)$ is shifted up from $g(x) = \frac{1}{2}\sin x$ by π

12. Which of the following equations is equal to the function graphed below?

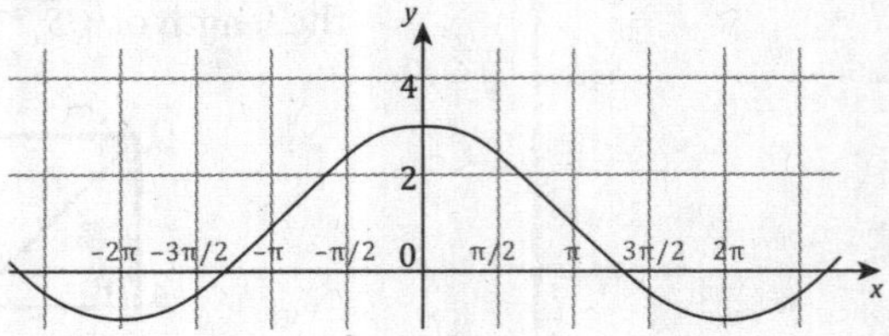

F. $2\sin x$

G. $\cos\frac{x}{2}$

H. $1 + \sin 2x$

J. $1 + 2\cos\frac{x}{2}$

K. $1 + 2\cos x$

Throwback to Math Class

You should be familiar with the graphs of the sine function and the cosine function.

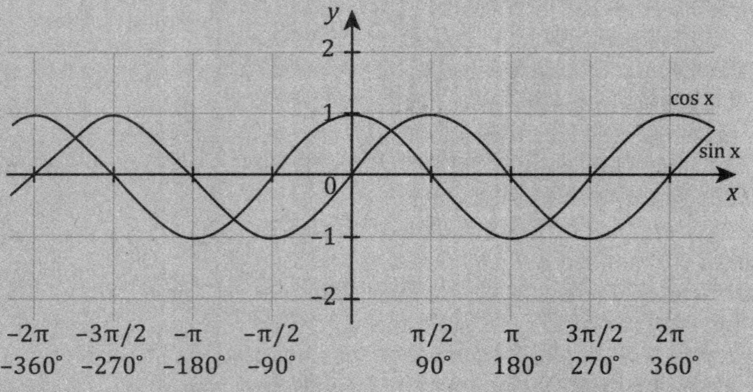

Remember, the amplitude is the maximum height of the function from the *x*-axis (which is half the total range) and the period is the distance on the *x*-axis over which the function repeats.

LESSON 6

Statistics, Probability, and Data Representation

MEASURES OF CENTER

> *Throwback to Math Class*
>
> Here are the steps to find a *missing element* of an average:
>
> 1. Multiply the average by the total number of quantities.
> 2. Add together the known quantities.
> 3. Subtract the result of Step 2 from the result of Step 1.

1. If the average of 35, 38, 41, 43, and x is 37, what is x?

A. 28
B. 30
C. 31
D. 34
E. 36

2. The average weight of 6 packages is 50 pounds per package. Another package is added, making the average weight of the 7 packages 52 pounds per package. What is the weight, in pounds, of the additional package?

F. 2
G. 7
H. 52
J. 62
K. 64

3. The average of 10 test scores is 80. If the high and low scores are dropped, the average is 81. What is the average of the high and low scores?

A. 76
B. 78
C. 80
D. 81
E. 82

4. In Latin 101, the final exam grade is weighted two times as heavily as the mid-term grade. If Leo received a score of 84 on his final exam and 90 on his mid-term, what was his course average?

F. 88
G. 87.5
H. 86.5
J. 86
K. 85

> *The Cambridge Edge*
>
> When computing weighted averages, don't check your calculations, but do check that:
>
> 1. The average weights the components properly.
> 2. The correct number of quantities is used.

> *The Cambridge Edge*
>
> For item #1, instead of working with the given values, work with the "aboves" and the "belows." There are three numbers above the average: 38 (1 above), 41 (4 above), and 43 (6 above). There is one number below: 35 (2 below). These two groups need to balance. Right now, the above group totals 11 above the average and the below group totals 2 below, so we need to add a value to the below group that is 9 below the average, to balance the two groups.
>
> If this seems too complicated, just use the first part of the strategy. Clearly we need a number less than 37 in the "belows" group. And it probably needs to be less than 36 or 34. This helps you quickly eliminate a few choices without doing any math.

Throwback to Math Class

The *median* is the middle value (or the average of the two middle values) when the data are arranged in ascending or descending order.

The *mode* is the data value that occurs with the greatest frequency.

5. In a group of children, 3 children are 10 years old and 2 children are 5 years old. What is the average age, in years, of the children in the group?

A. 6
B. 6.5
C. 7
D. 7.5
E. 8

6. The number of employment applications received by All-Star Staffing each month during 2016 was as follows: 8, 4, 5, 3, 4, 3, 1, 0, 3, 4, 0, and 7. What was the median number of applications received per month in 2016?

F. 2.5
G. 3
H. 3.5
J. 4
K. 4.5

7. William's monthly electric bills for last year were as follows: $40, 38, 36, 38, 34, 34, 30, 32, 34, 37, 39, and 40. What is the mode of the bills?

A. $33
B. $34
C. $35
D. $36
E. $37

COUNTING METHODS

8. The combination for screen lock consists of four numbers taken from 10 digits, 0 through 9. Which of the following expressions gives the number of distinct screen lock combinations that are possible given that repetition of digits is allowed?

F. 40
G. $\frac{10!}{10^4}$
H. 10^4
J. $4(10)^4$
K. $10!$

9. A committee of 4 members is chosen from a list at random. If the list has 6 names, in how many different sequences can the 4 member names be drawn?

A. 60
B. 120
C. 240
D. 360
E. 480

SETS

Throwback to Math Class

A set is a collection of things, people, numbers, or even concepts. Brackets are used to indicate set membership. For example, $\{2, 4, 6, 8\}$ is the set of all even numbers greater than 0 and less than 10.

Throwback to Math Class

The intersection of two sets P and Q, $P \cap Q$, is the set of all elements that are in both sets P and Q.

The null set, or empty set, is the set that contains no elements. The null set is symbolized as $\{\}$ or $\emptyset$.

The union of two sets P and Q, $P \cup Q$, is the set of all elements that are in either set P or Q or both sets P and Q.

10. If set $S = \{2, 3, 4\}$ and set P is the set of all products of different elements in set S, then set $P = ?$

F. $\{6, 8, 12\}$
G. $\{6, 8, 18\}$
H. $\{6, 8, 12, 24\}$
J. $\{6, 8, 12, 18, 24\}$
K. $\{6, 8, 12, 18, 24, 36\}$

11. If set X is the set of all integers between 1 and 24, inclusive, that are evenly divisible by 3, and set Y is the set of all integers between 1 and 24, inclusive, that are evenly divisible by 4, what is the set of all elements in both sets X and Y?

A. $\{12\}$
B. $\{3, 4\}$
C. $\{12, 24\}$
D. $\{4, 12, 24\}$
E. $\{3, 4, 12, 24\}$

12. If x is an element of set X, in which set X is the set of integers evenly divisible by 3 such that $6 < x < 11$, and y is an element of set Y, where set Y is the set of integers evenly divisible by 4 such that $7 < y < 12$, what is the intersection of sets X and Y?

F. $\{\}$
G. $\{8\}$
H. $\{9\}$
J. $\{12\}$
K. $\{8, 12\}$

13. If set S is the set of all positive odd integers and set T is the set of all positive even integers, then the union of sets S and T (the set of all elements that are in either set or both sets) is the set of:

A. positive integers.
B. integers.
C. even integers.
D. odd integers.
E. real numbers.

14. In a certain school, each of the 72 music majors must participate in the marching band, the orchestra, or both. If only music majors participate, 48 students total participate in the marching band, and 54 students total participate in the orchestra, how many students participate in both programs?

F. 6
G. 18
H. 24
J. 30
K. 36

15. There are 22 students at the immunization clinic, 15 of who need their measles booster shot and 19 of who need their polio booster shot. Assuming all the students need at least one of the two shots, how many students in the clinic need both shots?

A. 7
B. 9
C. 11
D. 12
E. 15

PROBABILITY

Throwback to Math Class

Probability = $\dfrac{\text{\# of desired outcomes}}{\text{\# of possible outcomes}}$

16. If set $A = \{1, 2, 3, 4, 5, 6\}$ and set $B = \{1, 2, 3, 4, 5, 6\}$, what is the probability that the sum of one number from set A and one number from set B will total 7?

F. $\frac{1}{12}$
G. $\frac{5}{36}$
H. $\frac{1}{6}$
J. $\frac{1}{5}$
K. $\frac{1}{3}$

17. If a book is selected at random from the collection shown below, which of the following has the greatest probability of being selected?

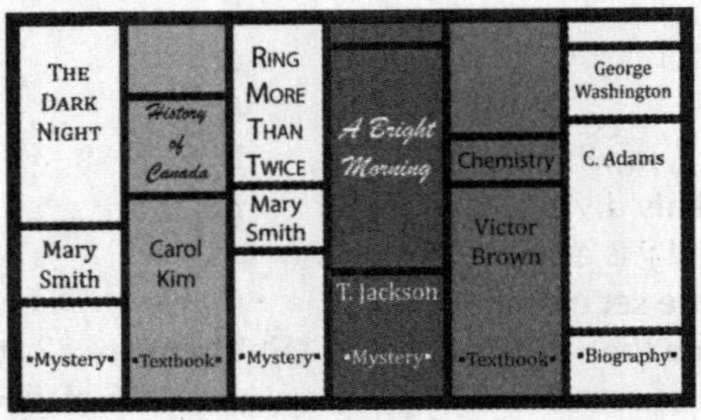

A. A book by Mary Smith
B. A textbook
C. A mystery
D. A book written by either Carol Kim or Victor Brown
E. A biography

18. If a jar contains r red marbles, b blue marbles, and g green marbles, which of the following expresses the probability that a marble drawn at random will NOT be red?

F. $\frac{-r}{r+b+g}$
G. $\frac{r}{r+b+g}$
H. $\frac{b+g-r}{b+g+r}$
J. $\frac{r}{b+g}$
K. $\frac{b+g}{b+g+r}$

19. The figure below shows a dartboard consisting of two concentric circles with center O. The radius of the larger circle is equal to the diameter of the smaller circle. What is the probability that a randomly thrown dart striking the board will score a 3?

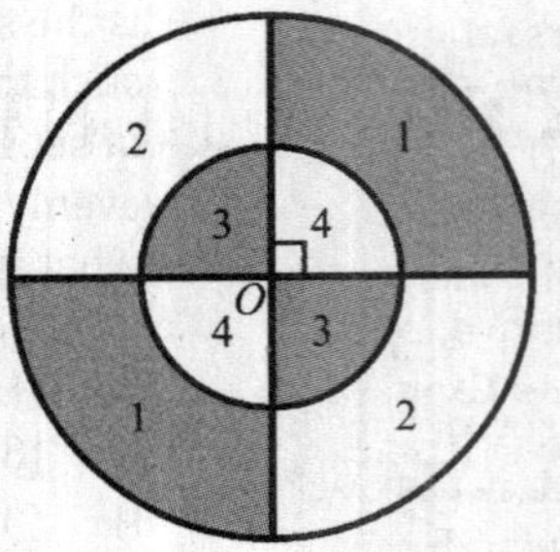

A. $\frac{1}{16}$
B. $\frac{1}{8}$
C. $\frac{1}{4}$
D. $\frac{1}{2}$
E. $\frac{3}{4}$

20. An underwater salvage team is searching the ocean floor for a lost signal device using a large circular search pattern and a smaller circular search pattern with a radius equal to one-third that of the larger pattern. If the device is known to be inside the boundary of the larger search area, what is the probability that it is NOT located in the shaded portion of the figure?

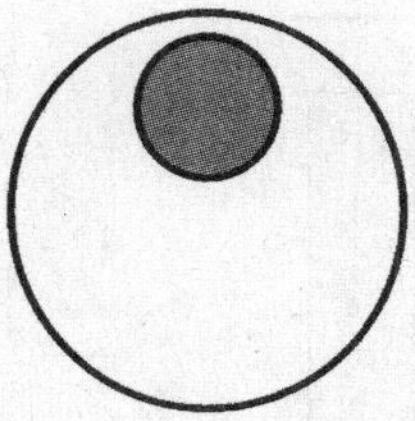

F. $\frac{1}{9}$
G. $\frac{1}{6}$
H. $\frac{1}{3}$
J. $\frac{4}{9}$
K. $\frac{8}{9}$

DATA REPRESENTATION

Bar, Cumulative, and Line Graphs
Items #21–25

The Cambridge Edge

Preview the data presented in graphs, charts, and tables before reading the accompanying item(s). Pay careful attention to any titles or labels, note the units, check the scale, and read any special notes. Any information that you need to answer the item will be provided in the data presentation.

21. During the week shown in the graph below, what was the greatest increase in sales from one day to the next?

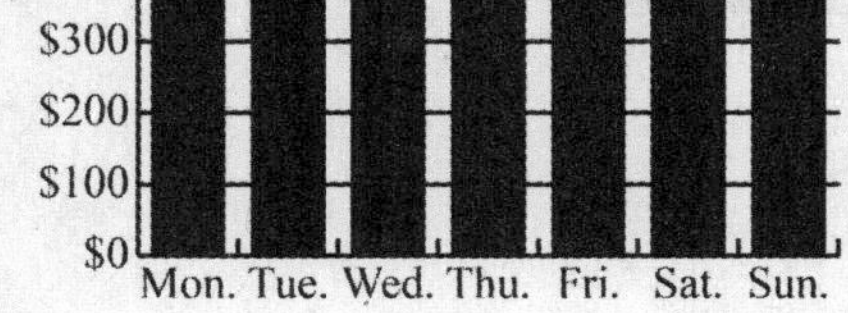

A. $50
B. $100
C. $150
D. $200
E. $250

22. If the graph below represents expenditures by Corporation X in two different years, what was the approximate ratio of expenditures in 2006 to those in 2007?

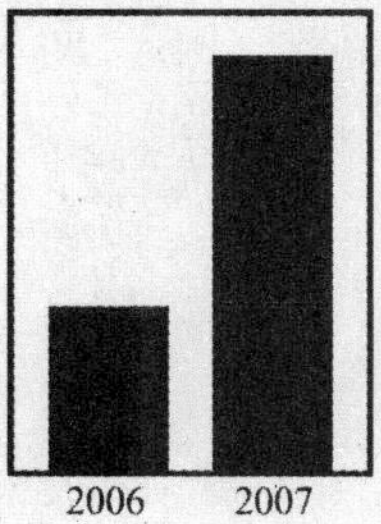

F. $\frac{1}{5}$
G. $\frac{2}{5}$
H. $\frac{1}{2}$
J. $\frac{2}{3}$
K. 2

The Cambridge Edge

Here are some tips for working with bar and line graphs.

1. Add quantities by adding bar lengths (or vertical line distances).
2. Subtract quantities by finding the difference between bar lengths (or vertical line distances).
3. Find ratios and fractions by dividing one bar length (or vertical line distance) by another.

Pie Charts
Items #26–27

23. Based on the data presented below, what was the difference, if any, between the number of permanent workers employed by Corporation X on March 1st and the number of permanent workers employed by Corporation X on April 1st?

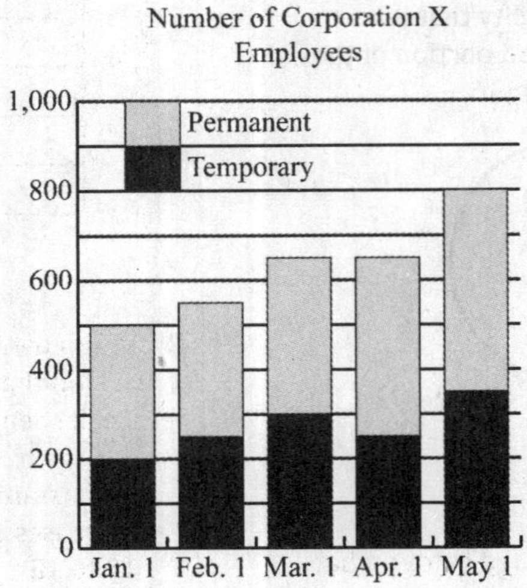

A. 0
B. 50
C. 100
D. 150
E. 200

24. Based on the data presented below, what was the difference in the value of foreign sales by Company T between 2003 and 2005?

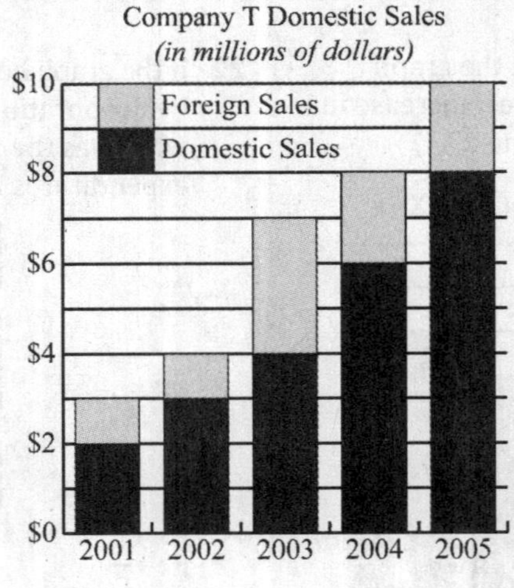

F. $1,000,000
G. $2,000,000
H. $3,000,000
J. $5,000,000
K. $6,000,000

25. Based on the data presented below, what was the approximate total number of packages shipped by PostExpress for the months January, February, and March, inclusive?

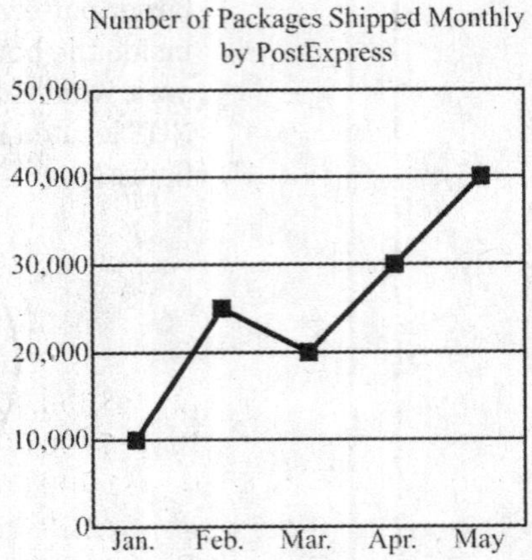

A. 40,000
B. 55,000
C. 60,000
D. 70,000
E. 85,000

26. Based on the data presented below, approximately how much money was spent on the Air Force?

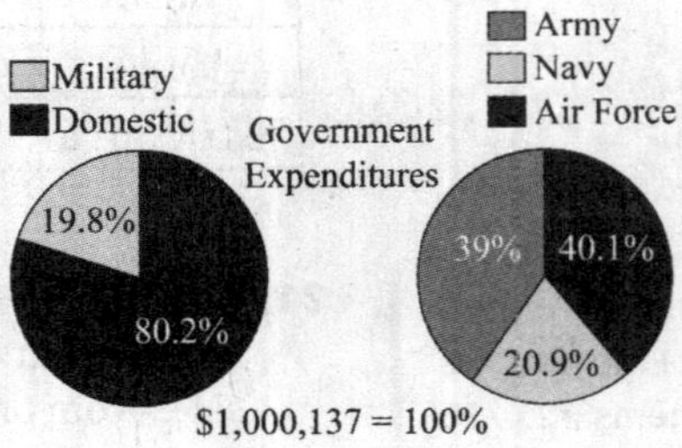

F. $39,704
G. $79,409
H. $96,123
J. $198,027
K. $401,054

27. Based on the data presented below, what was the dollar value of foreign sales to Europe by PetProducts in 2002?

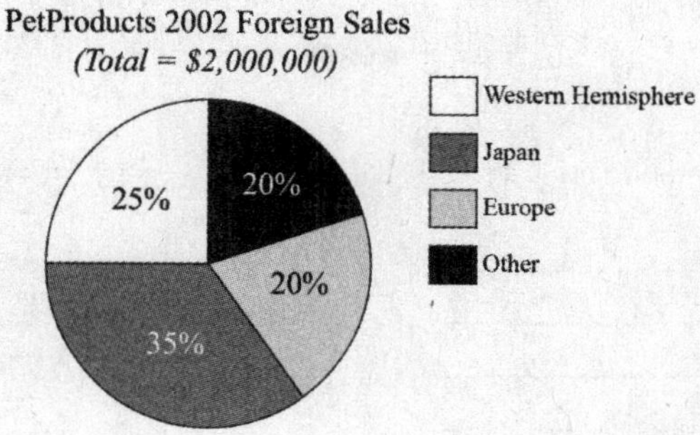

A. $200,000
B. $400,000
C. $1,200,000
D. $1,600,000
E. $2,000,000

Tables
Item #28

Scatterplots
Item #29

28. Based on the data presented below, what is the total cost of 5 large blue t-shirts, 8 small red t-shirts, and 4 extra large white t-shirts?

T-SHIRT PRICES			
	Blue	Red	White
Small	$5.00	$6.00	$7.00
Large	$5.75	$6.50	$7.25
Extra Large	$6.50	$7.25	$8.00

F. $56.00
G. $88.25
H. $105.50
J. $108.75
K. $135.00

29. The following scatterplot shows the video-game playing habits of 20 students.

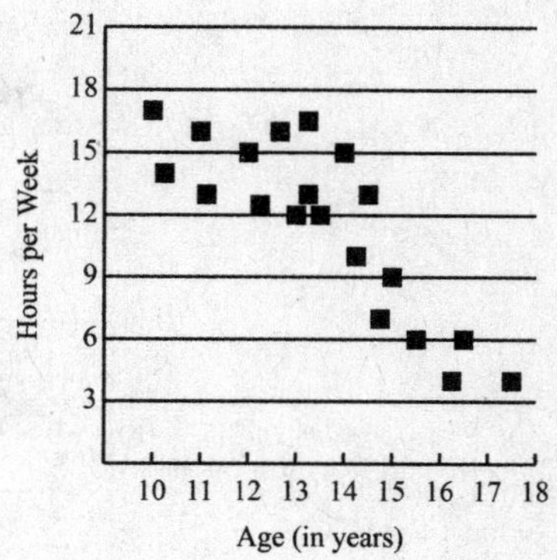

The graph most strongly supports the conclusion that the number of hours per week spent playing video-games:

A. is constant from age 10 to age 18.
B. increases as age increases from 10 to 18.
C. decreases as age increases from 10 to 18.
D. decreases as age increases from 10 to 14 and then remains approximately constant.
E. is approximately constant for ages 14 through 18.

MATH QUIZZES

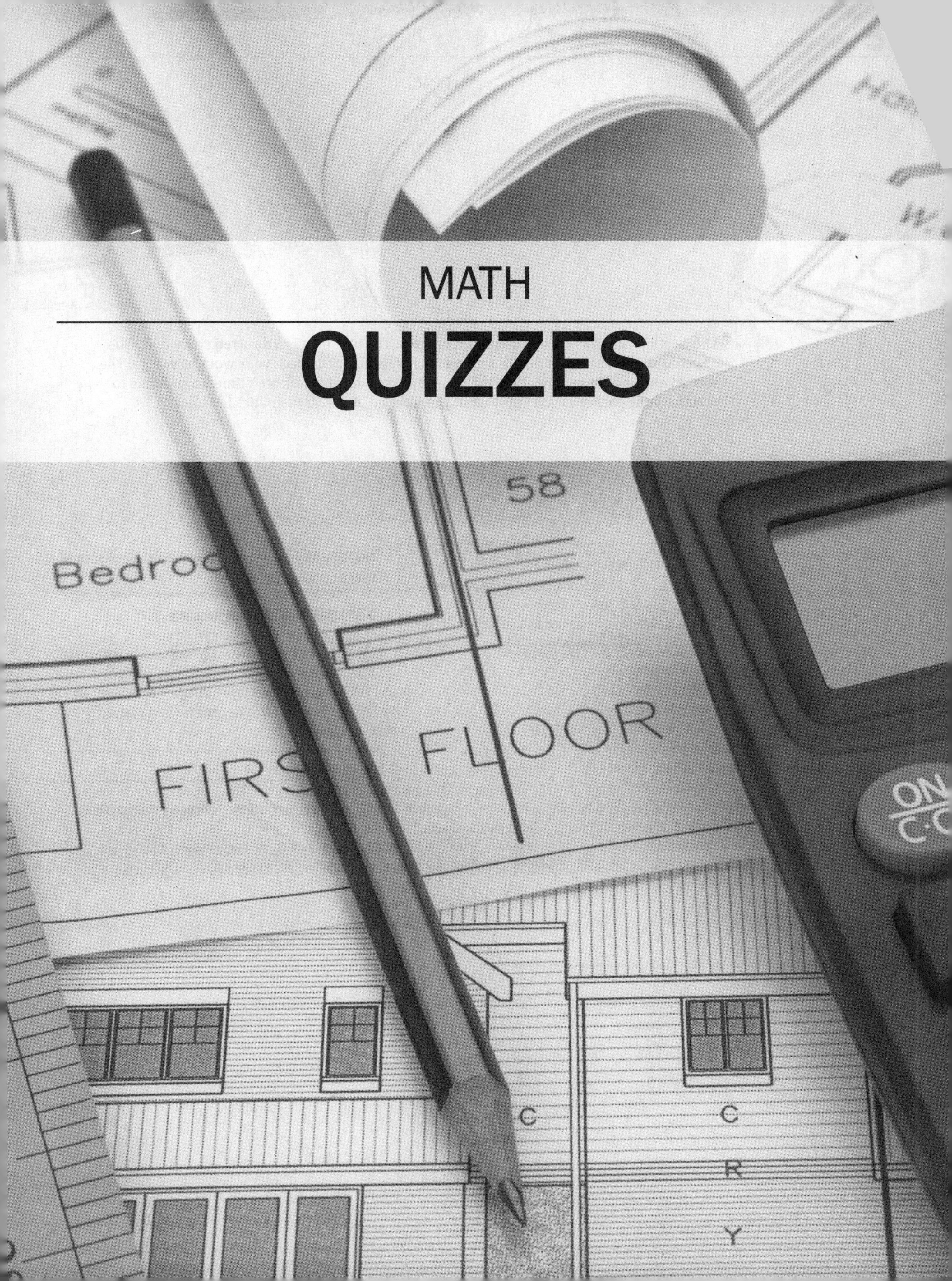

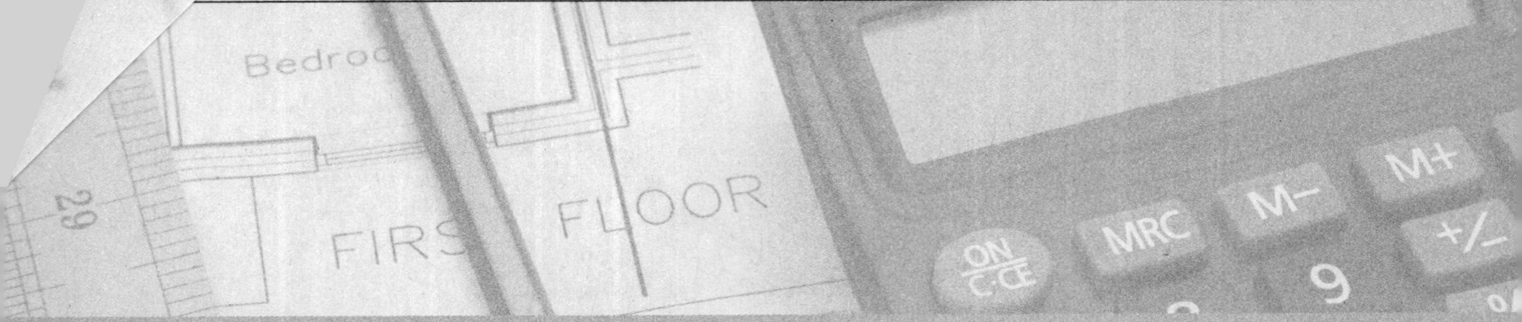

This section contains two Mathematics quizzes. The first quiz is a directed study quiz. The directed study quiz is not timed. Answer each question and check your work as you go. The second quiz is a timed quiz. Take the second quiz under the indicated timed conditions to practice your pacing as you apply what you learned in the Mathematics Lessons.

DIRECTED STUDY QUIZ *(20 items; 20 minutes)*

DIRECTIONS: Solve each item and choose the correct answer choice. Calculator use is permitted; however, some items are best solved without the use of a calculator.

NOTES: All of the following should be assumed, unless otherwise stated.

1. Illustrative figures are NOT necessarily drawn to scale.
2. The word *average* indicates arithmetic mean.
3. The word *line* indicates a straight line.
4. Geometric figures lie in a plane.

Throwback to Math Class

Remember the angles in a triangle must sum to 180°. In general, for a polygon with n sides, the sum of its interior angles must sum to: $(n-2)\times 180°$.

1. In the triangle below, $x = ?$

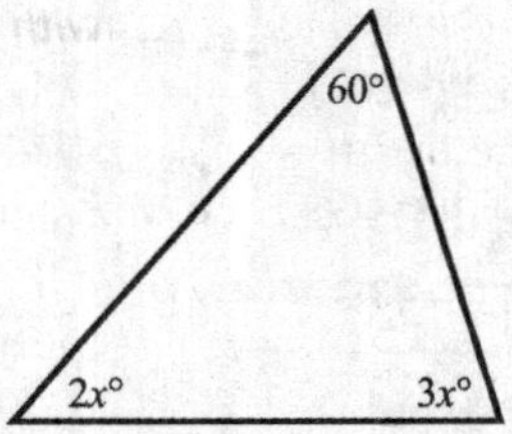

A. 24
B. 20
C. 16
D. 12
E. 10

EXPLANATIONS

1. (A) ***Mathematics/Geometry/Lines and Angles***
$60 + 2x + 3x = 180 \Rightarrow 5x = 120 \Rightarrow x = 24.$

EXPLANATIONS

2. A normal dozen contains 12 items, and a baker's dozen contains 13 items. If x is the number of items that could be measured either in a whole number of normal dozens or in a whole number of baker's dozens, what is the <u>minimum</u> value of x?

F. 1
G. 12
H. 13
J. 25
K. 156

2. (K) ***Mathematics/Number and Quantity/ Basic Arithmetic Manipulations***
The answer is the first number that is divisible by both 12 and 13: 156 $(156 = 12 \cdot 13)$.

The Cambridge Edge

The directions on the ACT clearly state that illustrative images are NOT necessarily drawn to scale. But if you are truly stuck on a problem with an image, go ahead and assume the image is drawn to scale. The images are provided to assist you, and most of the time they are drawn to scale or drawn accurately enough so that you can at least eliminate some answer choices.

3. In the figure below, what is the degree measure of the <u>smaller</u> of the two angles formed by the hour and minute hands of the clock?

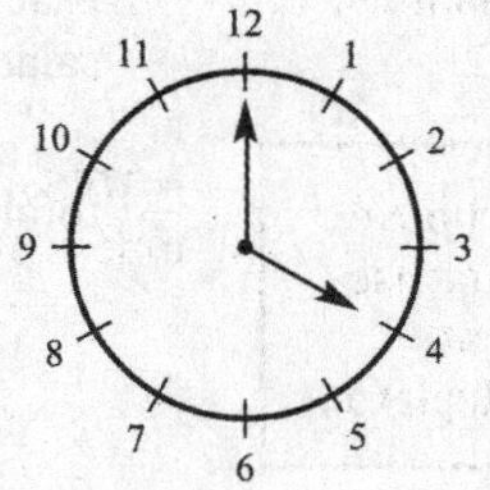

A. 45
B. 60
C. 90
D. 120
E. 240

3. (D) ***Mathematics/Geometry/Lines and Angles***
The numerals on the face of the clock divide the circumference of the circle into twelve equal 30°-arcs $(360 \div 12 = 30)$. Therefore, the degree measure of the arc from 12 to 4 is 120.

Alternatively, simply estimate. The angle is clearly greater than 90°, so eliminate (A), (B), and (C). This leaves (D), 120, as the only possible choice, since 240, (E), corresponds to an angle greater than a straight line.

4. Starting from points that are 200 kilometers apart, two trains travel toward each other along two parallel tracks. If one train travels at 70 kilometers per hour and the other travels at 80 kilometers per hour, how much time, in hours, will elapse before the trains pass each other?

F. $\frac{3}{4}$
G. 1
H. $\frac{4}{3}$
J. $\frac{3}{2}$
K. 2

4. (H) ***Mathematics/Algebra and Functions/ Solving Algebraic Equations or Inequalities with One Variable/Simple Equations***
This item is solved by realizing that the total distance traveled by the two trains, wherever the trains meet, will equal 200 kilometers. Thus, if x is the time the trains travel,

$$70\frac{\text{km}}{\text{hr}}x + 80\frac{\text{km}}{\text{hr}}x = 200 \Rightarrow x = \frac{4}{3} \text{ hours.}$$

Alternatively, "test-the-test," beginning with (H): if both trains run for $\frac{4}{3}$ hours, then the total distance traveled is 200 kilometers.

Throwback to Math Class

When setting up proportions, a common technique to solving for an unknown is cross-multiplying, Cross-multiplying is when you multiply the numerator of the first fraction with the denominator of the second and denominator of the first fraction with the numerator of the second and set both products equal to each other. Cross-multiplying eliminates the fractions and returns an equation that is easy to solve algebraically.

5. A student begins heating a certain substance with a temperature of 50°C over a Bunsen burner. If the temperature of the substance will rise 20°C for every 24 minutes it remains over the burner, what will be the temperature, in degrees Celsius, of the substance after 18 minutes?

A. 52
B. 56
C. 60
D. 65
E. 72

6. If the ratio of apples to oranges in a fruit salad made of only those two fruits is 8 to 7, what fractional part of the salad is oranges?

F. $\frac{1}{56}$
G. $\frac{1}{15}$
H. $\frac{1}{7}$
J. $\frac{7}{15}$
K. $\frac{8}{7}$

7. A local cafe has a soup and salad lunch special. There are three soups and six sandwichs available. How many different soup and salad combinations are possible?

A. 2
B. 3
C. 9
D. 12
E. 18

8. The average weight of three boxes is $25\frac{1}{3}$ pounds. If each box weighs at least 24 pounds, what is the greatest possible weight, in pounds, of any one of the boxes?

F. 25
G. 26
H. 27
J. 28
K. 29

EXPLANATIONS

5. (D) ***Mathematics/Number and Quantity/ Rates and Proportions***
The longer the substance is heated, the hotter it will be, so the quantities demonstrate direct variation:
$$\frac{x_1}{y_1}=\frac{x_2}{y_2} \Rightarrow \frac{20°\text{C}}{24 \text{ minutes}}=\frac{x°\text{C}}{18 \text{ minutes}} \Rightarrow$$
$$\frac{20°\text{C} \times 18 \cancel{\text{minutes}}}{24 \cancel{\text{minutes}}} = 15°\text{C}.$$ Thus, the new temperature is $50° + 15° = 65°\text{C}$.

6. (J) ***Mathematics/Number and Quantity/ Rates and Proportions***
Simplify the item by assuming there are exactly 8 apples and 7 oranges in the salad. Therefore, 15 pieces of fruit are in the salad, and the oranges are $\frac{7}{15}$ of the total number.

7. (E) ***Mathematics/Statistics and Probability/Counting Methods***
For each of the three soups, there are six possible sandwiches—the total number of combinations is $3 \cdot 6 = 18$.

8. (J) ***Mathematics/Statistics and Probability/Measures of Center***
The average weight of the three boxes is $25\frac{1}{3}$ pounds, so the total weight of the boxes is 76 pounds. If each box weighs at least 24 pounds, then the minimum weight of two boxes is 48 pounds, and the maximum weight of any one box is $76 - 48 = 28$ pounds.

Test-the-Test

When you can't solve the problem directly, use the answer choices. Remember, one of the answer choices is correct, all you have to do is find it. In problem 9, use test-the-test by assuming n is equal to each answer choice. The correct answer choice is the one where n subtracted from $\frac{13}{2}$ is equal to n divided by $\frac{2}{13}$.

9. If n subtracted from $\frac{13}{2}$ is equal to n divided by $\frac{2}{13}$, what is the value of n?

A. $\frac{2}{3}$
B. $\frac{13}{15}$
C. 1
D. $\frac{13}{11}$
E. 26

10. In the figure below, what is the area of the quadrilateral?

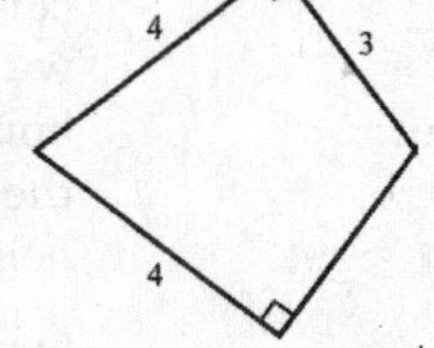

F. 18
G. 15
H. 12
J. 9
K. 8

Throwback to Math Class

A Pythagorean triple is a set of three positive integers that satisfy the Pythagorean theorem, $a^2 + b^2 = c^2$. The most common Pythagorean triples are 3-4-5, 5-12-13, and 8-15-17.

EXPLANATIONS

Alternatively, "test-the-test," starting with (H): a maximum box weight of 27 pounds means the average box weight is 25 pounds—too low. Try the next larger answer choice: (J). Substituting 28 pounds for the maximum box weight proves the answer is (J).

9. (B) ***Mathematics/Algebra and Functions/ Solving Algebraic Equations or Inequalities with One Variable/Simple Equations***
Write an equation for n as described in the item: $\frac{13}{2} - n = \frac{n}{\frac{2}{13}} \Rightarrow \frac{13}{2} - \frac{2n}{2} = \frac{13n}{2} \Rightarrow$

$\frac{13-2n}{2} = \frac{13n}{2} \Rightarrow$

$13 - 2n = 13n \Rightarrow$

$13 = 15n \Rightarrow n = \frac{13}{15}$.

The "test-the test" strategy can also be used to solve this item.

10. (H) ***Mathematics/Geometry/Complex Figures and Triangles/Properties of Triangles***
The figure is made up of two triangles with a common hypotenuse:

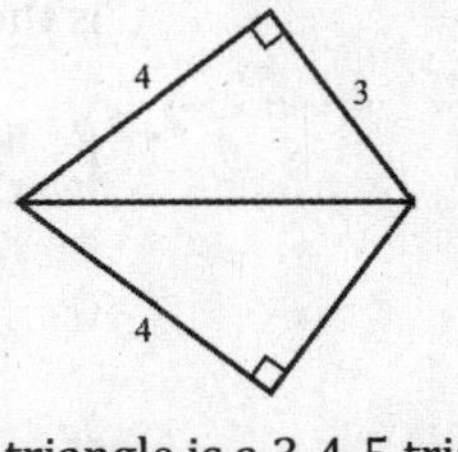

The top triangle is a 3-4-5 triangle with a hypotenuse of 5, so the bottom triangle, with a hypotenuse of 5 and one leg of 4, must also be a 3-4-5 triangle. Thus, the unlabeled side has a length of 3. The area of one 3-4-5 triangle is: $\text{area}_{\text{triangle}} = \frac{b \cdot h}{2} = \frac{3 \cdot 4}{2} = 6$. Thus, $\text{area}_{\text{quadrilateral}} = 2(\text{area}_{\text{triangle}}) = 2(6) = 12$.

The Cambridge Edge

Questions testing basic knowledge of the trigonometric functions are often found on the ACT. You can easily remember sine, cosine, and tangent using the mnemonic SOH-CAH-TOA.

$$\sin = \frac{\text{opp}}{\text{hyp}}$$

$$\cos = \frac{\text{adj}}{\text{hyp}}$$

$$\tan = \frac{\text{opp}}{\text{adj}}$$

11. In the figure below, what is the length of $\overline{BC}$? $\left(\sin 30^\circ = \frac{1}{2}\right)$

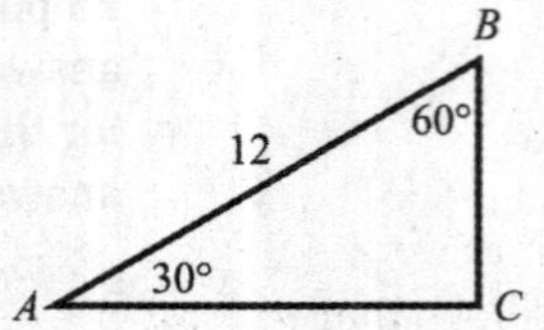

A. 2
B. 3
C. $3\sqrt{3}$
D. 6
E. $6\sqrt{3}$

12. After being dropped from a height of *h* meters, a ball bounces 3 meters high on the third bounce and $\frac{4}{3}$ meters high on the fifth bounce. The height of each bounce is lower by a constant factor. What is the value, in meters, of *h*?

F. $\frac{27}{8}$
G. $\frac{9}{2}$
H. $\frac{27}{4}$
J. $\frac{81}{8}$
K. $\frac{27}{2}$

EXPLANATIONS

11. (D) ***Mathematics/Geometry/Triangles/30°-60°-90° Triangles and Trigonometry/Definitions of the Six Trigonometric Functions***

You can solve this item using the special properties of 30°-60°-90° triangles. The length of the side opposite the 30° angle is equal to the hypotenuse length multiplied by $\frac{1}{2}$; the length of the side opposite the 60° angle is equal to the hypotenuse length multiplied by $\frac{\sqrt{3}}{2}$. Therefore, $\overline{BC} = \frac{\overline{AB}}{2} = \frac{12}{2} = 6$.

Alternatively, you can use the trigonometric identity for sine: $\sin \angle A = \frac{\text{side opposite } \angle A}{\text{hypotenuse}} \Rightarrow$ $\sin 30^\circ = \frac{\overline{BC}}{\overline{AB}} \Rightarrow \frac{1}{2} = \frac{\overline{BC}}{12} \Rightarrow \overline{BC} = 6$.

12. (J) ***Mathematics/Algebra and Functions/Evaluating Sequences***

The rebound of the ball's subsequent bounces constitutes a geometric sequence, so each successive term is equal to the previous term multiplied by a constant or common ratio, *r*: $b_n = rb_{n-1}$. In this case, we can use the given heights after the third bounce and the fifth bounce to determine the common ratio, *r*. If b_4 represents the height reached by the ball after the fourth bounce, then $b_4 = rb_3 \Rightarrow r = \frac{b_4}{b_3} = \frac{b_4}{3}$ and $b_5 = rb_4 \Rightarrow r = \frac{b_5}{b_4} = \frac{\frac{4}{3}}{b_4}$. Now, set these two equations for *r* equal to each other and solve for b_4:

$$\frac{b_4}{3} = \frac{\frac{4}{3}}{b_4} \Rightarrow (b_4)^2 = 3\left(\frac{4}{3}\right) = 4 \Rightarrow b_4 = 2.$$

Finally, plug this value for b_4 back into the simpler equation and solve for *r*:

$r = \frac{b_4}{3} = \frac{2}{3}$. And it is just a matter of working backward from the height after the 3rd bounce to the original *h*:

EXPLANATIONS

$$b_3 = rb_2 \Rightarrow 3 = \frac{2}{3}b_2 \Rightarrow b_2 = \frac{9}{2},$$
$$b_2 = rb_1 \Rightarrow \frac{9}{2} = \frac{2}{3}b_1 \Rightarrow b_1 = \frac{27}{4},$$
$$b_1 = rb_0 \Rightarrow \frac{27}{4} = \frac{2}{3}b_0 \Rightarrow b_0 = \frac{81}{8}.$$

13. Set $A = \{-2, -1, 0\}$, and set $B = \{-1, 0, 1\}$. If a is an element of set A and b is an element of set B, for how many pairs (a,b) is the product ab a member of both set A and set B?

A. 0
B. 2
C. 5
D. 6
E. 7

Throwback to Math Class

A set is a collection of things, people, numbers, or even concepts. Brackets are used to indicate set membership.

13. (D) *Mathematics/Statistics and Probability/Sets*

List all of the possible pairings for (a,b) and check each product, ab, for membership in both sets A and B:

(−2,−1): $-2 \cdot -1 = 2$ (neither set)
(−2,0): $-2 \cdot 0 = 0$ (both sets)
(−2,1): $-2 \cdot 1 = -2$ (set A only)
(−1,−1): $-1 \cdot -1 = 1$ (set B only)
(−1,0): $-1 \cdot 0 = 0$ (both sets)
(−1,1): $-1 \cdot 1 = -1$ (both sets)
(0,−1): $0 \cdot -1 = 0$ (both sets)
(0,0): $0 \cdot 0 = 0$ (both sets)
(0,1): $0 \cdot 1 = 0$ (both sets)

Therefore, 6 possible combinations of a and b return a product that is a member of both sets.

14. Which of the following is the complete solution set for $|2x+4| = 12$?

F. $\{-8, 4\}$
G. $\{-4, 8\}$
H. $\{0, 8\}$
J. $\{4, 8\}$
K. $\{6, 8\}$

Test-the-Test

Can't remember how to solve absolute value equations? Don't worry, you can still get this problem correct! Simply plug in the answer choices into the absolute value equation to determine which values yield a mathematically correct statement.

14. (F) *Mathematics/Algebra and Functions/Solving Algebraic Equations or Inequalities with One Variable/Equations Involving Absolute Value*

Solve the derived equations for x: $2x + 4 = 12 \Rightarrow 2x = 8 \Rightarrow x = 4$, and $-(2x+4) = 12 \Rightarrow -2x = 16 \Rightarrow x = -8$. Check $x = 4$ and $x = -8$ in the original equation: $|2(4)+4| = 12$ and $|2(-8)+4| = |-12| = 12$. Therefore, the complete solution set is $\{-8, 4\}$.

15. If $f(x) = \frac{(x-1)^2}{(-2-x)}$, for what value of x is $f(x)$ undefined?

A. −2
B. −1
C. 0
D. 1
E. 2

15. (A) *Mathematics/Algebra and Functions/Evaluating, Interpreting, and Creating Algebraic Functions/Concepts of Domain and Range*

Division by zero is undefined, so $f(x)$ is undefined for any value of x that results in a zero in the denominator of the rational expression. Set the denominator equal to zero and solve for x: $-2 - x = 0 \Rightarrow x = -2$. Therefore, $f(x)$ is undefined for $x = -2$.

Items #16–17 refer to the following table.

ANNUAL EXPENDITURES FOR THE JONES FAMILY (percent of annual expenditures) Category	2006	2007
Rent	23.0%	19.3%
Food	17.6%	18.2%
Clothing	14.2%	15.1%
Automobile	11.3%	12.3%
Utilities	10.9%	10.2%
Savings	6.2%	5.1%
Entertainment	5.2%	5.3%
Medical and Dental Care	4.0%	3.7%
Charitable Contributions	3.2%	3.9%
Household Furnishings	2.9%	3.1%
Other	1.5%	3.8%
Total	100.0%	100.0%
Total Expenditures	$34,987.00	$40,012.00

16. Approximately how much money did the Jones family spend on medical and dental care in 2006?

F. $1,200
G. $1,400
H. $1,520
J. $2,250
K. $4,000

17. If the categories in the table are rank ordered from one to eleven in each year, how many categories would have a different rank from 2006 to 2007?

A. two
B. three
C. four
D. five
E. six

The Cambridge Edge

Item #16 is best solved by quickly punching the arithmetic into a calculator. But here's a mental math trick for percentages that could come in handy later for approximations:

1% of a number is simply the number with the decimal shifted twice to the left. So 1% of $35,000 is $350.00. Now, to compute 4% of $35,000, multiply the value of 1% by 4: 4 × $350.00 = $1,400.

EXPLANATIONS

16. (G) ***Mathematics/Statistics and Probability/Data Representation/Tables and Number and Quantity/Percentages*** In 2006, medical and dental care accounted for 4.0% of expenditures. Since the item specifically asks for an approximation, use $35,000 as the value of expenditures in 2006: $0.04 \cdot \$35{,}000 = \$1{,}400$.

17. (E) ***Mathematics/Statistics and Probability/Data Representation/Tables*** Notice that the categories for 2006 are already in order, from greatest to least. Observing the 2007 column, Savings and Entertainment have flipped, Medical and Dental Care and Charitable Contributions have flipped, and Household Furnishings and Other have flipped, for a total of six categories that have changed position.

Throwback to Math Class

$\sec = \frac{1}{\cos} = \frac{\text{hyp}}{\text{adj}}$

$\csc = \frac{1}{\sin} = \frac{\text{hyp}}{\text{opp}}$

$\cot = \frac{1}{\tan} = \frac{\text{adj}}{\text{opp}}$

18. For the figure below, which of the following statements is INCORRECT?

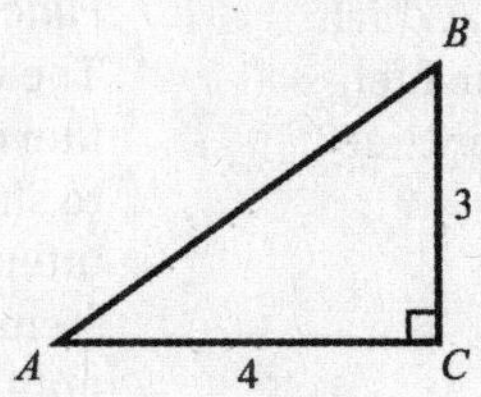

F. $\sin A = \frac{5}{13}$

G. $\cos A = \frac{12}{13}$

H. $\tan A = \frac{5}{12}$

J. $\cot A = \frac{13}{5}$

K. $\sec A = \frac{13}{12}$

EXPLANATIONS

18. (J) ***Mathematics/Geometry/Definitions of the Six Trigonometric Functions***
Since the figure is a right triangle with sides that are 5 and 12 units long, the hypotenuse must be 13 units long. The values of the six trigonometric functions for $\angle A$ are:

$\sin A = \frac{\overline{BC}}{\overline{AB}} = \frac{5}{13}$; $\cos A = \frac{\overline{AC}}{\overline{AB}} = \frac{12}{13}$;

$\tan A = \frac{\overline{BC}}{\overline{AC}} = \frac{5}{12}$; $\cot A = \frac{\overline{AC}}{\overline{BC}} = \frac{12}{5}$;

$\csc A = \frac{\overline{AB}}{\overline{BC}} = \frac{13}{5}$; $\sec A = \frac{\overline{AB}}{\overline{AC}} = \frac{13}{12}$. All of the answer choices are true except (J): $\cot A \neq \frac{13}{5}$.

Throwback to Math Class

The key phrase in this problem is "constant rate." This indicates that for every unit increase of the input (time), the output (fuel consumption) increases by a constant amount. This is a linear relationship, so the corresponding graph will also be linear.

19. When the 10-gallon tank of an emergency generator is filled to capacity, the generator operates without interruption for 20 hours, consuming fuel at a constant rate until all the fuel is consumed. Which of the graphs below represents the fuel consumption of the generator over time?

A.

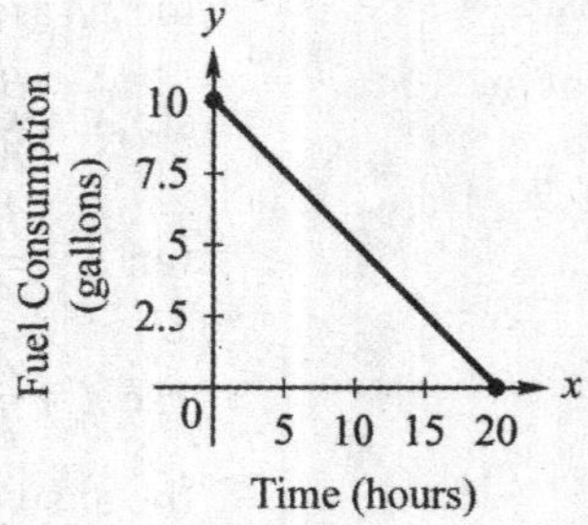

B.

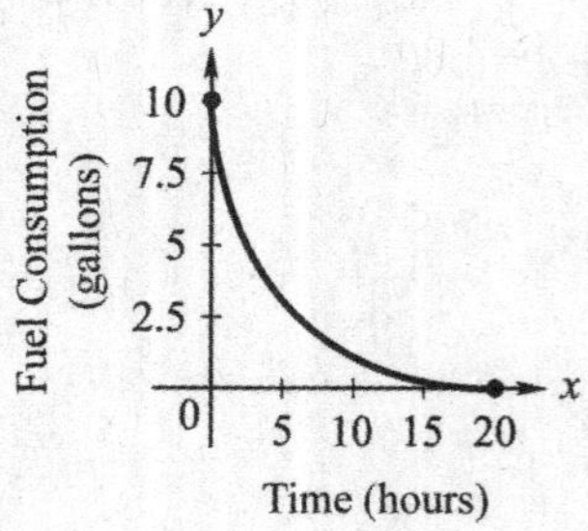

C.

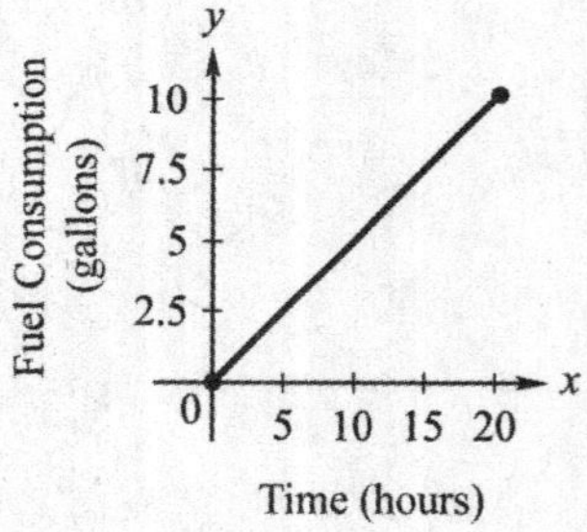

D.

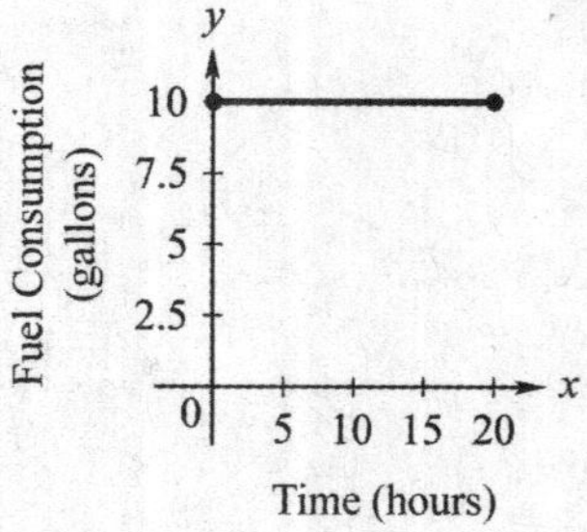

E.

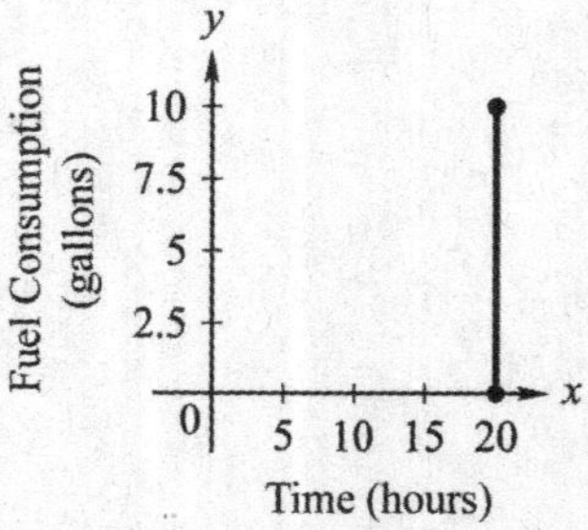

EXPLANATIONS

19. (C) ***Mathematics/Algebra and Functions/ Qualitative Behavior of Graphs of Functions***

The longer the generator runs, the more fuel it uses, and (C) is the only graph to show such a relationship. (A) is an interesting possibility, but (A) shows "remaining fuel" over time of operation, not the fuel already consumed.

20. In the figure below, $\overline{PQ}$ is tangent to circle O at point S and $\overline{QR}$ is tangent to circle O at point T. If the radius of circle O is 2, what is the area of the shaded portion of the figure?

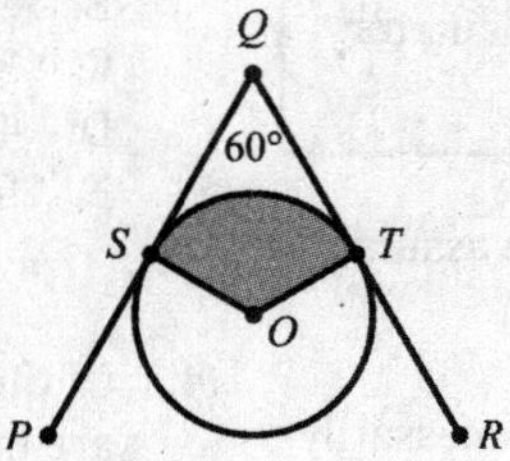

F. $\frac{\pi}{3}$
G. $\frac{2\pi}{3}$
H. π
J. $\frac{4\pi}{3}$
K. 2π

EXPLANATIONS

20. (J) ***Mathematics/Geometry/Complex Figures and Lines and Angles and Circles*** The radii $\overline{OS}$ and $\overline{OT}$ form right angles with $\overline{PQ}$ and $\overline{QR}$, respectively. Consequently, we know the measures of three of the angles in the quadrilateral *SQTO*: 90°, 90°, and 60°. Since the sum of the interior angles of a quadrilateral total 360°, $90° + 90° + 60° + \angle SOT = 360° \Rightarrow \angle SOT = 120°$. Since $\frac{120°}{360°} = \frac{1}{3}$, the shaded area is equal to one-third of the area of the circle: $\frac{1}{3}\pi(2)^2 = \frac{4\pi}{3}$.

TIMED QUIZ *(20 items; 20 minutes)*

DIRECTIONS: Solve each item and choose the correct answer choice. Calculator use is permitted; however, some items are best solved without the use of a calculator. Answers are on p. 440.

NOTES: All of the following should be assumed, unless otherwise stated.

1. Illustrative figures are NOT necessarily drawn to scale.
2. The word *average* indicates arithmetic mean.
3. The word *line* indicates a straight line.
4. Geometric figures lie in a plane.

1. The figure below is a plan that shows a solid set of steps to be constructed from concrete blocks of equal size. How many blocks are needed to construct the steps?

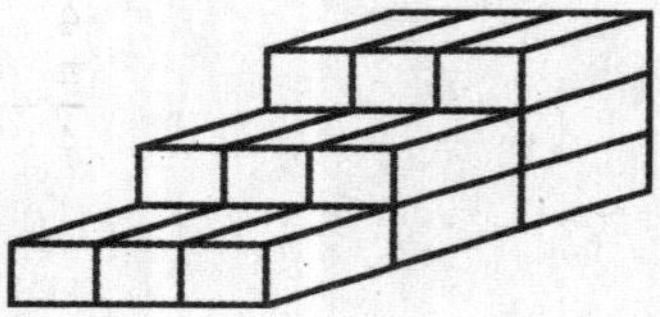

A. 12
B. 15
C. 18
D. 21
E. 24

2. In the figure below, what is the value of x?

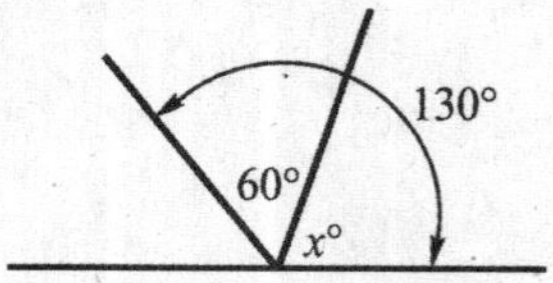

F. 70
G. 60
H. 50
J. 40
K. 30

3. If $2^{x+1} = 4^{x-1}$, what is the value of x?

A. 1
B. 2
C. 3
D. 4
E. 5

4. Of the actors in a certain play, five actors are in Act I, 12 actors are in Act II, and 13 actors are in Act III. If 10 of the actors are in exactly two of the three acts and all of the other actors are in just one act, how many actors are in the play?

F. 17
G. 20
H. 24
J. 30
K. 38

5. In the figure below, $\overline{AB} \cong \overline{BC} \cong \overline{CA}$. What is the value of y?

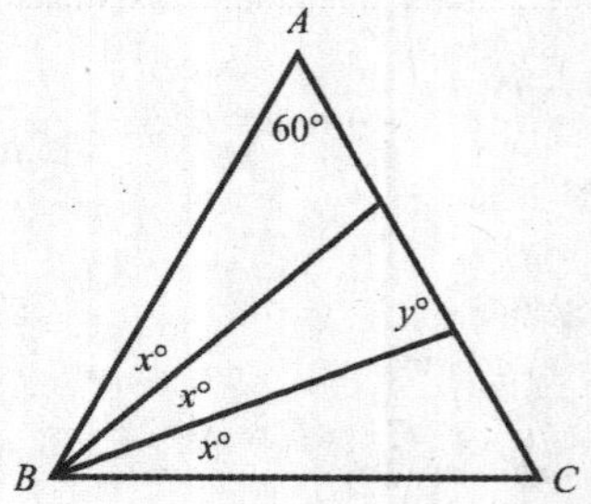

A. 20
B. 60
C. 80
D. 100
E. 120

6. Under certain conditions, a bicycle traveling k meters per second requires $\frac{k^2}{20} + k$ meters to stop. If $k = 10$, how many meters does the bicycle need to stop?

F. 10
G. 12
H. 15
J. 20
K. 30

Throwback to Math Class

The symbol $\cong$ means "congruent." Two geometric figures are congruent if they have the same size and the same angles. This is not to be confused with *similar* geometric figures, which means that the geometric figures are *proportional* in size.

> **Throwback to Math Class**
>
> 1. The radius of a circle is equal to one-half of the diameter: $r = \frac{1}{2}d$
> 2. The circumference of a circle is equal to the diameter multiplied by π: $C = \pi d$
> 3. The area of a circle is equal to the radius squared multiplied by π: $A = \pi r^2$

> **Throwback to Math Class**
>
> The slope of a line is one of the most important concepts to master for the ACT. The slope of the line that contains two points (x_1, y_1) and (x_2, y_2) is computed using the following formula:
>
> $$\frac{y_2 - y_1}{x_2 - x_1}$$

7. $\frac{2-i}{6+i} = ?$

A. $\frac{13-8i}{35}$
B. $\frac{11-8i}{35}$
C. $\frac{13-8i}{37}$
D. $\frac{11-8i}{37}$
E. $\frac{1}{3}$

8. An album contains x black-and-white photographs and y color photographs. If the album contains 24 photographs, then which of the following CANNOT be true?

F. $x = y$
G. $x = 2y$
H. $x = 3y$
J. $x = 4y$
K. Cannot be determined from the given information

9. If $2a = 3b = 4c$, then what is the average (arithmetic mean) of a, b, and c, in terms of a?

A. $\frac{13a}{18}$
B. $\frac{4a}{3}$
C. $\frac{13a}{9}$
D. $2a$
E. $\frac{8a}{3}$

10. If $x = 6 + y$ and $4x = 3 - 2y$, what is the value of x?

F. 4
G. $\frac{11}{3}$
H. $\frac{5}{2}$
J. $-\frac{2}{3}$
K. $-\frac{7}{2}$

11. If $\frac{2}{3}$ is written as a decimal to 101 places, what is the sum of the first 100 digits to the right of the decimal point?

A. 66
B. 595
C. 599
D. 600
E. 601

12. In the figure below, O is the center of the circle with radius 1. What is the area of the shaded region?

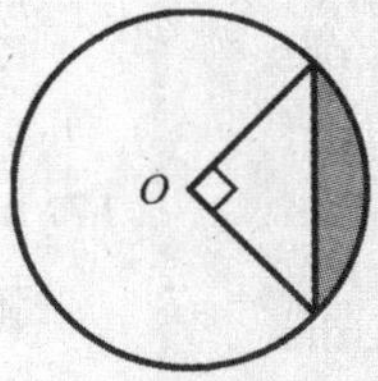

F. $\frac{3\pi}{4} + \frac{1}{2}$
G. $\frac{3\pi}{4} - \frac{1}{2}$
H. $\frac{\pi}{4} + \frac{1}{2}$
J. $\frac{\pi}{4} - \frac{1}{2}$
K. $\pi - 1$

13. If $f(3) = 5$ and $f(7) = 7$, what is the slope of the graph of $f(x)$ in the coordinate plane?

A. -2
B. $\frac{1}{2}$
C. 1
D. $\frac{1}{2}$
E. 2

14. In a list of the first 100 positive integers, the digit 9 appears how many times?

F. 9
G. 10
H. 11
J. 19
K. 20

15. If $\frac{x}{x+3}=\frac{3}{4}$, and $x \neq -3$, then $x = ?$

A. 3
B. 4
C. 5
D. 7
E. 9

16. Which of the following is the complete solution set for $\sqrt{2x+3}+2=5$?

F. {}
G. {−1}
H. {3}
J. {−1, 3}
K. {1, 2}

17. In the figure below, what is the length of $\overline{AC}$? $\left(\sin\angle ABD = \frac{\sqrt{7}}{4}\right)$

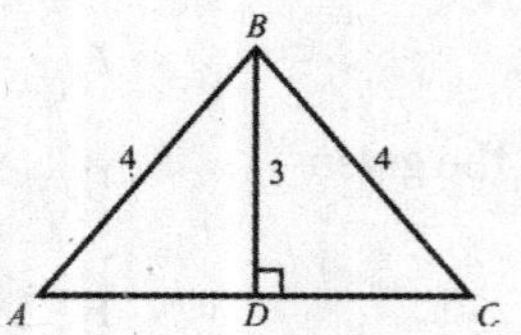

A. 5
B. $2\sqrt{7}$
C. $4\sqrt{3}$
D. 7
E. 10

18. A dartboard has four concentric circles. If the diameter of each circle except for the smallest is twice that of the next smaller circle, what is the probability that a randomly thrown dart that strikes the figure will strike the shaded portion of the figure?

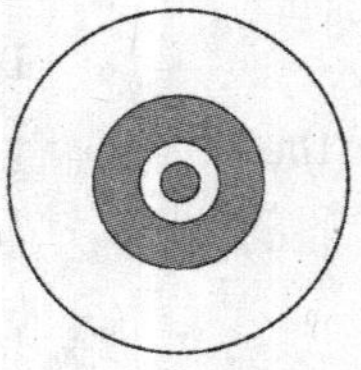

F. $\frac{3}{16}$
G. $\frac{13}{64}$
H. $\frac{1}{4}$
J. $\frac{17}{64}$
K. $\frac{1}{2}$

Throwback to Math Class

Steps for solving radical equations:

1. Isolate the radical expression.
2. Eliminate the radical sign by squaring (or cubing, etc.) both sides of the equation.
3. Solve for the unknown variable.
4. Check the solution(s) in the equation.

It is extremely important that you check your answers when dealing with radical equations. Squaring both sides of an equation while solving for *x* can generate extraneous solutions.

19. If $f(3)=4$ and $f(-3)=1$, what is the *y*-intercept of the graph of $f(x)$ in the coordinate plane?

A. $-\frac{5}{2}$
B. $-\frac{2}{5}$
C. 0
D. $\frac{2}{5}$
E. $\frac{5}{2}$

20. A tissue box has dimensions shown below. What is the total surface area of the box, in square inches?

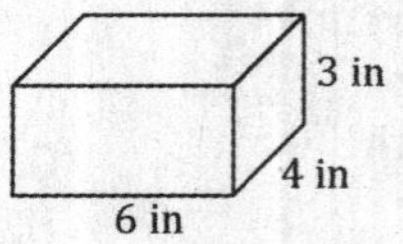

F. 24
G. 36
H. 48
J. 54
K. 108

MATH

REVIEW

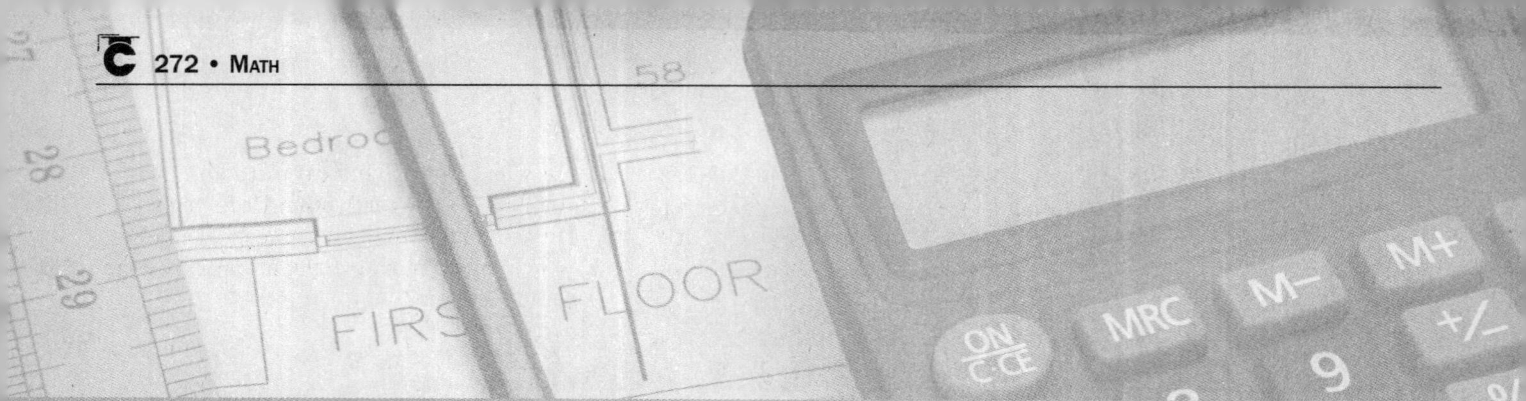

This section contains additional Mathematics items for further practice. Answers are on page 440.

DIRECTIONS: Solve each item and choose the correct answer choice. Calculator use is permitted; however, some items are best solved without the use of a calculator.

NOTES: All of the following should be assumed, unless otherwise stated.

1. Illustrative figures are NOT necessarily drawn to scale.
2. The word *average* indicates arithmetic mean.
3. The word *line* indicates a straight line.
4. Geometric figures lie in a plane.

The Cambridge Edge

Know how to use your calculator to do scientific notation problems. Some calculators allow you to input the numbers in scientific notation and return the product in scientific notation as well. Know the capabilities of your calculator. If you don't have a calculator that takes scientific notation inputs, then use the calculator to multiply the coefficients.

1. The approximate distance from the earth to the moon is 1,261,392,000 feet. If an astronaut has made three trips to the moon (and back), what is the approximate total distance he has traveled between the earth and the moon?

A. 1.26×10^6
B. 7.57×10^6
C. 1.26×10^9
D. 7.57×10^9
E. 7.57×10^{12}

2. If each of the dimensions of a rectangle is increased by 100%, by what percent is the area increased?

F. 100%
G. 200%
H. 300%
J. 400%
K. 500%

3. What is 10% of $\frac{x}{3}$ if $\frac{2x}{3}$ is 10% of 60?

A. 0.1
B. 0.2
C. 0.3
D. 0.4
E. 0.5

4. In the figure below, *M* and *N* are midpoints of sides $\overline{PR}$ and $\overline{PQ}$, respectively, of ΔPQR. What is the ratio of the area of ΔMNS to that of ΔPQR?

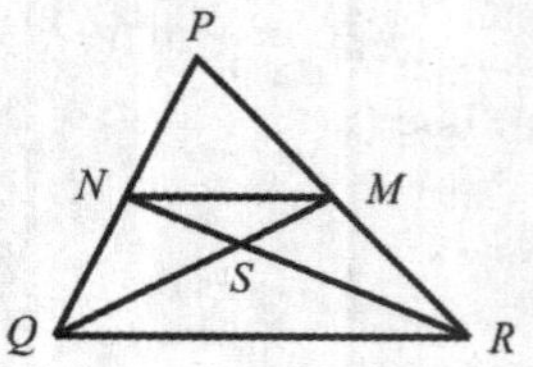

F. 2:5
G. 1:4
H. 2:9
J. 1:8
K. 1:12

5. A cube has an edge that is 4 inches long. If the edge is increased by 25%, which of the following is the best approximation of the percent increase in the volume of the cube?

A. 25%
B. 48%
C. 73%
D. 95%
E. 122%

6. In the figure below is a portion of the (x,y) coordinate plane. If each small square has an area of 1 and the coordinates of point P are (3,7), what are the (x,y) coordinates of point Q?

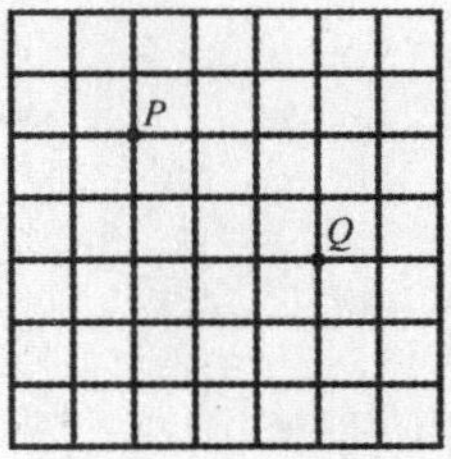

F. (5,6)
G. (1,10)
H. (6,9)
J. (6,5)
K. (5,10)

7. The average of 8 numbers is 6; the average of 6 other numbers is 8. What is the average of all 14 numbers?

A. 6
B. $6\frac{6}{7}$
C. 7
D. $7\frac{2}{7}$
E. $8\frac{1}{7}$

8. Which of the following is the matrix product of $\begin{bmatrix} 0.5 & -3 & 0.25 \\ -1 & 2 & 1.5 \end{bmatrix}$ and $\begin{bmatrix} 8 & 0 \\ -1 & 2 \\ 12 & 6 \end{bmatrix}$?

F. $\begin{bmatrix} 10 & -4.5 \\ 8 & 13 \end{bmatrix}$
G. $\begin{bmatrix} 10 & 0 \\ 1 & 4 \end{bmatrix}$
H. $\begin{bmatrix} 10 & -24 & 2 \\ -2.5 & 7 & 2.75 \\ 0 & -24 & 12 \end{bmatrix}$
J. $\begin{bmatrix} 4 & 0 & 0.25 \\ 1 & 4 & 1.5 \\ 12 & 6 & 0 \end{bmatrix}$
K. $\begin{bmatrix} 8.5 & -3 & 0.25 \\ -2 & 4 & 1.5 \\ 12 & 6 & 0 \end{bmatrix}$

The Cambridge Edge

When multiplying matrices, don't do more work than is necessary to answer the item. If matrix A has dimensions $m \times n$ and matrix B has dimensions $p \times q$, the product AB will have dimensions $m \times q$. The product BA will have dimensions $p \times n$. Eliminate any choices that don't contain the correct number of columns or rows. Then, determine only as many elements in the product matrix necessary to choose between the remaining choices.

9. Doreen can wash her car in 15 minutes, while her younger brother Dave takes twice as long to do the same job. If they work together, how many minutes will the job take them?

A. 5
B. $7\frac{1}{2}$
C. 10
D. $22\frac{1}{2}$
E. 30

10. In the figure below, the sides of the large square are each 14 inches long. Joining the midpoints of each opposite side forms 4 smaller squares. What is the value of y, in inches?

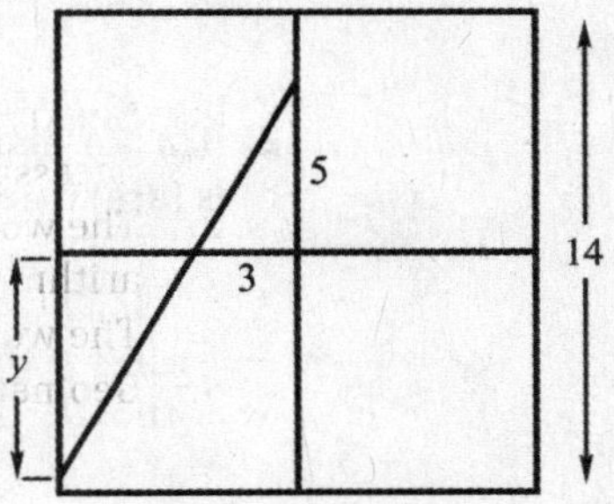

F. 5
G. 6
H. $6\frac{5}{8}$
J. $6\frac{2}{3}$
K. $6\frac{4}{5}$

11. In the figure below, $PQRS$ is a parallelogram, and $\overline{ST} = \overline{TV} = \overline{VR}$. If $\angle PTS = 90°$, what is the ratio of the area of ΔSPT to the area of the parallelogram?

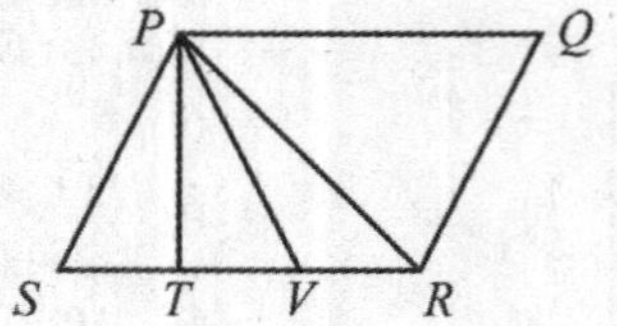

A. $\frac{1}{6}$
B. $\frac{1}{5}$
C. $\frac{2}{7}$
D. $2\frac{1}{3}$
E. Cannot be determined from the given information

12. If $p > q$ and $r < 0$, which of the following is (are) true?

I. $pr < qr$
II. $p + r > q + r$
III. $p - r < q - r$

F. I only
G. II only
H. I and III only
J. I and II only
K. I, II, and III

Throwback to Math Class

Cylinder volume:

$\pi r^2 h$

Cylinder lateral surface area:

πdh

Cylinder total surface area:

$\pi dh + 2\pi r^2$

13. A pound of water is evaporated from 6 pounds of seawater that is 4% salt. What is the percentage of salt in the remaining solution?

A. 3.6%
B. 4%
C. 4.8%
D. 5.2%
E. 6%

14. Which of the following expressions correctly describes the mathematical relationship below?

3 less than the product of 4 and x

F. $4x - 3$
G. $3x - 4$
H. $4(x - 3)$
J. $3(4x)$
K. $\frac{4x}{3}$

15. In the figure below, what percentage of the area of rectangle $PQRS$ is shaded?

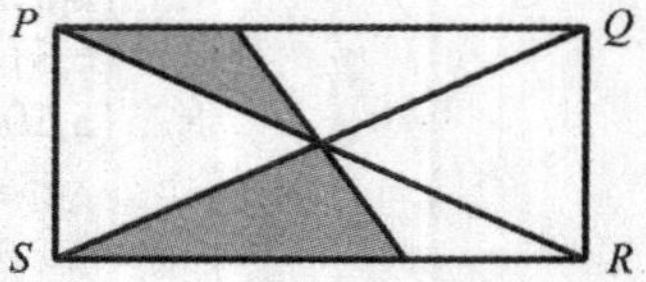

A. 20%
B. 25%
C. 30%
D. $33\frac{1}{3}\%$
E. 35%

16. A cylindrical container has a diameter of 14 inches and a height of 6 inches. Since one gallon equals 231 cubic inches, what is the approximate capacity, in gallons, of the tank?

F. $\frac{2}{3}$
G. $1\frac{1}{7}$
H. $2\frac{2}{7}$
J. $2\frac{2}{3}$
K. 4

17. If $12 + x = 36 - y$, then $x + y = ?$

A. -48
B. -24
C. 3
D. 24
E. 48

18. In the figure below, *PQRS* is a square and *PTS* is an equilateral triangle. What is the degree measure of $\angle TRS$?

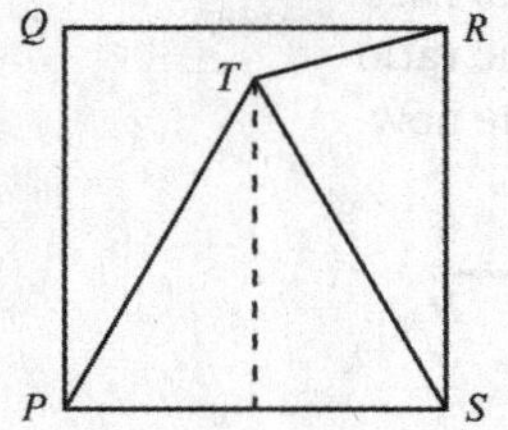

F. 60
G. 75
H. 80
J. 90
K. Cannot be determined from the given information

19. A line segment in the (*x*,*y*) coordinate plane has endpoints $(-4, -2)$ and $(6, 7)$. What is the midpoint of the line segment?

A. (2, 5)
B. (10, 9)
C. (−10, −9)
D. (1, 2.5)
E. (1.5, 5)

20. Paul can paint a fence in 2 hours and Fred can paint the same fence in 3 hours. If Paul and Fred work together, how many hours will it take them to paint the fence?

F. 5
G. $2\frac{1}{2}$
H. $1\frac{1}{5}$
J. 1
K. $\frac{5}{6}$

Throwback to Math Class

Memorize these properties:

$\log_a(x) = y \Leftrightarrow a^y = x$

$\log_a(xy) =$
$\log_a(x) + \log_b(y)$

$\log_a\left(\frac{x}{y}\right) =$
$\log_a(x) - \log_b(y)$

Be careful: a common mistake students make is assuming that
$\log_a(x+y) =$
$\log_a(x) + \log_b(y)$.

This is incorrect!

21. A motorist drives 60 miles to her destination at an average speed of 40 miles per hour and makes the return trip at an average speed of 30 miles per hour. What is her average speed, in miles per hour, for the entire trip?

A. 17
B. $34\frac{2}{7}$
C. 35
D. $43\frac{1}{3}$
E. 70

22. If $\log_3 a = x$ and $\log_3 b = y$, what is the value of $\log_3(ab^2)$?

F. xy^2
G. $x + y^2$
H. $x + 2y$
J. $a + b^2$
K. $a + 2b$

23. A sphere with a diameter of 18 feet sits inside of a cylinder. It is tangent to the top and bottom of the cylinder and has the same diameter as the cylinder. What is the volume of the space outside of the sphere but inside of the cylinder?

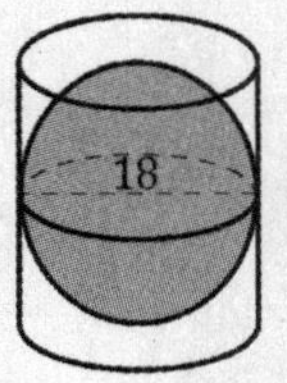

A. 486
B. 486π
C. 972π
D. 1,458π
E. 2,430π

24. Which of the following values of *x* satisfies the equation $\log_6 x = 3$?

F. 9
G. 18
H. 36
J. 216
K. 729

25. In the figure below, $\overline{AB}$ is three times longer than $\overline{BC}$, and $\overline{CD}$ is two times longer than $\overline{BC}$. If $\overline{BC}$ is removed from the line and the other two segments are joined to form one line, what is the ratio of the original length of $\overline{AD}$ to the new length of $\overline{AD}$?

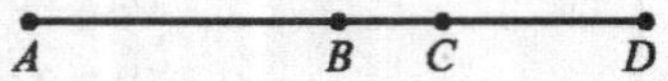

A. 3:2
B. 6:5
C. 5:4
D. 7:6
E. 11:10

26. If $(x+1)(x-2)$ is positive, then which of the following statements is true?

F. $x < -1$ or $x > 2$
G. $x > -1$ or $x < 2$
H. $-1 < x < 2$
J. $-2 < x < 1$
K. $x = -1$ or $x = 2$

27. In the table below, which yearly period had the smallest percent increase in sales?

ABC SOUND STORES Annual Sale of Compact Discs	
Year	Number Sold
2002	7,000
2003	9,000
2004	12,000
2005	16,000
2006	20,000
2007	24,000

A. 2002–2003
B. 2003–2004
C. 2004–2005
D. 2005–2006
E. 2006–2007

Throwback to Math Class

To find percent change, put the change in the quantity over the original amount. Multiply this fraction by 100 to change the fraction to a percent.

If the change in the quantity is positive (new value − original > 0), you are computing the percent increase. If the change is negative (new value − original < 0), you are computing the percent decrease.

28. For the figure below, which one of the following statements is true?

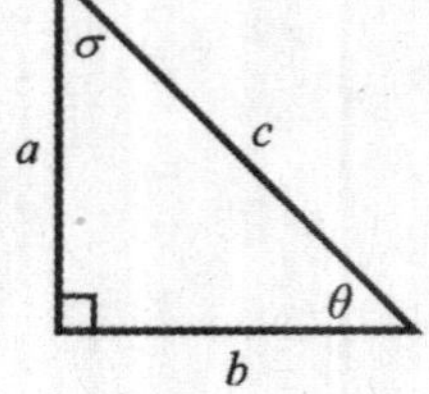

F. $\sin\theta = \frac{b}{c}$
G. $\tan\sigma = \frac{a}{b}$
H. $\cos\theta = \frac{c}{a}$
J. $\sin\theta = \cos\sigma$
K. $\cot\sigma = \tan\sigma$

29. In the figure below, if $\arcsin s = 2(\arcsin d)$, then $x = ?$

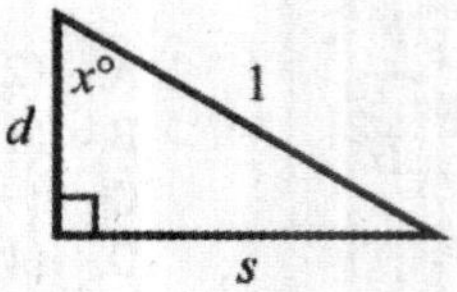

A. 15
B. 30
C. 45
D. 60
E. 75

30. In the figure below, if $\overline{AC}$ is the diameter of the circle, B is a point on the circle, and $\sin\theta = \frac{1}{2}$, then $\sin\phi = ?$

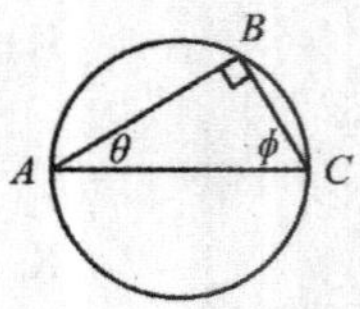

F. $\frac{\sqrt{2}}{3}$
G. $\frac{\sqrt{3}}{3}$
H. $\frac{\sqrt{3}}{2}$
J. $\frac{2\sqrt{2}}{3}$
K. $\frac{2\sqrt{3}}{2}$

31. The figure below is a possible graph of which of the following equations?

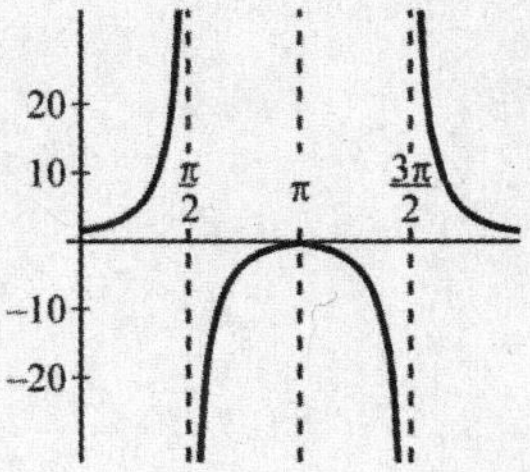

A. $y = 2(\sin x)$
B. $y = \sin x + 2$
C. $y = \csc x + 1$
D. $y = \csc x - 1$
E. $y = \sec x + 1$

32. If θ is an acute angle and $\cos\theta = \frac{b}{c}$, $b > 0$ and $c > 0$ and $b \neq c$, then $\sin\theta$ is equal to which of the following?

F. $\frac{b}{\sqrt{b^2 - c^2}}$

G. $\frac{c}{\sqrt{b^2 - b^2}}$

H. $\frac{\sqrt{b^2 - c^2}}{b}$

J. $\frac{\sqrt{b^2 - c^2}}{c}$

K. $\frac{\sqrt{c^2 - b^2}}{c}$

STRATEGY SUMMARY

MATH STRATEGIES

When approaching a Mathematics item, there are several things to which you should pay careful attention:

Figures

Figures are usually, but not always, drawn to scale. When all other options for answering the item fail, try the strategy of assuming the figure *is* drawn to scale. Then, use the figure to help you answer the item.

Answer Choices

Most answer choices are arranged in order of ascending or descending value and many incorrect answer choices correspond to conceptual errors.

"Signal" Words

Typically, "signal" words are capitalized (e.g., thought-reversers, such as "NOT," "CANNOT," and "EXCEPT"); however, they may sometimes be underlined or italicized (e.g., specified units). While the specific formatting of these words may vary, they can be critical to correctly understanding the item. Pay careful attention to thought-reversers, as they reverse the apparent meaning of an item.

Ladder of Difficulty

Difficult Mathematics items tend to be clustered near the end of the section. When solving items that are high on the ladder of difficulty, be wary of simplistic answers and the "Cannot be determined..." response. Remember to pace yourself—difficult, time-consuming items have the same value as the easy items.

Item Stems

Read the item stem first. Only then should you read the details of the item, keeping this item stem in mind.

Solutions

Double-check the solution by confirming that it answers the particular question that is being asked. When applicable, this confirmation includes verifying that the solution is given in the units specified by the item stem.

If you are unable to either find an elegant (quick) solution or solve the item directly based on subject knowledge, the following alternative solutions strategies can be extremely helpful:

"Test-the-Test" Strategy

The correct answer to any item is always one of five given choices. Sometimes, the easiest and quickest way to solve an item is to test each of the answer choices. The "test-the-test" strategy can mean plugging answer choices back into the item (starting with the middle answer choice) to test the validity of an expression, or it can mean checking each answer choice against any stated conditions. The "test-the-test" strategy is typically useful for items with numerical solutions or variables and values that meet stated conditions.

"Plug-and-Chug" Strategy

This strategy is similar to the "test-the-test" strategy in that the item stem and answer choices (rather than direct mathematical solution strategies) are used to isolate the correct answer. The difference is that rather than testing the validity of each answer choice against the item stem conditions, the item stem and/or answer choices are evaluated by plugging in chosen numbers: "plug-and-chug." This strategy is especially helpful when solving Algebra items.

"Eliminate-and-Guess" Strategy

If unable to determine the correct answer directly by using mathematical methods or indirectly by using either the "test-the-test" or "plug-and-chug" strategy, eliminate as many answer choices as possible and then guess from the remaining answer choices. For difficult mathematics items, eliminate answer choices that can be reached either by a single step or by copying a number from the item.

CHECKLIST OF SKILLS AND CONCEPTS

Number and Quantity

___ Basic Arithmetic Manipulations
___ Properties of Numbers (Odd, Even, Negative, Positive, Consecutive)
___ Scientific Notation
___ Complex Numbers
___ Matrices and Vectors
___ Ratios (Two-Part, Three-Part, Weighted), Rates, and Proportions (Direct, Indirect)
___ Percentages (Change, Original Amount, Price Increase)

Algebra and Functions

___ Evaluation of Expressions (Rational, Radical)
___ Exponents (Integer, Rational, Negative)
___ Factoring
___ Sequence
___ Solving Single Variable Equations and Inequalities
___ Absolute Value
___ Function Math
___ Domain and Range
___ Solving Equations (Multi-Variable, Linear, Simultaneous, Quadratic)
___ Story Problems: Work (Joint Effort), Averages

Coordinate Geometry

___ Coordinate Plane
___ Slope of a Line
___ Slope-Intercept Form of a Linear Equation
___ Distance Formula
___ Graphing Linear Equations
___ Graphing First-Degree Inequalities
___ Graphing Quadratic Equations
___ Permutations of Equations and Graphs

Geometry

___ Lines and Angles (Perpendicular, Parallel, Intersecting, Big Angle/Little Angle Theorem)
___ Triangles (Equilateral, Isosceles, Acute, Obtuse, Perimeter, Area, Altitudes, Angles, Bisectors, Pythagorean Theorem)
___ Quadrilaterals (Squares, Rectangles, Rhombuses, Parallelograms, Trapezoids, Perimeter, Area)
___ Polygons (Sum of Interior Angles)
___ Circles (Chords, Tangents, Radius, Diameter, Circumference, Area)
___ Solids (Cubes, Cylinders, Spheres, Volumes, Surface Areas)
___ Complex Figures

Trigonometry

___ Trigonometric Functions
___ Trigonometric Values
___ Trigonometric Relationships

Statistics and Probability

___ Measures of Center (Average, Median, Mode)
___ Probability
___ Counting Methods (Combinations, Permutations)
___ Sets (Union, Intersection, Elements)
___ Graphs (Bar, Cumulative, Line)
___ Pie Charts
___ Tables
___ Scatterplots

SCIENCE

Course Concept Outline

I. TEST MECHANICS 283

- **A. Overview** 284
- **B. Anatomy** *(Items #1–4)* 285–287
- **C. Pacing** 287
- **D. Time Trial** *(Items #1–5)* 288–290
- **E. Game Plan** 290
  1. Quickly Preview the Test Section, but Skip the Directions 290
  2. Personalize the Passage Order 290
  3. Read the Passage 291
  4. Answer the Items 291
  5. Use the Answer Choices 292
  6. Eliminate Choices, Guess (If Necessary), and Move On 292

II. LESSON | PRELIMINARIES[1]

- **A. Item Profiles**
- **B. Facts about the Science Test**
  1. Three Types of Passages
     - a) Data Representation
     - b) Research Summary
     - c) Conflicting Viewpoints
  2. Science Items Test Reasoning, Not Knowledge
- **C. Item-Types**
  1. Comprehension
  2. Analysis
  3. Application
- **D. General Strategies**
  1. Plan Your Attack—Easiest Passages First
  2. Do Not Preview Item Stems before Reading a Passage
  3. Underline Key Words and Phrases
  4. Pay Attention to What Is There, Not What Isn't There

1 Some concepts in this Course Concept Outline are not illustrated through examples in your student text but may be covered by your instructor in class. They are included here to provide a complete outline of your course.

5. Pay Attention to Differences
6. Watch for Assumptions
7. Look for Trends
8. Transcribe Answers in Groups
9. Answer the Question That Is Being Asked
10. Work Out the Answer First
11. Make Notes to Clarify Viewpoints

III. LESSON 1 | DATA REPRESENTATION 294

A. Graphs 294

1. Straight Lines
2. Parabolic Curves
3. Graph Reading Strategy *(Items #1–3)* 294–295

B. Tables 294

1. Understanding the Nature of Data *(Items #4–5)* 295
2. Recognizing Trends *(Items #6–8)* 296
3. Drawing Conclusions *(Item #9)* 296

C. Typical Data Representation Items *(Items #10–22)* **296–299**
D. Data Representation Strategies *(Items #23–40)* **300–305**

IV. LESSON 2 | RESEARCH SUMMARY 306

A. Understanding Experimental Design
B. Predicting Results
C. Evaluating Data
D. Typical Research Summary Items *(Items #1–11)* **306–310**
E. Research Summary Strategies *(Items #12–34)* **310–319**

V. LESSON 3 | CONFLICTING VIEWPOINTS 320

A. Predicting Results
B. Spotting the Assumptions
C. Picking the Best Argument
D. Typical Conflicting Viewpoints Items *(Items #1–11)* **320–323**
E. Conflicting Viewpoints Strategies *(Items #12–29)* **323–327**

VI. QUIZZES 329

A. Directed Study Quiz *(Items #1–16)* **330–336**
B. Timed Quiz *(Items #1–16)* **337–340**

VII. REVIEW 341–358

VIII. STRATEGY SUMMARY 359

SCIENCE

TEST MECHANICS

OVERVIEW

> **Ace the Pace**
>
> You may be better at certain problem types or groups of questions. All questions are worth the same number of points, so finish those you are best at first and then work on harder problems.

The ACT Science Test consists of 40 multiple-choice items divided into six or seven groups. Each group of items is based on a report of data findings, a description of an experiment, or the presentation of a debate on different scientific theories. The time limit for the Science Test is 35 minutes. Calculators are NOT allowed on the Science Test.

We'll call the initial presentation a "passage," whether it is a report of data (Data Representation), a description of an experiment (Research Summary), or a debate of a theory (Conflicting Viewpoints). So, just as the English and Reading Tests have passages with associated items, the Science Test has passages (of the three types) with associated items. We'll use this terminology even though "passage" doesn't quite fit here since the Science Test uses a lot of diagrams, pictures, tables, and graphs.

The Science Test roughly follows the content of science courses taught in grades 7 through 12. Passages use content from the following areas:

- **Biology:** botany, cellular biology, ecology, evolution, genetics, microbiology, zoology
- **Chemistry:** biochemistry, organic chemistry, nuclear chemistry, thermochemistry, acids and bases, kinetics and equilibria, properties of matter
- **Earth/Space Sciences:** astronomy, environmental science, geology, meteorology, oceanography
- **Physics:** mechanics, thermodynamics, fluids, solids, electromagnetism, optics

Although these are obviously "science" subjects, you don't really need to know any science—beyond some basic concepts—to do well on this part of the exam. In fact, the ACT Science Test would be more accurately labeled "Science Reasoning" Test because that phrase would emphasize that the items test reasoning ability and not the mastery of some specific body of scientific knowledge.

ANATOMY

DIRECTIONS: The passage below is followed by several items. After reading the passage, choose the best answer to each item. You may refer to the passage as often as necessary. You are NOT permitted the use of a calculator.

PASSAGE I

Passage Perfect

Remember, you do not need to know anything about particular chemicals or equations to correctly answer questions like this. In fact, you can replace the chemical name with its first letter to avoid confusion and focus on the problem.

A student studied the process by which malodorzane is produced by heating protocrud in a closed system and then releasing it into the surrounding atmosphere.

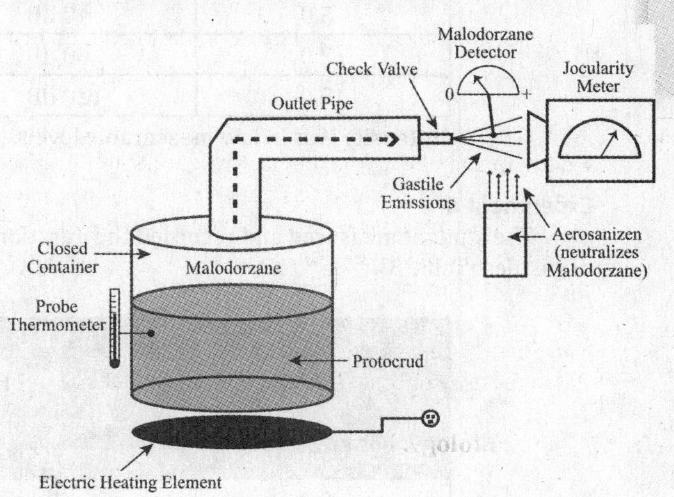

Experiment 1

The concentration of malodorzane produced by the protocrud at various temperatures was measured by determining how much aerosanizen was needed to neutralize the malodorzane (Table 1).

Now that you've read the directions, you don't need to read them again, especially not during the test. The only thing of real significance is that you CANNOT use your calculator on this part, even though you might think it would be nice. But you should be able to remember that one point without re-reading the directions.

In this Science passage, there is a single device and a series of tables that report data from the operation of the device. You'll see examples of other types of passages later in the Science Lessons.

TABLE 1

Temperature of Protocrud	Aerosanizen (spritz/minute)
20.0°C	46–198
22.5°C	199–377
25.0°C	378–612

Experiment 2

The student observed that the release of gastiles, whether or not the malodorzane was counteracted by aerosanizen, produced primary and secondary jocularities. The intensity of the jocularities was measured and recorded for different durations of gastiles (Table 2).

TABLE 2

Gastiles (seconds)	Intensity of Jocularities	
	Primary Jocularities (decibels)	Secondary Jocularities (decibels)
1.0	30 dB	—*
2.0	35 dB	—*
5.0	40 dB	30 dB
12.0	60 dB	40 dB
19.0	120 dB	60 dB

*Intensity was below measurable levels.

Experiment 3

The student measured and recorded the duration of the jocularities for different durations of gastiles (Table 3).

TABLE 3

Gastiles (seconds)	Duration of Jocularities	
	Primary Jocularities (seconds)	Secondary Jocularities (seconds)
0.2	3	—*
1.0	7	—*
2.5	13	11
5.0	25	9
12.0	51	4

*Duration was below measurable levels.

Passage Perfect

Think about what specific information you need before returning to the passage to look at the data. This will allow you to quickly find what you are looking for so that you can answer questions efficiently and accurately.

1. Data from the passage indicate that duration was greatest for secondary jocularities produced by gastiles of what duration?

A. 1.0 seconds
B. 2.5 seconds
C. 5.0 seconds
D. 12.0 seconds

1. **(B)** *Data for the duration of jocularities is given in Table 3, and the greatest entry, 11 seconds, corresponds to gastiles of duration 2.5 seconds.*

2. Gastiles with a duration of 13.0 seconds would probably produce primary jocularities of a duration:

F. between 3 and 7 seconds.
G. between 7 and 13 seconds.
H. between 13 and 25 seconds.
J. greater than 51 seconds.

2. **(J)** *Again, the answer is in Table 3, but this time there is no entry for 13 seconds. The largest entry is 12.0 seconds. Because primary jocularity duration increases as gastile duration increases, the corresponding entry in the "Primary Jocularities" column, if one existed, would likely be greater than 51 seconds.*

3. A primary jocularity of 90 decibels would most likely be produced by a gastile of:

A. less than 1.0 seconds.
B. between 1.0 and 2.0 seconds.
C. between 12.0 and 19.0 seconds.
D. greater than 19.0 seconds.

3. (C) *The relevant information is located in Table 2, but there is no entry in the table for 90 dB. However, 90 dB is between 60 dB and 120 dB. The most likely conclusion, then, is that the corresponding entry in the first column, if one existed, would be between 12.0 and 19.0 seconds.*

4. The data in Table 1 would be most useful in determining whether:

F. the temperature of aerosanizen affects the chemical's ability to neutralize malodorzane.
G. the volume of malodorzane varies with the chemical composition of the protocrud.
H. the closed system produces a greater volume of malodorzane than aerosanizen.
J. the temperature of the protocrud affects the rate of malodorzane production.

4. (J) *Table 1 shows the amount of aerosanizen needed to neutralize the quantity of malodorzane at various temperatures. So, the data in that table would provide information about how the temperature of the protocrud affects the rate of malodorzane production.*

PACING

Ace the Pace

Before you start answering any questions, preview the test to see how many passages it includes. Then adjust your pacing expectations accordingly.

The Science Test presents six or seven passages, with a total of 40 items, to be completed in 35 minutes. The table below establishes the time that you can afford to spend on various parts of the Science Test if your goal is to complete the entire test. For many people, completing the entire test may be an unrealistic goal, and a better goal for a test with seven passages is to complete six of the seven passages. Or perhaps even only five passages. If you choose to define your goal differently than completing the entire test, then you can adjust the timing for the remaining passages so that you'll have more time (e.g., four minutes for five items equals 48 seconds per item).

TESTS WITH SIX PASSAGES		
PASSAGE	TIME TO SPEND	TOTAL TIME SPENT
I	5 minutes	5 minutes
II	6 minutes	11 minutes
III	6 minutes	17 minutes
IV	6 minutes	23 minutes
V	6 minutes	29 minutes
VI	6 minutes	35 minutes

TESTS WITH SEVEN PASSAGES		
PASSAGE	TIME TO SPEND	TOTAL TIME SPENT
I	5 minutes	5 minutes
II	5 minutes	10 minutes
III	5 minutes	15 minutes
IV	5 minutes	20 minutes
V	5 minutes	25 minutes
VI	5 minutes	30 minutes
VII	5 minutes	35 minutes

You should begin work on each passage by reading the passage itself and familiarizing yourself with the main purpose of the data reports or experiments or the focus of the debate. This should be an overview of the information, not a detailed study. You are reading primarily to learn where information is located so that you can retrieve it—if an item asks about it.

Preview the number of questions associated with each passage. Allow yourself one minute to learn about the passage, then spend between 40 and 50 seconds answering each item. Thus, the time you spend on each passage will vary depending on the number of items associated with that passage. So, on the Science Test (perhaps more so than on any other test), time is of the essence.

TIME TRIAL *(5 items; 5 minutes)*

DIRECTIONS: The passage below is followed by several items. After reading the passage, choose the best answer to each item. You may refer to the passage as often as necessary. You are NOT permitted the use of a calculator.

PASSAGE I

The bacteria *Campylobacter jejuni* is one of the most common causes of food poisoning worldwide. The vast majority of cases occur as isolated events, not as part of recognized outbreaks. Food poisoning caused by *C. jejuni* can be severely debilitating but is rarely life-threatening. Table 1 shows the health risk from *C. jejuni* in liquid.

Table 1	
Bacteria Count/milliliter	Risk Factor
$0–10^2$	Virtually no count, no concern
$10^2–10^3$	Low count, little concern
$10^3–10^4$	Intermediate count, some concern
Above 10^4	High count, danger

C. jejuni is unable to grow and multiply at the temperatures normally used to store food. The temperature range for growth is 30°C–45°C, with an optimum of 42°C. Survival at room temperature is poor, but *C. jejuni* can survive for a short time at refrigeration temperatures—up to 15 times longer at 2°C than at 22°C. The bacteria die out slowly at freezing temperatures. Figure 1 shows the growth rate of *C. jejuni* at 42°C over time.

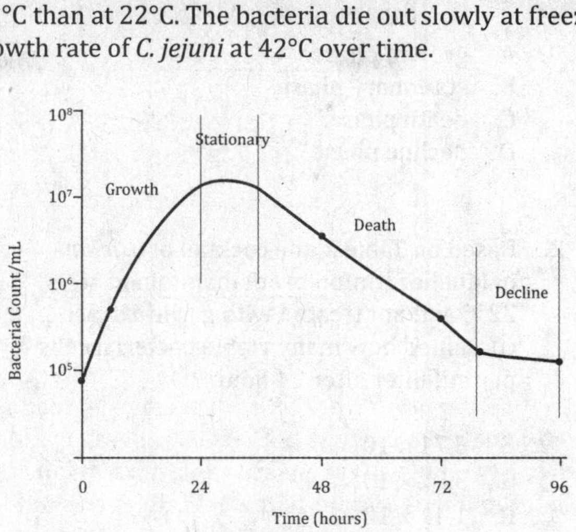

Figure 1

Garlic (*Allium sativum*) has been recognized as a food that has broad-spectrum antimicrobial potential against many genera of bacteria. Researchers treated cocktails of four strains of *C. jejuni* in Mueller Hinton broth at different temperatures with varying concentrations of garlic extract. Counts of the number of viable cells were made at intervals and recorded in Table 2.

Table 2

Temp (°C)	Concentration of garlic extract (μl/ml)*	Number of viable bacterial cells/ml		
		0 hours	24 hours	36 hours
2	0	9.95×10^4	3.01×10^4	3.69×10^3
	25	1.12×10^5	1.00×10^3	3.46×10^2
	50	9.33×10^4	1.50×10^2	1.20×10^2
	75	1.04×10^5	4.37×10^2	8.51×10
	100	1.25×10^5	5.13×10^2	3.63×10
22	0	8.32×10^4	8.71×10^3	8.91×10^2
	25	1.31×10^5	4.78×10^2	0
	50	9.55×10^4	0	0
	75	8.31×10^4	0	0
	100	1.23×10^5	0	0
42	0	7.94×10^4	3.90×10^7	1.41×10^7
	25	7.76×10^4	0	0
	50	9.77×10^4	0	0
	75	1.02×10^5	0	0
	100	1.31×10^5	0	0

*$\mu = 0.000001 = 10^{-6}$

1. The number of *C. jejuni* bacterial cells per milliliter increases most rapidly during the:

A. growth phase.
B. stationary phase.
C. death phase.
D. decline phase.

2. Based on Table 2, the cocktail of *C. jejuni* in Mueller Hinton broth maintained at 22°C and not treated with garlic extract contained how many viable bacterial cells per milliliter after 24 hours?

F. 8.71×10^3
G. 3.01×10^4
H. 1.41×10^7
J. 3.90×10^7

3. Which of the following best describes the relationship between the number of viable bacterial cells per milliliter after 36 hours and the concentration of garlic extract used to treat the cocktails of *C. jejuni* in Mueller Hinton broth that were maintained at 2°C?

A. The number of viable bacterial cells per milliliter is the same regardless of the concentration of garlic extract.
B. The number of viable bacterial cells per milliliter is different for each level of garlic extract concentration but shows no pattern.
C. The number of viable bacterial cells per milliliter increases with increased concentrations of garlic extract.
D. The number of viable bacterial cells per milliliter decreases with increased concentrations of garlic extract.

4. Which of the following hypotheses about a cocktail of *C. jejuni* in Mueller Hinton broth is supported by the data in Table 2?

F. Treatment of the cocktail with garlic extract in a concentration of 25 μl/ml or greater will result in a decrease in the number of bacterial cells per milliliter during the 24 hours immediately following treatment.
G. If the cocktail is held at a constant 42°C, the number of bacterial cells per milliliter will decrease regardless of the presence of or concentration of garlic extract.
H. Treatment of the cocktail with garlic extract in a concentration of 25μl/ml or greater will result in a rapid increase in the number of bacterial cells per milliliter followed by a rapid decrease.
J. If the cocktail is held at a constant 2°C, the number of bacterial cells per milliliter will increase over the 36 hours following treatment regardless of the presence of any garlic extract.

5. What risk factor should be assigned to a food containing the same viable bacteria count as that of the sample at 22°C and treated with a 25 μl/ml solution of garlic extract after 24 hours?

A. No concern
B. Little concern
C. Some concern
D. Danger

GAME PLAN

Quickly Preview the Test Section, but Skip the Directions

Last-minute adjustments to the test format are theoretically (but not practically) possible, so check the subject test before you start to work, especially the number of passages, the number of items, and the time limit. And yes, the test-writers always tell you to "read the directions carefully." But they don't tell you that you have to read them during the test. Instead, become familiar with them <u>before</u> test day. That way, you won't waste 30 seconds or more (enough time to answer an item) re-reading directions you are already familiar with.

Personalize the Passage Order

You are not required to do the passages in the order in which they appear in the test booklet. You can do the first passage second, or fourth, or last; and you can do the last passage first or third. So, you have the flexibility of choosing which ones you will do before the others, and you'll want to do first those passages that seem easier. "Easier," in this context, is really a subjective matter; it means the ones with which you are most comfortable, either because of the type of presentation or the subject matter.

- First, do those passage formats that you find easiest to handle.
- Then, of the remaining passages, do the familiar ones.
- Finally, do the rest of the passages, from the simplest to the most complicated.

Put large numbers in the margins of the test booklet beside each passage to indicate where the passage comes in the order you have chosen.

Read the Passage

For the Science Test, "reading the passage" means "reading through" the passage. You can't afford to study the passage, and don't forget that this is an "open-book" test. So, learn generally what is going on and where things are located. Then, let the items tell you where to look in the passage more carefully.

- Read any introductory paragraph(s). Not only does this material usually explain why an experiment is being conducted or data are being collected, but it often defines a key term that is essential to understanding the connections between the various parts of the passage.
- Examine any diagrams or schematics. The focus of a passage is often a device that includes beakers, tubing, switches, pulleys, test tubes, or any other paraphernalia associated with science. Try to understand what the device is designed to accomplish and how the various parts work together.
- Look at the various subparts of the passage. The subparts are things such as experiments that change initial conditions, tables of data, and graphs. Do not try to fully understand these subparts of the passage. Just get a general notion of what they do. For example, for a graph, read the title and the labels of the *x*- and *y*-axes. For tables, read the column heads and the titles of the rows. Do not, however, read specific values on a graph or in a table. There are too many of them, and only one or two are likely to be relevant to answering one of the few items based on that passage (compared to all the different questions that the test-writers could have chosen).

Passage Perfect

Reading the introductory paragraph is a powerful way to focus your mind on key parts of the science passage. By knowing the gist of an experiment before you read specifics, you will be able to underline and circle key information that allows you to quickly answer accompanying questions.

The Cambridge Edge

When overviewing a graph, look at the general trend of points, rather than specific, point-by-point data. Note whether the data points are increasing, decreasing, or remaining constant. This can help you quickly answer general questions about the graph, as well as give you background knowledge that may help you with more specific questions.

Answer the Items

Answer the question that is being asked. One of the most common mistakes is to read the item stem carelessly and then answer the wrong question. It's just a matter of inattention, in which you respond to what you think you read rather than what is actually there on the page. Since wrong answers often correspond to wrong readings, if you make this mistake, you are probably going to find a pretty good answer—to the wrong question.

Pay attention to thought-reversers. "Thought-reversers" are words in the item stem like "NOT," "BUT," and "EXCEPT." These words turn the question upside-down. What is normally the right answer is now a wrong answer, and what is normally a wrong answer is the right answer. Circle these words or put stars beside them so that they keep your attention while you answer the question.

Locate the relevant information. The first and often last step in answering an item is to locate the information you need. Most item stems use a key word or phrase to tell you where to look. For example, "in Table 2" tells you that the information you need is located in Table 2; "the troposphere" tells you that you need the graph, table, or description that supplies information about the troposphere; and "lowering the temperature" indicates that the answer is in the subpart of the passage that provides information about temperature.

Use the Answer Choices

Study the answer choices for guidance. The answer choices, like an item stem, can direct you to the subpart of the passage that contains the information you need. Consider the following item, in which only the answer choices are visible:

Example:

A. Sodium
B. Potassium
C. Lithium
D. Oxygen

With this array, you know to look at that table or graph or paragraph that includes the given list of terms. The choices will also give you guidance as to what degree of precision is required by the item.

Often, the choices are ranges of values, such as $0.015w$ to $0.018w$, rather than specific values, such as simply $0.018w$. Do not look for more precision than the choices allow.

Read the answer choices carefully. The test-writers love to put in wrong answers that look right. For example, if a particular value doubles with a decrease in temperature from 40°C to 20°C, a question might ask, "Assuming the temperature rises from 20°C to 40°C, what happens to the value?" The correct answer is, of course, "The value is reduced by half." But you can bet that the wrong answers will include ideas like "doubles," "increases by one-fourth," and "decreases by four," or some other variation on those ideas.

Eliminate Choices, Guess (If Necessary), and Move On

Do NOT spend too much time on any one item. Remember that you get +1 for the hardest item and +1 for the easiest item. The items that correspond to a Science passage tend to be arranged from easiest to most difficult. (This is not an absolute rule; it is just the typical arrangement.) The first item may ask you to find a single number in a table. The second item may ask for a value that is the largest or smallest in a series. And the third item may require you to interpolate a value. Then, the going might get considerably more difficult. So, try the next item, and if it is totally confusing, skip the rest of the questions and go to the next passage where the difficulty resets to the lowest setting. And don't forget: the ACT test has no penalty for guessing. If you find yourself stuck on a difficult item, eliminate as many choices as possible, guess, and move on!

SCIENCE

LESSONS

LESSON 1

Data Representation

Ditch the Directions

Make sure you are familiar with the directions before test day. You can be confident that you know what to do when you open your test booklet and save yourself 30 seconds by skipping the directions.

The passages and items in this section accompany the in-class review of the skills and concepts tested by Data Representation items on the ACT Science Test. You will work through the items with your instructor in class. Answers are on page 441.

DIRECTIONS: Each passage below is followed by several items. After reading a passage, choose the best answer to each item. You may refer to the passages as often as necessary. You are NOT permitted the use of a calculator.

GRAPHS

PASSAGE I

The kinetic energy of an object with mass *m* (measured in grams) after a fall from a height *h* (measured in centimeters) was recorded for different heights. A graph was made representing the kinetic energy versus height.

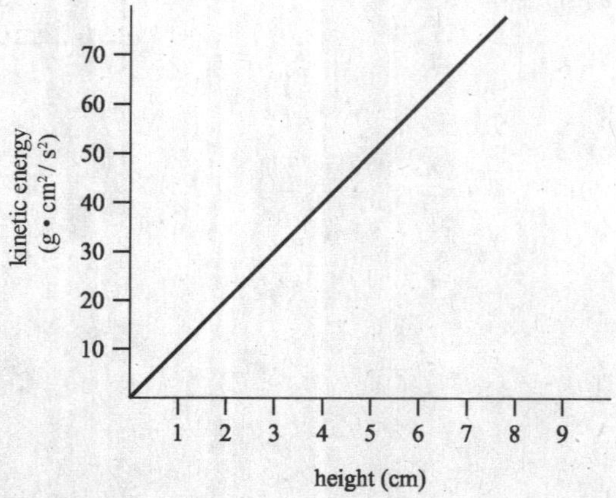

1. What would be the approximate kinetic energy (in $g \cdot cm^2 / s^2$) of an object of mass *m* if it were dropped from a height of 4.5 cm?

A. 4.5
B. 9.0
C. 45
D. 90

Closer Look

You aren't allowed to use a calculator on the test, which means you won't be asked to do complicated manipulations. Any questions involving math will only require straightforward calculations.

2. In the graph, if the kinetic energy is given in units of $g \cdot cm^2 / s^2$, what units must the slope have?

F. $g \cdot cm / s$
G. $g \cdot cm / s^2$
H. $s \cdot cm / g$
J. $s^2 / (g \cdot cm)$

3. It is discovered that if the experiment is repeated for an object with twice the mass, the kinetic energy obtained for every height is doubled. The slope of the new set of experiments can be obtained by doing what to the old slope?

A. Multiplying by 2
B. Dividing by 2
C. Squaring
D. Taking the square root

TABLES

Understanding the Nature of Data
Items #4–5

PASSAGE II

A scientist investigated the variables that affect the age at which a female of the animal species *Taedi periculum* first gives birth. Some of the results of this study are summarized in the table below.

EXPERIMENT	TEMPERATURE (°C)	AVERAGE FOOD INTAKE (grams)	AGE WHEN FIRST GAVE BIRTH (months)
1	25	15	7
2	25	30	6
3	25	45	4
4	35	15	5
5	35	30	3
6	35	45	3

The Cambridge Edge

Sometimes if you are confused by a table, it can help to quickly sketch a graph to recognize trends.

Throwback to Science Class

Remember, you can only compare two trials or experiments if they differ in just one respect. For instance, if you want to study the effect of temperature on reproductive age, you would compare two trials with the same food consumption but different temperatures.

4. Which of the following would be good animals to use for the experiment?

F. Adult females
G. Newborn females
H. Newborn males
J. Adult males

5. Which of the following pairs of experiments would be useful for studying the effect of temperature on the age of first birth?

A. Experiments 1 and 2
B. Experiments 1 and 5
C. Experiments 1 and 4
D. Experiments 2 and 6

Recognizing Trends
Items #6–8

Drawing Conclusions
Item #9

6. If all other variables are kept constant, which of the following will result in an increase in the age at which the animals give birth?

F. Increase in temperature from 25°C to 35°C
G. Increase in food from 15 grams to 45 grams
H. Decrease in food from 30 grams to 15 grams
J. Increase in temperature from 25°C to 30°C

7. Which of the following experiments was a control for temperature in Experiment 5?

A. Experiment 1
B. Experiment 2
C. Experiment 3
D. Experiment 6

8. If an experiment was set up with the temperature set at 30°C and the food intake at 30 grams, which of the following would be a reasonable prediction of the age in months of the animals when they first gave birth?

F. 7.5
G. 6.5
H. 4.5
J. 2.5

9. Which of the following conclusions is consistent with the data presented in the table?

A. The weight of the firstborn is proportional to the food intake.
B. The weight of the firstborn is related to the temperature.
C. The age of the mother at time of first offspring's birth increases with decreasing food intake.
D. The age of the mother at time of first offspring's birth decreases with decreasing food intake.

TYPICAL DATA REPRESENTATION ITEMS

The Cambridge Edge

With so much information going on at once, graphs like this can be confusing. When a graph is this complicated, preview it and then head straight into questions. Questions will ask for specific information, which you can pick out of this complex graph.

PASSAGE III

The chart below shows the average blood pressure and relative total surface area associated with the different types of human blood vessels.

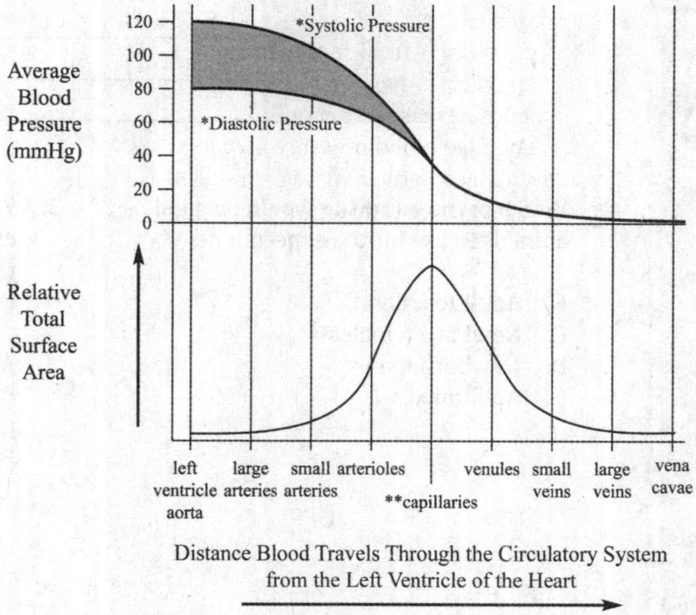

*Pulse pressure is the difference between systolic and diastolic pressure.
**Blood velocity is lowest in the capillaries (averaging 3 cm/sec).

10. According to the diagram, pulse pressure can be detected:

F. in large arteries only.
G. in large arteries as well as in large veins.
H. in blood vessels between the aorta and the capillaries.
J. primarily in the arterioles, capillaries, and venules.

11. Based on the information in the diagram, average blood pressure:

A. decreases with increasing blood vessel distance from the left ventricle.
B. remains approximately constant regardless of blood vessel distance from the left ventricle.
C. first increases, then decreases with increasing blood vessel distance from the left ventricle.
D. is highest in blood vessels with the greatest relative total surface area.

12. Which of the following correctly states the relationship between the relative total surface area of blood vessels and the average blood pressure?

F. As relative total surface area decreases, average blood pressure increases.
G. As relative total surface area decreases, average blood pressure decreases.
H. As relative total surface area decreases, average blood pressure may increase or decrease.
J. Average blood pressure always changes in the opposite direction as the relative total surface area changes.

13. Based on the information in the diagram, which of the following conclusions is correct?

A. As blood vessel distance from the left ventricle increases, relative total surface area decreases.
B. As blood vessel distance from the left ventricle increases, pulse pressure increases.
C. Blood vessels with the greatest relative total surface area have the highest pulse pressure.
D. Blood vessels closest to and farthest from the left ventricle have the smallest relative total surface area.

14. A physician examining a newly discovered tribe of people deep in the Amazon jungles found that the relative total surface area of their capillaries was greater than that previously reported for any other group of people. If the physician were to predict the average velocity of blood through the capillaries of these people, which of the following values would be most reasonable?

F. 2 cm/sec
G. 3 cm/sec
H. 4 cm/sec
J. 5 cm/sec

PASSAGE IV

In 1933, Dr. Fletcher and Dr. Munson of Bell Labs discovered that the sensitivity of the human ear varies with frequency. The Fletcher-Munson equal-loudness contours (Figure 1) show how the human ear's sensitivity to sound pressure level (SPL) varies with frequency. Each contour represents the loudness level as perceived by the human ear. Loudness is subjective but related to sound pressure level as measured by a sound level meter.

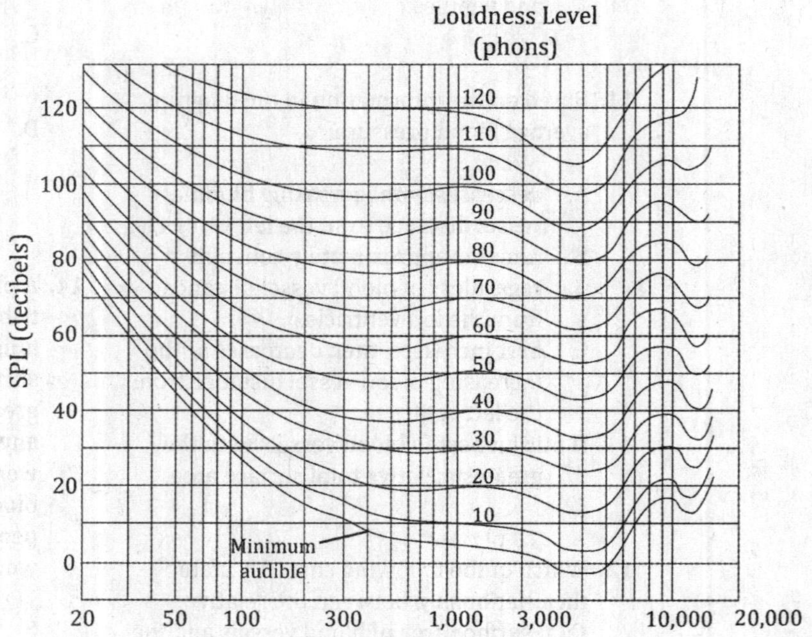

Figure 1

The bottom contour (minimum audible) represents the hearing threshold of the human ear, that is, the minimum SPL of a pure tone that the average human ear with normal hearing can hear with no other sound present. The top contour (120 phons) represents the pain threshold of the human ear, that is, the SPL beyond which sound becomes unbearable to the average listener. Prolonged exposure to sound pressure levels in excess of the pain threshold can cause physical damage.

15. The Fletcher-Munson contours indicate that the human ear is:

A. equally sensitive to all frequencies.
B. less sensitive to low and high frequencies and more sensitive to mid-range frequencies.
C. most sensitive to low and high frequencies and less sensitive to mid-range frequencies.
D. capable of hearing sounds below 20 hertz.

16. The threshold of human hearing:

F. does not depend on sound frequency.
G. is sometimes equal to the threshold of pain.
H. is based on an average ear with normal hearing.
J. is represented by the 10-phon Fletcher-Munson contour.

The Cambridge Edge

How can you recognize a data representation item? Here are some sample items to help you recognize what these questions ask:

1. *Select a conclusion that can be supported by Figure X.*
2. *Determine what the slope of a given line represents in Figure X.*
3. *Predict the results given an assumption or a new situation.*
4. *Select a statement that is best supported by the data represented in Graph X.*
5. *Determine the results based on the difference of time or location.*
6. *Determine the relationship between the two variables.*
7. *Determine which conclusion is NOT consistent with the information given in Graph X.*
8. *Select an explanation for a given outcome.*
9. *Identify the LEAST significant assumption made when determining a particular outcome.*

17. The range of maximum sensitivity for human hearing is approximately:

A. 50 to 100 hertz.
B. 100 to 500 hertz.
C. 500 to 5,000 hertz.
D. 4,000 to 6,000 hertz.

18. Which of the following is a true statement regarding loudness and SPL?

F. Loudness is measured in decibels; SPL is measured in phons.
G. SPL is a measure of subjective quantity; phons may be measured with a sound level meter.
H. Loudness is subjective, but related to SPL.
J. For any given SPL, loudness remains constant for all frequencies.

19. A 300-hertz sound with an SPL of 15 decibels has a loudness of:

A. 10 phons.
B. 20 phons.
C. 30 phons.
D. 40 phons.

20. For the human ear to hear a 20-hertz sound at a loudness of 70 phons, the SPL must be:

F. 50 decibels.
G. 75 decibels.
H. 100 decibels.
J. 110 decibels.

21. For the human ear to hear a minimum audible 30-hertz sound, the SPL must be:

A. 20 decibels.
B. 40 decibels.
C. 60 decibels.
D. 80 decibels.

22. The perceived loudness of a 300-hertz sound with an SPL of 15 decibels is the same as a 30-hertz sound with an SPL of:

F. 50 decibels.
G. 55 decibels.
H. 62 decibels.
J. 150 decibels.

DATA REPRESENTATION STRATEGIES

The Cambridge Edge

Use the following approach for Data Representation passages:

1. Preview the passage and items
2. Underline and circle key words
3. Pay attention to scales, units, legends, and other keys to understanding graphs and charts
4. Pay attention to axes on graphs
5. Pay attention to data trends

Passage Perfect

When a passage includes two graphs, you may be asked to use information from both graphs to answer a single question. As you preview the graphs, pay attention to any similarities and differences between them.

PASSAGE V

Seawater contains dissolved salts. As a result, seawater freezes at a lower temperature than freshwater (Figure 1).

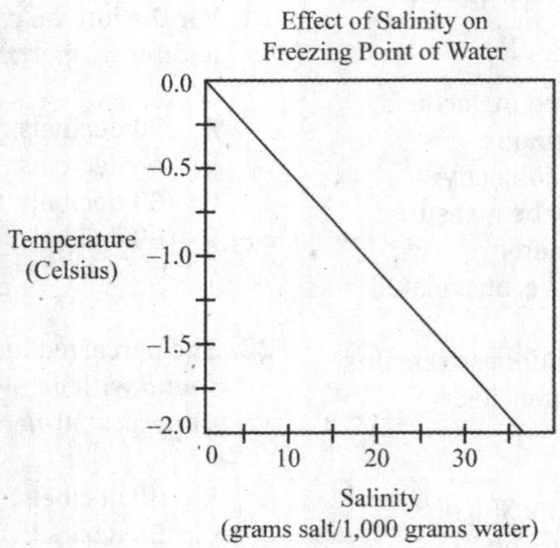

Figure 1

When seawater freezes, as the water molecules begin to form their characteristic ring-like structures, the salt ions, primarily sodium and chloride, are forced out of solution and form pockets of salt. The brine (salty water) leaches out of the bottom of the ice into the water below. Thus, sea ice, when melted, is generally considerably less saline than the original seawater. The solid-line graph below indicates the percentage of salt in a slab of ice that lies over seawater on a cold ocean surface (Figure 2).

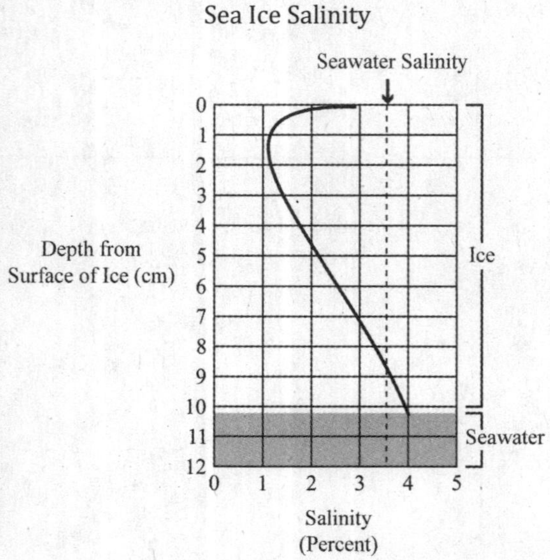

Figure 2

23. Compared to the ocean water below it, the salinity of sea ice in contact with seawater is:

A. higher than that of the seawater.
B. about the same as that of the seawater.
C. lower than that of the seawater.
D. sometimes lower and sometimes higher than that of the seawater.

24. The salinity of the ice at the surface of the slab is equal to the salinity of the:

F. sea ice at a depth of approximately 1.5 cm.
G. sea ice at a depth of approximately 7.0 cm.
H. sea ice at a depth of approximately 9.0 cm.
J. water beneath the sea ice.

25. According to the information provided, the freezing temperature of pure water is approximately:

A. 2 degrees lower than that of seawater.
B. 0.2 degrees lower than that of seawater.
C. 3.5 degrees higher than that of seawater.
D. 2 degrees higher than that of seawater.

26. According to Figure 2, the salt content of the sea ice:

F. equals 0.
G. is constant at all depths.
H. decreases, then increases with depth.
J. increases, then decreases with depth.

27. The researcher takes a 1 gram sample of ice from a depth of 10 cm, and wishes to take a sample of ice from a depth of 1.3 cm that will contain the same weight of total salts. Approximately how large a sample is needed?

A. 0.25 grams
B. 1.0 gram
C. 4.0 grams
D. 10.0 grams

PASSAGE VI

According to the kinetic molecular theory of gases, all gases consist of particles (atoms or molecules) in continuous, random motion. In an ideal gas, particles move freely without interacting with one another except for brief elastic collisions. Particles of a gas at a particular temperature will have a range of different speeds. The distribution of particle speeds, that is, the number of particles moving with a certain speed, is given by the Maxwell-Boltzmann distribution curves. The most probable speed for the particles is represented by the peak of the curve. For a given distribution, the area under the curve corresponds to the total number of particles of a gas sample.

To illustrate how mass affects molecular speed, Figure 1 gives the Maxwell-Boltzmann distributions for the common gases listed in the table at a fixed temperature (300 K). To illustrate how temperature affects molecular speed, Figure 2 gives the Maxwell-Boltzmann distributions for nitrogen gas (N_2) at several temperatures.

Table 1: Molar Mass of Common Gases (grams/mole)	
H_2 (hydrogen)	2.02
He (helium)	4.00
N_2 (nitrogen)	28.01
O_2 (oxygen)	32.00
Cl_2 (chlorine)	70.91
Kr (krypton)	83.80

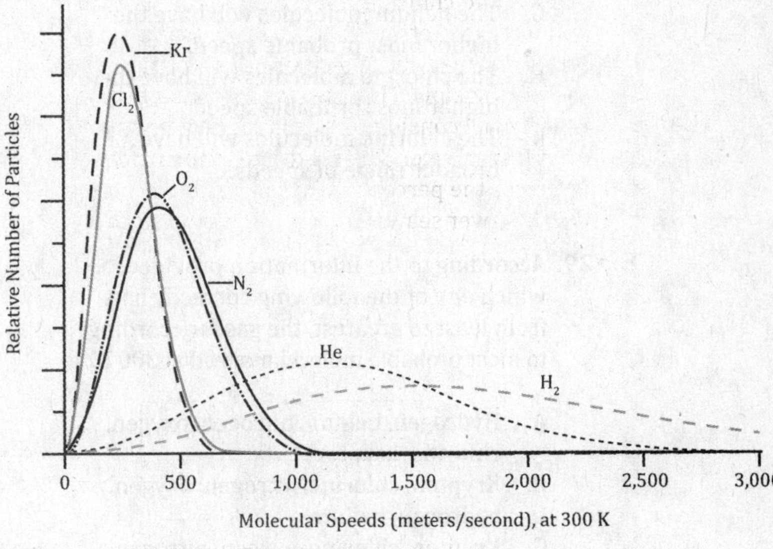

Figure 1

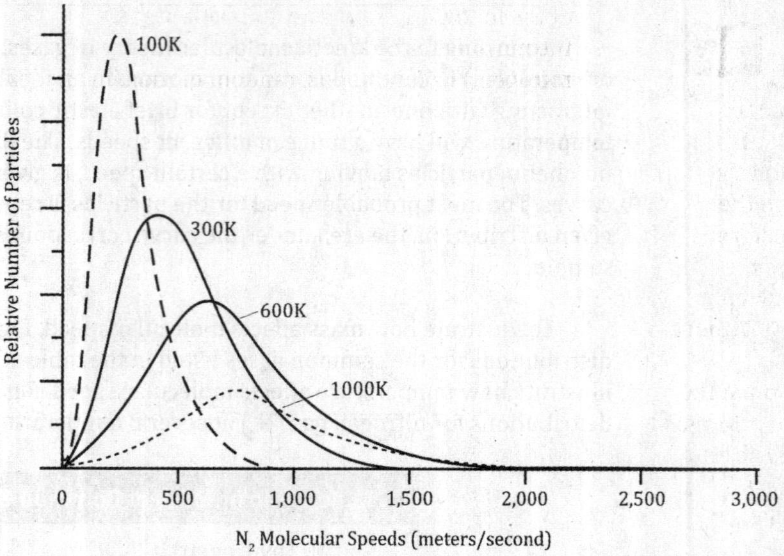

Figure 2

28. A scientist fills one metal cylinder with helium gas and a second metal cylinder with chlorine gas. After the scientist heats both gases to 300 K, which of the following will be true?

F. The molecules in both gases will have the same most probable speed.
G. The helium molecules will have the higher most probable speed.
H. The chlorine molecules will have the higher most probable speed.
J. The chlorine molecules will have a broader range of speeds.

29. According to the information provided, which one of the following correctly lists, from least to greatest, the gases according to most probable molecular speed at 300 K?

A. Hydrogen, helium, nitrogen, oxygen, chlorine, krypton
B. Krypton, chlorine, nitrogen, oxygen, hydrogen, helium
C. Krypton, chlorine, oxygen, nitrogen, hydrogen, helium
D. Krypton, chlorine, oxygen, nitrogen, helium, hydrogen

30. Based on the information provided, it is inferable that as the temperature of a gas increases:

F. The molecular weight of the gas increases.
G. the relative number of particles at the most probable speed decreases.
H. the total number of particles in the gas decreases.
J. the most probable molecular speed decreases.

Passage Perfect

Don't forget to preview both the text and the graphics in the passage before answering the accompanying questions. Without the critical information in the text of the passage it is impossible to answer item #31, for example.

31. Based on the information provided, which of the following graphs best represents the most probable molecular speed for nitrogen as a function of gas temperature?

A.

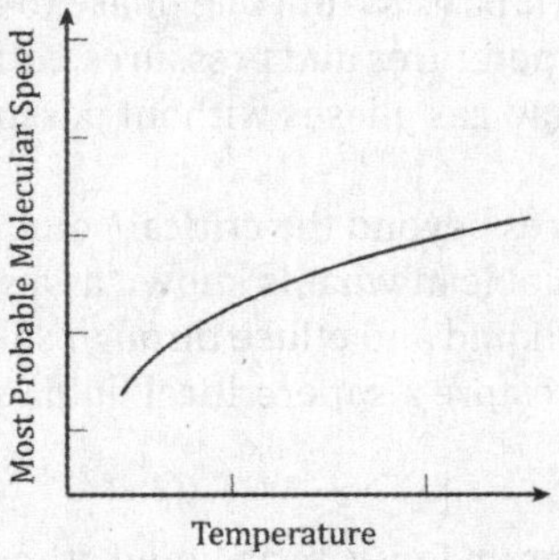

B.

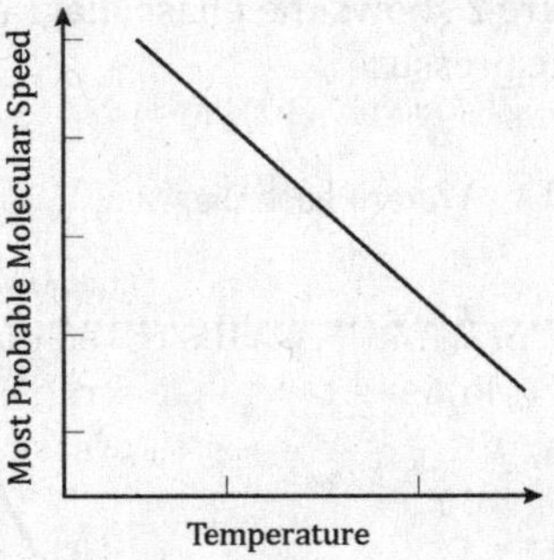

C.

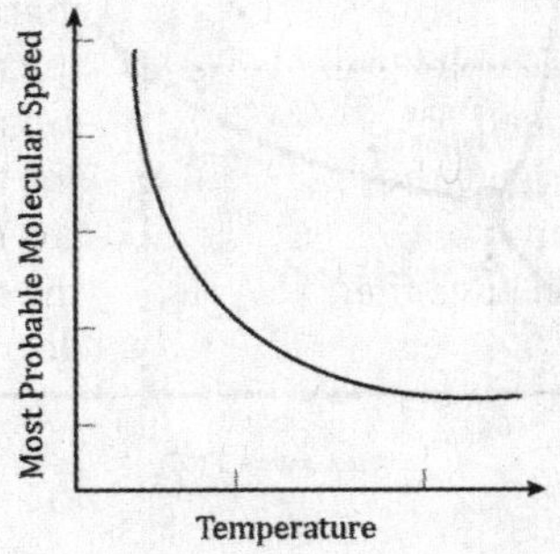

D.

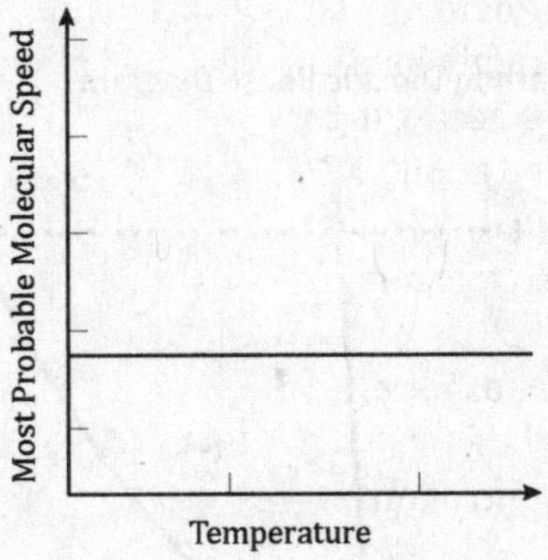

32. Which of the following statements best describes the relationship between nitrogen gas molecule speeds and the temperature of the gas?

F. As gas temperature increases, the range of molecular speeds increases and the most probable speed decreases.
G. As gas temperature decreases, the range of molecular speeds decreases and the most probable speed decreases.
H. As molar mass of gas increases, the range of molecular speeds decreases and the most probable speed decreases.
J. As molar mass of gas decreases, the range of molecular speeds increases and the most probable speed increases.

33. According to the information provided, as the molar mass of a gas increases:

A. the number of particles at greater speeds increases.
B. the number of particles in the gas increases.
C. the most probable molecular speed decreases.
D. the most probable molecular speed increases.

34. Argon is a gas with molar mass of 39.95 grams/mole. Based on the information provided, the most probable molecular speed of argon molecules at 100 K is:

F. less than 250 meters/second.
G. between 250 and 450 meters/second.
H. between 450 and 800 meters/second.
J. over 800 meters/second.

PASSAGE VII

Phase diagrams illustrate the relationship between temperature, pressure, and the phases of matter. Each of the three phases—solid, liquid, and gas—is represented by a section of the phase diagram. The curves represent states of equilibrium between two phases—the substance is present in two phases at once as it passes from one phase to the next. All three phases are present at the triple point. For temperatures and pressures both below the triple point, matter passes directly between the solid and gas phases without passing through the liquid phase.

For pressures and temperatures beyond the critical point, the liquid and gas phases converge and become indistinguishable in what is known as a *supercritical fluid*. Supercritical fluids can dissolve materials like a liquid and effuse through solids like a gas. Beyond the critical point, no amount of pressure will restore a supercritical fluid to its liquid or solid phase without decreasing the temperature.

Figure 1 shows the phase diagram for water, a liquid at room temperature (21°C) and atmospheric pressure (1 atm). Figure 2 shows the phase diagram for carbon dioxide, a gas at room temperature and atmospheric pressure.

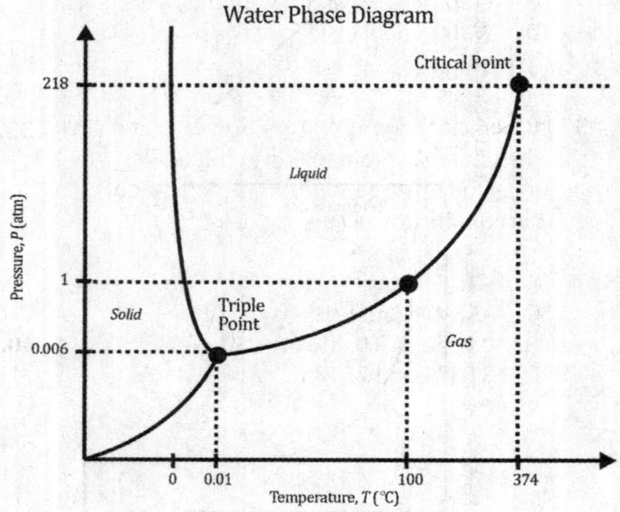

Figure 1

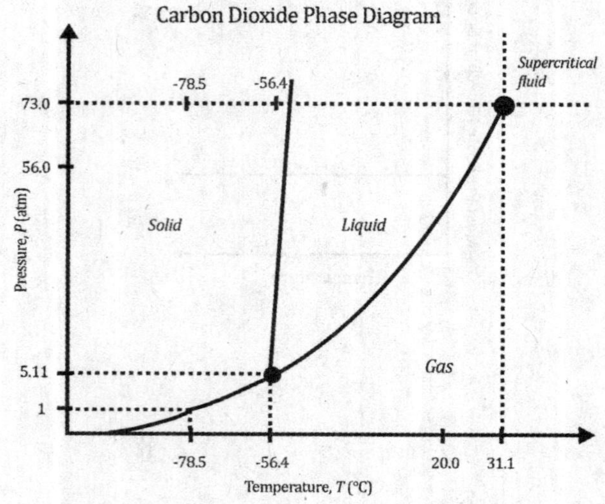

Figure 2

35. According to the information provided and Figure 1, water becomes a supercritical fluid when the temperature and pressure exceed:

F. 0.006°C and 0.01 atm.
G. 0.01°C and 0.006 atm.
H. 218°C and 374 atm.
J. 374°C and 218 atm.

36. At 100°C, as pressure is decreased from 1.5 atm to 0.006 atm, which of the following is true?

A. Carbon dioxide changes from a gas to a liquid.
B. Carbon dioxide changes from a liquid to a gas.
C. Water changes from a liquid to a gas.
D. Water changes from a gas to a liquid.

37. Based on the information provided and the phase diagram for carbon dioxide, it can be inferred that the triple point of carbon dioxide occurs at:

F. −78.5°C and 1 atm.
G. −56.4°C and 5.11 atm.
H. 0.01°C and 0.006 atm.
J. 31.1°C and 73 atm.

38. According to the information provided, both water and carbon dioxide exist solely as liquids at which of the following pressure and temperature combinations?

A. 10°C and 56 atm.
B. 0°C and 1 atm.
C. 30°C and 10 atm.
D. There is no point at which both water and carbon dioxide exist solely as liquids.

39. In Figure 1, the line indicating equilibrium between solid water (ice) and liquid water has a negative slope. This indicates that to maintain equilibrium between the two states:

A. as the temperature is decreased, the pressure must be decreased.
B. as the temperature is increased, the pressure must be decreased.
C. as the temperature is increased, the pressure must remain constant.
D. as the temperature is increased, the pressure must be increased, then decreased.

40. Sublimation occurs when a solid changes to a gas without going through a liquid phase. Under which of the following conditions can sublimation occur?

F. Water at 0°C and 0.80 atm.
G. Water at 80°C and 0.006 atm.
H. Carbon dioxide at −78.5°C and 1 atm.
J. Carbon dioxide at 0°C and 5.11 atm.

LESSON 2

RESEARCH SUMMARY

The passages and items in this section accompany the in-class review of the skills and concepts tested by Research Summary passages on the ACT Science Test. You will work through the items with your instructor in class. Answers are on page 441.

DIRECTIONS: Each passage below is followed by several items. After reading a passage, choose the best answer to each item. You may refer to the passages as often as necessary. You are NOT permitted the use of a calculator.

TYPICAL RESEARCH SUMMARY ITEMS

Use Your Test Booklet Tools

When specific experiments are being described in a science passage, especially if these experiments are being compared to one another, underline or circle key features of each experiment. This will help you answer your questions quickly and correctly.

PASSAGE I

To test the hypothesis that all antibiotics are equally effective in preventing bacterial growth, the following three experiments were carried out using clear plastic plates filled with nutrient agar (a mixture of ingredients that supports the growth of bacteria). When bacteria reproduce successfully, colonies form on the agar, giving it a cloudy appearance.

Experiment 1

Three plates (A, B, and C) of agar were set up, each with an equal amount of bacterial culture (Bacterium X) spread over the agar surface and with a paper disk placed in the center. Plate A's disk was soaked in Antibiotic I; Plate B's disk was soaked in Antibiotic II; Plate C's disk was soaked in plain water. After incubation overnight at 37°C (body temperature), Plates A and B had a clear area, 2" in diameter surrounding the paper disk, but beyond this 2" region, the plates were cloudy. Plate C was entirely cloudy, including the area adjacent to the paper disk.

Experiment 2

Identical procedures were followed except that Plates A, B, and C were incubated overnight at 22°C (room temperature). After incubation, Plate A had a clear area, 2" in diameter, surrounding the paper disk. Plates B and C were entirely cloudy.

Experiment 3

Identical procedures were followed except that the concentrations of Antibiotic I (Plate A) and Antibiotic II (Plate B) were made twice as strong. After incubation overnight at 22°C, Plates A and B both had clear, 2" areas around the paper disk, while Plate C remained entirely cloudy.

1. After incubation, a clear area around a previously soaked paper disk represents a region where:

A. agar had washed away.
B. decomposition had occurred due to high incubation temperatures.
C. bacterial growth did not occur.
D. bacteria grew best.

The Cambridge Edge

How can you recognize a Research Summary item? Here are some sample items to help you recognize what these questions ask:

1. *Identify the difference in the experimental design of the two experiments.*
2. *Predict an outcome based on the results of Experiment 2.*
3. *Predict the outcome of Experiment 1 when one of the variables is altered.*
4. *Identify an assumption of Experiment 2 based on the results.*
5. *Identify a conclusion supported by the results of Experiment 1.*
6. *Select an experiment that should be conducted in order to test another hypothesis.*
7. *Identify a hypothesis that was investigated in Experiment 1.*

2. Which of the following results would indicate that the antibiotics being tested have nothing to do with the control of bacterial growth?

F. A clear, 2" region was always observed around the disks soaked in water.
G. All results remained the same at the two experimental temperatures and at the two antibiotic concentration levels.
H. Plates A and B always remained clear.
J. The disks soaked in water were not used in the experiments at all.

3. Which statement is supported by the results of Experiment 1 alone?

A. Antibiotic I, Antibiotic II, and water are equally effective as inhibitors (preventers) of bacterial growth at 37°C.
B. Dry paper disks can be effective in controlling bacterial growth at 37°C.
C. The concentration of an antibiotic may influence its effectiveness in controlling bacterial growth at 37°C.
D. Both Antibiotics I and II can inhibit bacterial growth at 37°C.

4. The results of both Experiment 2 and Experiment 3 lead to which of the following conclusions?

F. Antibiotics I and II have similar effects on bacterial growth, regardless of concentrations.
G. Antibiotic II and water have similar effects on bacterial growth, regardless of concentrations.
H. The effectiveness of Antibiotic I at 22°C depends on its concentration.
J. The effectiveness of Antibiotic II at 22°C depends on its concentration.

5. Which hypothesis best explains the observation that the agar plates never appear clear beyond a 2" area surrounding the soaked paper disks?

A. The bacteria cannot grow well within 2" of any moist paper disks.
B. The antibiotics cannot seep through the agar beyond a distance of 2".
C. At the experimental incubation temperatures used, the two antibiotics interfere with each other's effectiveness.
D. The paper disks can absorb nutrients out of the agar from the distance of 2".

6. If either Antibiotic I or II could be prescribed for internal use to prevent the spread of Bacterium X infections, which recommendation, based on the experimental results, is appropriate if the cost due to the amount of antibiotic used per dose is the most critical factor (the antibiotics are equal in cost for equal concentrations)?

F. Either Antibiotic I or II can be taken at equal cost.
G. Antibiotic I would be less expensive.
H. Antibiotic II would be less expensive.
J. Neither Antibiotic I nor II would be effective in preventing the spread of Bacterium X.

PASSAGE II

Simple carbohydrates can form either a *single* ring structure called a *mono*saccharide or a *double* ring structure called a *di*saccharide. Familiar sugars include the monosaccharides glucose (the basic fuel of cells) and fructose (found in fruits) and the disaccharides sucrose (table sugar) and lactose (the sugar in milk).

Benedict's solution is a chemical reagent commonly used to detect the presence of reducing sugars. The reducing sugars include all monosaccharides such as glucose and some disaccharides such as lactose. Sucrose is not a reducing sugar.

The principle of Benedict's test is that when reducing sugars are heated in the presence of an alkali, they reduce the cupric compounds (Cu^{++}) present in the Benedict's reagent to cuprous compounds (Cu^{+}) which are precipitated as insoluble red copper oxide (Cu_2O). The color of the precipitate gives an approximation of the quantity of sugar present in the solution.

Table 1

Result of Benedict's Test	Concentration of Reducing Sugar (by weight)
Blue (unchanged)	0.0%
Green	0.1%–3.5%
Yellow	3.6%–5.0%
Red-Brown	>5.0%

Experiment 1

A group of students prepared test samples by measuring 40 drops of seven different liquids—distilled water, 10% sucrose solution, 6%-glucose solution, heavy cream, whole milk, no-fat milk, and unsweetened soy milk—into pre-labeled test tubes. To each test tube, the students added 10 drops of Benedict's solution. The test tubes were agitated and then placed in racks and immersed in a water bath at 95°C for 10 minutes. The students observed any color changes in the solutions and interpreted the changes using Table 1. The students recorded the results in Table 2.

Table 2

Substance	Initial Color	Final Color
Distilled Water	Blue	Blue
Sucrose Solution	Blue	Blue
Glucose Solution	Blue	Red-Brown
Heavy Cream	Blue	Yellow
Whole Milk	Blue	Yellow
No-Fat Milk	Blue	Yellow
Unsweetened Soy Milk	Blue	Blue

Experiment 2

Lipids are a class of organic compounds that are fatty acids or their derivatives. They are soluble in organic solvents but insoluble in water. *Sudan red* is a dye that attaches to lipids. The students performed a second experiment in which 1 milliliter of each of the liquids used in Experiment 1 was pipetted into pre-labeled test tubes. Two drops of Sudan red were added to each test tube, and the students recorded the results in Table 3.

Table 3	
Substance	Presence of Lipids
Distilled Water	Negative
Sucrose Solution	Negative
Glucose Solution	Negative
Heavy Cream	Positive
Whole Milk	Positive
No-Fat Milk	Positive
Unsweetened Soy Milk	Negative

Experiment 3

Starch is a molecule found only in plants. *Lugol's iodine* is used as an indicator test for the presence of starch in organic compounds, with which it reacts by turning a blue-black color. The students performed a third experiment in which 2 milliliters of each of the liquids used in Experiments 1 and 2 were pipetted into pre-labeled test tubes. Three drops of Lugol's solution were added to each test tube, and the students recorded the results in Table 4.

Table 4	
Substance	Presence of Starch
Distilled Water	No Change
Sucrose Solution	No Change
Glucose Solution	No Change
Heavy Cream	No Change
Whole Milk	No Change
No-Fat Milk	No Change
Unsweetened Soy Milk	Turned Blue-Black

7. According to the information provided, whole milk contains what percentage lactose by weight?

A. 0.0%
B. Between 0.2% and 3.5%
C. Between 3.6% and 5.0%
D. More than 5.0%

8. Which of the test substances in Experiment 2 functioned as a control?

F. Distilled water
G. Heavy cream
H. No-fat milk
J. Unsweetened soy milk

9. Which substances tested positive for both lipids and reducing sugars?

A. Glucose only
B. Whole milk and heavy cream only
C. Whole milk, heavy cream, and no-fat milk only
D. Whole milk, heavy cream, no-fat milk, and unsweetened soy milk only

10. According to reliable scientific research, dry whole milk contains approximately 38% lactose by weight and liquid whole milk contains between 3.6% and 5.0% lactose by weight. Which of the following best explains why dry whole milk has a much higher lactose content than liquid whole milk?

F. Removing water from whole milk greatly reduces the weight of the product while the amount of lactose remains the same.
G. The process of removing water from whole milk to produce dry whole milk also removes an equal weight of lactose.
H. When whole milk is processed into dry milk, the loss of liquid weight is balanced by the addition of an equal weight of lipids.
J. Removing water from whole milk to produce dry milk concentrates the starch content in the dry milk left behind.

11. The students created an additional test substance by mixing whole milk with sucrose and then testing the mixture with Benedict's solution following the procedures used in Experiment 1. The expected color of the liquid is:

A. blue.
B. green.
C. yellow.
D. red-brown.

RESEARCH SUMMARY STRATEGIES

The Cambridge Edge

Use the following strategies for Research Summary passages:

1. Identify the controls and the variables.
2. Anticipate how to alter experimental variables to support alternative hypotheses and predict the results of these new experiments.
3. For depicted data trends, determine any proportional or inverse relationships.
4. Question the validity of any assumptions.

PASSAGE III

Erosion refers to processes that wear down rocks and soil, as well as processes that transport the worn-away materials to other locations. Although these processes usually cause effects gradually (over geologic time), laboratory models can be designed to investigate which environmental factors affect erosion rate.

Three experimental sandboxes were set up that were identical in size (10-by-10-foot), had identical types of soil and rocks, and were filled to equal depths (3 feet). The sandboxes were kept for two weeks in large environmental chambers, each maintained at a constant temperature, with a continuous wind flow of 5 mph.

Sandbox 1

One-half of Sandbox 1 was kept bare (just soil and rocks), while the other half had a variety of grasses and weeds planted among the soil and rocks. After two weeks, the bare half had small channels (ruts) running along its length that averaged 1 inch in width. The planted half had few channels, and those that were found averaged less than 1 inch wide.

Sandbox 2

The conditions of Sandbox 2 were identical to those of Sandbox 1, with the addition that both halves were subjected to light, 15-minute showers of water every 12 hours. After two weeks, the bare half had channels averaging 4 inches wide, while the planted half had fewer channels, averaging 2 inches wide.

Sandbox 3

The conditions of Sandbox 3 were identical to those of Sandbox 2, but the entire box was mechanically raised to rest at an angle of 15° to simulate a steep slope. After two weeks, the bare half had channels averaging 7 inches wide, while the planted half had fewer channels, averaging 4 inches wide.

12. Results from all three sandboxes indicate that:

F. different types of soils and rocks are affected differently by environmental factors.
G. under all tested conditions, plants reduce erosion.
H. changing wind and temperature conditions can affect erosion patterns.
J. water from short periods of rain has little or no effect on erosion patterns.

13. The experimental design and results do NOT support which of the following claims?

A. Light winds have no erosive effect.
B. Slopes have more erosion than level surfaces.
C. Water has major erosive effects.
D. The effects of changing temperature remain unanswered.

14. Sudden cloudbursts are known to cause more erosion than longer periods of mild rains. How could the present experiments be changed to examine this idea?

F. Raise the angle in Sandbox 3 to produce a steeper slope.
G. Add the "rain conditions" from Sandbox 2 to the conditions in Sandbox 1.
H. Include light, 15-minute showers every 6 hours instead of every 12 hours.
J. Every 12 hours, allow the same total volume of water to fall in a 5-minute span rather than in a 15-minute span.

15. Should the investigator have used different soil types in each sandbox experiment?

A. Yes, because different soils may erode differently.
B. Yes, because a different group of plants could have been used in each sandbox as well.
C. No, because some soils can be washed completely away within the two-week experiment.
D. No, because the soil type was a controlled variable in all three experiments.

16. Sandbox 3 specifically demonstrates the role of which particular variable in the set of experiments?

F. Rain
G. Wind
H. Gravity
J. Temperature

17. If another sandbox were set up, which of the following conditions would probably cause wider and deeper channels in the soil of the new sandbox than those in Sandbox 3?

I. Steeper angles for the sandbox
II. A greater volume of water during the 15-minute showers every twelve hours
III. Removal of plants from soil

A. I only
B. I and II only
C. II and III only
D. I, II, and III

PASSAGE IV

Throwback to Science

Remember what it means for two variables to be proportional. As one variable goes up, the other goes up as well. Similarly, when two variables are inversely proportional, when one variable goes up, the other goes down. It can be helpful to draw arrows so that you can easily and quickly remember this concept while testing. For example: For Charles's law, ↑*V* and ↑*T*, and for Boyle's law, ↑*V* and ↓*P*.

Charles's law states that the volume, *V*, of a gas at constant pressure is proportional to its absolute temperature *T* (temperature in kelvins, K):

$$V \propto T \qquad \text{(Equation 1)}$$

Boyle's law states that the volume of a gas at constant temperature is inversely proportional to its pressure *P*:

$$V \propto 1/P \qquad \text{(Equation 2)}$$

Experiment 1

Students inserted a 100-mL syringe and a thermometer through holes in a rubber stopper and placed the stopper into a flask that had been cooled in an ice bath to 273 K (Figure 1). They then removed the flask from the ice bath and placed it on a hot plate. The gas in the flask expanded as it warmed, slowly pushing the piston up the syringe. Students recorded the temperature and corresponding syringe volume readings as the gas expanded at a constant atmospheric pressure (100 kPa). To obtain the total volume of the gas in the system, they added the volume of the syringe to the volume of the flask. The students created a graph of the experimental data (Figure 2).

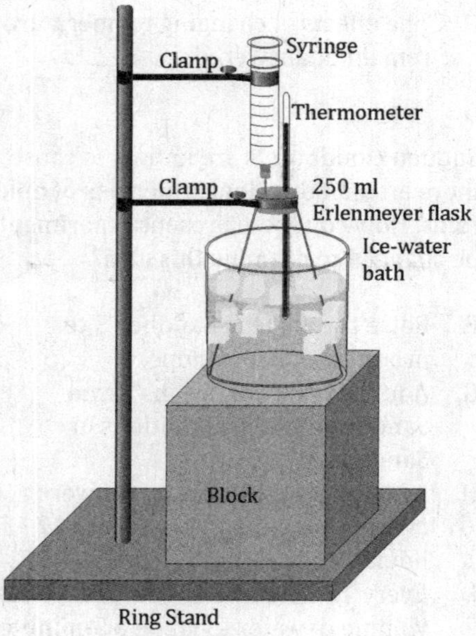

Figure 1

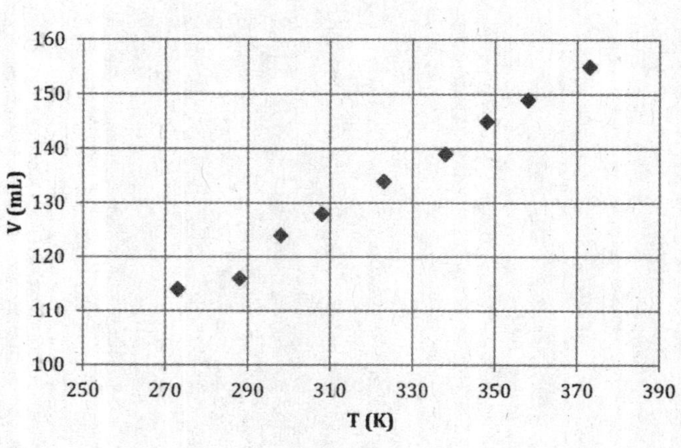

Figure 2

Experiment 2

The students investigated the change in the volume of a gas at room temperature (294 K) at different pressures using the apparatus shown in Figure 3. A glass tube contained a pure nitrogen gas sample (a), and its volume (in mL) was read from the scale. A column of oil (c) transmitted pressure from the reservoir (b), and the pressure value was read on the gauge (d). Table 1 summarizes the data.

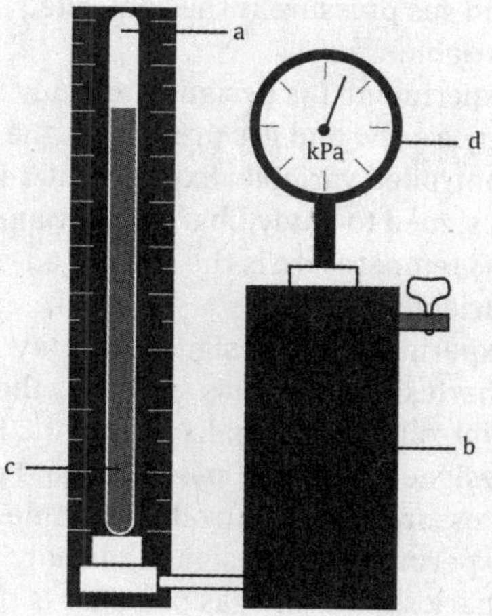

Figure 3

Table 1

Pressure, P (kPa)	Gas Volume, V (mL)
40	160
50	128
60	107
70	91
80	80
100	64
120	53
140	46
160	40
180	35
200	32

Debrief

Notice the trend in this chart and think back to the arrows you drew describing Boyle's and Charles's laws. Which law (and arrow set) fits with this information?

18. Which of the following correctly describes Experiments 1 and 2?

F. Experiment 1 is designed to study Boyle's law and gas temperature is the controlled variable; Experiment 2 is designed to study Charles's law and gas pressure is the controlled variable.
G. Experiment 1 is designed to study Boyle's law and gas pressure is the controlled variable; Experiment 2 is designed to study Charles's law and gas temperature is the controlled variable.
H. Experiment 1 is designed to study Charles's law and gas volume is the controlled variable; Experiment 2 is designed to study Boyle's law and gas pressure is the controlled variable.
J. Experiment 1 is designed to study Charles's law and gas pressure is the controlled variable; Experiment 2 is designed to study Boyle's law and gas temperature is the controlled variable.

19. In the experiment demonstrating Boyle's law, the volume of gas at atmospheric pressure was:

A. 32 mL.
B. 64 mL.
C. 100 mL.
D. Cannot be determined from the given information.

20. In Experiment 2, the function of the column of oil in the experimental apparatus is to:

F. measure the pressure of the air in the glass tube as it expands or contracts.
G. measure the temperature of air in the glass tube as it expands or contracts.
H. transmit pressure from the reservoir to the gas in the glass tube.
J. transmit air to the gas in the glass tube.

21. Does the data graph from Experiment 1 support Charles's law?

A. No; the graph supports Boyle's law because the data demonstrates that volume and temperature are directly proportional.
B. No; the graph does not support Charles's law because the data demonstrates that volume and pressure are inversely proportional.
C. Yes; the graph supports Charles's law because the data demonstrates that volume and temperature are directly proportional.
D. Yes; the graph supports Charles's law because the data demonstrates that volume and temperature are equal.

22. To test the validity of Boyle's law, the students should graph gas volume as a function of:

F. temperature using the data from Experiment 1.
G. temperature using the data from Experiment 2.
H. pressure using the data from Experiment 1.
J. pressure using the data from Experiment 2.

23. Based on the information provided, which of the following is true for the pressure, *P*, temperature, *T*, and/or volume, *V*, of a sample of gas?

A. PV is constant for the same temperature.
B. VT is constant for the same pressure.
C. $\frac{V}{P}$ is constant for the same temperature.
D. PVT is constant for all pressures, volumes, and temperatures.

PASSAGE V

Freezing point depression occurs when a non-volatile solute is added to a pure solvent, resulting in a solution with a lower freezing point than that of the pure solvent. The freezing point depression, ΔT, is roughly proportional to the concentration of the solute in the solution (as measured by molality):

$$\Delta T = K_f \times m \times i \qquad \text{(Equation 1)}$$

K_f is the freezing point depression constant for the solvent, m is the molality of the solution (moles of solute per kilogram of solvent), and i is the van't Hoff factor, which is equal to the number of particles produced by dissolving one unit of solute.

A chemistry student uses the phenomenon of freezing point depression to determine the molar mass and identification of an unknown substance from Table 1.

Table 1

Chemical	Molar Mass (grams/mole)
Sodium iodide (NaI)	150
Calcium sulfate ($CaSO_4$)	136
Sodium nitrate ($NaNO_3$)	85
Sodium chloride (NaCl)	58
Sodium fluoride (NaF)	42

Throwback to Science

If you are confused about how the units work out in Equation 2, you can set up the units in a dimensional analysis equation. Just take the unit fractions of the numerator and denominator, making sure to flip the fraction of the denominator since it is on bottom, and multiply them together. Then cancel out the matching units, which will leave you with the units of the final answer. For example:

$$\frac{\text{g}}{\cancel{\text{kg of water}}}\left(\frac{\cancel{\text{kg of water}}}{\text{mol}}\right) = \frac{\text{g}}{\text{mol}}$$

Part 1

A test tube filled with distilled water is placed in a salt/ice water bath at below –10°C and constantly stirred until crystals begin to form, at which point the distilled water temperature is recorded.

The procedure is repeated for a sugar-water solution of molality 1.0 m (1.0 mol sugar/1 kg water) and van't Hoff factor of 1. The student uses the freezing point depression for the sugar-water solution to calculate the freezing point depression constant for water (Table 2).

Table 2

1. Freezing point of distilled water	–0.04°C
2. Freezing point of 1.0 m sugar-water solution	–1.91°C
3. ΔT for sugar-water solution	–1.87°C
4. K_f value for distilled water	-1.87°C/(mol/kg)

Part 2

A beaker is weighed before and after the addition of approximately 100 mL of distilled water. The beaker is weighed again after the addition of a sample of an unknown substance from Table 1 known to have a van't Hoff factor of 2. The student calculates the solution concentration (grams of solute per kilogram of water).

The freezing point depression of the unknown solution is determined as in Part 1, and the solution molality is calculated. Finally, the student calculates the molar mass of the unknown solute using Equation 2.

$$\text{molar mass (grams/mole)} = \frac{\text{concentration (grams/kilogram of water)}}{\text{molality (moles/kilogram of water)}} \qquad \text{(Equation 2)}$$

The experimental data and calculation results are recorded in Table 3.

Table 3	
1. Mass of empty 250 mL beaker	125.45 g
2. Mass of beaker + water	225.86 g
3. Mass of water in beaker	100.41 g
4. Mass of beaker + water + unknown solute	239.11 g
5. Mass of unknown solute	13.25 g
6. Concentration of unknown solution	131.96 g solute/kg water
7. Freezing point of unknown solution	−8.49°C
8. ΔT for unknown solution	−8.45°C
9. Molality of unknown solution	2.26 mol/kg
10. Molar mass of the unknown solute	?

24. According to the information provided, the ultimate purpose of Part 1 was to experimentally determine:

F. the freezing point of distilled water.
G. the freezing point depression of distilled water.
H. the freezing point depression constant of sugar-water.
J. the freezing point depression constant for distilled water.

25. According to the information provided, which of the following entries in Table 3 were experimental observations?

A. 1, 2, and 7 only
B. 1, 2, and 4 only
C. 1, 2, 4, and 7 only
D. 1, 2, 3, 4, and 7 only

26. The student repeats Part 1 with a 2.0 *m* sugar-water solution. Based on the information provided, the student can expect that:

F. the freezing point depression for the 2.0 *m* sugar solution will be half that of the 1.0 *m* sugar solution.
G. the freezing point depression for the 2.0 *m* sugar solution will be twice that of the 1.0 *m* sugar solution.
H. the freezing point depression constant for distilled water will be twice that found using the 1.0 *m* sugar solution.
J. freezing point depression constant for distilled water will be half that found using the 1.0 *m* sugar solution.

27. Based on the information provided, it can be concluded that the unknown solute tested in Part 2 was most likely:

A. sugar.
B. calcium fluoride.
C. sodium chloride.
D. sodium fluoride.

28. Based on the information provided, decreasing the amount of salt in a salt-water solution will cause the freezing point of the solution to:

F. increase only.
G. decrease only.
H. decrease, then increase.
J. remain the same.

29. The student discovered that the scale was not calibrated properly (set to zero) before it was used in Part 2. Which of the following is the simplest way to correct this mistake?

A. Determine how much mass was added to the measurements from not zeroing the scale and subtract this value from entry 5 in Table 2.
B. Determine how much mass was added to the measurements from not zeroing the scale and subtract this value from entries 3 and 5 in Table 2.
C. Determine how much mass was added to the measurements from not zeroing the scale and subtract this value from entries 1, 2, and 5 and recalculate entries 3 and 5 in Table 2
D. No correction is necessary because any added mass from not zeroing the balance would cancel out in the calculations leading to entries 3 and 5.

PASSAGE VI

A useful property of lenses is their ability to form images of objects due to the refraction of light as it passes from one medium to another. *Focal length* is the distance between the center of a lens and the point at which a clear image of a very distant object is formed. If the object and image sizes are *h* and *h'*, respectively, the magnification of the lens is the ratio of the image size to object size, or:

$$\frac{h'}{h} = -\frac{i}{o} \qquad \text{(Equation 1)}$$

In Equation 1, *o* represents the distance between the center of the lens and the object and *i* represents the distance between the center of the lens and the image. The magnification is represented as a negative number to indicate that an inverted image has a negative height and an upright image has a positive height.

Experiment 1

A student places an LED candle 100 centimeters from a thin converging lens. A paper screen on the other side of the lens is moved until a sharply focused image of the candle light appears on the screen (Figure 1). The image distance and height are measured. The candle is moved 20 centimeters closer to the lens and the experiment repeated until an object distance of 20 centimeters is reached. For each data set, the magnification is calculated (Table 1).

Table 1

Object Distance, *o* (cm)	Image Distance, *i* (cm)	Image Height, *h'* (cm)	Magnification
100.0	11.1	−0.55	−0.11
80.0	11.4	−0.71	−0.14
60.0	12.0	−1.00	−0.20
40.0	13.3	−1.66	−0.33
20.0	20.0	−5.00	−1.00

Experiment 2

The student repeats Experiment 1 after replacing the single lens with two identical lenses side-by-side and in contact with each other. Table 2 summarizes the results.

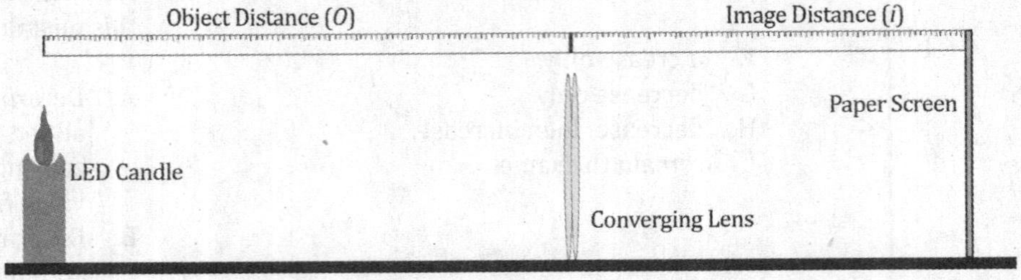

Figure 1

Table 2

Object Distance, o (cm)	Image Distance, i (cm)	Image Height, h′ (cm)	Magnification
100.0	5.3	−0.27	−0.05
80.0	5.3	−0.33	−0.07
60.0	5.5	−0.46	−0.09
40.0	5.7	−0.71	−0.14
20.0	6.7	−1.68	−0.34

Experiment 3

Using a similarly sized waterproofed LED candle and white plastic screen, the student repeats Experiment 1 in a water-filled tank until the length of the tank prevents further measurements. Table 3 summarizes the results.

Table 3

Object Distance, o (cm)	Image Distance, i (cm)	Image Height, h′ (cm)	Magnification
100.0	63.9	−3.20	−0.64
80.0	76.1	−4.76	−0.95
60.0	88.1	−7.34	−1.47

Use POE

Notice that each of the answer choices for item #30 mentions a different independent variable. Use the process of elimination to identify the independent variable in Experiment 3 and rule out the wrong answers.

30. Which of the following best describes the purpose of Experiment 3?

F. To study how focal length is affected by changing the medium surrounding a pair of converging lenses
G. To study how image formation is affected by combining converging lenses
H. To study how image formation is affected by changing the medium surrounding a converging lens
J. To study how image formation is affected by changing the position of an object relative to a converging lens

31. According to the experimental results, for the same object distance, the paired converging lenses in air produces a magnification:

A. less than that of a single converging lens in air.
B. greater than that of a single converging lens in air.
C. equal to that of a single converging lens in air.
D. greater than that of a single converging lens in water.

32. Which of the following graphs best represents the relationship between object distance and image distance for a thin converging lens in air?

F.

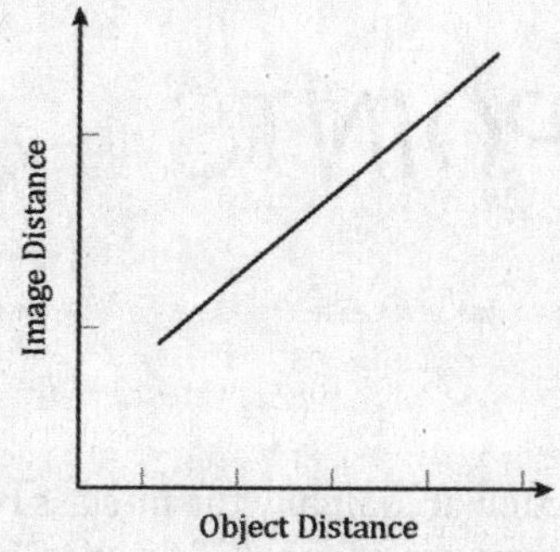

G.

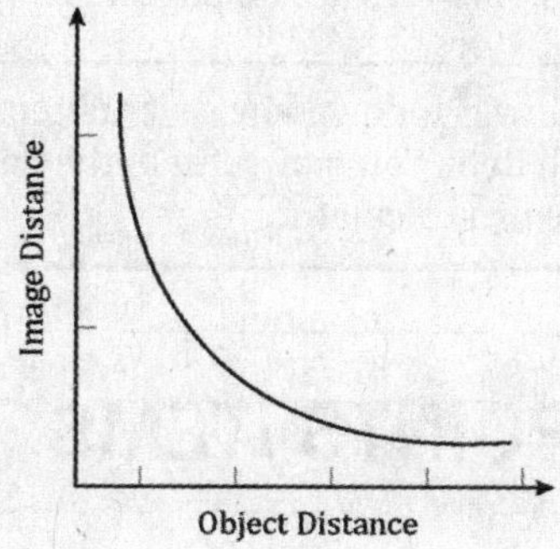

H.

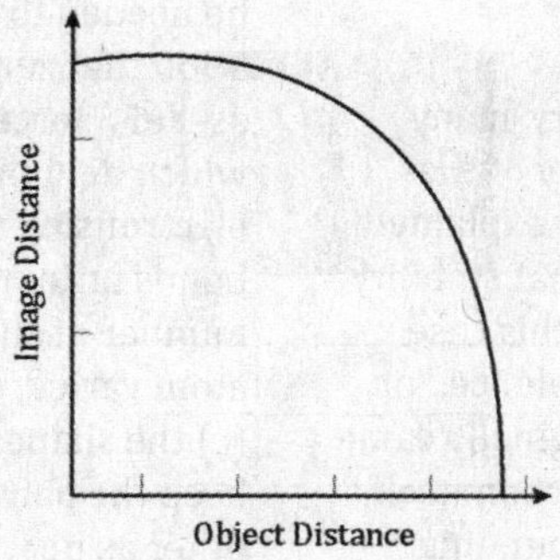

J.

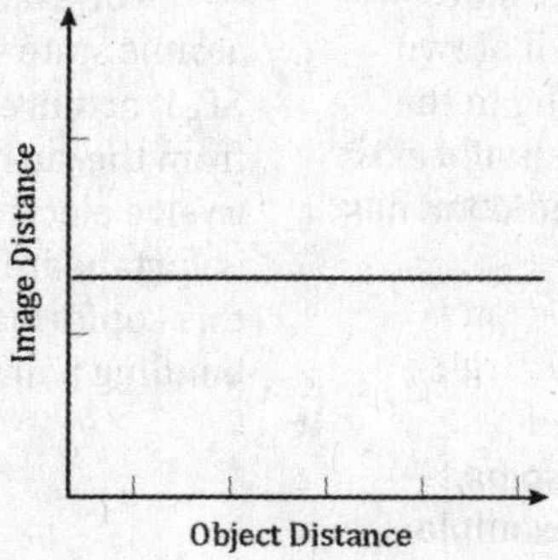

33. Based on the information provided, approximately how tall are the LED candles used in these experiments?

A. 5 cm
B. 10 cm
C. 20 cm
D. Cannot be determined from the given information

34. For a thin converging lens in air, the lens formula relates focal length, f, to object distance, o, and image distance, i:

$$\frac{1}{f} = \frac{1}{i} + \frac{1}{o}$$

Using this information, what is the focal length of the lens used in Experiment 1?

F. 33.3 cm
G. 40 cm
H. 10 cm
J. 5 cm

LESSON 3

CONFLICTING VIEWPOINTS

The passages and items in this section accompany the in-class review of the skills and concepts tested by Conflicting Viewpoints passages on the ACT Science Test. You will work through the items with your instructor in class. Answers are on page 441.

DIRECTIONS: Each passage below is followed by several items. After reading a passage, choose the best answer to each item. You may refer to the passages as often as necessary. You are NOT permitted the use of a calculator.

TYPICAL CONFLICTING VIEWPOINTS ITEMS

Passage Perfect

Circle or underline key information as you read the passage. This will allow you to easily locate key points in each theory.

PASSAGE I

Theory 1

Early in the twentieth century, many chemists believed that the stability of the molecule methane, CH_4, could be explained by the "octet" rule, which states that stability occurs when the central atom, in this case carbon, is surrounded by eight "valence," or outer, electrons. Four of these originally came from the outer electrons of the carbon itself, and four came from the four surrounding hydrogen atoms (the hydrogen atom was considered an exception to the rule since it was known to favor a closed shell of two electrons, as helium has). According to the octet rule, neither CH_3 nor CH_5 should exist as stable compounds, and this prediction has been borne out by experiment.

Theory 2

While the octet rule predicted many compounds accurately, it also had shortcomings. Ten electrons, for example, surround the compound PCl_5. The greatest shock to the octet rule concerned noble gases such as krypton and xenon, which have eight electrons surrounding them in their atomic states, and therefore should not form compounds since no more electrons would be needed to make an octet. The discovery in 1960 that xenon could form compounds such as XeF_4 forced consideration of a new theory, which held that (a) compounds formed when electrons were completely paired, either in bonds or in non-bonded pairs; (b) the total number of shared electrons around a central atom varied, and could be as high as twelve; (c) the shapes of compounds were such as to keep the pairs of electrons as far from each other as possible.

For example, since six electrons in the atomic state surround sulfur, in the compound SF_6 it acquired six additional shared electrons from the surrounding fluorines for a total of twelve electrons. The shape of the compound is "octahedral," as shown in Figure 1, since this conformation minimizes the overlap of bonding pairs of electrons.

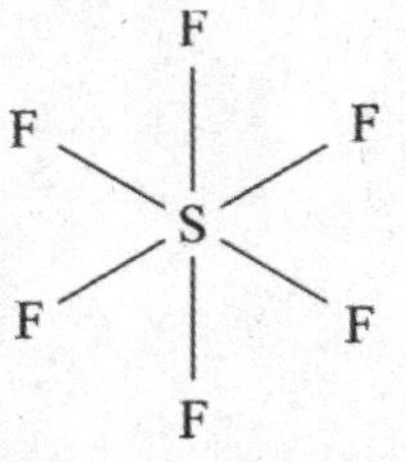

Figure 1

1. According to Theory 1, the compound CH_2Cl_2:

A. should have eight electrons surrounding the carbon atom.
B. cannot exist since the original carbon atom does not have eight electrons.
C. should have eight electrons surrounding each hydrogen atom.
D. requires more electrons for stability.

2. According to Theory 1, the compound XeF_4:

F. exists with an octet structure around the xenon atom.
G. should not exist since more than eight electrons surround the xenon atom.
H. will have chemical properties similar to those of CH_4.
J. exists with the xenon atom surrounded by twelve electrons.

3. The boron atom has three outer electrons, and in bonding to boron, a fluorine atom has a single, unpaired electron to bond with a boron atom. The BF_3 molecule is known to exist. Which of the following is true?

A. BF_3 obeys Theory 1.
B. The existence of BF_3 contradicts Theory 2.
C. According to Theory 2, the structure of BF_3 is a pyramid:

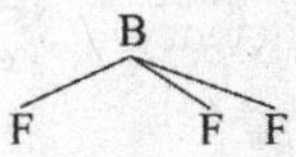

D. According to Theory 2, the structure of BF_3 is triangular and planar:

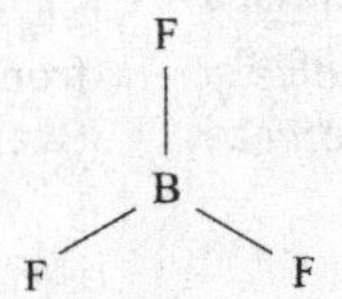

4. A scientist seeking to explain why Theory 2 has more predictive power than Theory 1 might argue that:

F. eight electrons shall represent a "closed shell."
G. while eight electrons represent a "closed shell" for some atoms, for others the closed shell may be six, ten, or twelve.
H. it is incorrect to assume that a given atom always has the same number of electrons around it.
J. CH_4 is not as important a compound as XeF_4.

5. Theory 2 could be threatened by evidence of:

A. the existence of SF_4.
B. the existence of XeF_5.
C. molecules with stable octets.
D. the existence of SF_6.

The Cambridge Edge

How can you recognize a Conflicting Viewpoints item? Here are some sample items to help you recognize what these questions ask:

1. *Predict results based on Scientist 1's argument.*
2. *Select a generalization that is most accurate given that Scientist 1's argument is correct.*
3. *Select the findings upon which Scientist 1 and Scientist 2 would NOT agree.*
4. *Predict which observations support Scientist 1's argument.*
5. *Select the weakest link in one of the arguments.*
6. *Select the findings that support the interpretations of both scientists.*
7. *Select a criticism that Scientist 2 would make about Scientist 1's conclusion.*

PASSAGE II

Scientist 1

The atmosphere of Earth was at one time almost totally lacking in oxygen. One piece of evidence supporting this assertion is the very fact that life got started at all. The first chemical reactions that are necessary for the origin of life, the formation of amino acids, require ultraviolet light. Most of the ultraviolet light coming from the sun is now absorbed by oxygen in the atmosphere. If there were as much oxygen in the atmosphere then as there is now, there would have been too little ultraviolet light available to enable life to begin. Also, the oldest bacteria, the ones that have the shortest DNA, are almost all anaerobes—they either do not need oxygen or die if exposed to oxygen. Most of the oxygen that exists now entered the atmosphere later from volcanic fumes, which continue to occur.

Scientist 2

The prevailing opinion is that the atmosphere, though thicker now than it was in the past, is not essentially different in composition. The argument that Earth must originally have been deficient in oxygen is flawed. First of all, the presence of iron and other oxides in the rocks from this time indicates that there was oxygen available. Secondly, the requirement for a great deal of ultraviolet light holds only if there is a low concentration of the starting materials in the water. If the water in some prehistoric lake began to freeze, the starting materials would be concentrated in a small volume of unfrozen water. The high concentration of the starting materials would offset the so-called deficiency of ultraviolet light, and life could begin.

6. According to the hypothesis of Scientist 1, which of the following would have been among the last living things to evolve?

F. Anaerobes
G. Amino Acids
H. Insects
J. Viruses

7. According to the information presented by Scientist 1, if his theory of the origin of oxygen in the atmosphere is correct, the total amount of oxygen in the air over the next million years, on the average, should:

A. decrease, then increase.
B. increase, then decrease.
C. increase only.
D. decrease only.

8. Underlying the argument of Scientist 2 is the assumption that the oxygen in the oxides in the rocks was:

F. always tied up in the rocks.
G. involved in biological reactions.
H. completely gaseous during the early days of the atmosphere.
J. proportional to the oxygen in the atmosphere at the time.

9. Underlying Scientist 1's suggestion that the evolutionary record supports the idea of an oxygen deficiency on early Earth is the assumption that the oldest living things:

A. have the shortest DNA.
B. have the most fragmented DNA.
C. have changed radically.
D. must have died out.

10. Which of the following is the strongest argument Scientist 1 could use to counter Scientist 2's suggested mechanism for the origin of life?

F. There was not enough ultraviolet light available.
G. Chemical reactions occurred differently then.
H. The temperature at the surface of Earth at that time was always above 35°C because of geothermal heat release.
J. Most lakes would not have covered large enough areas to guarantee that all the essential building blocks were present.

11. To refute Scientist 1's hypothesis, Scientist 2 might best show that:

A. the amount of oxide in rocks has changed little over the past four billion years.
B. there are ways of making the biologically important molecules without ultraviolet light.
C. there are complex anaerobic bacteria.
D. the atmospheric pressure has not changed over Earth's history.

Master Moves

If you can't automatically see the assumption in the scientist's argument, try thinking about which answer choice, if removed from the passage, would make the scientist's statement seem weak or even false. You can also use the converse of this method. Which answer choice, if put into the passage, makes the scientist's argument stronger and more logical?

Master Moves

Items like #6 rely on your ability to pick up on clues in the passage and then use these clues to infer the correct answer. For example, this question is checking to see whether you could infer the correct answer from the line"the oldest bacteria, the ones that have the shortest DNA, are almost all anaerobes." When tackling these questions, look for similarities in clues and the item stem.

CONFLICTING VIEWPOINTS STRATEGIES

The Cambridge Edge

Use the following strategies for Conflicting Viewpoints passages:

1. Be prepared to predict results.
2. Watch for assumptions in each viewpoint.
3. Be prepared to identify which argument best addresses the issue.
4. Identify the viewpoints' main point(s) and logical value; identify the differences.
5. Read the viewpoints, but do NOT dwell on the details.
6. Read the answer choices carefully.

PASSAGE III

In the 1940s, 1950s, and 1960s, the growing field of animal behavior maintained an ongoing debate about the origin of observed behavior in many different animal species. Two extreme viewpoints were at the center of this "Nature vs. Nurture" debate.

Viewpoint 1 (Nature)

Many behaviors or instincts are literally programmed by one or more genes. Genes serve as "blueprints" that enable an individual to carry out a particular stereotyped behavior (Fixed Action Pattern) as soon as the appropriate stimulus (releaser) is observed. Other individuals do not have to be observed performing the behavior. The releasing stimulus need never have been seen before. At first view of the releaser and every time thereafter, the Fixed Action Pattern will be carried out to completion in the exact same way—even if the releaser is removed before the Fixed Action Pattern is completed. Examples include a) the pecking of baby gulls at the red spot on their mother's bill (which causes the mother gull to regurgitate food), b) song birds producing their species song without ever having heard it before, and c) a male stickle-back fish defending its territory by attacking anything red because other breeding males have red underbellies.

Viewpoint 2 (Nurture)

Many behaviors are determined by experience and/or learning during an individual's lifetime. Genes provide the limits of the "blank slate" that each individual starts out as, but then various experiences will determine the actual behavior patterns within the individual genetic range of possibilities. In other words, behavior can be modified. Examples include a) positive ("reward") reinforcement and punishment causing a behavior to increase and decrease (respectively), and b) songbirds producing their species song only after having heard it performed by other individuals of their species.

12. The red spot on a mother gull's bill is called a(n):

F. Fixed Action Pattern.
G. instinct.
H. releaser.
J. stereotyped response.

The Cambridge Edge

Item #15 is testing your ability to identify examples of a concept. Sometimes this type of question can be tricky, but if you break the question down into its basic components, the answer can be found. Ask yourself, "What action is being completed? Is this action something the animal is learning, or is it something the animal already knew?"

13. To refute the strict "genetic blueprint" ideas of Viewpoint 1, a scientist could show that:

A. baby gulls peck at a stick with a red spot.
B. baby gulls will peck at mother gulls' red spot as soon as they hatch out of their eggs.
C. baby gulls pecking at the red spot happens exactly the same way each time.
D. baby gulls' accuracy in pecking at mother gulls' red spot improves with practice.

14. A food-seeking blue jay captured a distinctively colored butterfly that had a bad-tasting substance in its tissues. After spitting out the butterfly, it never again tried to capture a similarly colored butterfly. This incident seems to support:

F. Viewpoint 1.
G. Viewpoint 2.
H. both viewpoints.
J. neither viewpoint (the incident is irrelevant).

15. Which of the following supports Viewpoint 1?

A. A rat reaches the end of a maze by the same route, but finishes faster after each trip.
B. A monkey watches other monkeys wash sweet potatoes before they eat them; then, he washes sweet potatoes before he eats them.
C. A male stickleback fish attacks a picture of a red mailbox held in front of his aquarium.
D. A bird performs its species song after hearing the song only once.

16. If a female goose uses a repeated beak and neck movement to return an egg to her nest, continuing the movement even when the egg slides off course or is removed, then this:

F. supports Viewpoint 1.
G. supports Viewpoint 2.
H. does not refer to behavior.
J. is irrelevant to the Nature vs. Nurture debate.

17. It is thought that some species of birds "learn" to fly. This belief is based on observations of young birds fluttering and flapping their wings at the nest until they reach the age when flight is possible. In Species X, nestlings were kept in harmless, but tight plastic tubes in which they could not carry out such "practice movements." They were released when they reached the age of flight. Viewpoint 1 predicts that the birds will fly:

A. after fluttering their wings for a time.
B. after watching other birds flutter their wings.
C. after watching other birds flutter and fly.
D. immediately.

18. A songbird can sing its species song after it hears other birds of its own species singing. Yet, if it hears the song from another species, the bird will not sing the "foreign" song. This suggests that:

F. genetic "programming" and experience play a role in this species' ability to sing its song.
G. this species' song is a Fixed Action Pattern.
H. song development in this species is strictly a learned behavior with no genetic component.
J. genes appear to be far more important than experience in this example.

Passage Perfect

For a graph like this where distinct regions are described, it can be helpful to mark up the graph with information from the passage. For example, in the photosphere region you might write "densest," and in the corona region you might write "least dense and hottest."

PASSAGE IV

The sun's atmosphere is divided into three major regions: the photosphere, the chromosphere, and the corona. The photosphere is the visible region of the sun. Just above the photosphere is the chromosphere which is far less dense, but hotter. Consisting of low-density plasma, the corona is the thin, outermost atmosphere of the sun that extends for millions of kilometers above the sun's surface.

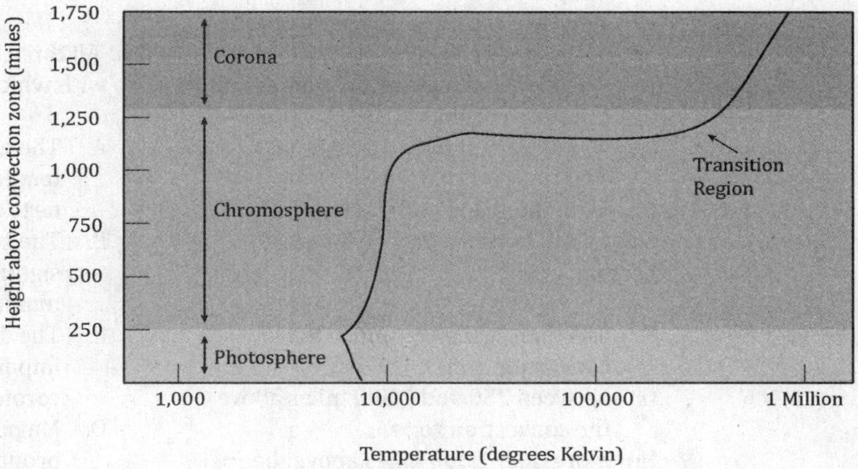

One would expect that the atmosphere of the sun should become cooler with increasing distance from its surface. To the contrary, as the graph above shows, coronal temperatures increase with increasing distance from the sun's visible photosphere, rising to over a million degrees. The mechanism responsible for this heating remains a fundamental question of modern astrophysics.

Three scientists discuss the heating mechanism.

Scientist 1

Just above the surface of the sun, in the chromosphere, there are approximately 10,000 regions of violently rotating columns of hydrogen and helium gas, or vortices. These vortices are likely produced by magnetic activity within the sun that exerts pressure on the plasma in the atmosphere. Computer simulations suggest that plasma particles trapped within the vortices are accelerated as they spiral toward the corona. The accelerated plasma particles greatly increase the average speed of the coronal particles, which translates into higher coronal temperatures.

Scientist 2

Solar telescopes have detected millions of magnetic patches on the sun's photosphere. The patches, between 50 and 1,000 kilometers wide, are constantly changing in size and shape due to the turbulent movement of the plasma in the chromosphere. The magnetic fields in the sun's corona constantly change as they respond to changes in the photosphere magnetic patches. As magnetic field lines in the corona interact, they undergo a process called reconnection: they snap apart and then reconnect. The reconnection releases a tremendous amount of heat and wave energy, causing the high coronal temperatures.

Scientist 3

Neutrons are produced in the sun's interior through thermonuclear reactions in the core and the stripping of complex particles at the surface. Due to solar flares and other magnetic phenomena, some of these neutrons reach the base of the sun's corona. Free neutrons last about 15 minutes before they undergo radioactive decay, creating electrons as energetic as 0.78 MeV. When these fast moving electrons collide with particles in the corona, they transfer some of their energy, causing the high coronal temperatures.

19. Which of the following best describes the question the three scientists attempt to answer?

A. What is the cause of vortices on the surface of the sun?
B. What is the cause of high coronal temperatures?
C. What are the physical characteristics of the sun's corona?
D. What is the temperature gradient of the sun's corona?

20. Based on the graph and the views of Scientist 1, vortices may be found at heights:

F. less than 250 miles above the convection zone.
G. between 250 and 1,300 miles above the convection zone.
H. more than 1,300 miles above the convection zone.
J. more than 10,000 miles above the convection zone.

21. Scientist 2 states that the changing magnetic patches on the sun's photosphere are due to:

A. the radioactive decay of neutrons.
B. plasma particles trapped within vortices.
C. the movement of the plasma in the chromosphere.
D. fast moving electrons colliding with particles in the corona.

22. Magnetism plays a role in the explanation of the coronal heating in the views of:

F. Scientists 1 and 2 only.
G. Scientists 1 and 3 only.
H. Scientists 2 and 3 only.
J. all three scientists.

23. All three scientists would likely agree with which of the following statements?

A. The energy source for high coronal temperatures in the corona originates near or in the sun.
B. The coronal temperatures do not vary significantly from the average surface temperature of the sun.
C. The decay of neutrons plays an important role in the creation of high coronal temperatures.
D. Magnetic-generated tornadoes produce neutrons that decay, creating energetic electrons.

> *The Cambridge Edge*
>
> Don't forget to pay close attention to this passage introduction! It can give you insights into the comparative passages that follow and can also give you helpful hints to solve accompanying questions.

PASSAGE V

Space probes have imaged thousands of gullies on Mars—channels, or ravines, worn into the surface of the planet. On Earth, gullies form as running water erodes soil. Mars, however, is currently a frigid planet without rain or liquid water on the surface. Interestingly, some of the Martian gullies appear to have formed very recently. Three planetary scientists discuss the origins of gullies on Mars.

Scientist 1

Mars contains many deposits of solid carbon dioxide, or dry ice, buried under the dust and sand found on the slopes of hills and craters. When sunlight warms these deposits, the dry ice converts directly into a gas through the process of sublimation. As the carbon dioxide gas blows out of the ground, the surrounding dust and sand flow like a liquid in a process called fluidization.

An experiment conducted on Earth supports this mechanism for gully formation. A tub was filled with Mars-like dust and sand shaped into a small mound. An air pump buried beneath the mound forced air up toward the surface. The dust and sand flowed down the mound, creating gullies similar to those imaged on Mars.

Scientist 2

The gullies on Mars form when water from shallow aquifers seeps onto the surface and flows downslope. Although the surface of Mars is dry today, there is abundant evidence that at one time water flowed on its surface. Some of that water likely still exists in underground aquifers. Liquid water is unstable on the surface of Mars due to low temperatures and low atmospheric pressure. However, computer models indicate that liquid water could be discharged onto the surface of Mars in two situations: the liquid in a shallow aquifer is water with a temperature of at least 350 K, or if the liquid is a water-based brine with a freezing point of no more than 250 K. In either scenario, the flow of water onto the surface is likely triggered by the melting of surface ice plugs, which otherwise act like caps for the water in the aquifers. Once the ice plugs melt, the sub-surface water gushes to the surface, forming gullies as the water flows downslope.

Scientist 3

The gullies on Mars form when snow packs melt. The melted snow (liquid water) at the bottom of snow packs does not undergo rapid evaporation due to the low atmospheric pressure on Mars. This water carves the gullies as it flows downslope. This theory is supported by the fact that most gullies found on Mars are on the cold, pole-facing slopes of hills and craters. These colder conditions allow for the accumulation of snow on these slopes, which with warmer temperatures, begin to melt, initiating the formation of gullies.

24. According to the information provided, which of the following accurately describes the current environmental conditions on Mars?

F. High temperatures and high atmospheric pressure
G. High temperatures and low atmospheric pressure
H. Low temperatures and high atmospheric pressure
J. Low temperatures and low atmospheric pressure

25. Which scientist's argument presents water as the primary agent in gully formation on Mars?

A. Scientist 1 only
B. Scientist 2 only
C. Scientists 1 and 3 only
D. Scientists 2 and 3 only

26. Which scientist's argument does NOT require the flow of a liquid to explain gully formation on Mars?

F. Scientist 1
G. Scientist 2
H. Scientist 3
J. None of the scientists

27. All three scientists agree that gully formation on Mars is triggered by:

A. the flow of a liquid on the surface.
B. surface warming.
C. sublimation of sub-surface ices.
D. a drop in atmospheric pressure.

28. Which scientist's argument is best supported by the fact that most gullies on Mars are found on cold, pole-facing slopes?

F. Scientist 1 only
G. Scientist 2 only
H. Scientist 3 only
J. All three scientists

29. The gamma ray spectrometer (GRS) on-board the space probe Mars Odyssey detects water on the surface of Mars down to a depth of several meters. A strong correlation is found between areas on Mars where the GRS detected high levels of water and where the majority of gullies are found. That most gullies are found in water-rich areas supports the position(s) of:

A. Scientist 1 only.
B. Scientist 3 only.
C. Scientists 1 and 3 only.
D. Scientists 2 and 3 only.

SCIENCE
QUIZZES

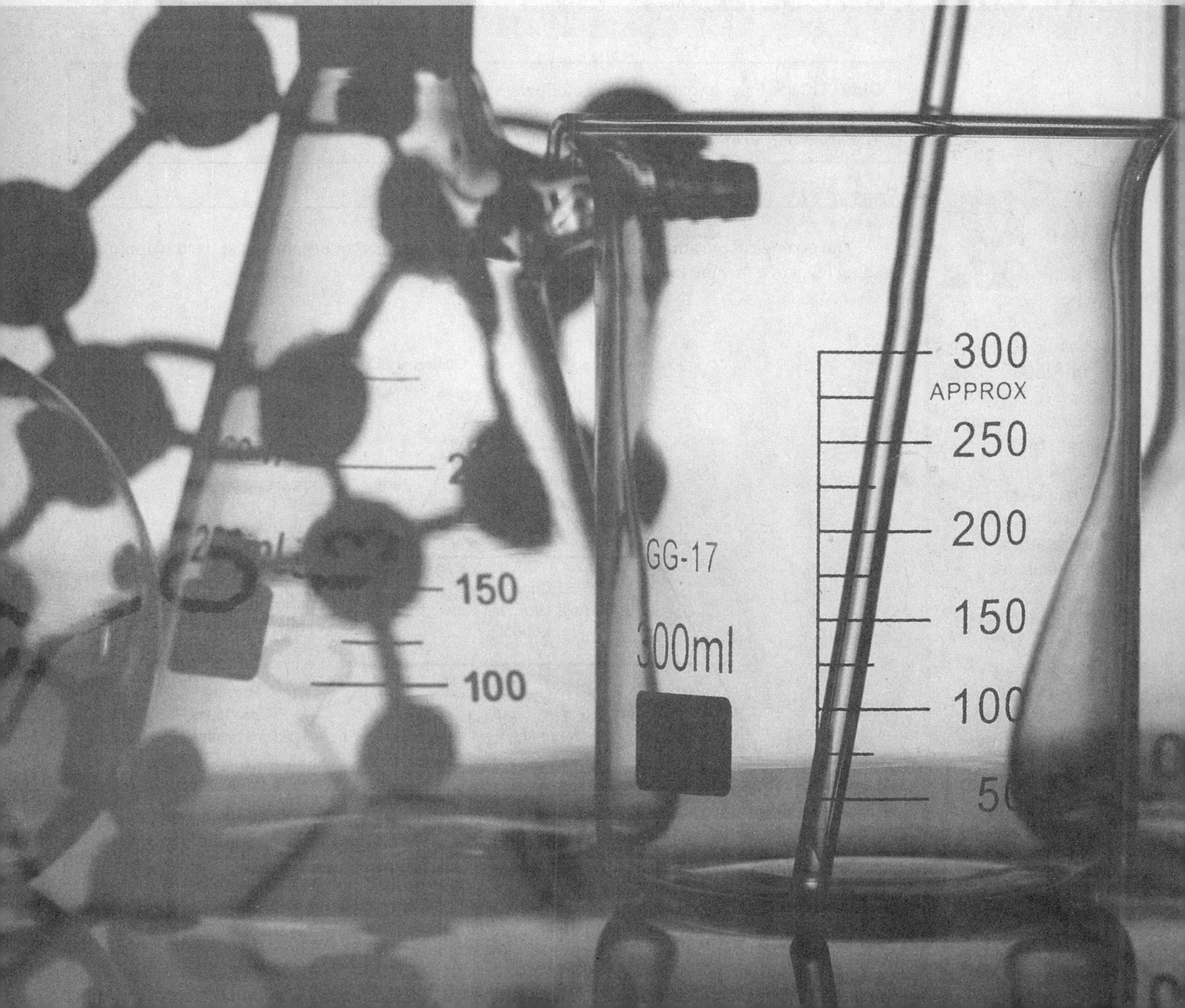

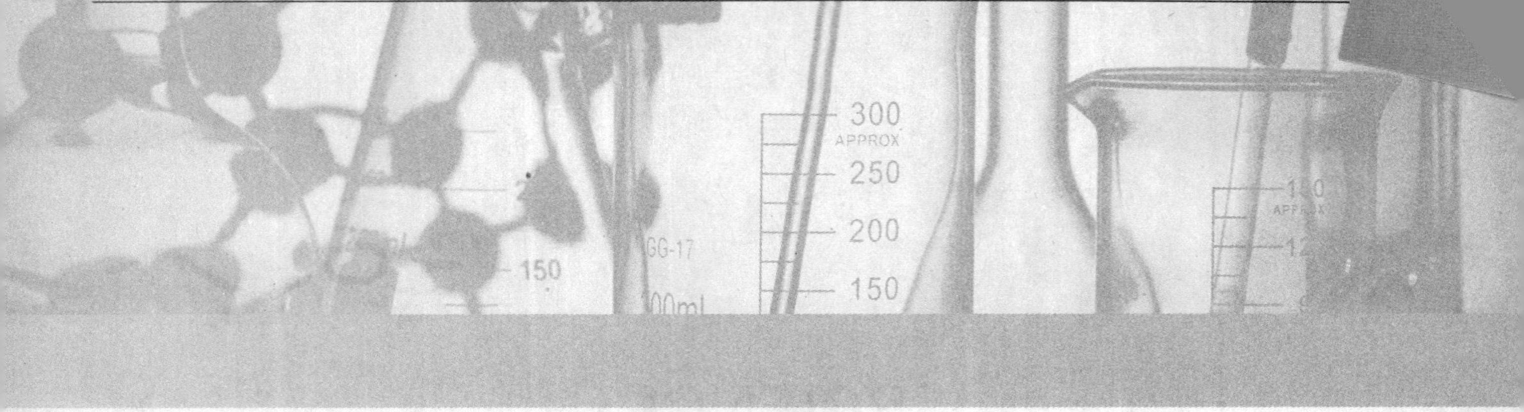

This section contains two Science quizzes. The first quiz is a directed study quiz. The directed study quiz is not timed. Answer each question and check your work as you go. The second quiz is a timed quiz. Take the second quiz under the indicated timed conditions to practice your pacing as you apply what you learned in the Science Lessons.

DIRECTED STUDY QUIZ *(16 items)*

DIRECTIONS: Each passage below is followed by several items. After reading a passage, choose the best answer to each item. You may refer to the passages as often as necessary. You are NOT permitted the use of a calculator.

Master Moves

When you see a diagram like this, with the same information given for each scientific concept, it is helpful to spend a few moments trying to understand the relationship between all of these concepts. This can help you speed through later questions. For example, in this passage, understanding the relationship between each trophic feeding level helps you quickly answer questions 2, 4, and 5.

Passage I

The ecological pyramid below shows the relative biomass* of organisms at each trophic feeding level of a marine food chain.

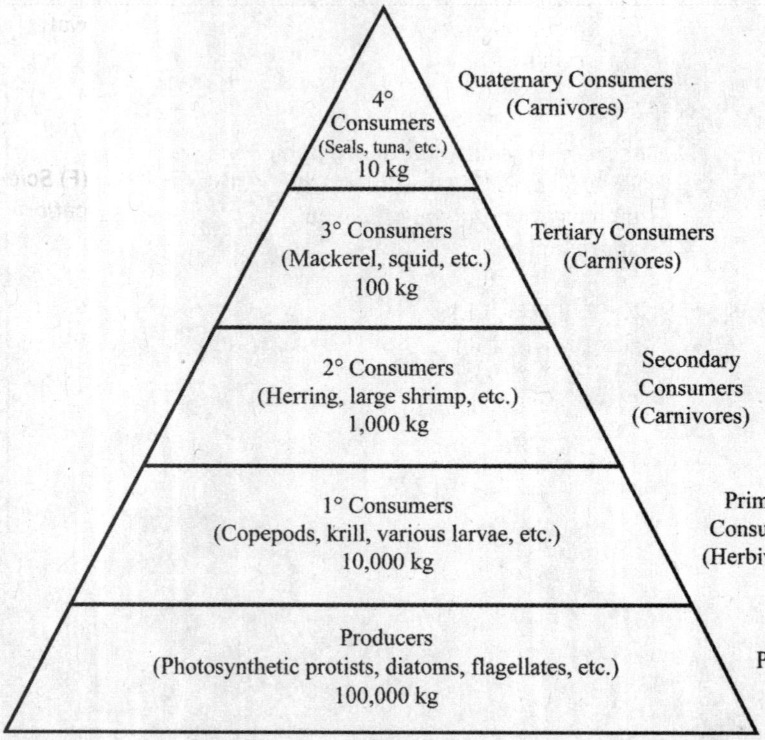

*Biomass is the total dry weight of organisms (usable chemical energy stored in organic matter) at each trophic level at any given time.

1. According to the diagram, the trophic level with the largest relative biomass is the:

A. 4° consumers.
B. 3° and 2° consumers.
C. 1° consumers.
D. producers.

2. From the information in the diagram, one can conclude that at any given time:

F. 10 seals may be found for every mackerel.
G. the relative dry weight of all carnivores combined is far greater than that of the herbivores alone.
H. only 1 percent of all producers live long enough to be eaten by a mackerel.
J. the relative dry weight of every consumer trophic level is less than that of the trophic level on which they feed.

3. Organisms from which trophic level are most likely to be found near the water surface where light can penetrate?

A. 4° consumers
B. 2° consumers
C. 3° consumers
D. producers

4. If there were an additional trophic level of carnivores (5° consumers), its relative biomass at any given time would be approximately:

F. 0.1 kg.
G. 1 kg.
H. 9 kg.
J. 1,000,000 kg.

EXPLANATIONS

1. (D) ***Science/Interpretation of Data/ Comprehension***
The trophic level with the largest biomass is at the base of the pyramid: producers (100,000 kg).

2. (J) ***Science/Evaluation of Models/Analysis***
The relative dry weight of the organisms in each trophic level decreases from bottom to top. That is, the relative weight of each level's organisms is smaller than the relative weight of the food it eats in the next lower level.

3. (D) ***Science/Evaluation of Models/Analysis***
Light is always needed by the photosynthetic organisms of any ecosystem. Since light does not penetrate into the deeper waters, producers must remain near the water surface.

4. (F) ***Science/Scientific Investigation/Application***
Each trophic level supports 10% of the biomass found in the previous trophic level. Therefore, since the 4° consumer trophic level has a relative biomass totaling 10 kg, it will support $\frac{1}{10}$ of 10 kg = 1 kg of relative biomass

in the next trophic level.

5. The best explanation for biomass being measured as dry weight is:

A. if water weight were included, efficiency ratios at each trophic level would be unpredictable.
B. body fluids contribute little to the mass of marine organisms.
C. water molecules contain little or no usable chemical energy.
D. each trophic level contains a different amount of water.

EXPLANATIONS

5. **(C)** ***Science/Evaluation of Models/Analysis*** The definition of biomass, as indicated in the footnote, states that dry weight reflects the usable chemical energy stored at each trophic level. Since water weight represents no additional usable energy, it is not included in measures of biomass.

Passage II

The graph below shows various characteristics of the different layers of the atmosphere and the boundaries between layers.

The Cambridge Edge

Graphs with this much information can be difficult to understand. Breaking the graph down step by step can help you master the graph and answer any accompanying questions. Start by understanding the relationship between the *x*- and *y*-axes. Then add in each additional layer of information, keeping in mind how these pieces fit in with the *x*- and *y*-axes.

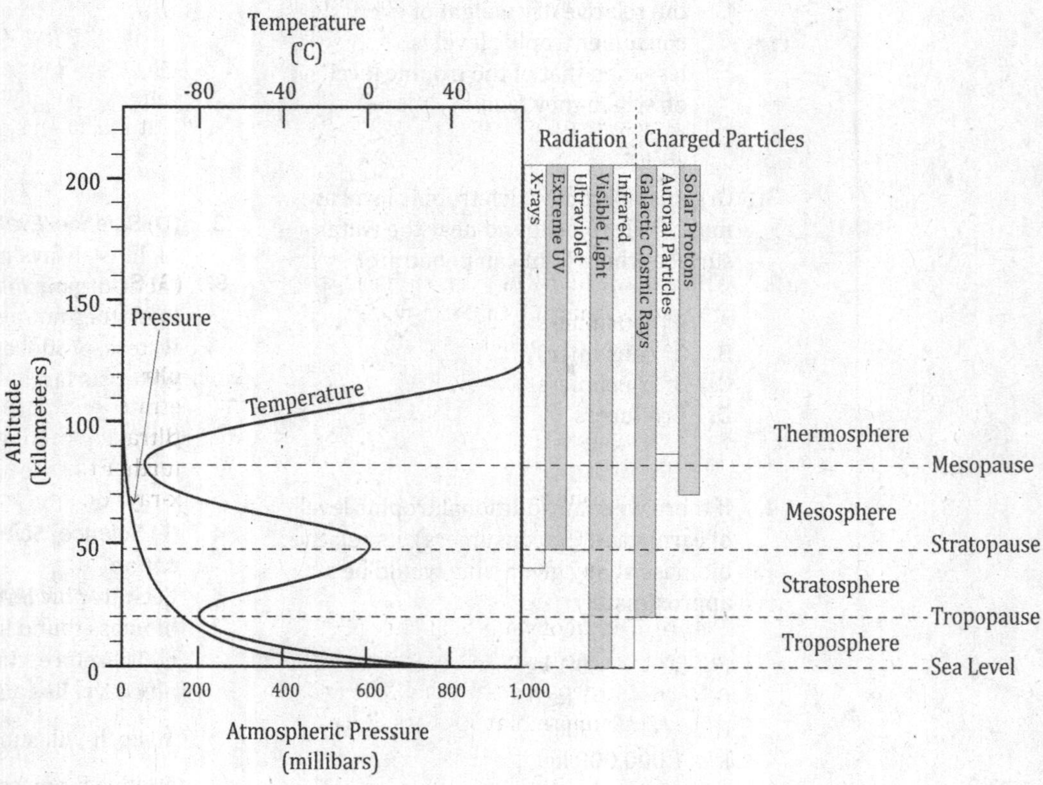

6. Which statement accurately describes the relationship between the approximate altitude and the approximate mean temperature of the layers of the atmosphere?

F. As altitude increases, temperature increases.
G. As altitude increases, temperature decreases.
H. As altitude increases, temperature first decreases then continuously increases.
J. As altitude increases, temperature first decreases, then increases, then decreases, and then increases.

7. According to the diagram, the atmospheric layer with the narrowest range of altitude is the:

A. thermosphere.
B. troposphere.
C. mesosphere.
D. stratosphere.

8. Which of the following atmospheric layers can x-rays penetrate that ultraviolet radiation can not penetrate?

F. troposphere
G. stratosphere
H. mesosphere
J. thermosphere

9. The absorption of solar heat energy increases as the gases of the atmosphere become less dense, or rarefied. The layer of the atmosphere that appears most rarefied is the:

A. thermosphere.
B. mesosphere.
C. stratosphere.
D. troposphere.

EXPLANATIONS

6. (J) *Science/Interpretation of Data/Analysis*
In the graph, the temperature data corresponds to the axis at the top of the diagram. The general trend of the temperature data is to decrease (from about 30°C at sea level), then increase, then decrease, and then increase again to nearly 80°C.

7. (B) *Science/Interpretation of Data/ Comprehension*
Altitude is shown by the left-hand axis of the graph. The troposphere is the atmospheric layer with the smallest range of altitude, from sea level to about 12 km.

8. (G) *Science/Evaluation of Models/ Comprehension*
According to the right side of the diagram, ultraviolet radiation and x-rays both penetrate the thermospere and mesosphere. Ultraviolet radiation does not penetrate further than the mesosphere. However, x-rays do penetrate the stratosphere.

9. (A) *Science/Interpretation of Data/ Analysis*
The greater the amount of solar heat absorbed by an atmospheric layer, the hotter and more rarefied that layer will become. According to the diagram, the hottest layer is the thermosphere.

10. According to the diagram, which atmospheric layer shows the greatest decrease in temperature per unit increase in altitude?

F. thermosphere
G. mesosphere
H. stratosphere
J. troposphere

EXPLANATIONS

10. (J) *Science/Interpretation of Data/Analysis*
According to the diagram, the temperature decreases with increasing altitude in the mesosphere and troposphere only, so eliminate (F) and (H). To choose between (G) and (J), compare the slopes of the data lines. The temperature decreases by about 120°C per an increase of 20 kilometers in the troposphere, while the temperatures decreases by about 100°C per 35 kilometers in the mesosphere. So the greatest decrease in temperatures per unit increase in altitude happens in the troposphere, (J).

The Cambridge Edge

For speed and accuracy, it is helpful to draw diagrams of Experiments 1, 2, and 3. This method helps you quickly answer questions that ask you to manipulate parts of each experiment, such as questions 11, 12, and 15. Also, any questions about experimental set-up can be easily tackled using this method.

Passage III

Using electrical circuits, three experiments were performed to investigate the relationship between voltage (in volts), resistance (in ohms), and current (in amperes). Each experiment was set up with the following circuit design:

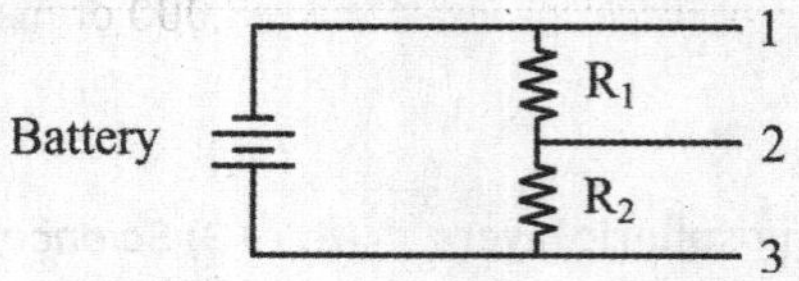

Experiment 1

Using a 6-volt battery and two 1,000-ohm resistors (R_1 and R_2), the measured voltages between points 1 and 2 and between points 2 and 3 were 3 volts each.

Experiment 2

Using a 12-volt battery and the same resistors as in Experiment 1, the measured voltages between points 1 and 2 and between points 2 and 3 were 6 volts each.

Experiment 3

Using the battery from Experiment 1 and a 1,000-ohm resistor and a 2,000-ohm resistor, the measured voltages between points 1 and 2 and between points 2 and 3 were 4 volts and 2 volts, respectively.

11. Judging from the results in Experiment 1 and Experiment 2, if the battery voltage were changed to 1.5 volts and both resistors were 1,000 volts, what voltage would be expected between point 1 and point 2?

A. 0.75 volts
B. 1.5 volts
C. 3.0 volts
D. 6.0 volts

EXPLANATIONS

11. (A) *Science/Scientific Investigation/Application*
The experiments show that the measured voltages are one-half of the battery voltage.

12. After studying the measurement made in the previous question, as well as those made earlier in Experiments 1, 2, and 3, the experimenter could reasonably hypothesize that:

F. voltage measured across a resistor is inversely proportional to the value of that resistor.
G. voltage measured across a resistor is directly proportional to the value of that resistor.
H. voltage measured across a resistor is not related to the value of that resistor.
J. voltage measured across a resistor equals the battery voltage.

13. When the experimenter recorded the current in the circuit of Experiment 1, it measured 0.003 amperes. In Experiment 3, however, the current measured 0.002 amperes. These results show that current and total resistances are:

A. directly proportional.
B. inversely proportional.
C. equal.
D. unrelated.

14. Which of the following expressions for the current in the circuit best summarizes the results of all three experiments? (The battery voltage is given by V_b and the total resistance is given by R.)

F. $V_b R$
G. $\frac{R}{V_b}$
H. $\frac{V_b}{R}$
J. $V_b + R$

EXPLANATIONS

12. (G) ***Science/Evaluation of Models/Analysis***
A directly proportional relationship between voltage and resistance is shown in all three experiments:

$$\frac{R_1}{R_2} = \frac{1{,}000 \text{ ohms}}{1{,}000 \text{ ohms}} \Rightarrow \frac{V_1}{V_2} = \frac{3 \text{ volts}}{3 \text{ volts}},$$

$$\frac{R_1}{R_2} = \frac{1{,}000 \text{ ohms}}{1{,}000 \text{ ohms}} \Rightarrow \frac{V_1}{V_2} = \frac{6 \text{ volts}}{6 \text{ volts}}, \text{ and}$$

$$\frac{R_1}{R_2} = \frac{2{,}000 \text{ ohms}}{1{,}000 \text{ ohms}} \Rightarrow \frac{V_1}{V_2} = \frac{4 \text{ volts}}{2 \text{ volts}}.$$

13. (B) ***Science/Interpretation of Data/Analysis***
Experiments 1 and 3 demonstrate that if the resistance is increased, the current decreases (2,000 ohms/0.003 amperes; 3,000 ohms/0.002 amperes).

14. (H) ***Science/Interpretation of Data/ Analysis***
Based on the experimental results, current and resistance are inversely proportional $\left(\text{current} \propto \frac{1}{\text{resistance}}\right)$, and current and voltage are directly proportional (current $\propto$ voltage). Thus, the formula relating the three variables is: $\text{current} \propto \frac{\text{voltage}}{\text{resistance}} \propto \frac{V_b}{R}$.

15. A new circuit is set up, similar in design to those in the experiments. The battery voltage and the size of the resistors are unknown, but the current measures 0.001 amperes. If the battery voltage is doubled and one of the two resistors is replaced with one having a smaller value, which of the following most accurately describes the new current?

A. It will be smaller than 0.001 amperes.
B. It will be unchanged.
C. It will be greater than 0.001 amperes.
D. Cannot be determined from the given information.

16. Which of the following single changes to Experiment 2 would produce a current of 0.004 amperes?

F. Decrease the voltage to 8 volts.
G. Increase the resistance to 3,000 ohms.
H. Neither (F) nor (G) will create a current of 0.004 amperes.
J. Either (F) or (G) will create a current of 0.004 amperes.

EXPLANATIONS

15. (C) ***Science/Scientific Investigation/Application***

Again, increasing the voltage or decreasing the resistance will cause an increase in current.

16. (J) ***Science/Scientific Investigation/Application***

The current in Experiment 2 is 0.006 amperes (12 volts/2,000 ohms). To decrease the current to 0.004 amperes, use either an 8-volt battery (8 volts/2,000 ohms) or resistors totaling 3,000 ohms (12 volts/3,000 ohms).

TIMED QUIZ *(16 items; 15 minutes)*

DIRECTIONS: Each passage below is followed by several items. After reading a passage, choose the best answer to each item. You may refer to the passages as often as necessary. You are NOT permitted the use of a calculator. Answers are on p. 442.

Passage I

The chart below shows an outline for a common means of analyzing a sample solution for various dissolved cations (positive ions). Ions above the horizontal arrows are those that are suspected to be present in the sample solution; the substances in the boxes are the reagents added as tests (0.3 M H^+ is acidic, NH_4OH is alkaline); the products shown next to the arrows pointing downward are solid precipitates resulting from the tests. Tests for specific ions need not always start from the beginning of the sequence.

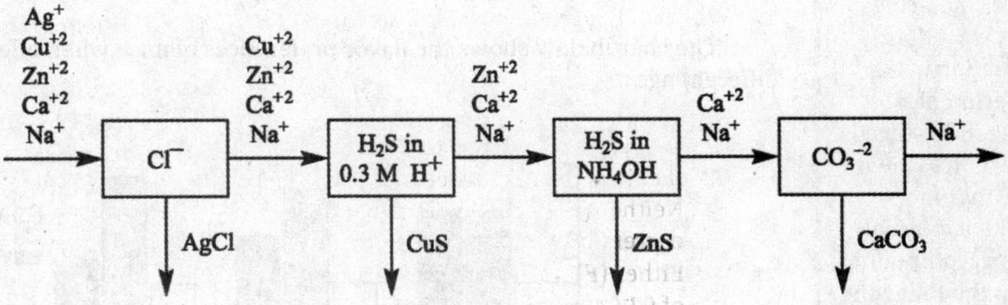

1. According to the chart, which precipitate indicates if silver (Ag^+) is present in the sample?

A. AgCl
B. Ag
C. CuS
D. ZnS

2. If a solution containing silver (Ag) nitrate and cupric (Cu) nitrate, both compounds known to dissociate into ions in solution, is tested according to this scheme, an experimenter will:

F. first observe AgCl on treatment with Cl^-, and next observe CuS on treatment with acidic H_2S.
G. first observe CuS on treatment with Cl^-, and next observe AgCl on treatment with acidic H_2S.
H. first observe $CaCO_3$ on treatment with CO_3^{-2}, and next observe AgCl on treatment with Cl^-.
J. observe no reactions, since the scheme does not test for nitrate.

3. What is the minimum number of tests necessary to confirm the composition of an unknown solution that contains either Cu^{+2} or Zn^{+2}, but not both?

A. One
B. Two
C. Three
D. Four

Throwback to Science

Remember, when positive and negative ions are placed in the same solution, they will become an ionic compound if the attraction between the two oppositely charged ions is greater than the attraction of the ions to the water molecule. This is what is occurring in the experimental chart in Passage I. To predict which negative and positive ions will form a compound, keep the following rule in mind: An ionic compound is always neutral, meaning that the charges of the ions must balance out. This means an ion with a positive charge of two can bond with another ion that has a negative charge of two or two ions with negative charges of one each.

4. Which statement is most correct concerning the separation of Cu^{+2} from Zn^{+2} in the same solution?

F. Completely different test reagents are used in each of the two steps.
G. The same test reagents are used under the same conditions in each of the two steps.
H. The same test reagents are used, but the first step must be in an alkaline environment while the second step must be in an acidic environment.
J. The same test reagents are used, but the first step must be in an acidic environment while the second step must be in an alkaline environment.

5. A clear solution is found, by a method not discussed here, to contain chloride ions (Cl^-). Based on the information provided, what ion could not be present in the solution?

A. Carbonate (CO^{-2})
B. Cupric (Cu^{+2})
C. Silver (Ag^+)
D. Zinc (Zn^{+2})

Passage II

The chart below shows the flavor preferences of mice when offered various fluids to drink at different ages.

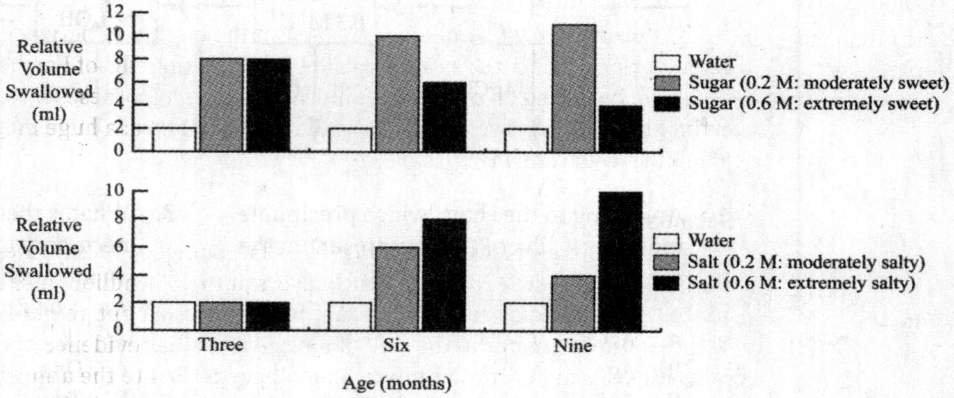

6. Which category on the chart shows no preference between water and the tested flavor?

F. Three months of age/sugar
G. Six months of age/salt
H. Three months of age/salt
J. Nine months of age/sugar

7. Which statement about mice is supported by the information in the chart?

A. As age increases, the preference for all tested sugars increases.
B. As age increases, the preference for all tested salts increases.
C. As age increases, differences between sugars cannot be detected, and differences between salts cannot be detected.
D. As age increases, differences between sugars can be detected, and differences between salts can be detected.

Master Moves

Before answering any questions, spend a few moments interpreting the given graphs. Note the trends within each graph and draw a few conclusions. In this case, after briefly looking at the top graph, it is clear that mice prefer moderately sweet water as they age. Making a few quick conclusions like this can help you speed through any accompanying questions.

8. The flavor preference that fluctuates most irregularly with age is:

F. moderately salty.
G. moderately sweet.
H. extremely salty.
J. extremely sweet.

9. Based on the trends shown in the chart, which of the following predictions is most reasonable for one-year-old mice?

A. Moderately sweet and moderately salty will be most preferred.
B. Extremely sweet and extremely salty will be most preferred.
C. Moderately sweet and extremely salty will be most preferred.
D. Extremely sweet and moderately salty will be most preferred.

10. Which of the following conclusions about water is NOT consistent with the data in the chart?

F. Water is never preferred over any tested flavors.
G. Before the age of six months, mice cannot taste the difference between water and sugar or between water and salt.
H. At the age of three months, both salty fluids are equal to the water swallowed.
J. As age increases, the volume of water swallowed remains the same.

Passage III

Approximately 65 million years ago, at the boundary between the Cretaceous and Paleogene geologic periods, a mass extinction of about three-fourths of Earth's plant and animal species occurred, including all non-flying dinosaurs. Many hypotheses have been proposed to explain the extinction, but only two have received great acceptance: a huge meteorite impact and an episode of intensive volcanism.

Scientist 1

The evidence is overwhelming that a large meteorite hit the earth at the end of the Cretaceous period. Sedimentary rock layers at the 65-million-year mark reveal a high concentration of iridium, which is rare in Earth's crust but abundant in meteorites. The discovery of the Chicxulub crater in the Gulf of Mexico is further evidence of a major meteor strike. The impact of this meteorite sent up a cloud of particles into the atmosphere, blocking sunlight and drastically reducing solar energy and hence photosynthesis. Plants and marine algae withered and died, followed by the plant-eating herbivores. This reverberated up the food chain to include the predators that depended on the plant-eating animals for food.

Passage Perfect

While reading passages with conflicting viewpoints, especially those with detailed information, it is important to circle and underline key ways in which the passages differ. This allows you to quickly answer accompanying questions, since most questions on this passage type focus on differences in the presented viewpoints.

Scientist 2

Granted, a meteorite hit Earth 65 million years ago. However, the planet was already an overheated greenhouse snuffing out life before the meteorite's arrival. A major volcanic event occurred around the same time as the Cretaceous-Paleogene boundary extinction. The Deccan Traps in India represent one of the largest volcanic features on Earth today. Formed between 60 and 68 million years ago from a series of volcanic eruptions, the Deccan Traps consist of multiple layers of solidified basalt lava. It is one of the biggest flood basalts in the history of the planet. The massive release of volcanic gases, particularly carbon dioxide, from the eruptions that created the Deccan Traps caused a greenhouse effect. It heated up the planet and stressed the land-dwelling dinosaurs and many other animal and plant species to extinction. Five major extinctions have occurred in the past 500 million years: the Ordovician, the Devonian, the Permian, the Triassic, and the Cretaceous. All of these extinctions are greenhouse extinctions associated with flood basalts.

11. Which of the following best describes the cause of the Cretaceous-Paleogene boundary extinction according to Scientist 2?

A. A huge meteorite impact
B. An abundance of iridium in Earth's crust
C. A massive release of volcanic gases
D. A flood covering three-fourths of Earth's surface

12. According to Scientist 1, a meteorite impact could cause a major extinction due to the resulting:

F. shockwaves that limited photosynthesis.
G. sunlight-blocking cloud of particles.
H. unusually high concentration of the element iridium.
J. release of toxic gases.

13. According to the information provided, evidence of a meteorite strike at the end of the Cretaceous period includes:

A. high concentrations of iridium in sedimentary rock.
B. major extinctions at other times in history.
C. massive releases of gases, particularly carbon dioxide.
D. multiple layers of solidified basalt in the Deccan Traps.

14. According to the information provided, both scientists agree that:

F. volcanic activity occurred at the Cretaceous-Paleogene boundary.
G. a meteorite hit Earth 65 million years ago.
H. a meteorite was the cause of the Cretaceous-Paleogene boundary extinction.
J. the Cretaceous-Paleogene boundary extinction is a greenhouse extinction associated with flood basalts.

15. According to Scientist 2, the Deccan Traps:

A. led to a reduction in solar energy and photosynthesis.
B. caused greenhouse warming.
C. resulted from a series of volcanic eruptions.
D. occurred roughly around the same time as the Permian-Triassic boundary extinction.

16. Both scientists would most likely agree that:

F. there were multiple major extinctions throughout history.
G. extinctions impact dinosaurs and other animal species but not plants.
H. the Deccan Traps impacted the major extinction between the Cretaceous and Paleogene periods.
J. a change in Earth's atmosphere led to the extinction between the Cretaceous and Paleogene periods.

SCIENCE

REVIEW

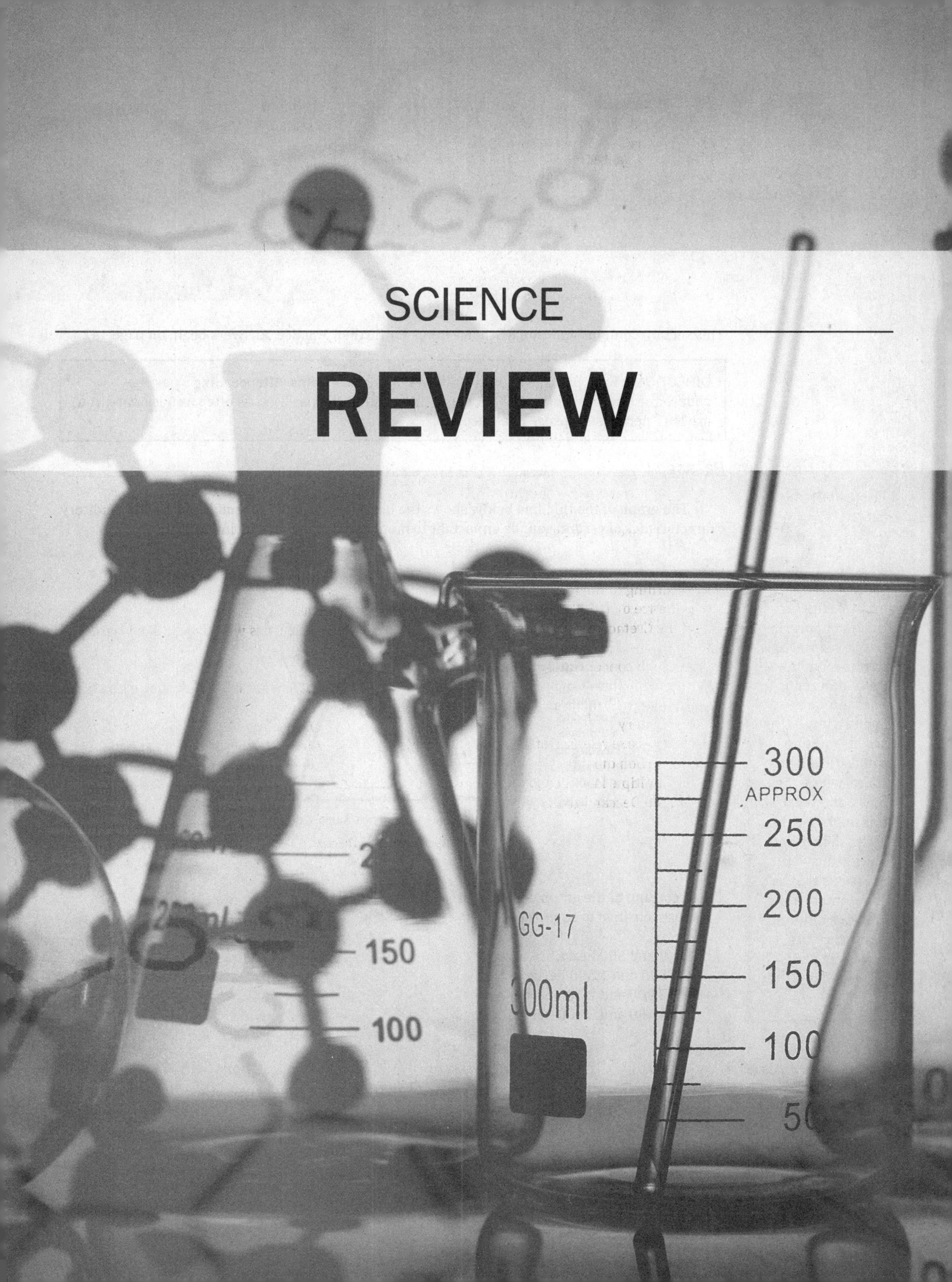

This section contains additional Science items for further practice. Answers begin on page 442.

DIRECTIONS: Each passage below is followed by several items. After reading a passage, choose the best answer to each item. You may refer to the passages as often as necessary. You are NOT permitted the use of a calculator.

The Cambridge Edge

When a graph shows multiple lines or curves at once, it can be helpful to think about how these different lines interact. Spend a few seconds noting trends the lines share, where they cross, and what this might mean. This can help you quickly answer questions that ask about interactions between different characteristics, such as in items #3, 4, and 5.

Passage I

The graph of the thin line below shows the hearing sensitivity of female moths. The auditory characteristics of certain sounds important to moth survival are also included.

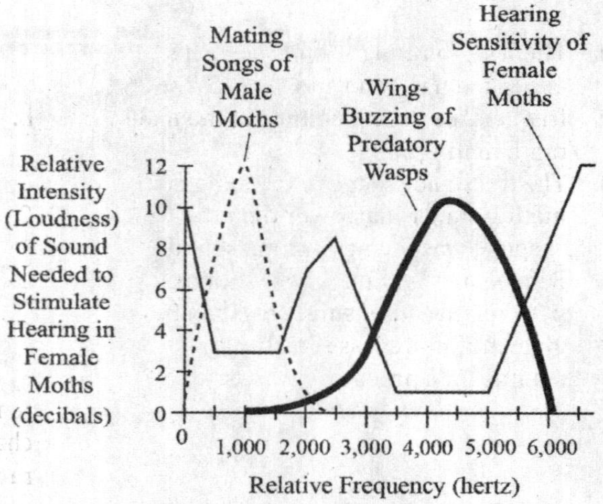

1. According to the graph, female moths are most sensitive to sounds between:

A. 0 and 500 hertz.
B. 500 and 1,500 hertz.
C. 2,000 and 2,500 hertz.
D. 3,500 and 5,000 hertz.

2. The nervous system of female moths may be set up to allow them to respond differently to sounds of different frequencies. Based on the information in the graph, which statement best describes the appropriate responses of female moths?

F. Approach sounds between 500 and 1,500 hertz, withdraw from sounds between 3,500 and 5,000 hertz
G. Approach sounds between 3,500 and 5,000 hertz, withdraw from sounds between 500 and 1,500 hertz
H. Approach sounds between 500 and 1,500 hertz and between 3,500 and 5,000 hertz
J. Withdraw from sounds between 500 and 1,500 hertz and between 3,500 and 5,000 hertz

3. Which of the following statements is supported by the information in the graph?

A. The wing-buzzing sounds of wasps occur at a narrower range of frequencies than the range of the male moth mating song.
B. The frequency range of the male moth mating song is narrower than the range of wasp wing-buzzing sounds.
C. Female moths cannot hear sounds with relative intensities less than 3.
D. Male moths are less sensitive to sounds than predatory wasps.

4. Which of the following statements accurately describes the relationship between the male moth mating song and female moth hearing sensitivity?

F. The frequency range of the male song coincides with the frequency range at which females are maximally sensitive to any sound.
G. Females need not be maximally sensitive at the frequency range of the male song because of the extremely high intensity of the song.
H. Females cannot hear the male song if its intensity level is less than 10.
J. The male song does not extend to an intensity level above 10.

5. If a new species of wasp were introduced into the moths' environment, which of the following wing-buzzing characteristics would make it the most successful predator of female moths?

A. Extremely high intensity at relative frequencies between 3,500 and 5,000 hertz
B. An intensity level of 7 to 8 dB at relative frequencies between 2,000 and 2,500 hertz
C. Low intensity at relative frequencies above 6,000 hertz
D. Extremely high intensity at relative frequencies above 6,000 hertz

6. A male is born with a mutation that changes his mating song to a frequency range between 2,000 and 2,500 hertz and an intensity level of 4 dB. What are his chances of finding a mate?

F. Excellent
G. Poor
H. Good, if no wasps are present
J. Cannot be determined from the given information

Passage II

A chemistry student wishes to study weight relationships between compounds before and after reactions involving the compounds. Two experiments were conducted to investigate two different reactions. The reactions are shown below, together with the amount (grams) of each substance before and after each reaction has proceeded. Equations are balanced to show the ratio of each type of atom before and after the reactions.

EXPERIMENT 1				
	$NaBr$ +	$AgNO_3 \Rightarrow$	$AgBr$ +	$NaNO_3$
Initial Mass (g)	103	170	0	0
Final Mass (g)	0	0	188	85

EXPERIMENT 2					
	Na_2CO_3 +	$2HCl \Rightarrow$	$2NaCl$ +	H_2O +	CO_2
Initial Mass (g)	106	73	0	0	(?)
Final Mass (g)	0	0	117	18	(?)

(The student has measured the quantities he could, but was unable to weigh the CO_2 because it is a gas. Since it is a gas, he assumes it has negligible mass.)

7. In Experiment 1, the data indicate that after the reaction has proceeded:

A. all of the Na originally present has been converted to Ag.
B. there are more molecules of $NaNO_3$ than there were molecules of $AgNO_3$ at the outset.
C. no NaBr remains.
D. no AgBr remains.

8. Which of the following is (are) conserved in the reaction in Experiment 1?

I. mass
II. number of atoms
III. amount of $AgNO_3$

F. I only
G. I and II only
H. I and III only
J. I, II, and III

9. In Experiment 2, the mass of the weighed products is:

A. zero.
B. less than the mass of reactants.
C. equal to the mass of reactants.
D. greater than the mass of reactants.

10. Experiment 2 differs from Experiment 1 in that:

F. the number of atoms is not conserved.
G. the reaction does not go to completion.
H. there are no compounds involved.
J. gas is produced.

11. The student's assumption in neglecting the mass of one of the products in Experiment 2 would most likely lead him to draw which of the following conclusions?

A. Mass is consumed as the reaction proceeds.
B. Mass is produced as the reaction proceeds.
C. Energy is consumed as the reaction proceeds.
D. Mass is conserved as the reaction proceeds.

12. The student is advised of a means to weigh the CO_2 gas produced in the reaction and finds the mass to be 44 grams. The student can now state that the two experiments:

F. lead to similar conclusions: neither mass nor atoms are conserved.
G. lead to similar conclusions: both mass and atoms are conserved.
H. lead to different conclusions: the number of molecules is not the same for the reactants as for the products.
J. lead to different conclusions: gases have negligible mass.

Passage III

Jean Baptiste Lamarck hypothesized the process of biological evolution before Charles Darwin was born. Some aspects of Lamarck's ideas and Darwin's ideas are presented below.

Lamarckism

Observations of the fossil record led Lamarck to believe that several lines of descent led to nature's broad diversity of organisms. Old fossils and recent fossils showed patterns leading to the characteristics of modern species. He believed that newer forms were more complex and more "perfectly" adapted to their environment. New adaptations could arise as the environment changed. Body organs that were used to cope with the environment became stronger and larger, while those not used deteriorated. For example, giraffes stretching their necks to reach higher leaves would develop longer necks. In addition, such changes in structure could then be passed on to offspring (these acquired characteristics could be inherited).

Darwinism

Based on the fossil and geologic record, Darwin also came to believe that various modern species were related through descent from common ancestors. He also noted that the great diversity of organisms that he observed during his travels were all very well-adapted to their environments. The adaptations, however, did not come about through "coping" or usage. Instead, individuals from a population can each show slight genetic or "heritable" differences (variability) in a trait. If such differences, by chance alone, give the individual some reproductive advantage (he or she can successfully produce more offspring than other members of the population), then more individuals with that trait will make up the next generation. Through this "natural selection" of individuals with characteristics that give them a slight advantage in their particular environment, species appear to become very well-suited to their natural world. However, "perfection" is not a useful term since the environment is constantly changing. The adaptations that are advantageous "today" may not be advantageous "tomorrow" under different conditions.

Passage Perfect

Be sure to circle or underline the key concepts of Lamarckism and Darwinism so that you can easily compare the two while answering questions. Also, when answering a comparison question about a particular scientific discipline, it is important to understand the mechanism each viewpoint believes is responsible for the phenomenon as this is likely to be questioned.

13. A major difference between Lamarck and Darwin relates to their views on:

A. the diversity of organisms in the natural world.
B. the significance of fossils.
C. the importance of adaptations to the environment.
D. the way adaptations come about.

14. Which viewpoint supports the idea that present-day species are descended from earlier forms?

F. Lamarckism
G. Darwinism
H. Both viewpoints
J. Neither viewpoint

15. Which statement might be used by a Darwinist to explain the extinction of a species?

A. The environment changed, and not enough individuals had traits or adaptations well-suited to the new conditions.
B. The environment changed, and body parts could not be manipulated enough to adapt to new conditions.
C. As the environment changed, the individuals present were not "perfect" enough.
D. As the environment changed, there was no "natural selection."

16. Darwin might dispute the Lamarckian idea of inheriting acquired characteristics by pointing out that:

F. giraffes with short necks may do just as well as those with long necks.
G. giraffes that break a leg and walk around on three legs still do not produce three-legged offspring.
H. giraffes had shorter necks millions of years ago.
J. giraffes that break a leg would not be able to reach the highest leaves.

17. Many species of moles live underground in the dark. These species often have small, almost dysfunctional, eyes. Which of the following statement(s) would a Lamarckian use to explain this phenomenon?

I. Moles without eyesight are better adapted for survival underground and therefore produce more offspring.
II. Disuse of eyes in the dark led to their deterioration in mole species.
III. Eye deterioration can be transferred to a mole's genes, which are then passed on to the next generation.

A. I only
B. II only
C. II and III only
D. I, II, and III

18. Which factor is vital to Darwin's ideas, but not to those of Lamarck?

F. The fossil record
G. An examination of modern species
H. The inheritance of adaptations
J. Chance

19. A few individuals in a population have an adaptation that enables them to tolerate extremely cold temperatures. In their lifetimes, the environment never reaches such extremes. If all other traits are approximately the same among individuals, which of the following best represents the prediction of a Darwinist regarding the number of offspring left in the next generation by these individuals, compared to the number left by other members of the population?

A. These individuals will leave approximately the same number of offspring.
B. These individuals will leave more offspring.
C. These individuals will leave fewer offspring.
D. These individuals will probably not leave any offspring.

Passage IV

Graph I shows the relationship between the relative rates of activity of enzymes A and B and temperature, with pH held constant. Graph II shows the relationship between the relative rates of activity of enzymes A and B and pH, with temperature held constant.

Passage Perfect

Quickly comparing the similarities and differences of these two graphs can give you an edge when answering accompanying questions. You'll understand the experiment more, and it's likely the relationship between the graphs will be questioned.

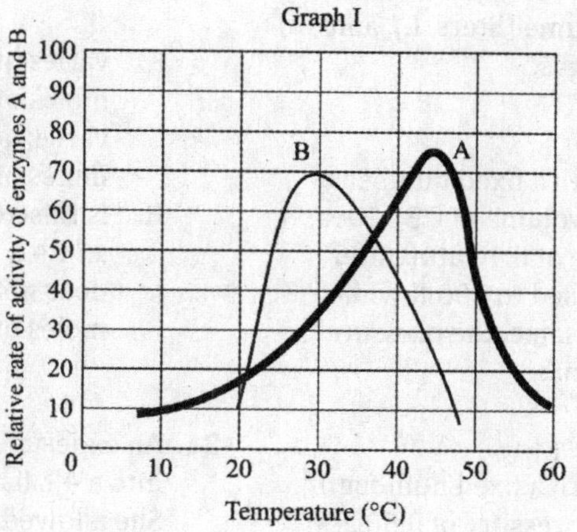

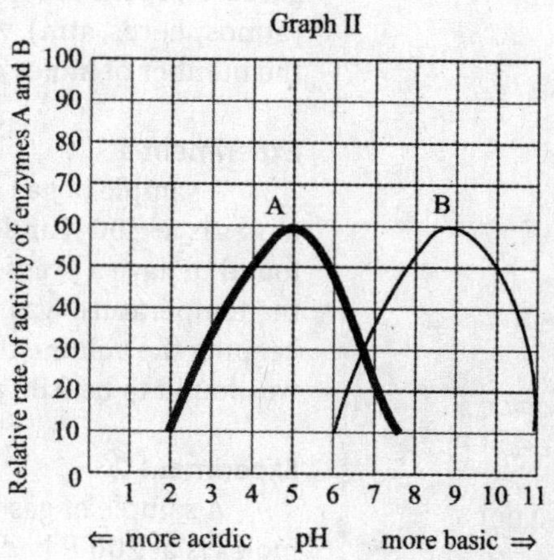

20. Under which conditions is enzyme A most active?

F. 40°C and a pH of 5
G. 45°C and a pH of 5
H. 45°C and a pH of 9
J. 50°C and a pH of 9

21. The optimum environment for enzyme B is:

A. acidic.
B. basic.
C. either acidic or basic.
D. neutral.

22. At which of the following temperatures do enzymes A and B exhibit approximately the same relative rate of activity?

F. 6.9°C
G. 10°C
H. 37°C
J. 47°C

23. At which pH do both enzymes A and B exhibit approximately the same relative rate of activity?

A. 6.7
B. 10
C. 37
D. 60

24. At what temperature does enzyme A have about half the activity of enzyme B?

F. 20°C
G. 30°C
H. 42°C
J. 53°C

25. At what temperature does enzyme B have about half the activity of enzyme A?

A. 20°C
B. 30°C
C. 42°C
D. 53°C

26. Over which of the following pH ranges will both enzymes A and B be active?

F. 1 to 3
G. 3 to 6
H. 6 to 7.5
J. 7.5 to 10

27. At what pH will both enzymes A and B be at their maximum activity?

A. 2
B. 5
C. 8.5
D. No such pH exists.

Passage V

A series of three experiments was designed to investigate the interrelationships between various factors known to influence gases: temperature (kelvin, K), pressure (atmospheres, atm), volume (liters, L), and the number of moles of gas.

Experiment 1

A sample of gas with a fixed number of moles is at 200 K and a volume of 0.30 L was found to have a pressure of 0.40 atm. After the temperature was raised to 400 K while keeping the volume the same, the pressure was found to be 0.80 atm.

Throwback to Science

You are not required to know any specific chemical formulas for the ACT, but any question dealing with the volume, temperature, and pressure of a gas it is helpful to remember the ideal gas law: $PV = nRT$, where P = pressure (in atm), V = volume (in liters), n = moles, R = universal gas constant (.08206 L atm mol^{-1} K^{-1}), and T = temperature (in Kelvin).

Experiment 2

A sample of gas with a fixed number of moles is at 200 K had a pressure of 0.50 atm when its volume was 1 L. Its volume was then increased to 2 L at constant temperature. The resulting pressure was 0.25 atm.

Experiment 3

Two moles of a gas were found to occupy 44.8 L at 1 atm and 273 K. Four moles of the same gas are added to the system with temperature and pressure held constant, resulting in a new volume of 89.6 L.

28. Which of the following hypotheses is (are) supported by the results of Experiment 1?

I. The pressure of the gas is proportional to its volume at constant temperature.
II. The volume of the gas is proportional to its temperature at constant pressure.
III. The pressure of the gas is proportional to its temperature at constant volume.

F. I only
G. I and II only
H. III only
J. II and III only

29. The results of Experiment 2 support the hypothesis that if the temperature of a gas is held constant, then the pressure:

A. increases as the volume increases.
B. decreases as the volume increases.
C. does not depend strongly on the volume.
D. Cannot be determined from the given information

30. The result of Experiment 3 supports the hypothesis that if both the pressure and the temperature of a gas are held constant, then the volume:

F. varies inversely with the number of moles of gas.
G. varies directly with the number of moles of gas.
H. is raised to a maximum value of 134.4 L when additional gas is added.
J. does not depend on the number of moles of gas.

31. An experimenter put 0.08 moles of gas into a 4 L flask at 273 K and 0.448 atm. She allowed 0.02 moles of the gas to escape, and she put the remaining gas into a smaller flask that caused the pressure to remain at 0.448 atm, while the temperature was kept constant as well. According to Experiment 3, the volume of the smaller flask must be:

A. 0.06 L.
B. 2 L.
C. 3 L.
D. 5 L.

32. In an additional experiment, 0.06 moles of a gas originally at 0.1 atm and 273 K occupy a volume of 13.4 L. The temperature is then changed to 300 K and the volume is changed to 10.0 L. To predict the final pressure on the 0.06 moles of gas, a student should use the results of:

I. Experiment 1.
II. Experiment 2.
III. Experiment 3.

F. I only
G. II only
H. I and II only
J. I and III only

33. The final pressure of the gas described in the previous question will be:

A. less than 0.1 atm.
B. equal to 0.1 atm.
C. greater than 0.1 atm.
D. Cannot be determined from the given information

Passage VI

How did life originate on planet Earth? Two opposing views are presented.

Passage Perfect

For strengthen-the-argument questions, it is important to think about the central assumption of the argument. Which statement most validates this assumption? For example, in Scientist 2's argument, the assumption is that meteorites actually *could* bring life with them. Which statement addresses this assumption?

Scientist 1

The idea that Earth could have given rise to life independently is incorrect. Life on this planet must have come from elsewhere for several reasons. First of all, complex life appears very suddenly in the geological record. Secondly, all life on Earth has a very similar biochemistry. If life originated on Earth, one would expect regional variations in biochemistry, similar to the variations in species spread over large areas. Finally, the time when life first appeared in the geological record was also a time when large numbers of meteorites struck Earth. The meteorites must have caused life to appear on Earth. The simplest hypothesis is that the meteorites brought life with them.

Scientist 2

Life need not have been imported from outer space. The chemicals required for life existed on the surface of Earth at the time life first appeared. The fact that all life has a similar biochemistry can be explained because any group of chemicals that won the race to life would probably have used the same "almost-living" chemicals as food. Since we can offer explanations for what happened without relying on a meteorite of unknown composition that might have fallen to Earth, we should stick to hypotheses that have fewer unknowns.

34. Which of the following is an assumption of Scientist 1?

F. Complex life forms can develop quickly.
G. Meteorites burn up as soon as they hit Earth's atmosphere.
H. There is a cause-and-effect relationship between meteors falling and the origin of life.
J. The changes on Earth's surface due to the presence of life attracted meteor showers.

35. Which of the following, if true, most strengthens Scientist 2's argument?

A. Only five percent more meteors than normal fell on Earth during the time life began.
B. Only five percent of the meteorites studied contained organic molecules.
C. A simulation of early Earth chemistry showed the spontaneous formation of complex biomolecules.
D. Meteorites containing amoebas have been found.

36. Which of the following, if true, most strengthens Scientist 1's argument?

F. No meteors fell to Earth during the time life began.
G. Meteorites studied did not contain molecules necessary to form life.
H. A simulation of early Earth chemistry showed the spontaneous formation of complex biomolecules.
J. Meteorites containing amino acids have been found.

37. With which explanation of the similar biochemistry of all life on Earth would Scientist 1 most likely agree?

A. A single chemical pathway to life exists.
B. Life on Earth arose from a single source.
C. Life on Earth is not varied.
D. Meteors are simple.

38. With which explanation of the similar biochemistry of all life on Earth would Scientist 2 most likely agree?

F. A single chemical pathway to life exists.
G. Life on Earth arose from a single source.
H. Life on Earth is not varied.
J. Meteors are simple.

39. Which scientist would be likely to disagree with the idea that life on planets other than Earth could have different biochemistries?

A. Scientist 1
B. Scientist 2
C. Both scientists
D. Neither scientist

40. Which of the following questions would be the most difficult for Scientist 1 to defend his theory against?

F. Why was there more meteorite activity earlier in Earth's history?
G. Why have other meteors not brought other life based on a different biochemistry?
H. Why did complex life emerge suddenly?
J. Why should meteor activity have any connection to the origin of life?

41. Could Scientist 2 believe that life exists on other planets without affecting his hypothesis?

A. Yes, as long as he believes that life elsewhere has a different biochemistry.
B. Yes, because wherever the chemicals required for life exist, life can begin.
C. No, because then he has to admit that meteorites brought life from these planets.
D. No, because then he has to admit that meteorites that came from pieces of similar planets brought life to Earth.

Passage VII

A seismographic station can detect how far away an earthquake occurred, but it cannot determine the direction of the earthquake. Any given station can therefore report that the epicenter of an earthquake occurred somewhere on the circumference of a circle a certain distance around the station with the seismograph in its center. The map below shows the data recorded for an earthquake at three different seismic stations (A, B, and C). Intersections of the three seismic stations' curves are marked by roman numerals.

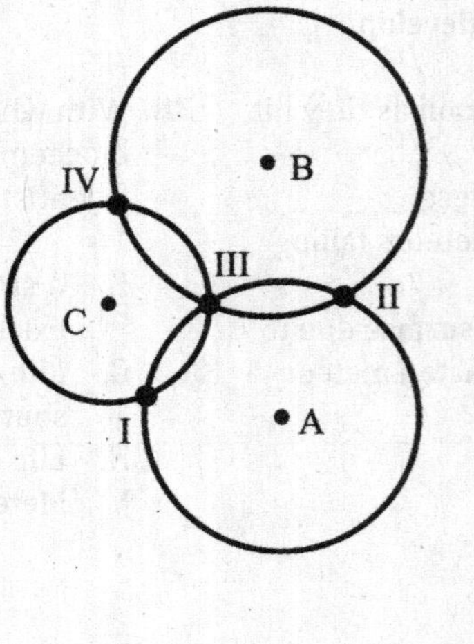

42. Which station was closest to the earthquake epicenter?

F. A
G. B
H. C
J. Cannot be determined from the given information

43. Given the information from stations A and B only, which site(s) is (are) possible for the earthquake epicenter?

A. I only
B. III only
C. II and III only
D. I and III only

44. Given the information from stations A and C only, which site(s) is (are) possible for the earthquake epicenter?

F. I only
G. III only
H. II and III only
J. I and III only

45. Given the information from all three stations, which site(s) is (are) possible for the epicenter?

A. I only
B. III only
C. I and III only
D. II and III only

46. If a fourth seismic station gave a report on this earthquake, at what point must its circle meet station A's circle?

F. I
G. II
H. III
J. IV

47. If a fourth seismic station gave a report on this earthquake, at what point must its circle meet station C's circle?

A. I
B. II
C. III
D. IV

48. What is the minimum number of points where two circumferences from two seismic stations, both measuring the same earthquake, can meet?

F. One
G. Two
H. Three
J. Infinite

Throwback to Science

While reading an extended experiment like this one, it is helpful to note which factors play which roles during the experiment. Remember, a control is a factor that gives a source of comparison to the single independent variable so it is clear that the effects seen are coming from the independent variable. And an independent variable is the variable scientists change to see the effect on the dependent variable. Understanding these differences in the experiment can help you gain a better grasp of what is going on and can allow you to more quickly and accurately answer accompanying questions.

Passage VIII

To investigate the factors affecting the rate at which starch is broken down to sugar by the digestive enzyme salivary amylase, two experiments were performed. In both experiments, starch (in the form of a cracker) was mixed in a beaker with the enzyme, and samples were removed and tested every 3 minutes. Special indicators were dipped in the sample to determine the presence of starch or sugar.

Experiment 1

To test the effects of different pH levels on enzyme activity rate, one cracker and a standard amount of enzyme were placed in three beakers, each containing buffers of different pH. This procedure was repeated using standard amounts of water in place of the enzyme. All tests were carried out at optimal temperature. Starch and sugar levels (starch/sugar) from selected samples are shown in Table 1.

TABLE 1

Contents of Beakers	Approximate pH Levels	Levels of Starch/Sugar: After 3 minutes	After 9 minutes	After 15 minutes	After 60 minutes
cracker + enzyme + buffer	5	high/none	high/none	high/low	moderate/moderate
	7	moderate/moderate	low/high	none/high	none/high
	9	high/none	high/none	high/low	moderate/moderate
cracker + water + buffer	5	high/none	high/none	high/none	high/none
	7	high/none	high/none	high/none	high/none
	9	high/none	high/none	high/none	high/none

Experiment 2

To test the effects of temperature on enzyme activity rate, one cracker and a standard amount of enzyme were placed in three beakers, each kept at different temperatures. This was also repeated using standard amounts of water in place of the enzyme. All tests were carried out at optimal pH. Starch and sugar levels (starch/sugar) from selected samples are shown in Table 2.

TABLE 2

Contents of Beakers	Temperatures	Levels of Starch/Sugar			
		After 3 minutes	After 9 minutes	After 15 minutes	After 60 minutes
cracker + enzyme	25°C 37°C 45°C	high/none moderate/moderate high/none	high/none low/high high/none	high/low none/high high/low	moderate/moderate none/high moderate/moderate
cracker + water	25°C 37°C 45°C	high/none high/none high/none	high/none high/none high/none	high/none high/none high/none	high/none high/none high/none

49. Under what conditions does salivary amylase appear to work best?

A. Any pH level greater than 5 and any temperature greater than 25°C
B. Any pH level greater than 5 and any temperature less than 45°C
C. pH level of 9 and temperature equals 37°C
D. pH level of 7 and temperature equals 37°C

50. The ingredient used as a control for both experiments is the:

F. cracker.
G. water.
H. enzyme.
J. starch/sugar level.

51. Which of the following hypotheses is supported by the results of Experiment 1?

A. At the appropriate pH level, water can break down starch, but at a slower rate than salivary amylase can.
B. After any given time interval, no differences in the effects of the three buffers on salivary amylase activity should be detectable.
C. Salivary amylase can show activity at each of the three pH levels tested.
D. The duration of time in which starch and enzyme remain in the beakers should have no effect on the amount of sugar produced.

52. Which of the following experimental designs would test the hypothesis that enzyme concentration can affect the rate of starch digestion?

F. Using the same pH, temperature, and enzyme levels in all beakers, test additional samples at 90 minutes, 120 minutes, and 240 minutes.
G. Using different pH, temperature, and enzyme levels in all beakers, test additional samples at 90 minutes, 120 minutes, and 240 minutes.
H. Using the same pH and temperatures in all beakers, test additional samples with the enzyme at one-half the strength, two times the strength, and four times the strength.
J. Using the same pH, temperature, and enzyme levels in all beakers, test additional samples after stirring for 3 minutes, 9 minutes, 15 minutes, and 60 minutes.

53. In Experiment 2, an additional beaker was tested at 70°C (cracker + enzyme). After 60 minutes, the sample showed high levels of starch and no sugar. Which of the following best explains this result?

A. All the starch was destroyed at this high temperature.
B. The enzyme does not work at all at this high temperature.
C. Starch cannot be detected at this high temperature.
D. Iodine and sugar indicators cannot function properly at this high temperature.

54. On the basis of the results of Experiment 1, what would probably occur if Experiment 2 were carried out at a pH level of 5?

F. Digestion of starch to sugar would slowly begin in the beakers containing crackers plus water.
G. Overall, digestion of starch to sugar would probably take place less efficiently.
H. Overall, digestion of starch to sugar would probably take place more efficiently.
J. The experimental results would not change.

Passage IX

The *blast wave* of compressed air created by an aerial explosion propagates in a spherical pattern from the center of the detonation and loses force with the distance traveled from the center. *Overpressure* is the difference between the air pressure at the leading edge of the blast wave and the ambient air pressure before the arrival of the blast wave. Figure 1 shows the typical overpressure history of a blast wave at locations distant from the center of the explosion.

> **Passage Perfect**
>
> To answer an assumption question, you can take several different routes. The fastest would be to see if you can automatically recognize what part of the argument has a logical gap. If you cannot automatically see the gap in reasoning, you can substitute each answer into the argument and see which strengthens the line of reasoning most. This will show you which answer choice is the argument's major assumption.

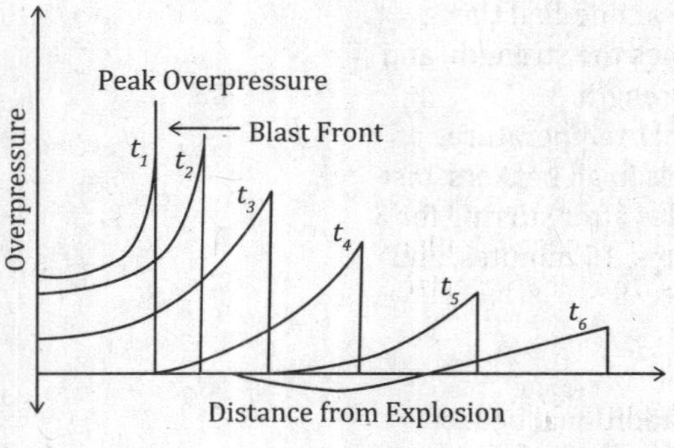

Figure 1

After the passage of the blast front, air pressure drops abruptly and eventually comes back into equilibrium with the ambient pressure. Figure 2 shows the overpressure and *dynamic pressure* (a measure of the wind gust force per unit area) at the blast front as a function of time following an explosion.

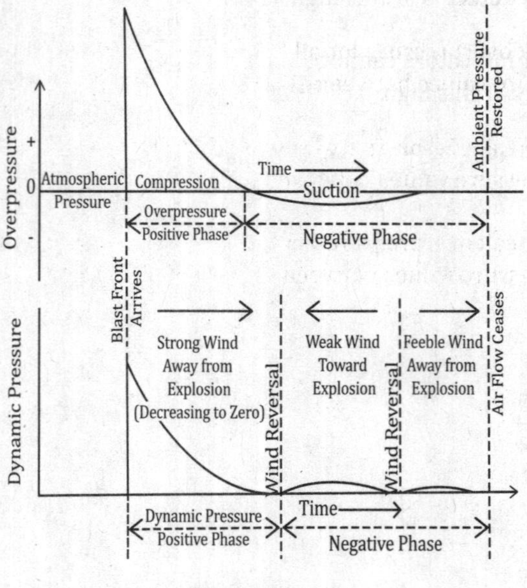

Figure 2

For a *ground level explosion*, a portion of the blast wave is reflected back by Earth's surface. When the reflected blast wave merges with the initial wave impulse, the result is a shock wave with overpressure that may be 12 times more than twice that of the initial impulse. The various aspects of the blast wave are a function of the peak overpressure (see Figure 3), which is dependent on the amount and type of explosive.

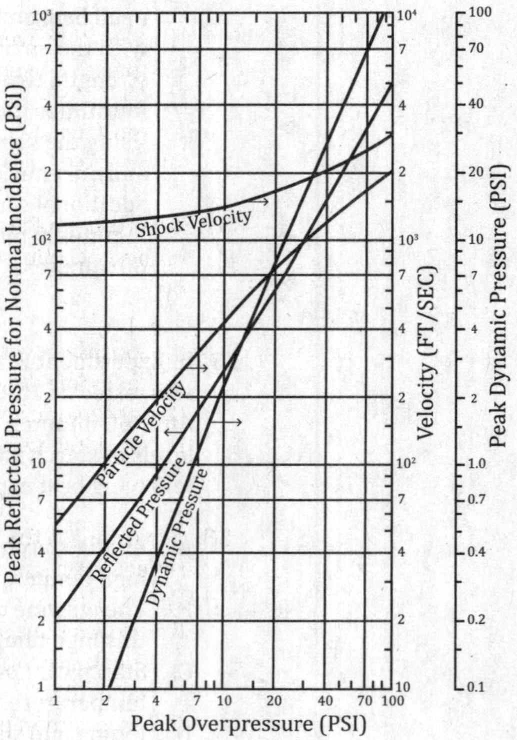

Figure 3

55. In Figure 1, the successive peaks of the diagram represent overpressure readings that are separated by:

A. time only.
B. distance only.
C. both time and distance.
D. neither time nor distance.

56. According to Figure 2, conditions during the time lag between the explosion and the arrival of the blast front are characterized by:

F. negative overpressure.
G. positive overpressure.
H. atmospheric pressure.
J. positive dynamic pressure.

57. According to Figure 2, the negative phase of the dynamic pressure is characterized by:

A. positive overpressure.
B. negative dynamic pressure.
C. atmospheric pressure.
D. variable winds.

58. According to the data provided in Figure 3, reflected pressure:

F. is less than peak overpressure only for peak overpressure values between 1 and 10 PSI.
G. is less than peak overpressure for all peak overpressure values between 1 and 100 PSI.
H. is greater than peak overpressure only for peak overpressure values between 10 and 100 PSI.
J. is greater than peak overpressure for all peak overpressure values between 1 and 100 PSI.

59. According to the data provided in Figure 3, the difference in the velocity of a shock wave for a peak overpressure of 1 PSI and the velocity of a shock wave for a peak overpressure of 100 PSI is approximately:

A. 18 feet per second.
B. 180 feet per second.
C. 1,800 feet per second.
D. 18,000 feet per second.

Passage X

Radiometric dating is the process of determining the age of rocks from the *decay* of a radioactive element (decay is the spontaneous disintegration of a nucleus into a slightly lighter nucleus with the emission of subatomic particles, electromagnetic radiations, or both). The original element is called the *parent isotope*, and the element left behind after decay is called the *daughter product.*

Rubidium-87, with a half-life of 48.8 billion years, decays into strontium-87, a stable isotope:

PARENT DAUGHTER

$$^{87}_{37}Rb \rightarrow {}^{87}_{38}Sr + {}^{0}_{-1}\beta$$

Strontium has several other isotopes that are also stable and do not decay, including strontium-86. Therefore, the ratio of strontium-87 to strontium-86 (Sr-87/Sr-86) in a rock increases over time as rubidium-87 decays into strontium-87.

When *magma* (molten rock) cools and forms a rock, all parts of the rock have the same initial Sr-87/Sr-86 ratio because the two isotopes are uniformly mixed during the fluid magma stage. However, the different minerals that form in rock accommodate varying quantities of rubidium, so different minerals will have different initial ratios of rubidium to strontium. With the passage of time, rubidium atoms frozen in place in mineral *inclusions* decay into strontium, so any increase in the quantity of strontium in a rock is attributable to an equal decrease in the quantity of rubidium (see Figure 1).

Since the decrease in rubidium-87 is matched exactly by an increase in strontium-87, any decrease in the Rb-87/Sr-87 ratio over time due to decay is proportional to the amount of rubidium-87 in the mineral at the time it froze into rock. Therefore, a line drawn through the points of the Rb-87/Sr-87 ratios for the mineral inclusion samples at a given time, called an *isochron*, is linear. The greater the *slope* of an isochron (the steeper the rate of climb), the older the minerals and therefore the rock that contains them.

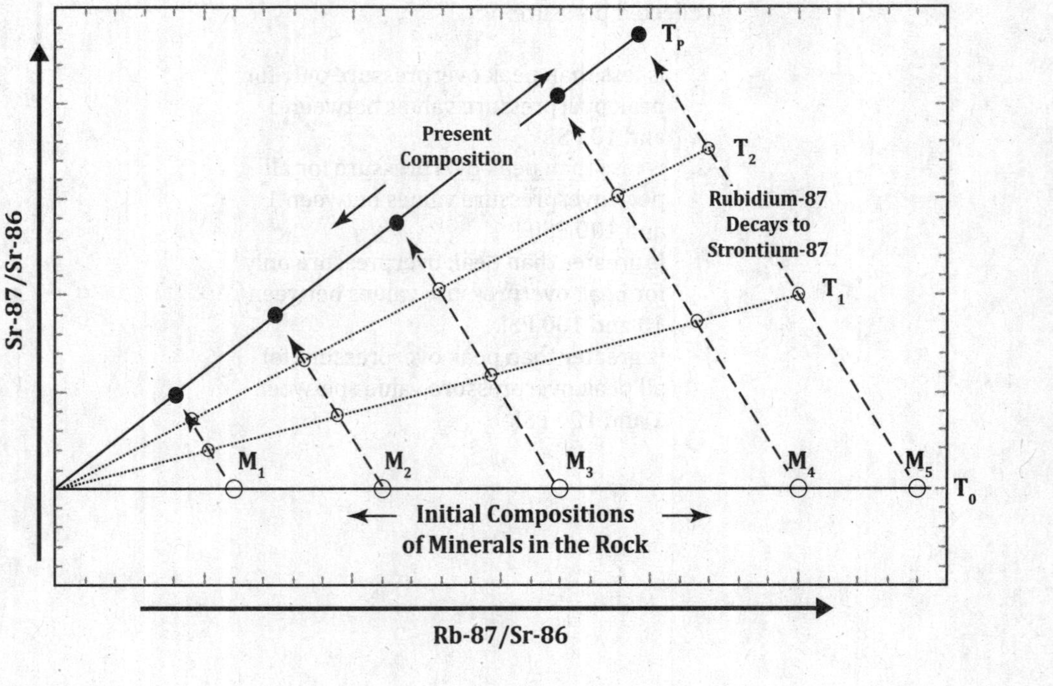

Figure 1

Experiment 1

Scientists tested the mineral samples in a basalt rock to determine its age. The results are shown in Figure 2.

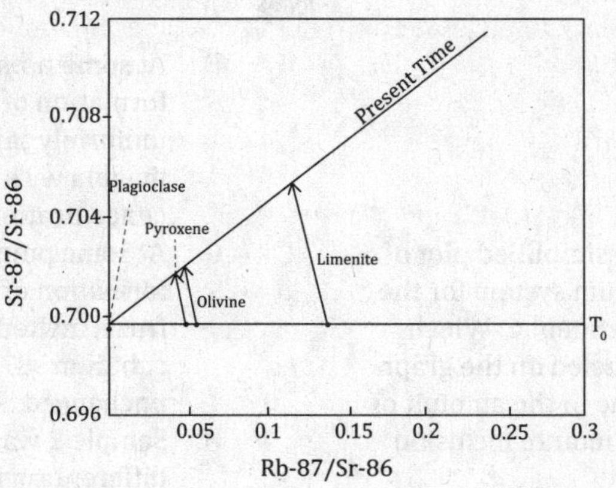

Figure 2

Experiment 2

Scientists tested the mineral samples in a second basalt rock. The results are shown in Figure 3.

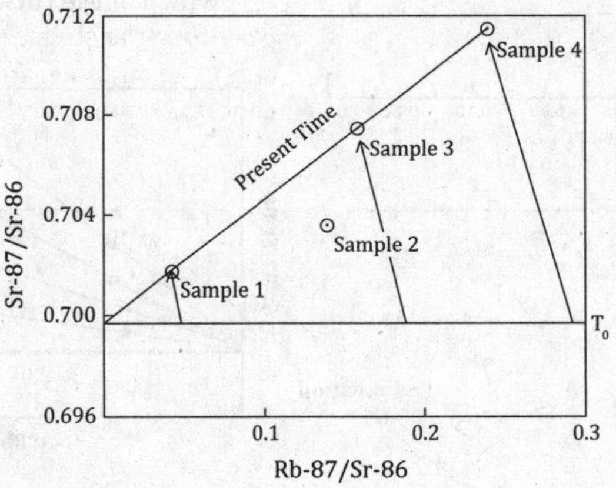

Figure 3

60. In Figure 1, the line for T_0 is horizontal to the *x*-axis because:

F. all radioactive elements decay from parent to daughter isotopes at the same rate.
G. the quantities of strontium-87 and strontium-86 exist in a fixed ratio throughout the life of the rock.
H. the rubidium-87 in the magma does not begin to decay until the rock is thoroughly cooled.
J. the Sr-87/Sr-86 ratio was the same throughout the magma when it froze into rock.

61. According to Figure 1, which of the following best describes the composition of the M_5 inclusion sample at T_0 compared with its composition at T_1?

A. M_5 has more strontium-87 at T_0 than at T_1.
B. M_5 has more strontium-86 at T_0 than at T_1.
C. M5 has more rubidium-87 at T_0 than at T_1.
D. M_5 has less strontium-86 at T_0 than at T_1.

62. Based on the results of Experiment 1, what was the approximate Rb-87/Sr-86 ratio in the olivine inclusion sample at the time the rock froze from magma?

F. 0.03
G. 0.06
H. 0.07
J. 0.13

63. The graph below is a simplified plot of the rubidium-strontium system for the rock studied in Experiment 1. Which of the dimensions labeled on the graph represents the decline in the amount of rubidium-87 in the limonite inclusion sample over time?

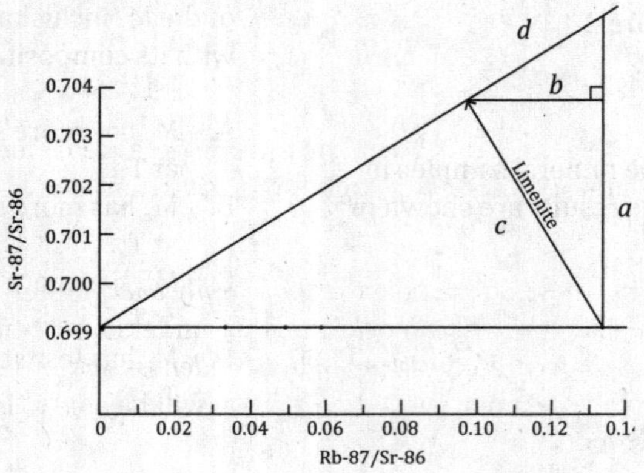

A. *a*
B. *b*
C. *c*
D. *d*

64. Which of the following provides the best explanation for why the Sample 2 data point in Experiment 2 does not align with the other three sample data points on the isochron in Figure 3?

F. At some point after the initial formation of the rock, it melted, uniformly mixed with other molten magma with a higher rubidium-87 concentration, and then refroze.
G. At some point before the initial formation of the rock, it partially froze, melted, and then refroze with rubidium-87 to strontium-86 ratios unchanged.
H. Sample 2 was collected from a different rock than Samples 1, 3, and 4.
J. Each of the four samples was collected from a different rock.

65. The graph below shows isochrones of mineral inclusion samples taken from four different rocks today. Based on the graph, which of the rocks is the oldest?

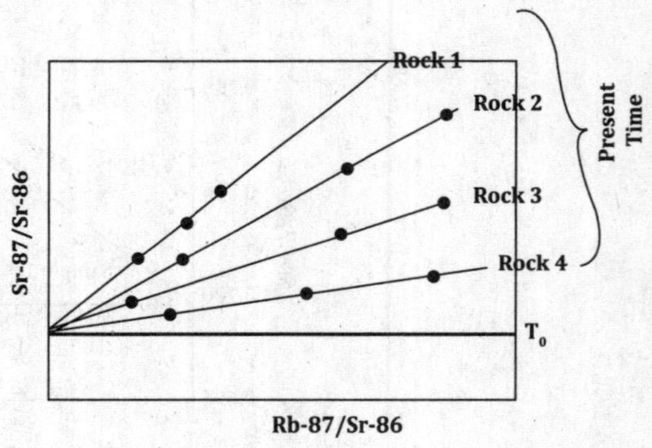

A. Rock 1
B. Rock 2
C. Rock 3
D. Rock 4

STRATEGY SUMMARY

SCIENCE STRATEGIES

Science items test your reasoning skills, not your scientific knowledge. So, most of the passages have all of the information that you will need to answer the items. In some cases, background information at the level of your high school general science courses is required, but *do not assume* data that is not given. The following are general strategies for the Science Test:

1. Before reading any Science passage, *quickly glance over all of the passages and code them according to passage-type* in order to determine the order in which you will attack them. Identifying and coding the passages should take no more than five seconds each.

2. *Do NOT preview the item stems.* Since the Science item stems tend to be confusing without having first read the corresponding passage, previewing them will only confuse you and slow you down.

3. It is important to only *read the passage thoroughly once*, rather than to skim over it several times. The material can be difficult to understand; thus, it is important to read thoughtfully and carefully. *Be an active reader.* Use your pencil to underline key words and points of information. That way, you will be able to locate them easily when answering the items.

4. When a Science passage includes tables or graphs, make sure that you *read and understand the labels* on axes, columns, and rows. You need to know what information is being presented and what units of measure are being used.

5. Many passages will contain much more information than you need to answer a particular item. In your search for a logical conclusion, *do not be misled by data that does not relate to the item at hand.*

6. In Data Representation passages, tables and graphs present results, often of observations or experiments. Corresponding items will usually ask you to spot patterns in the data, so *look for trends*, such as upward movement, downward movement, inverse variation, etc.

7. The experiments described in Research Summary passages are based on scientific assumptions. However, if an assumption is faulty, the experiment may not prove what it claims, and conclusions drawn from it may therefore be invalid. So, for items that ask about the validity of a scientific conclusion, *consider the validity of any underlying assumptions.*

8. The arguments presented in Conflicting Viewpoints passages are also based on scientific assumptions. Again, *if the assumption is wrong, the entire argument is open to challenge.* Assumptions that are based on scientific fact add strength to an argument; faulty assumptions weaken an argument.

9. Offering the assumptions that you started with as proof of your argument is called circular reasoning, and this type of proof is not acceptable. For that reason, any conclusions discussed in Science passages or offered as answer choices must be based on additional evidence (e.g., experiments) to be valid. *Beware of any conclusions that are nothing more than a restatement of an underlying premise.*

10. All of the information that you need to answer the items is provided in the passage—do not infer any information that is not given or relate any previous experience to the passage. *Pay attention to material noted with an asterisk.*

11. Transcribe your answers from the test booklet to the answer sheet *in groups* (by passage). However, when you arrive at the last passage, transcribe each answer as it is determined.

STRATEGIES FOR EACH PASSAGE-TYPE

- ***Data Representation Passages:*** When given data in the form of a graph or a chart, pay particular attention to the scale, units, legend, and other noted information.
- ***Research Summary Passages:*** When given multiple experiments, identify the controls and variables. Note that the controls must remain the same and that variables can only change *one at a time* in all experiments.
- ***Conflicting Viewpoints Passages:*** When given two points of view on a topic, identify the main points of difference and the logical value of each argument. After you understand the nature of the passage, attack the items.

STRATEGIES FOR EACH ITEM-TYPE

- ***Comprehension Items:*** Recognize basic concepts. Read carefully. Make sure that your answers consider appropriate scales and units. Also, note the difference between absolute and percentage changes.
- ***Analysis Items:*** Identify relationships and trends. Pay particular attention to direct and inverse relationships.
- ***Application Items:*** Draw conclusions, predict outcomes, and synthesize new information. In answering Application items, beware of the following terms: "all," "none," "always," and "never." Remember that a single case of contradictory evidence is all that is necessary to disprove an absolute theory.

PRACTICE TEST REINFORCEMENT

VICTORY PRACTICE TEST

DIRECTIONS

The Victory Practice Test includes five subject tests: English, Mathematics, Reading, Science, and Writing. Calculator use is permitted on the Mathematics Test only.

Cambridge offers several services for schools utilizing our practice tests. Ask your teacher whether your school has decided to send your answers to Cambridge for scoring or to score your answers at your school. If Cambridge is scoring your test, you will use a Scantron™ form provided by your teacher, or you will enter your answers online. If your school is scoring your test, you may use a Scantron™ form provided by your teacher, or you may write your answers on paper.

If you are entering your test answers on a Scantron™ form, please be sure to include the following information on the Scantron™:

Book and Edition	*Victory for the ACT Test, 15th Edition*
Practice Test Name	**Victory Practice Test**

If you are only completing a single section of this practice test, make sure to also include the following information:

Subject	English, Mathematics, Reading or Science
Section Number	**Section 1, 2, 3** or **4**

The items in each multiple-choice test are numbered and the answer choices are lettered. The Scantron™ form has numbered rows that correspond to the items on the test. Each row contains lettered ovals to match the answer choices for each item on the test. Each numbered row has a corresponding item on the test.

For each item, first decide on the best answer choice. Then, locate the row number that corresponds to the item. Next, find the oval in that row that matches the letter of the chosen answer. Then, use a soft lead pencil to fill in the oval. DO NOT use a ballpoint pen.

Mark only one answer for each item. If you change your mind about an answer choice, thoroughly erase your first mark before marking your new answer.

Note that only responses marked on your Scantron™ form or written on your paper will be scored. Your score on each test will be based only on the number of items that are correctly answered during the time allowed for that test. You will not be penalized for guessing. Therefore, it is in your best interest to answer every item on the test, even if you must guess.

On the Writing Test, write your response to the prompt using the essay response sheets or loose-leaf paper provided by your teacher. Your teacher might also direct you to enter your essay response online. (Note that the Writing Test is optional.)

You may work on each test only during the time allowed for that test. If you finish a test before time is called, use the time to review your answer choices or work on items about which you are uncertain. You may not return to a test on which time has already been called, and you may not preview another test. You must lay down your pencil immediately when time is called at the end of each test. You may not for any reason fill in or alter ovals for a test after time has expired for that test. Violation of these rules will result in immediate disqualification from the exam.

1 1 1 1 1 1 1 1 1 1 1 1

SECTION 1: ENGLISH TEST

45 Minutes—75 Items

DIRECTIONS: In the passages below, certain parts of the sentences have been underlined and numbered. In the right-hand column, you will find different ways of writing each underlined part; the original version is indicated by the "NO CHANGE" option. For each item, select the choice that best expresses the intended idea, is most acceptable in standard written English, or is most consistent with the overall tone and style of the passage.

There are also items that ask about a section of the passage or the passage as a whole. These items do not refer to an underlined portion of the passage; these items are preceded by statements that are enclosed in boxes.

Read the passage through once before you begin to answer the accompanying items. Finding the answers to certain items may depend on looking at material that appears several sentences beyond the item. So, be sure that you have read far enough ahead before you select your answer choice. Answers are on page 445.

PASSAGE I

La Bohème—Spoiler Alert

La Bohème is an opera set in the Latin Quarter of Paris around 1830. The cast includes four friends, Rodolfo, Marcello, Schaunard, and Colline, who are respectfully, [1] a poet, a painter, a musician, and a philosopher; the consumptive Mimi, who is a seamstress; and the frivolous Musetta, who is a singer.

The curtain rises on a *garret* [A] shared by the four friends, who are destitute. It is a frigid Christmas Eve, and Rodolfo and Marcello burn Rodolfo's manuscript for heat. Colline arrives, then Schaunard, who bringing [2] provisions and money. During the ensuing festivities, the landlord comes for the rent [B], but the four trick him into leaving without the money, which they divvy up. [3]

1. A. NO CHANGE
   B. who are, respectfully,
   C. who are, respectively,
   D. who, are respectively,

2. F. NO CHANGE
   G. that bringing
   H. who brings
   J. that brings

3. A. NO CHANGE
   B. divide among themselves
   C. divide between them
   D. apportion

GO ON TO THE NEXT PAGE.

All except Rodolfo go out for the evening, who is [4] soon disturbed by Mimi, another tenant in the building [C]. Mimi needs a match to light her candle, and the pair are soon in darkness. The couple later leave the apartment [D] singing about their [5] new love. [6]

Act 2 takes place in a café. It's still Christmas Eve, and Musetta, whom has come [7] with an older man, joins the party. Marcello wants to rekindle a relationship with Musetta if [8] the older man is tricked into leaving. When the older man returns, the others have gone, and he pays [9] the bill.

Several weeks have passed when Act 3 begins; while coughing uncontrolled, [10] Mimi tells Marcello that Rodolfo left her. Rodolfo arrives unexpectedly; Mimi hides and eavesdrops [11] Rodolfo saying that he left because Mimi is dying and he hopes that she

4. F. NO CHANGE
G. except Rodolfo goes out for the evening and
H. go out for the evening, except Rodolfo
J. go out for the evening except Rodolfo, who

5. A. NO CHANGE
B. they're
C. there
D. that

6. The author wants to insert the following into the second paragraph:

(dismal attic apartment)

The parenthetical remark could most logically be placed at:

F. Point A
G. Point B
H. Point C
J. Point D

7. A. NO CHANGE
B. who has come
C. who have come
D. whom came

8. F. NO CHANGE
G. because
H. so
J. due to

9. A. NO CHANGE
B. gets
C. is given
D. is stuck with

10. F. NO CHANGE
G. coughing uncontrollably
H. out of control coughing
J. out of controlled coughing

11. A. NO CHANGE
B. hears
C. watches
D. overhears

GO ON TO THE NEXT PAGE.

could find a wealthy suitor who will pay for her medical treatment.
12

Act 4 takes place months later in the *garret* where the four friends share a little food but pretending it is a magnificent feast. Musetta arrives with Mimi, who must be helped to a chair. People leave to pawn items to buy medicine for Mimi, and Mimi and Rodolfo reminisce about their first meeting until Mimi is overwhelmed by a coughing fit. The others return with medicine and send for a doctor. It's too late. [14]
13

12. F. NO CHANGE
G. can find
H. is finding
J. had found

13. A. NO CHANGE
B. but pretends
C. but pretend
D. yet pretending

14. At this point, the writer is thinking of adding:

Mimi dies.

If the writer adds this sentence, the effect will be to:

F. restate the main idea of the final paragraph.
G. summarize the development of the entire essay.
H. contradict what is said in the preceding sentence.
J. make explicit the meaning of the preceding sentence.

Item #15 asks about the preceding passage as a whole.

15. Suppose that the writer's goal was to help a reader who is unfamiliar with *La Bohème* understand the action before attending a performance. Did the writer accomplish this goal?

A. No, because the writer does not discuss other operas by other composers that are also popular.
B. No, because the essay presents the events described in chronological sequence.
C. Yes, because the writer summarizes the important action in each of the four acts of the opera.
D. Yes, because *La Bohème* was composed over 100 years ago and describes events in another country.

GO ON TO THE NEXT PAGE.

PASSAGE II

A Cheap, One-Day Tour of New York City

I live in Greenwich Village in New York City, and <u>from time to time,</u> [16] I entertain visitors from back home. <u>They all of them</u> [17] want to see every one of the sights, but there <u>is too much</u>. [18] Plus, New York is expensive. So I listen to their impossibly long <u>list</u> [19] while silently rehearsing my standard cheap, one-day tour. We start with a classic New York breakfast of bagels with cream cheese and then strike out <u>walking on foot</u> [20] to the Brooklyn Bridge. From mid-span, we admire tall buildings, survey the riverfront, and <u>would watch</u> [21] the boat traffic.

The Statue of Liberty is at the top of <u>everyone's</u> [22] list, but Liberty Island is accessible only by boat, the ticket line is long, and the tour requires four hours. Plus, the ticket is costly. <u>Instead,</u> [23] we take the nearby Staten Island Ferry because the route passes near the monument, a ferry leaves every 15 minutes, and

16. F. NO CHANGE
G. once
H. in the meantime
J. initially

17. A. NO CHANGE
B. They all of those
C. All of them
D. All of those

18. F. NO CHANGE
G. is too many
H. are too many
J. are too much

19. A. NO CHANGE
B. lists
C. listing
D. listings

20. F. NO CHANGE
G. walking afoot
H. on feet
J. walking

21. A. NO CHANGE
B. watching
C. watch
D. OMIT the underlined portion.

22. F. NO CHANGE
G. everyones'
H. everyones
J. every ones

23. A. NO CHANGE
B. However,
C. Subsequently,
D. Surprisingly,

GO ON TO THE NEXT PAGE.

the roundtrip takes only 50 minutes. <u>The Staten Island Ferry is operated by the New York City Department of Transportation and is one of several ferry systems in the metropolitan area.</u> 24

The New York Subway is the granddaddy of them all, so we take a ride uptown to Central Park, where, if the weather is <u>acceptable,</u> 25 a sandwich eaten on a bench is high dining at low price. Then we make a detour through the lobby of an elegant hotel for a restroom <u>break, continuing</u> 26 on to Rockefeller Center.

After eight more blocks, we're inside the cavernous Grand Central Terminal where the current ceiling mural obscures an earlier version. <u>When the first artists looked up from the plan and transferred figures of the zodiac to the ceiling-canvas, they painted the mirror image of the night-time sky.</u> 27

24. Given that all the statements are factually correct, which one adds the most relevant detail at this point in the passage?

F. NO CHANGE
G. The Staten Island Ferry began service in 1817, when the Richmond Turnpike Company started a steamboat service from Manhattan to Staten Island.
H. The Staten Island Ferry is the single busiest ferry route in the United States as well as the world's busiest passenger-only ferry.
J. The Staten Island Ferry is fare-free, and after riding the ferry, passengers can transfer to the subway or a bus in Manhattan at no cost.

25. Which choice best describes weather in a way that adds sensory detail to the reference to lunch in the park?

A. NO CHANGE
B. warm and sunny
C. inviting
D. predictable

26. F. NO CHANGE
G. break before continuing
H. break, while continuing
J. break so continue

27. The writer is thinking of replacing this sentence with:

When the first artists look up from the plan and transfer figures of the zodiac to the ceiling-canvas, they paint the mirror image of the night-time sky.

Should the writer make the change?

A. No, because the murals were painted in the past before the writer and visitors visit the terminal.
B. No, because both versions of the mural continue to exist even though one is not visible to the public.
C. Yes, because the narrator is describing events as they are occurring in real time.
D. Yes, because the original mural was painted before the second version which replaced it.

GO ON TO THE NEXT PAGE.

Times Square, the scene of the annual New Year's Eve <u>celebration every year,</u> [28] is just a major traffic intersection, but the name is magical and the stop required. [29] After so much walking, we splurge on a cab and ride in style to the Village to eat supper at John's, a pizzeria serving traditional New York pies. Then it is back to my apartment to catch up on hometown news.

28. F. NO CHANGE
G. celebrating every year
H. celebration
J. celebrating

29. Should the writer begin a new paragraph at this point?

A. Yes, because the discussion shifts from a walking tour to a cab ride and the end of the day's activities.
B. Yes, because earlier in the essay the writer has used new paragraphs to introduce the meals included on the tour.
C. No, because the tour does not come to an end until the writer and visitors return to the apartment.
D. No, because the supper at John's is just another event on the tour that has already been scheduled by the writer.

Item #30 asks about the preceding passage as a whole.

30. The passage is primarily organized according to the:

F. historical importance of the locations visited.
G. popularity of the sites by number of visitors.
H. sequence in which the writer and visitors see places.
J. proximity of attractions to the writer's apartment.

PASSAGE III

Violence in the Park

Yellowstone Park tells a remarkable story of three <u>big</u> [31] events that occurred over the past 2.1 million years. Each climaxed in a violent volcanic

31. Which choice best conveys the idea that the events described were both sudden and devastating?

A. NO CHANGE
B. enormous
C. precipitous
D. cataclysmic

eruption accompanied by [32] an enormous volume of hot, fragmented volcanic rocks followed by [A] the formation of a [B] giant caldera and, all [33] occurring within weeks or even days. [C] The hot ash, pumice, and other rock fragments welded together by the heat and the weight [34] of overlying material formed extensive sheets of hard lava-like rock. In some sections, these ash-flow tuffs are more than 400 yards thick. [D] [35]

[1] The Huckleberry Ridge Tuff erupted about 2.1 million years ago, creating a caldera approximately 47 miles wide. [2] A second episode concluded with the eruption of the much smaller Mesa Falls Tuff around 1.3 million years ago. [3] Activity culminated 640,000 years ago with the eruption of the Lava Creek Tuff and fortunate [36] formation of a 28-mile by 53-mile caldera. [37]

In each case, the sequence of events were [38] the same. Rocks of the lower continental shelf melted, and the newly formed magma rose toward the

32. F. NO CHANGE
G. accompanied
H. accompanying
J. in the company of

33. A. NO CHANGE
B. caldera and all,
C. caldera, the total
D. caldera, all

34. F. NO CHANGE
G. weighing
H. weighing out
J. clout

35. The writer plans to add the following parenthetical statement to paragraph 1:

(A caldera is a cauldron-like depression in the ground.)

What is the most appropriate location for the addition?

A. Point A
B. Point B
C. Point C
D. Point D

36. F. NO CHANGE
G. fortunately
H. consequent
J. subsequently

37. What is the most logical order for the three sentences of paragraph 2?

A. 1, 2, 3
B. 1, 3, 2
C. 2, 3, 1
D. 3, 2, 1

38. F. NO CHANGE
G. was
H. being
J. will be

surface but is trapped below ground in a magma chamber. The volume of magma eventually exceeded the capacity of the chamber and stretched the overlying crust, caused fracturing in the surface. At the critical stage, the magma busted through the fracture zone, producing extensive ash-flow sheets and emptying the chamber. The rapid evacuation of magma led to the collapse of the magma-chamber roofs, causing the ground above to subside by many hundreds of yards, thus forming the calderas.

(39: is trapped; 40: crust, caused; 41: busted)

There have been no major eruptions since Lava Creek, but smaller eruptions occurred between 180,000 and 70,000 years ago, and huge hydrothermal explosions have taken place since the last 12,000 years. The long history of volcanism in this region suggests that additional eruptions can be expected, but they're likely to be less violent and expel only moderate quantities of lava. A fourth massive explosion with extensive lava flow and a new caldera is unlikely.

(42: since; 43: they're; 44: A fourth massive explosion with extensive lava flow and a new caldera is unlikely.)

39. A. NO CHANGE
B. was trapped
C. could be trapped
D. is trapping

40. F. NO CHANGE
G. crust caused
H. crust, causing
J. crust, causes

41. A. NO CHANGE
B. burst
C. blowed up
D. blown up

42. F. NO CHANGE
G. after
H. over
J. following

43. A. NO CHANGE
B. their
C. its
D. it is

44. Assuming that all of the following statements are accurate, which one would be the best conclusion for the final paragraph and the essay as a whole?

F. NO CHANGE
G. A volcano observatory monitors seismic activity and volcanic gas within the park.
H. The Earth is like a ball with a central core that is surrounded by concentric layers.
J. While the mountains and valleys of Yellowstone Park may appear to be stable, they change over time.

GO ON TO THE NEXT PAGE.

Item #45 asks about the preceding passage as a whole.

45. Suppose the writer wanted to highlight outdoor activities that make Yellowstone Park a popular tourist destination. Would the essay succeed in achieving that goal?

A. No, because most tourists would be reluctant to visit a region that has been the center of volcanic activity in the remote past.
B. No, because the essay is primarily concerned with geological events that occurred in the past and not with present conditions in the park.
C. Yes, because the geological events that shaped the present landscape determine what outdoor activities are currently available.
D. Yes, because many of the tourists who visit the park may be interested in the geological history of the surrounding region.

PASSAGE IV

Chicago versus New York: The Sky Is Not the Limit

Low-rise buildings characterized New York and Chicago, so [46] inventions like elevators made taller buildings possible. Initially, [47] Chicago led in the construction of high-rises and by 1890 had 12 skyscrapers in its financial district. Critics, however, complained that the tall buildings caused traffic congestion and degrading [48] air quality. In 1892, Chicago banned new buildings as tall as [49] 150 feet.

So New York took the lead in skyscraper construction. The distinctive Flatiron Building with its triangle shape was completed in 1902, the Singer

46. F. NO CHANGE
G. Chicago, if
H. Chicago because of
J. Chicago until

47. A. NO CHANGE
B. Accordingly,
C. Moreover,
D. Besides,

48. F. NO CHANGE
G. when degrading
H. and degraded
J. to degrade

49. A. NO CHANGE
B. tall as
C. taller as
D. taller than

GO ON TO THE NEXT PAGE.

Tower in 1908, and the Woolworth Building in 1912. Ironically, [50] the Flatiron Building has all the characteristics of a Chicago structure <u>instead of</u> [51] a typical New York building with a tower rising from a massive block of lower stories.

<u>Advances</u> [52] in building techniques and improvements to elevators, technical constraints on building height diminished. The 42-story Equitable Building in Lower Manhattan, completed in 1916, <u>casting</u> [53] a seven-acre shadow over the neighborhood. The <u>antis</u> [54] set the stage for the nation's first comprehensive zoning plan.

50. The writer is considering deleting the word "Ironically" (and capitalizing "The"). Should the writer make this change?

F. Yes, because in the 1800s Chicago had more skyscrapers than New York.
G. Yes, because the Flatiron Building is only one of the examples mentioned in the paragraph.
H. No, because finding a Chicago-style building in New York is unexpected.
J. No, because the Flatiron Building is not identified as the tallest building of its era.

51. A. NO CHANGE
B. instead
C. instead of those of
D. instead of that of

52. F. NO CHANGE
G. Advancing
H. With advances
J. By advancing

53. A. NO CHANGE
B. cast
C. would cast
D. had cast

54. F. NO CHANGE
G. adverse public reaction
H. resistant public reaction
J. averse public

GO ON TO THE NEXT PAGE.

(1) Chicago altered its laws in the 1920s to allow the main portion of a skyscraper to reach 264 feet and a tower on top of that up to 20 additional stories. (2) New York's Zoning Resolution of 1916 established setback standards. (3) Still, New York continued to lead with more than ten times the number of tall buildings as Chicago. (4) Typically, a building could rise directly from the sidewalk to a height of <u>only</u> 100 feet; after that, the exterior walls had to be set back from the property lines to allow
55

sunlight to reach the street below. [56]

<u>For many years,</u> the two cities have vied for
57

the honor of being home to the <u>countries</u> tallest
58

55. What is the most logical placement for the word *only* in this sentence?

A. where it is now
B. before *a building*
C. after *rise*
D. after *directly*

56. Which of the following represents the most logical order for the sentences in the paragraph?

F. 1, 2, 3, 4
G. 2, 3, 1, 4
H. 2, 4, 3, 1
J. 3, 1, 2, 4

57. A. NO CHANGE
B. Every year
C. Yearly
D. Most years

58. F. NO CHANGE
G. countries'
H. country's
J. countrys'

GO ON TO THE NEXT PAGE.

building. Trinity Church gave up the title to Chicago's Saint Michael's Church in 1869; the Chicago Board of Trade Building fell to the Singer Building in 1908; and the ill-fated Twin Towers lost to Chicago's Willis Tower in 1974. [59] Is New York's One World Trade Center now the tallest? The answer depends on whether its mast is a true spire or just an antenna. [60]

59. If the writer deleted the preceding sentence, the passage would primarily lose:

A. the name of the first skyscraper to be built in New York.
B. examples of the inter-city competition for tallest building.
C. information about techniques for constructing tall buildings.
D. background on the impact of zoning on high-rise construction.

60. The writer is thinking of adding the following sentence at this point:

> The Council on Tall Buildings and Urban Habitat, an international body that determines the heights of skyscrapers, has seemingly settled the issue with its ruling that the spire is an architecturally significant feature of the building and not an antenna.

Would the addition be appropriate?

F. No, because the sentence does not put quotation marks around the organization's finding.
G. No, because the question asked is rhetorical and does not have an answer.
H. Yes, because a writer should not raise a question unless an answer can be provided.
J. Yes, because the sentence provides a possible answer to the question raised earlier.

GO ON TO THE NEXT PAGE.

PASSAGE V

Vice-President Shoots Secretary of Treasury

Alexander Hamilton, one of the nation's founders and its first Secretary of the Treasury, and Aaron Burr, the sitting Vice-President, fought a duel of honor. That killed [61] Hamilton and ended the political career of Burr. The duel arose from personal animosity that had simmered for years and boiled over caused by [62] Hamilton engineered Burr's defeat in the race for New York governor. Following an exchange of increasingly belligerent [63] letters: Burr [64] issued a formal challenge that Hamilton, which had [65] previously resisted, finally accepted. [66]

61. A. NO CHANGE
B. honor what killed
C. honor that killed
D. honor that killed,

62. F. NO CHANGE
G. by reason of
H. for the reason that
J. because

63. Which choice best reflects the idea expressed by *simmering* and *boiled over* in the preceding sentence?
A. NO CHANGE
B. hateful
C. ill-conceived
D. heated

64. F. NO CHANGE
G. letters—Burr.
H. letters. Burr
J. letters, Burr

65. A. NO CHANGE
B. Hamilton, who had
C. Hamilton had
D. OMIT the underlined phrase.

66. F. NO CHANGE
G. excepted
H. expected
J. given

Dueling had been outlawed in both New York and New Jersey, but New Jersey was not as aggressive in prosecuting dueling participants as New York. [67] So early on July 11, 1804, Burr and Hamilton departed Manhattan by separate boats and crossed the Hudson River to New Jersey. The duel took place in Weehawken by the cliffs of the Palisades and near the spot where Hamilton's son

Philip had died in a duel three years <u>ago.</u> 68

At the <u>beginning</u> 69, it was common for both participants in a duel to fire initial shots into the ground. By leaving themselves vulnerable, they satisfied the demands of honor, and the duel could end without the necessity of <u>either party's</u> 70 firing a second shot. Hamilton confided to friends in the days before the confrontation that he intended to follow this course.

It is unclear what actually happened in this case. All first-hand reports agreed that two shots

67. The writer is thinking of adding this sentence at this point:

> Many other states had also banned dueling, though the practice survived until the mid-1800s in the South and West where the social status of individuals was more often at issue.

Should the writer make this addition?

A. No, because the focus of the essay is the Hamilton-Burr duel fought in New Jersey in 1804.
B. No, because the Hamilton-Burr duel grew out of a political, not a social, dispute.
C. Yes, because duelists were more likely to be prosecuted in New York than New Jersey.
D. Yes, because the writer mentions in the next sentence the duel involving Hamilton's son.

68. F. NO CHANGE
G. earlier
H. in advance
J. hence

69. A. NO CHANGE
B. end
C. start
D. time

70. F. NO CHANGE
G. both party's
H. either parties
J. one parties

GO ON TO THE NEXT PAGE.

were fired, one by each duelist no one could say for (71) certain who had fired first. According to a common (72) accepted theory, however, Hamilton fired first but in vain, (73) and the ball passed over Burr's head. Burr returned fire, hitting Hamilton in the abdomen, and Hamilton immediately fell to the ground unconscious.

Regaining consciousness, the attending physician heard Hamilton say, (74) "This is a mortal wound." He died the next day and was buried in the Trinity Church Cemetery. Burr was charged with murder but never went to trial. He served out his term as Vice-President and faded from public view.

71. A. NO CHANGE
B. duelist, no one
C. duelist, so no one
D. duelist, but no one

72. F. NO CHANGE
G. commonly
H. ordinary
J. usual

73. The writer believes that Hamilton fired before he intended to. Which word would best convey that belief to the reader?

A. NO CHANGE
B. inaccurately
C. unsuccessfully
D. prematurely

74. F. NO CHANGE
G. Regaining consciousness, the physician who was attending heard Hamilton say,
H. As he regained consciousness, the attending physician heard Hamilton saying,
J. Regaining consciousness, Hamilton said to the attending physician,

Item #75 asks about the preceding passage as a whole.

75. Suppose that the goal of the writer was to produce an essay that provided a detailed explanation of the rules for dueling with pistols. Does the essay accomplish this goal?

A. No, because the details given about the procedures followed are not the focus of the essay.
B. No, because the description of the events in the passage cannot be independently verified.
C. Yes, because the writer states that duelists could fire into the ground, thereby ending the duel.
D. Yes, because the rules for dueling are open to interpretation by the parties fighting a duel.

END OF TEST 1
STOP! DO NOT TURN THE PAGE UNTIL TOLD TO DO SO.

2 2 2 2 2 2 2 2 2 2 2 2

SECTION 2: MATHEMATICS TEST

60 Minutes—60 Items

DIRECTIONS: Solve each item and choose the correct answer choice. Then, fill in the corresponding oval on the bubble sheet.

Allocate time wisely. Try to solve as many items as possible, returning to skipped items if time permits.

Calculator use is permitted on this test; however, some items are best solved without the use of a calculator.

NOTE: All of the following should be assumed, unless otherwise stated.

1. Illustrative figures are NOT necessarily drawn to scale.
2. The word *average* indicates arithmetic mean.
3. The word *line* indicates a straight line.
4. Geometric figures lie in a plane.

Answers are on page 452.

DO YOUR FIGURING HERE.

1. What is the additive inverse of $-\frac{2}{3}$?

A. $-\frac{3}{2}$
B. 0
C. $\frac{2}{3}$
D. 1
E. $\frac{3}{2}$

2. In the figure below, if O is the center of the circle and $\angle AOC$ is a central angle equal to 70°, what is the measure of $\angle ABC$?

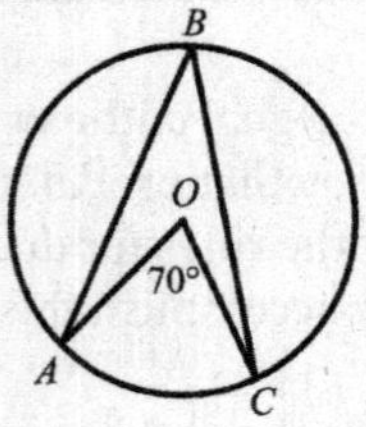

F. 140°
G. 70°
H. 50°
J. 35°
K. 22°

3. Which of the following is a solution to the equation $x^2 + 6x + 8 = 0$?

A. 8
B. 6
C. 4
D. −2
E. −8

GO ON TO THE NEXT PAGE.

DO YOUR FIGURING HERE.

4. In the figure below $l_1 \parallel l_2$. If $x = 70$ and $y = 105$, what is the value of r?

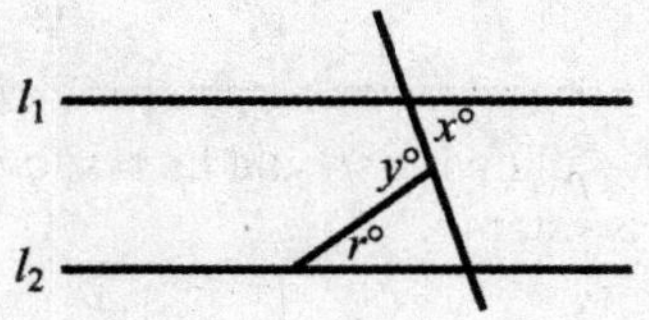

F. 35
G. 45
H. 85
J. 145
K. 175

5. If $A = \frac{2gr}{g+r}$, what is the value of g when $r = 1$ and $A = 4$?

A. -2
B. $\frac{4}{7}$
C. $\frac{8}{5}$
D. 2
E. 4

6. The figure below represents which of the following equations?

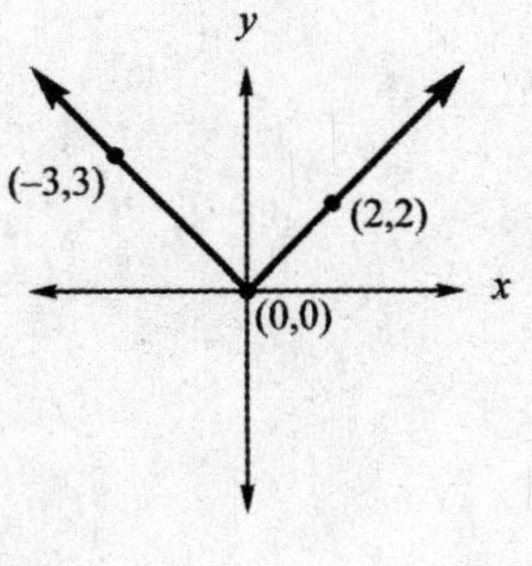

F. $y = x$
G. $y = -x$
H. $y = |x|$
J. $|y| = x$
K. $y = x^2$

7. Which of the following is an illustration of the distributive property?

A. $(12 \cdot 25)(4) = 12(25 \cdot 4)$
B. $7n + 2 - 3n = 7n - 3n + 2$
C. $(17)(b^2)(5) = (17)(5)(b)^2$
D. $x(x+2) = x^2 + 2x$
E. $ab + ac = ba + ca$

GO ON TO THE NEXT PAGE.

DO YOUR FIGURING HERE.

8. Joshua buys a television that costs $600. If the sales tax is 7%, what is the total cost of the purchase?

F. $4.20
G. $42.00
H. $420.00
J. $604.20
K. $642.00

9. What is the value of $-x^2 - 2x^3$ when $x = -1$?

A. -3
B. -1
C. 0
D. 1
E. 3

10. What is the average of $n+3$, $2n-1$, and $3n+4$?

F. $\frac{5n+6}{3}$
G. $2n+2$
H. $3n+3$
J. $\frac{6n+7}{3}$
K. $6n+6$

11. If $x = 9$, what is the value of $x^0 + x^{\frac{1}{2}} + x^{-2}$?

A. $77\frac{1}{2}$
B. $76\frac{1}{2}$
C. $5\frac{7}{18}$
D. $4\frac{1}{81}$
E. $3\frac{1}{81}$

12. $4\sqrt{3} + 3\sqrt{27} = ?$

F. $10\sqrt{3}$
G. $13\sqrt{3}$
H. $7\sqrt{30}$
J. 63
K. 108

DO YOUR FIGURING HERE.

13. Jessica Dawn received marks of 87, 93, and 86 on 3 successive tests. What grade must she receive on a fourth test in order to have an average grade of 90?

A. 90
B. 92
C. 93
D. 94
E. 95

14. In terms of x, what is the total number of cents in $4x$ dimes?

F. $0.04x$
G. $0.4x$
H. $4x$
J. $40x$
K. $400x$

15. Which of the following is shown by the graph below?

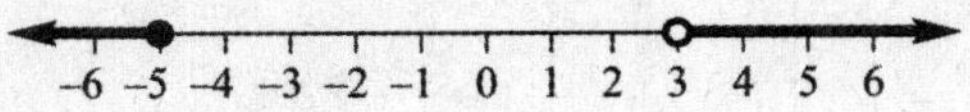

A. $-5 \leq x < 3$
B. $-5 < x$ or $x < 3$
C. $-5 \leq x$ or $x > 3$
D. $-5 \leq x \leq 3$
E. $-5 \geq x$ or $x > 3$

16. $2\frac{2}{5} - 1\frac{7}{8} = ?$

F. $\frac{11}{40}$
G. $\frac{19}{40}$
H. $\frac{21}{40}$
J. $\frac{7}{13}$
K. $1\frac{5}{40}$

DO YOUR FIGURING HERE.

17. In a circle with a radius of 6, what is the degree measure of an arc whose length is 3π?

A. 20°
B. 30°
C. 60°
D. 90°
E. 120°

18. If $\frac{2x}{3\sqrt{2}} = \frac{3\sqrt{2}}{x}$, what is the positive value of x?

F. $\sqrt{3}$
G. $\sqrt{6}$
H. $2\sqrt{3}$
J. 3
K. 9

19. If $f(x) = 2x - x^2$ and $g(x) = x - 4$, what is the value of $g(f(2))$?

A. −8
B. −4
C. −2
D. 0
E. 3

20. What is the solution set of the equation $|5 - 2x| = 7$?

F. $\{-1, 6\}$
G. $\{-1\}$
H. $\{1\}$
J. $\{6\}$
K. The empty set

21. When $\frac{3 - \frac{3}{x}}{x(x-1)}$ is defined, it is equivalent to which of the following expressions?

A. $\frac{1}{x-1}$
B. $\frac{1}{3}$
C. $x+1$
D. $\frac{3}{x^2}$
E. 3

GO ON TO THE NEXT PAGE.

DO YOUR FIGURING HERE.

22. What is the slope of the line that passes through the points $(-3,5)$ and $(4,7)$?

F. $\sqrt{53}$

G. $\frac{7}{2}$

H. 2

J. $\frac{1}{2}$

K. $\frac{2}{7}$

23. In the circle below with center O, diameter $\overline{AB}$ is perpendicular to chord $\overline{CD}$ at point E. If chord $\overline{CD} = 8$ inches and $\overline{OE} = 3$ inches, what is the length of the radius of the circle, in inches, if O is the center of the circle?

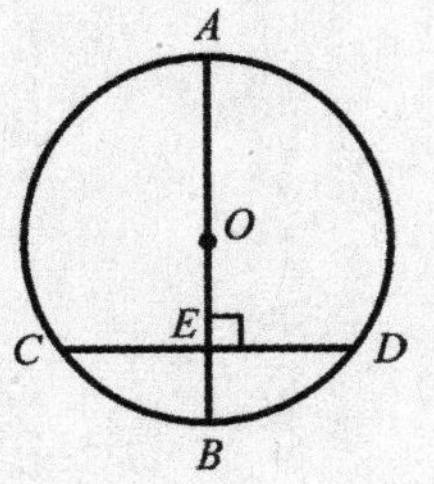

A. $\sqrt{3}$
B. $\sqrt{5}$
C. $\sqrt{7}$
D. $\sqrt{15}$
E. 5

24. In the figure below, the diagonals of parallelogram $ABCD$ intersect at point E. If $\overline{DB} = 4x + 2$ and $\overline{DE} = x + 4$, what is the value of x?

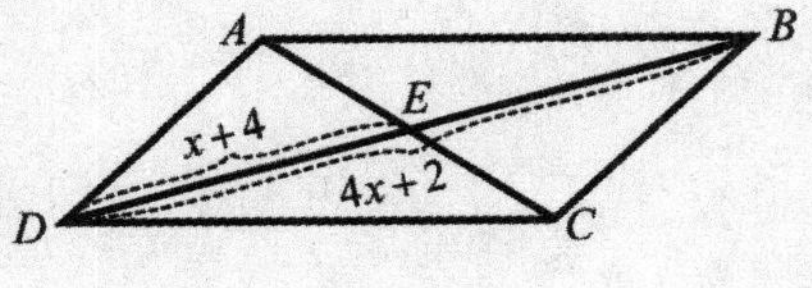

F. 3
G. 2
H. 1
J. $\frac{2}{3}$
K. 0

DO YOUR FIGURING HERE.

25. If the measure of the central angle of a sector of a circle is 120°, what is the area, in square units, of the sector if the radius is 6 units long?

A. 4π
B. 6π
C. 8π
D. 10π
E. 12π

26. If the statement "if two triangles are red, then they are equal in area" is true, then which of the following *must* be true?

F. If the two triangles are not equal in area, then they are not red.
G. If the two triangles are equal in area, then they are red.
H. If the two triangles are equal in area, then they are not red.
J. If the two triangles are not red, then they are not equal in area.
K. If the two triangles are red, then they are not equal in area.

27. If $\frac{a}{b}=\frac{r}{t}$, then which of the following is NOT necessarily true?

A. $\frac{a}{r}=\frac{b}{t}$
B. $\frac{a}{t}=\frac{b}{r}$
C. $\frac{a+b}{b}=\frac{r+t}{t}$
D. $\frac{b}{a}=\frac{t}{r}$
E. $at=br$

28. If $-2x+5=2-(5-2x)$, then $x=$?

F. 6
G. 5
H. 4
J. 3
K. 2

GO ON TO THE NEXT PAGE.

29. $\frac{(1+\sin x)(1-\sin x)}{(1+\cos x)(1-\cos x)}$ is equivalent to which of the following?

DO YOUR FIGURING HERE.

A. $\cos x$
B. $\tan x$
C. $\tan^2 x$
D. $\cos^2 x$
E. $\cot^2 x$

30. In the figure below, ΔACB is a right triangle. $\overline{CE}$ is the median to hypotenuse $\overline{AB}$, and $\overline{AB} = 14$ centimeters. What is the length, in centimeters, of $\overline{CE}$?

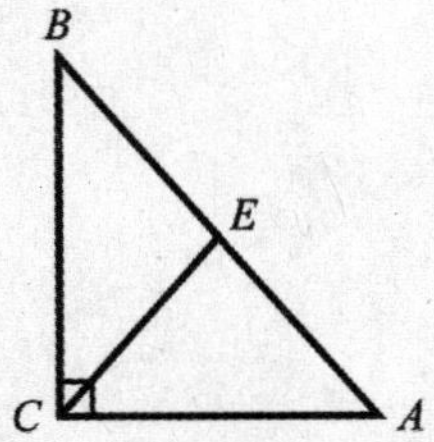

F. 5
G. 6
H. 7
J. 8
K. Cannot be determined from the given information

31. If y varies directly as x, and $y = 10$ when $x = \frac{1}{5}$, what is the value of y when $x = \frac{1}{2}$?

A. 1
B. 4
C. 7
D. 16
E. 25

32. $\frac{(-1)(2)(-3)(4)(-5)}{(5)(-4)(3)(-2)(1)} = ?$

F. −2
G. −1
H. 1
J. 2
K. 3

DO YOUR FIGURING HERE.

33. How many positive prime factors does the number 36 have?

A. One
B. Two
C. Three
D. Five
E. Six

34. The measure of the vertex angle of an isosceles triangle is 50°. What is the degree measure of each base angle?

F. 40°
G. 50°
H. 65°
J. 75°
K. 130°

35. Using the table below, what is the median of the following data?

Score	Frequency
20	4
30	4
50	7

A. 20
B. 30
C. 40
D. 50
E. 60

36. Which of the following number lines represents the solution set of $x^2 - 2x - 3 > 0$?

F.
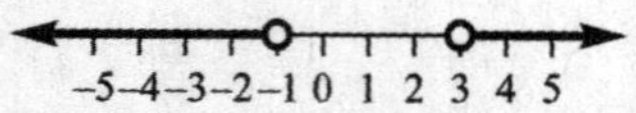

G.
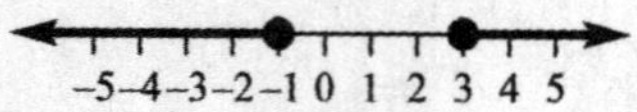

H.
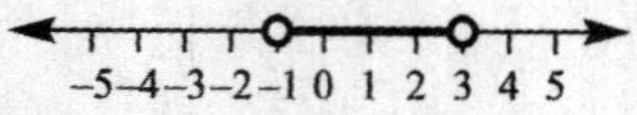

J.
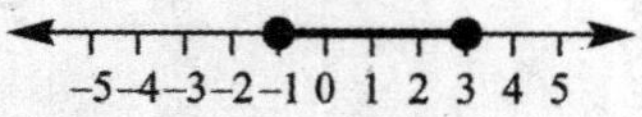

K.
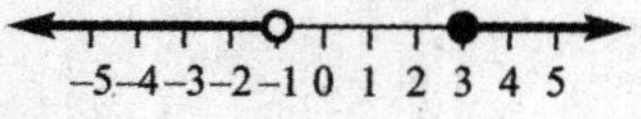

DO YOUR FIGURING HERE.

37. The expression $\sin x + \frac{\cos^2 x}{\sin x}$ is equal to which of the following?

A. 1
B. $\sin x$
C. $\cos x$
D. $\frac{1}{\sin x}$
E. $\frac{1}{\cos x}$

38. The value of $(2.5 \times 10^5)^2$ is equal to which of the following?

F. 2.5×10^7
G. 5×10^7
H. 6.25×10^7
J. 2.5×10^{10}
K. 6.25×10^{10}

39. If $f(x) = \frac{-2x - x}{-x}$, what is the value of $f(2)$?

A. -3
B. -1
C. 0
D. 1
E. 3

40. If one of the roots of the equation $x^2 + kx - 12 = 0$ is 4, what is the value of k?

F. -1
G. 0
H. 1
J. 3
K. 7

41. In the figure below, D is a point on $\overline{AB}$ and E is a point on $\overline{BC}$ such that $\overline{DE} \parallel \overline{AC}$. If $\overline{DB} = 4$ units long, $\overline{AB} = 10$ units long, and $\overline{BC} = 20$ units long, how many units long is $\overline{EC}$?

DO YOUR FIGURING HERE.

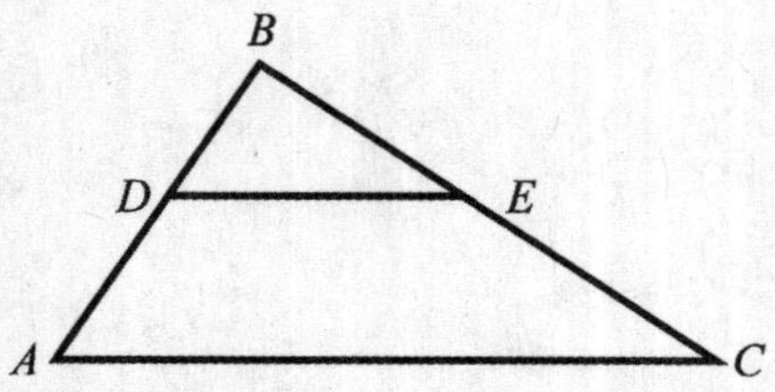

A. 4
B. 6
C. 8
D. 10
E. 12

42. $(x+2)(x-4)-(x+4)(x-2) = ?$

F. 0
G. $2x^2 + 4x - 16$
H. $-4x$
J. $4x$
K. $-4x - 16$

43. If the sum of the measures of the interior angles of a polygon equals the sum of the measures of the exterior angles, how many sides does the polygon have?

A. Three
B. Four
C. Five
D. Six
E. Seven

44. If the perimeter of an equilateral triangle is 12 inches, what is its area, in square inches?

F. $2\sqrt{3}$
G. $4\sqrt{3}$
H. 8
J. $6\sqrt{3}$
K. $36\sqrt{3}$

DO YOUR FIGURING HERE.

45. If the ratio of two complementary angles is 8:1, what is the degree measure of the smaller angle?

A. 10°
B. 20°
C. 30°
D. 40°
E. 80°

46. Given a square, a rectangle, a trapezoid, and a circle, if one figure is selected at random, what is the probability that the figure has four right angles?

F. 1
G. $\frac{3}{4}$
H. $\frac{1}{2}$
J. $\frac{1}{4}$
K. 0

47. A man travels 320 miles in 8 hours. If he continues at the same rate, how many miles will he travel in the next 2 hours?

A. 6
B. 40
C. 80
D. 120
E. 240

48. $\frac{\sin x}{\cos x} + \frac{\cos x}{\sin x} = ?$

F. 1
G. $\sin x$
H. $\frac{1}{(\sin x)(\cos x)}$
J. $\tan x$
K. $\frac{\sin x + \cos x}{(\sin x)(\cos x)}$

DO YOUR FIGURING HERE.

49. The average temperatures for 5 days were 82° F, 86° F, 91° F, 79° F, and 91° F. What is the mode of these temperatures?

A. 79° F
B. 82° F
C. 85.8° F
D. 86° F
E. 91° F

50. A booklet contains 30 pages. If 9 pages in the booklet have drawings, what percentage of the pages in the booklet have drawings?

F. 30%
G. 9%
H. 3%
J. 1%
K. $\frac{3}{10}$%

51. Which of the following represents $-7t+6t^2-3$ when it is completely factored?

A. $(3t-1)(2t+3)$
B. $(3t+1)(2t-3)$
C. $(6t-1)(t+3)$
D. $(6t+1)(t-3)$
E. $(2t-1)(3t+3)$

52. What is the solution set of $2^{x^2+2x}=2^{-1}$?

F. {1}
G. {−1}
H. {1, −1}
J. {2}
K. The empty set

53. Jessica is 3 years younger than Joshua. If x represents Joshua's age now, what was Jessica's age four years ago in terms of x?

A. $x-1$
B. $x-3$
C. $x-4$
D. $x-6$
E. $x-7$

DO YOUR FIGURING HERE.

54. In a drama club, *x* students contributed *y* dollars each to buy an $18 gift for their advisor. If three more students had contributed, each student could have contributed one dollar less to buy the same gift. Which of the following sets of equations expresses this relationship?

F. $xy = 18$ and $(x+3)(y-1) = 18$
G. $xy = 18$ and $(x-3)(y+1) = 18$
H. $xy = 18$ and $(x+3)(y+1) = 18$
J. $xy = 18$ and $(x-3)(y-1) = 18$
K. $xy = 18$ and $(x+1)(y-3) = 18$

55. $\frac{1}{2}\sqrt{112} - \sqrt{28} + 2\sqrt{63} = ?$

A. $6\sqrt{7}$
B. $7\sqrt{7}$
C. $8\sqrt{7}$
D. $9\sqrt{7}$
E. $10\sqrt{7}$

56. What is the value of *x* for the following set of simultaneous equations?

$$\frac{1}{x} + \frac{1}{y} = \frac{1}{4}$$
$$\frac{1}{x} - \frac{1}{y} = \frac{3}{4}$$

F. 4
G. 2
H. $\frac{1}{2}$
J. $\frac{1}{4}$
K. -4

57. Which set could represent the lengths of the sides of a triangle?

A. {1, 3, 6}
B. {2, 4, 7}
C. {2, 10, 12}
D. {4, 6, 8}
E. {4, 4, 10}

DO YOUR FIGURING HERE.

58. What is the solution set $\{x, y\}$, in terms of a and b, for the following system of equations?

$$ax + y = b$$
$$2ax + y = 2b$$

F. $\left\{-\frac{b}{a}, -1\right\}$
G. $\{-a, b\}$
H. $\left\{\frac{b}{a}, 0\right\}$
J. $\left\{\frac{b}{a}, \frac{a}{b}\right\}$
K. $\left\{\frac{2a}{b}, \frac{2b}{a}\right\}$

59. In the figure below, $\sin\theta = \frac{r}{4}$. What is the value of $\cos\theta$?

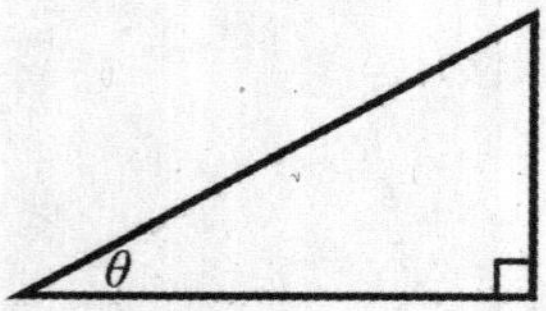

A. $\frac{\sqrt{16-r^2}}{4}$
B. $\frac{4-r}{4}$
C. $\frac{16-r^2}{2}$
D. $\frac{4-r}{2}$
E. $\frac{16-r^2}{r}$

60. If 3 copier machines can copy 300 sheets in 3 minutes, assuming the same rate, how long, in minutes, will it take 6 such copiers to copy 600 sheets?

F. 2
G. 3
H. 4
J. 6
K. 9

END OF TEST 2
STOP! DO NOT TURN THE PAGE UNTIL TOLD TO DO SO.
DO NOT RETURN TO THE PREVIOUS TEST.

NO TEST MATERIAL ON THIS PAGE

3 3 3 3 3 3 3 3 3 3 3 3

SECTION 3: READING TEST

35 Minutes—40 Items

DIRECTIONS: Each passage below is followed by a set of items. Read each passage and choose the best answer for each item. Fill in the corresponding oval on your bubble sheet. You may refer to the passage as often as necessary to answer the items. Answers are on page 466.

PASSAGE I

PROSE FICTION: This passage is adapted from the short story "Paul's Case: A Study in Temperament" by Willa Cather.

It was Paul's afternoon to appear before the faculty of Pittsburgh High School to account for his various misdemeanors. He had been suspended a week ago. His father had visited the principal's office and confessed his perplexity about his son. Paul entered the faculty room suave and smiling. His clothes were a trifle outgrown. The tan velvet on the collar of his open overcoat was frayed and worn. But for all that there was something of the dandy in him. He wore an opal pin in his neatly knotted black four-in-hand, and a red carnation in his buttonhole. This latter adornment the faculty somehow felt was not properly significant of the contrite spirit befitting a boy under the ban of suspension.

Paul was tall for his age and very thin. He had high, cramped shoulders and a narrow chest. His eyes were remarkable for a certain hysterical brilliancy. He continually used them in a conscious, theatrical sort of way, peculiarly offensive in a boy. The pupils were abnormally large, as though he was addicted to belladonna. But there was a glassy glitter about them, which that drug does not produce.

When questioned by the principal as to why he was there Paul stated, politely enough, that he wanted to come back to school. This was a lie, but Paul was quite accustomed to lying; he found it, indeed, indispensable for overcoming friction. His teachers were asked to state their respective charges against him. They did so with such a rancor and aggrievement as evinced that this was not a usual case. Disorder and impertinence were among the offenses named. Yet each of his instructors felt that it was scarcely possible to put into words the real cause of the trouble, which lay in a sort of hysterically defiant manner of the boy's, in the contempt which they all knew he felt for them, and which he seemingly made not the least effort to conceal. Once, when he had been making a synopsis of a paragraph at the blackboard, his English teacher had stepped to his side and attempted to guide his hand. Paul had started back with a shudder and thrust his hands violently behind him. The astonished woman could scarcely have been more hurt and embarrassed had he struck at her. The insult was so involuntary and definitely personal as to be unforgettable. In one way or another he had made all his teachers, men and women alike, conscious of the same feeling of physical aversion. In one class he habitually sat with his hand shading his eyes; in another he always looked out of the window during the recitation; in another he made a running commentary on the lecture, with humorous intention.

His teachers felt this afternoon that his whole attitude was symbolized by his shrug and his flippant red carnation flower. They fell upon him without mercy, his English teacher leading the pack. He stood through it smiling. His pale lips parted over his white teeth. (His lips were continuously twitching, and he had a habit of raising his eyebrows that was contemptuous and irritating to the last degree.) Older boys than Paul had broken down and shed tears under that baptism of fire, but his set smile did not once desert him. His only sign of discomfort was the nervous trembling of the fingers that toyed with the buttons of his overcoat, and an occasional jerking of the other hand that held his hat. Paul was always smiling, always glancing about him, seeming to feel that people might be watching him and trying to detect something. This conscious expression, since it was as far as possible from boyish mirthfulness, was usually attributed to insolence or "smartness."

As the inquisition proceeded, one of his instructors repeated an impertinent remark of the boy's, and the principal asked him whether he thought that a courteous speech to have made a woman. Paul shrugged his shoulders slightly and his eyebrows twitched.

"I don't know," he replied. "I didn't mean to be polite, or impolite, either. I guess it's a sort of way I have of saying things, regardless."

GO ON TO THE NEXT PAGE.

The principal, who was a sympathetic man, asked him whether he thought he ought to change his way of saying things. Paul grinned and said he guessed so. When he was told that he could go, he bowed gracefully and went out. His bow was but a repetition of the scandalous red carnation.

His teachers were in despair, and his drawing-master voiced the feeling of them all when he declared there was something about the boy which none of them understood. He added: "I don't really believe that smile of his comes altogether from insolence; there's something sort of haunted about it. The boy is not strong, for one thing. I happen to know that he was born in Colorado, only a few months before his mother died out there of a long illness. There is something wrong about the fellow."

1. This short story is subtitled "A Study in Temperament," which suggests that the author wants to examine:

   A. a certain type of character.
   B. reactions under pressure.
   C. how people change over time.
   D. people and their settings.

2. The phrases "something of the dandy" (line 9), "hysterical brilliancy" (lines 17–18), and "peculiarly offensive" (line 19):

   I. describe Paul's reaction to his peers.
   II. show the narrator's distaste for Paul.
   III. reveal Paul as an unpleasant character.

   F. I only
   G. III only
   H. I and II only
   J. II and III only

3. The passage makes it clear in the first paragraph that the faculty of the high school:

   A. is sympathetic to Paul's situation.
   B. considers Paul's dress objectionable.
   C. cannot understand Paul's words.
   D. wants only the best for Paul.

4. The words *hysterical* and *hysterically*, as used in lines 17 and 35, respectively, seem to imply:

   F. delirium.
   G. raving.
   H. uncontrolled behavior.
   J. frothing.

5. The author implies that the most serious flaw Paul has is his:

   A. inability to complete his work.
   B. flippant sense of humor.
   C. surreptitious use of drugs.
   D. failure to hide his contempt for others.

6. In lines 56–57, the author indicates that the faculty behaved like a pack of:

   F. cowards.
   G. predators.
   H. liars.
   J. scholars.

7. The author uses the phrase "baptism of fire" (line 63) to denote the:

   A. challenge faced by students in a faculty inquisition.
   B. youthfulness of Paul and his fellow students.
   C. obstacles adolescents confront while growing up.
   D. fury with which Paul faced up to the faculty.

8. The word *smartness* (line 73) is used to mean:

   F. wit.
   G. intelligence.
   H. impudence.
   J. reasonableness.

9. Which adjective does NOT describe Paul as he is presented in this story?

   A. Defiant
   B. Proud
   C. Flippant
   D. Candid

10. The remarks of the drawing-master (lines 89–98) are an attempt to:

   F. show that Paul's behavior is a reaction to his difficult circumstances.
   G. exonerate Paul of the specific allegations made against him.
   H. demonstrate that Paul should be permanently expelled.
   J. mitigate the severity of the faculty's judgment of Paul.

GO ON TO THE NEXT PAGE.

PASSAGE II

SOCIAL SCIENCE: This passage discusses the history of African Americans in Congress.

Only with the enforcement of the Reconstruction Act of 1867 and the ratification of the Fifteenth Amendment to the Constitution did African Americans first win seats in Congress. Hiram Revels of Mississippi became the first African American to serve. He took his seat in the Senate on February 25, 1870. Joseph Rainey of South Carolina became the first African American member of the House of Representatives later in 1870. In the next 80 years, nearly seventy African Americans served in Congress.

African Americans throughout the South became politically active soon after the close of the Civil War. State conventions and local political groups such as the Union League provided an opportunity for freed African Americans to convey their vision of full participation in the political and economic life of the former slave states. Out of this broad-based mobilization came a generation of African American leaders who nearly all adhered to the Republican Party because it had championed the rights of African Americans. Those elected to Congress during Reconstruction found the legislature an effective forum for the promotion of political equality. Following the end of Reconstruction in 1877, African Americans continued to win election to Congress. Their struggle for civil rights and economic opportunity also continued. The African American congressional representatives of the late nineteenth century were the most prominent indication of the persistence of political organization on a local level in the South.

During the 1890s and early 1900s, no African American won election to Congress. This was in part due to restrictive state election codes in some southern states. During World War I and in the following decade, however, African American migration to northern cities established the foundation for political organization in urban centers. Oscar DePriest's election in 1928 as a representative from Chicago began a slow but steady succession of victories in the North. Over the next three decades African Americans won seats in New York City, Detroit, and Philadelphia. In the wake of the civil rights movement and the Voting Rights Act of 1965, African Americans regained seats in the South. Since the 1930s, nearly all African American representatives have been Democrats.

Since the nineteenth century, African American members of Congress have served as advocates for all African Americans as well as representatives for their constituencies. During Reconstruction and the late nineteenth century, African American representatives called on their colleagues to protect the voting rights of African Americans. These members of Congress, many of them former slaves, also called for more educational opportunities and land grants for freed African Americans. In the mid-twentieth century, African American representatives turned to the needs of urban areas. They asked for improved housing and job training. As the most prominent African American office-holders of the time, these representatives served as defenders of the civil rights movement and proponents of laws to end segregation. In 1971, the formation of the Congressional Black Caucus offered a formal means of representing the combined interests of African Americans. The caucus has shown a special concern for the protection of civil rights: the guarantee of equal opportunity in education, the workplace, and housing, and a broad array of foreign and domestic policy issues.

African Americans in Congress have been further united by their shared experience in the African American community. Many of the early Black representatives were born in slavery. The opportunities of Reconstruction gave these representatives the hope that African Americans might gain genuine equality in American society. However, the opposition of some white Southerners reminded them of the need for federal protection of the liberties won in the aftermath of the Civil War.

Since the victories of the civil rights movement in the 1960s, African American men and women have won election to Congress from more diverse regions of the country. Whether from urban districts, suburban areas, or—more recently—from rural Mississippi, these members of Congress have kept their common concern with economic issues that affect African Americans and with the protection of civil rights.

The biographies of African Americans who served in the House and Senate provide a unique perspective on the history of the Congress and the role of African Americans in politics. Their stories offer testimony to the long struggle to extend the ideals of the founders to include all citizens of the United States.

GO ON TO THE NEXT PAGE.

11. According to the passage, the first African American to serve in the House of Representatives was:

A. Hiram Revels.
B. Joseph Rainey.
C. from Chicago.
D. a former slave.

12. The passage suggests that, in contrast to African Americans elected to Congress during and shortly after Reconstruction, African Americans elected to Congress today are more likely to:

F. be Democrats.
G. be members of the Republican Party.
H. work for full political equality for all African Americans.
J. come from districts in which the majority is African American.

13. One difference between African American congressional representatives in the nineteenth century and those in the mid-twentieth century was:

A. the political party to which they were likely to belong.
B. their commitment to education for African Americans.
C. the strength of their ties to the African American community as a whole.
D. the extent to which they represented all African Americans and not just their constituents.

14. When the African American representatives "turned to" (line 60) certain issues in the mid-twentieth century, they:

F. became antagonistic toward those issues.
G. reversed their positions on those issues.
H. devoted themselves to those issues.
J. referred to those issues.

15. According to the passage, one reason African Americans began to be elected to Congress from cities in the northern United States after the 1930s was that:

A. more African Americans lived in northern cities at that time than had been the case previously.
B. African Americans in northern cities had better political organizations than did African Americans in the rural South.
C. African American politicians in the North were more likely to be members of the Democratic Party than were those in the South.
D. African American politicians in the North were more likely to focus on voting rights for African Americans than were those in the South.

16. Which one of the following is NOT mentioned in the passage as a common concern of African American congressional representatives?

F. Enforcing voting rights for African Americans
G. Increasing educational opportunities for African Americans
H. Ensuring opportunities for employment for African Americans
J. Protecting people of African descent in other countries

17. One reason cited in the passage for the election of African Americans to Congress from both southern states after Reconstruction and northern states after World War I is the:

A. success of the civil rights movement.
B. passage and enforcement of the Fifteenth Amendment.
C. strength of local African American political organizations.
D. predominance of African Americans in certain districts.

GO ON TO THE NEXT PAGE.

18. According to the passage, the Congressional Black Caucus:

F. focused its attention almost exclusively on domestic issues.
G. was the first organization founded exclusively for African American congressional representatives.
H. was intended to replace local African American political organizations with one large national organization.
J. provided a forum in which African American representatives could deal with issues of concern to all African Americans.

19. The last paragraph suggests that this passage might serve as:

A. a call to political involvement on the part of African Americans.
B. an introduction to biographies of African American members of Congress.
C. the conclusion of a history of African Americans in the United States.
D. part of a longer work on the history of the United States Congress.

20. The author expresses admiration toward the African American congressional representatives discussed in the passage for their:

F. political acumen.
G. attempts to ensure the rights of all Americans.
H. single-minded devotion to the struggle for civil rights.
J. focus on providing economic opportunity for African Americans.

GO ON TO THE NEXT PAGE.

PASSAGE III

HUMANITIES: This passage is adapted from Thomas Bulfinch's *Mythology*.

Minerva was the goddess of wisdom, but on one occasion she did a very foolish thing; she entered into competition with Juno and Venus for the prize of beauty. It happened thus: at the nuptials of Peleus and Thetis all the gods were invited with the exception of Eris, or Discord. Enraged at her exclusion, the goddess threw a golden apple among the guests, with the inscription, "For the fairest." Thereupon Juno, Venus, and Minerva each claimed the apple. Jupiter, not willing to decide in so delicate a matter, sent the goddesses to Mount Ida, where the beautiful shepherd Paris was tending his flocks. To him was committed the decision. The goddesses accordingly appeared before him. Juno promised him power and riches. Minerva promised glory and renown in war. Venus offered the fairest of women for his wife. Each attempted to bias his decision in her own favour. Paris decided in favour of Venus and gave her the golden apple, thus making the two other goddesses his enemies. Under the protection of Venus, Paris sailed to Greece. He was hospitably received by Menelaus, king of Sparta. Now Helen, the wife of Menelaus, was the very woman whom Venus had destined for Paris, the fairest of her sex. She had been sought as a bride by numerous suitors. Before her decision was made known, they all, at the suggestion of Ulysses, one of their number, took an oath that they would defend her from all injury and avenge her cause if necessary. She chose Menelaus, and was living with him happily when Paris became their guest. Paris, aided by Venus, persuaded her to elope with him. He carried her to Troy, whence arose the famous Trojan War, the theme of the greatest poems of antiquity, those of Homer and Virgil.

Menelaus called upon his brother chieftains of Greece to fulfill their pledge, and join him in his efforts to recover his wife. They generally came forward, but Ulysses, who had married Penelope, and was very happy in his wife and child, had no disposition to embark in such a troublesome affair. He therefore hung back and Palamedes was sent to urge him. When Palamedes arrived at Ithaca, Ulysses pretended to be mad. He yoked an ass and an ox together to the plough and began to sow salt. Palamedes, to try him, placed the infant Telemachus before the plough, whereupon the father turned the plough aside, showing plainly that he was no madman, and after that could no longer refuse to fulfill his promise. Being now himself gained for the undertaking, he lent his aid to bring in other reluctant chiefs, especially Achilles. This hero was the son of that Thetis at whose marriage the apple of Discord had been thrown among the goddesses. Thetis was herself one of the immortals, a sea-nymph. Knowing that her son was fated to perish before Troy if he went on the expedition, she endeavored to prevent his going. She sent him away to the court of King Lycomedes, and induced him to conceal himself in the disguise of a maiden among the daughters of the king. Ulysses, hearing he was there, went disguised as a merchant to the palace and offered for sale female ornaments, among which he had placed some arms. While the king's daughters were engrossed with the other contents of the merchant's pack, Achilles handled the weapons and thereby betrayed himself to the keen eye of Ulysses, who found no great difficulty in persuading him to disregard his mother's prudent counsels and join his countrymen in the war.

The Greeks laid siege to Troy, but after ten years the city still held out. The Greeks began to despair of ever subduing it by force, so upon the advice of Ulysses, they resorted to stratagem. The Greeks constructed an immense wooden horse, which was intended as a propitiatory offering to Minerva, but in fact was filled with armed men. The remaining Greeks then sailed away, as if for a final departure. The Trojans, seeing the encampment broken up and the fleet gone, concluded the enemy to have abandoned the siege, and the gates were thrown open. The great horse was an object of great curiosity. After much debate, the structure was dragged inside the city. In the night, the armed men who were enclosed in the body of the horse opened the gates of the city to their friends, who had returned under cover of the night. The city was set on fire; the people, overcome with feasting and sleep, were put to the sword, and Troy was completely subdued.

21. By describing Jupiter as "not willing to decide in so delicate a matter" (lines 10–11), the author implies that:

A. Jupiter is usually heavy-handed.
B. any decision is bound to offend someone.
C. Jupiter is overly sensitive.
D. the problems are so obscure that no one can judge them.

GO ON TO THE NEXT PAGE.

22. The word *disposition* (line 40) is used to mean:

F. inclination.
G. nature.
H. integrity.
J. value.

23. All of the following assertions are examples of the author's inserting himself into the narrative EXCEPT:

A. Minerva did a foolish thing.
B. The poems of Homer and Virgil were great.
C. Helen was the fairest of her sex.
D. The greatest poems of antiquity were about the Trojan War.

24. Ulysses pretended to be mad by planting salt because salt:

F. does not grow.
G. is nearly worthless.
H. was used for money.
J. is used in battle.

25. When Palamedes tries Ulysses (lines 45–49), he:

A. finds him guilty.
B. judges him.
C. tests him.
D. attempts to help him.

26. The author reveals that Thetis is a sea-nymph in order to explain:

F. why she married Peleus.
G. why she dislikes the idea of war.
H. the effect of the apple of Discord.
J. her ability to predict the future.

27. Among the chieftains of Greece apparently are:

A. Juno, Venus, and Minerva.
B. Paris and Lycomedes.
C. Ulysses, Achilles, and Menelaus.
D. Eris and Thetis.

28. Why does Ulysses display arms among the ornaments?

F. To trick Achilles into revealing himself
G. As a declaration of war
H. To mislead the daughters of the king
J. To complete his disguise as a merchant

29. According to the passage, the events described will ultimately lead to:

I. the death of Achilles.
II. the advent of war.
III. the downfall of Paris.

A. I only
B. II only
C. I and II only
D. II and III only

30. One of the main themes of the literature discussed in this passage is the:

F. violence that characterized warfare of the ancient Greeks.
G. use of clever tricks rather than direct action to attain goals.
H. similarity of the character flaws of humans and Greeks gods.
J. comparison of the power of women to the relative weakness of men.

GO ON TO THE NEXT PAGE.

PASSAGE IV

NATURAL SCIENCE: This passage discusses the production of electromagnetic radiation.

The constellation of Orion, named for the Greek hunter, is visible in the skies of both the northern and southern hemispheres. If you peer closely at the stars in Orion, you will see that they are not all the same color. Betelgeuse, found at the upper left corner of the constellation, is very red, while Rigel, in the lower right, is blue. The difference in color is explained by the difference in temperature of the two stars.

The mechanism by which starlight is produced is the same one that causes horseshoes in the blacksmith's forge to glow: heat. As the metal begins to heat, it will first glow red, then yellow, and then, if very, very hot, white. The light is produced by the acceleration of charged particles, most often electrons as they have little mass and are positioned at the periphery of atoms. So electrons are easy to set into motion. To prove this, simply run a comb through your hair. You produce static electricity when you disturb electrons in both your hair and the comb. Stand near an AM radio and comb your hair. You'll hear static. The scientific principle that you've just proved is that whenever you disturb electrons, you generate electromagnetic waves.

The atoms in a heated object are vibrating rapidly, and the hotter the object becomes, the faster the atoms vibrate. The vibrating atoms collide with the electrons in the material. Each time the motion of an electron is disturbed, it emits a photon. Therefore, heated objects emit electromagnetic radiation. This type of radiation, called black body radiation, is very common and is responsible for the light emitted from an ordinary incandescent light bulb.

The light coming from the bulb that your eye can detect is called visible light, but the visible spectrum is just a small segment of the much larger electromagnetic spectrum. The average wavelength of visible light is about 0.0005 mm, so small that 50 light waves could be lined up end to end across the thickness of ordinary plastic wrap. For this reason, scientists measure wavelengths in Angstroms. One Angstrom (Å) is 10^{-10} meters or 0.0000000001 meters.

Visible light ranges from 4,000 Å to 7,000 Å. Light near the short wavelength end of the visible spectrum (4,000 Å) looks violet, and light near the long wavelength end (7,000 Å) looks red. Beyond the red end of the visible spectrum lies infrared radiation, where wavelengths range from 7,000 Å to 1 mm. At wavelengths shorter than violet, there is ultraviolet radiation. These wavelengths range from 4,000 Å down to about 100 Å. At wavelengths shorter than these are X-rays and gamma rays.

Although we cannot see it, our skin senses long wavelength radiation (7,000 Å to 1 mm) as warmth. This is the principle on which heat lamps work. These lower-energy photons can warm us without being dangerous. In contrast, the short wavelengths contain a large amount of energy, and these wavelengths can be quite dangerous.

When a bulb's filament is heated, three sorts of collisions take place among the electrons. Gentle collisions produce low-energy photons with long wavelengths, and violent collisions produce high-energy photons with short wavelengths. Most collisions are of moderate intensity, producing photons of intermediate wavelengths.

The wavelength at which an object emits the maximum amount of energy is called the wavelength of maximum. The wavelength of maximum depends on the object's temperature. As an object is heated, the average collision between electrons becomes more violent, producing high-energy, shorter-wavelength photons. The hotter the object is, the shorter the wavelength of maximum.

This is a very important point in astronomy, since it is possible to determine the temperature of a star from its light. It is also possible to estimate the temperature of a star from the color of light it emits. For a hot star, the wavelength of maximum lies in the ultraviolet spectrum and most of the radiation cannot be seen, but in the visible range, the star emits more blue than red. Thus, a hot star looks blue. In contrast, a cooler star radiates its maximum energy in the infrared. In the visible range of the spectrum it radiates more red than blue and, therefore, looks red.

Objects much cooler than stars don't glow at visible wavelengths but still emit blackbody radiation. The human body, for example, has a temperature of 310K and emits blackbody radiation, mostly in the infrared part of the spectrum. This is the principle on which infrared security cameras are built. They detect the human body's heat signature rather that visible light.

GO ON TO THE NEXT PAGE.

31. According to the passage, which of the following types of radiation has the shortest wavelength?

A. Infrared light
B. Visible light
C. Ultraviolet light
D. X-rays

32. It can be inferred that radiation of very short wavelengths can be dangerous because the radiation:

F. has no wavelength of maximum.
G. has very high energy.
H. originated in a black body.
J. is visible to the eye.

33. According to the passage, the wavelength of maximum is:

A. the maximum temperature at which an object emits light.
B. visible radiation with the longest wavelength.
C. the wavelength of light at the red end of the spectrum.
D. the wavelength at which an object emits the maximum amount of energy.

34. The main purpose of the third paragraph is to:

F. introduce a new theory of electromagnetic radiation.
G. define the scientific concept of black body radiation.
H. contrast black body radiation with incandescence.
J. illustrate the different kinds of radiation that make up the spectrum.

35. According to the passage, ultraviolet radiation has wavelengths:

A. shorter than 100 Å.
B. between 100 Å and 4,000 Å.
C. between 4,000 Å and 7,000 Å.
D. longer than 7,000 Å.

36. The passage implies that heat lamps utilize:

F. X-rays.
G. gamma rays.
H. visible wavelengths.
J. infrared radiation.

37. An astronomer views two stars of different temperatures. Which is hotter?

A. The one that is larger.
B. The one that is smaller.
C. The one that is redder.
D. The one that is bluer.

38. According to the seventh paragraph (lines 62–68), most of the electron collisions in the filament of a light bulb are:

F. gentle and emit photons with long wavelengths.
G. violent and emit photons with short wavelengths.
H. violent and emit photons with long wavelengths.
J. moderate and emit photons of intermediate wavelengths.

39. It can be inferred from the information that an incandescent bulb emits light because:

A. electricity heats the bulb's filament.
B. high-energy radiation surrounds the filament.
C. non-visible radiation bombards the filament.
D. high-energy photons collide with the atoms.

40. The information provided in the passage indicates that night vision goggles would be most useful in locating:

F. the rotating beam of a high-powered lighthouse.
G. the dying embers of a campfire.
H. the bright perimeter lights of a high-security facility,.
J. a high intensity searchlight.

END OF TEST 3
STOP! DO NOT TURN THE PAGE UNTIL TOLD TO DO SO.
DO NOT RETURN TO THE PREVIOUS TEST.

NO TEST MATERIAL ON THIS PAGE

4 4 4 4 4 4 4 4 4 4 4 4 4

SECTION 4: SCIENCE TEST

35 Minutes—40 Items

DIRECTIONS: Each passage below is followed by several items. After reading a passage, choose the best answer for each item. Fill in the corresponding oval on your bubble sheet. You may refer to the passage as often as necessary. You are NOT permitted the use of a calculator on this test. Answers are on page 469.

PASSAGE I

The solubility of materials in liquids depends not only on the nature of the solute and the solvent, but also on temperature. Above the solubility point for each temperature, excess grams of solute will be unable to dissolve in a solution. A graph showing the solubilities of several substances in water is presented below.

Solubility Curves

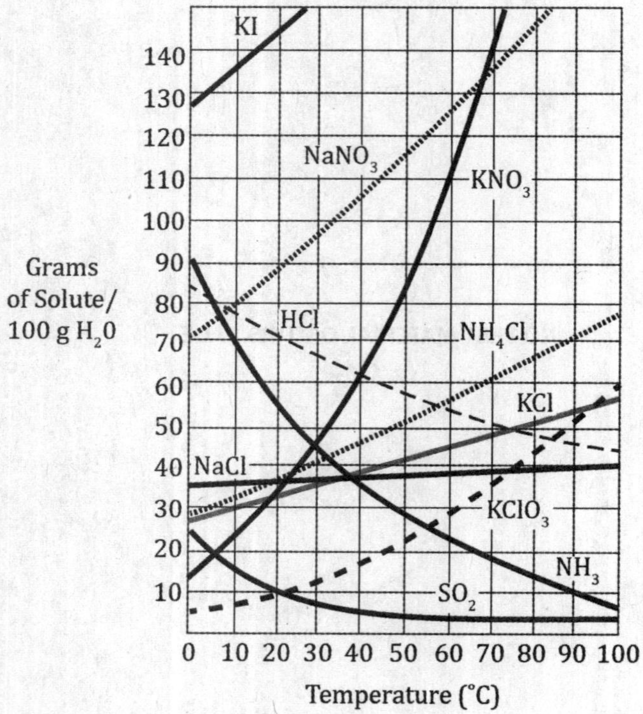

Note: NH_3, SO_2, and HCl are gases at room temperature.

GO ON TO THE NEXT PAGE.

1. Which of the following has the most temperature sensitive solubility in water throughout the range shown?

A. KNO_3
B. $NaNO_3$
C. NaCl
D. NH_3

2. The solubility of sodium (Na) salts is:

F. high because sodium is an alkali metal.
G. low because sodium combines with anions to make salts.
H. dependent on what salt it forms.
J. always greater than 40 grams per 100 grams of water.

3. A 250 ml alcoholic solution of KNO_3 at 50°C contains approximately how many grams KNO_3 at saturation?

A. 200
B. 85
C. 30
D. Cannot be determined from the given information

4. An aqueous solution at 100°C containing equal amounts of $NaNO_3$ and KNO_3 is allowed to cool until a white powder begins to appear at the bottom of the flask. That powder is:

F. KNO_3.
G. $NaNO_3$.
H. a mixture of both.
J. Cannot be determined from the given information

5. The solubility curves of the gases suggest an explanation of why:

A. divers get the bends (nitrogen bubbles in the blood) if they rise too quickly.
B. warm soda is less fizzy than cold soda.
C. warm lemonade is sweeter than cold lemonade.
D. hot air balloons rise.

GO ON TO THE NEXT PAGE.

PASSAGE II

Part of our understanding of Earth comes from a consideration of its physical properties. Selected properties of Earth are presented in Table 1.

Table 1

Property	*Value*
Mass	6×10^{24} kg
Radius	6×10^{6} m
Orbital Radius	1.5×10^{11} m
Period of Revolution	365.3 days
Period of Rotation	24 hours

Table 2 compares the properties of the other planets of the solar system relative to Earth's properties, shown in proportion to the same property as it applies to Earth.

Table 2

Property	Mercury	Venus	Earth	Mars	Jupiter	Saturn	Uranus	Neptune
Radius	0.387	0.949	1	0.532	11.21	9.449	4.007	3.86
Mass	0.055	0.815	1	0.107	317.87	95.159	14.536	17.147
Surface Gravity	0.378	0.905	1	0.379	2.53	1.065	0.905	1.14
Volume	0.056	0.857	1	0.151	1,321.37	763.59	63.08	57.74
Average Distance to Sun	0.39	0.723	1	1.524	5.204	9.582	19.201	30.047
Period of Revolution	0.24	0.615	1	1.881	11.862	29.457	84.01	164.79
Period of Rotation	58.79	243.686	1	1.029	0.415	0.445	0.720	0.673

The following are a few basic equations:

(1) $\text{density} = \dfrac{\text{mass}}{\text{volume}}$

(2) $\text{distance} = \text{rate}(\text{time})$

(3) $\text{volume}_{\text{sphere}} = \dfrac{4}{3}\pi r^3$, where r is the radius of the sphere

6. Based on the information given in Table 1 and Table 2, what is the approximate ratio of the period of revolution in days to the period of rotation in days for Mercury?

F. 240

G. $\frac{3}{2}$

H. $\frac{2}{3}$

J. $\frac{1}{240}$

7. Which planet is approximately as dense as Earth?

A. Mercury
B. Jupiter
C. Mars
D. None

8. Which planet orbits the sun at the slowest rate?

F. Mercury
G. Jupiter
H. Saturn
J. Neptune

9. Analysis of Table 2 shows that surface gravity most likely depends on:

A. mass of the planet only.
B. radius and mass of the planet.
C. radius of the planet only.
D. density of the planet and proximity to the sun.

10. Assuming that both Earth and Neptune are spherical, the diameter of Neptune is:

F. 3.86 times Earth's radius.
G. 4.007 times Earth's radius.
H. 7.72 times Earth's radius.
J. 9.449 times Earth's radius.

11. What distance separates the orbits of the consecutive planetary neighbors that are farthest apart, based on their average distances to the sun?

A. 40 times Earth's average distance to the sun.
B. 11 times Earth's average distance to the sun.
C. 10 times Earth's average distance to the sun.
D. 9 times Earth's average distance to the sun.

PASSAGE III

Medical records for 4,000 men were compiled and analyzed. The men were sorted into four groups based on total blood cholesterol levels. The four groups' histories of illness are recorded below.

	Diagnosis rate, standardized/1,000			
Illness	<160 mg/dL	160–199 mg/dL	200–239 mg/dL	240+ mg/dL
Cancer				
Colon	0.01	0.03	0.04	0.02
Prostate	2.02	0.06	1.03	4.01
Lung	0.03	0.06	0.40	0.20
Coronary				
Thrombosis	5.02	1.01	4.00	10.05
Arrest	6.00	0.98	5.09	11.00
Cardiovascular	5.96	0.65	4.97	9.08
Cerebral Clot	4.01	0.02	0.50	4.01
Depression	5.01	0.30	0.30	0.30

12. Which of the following statements is best supported by the data?

F. A man with a total blood cholesterol level of less than 160 mg/dL is approximately twice as likely to be diagnosed with prostate cancer as a man with a total blood cholesterol level of 220 mg/dL.
G. A total blood cholesterol level of 160 mg/dL or more decreases the risk of being diagnosed with all three forms of cancer listed in the table.
H. At high levels, total blood cholesterol level seems unrelated to the probability of being diagnosed with coronary disease.
J. Cerebral clots are the most prevalent diagnosis among the group with the highest total blood cholesterol level.

13. What might one conclude about the relationship between total blood cholesterol levels and depression based on the information above?

A. Cholesterol causes depression.
B. Total blood cholesterol level has no effect on the diagnosis of depression.
C. Lower total blood cholesterol is most effective in combating depression.
D. Total blood cholesterol of 160–199 mg/dL and 240+ mg/dL are equally effective in reducing the depression diagnosis rate.

14. For which of the following illnesses does the highest total blood cholesterol increase the probability of diagnosis most, compared relatively to the lowest total blood cholesterol?

F. Cerebral clots
G. Coronary arrest
H. Cardiovascular disease
J. Coronary thrombosis

15. For which of the following groups of illnesses does a total cholesterol level of 160–199 mg/dL reduce the probability of diagnosis?

A. Cerebral clot, coronary thrombosis, and lung cancer
B. Cerebral clot, depression, and colon cancer
C. Cerebral clot, coronary arrest, and prostate cancer
D. Depression, coronary thrombosis, and colon cancer

GO ON TO THE NEXT PAGE.

16. What might be involved in determining a standardized diagnosis rate for men?

F. Ignoring diagnoses that do not conform to the average results
G. Adjusting diagnosis rates according to discrepancies in age
H. Assuming that the diagnosis rate disregarding effects of aging is 0 diagnoses per 1,000 men
J. Comparing data with a similar experiment involving women

PASSAGE IV

The resistance (*R*, measured in ohms) of a material is directly proportional ($\propto$) to the resistivity (*r*, measured in ohm-meters) of the material. The voltage (*V*, measured in volts) in a circuit is directly proportional to both the resistance and the current (*I*, measured in amperes). Resistors in series act as one resistor according to the following formula:

$$R_s = R_1 + R_2 + R_3 + \dots$$

Resistors in parallel act as one resistor according to the following formula:

$$\frac{1}{R_p} = \frac{1}{R_1} + \frac{1}{R_2} + \frac{1}{R_3} + \cdots$$

The resistivities of several materials at 20°C are listed in Table 1.

Table 1

Substance	Resistivity, *r* (ohm-meters)
Aluminum	2.63×10^{-8}
Copper	1.72×10^{-8}
Germanium	6.00×10^{-1}
Silicon	2.30×10^{3}
Silver	1.47×10^{-8}
Sulfur	1.00×10^{15}

17. According to the information provided, the best formula for the voltage in a circuit, where voltage is *V*, current is *I*, and resistance is *R*, is:

A. $V \propto \frac{I}{R}$.

B. $V \propto I + R$.

C. $V \propto IR$.

D. $V \propto I - R$.

18. Two resistors with a resistance of 2 ohms each are placed in series. How does the voltage in the circuit compare with the voltage in a circuit with only one resistor, with a resistance of 2 ohms? (Assume current remains constant.)

F. The voltage is doubled.
G. The voltage is halved.
H. The voltage is the same.
J. The voltage is zero.

19. According to the information provided, how would the voltage in a circuit with a silver resistor compare to the voltage in a circuit with a germanium resistor of the same length? (Current is the same in both circuits.)

A. The voltage in the germanium circuit would be greater.
B. The voltage in the silver circuit would be greater.
C. The voltage would be the same in both circuits.
D. Cannot be determined from the given information

GO ON TO THE NEXT PAGE.

20. A resistor with a resistance of 4 ohms is put in parallel with an identical resistor with a resistance of 4 ohms. What is R_p, in units of ohms?

F. 0
G. $\frac{1}{2}$
H. 2
J. 8

21. Power is defined as $P = I^2 R$. If R is a constant, then power would increase ____ with an increase in the current. (Fill in the blank space with the best answer choice.)

A. exponentially
B. logarithmically
C. directly
D. inversely

22. In order to keep the current in a circuit constant, if one increases the voltage, one must:

F. lengthen the circuit.
G. shorten the circuit.
H. decrease the resistance.
J. increase the resistance.

PASSAGE V

Some reactions occur in a series of steps referred to as a reaction mechanism. In order to discover the steps by which a chemical reaction occurs, the dependence of the initial rate of reaction on the concentration of the reactants is determined. Three experiments exploring the mechanism of a reaction are presented below.

Experiment 1

Chemical A is injected into a rapidly stirred solution of Chemical B in the solvent hexamethyl phosphoramide. As A and B react, they form a compound that absorbs light at a characteristic wavelength of 520 nm. The mixed solutions are quickly placed into a device for measuring light absorption of solutions such as a spectrophotometer. By using this device, the rate of product formation is determined. The results are presented in Table 1.

Table 1

Trial	Concentration A	Concentration B	Reaction Rate
1	4	4	60
2	2	2	30
3	4	2	30
4	4	8	120

Experiment 2

Chemical A is injected into a rapidly stirred solution of Chemical B in the solvent carbon tetrachloride. The product of the reaction is identical to the product in Experiment 1. The rate of reaction is followed using spectrophotometry as in Experiment 1. The results are presented in Table 2.

Table 2

Trial	Concentration A	Concentration B	Reaction Rate
1	3	3	27
2	6	6	108
3	6	3	54
4	12	6	216

Experiment 3

Chemical A is injected into a rapidly stirred solution of Chemical B in a 1:1-by-volume mixture of carbon tetrachloride and hexamethyl phosphoramide. The rate of reaction is followed using spectrophotometry as in Experiment 1. The results are presented in Table 3.

Table 3

Trial	Concentration A	Concentration B	Reaction Rate
1	9	9	54
2	9	4.5	27
3	4	4.5	18
4	4	9	36

23. Which of the following statements best describes the effect of the concentration of A on the rate of reaction in Experiment 1?

A. Rate increases in direct proportion with increasing concentration of A.
B. Rate decreases by the square root of A's concentration.
C. Rate decreases by the square of A's concentration.
D. Rate is independent of A's concentration.

24. Which of the following statements best describes the effect of the concentration of A on the rate of reaction in Experiment 2?

F. Rate increases in direct proportion with increasing concentration of A.
G. Rate increases by the square of A's concentration.
H. Rate decreases by the square root of A's concentration.
J. Rate is independent of A's concentration.

GO ON TO THE NEXT PAGE.

25. Which of the following statements best describes the effect of the concentration of A on the rate of reaction in Experiment 3?

A. Rate increases in direct proportion with increasing concentration of A.
B. Rate increases by the square of A's concentration.
C. Rate increases by the square root of A's concentration.
D. Rate is independent of A's concentration.

26. What is the likeliest explanation for the results obtained in Experiment 3?

F. A mechanism intermediates between the ones found in Experiments 1 and 2.
G. Some of the molecules react by Experiment 1's mechanism, others by Experiment 2's mechanism.
H. A different mechanism is responsible.
J. There is an averaging of the mechanisms.

27. What is the best conclusion that can be drawn from this set of experiments?

A. Rate is increased by changing solvents.
B. Reactions may depend on solvent effects as well as on the nature of the reactants.
C. Mechanisms can always be changed by use of an appropriate solvent.
D. Reactions depend on solvent effects as well as on the nature of the reactants.

PASSAGE VI

Acceleration is defined as the change in the velocity of an object divided by the length of time during which that change took place. In the following sets of experiments, a student studies the motion of bodies on an inclined plane.

For all of the following experiments, time is measured in seconds, distance in feet, and velocity in feet per second. The distance (d) an object travels at a constant acceleration (a) in time (t), assuming it starts from rest, is given by the equation $d = \frac{1}{2}at^2$.

Experiment 1

A student set up a smooth wooden board at an angle of 30° from horizontal. The board had a length of 10 feet. Using a series of photogates, the student was able to determine the position and velocity of a 100 gram steel ball that was rolled down the incline. The results are presented in Table 1.

Table 1

Time	Distance (ft)	Instantaneous Velocity (ft/sec)
0	0	0
0.5	0.44	1.75
1.0	1.75	3.50
1.5	3.94	5.25
2.0	7.00	7.00

Experiment 2

The same 10-foot wooden board was used at an angle of 30° from the horizontal. The object used this time was a 100-gram sled made of the same material as the ball in Experiment 1. The photogates were used to determine its position and velocity as it slid down the inclined plane. The results are presented in Table 2.

Table 2

Time	Distance (ft)	Instantaneous Velocity (ft/sec)
0	0	0
0.5	1.13	2.45
1.0	2.45	4.90
1.5	5.51	7.35
2.0	9.80	9.80

Experiment 3

The same board at the same angle was used in the third experiment as in the previous two. In this experiment, a 100-gram box made of the same material as the ball and the sled was used. The same recording devices were used. The results are presented in Table 3.

Table 3

Time	Distance (ft)	Instantaneous Velocity (ft/sec)
0	0	0
1.0	0.33	0.66
2.0	1.31	1.32
3.0	2.97	1.98
4.0	5.28	2.64
5.0	8.25	3.30

Experiment 4

The board in the previous experiments was carefully oiled to reduce friction. Once again, the board was placed at an angle of 30° from horizontal. Each of the objects was then allowed to move down the inclined plane, and the time required for each object to reach the bottom of the plane was recorded. Results are presented in Table 4.

Table 4

Object	Time
sled	2.02
ball	2.39
box	5.00

28. Which object in the first three experiments has the greatest acceleration?

F. Ball
G. Sled
H. Box
J. The three objects have equal acceleration.

29. The acceleration of the ball relative to that of the sled is due to the ball's:

A. rolling only.
B. friction only.
C. rolling and friction.
D. having the same mass as the sled and therefore having the same acceleration.

GO ON TO THE NEXT PAGE.

30. The acceleration of the ball relative to that of the box is due to the ball's:

F. rolling only.
G. friction only.
H. rolling and the box's friction.
J. having the same mass as the box and therefore having the same acceleration.

31. Based on these four experiments, the ratio of the acceleration of the ball to the acceleration of the sled is:

A. $\frac{5}{7}$.
B. 1.
C. $\frac{7}{5}$.
D. dependent on time.

32. Based on these four experiments, the ratio of the acceleration of the ball to the acceleration of the box is:

F. $\frac{5}{7}$.
G. 1.
H. dependent on the amount of friction.
J. dependent on time.

PASSAGE VII

What was the fate of Neanderthal man? Two differing views are presented below.

Scientist 1

Whenever two species compete for the same niche, there is a conflict. In this conflict the loser either moves to a different niche or dies out. It is unusual for two species to interbreed. The difference between early modern humans and Neanderthals physically may not appear great to an anatomist, but to those that are choosing a mate the differences would be significant. Even if early modern humans and Neanderthals did mate, the result—us—would look more like a mix of the two rather than like modern humans. Early modern humans and Neanderthals, because they were so close to each other physically, must have been deadly enemies. The population was thinly dispersed at that time because the resources available would not support a greater population density. There literally was not room enough on the planet for the two species. They could not combine because they were so different in appearance, so only one answer remained. We survived because we killed our cousin.

Scientist 2

Neanderthals were very similar to modern humans in appearance. It is true that Neanderthals were somewhat more muscular than modern humans and that the way the muscles seem to have been arranged on the skeleton was, in a few minor ways, different. This we are able to deduce from the places on the surviving bones that mark where the ligaments were once attached. For example, the neck and wrists of Neanderthals were far thicker than is natural to modern humans. Some of the facial structure was also different, especially the protrusion of the brow. But differences between the appearance of Neanderthals and modern humans have been exaggerated since they are based on the skeleton of one individual who was later discovered to have been suffering from severe arthritis. It is likely that, because of the low population density and the nomadic lifestyle that spread the few individuals over ever-larger areas, Neanderthal and early modern humans interbred and eventually merged into one species. The notion that some sort of "war" broke out between these different species (or, more likely, subspecies) of humans is a misguided attempt to look out of early human eyes with a modern perspective.

33. Underlying the hypothesis of Scientist 2 is the assumption that:

A. Neanderthals were more likely than early modern humans to suffer from diseases such as arthritis.
B. early modern humans and Neanderthals were sufficiently alike to allow them to interbreed.
C. Neanderthals and early modern humans lived in geographically distinct regions.
D. in combat, a group of Neanderthals was likely to defeat a similar grouping of early modern humans.

34. Underlying the hypotheses of both scientists is the assumption that:

F. early modern humans and Neanderthals understood the consequences of their actions.
G. early modern humans and Neanderthals both lived in exactly the same type of environment.
H. early modern humans and Neanderthals both lived in the same geographical regions.
J. early modern humans were more intelligent than Neanderthals.

35. If an isolated community of Neanderthals was discovered, whose hypothesis would be more damaged?

A. Scientist 2's because his theory does not allow for such a community to survive
B. Scientist 1's because the descendants of early modern humans inhabit all the earth and therefore there should be no community of Neanderthals
C. Both hypotheses are disproved.
D. Neither hypothesis is affected.

36. Which of the following, if true, would most support the hypothesis of Scientist 1?

F. The camps of early modern humans are often close to the camps of Neanderthals.
G. The camps of early modern humans are never close to Neanderthal camps.
H. Bones of Neanderthals and early modern humans are often found near each other.
J. Chipped Neanderthal bones are found with early modern human weapons.

GO ON TO THE NEXT PAGE.

37. The fact that lions and tigers fight when brought together artificially even though they can be interbred supports which hypothesis to the greater extent?

A. Scientist 2's hypothesis, because it proves two species can interbreed
B. Scientist 2's hypothesis, because two species still exist that share the same niche
C. Scientist 1's hypothesis, because it suggests that two species that can interbreed may not do so under natural conditions
D. Scientist 1's hypothesis, because lions and tigers fight when brought together artificially

38. According to the hypothesis of Scientist 1, what should be the result of interbreeding lions and tigers?

F. The offspring should be infertile.
G. The offspring will resemble one parent only.
H. The offspring will possess a mixture of traits.
J. Scientist 1's hypothesis makes no conjectures on the point because lions and tigers would not interbreed.

39. What assumption about Neanderthals and early modern humans is shared by both Scientist 2 and Scientist 1?

A. Early modern humans were one factor in the disappearance of Neanderthals as a separate species.
B. Early modern humans were more intelligent than Neanderthals thus enabling humans to prevail.
C. Early modern humans and Neanderthals differed little from one another in physical appearance.
D. Neanderthals occupied territories that were not suitable for early modern human habitations.

40. If a burial site containing over one hundred early modern humans and Neanderthal remains was discovered, and if two Neanderthal skeletons were found with early modern human spearpoints in them, which hypothesis would be the most strengthened?

F. Scientist 2's hypothesis, because spearpoints need not have been what killed the two Neanderthals
G. Scientist 1's hypothesis, because two Neanderthals were killed by early modern humans
H. Scientist 1's hypothesis, because the spearpoints prove that the early modern humans had more developed weapons
J. Scientist 2's hypothesis, because only a couple of the individuals buried together died violently

END OF TEST 4
STOP! DO NOT TURN THE PAGE UNTIL TOLD TO DO SO.
DO NOT RETURN TO THE PREVIOUS TEST.

5 5 5 5 5 5 5 5 5 5 5 5

SECTION 5: WRITING TEST (OPTIONAL)

40 Minutes—1 Essay Prompt

DIRECTIONS: Read the prompt carefully and make sure you understand the instructions. A successful essay will have the following features: it will take a position on the issue presented in the writing prompt; it will maintain a consistent focus on the topic; it will use logical reasoning and provide supporting ideas; it will present ideas in an organized manner; and, finally, it will include clear and effective language in accordance with the conventions of standard written English. Sample essay responses begin on page 474.

Campaign Funding

Political campaigns are part of the fabric of American life, and politicians invite the public to join in the process of selecting those who govern them in a variety of ways, including financial support. Some Americans think that there should be limits to how much any one person, group or corporation may contribute to any particular candidate. This view states that contribution limits allow for more equal participation by all citizens in the electoral process, regardless of their income. Others, however, believe that political campaign contributions should have no limits, that such limitations really abridge freedom of speech and thereby violate constitutionally protected freedoms. Do limits on campaign funding make elections a fairer process in which voters' incomes do not matter, or are such limits unfair to donors who wish to maximize their participation in elections? The issue of campaign funding is a high-profile debate in both state and national elections.

Perspective 1

Freedom of speech is an essential right for all Americans. The right to allow our hard-earned money to give voice to our choice for governance must be protected.

Perspective 2

There should be very real limits on the amount of contributions from any one individual or corporation. No one should be allowed to purchase democracy from the people, as self-governance is a right.

Perspective 3

Democratic participation must be protected at all costs, even if it costs our Treasury. Fair elections must be held on level financial playing fields in order to achieve our dreams. No individual contributions should be allowed, and all campaigns and candidates be funded from public money raised by taxation.

Essay Task

Write a unified, coherent essay in which you evaluate multiple perspectives on the impact of campaign funding. In your essay be sure to:

- Analyze and evaluate perspectives given
- State and develop your own perspective
- Explain the relationship between your perspective and those given

Your perspective may be in full agreement with any of the others, in partial agreement, or wholly different. Whatever the case, support your ideas with logical reasoning and detailed, persuasive examples.

END OF TEST 5

STOP! DO NOT TURN THE PAGE UNTIL TOLD TO DO SO.

DO NOT RETURN TO THE PREVIOUS TEST.

Take a Final Look with a Full-Length Test

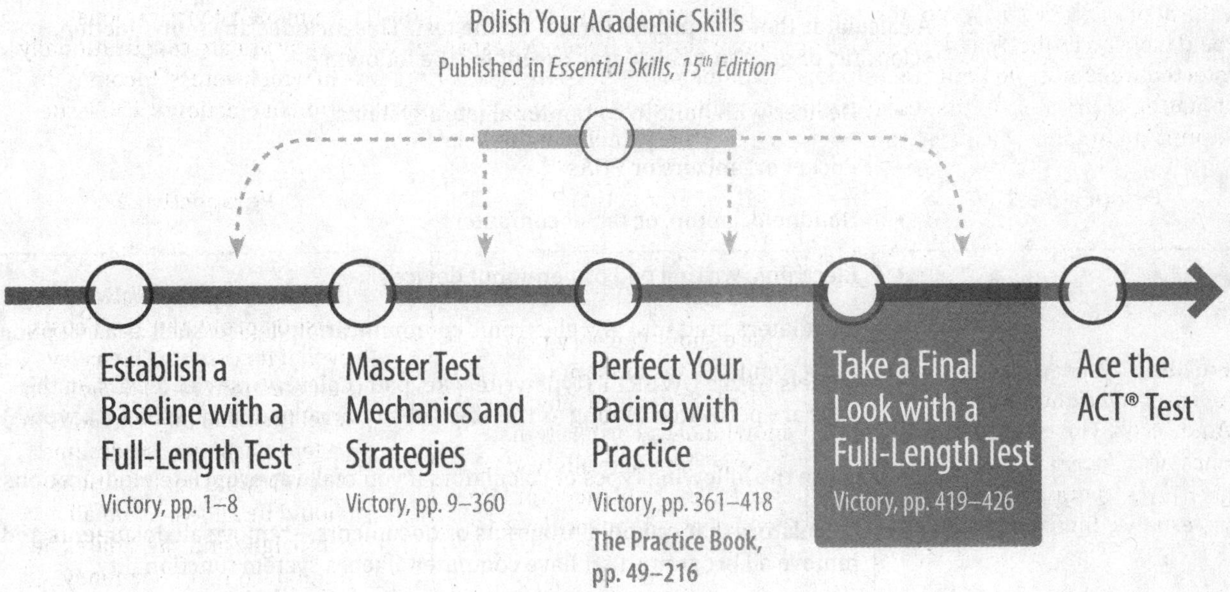

CAMBRIDGE
VICTORY FOR THE
ACT® TEST

POST-ASSESSMENT ADMINISTRATION

At the end of the course, you will take a post-assessment. This post-assessment consists of an ACT, Inc. ACT practice exam. When you take the post-assessment, you should bring the following items to the classroom, in addition to anything else your teacher instructs you to bring:

1. Sharpened, soft-lead No. 2 pencils
2. A calculator that is approved for use on the test. This includes any four-function, scientific, or graphing calculator, except for the following:
    - Devices with built-in computer algebra systems
    - Pocket organizers or PDAs
    - Handheld, laptop, or tablet computers
    - Electronic writing pad or pen-input devices
    - Calculators built into any electronic communication device, such as a cell phone
    - Models with a QWERTY (typewriter) keypad (Calculators with letters on the keys are permitted as long as the keys are not arranged in a QWERTY keypad.)

    You may use the following types of calculators if you make appropriate modifications:

    - Calculators that can hold programs or documents—remove all documents and remove all programs that have computer algebra system functionality.
    - Models with paper tape: the paper must be removed.
    - Models that make noise: the sound feature must be turned off.
    - Models that have an infrared data port: the port must be covered with duct tape, electrician's tape, or another heavy, opaque material.
    - Models that have a power cord: the power cord must be removed.
    (For more detailed information on calculator usage, go to http://www.act.org/content/dam/act/unsecured/documents/ACT-calculator-policy.pdf.)
3. A watch (to pace yourself as you work through each test section)

The Cambridge Edge

Remember the following points about marking the bubble sheet:

- Completely darken the bubble for each answer choice. If the letter within the bubble can be read through the pencil mark, then it is not dark enough. Mechanical pencils, even with No. 2 pencil lead, often fail to leave a dark mark.
- Stay within the lines.
- When erasing pencil marks, be sure to erase the marks completely. Do not leave any stray marks.
- Circle the answer choices in the test booklet. Towards the end of the section, or after each completed group of items, transfer the selected answers as a group to the answer form. Not only does this minimize erasing on the answer form, but it also saves time and minimizes transcription errors.
- When changing an answer, over-darken the final answer choice after completely erasing the original mark. This extra density tends to offset the residue left over from the original answer choice.

Strategic test-taking:

- Code items in the margin of the test booklet as easy or difficult before beginning to answer them. When pressed for time, skip to items that you are more likely to answer correctly.
- Make notes and calculations directly in the test booklet.
- Underline key words in Reading passages.

HOW TO USE THE POST-ASSESSMENT REPORTS

You will receive the results of your post-assessment in the form of Student Summary and Student Item Analysis reports approximately six days after taking the test. These reports provide details about your performance and will help you to determine where to focus your efforts from now until your test date by targeting skills, concepts, and strategies that will help you to improve in your areas of weakness. Just as you did with the pre-assessment, review the details of the sample reports on pages 4–5 of this book so that you are familiar with their contents.

Once you have received your post-assessment reports, you can develop a Personal Action Plan. Make connections between the reports and the specific skills, concepts, and strategies that you need to study, then complete the "to do" list on the following page.

TOPIC	START DATE	DATE TO BE COMPLETED	DATE COMPLETED

PLANNING FOR FURTHER STUDY

You have received the results of your post-assessment. You have finished the Cambridge *Victory for the ACT® Test* program. Now what?

In most cases you will have some spare time before the test day, so planning a study schedule for the time between the post-assessment and the real test is critical to reinforce and maintain the skills, concepts, and strategies that you have learned throughout the course. Below are three steps that will help you make the most of your time.

TAKE THE PRACTICE TESTS

Most students understand the concepts tested, but many struggle with time management. If you have not yet done so, take the practice tests in this book and *The Practice Book*. These practice tests:

1. reinforce skills and strategies,
2. simulate the experience of the real test by using time restrictions to emphasize time management, and
3. are an excellent guide to targeting your study plan.

CREATE A WRITTEN STUDY PLAN

Use the results of your post-assessment and the practice tests to determine a day-by-day schedule that will give you a clear and dependable guide for study. Create this plan based on the amount of time you have before the test day.

Several weeks before test day:

- Plan to review all material equally.
- As the test date approaches, devote your time to any particular areas of weakness.

Remember: picking a few subjects to focus on each week will help you manage your time between now and the test.

A few days before test day:

- Focus on core subjects that are giving you difficulty, or areas in which you would like to improve.
- Divide your time proportionally among these subjects based on your assessment of their difficulty.

Determine the topics you will study each day and allot the proper amount of time to study those sections of the book and complete relevant exercises.

STICK TO THE PLAN

Once you have determined your rubric for study, stick to it without fail. Such discipline will surely reward you on the day of the test. Follow these helpful hints:

- Ask your teacher for insight. He or she can help you set goals for each core subject and may be able to suggest further strategies or a re-allotment of your time.
- Do not study too much. An hour or two of studying each day will be more productive than a severe study schedule.
- Practice every day.

Appendix A: Answers and Explanations

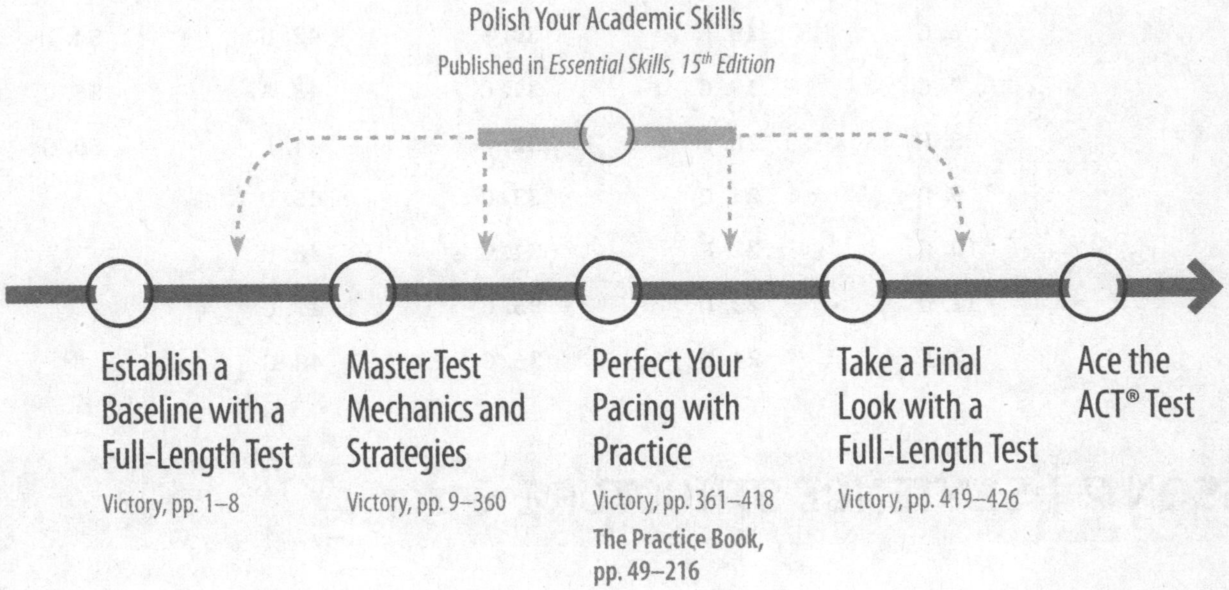

CAMBRIDGE
VICTORY FOR THE ACT® TEST

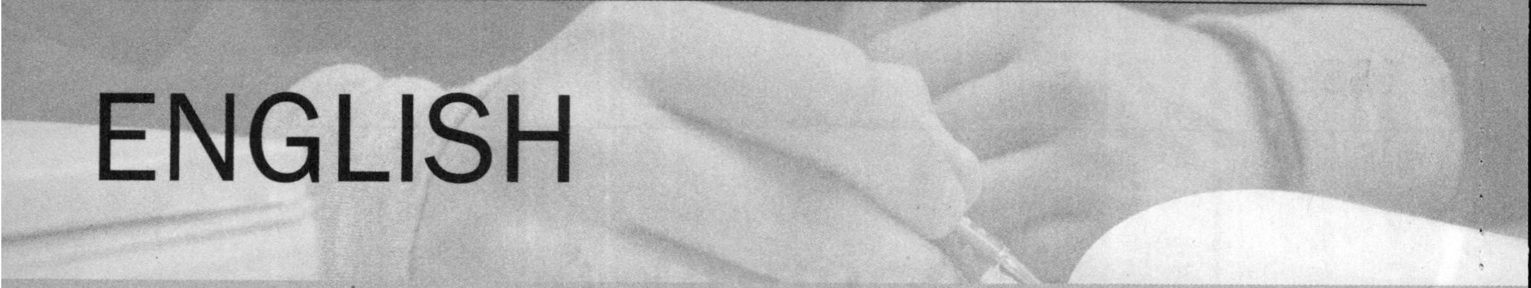

ENGLISH

LESSON 1 | GRAMMAR AND USAGE (p. 24)

1. B	**13.** D	**25.** D	**37.** D	**49.** D
2. G	**14.** H	**26.** G	**38.** G	**50.** J
3. C	**15.** D	**27.** C	**39.** B	**51.** C
4. G	**16.** H	**28.** G	**40.** F	**52.** G
5. D	**17.** B	**29.** C	**41.** B	**53.** D
6. G	**18.** J	**30.** J	**42.** G	**54.** H
7. C	**19.** C	**31.** C	**43.** A	**55.** C
8. H	**20.** J	**32.** J	**44.** J	**56.** G
9. D	**21.** C	**33.** C	**45.** D	
10. G	**22.** F	**34.** G	**46.** H	
11. D	**23.** D	**35.** C	**47.** C	
12. F	**24.** H	**36.** G	**48.** G	

LESSON 2 | SENTENCE STRUCTURE (p. 32)

1. C	**6.** J	**11.** B	**16.** G	**21.** C
2. G	**7.** B	**12.** H	**17.** D	**22.** J
3. C	**8.** J	**13.** D	**18.** H	**23.** B
4. H	**9.** A	**14.** H	**19.** C	**24.** H
5. B	**10.** H	**15.** B	**20.** H	

LESSON 3 | PUNCTUATION (p. 36)

1. B	**8.** H	**15.** B	**22.** F	**29.** B
2. F	**9.** A	**16.** H	**23.** B	**30.** J
3. A	**10.** H	**17.** D	**24.** J	**31.** A
4. F	**11.** B	**18.** J	**25.** C	**32.** H
5. A	**12.** H	**19.** D	**26.** G	**33.** A
6. F	**13.** A	**20.** G	**27.** B	**34.** J
7. B	**14.** F	**21.** A	**28.** J	

35. On Monday, Mark received a letter of acceptance from State College. He immediately called his mother—herself a graduate of State College—to tell her about his acceptance. When he told her he had also been awarded a scholarship, she was very excited. After hanging up, Mark's mother decided to throw a surprise party for Mark. She telephoned his brother, his sister, and several of his friends. Because the party was supposed to be a surprise, she made them all promise not to say anything to Mark. Mark, however, had a similar idea: a party for his mother to celebrate his acceptance at her alma mater. He telephoned his brother, his sister, and several of his parents' friends to invite them to a party at his house on Saturday night, and he made them all promise to say nothing to his mother. On Saturday night, both Mark and his mother were surprised.

LESSON 4 | PRODUCTION OF WRITING AND KNOWLEDGE OF LANGUAGE (p. 42)

1. D	**5.** B	**9.** A	**13.** C	**17.** B
2. J	**6.** F	**10.** F	**14.** G	**18.** J
3. D	**7.** B	**11.** B	**15.** D	**19.** B
4. G	**8.** J	**12.** G	**16.** J	**20.** G

LESSON 5 | GENERAL STRATEGIES (p. 47)

1. B	**3.** D	**5.** A	**7.** B	**9.** D
2. F	**4.** H	**6.** F	**8.** J	**10.** H

TIMED QUIZ (p. 64)

1. D
2. F
3. D
4. J
5. C
6. F
7. B
8. G
9. A
10. F
11. B
12. F
13. B
14. G
15. D
16. F
17. D
18. F
19. C
20. G
21. A
22. J
23. B
24. H
25. D
26. H
27. D
28. F
29. B

REVIEW (p. 69)

1. A
2. J
3. B
4. H
5. A
6. F
7. A
8. F
9. D
10. H
11. A
12. F
13. A
14. J
15. A
16. G
17. B
18. G
19. D
20. G
21. D
22. G
23. B
24. J
25. A
26. H
27. A
28. F
29. B
30. H
31. B
32. H
33. A
34. G
35. D
36. G
37. C
38. G
39. A
40. F
41. A
42. H
43. C
44. H
45. A
46. F
47. B
48. H

READING

LESSON 1 | ITEM-TYPES AND STRATEGIES (p. 96)

1. C	**8.** H	**15.** C	**22.** G	**29.** C	**36.** J
2. F	**9.** D	**16.** G	**23.** A	**30.** F	**37.** C
3. A	**10.** J	**17.** D	**24.** G	**31.** A	**38.** J
4. J	**11.** A	**18.** F	**25.** A	**32.** G	**39.** A
5. B	**12.** J	**19.** D	**26.** F	**33.** D	
6. J	**13.** A	**20.** H	**27.** A	**34.** G	
7. C	**14.** H	**21.** B	**28.** H	**35.** D	

LESSON 2 | PAIRED PASSAGES (p. 105)

1. A	**7.** D	**13.** D	**19.** A	**25.** A	**31.** B
2. G	**8.** G	**14.** J	**20.** J	**26.** J	**32.** H
3. D	**9.** B	**15.** B	**21.** D	**27.** B	**33.** D
4. H	**10.** F	**16.** G	**22.** F	**28.** G	
5. B	**11.** B	**17.** D	**23.** C	**29.** C	
6. J	**12.** F	**18.** G	**24.** H	**30.** G	

LESSON 3 | FURTHER USE OF READING STRATEGIES, PART 1 (p. 115)

1. C	**9.** A	**17.** C	**25.** C	**33.** A	**41.** D
2. F	**10.** J	**18.** F	**26.** F	**34.** J	**42.** G
3. C	**11.** D	**19.** D	**27.** C	**35.** D	**43.** A
4. J	**12.** H	**20.** H	**28.** H	**36.** H	**44.** J
5. B	**13.** B	**21.** D	**29.** B	**37.** B	**45.** B
6. F	**14.** J	**22.** J	**30.** G	**38.** J	**46.** F
7. D	**15.** A	**23.** A	**31.** B	**39.** A	
8. H	**16.** G	**24.** J	**32.** G	**40.** G	

LESSON 4 | FURTHER USE OF READING STRATEGIES, PART 2 (p. 125)

1. A	**9.** B	**17.** C	**25.** D	**33.** A	**41.** B
2. G	**10.** H	**18.** J	**26.** H	**34.** F	**42.** J
3. D	**11.** C	**19.** C	**27.** A	**35.** D	**43.** B
4. G	**12.** G	**20.** G	**28.** J	**36.** F	**44.** H
5. D	**13.** D	**21.** D	**29.** C	**37.** D	**45.** C
6. H	**14.** G	**22.** H	**30.** G	**38.** H	
7. C	**15.** D	**23.** C	**31.** C	**39.** B	
8. H	**16.** J	**24.** G	**32.** J	**40.** G	

TIMED QUIZ (p. 145)

1. B	**7.** A	**13.** B
2. G	**8.** F	**14.** H
3. B	**9.** C	**15.** A
4. F	**10.** G	**16.** J
5. D	**11.** D	**17.** C
6. H	**12.** G	

REVIEW (p. 149)

1. D	**8.** J	**15.** B	**22.** J	**29.** C	**36.** H	**43.** D
2. G	**9.** B	**16.** F	**23.** C	**30.** J	**37.** D	**44.** H
3. C	**10.** J	**17.** C	**24.** G	**31.** A	**38.** G	**45.** D
4. J	**11.** B	**18.** G	**25.** C	**32.** J	**39.** B	**46.** F
5. A	**12.** F	**19.** D	**26.** J	**33.** D	**40.** F	
6. F	**13.** C	**20.** F	**27.** A	**34.** F	**41.** B	
7. C	**14.** F	**21.** D	**28.** J	**35.** D	**42.** H	

WRITING

LESSON (p. 173)

Sample Essay Outline

I. Introduction

  A. My three supporting arguments relate to technology making it easier and faster to communicate, lack of meaningful content in quick, impersonal communication, and the need to use technology with care.

  B. Thesis statement: Technological advances have opened many possibilities for communication and are professionally and socially indispensable in today's world; however, one must use this technology wisely in order to build meaningful relationships.

II. Online communication has revolutionized professional and personal interactions, and it is essential for maintaining relationships in today's globalized society.

  A. Ease of communication for personal and business purposes

  B. You can keep in contact with people if you have to move

  C. You can learn about a greater diversity of people and places

III. There are some potential drawbacks of online communication.

  A. Since information is shared so quickly, there is a greater chance that it might not be accurate or express complex viewpoints

  B. In the workplace, close relationships are important for some tasks

IV. One can benefit the most from online communication by using it cautiously.

  A. Verify online information with other sources

  B. Use forms of technology that require closer communication, such as video chatting

V. Conclusion

  A. Restatement of thesis: To avoid the risks of online communication, one must assess the value of the information received and use technologies that allow for more personal interaction.

Sample Essay—Above Average Response

Thanks to online communication, you can share news, conduct meetings, or make friends across the globe. Technologies such as email and video chats allow you to contact others instantaneously and cheaply. However, some argue that the low cost of online communication isn't the only thing that's "cheapened" by the use of these technologies. When online interactions are quick and easy, they can lack deep and meaningful information and be insufficient to build relationships. Technological advances have opened many possibilities for communication and are professionally and socially indispensable in today's world; however, one must use this technology wisely in order to build meaningful relationships.

Online communication has revolutionized professional and personal interactions in the twenty-first century, and in today's increasingly globalized society, it is essential for maintaining relationships. As Perspective 3 states, communication has become instantaneous. Instead of waiting days or paying expensive phone bills to reach colleagues and friends abroad, businesses can hold online meetings between London and New York, and you can chat with a friend on another continent. Moving to another country or even another state used to isolate you from the people you had met, but now, it is possible to stay in close contact with people you cannot see on a regular basis. Furthermore, even if you never leave your hometown, you can be exposed to a diverse array of cultures and opinions across the globe.

Although technology has had a positive impact on the ease of communication, it comes with some potential dangers. For example, when information or opinions can be shared instantaneously, there is a temptation to post information without thoroughly checking for accuracy or developing a nuanced viewpoint. This leads to what Perspective 1 calls "fast food" information that is "empty of real depth." Additionally, it is harder to build significant, lasting relationships with people you only meet online. In a professional context, weak relationships could cause problems when one needs to negotiate with colleagues abroad. And while social networking allows one to have a wide range of personal contacts, commenting on someone's post or browsing through a friend's online photos does not require direct contact.

One can optimize the benefits of online communication by using it cautiously. For example, instead of reading news updates on social media and believing them at face value, one should verify the information with other sources. Furthermore, the type of technology that one uses can make a huge difference in the quality of communication. As Perspective 2 argues, "We have a need for closer contact with the people we know." Some technologies, such as video chats, facilitate closer communication. While talking to someone important, such as a colleague or a close friend, it is better to use this type of technology, rather than relying on instant messaging or social media.

Technology has made it easier to maintain communication that is crucial for conducting business and establishing relationships. However, reliance on these instantaneous interactions can compromise the accuracy of information shared, as well as the depth of one's relationships. To avoid these risks, one must assess the value of the information received and use technologies that allow for more personal interaction. And if it is possible, one should make an effort to see friends in person from time to time.

Sample Essay—Below Average Response

I agree with the third perspective that online communication is a positive change. You can read information from all over the world and keep in touch with family and friends who live far away. Some people argue that online communication is not real communication, I disagree.

When my family and I moved to another state, I was afraid that I would lose touch with all of my friends from home. However, thanks to email, and Facebook, we have stayed in contact. I think the smartphone is the most important piece of technology for staying connected with other people because you can take it with you everywhere. No matter where I am. I can text my friends, send them photos through Instagram, or see what their up to on social media. I know that commenting one someone's Twitter post isn't enough to stay friends with them, but for people who I really care about, I can always message them directly or video chat with them. The video chat makes it very easy to have a conversation.

Online communication also makes it easier to get information from all over the world. For example, if you need to do business with people from another country, you can contact them right away instead of waiting several days for a response. It's also easier to learn about global topics because there's so much information on the internet.

It's true that I would feel lonely, as perspective 2 says, if I only talked to people online. However, online communication makes it easier to talk to people who I can't see face to face.

TIMED QUIZ (p. 183)

Sample Essay—Above Average Response

With educational games on computers and tablets, technology can enhance students' learning experiences in Pre-K classrooms. Pre-K programs should foster a balance between technology-based and technology-free learning to develop different forms of creativity in children. Computer-based learning can make academic concepts fun for students and can make technology use intuitive for them, and technology in the classroom can be made more affordable through grants and educational discounts. However, it is important that they learn to appreciate other forms of entertainment and learning.

Learning basic concepts such as numbers and the alphabet may frustrate or bore children, but computer programs can make this process seem like a game. While parents may complain about their children's addiction to video games, educational games can harness the addicting nature of technology for a useful purpose. As Perspective 2 argues, when students are engaged with the graphics, characters, or story of a computer game, learning will seem like play, rather than a chore. Furthermore, computer games can be easily adapted to students' abilities, which can help teachers with a range of skill levels in the class. As a child, I enjoyed learning independently with computer games, which stimulated my curiosity and love of learning. Games helped me work with numbers and learn new words, and when I was a little older, they also introduced me to different historical periods and parts of the world.

In addition to engaging children in academic subjects, computer programs teach students another important skill: the use of technology. While I disagree with the idea of preparing four-year-olds for the workplace, as Perspective 3 mentions, children may have an educational disadvantage if they enter elementary school without basic technological skills. At the Pre-K level, it is more likely for technology use to become intuitive and habitual for children. One objection to technology in the classroom is its price, as Perspective 1 argues, but schools may be eligible for government grants, and companies often offer educational discounts for computers and software. Although technology changes rapidly, schools could invest in versatile devices such as desktops, laptops, or tablets that are still useful even if one does not own the latest version.

However, I also think preschools should give children time away from technology so that they do not become dependent on it for entertainment or creative stimulation. I have seen children who become bored or even angry when they do not have access to laptops or tablets. Although the addicting nature of computer games can be used to promote learning, children must also be able to put down their games and focus on other activities. Technology may stimulate children's minds, but it is important for their physical health to exercise and play outside, and they should also be offered more hands-on creative activities, such as art projects.

If used in moderation, technology can expand students' educational opportunities and make them excited about concepts such as numbers and letters. If schools have access to funding, the skills that students gain can outweigh the cost of computers. However, it is important to remember that technology can be "too much of a good thing" and that students must learn to function without it.

Sample Essay—Below Average Response

Technology has no place in pre-K classrooms. Children this young cannot use technology properly, and they will only break expensive products like computers and tablets. Technology actually might harm children's development. It can stifle kids creativity and individuality and makes them greedier and unable to work in groups.

I agree with Perspective 1 I think that the biggest reason not to use technology in the classroom is that it's too expensive and can brake easily. A desktop costs hundreds of dollars, and even though tablets are a little cheaper, they still cost at least $100. Kids are too young to appreciate how expensive these things are and can't learn to use them properly. Since it's impossible for a teacher to supervise so many students at once, kids might misuse and damage the technology, and it would be really expensive to repair or replace it.

Perspectives 2 and 3 argue that technology is good for making kids learn, but I think that it can actually make kids less creative. It might help them learn a certain skill, like counting, but it can stop kids from thinking for themselves. They depend on computers to create games for them, instead of using their imaginations and thinking of their own games.

I also think that technology is bad for kids' social skills. Instead of playing games with others, they are all alone on a computer game. They don't learn important skills like sharing and how to act in groups. This could make kids more materialistic they take technology for granted and expect their parents to buy them these expensive things.

Although I see how technology can be helpful in the classroom, I think it's better for older kids. Pre-K students are too young to use technology properly and should focus instead on building their creativity and social skills.

MATH

CALCULATOR EXERCISE (p. 198)

1. D; 1	**3.** B; 2	**5.** A; 1	**7.** D; 3	**9.** E; 3
2. K; 2	**4.** F; 3	**6.** H; 1	**8.** F; 3	**10.** H; 3

LESSON | PRELIMINARIES AND STRATEGIES (p. 202)

1. C	**8.** H	**15.** E	**22.** H	**29.** D
2. J	**9.** D	**16.** J	**23.** B	**30.** J
3. D	**10.** F	**17.** C	**24.** H	**31.** E
4. J	**11.** D	**18.** K	**25.** E	
5. C	**12.** J	**19.** C	**26.** H	
6. F	**13.** D	**20.** G	**27.** C	
7. E	**14.** J	**21.** D	**28.** G	

LESSON 1 | NUMBER AND QUANTITY (p. 208)

1. A	**9.** D	**17.** C	**25.** C	**33.** A	**41.** A
2. H	**10.** J	**18.** J	**26.** F	**34.** H	**42.** J
3. B	**11.** C	**19.** E	**27.** D	**35.** E	**43.** D
4. H	**12.** J	**20.** J	**28.** H	**36.** G	**44.** K
5. D	**13.** B	**21.** D	**29.** E	**37.** E	**45.** D
6. F	**14.** J	**22.** K	**30.** J	**38.** H	**46.** H
7. E	**15.** C	**23.** C	**31.** B	**39.** C	
8. F	**16.** K	**24.** F	**32.** J	**40.** F	

LESSON 2 | ALGEBRA AND FUNCTIONS (p. 216)

1. C	**14.** F	**27.** C	**40.** H	**53.** C	**66.** K
2. J	**15.** B	**28.** F	**41.** B	**54.** G	**67.** A
3. E	**16.** K	**29.** A	**42.** H	**55.** B	**68.** K
4. G	**17.** C	**30.** K	**43.** B	**56.** K	**69.** D
5. D	**18.** H	**31.** A	**44.** H	**57.** C	**70.** H
6. J	**19.** D	**32.** F	**45.** A	**58.** K	**71.** C
7. D	**20.** K	**33.** D	**46.** K	**59.** C	**72.** G
8. F	**21.** C	**34.** G	**47.** B	**60.** K	**73.** C
9. D	**22.** F	**35.** B	**48.** F	**61.** B	**74.** G
10. K	**23.** A	**36.** J	**49.** D	**62.** G	**75.** C
11. D	**24.** K	**37.** C	**50.** G	**63.** B	**76.** F
12. J	**25.** D	**38.** J	**51.** C	**64.** F	**77.** D
13. D	**26.** F	**39.** D	**52.** J	**65.** B	

LESSON 3 | COORDINATE GEOMETRY (p. 227)

1. B	**6.** G	**11.** B	**16.** K	**21.** A	**26.** K
2. K	**7.** C	**12.** J	**17.** B	**22.** H	**27.** C
3. C	**8.** H	**13.** B	**18.** K	**23.** D	**28.** J
4. J	**9.** C	**14.** H	**19.** A	**24.** H	
5. D	**10.** K	**15.** E	**20.** F	**25.** D	

LESSON 4 | GEOMETRY (p. 236)

1. E	**7.** A	**13.** E	**19.** C	**25.** D	**31.** D
2. K	**8.** G	**14.** J	**20.** K	**26.** G	**32.** J
3. C	**9.** C	**15.** E	**21.** C	**27.** C	**33.** B
4. H	**10.** H	**16.** H	**22.** H	**28.** G	**34.** G
5. C	**11.** A	**17.** E	**23.** D	**29.** A	**35.** C
6. H	**12.** H	**18.** K	**24.** H	**30.** H	**36.** H

LESSON 5 | TRIGONOMETRY (p. 245)

1. E	**4.** K	**7.** D	**10.** G
2. J	**5.** D	**8.** H	**11.** E
3. A	**6.** J	**9.** D	**12.** J

LESSON 6 | STATISTICS AND PROBABILITY (p. 249)

1. A	**6.** H	**11.** C	**16.** H	**21.** D	**26.** G
2. K	**7.** B	**12.** F	**17.** C	**22.** G	**27.** B
3. A	**8.** H	**13.** A	**18.** K	**23.** B	**28.** J
4. J	**9.** D	**14.** J	**19.** B	**24.** F	**29.** C
5. E	**10.** H	**15.** D	**20.** K	**25.** B	

TIMED QUIZ (p. 268)

1. C	**6.** H	**11.** D	**16.** H
2. F	**7.** D	**12.** J	**17.** B
3. C	**8.** J	**13.** D	**18.** G
4. G	**9.** A	**14.** J	**19.** E
5. C	**10.** H	**15.** E	**20.** K

REVIEW (p. 271)

1. D	**6.** J	**11.** A	**16.** K	**21.** B	**26.** F	**31.** E
2. H	**7.** B	**12.** J	**17.** D	**22.** H	**27.** E	**32.** K
3. C	**8.** F	**13.** C	**18.** G	**23.** B	**28.** J	
4. K	**9.** C	**14.** F	**19.** D	**24.** J	**29.** D	
5. D	**10.** J	**15.** B	**20.** H	**25.** B	**30.** H	

SCIENCE

LESSON 1 | DATA REPRESENTATION (p. 294)

1. C	**8.** H	**15.** B	**22.** H	**29.** D	**36.** C
2. G	**9.** C	**16.** H	**23.** A	**30.** G	**37.** G
3. A	**10.** H	**17.** D	**24.** G	**31.** A	**38.** A
4. G	**11.** A	**18.** H	**25.** D	**32.** G	**39.** B
5. C	**12.** H	**19.** A	**26.** H	**33.** C	**40.** H
6. H	**13.** D	**20.** J	**27.** C	**34.** F	
7. D	**14.** F	**21.** C	**28.** G	**35.** J	

LESSON 2 | RESEARCH SUMMARY (p. 306)

1. C	**7.** C	**13.** A	**19.** B	**25.** C	**31.** A
2. F	**8.** F	**14.** J	**20.** H	**26.** G	**32.** G
3. D	**9.** C	**15.** D	**21.** C	**27.** C	**33.** A
4. J	**10.** F	**16.** H	**22.** J	**28.** F	**34.** H
5. B	**11.** C	**17.** D	**23.** A	**29.** D	
6. F	**12.** G	**18.** J	**24.** J	**30.** H	

LESSON 3 | CONFLICTING VIEWPOINTS (p. 320)

1. A	**8.** J	**15.** C	**22.** J	**29.** D
2. G	**9.** A	**16.** F	**23.** A	
3. D	**10.** H	**17.** D	**24.** J	
4. G	**11.** B	**18.** F	**25.** D	
5. B	**12.** H	**19.** B	**26.** F	
6. H	**13.** D	**20.** G	**27.** B	
7. C	**14.** G	**21.** C	**28.** H	

TIMED QUIZ (p. 337)

1. A
2. F
3. A
4. J
5. C
6. H
7. D
8. F
9. C
10. G
11. C
12. G
13. A
14. G
15. C
16. J

REVIEW (p. 341)

1. D
2. F
3. B
4. G
5. C
6. G
7. C
8. G
9. B
10. J
11. A
12. G
13. D
14. H
15. A
16. G
17. C
18. J
19. A
20. G
21. B
22. H
23. A
24. G
25. C
26. H
27. D
28. H
29. B
30. G
31. C
32. H
33. C
34. H
35. C
36. J
37. B
38. G
39. D
40. G
41. B
42. H
43. C
44. J
45. B
46. H
47. C
48. F
49. D
50. G
51. C
52. H
53. B
54. G
55. C
56. H
57. D
58. J
59. C
60. J
61. C
62. G
63. B
64. H
65. A

PRACTICE TEST

MULTIPLE-CHOICE ANSWER KEYS

DIRECTIONS: For each correct answer, check the corresponding box. Then, total the number of checkmarks to determine the raw score for that test.

Section 1: English (Student Text, p. 363)

	Correct		Correct		Correct		Correct		Correct
1. C		**16.** F		**31.** D		**46.** J		**61.** C	
2. H		**17.** C		**32.** F		**47.** A		**62.** J	
3. B		**18.** H		**33.** D		**48.** H		**63.** D	
4. J		**19.** B		**34.** F		**49.** D		**64.** J	
5. A		**20.** J		**35.** C		**50.** H		**65.** B	
6. F		**21.** C		**36.** H		**51.** C		**66.** F	
7. B		**22.** F		**37.** A		**52.** H		**67.** A	
8. H		**23.** A		**38.** G		**53.** B		**68.** G	
9. D		**24.** J		**39.** B		**54.** G		**69.** D	
10. G		**25.** B		**40.** H		**55.** A		**70.** F	
11. B		**26.** G		**41.** B		**56.** H		**71.** D	
12. G		**27.** A		**42.** H		**57.** A		**72.** G	
13. C		**28.** H		**43.** A		**58.** H		**73.** D	
14. J		**29.** A		**44.** F		**59.** B		**74.** J	
15. C		**30.** H		**45.** B		**60.** J		**75.** A	

Raw Score: ______/75

Section 2: Mathematics (Student Text, p. 378)

	Correct		Correct		Correct		Correct
1. C		**16.** H		**31.** E		**46.** H	
2. J		**17.** D		**32.** G		**47.** C	
3. D		**18.** J		**33.** B		**48.** H	
4. F		**19.** B		**34.** H		**49.** E	
5. A		**20.** F		**35.** B		**50.** F	
6. H		**21.** D		**36** F		**51.** B	
7. D		**22.** K		**37.** D		**52.** G	
8. K		**23.** E		**38.** K		**53.** E	
9. D		**24.** F		**39.** E		**54.** F	
10. G		**25.** E		**40.** F		**55.** A	
11. D		**26.** F		**41.** E		**56.** G	
12. G		**27.** B		**42.** H		**57.** D	
13. D		**28.** K		**43.** B		**58.** H	
14. J		**29.** E		**44.** G		**59.** A	
15. E		**30.** H		**45.** A		**60.** G	

Raw Score: ______/60

Section 3: Reading (Student Text, p. 394)

	Correct		Correct		Correct		Correct
1. A		11. B		21. B		31. D	
2. J		12. F		22. F		32. G	
3. B		13. A		23. C		33. D	
4. H		14. H		24. F		34. G	
5. D		15. A		25. C		35. B	
6. G		16. J		26. J		36. J	
7. A		17. C		27. C		37. D	
8. H		18. J		28. F		38. J	
9. D		19. B		29. C		39. A	
10. F		20. G		30. G		40. G	

Raw Score:______/40

Section 4: Science (Student Text, p. 404)

	Correct		Correct		Correct
1. A		15. C		28. G	
2. H		16. G		29. A	
3. D		17. C		30. H	
4. J		18. F		31. A	
5. B		19. A		32. H	
6. G		20. H		33. B	
7. A		21. A		34. H	
		22. J			
8. J				35. D	
9. B		23. D		36. J	
10. H		24. F		37. C	
11. B		25. C		38. H	
12. F		26. H		39. A	
13. D		27. B		40. G	
14. J					

Raw Score: ______/40

MULTIPLE-CHOICE EXPLANATIONS

Section 1: English

1. **(C) (p. 363) *English/Knowledge of Language/Vocabulary.*** The most obvious problem with the original is the choice of the word "respectfully." The author really means to say "respectively," (C). As for the other choices, (B) fails to correct the error, and (D) incorrectly places a comma between the subject (who) of the relative clause and the verb (are).

2. **(H) (p. 363) *English/Conventions of Standard English/Grammar and Usage/Subject-Verb Agreement.*** "Who" introduces a relative clause, and the clause needs a main verb. "Bringing" is a participle, which can be used as an adjective but not a main verb. The main verb has to show tense. (H) makes the needed correction. "Who" is the subject, and "brings" is the verb. (G) fails to solve the problem, and (J) tries to use "that," a relative pronoun, but "who" is preferred as a pronoun to refer to people.

3. **(B) (p. 363) *English/Knowledge of Language/Style/Tone.*** While the passage is written in fairly direct prose (the language is not academic or otherwise ponderous), "divvy up" is informal usage that falls below the otherwise grammatically precise and correct level of the writing. (B) substitutes a neutral and grammatical phrase. (C) introduces a new error with "between." "Between" would be used if there were two people; "among" is needed for three or more. Finally, "apportion," (D), means to divide but not in equal parts.

4. **(J) (p. 364) *English/Conventions of Standard English/Sentence Structure/Misplaced Modifiers.*** The error in the original is not egregious, but the sentence is considerably improved by changing the wording to that given in (J). The problem with the original is the placement of "except Rodolfo." The relative clause that begins with "who is" is intended to modify "Rodolfo," but the clause is separated from the word it modifies by the main verb of the independent clause plus its prepositional modifier. (J) improves the structure by moving "Rodolfo" next to "who" so that the connection is obvious. (G) completely destroys the logic of the sentence: it is not Rodolfo who goes out with the others. And (H) eliminates the relative clause and tries to turn the word grouping into a main clause. But the result would be, at best, a comma-splice and, at worst, gibberish.

5. **(A) (p. 364) *English/Conventions of Standard English/No Change.*** "Their" is a plural possessive pronoun. It's used here to say whose love (their love). "They're," (B), and "there," (C), are words commonly confused with "their." "That," (D), is a demonstrative pronoun used to point out one among many, a usage not appropriate here.

6. **(F) (p. 364) *English/Production of Writing/Style/Appropriate Supporting Material.*** The information in parentheses is a definition of "garret," so it should be placed just following that word so the reader is given the information in a timely fashion. The other possible locations also relate to the idea of the apartment or building, but the parenthetical remark would not provide a definition of the word associated with those points. "(dismal attic apartment)" does not define or explain "rent" or "building" or "apartment."

7. **(B) (p. 364) *English/Conventions of Standard English/Grammar and Usage/Pronoun Usage and Subject-Verb Agreement.*** This item tests a couple of conventions of standard, written English. First, the test will occasionally throw at you the old who/whom problem. Just remember that "who" is used as the subject of a verb, and "whom" is used for objects of verbs and prepositions:

   Who is at the door?
   Jan is the one who is at the door.

   Whom do you prefer?
   I prefer the incumbent.

   Of *whom* are you speaking?
   I am speaking of the incumbent, Jan.

   So "who" is the correct pronoun here. Second, there is also a question of the agreement between subject and verb. In this sentence, "who" refers to "Musetta." "Musetta" is singular, so you need the singular verb "has."

8. **(H) (p. 364) *English/Knowledge of Language/Style/Effective Transitional Sentence.*** This item is asking about the right word to correctly describe the logical connection between the two ideas in the sentence: Marcello wants to see Musetta again, and the older man is tricked. The original suggests that the two are contingently related, but if the connection were only a probable one, the sentence would be worded: "Marcello wants to see Musetta again if the old man can be tricked." What the author means to say is that the trick is played because Marcello wants to see Musetta again, and that relation is best captured by "so," (H). As for (G), "because" would actually reverse this connection, suggesting that the trick caused Marcello's feelings. And (J) completely destroys the logic of the sentence.

9. **(D) (p. 364) *English/Knowledge of Language/Vocabulary.*** This item asks about the implicit value of language. All four options indicate that the old man pays the bill, but you want the one that suggests that the group has tricked him a second time. The phrase "is stuck with" conveys that idea.

10. **(G) (p. 364) *English/Conventions of Standard English/Grammar and Usage/Adjectives versus Adverbs.*** The original uses an adjective to modify the verb. Correct usage requires an adverb of the sort supplied by (G). (H) and (J) do not make coherent sentences.

11. **(B) (p. 364) *English/Conventions of Standard English/Grammar and Usage/Diction.*** Here is another item that asks about the implicit value of a word. Mimi is out of sight. She is listening to Rodolofo tell his story. Either "eavesdrop," (A), or "overhear," (D), could be used. But the original is not idiomatic; the correct phrasing would be "eavesdrops on." (B) and (C) avoid this problem, but to be as precise as possible, Mimi is hearing and not seeing Rodolfo, so (B) is correct.

12. **(G) (p. 365) *English/Conventions of Standard English/Grammar and Usage/Verb Tense.*** If you want a hypertechnical grammar explanation for this item, you should google "subjunctive" because the distinction between the indicative mood and the subjunctive mood is at the heart of this item. Verbs such as want, desire, hope, and so on—verbs that express contingency or possibility—require an unusual form to complete them: the subjunctive form. "Could" in the original indicates a past action that is inconsistent with the present tense "hopes." (G) corrects this problem.

13. **(C) (p. 365) *English/Conventions of Standard English/Sentence Structure/Faulty Parallelism.*** The original sentence suffers from a lack of parallelism. The verb form of "to pretend" should reflect the form of "share," and (C) makes the needed correction. (B) provides the correct form, but the number of the changed verb is inconsistent with the number of the subject. (They fail to agree.) (D) offers a new conjunction but fails to address the underlying problem of the original.

14. **(J) (p. 365) *English/Production of Writing/Strategy/Effective Concluding Sentence.*** The additional sentence would be like the landing in a gymnastics routine—the final dramatic move that ties everything together. Here "Mimi dies" is the climax of the drama, and the phrase makes clear what the writer only implies with the phrase "too late."

15. **(C) (p. 365) *English/Production of Writing/Strategy/Main Idea.*** The essay provides a very nice summary of the development of each of the four acts and therefore a good look at the plot development from start to finish. For someone not familiar with the story, this would be very helpful for understanding the performance. As for (A), while such discussion might deepen the reader's understanding of opera, it would not help in understanding the specifics of this particular play. As for (B), the passage does present the story in chronological order, but that is because the opera apparently develops the story in that way. (D) is an interesting observation but an answer to the wrong question. (D) would be a good answer to the question "What would make the opera difficult to understand?" but that is not the question actually asked.

16. **(F) (p. 366) *English/Production of Writing/Strategy/Effective Transitional Sentence.*** This item asks which adverb (technically, conjunctive adverb since the choices have elements of both conjunctions and adverbs) sets the appropriate timeframe for the visitors. The author wants to describe events that happen occasionally but not continuously, and "from time to time" is a good phrase for that purpose. "Once" does not create the idea of repeated events. "In the meantime" is used to describe two events that occur in one timeframe. And "initially" would be used to refer to an event that occurred but was followed by a different event or events.

17. (C) (p. 366) ***English/Conventions of Standard English/Sentence Structure.*** The error in the original is often described as a "double subject," that is, both "they" and "all of them" (or even just "all") could be the subject. But a sentence cannot have two subjects. (It can have a compound subject, but that is another matter.) (C) corrects the problem by providing one subject to go with the verb. (B) just makes matters worse, and as for (D), "those" is a demonstrative adjective that has nothing to modify.

18. (H) (p. 366) ***English/Conventions of Standard English/Grammar and Usage/Subject-Verb Agreement.*** The phrase is elliptical, that is, some words have been left out, and the reader is expected to fill in the blank. This is a perfectly acceptable practice in English—so long as the elliptical phrase is logically constructed. In this case, the writer means to say "but there are too many sights." The writer would not say "but there are too much sights." (H) makes the needed correction, but (J) does not. (G) tries to make the sentence correct, but the verb "is" does not agree with the plural "many."

19. (B) (p. 366) ***English/Conventions of Standard English/Grammar and Usage/Nouns and Noun Clauses.*** This is a fairly subtle question because it asks about noun number, that is, whether the noun should be singular or plural. The noun is modified by "their," which refers to "visitors," so the author is talking about more than one list. Each person has a list, but taken as a group, the visitors have lists (plural). (B) eliminates the inconsistency between the plural "visitors" and the singular "list." The meaning of "listing," whether singular or plural, doesn't fit with the author's intended meaning.

20. (J) (p. 366) ***English/Knowledge of Language/Style/Conciseness.*** The original is needlessly repetitious. In the context of this sentence, "walking" and "on foot" have the same meaning. (G) and (H) are just not idiomatic.

21. (C) (p. 366) ***English/Conventions of Standard English/Sentence Structure/Faulty Parallelism.*** Elements of a sentence that have similar functions need to have similar forms; that is, they should look like one another. Here you have a series: admire buildings, survey riverfront, are watching boat traffic. The third element sticks out like a sore thumb. "Watch" brings the element into line: admire, survey, and watch.

22. (F) (p. 366) ***English/Conventions of Standard English/No Change.*** The original shows the correct use of the apostrophe to create a possessive. The word is singular, so use the rule "Add an apostrophe and an 's.'"

23. (A) (p. 366) ***English/Production of Writing/Strategy/Effective Transitional Sentence.*** This item asks you to select a transitional word that express the logical relationship between the sentence introduced by the underlined word and the preceding group of sentences. The writer has just listed all of the disadvantages of visiting Liberty Island and proposes the Staten Island Ferry as an alternative. So "instead," (A), correctly expresses the logical relationship. "However," (B), is used to create a contrast, but its meaning doesn't fit here. Here you need the idea of an alternative or substitute. "Subsequently," (C), is used to describe an event that is later in time to an event that actually occurs, but in this case, "taking the Liberty Island Ferry" does not occur. Finally, though the visitor might be surprised, (D), to learn about the substitution, the writer is not because the switch has been part of the plan all along.

24. (J) (p. 367) ***English/Production of Writing/Strategy/Appropriate Supporting Material.*** One of the themes treated by the writer is cost: NYC is expensive, the ferry to Liberty Island is costly, lunch in the park is cheap, etc. So it would be appropriate for the writer to mention the cost of the Staten Island Ferry. And the position of the sentence is particularly suitable since the cost of the ticket is the last factor mentioned in connection with the trip to Liberty Island.

25. (B) (p. 367) ***English/Knowledge of Language/Vocabulary.*** Sometimes test questions have stems that are entirely formal, for example, "What is the value of *x*?" You'll see this stem, or some variation thereon, in the math section. The stem itself is suitable for almost any question that asks about *x* as an unknown. But sometimes the stem provides additional guidance for choosing the correct answer. Pay careful attention to such information. In this case, the stem asks for "sensory detail," so you need a choice that conveys information that suggests a physical feeling: warm and sunny.

26. (G) (p. 367) ***English/Conventions of Standard English/Sentence Structure.*** The logical and grammatical structure of the original is broken. The -ing form suggests an adjective, but the phrase does not modify anything. The problem could be corrected by using a main verb as (J) suggests, but "so" is not the right conjunction for the job. (H) seems to say that the writer and visitors take a restroom break while at the same time they are going on to the next attraction. (G) is an improvement. (G) uses the -ing form as a gerund or noun that is the object of the preposition "before" and the prepositional phrase is used as an adverb showing time to modify "make."

27. (A) (p. 367) ***English/Conventions of Standard English/Grammar and Usage/Verb Tense.*** The use of the present tense in the passage is called the "historical present" or the "narrative present" and sometimes the "dramatic present." It's often used to describe historical events: "The President learns of the planned invasion at noon and tells the generals to prepare. The next morning the enemy launches an all-out assault." And you can see why it might also be called the "dramatic present." It refers to tours the writer has conducted in the past and will conduct in the future. The painting of the murals is an action contained entirely in the past before the writer plans a tour.

28. (H) (p. 368) ***English/Knowledge of Language/Style/Conciseness.*** "Every year" is needlessly repetitious of "annual" and should be eliminated. While "celebration" and "celebrating" are both nouns, the gerund -ing is not idiomatic here, so (H) is correct.

29. (A) (p. 368) ***English/Production of Writing/Organization/Paragraph-Level Structure.*** The last two sentences have a different tone from the preceding ones. The phrase "after . . . walking" implies a different perspective; and, in fact, the writer is winding down the tour. So a new paragraph here would reinforce this distinction and alert the reader to the fact that this is the conclusion of the narrative.

30. (H) (p. 368) ***English/Production of Writing/Organization/Passage-Level Structure.*** This selection is entitled Tour for a reason. The narrative describes the order in which the writer shows visitors the various tourist attractions. Words and phrases such as "start," "then," and "after" characterize this arrangement, and the order of sentences also reinforces the order of the tour. There is no warrant in the text for any of the other choices. While you might have some notion about history or popularity, the writer does not include such clues in the passage, so (F) and (G) are wrong. And though the tour starts and ends at the apartment, there is nothing to indicate geographical positioning is a factor. Now, in reality, if you connect the dots on the map, you'll see that this fictional tour actually makes geographical sense. But that's movement, not proximity.

31. (D) (p. 368) ***English/Production of Writing/Strategy/Appropriate Supporting Material.*** There is no question that the events described in the selection were "big." A volcanic eruption could hardly be anything other than large or huge. But another important element of the eruptions is that they were also very destructive. "Cataclysm" is used to describe an event that is violent, sudden, and disastrous. So the best choice is (D).

32. (F) (p. 369) ***English/Conventions of Standard English/No Change.*** The original makes it clear that the big event is the eruption and the lava flow the extra phenomenon. (G) changes the priority between the two events by implying that the lava is the main event and the eruption a secondary development. Both (H) and (J) destroy the logic of the sentence.

33. (D) (p. 369) ***English/Conventions of Standard English/Punctuation/Commas.*** This item primarily tests punctuation. "Occurring" is the participle form of "to occur," and the word is used here as an adjective to modify the entire sequence of events described earlier in the sentence. To make the function of "occurring" clear to the reader, you need a comma to set off the modifying phrase, and the comma needs to be placed just after the end of the word group to be modified. A secondary issue is idiomatic expression, and (D), but not (C), passes the test.

34. (F) (p. 369) ***English/Conventions of Standard English/Sentence Structure/Faulty Parallelism.*** Sentence elements that have the same function should have similar forms. In this case, heat and weight both operate to cement the debris into rocks. So the two factors should have similar word forms, and the original is correct. (G) and (H) disrupt this parallelism, and (J) has a meaning that doesn't make sense here.

35. (C) (p. 369) ***English/Production of Writing/Organization/Sentence-Level Structure.*** This item asks you to place the parenthetical remark at the point where the logical flow of the paragraph will be best preserved. The one mention of caldera is made in the third sentence, so the information should be close by. If this were a parenthetical phrase as opposed to a complete sentence, the information could be inserted directly following the word caldera, but that is not an option you are given. The next best choice is (C), and this is a good location for the insert since it is a complete sentence.

36. (H) (p. 369) ***English/Conventions of Standard English/Grammar and Usage/Adjectives versus Adverbs.*** This item has two elements. One is the choice of the part of speech. Here you need an adjective to modify the noun "formation," so both (G) and (J) are wrong. Second, the chosen word must correctly express the relationship between the two events: eruption and formation. "Consequent," (H), shows the causal connection between the two, but there is nothing in the text to suggest that the connection is "fortunate," (F).

37. (A) (p. 369) ***English/Production of Writing/Organization/Paragraph-Level Structure.*** The original paragraph is organized chronologically, from earliest to latest events, and that ordering makes sense in describing the geological history of Yellowstone Park. Changing the order disrupts the story. Also, a different order creates different transitional problems. For example, the Mesa Falls Tuff is labelled as the "second" event to occur. That wording does not make sense if Sentence 2 is placed first or last in the paragraph.

38. (G) (p. 369) ***English/Conventions of Standard English/Grammar and Usage/Subject-Verb Agreement.*** The original has a problem with the agreement between subject and verb: "Sequence" is singular but "were" is plural. (G) eliminates the mistake. (H) reduces the word grouping to a fragment without a main verb, and as for (J), the future tense "will be" is inconsistent with the other tenses in the paragraph.

39. (B) (p. 370) ***English/Conventions of Standard English/Grammar and Usage/Verb Tense.*** The original uses the present tense "is trapped," but the other events in the sequence, which all occur in the same time frame, are described as events that occurred in the past using the past tense. (B) brings this part of the sentence into line with the tense in the rest of the sentence. (C) and (D) do not make the needed change.

40. (H) (p. 370) ***English/Conventions of Standard English/Sentence Structure/Faulty Parallelism.*** The structure of the original sentence is unclear. It's not obvious whether "caused" is intended to be a third element in a series including "exceeded," "stretched," and "caused" or an adjective modifying the sequence of events. (H) resolves the uncertainty. (G) also makes a clear choice between the two interpretations but is punctuated incorrectly. (G) would need a comma following "crust." And (J) seems to set up "causes" as the third element in the series but uses the wrong verb tense.

41. (B) (p. 370) ***English/Conventions of Standard English/Grammar and Usage/Verb Tense.*** "Burst," (B), and not "busted" is the past tense of "to burst."

42. (H) (p. 370) ***English/Conventions of Standard English/Grammar and Usage/Sequence and Verb Tense.*** This item is looking for the right word to create a logical connection between two ideas. The form "have taken place" is called the perfect (or present perfect) tense and implies that the action took place partly in the past but continues into the present, like "I have always enjoyed movies." "Since," however, implies a completed action, so the two are inconsistent. (G) and (J) make the same error, but "over," (H), indicates that the time period still continues.

43. (A) (p. 370) ***English/Conventions of Standard English/No Change.*** Here you have a test of usage. "They're" is a contraction of "they are," a plural pronoun that agrees with "eruptions" with its plural verb "are." "Their," (B), is a possessive pronoun and cannot be used as a subject, though "they're" and "their" are frequently confused. "Its," (C), is also a possessive pronoun and is singular, as is "it is," (D).

44. (F) (p. 370) ***English/Production of Writing/Strategy/Effective Concluding Sentence.*** (F) provides the best conclusion both for the final paragraph and the essay as a whole because it addresses the possible next event in the geological sequence. The other choices make statements that are generally related to the essay topic but don't specifically fit in with the development of the piece and especially do not fit as possible conclusions.

45. (B) (p. 371) ***English/Production of Writing/Strategy/Main Idea.*** The essay is a quasi-academic paper about geology. It doesn't mention activities such as hiking or camping.

46. (J) (p. 371) ***English/Production of Writing/Strategy/Effective Transitional Sentence.*** The original does not reflect the logical connection between the "old" and the "new." The necessity of constructing low-rise structures did not cause the inventions mentioned. The writer means to say that the "old" situation existed but the "new" replaced it. "Until," (J), has this meaning. "If," (G), expresses contingency or possibility, but the writer intends to show a sequence. "Because of," (H), implies that the "old" is somehow dependent on the "new," an illogical proposition.

47. (A) (p. 371) ***English/Conventions of Standard English/No Change.*** The original correctly states that Chicago took the early lead over New York, as the writer explains later in the essay. But you don't really have to wait that long to confirm the correctness of "initially," (A). The other choices are definitely wrong. "Accordingly," (B), implies a causal or at least a logical connection between two events or ideas; "moreover," (C), is used to extend or provide detail to an earlier idea; and "besides," (D), is used to create additional emphasis for a second point.

48. (H) (p. 371) ***English/Conventions of Standard English/Sentence Structure/Faulty Parallelism.*** This item tests parallelism. The sentence presents two problems associated with tall buildings: traffic and air pollution. They are, in a sense, equal ideas, so they should have equivalent forms: caused and degraded. (B) and (D) just add to confusion of the original by implying a dependence of one of the two on the other.

49. (D) (p. 371) ***English/Conventions of Standard English/Grammar and Usage/Faulty or Illogical Comparisons.*** The problem here is an illogical assertion. "As [comparative adjective] as" is a phrase to say that one thing has a magnitude that is equal to that of another thing. Examples are "as heavy as" or "as sweet as." The writer means to say, however, that buildings equal to or greater than 150 feet were banned, and for that, "[adjective]er than," (D), is needed. (B) and (C) are not properly formed English expressions.

50. (H) (p. 372) ***English/Knowledge of Language/Vocabulary.*** Irony refers to an event or state of affairs that is contrary to what one expects, so the word is used correctly here. The writer is describing what is almost a contest between Chicago and New York, so it is surprising to learn that one of the New York entrants seems to be from Chicago.

51. (C) (p. 372) ***English/Conventions of Standard English/Grammar and Usage/Faulty or Illogical Comparisons.*** The error in the original is fairly subtle. As written, the sentence seems to create an equivalence between "characteristics" and "a typical New York building." (C) corrects the problem by making it clear that the comparison is between "characteristics" and "those." In this case, "those" is a demonstrative pronoun that references "characteristics." (B) completely disrupts the logic of the sentence. And in (D), the singular "that" fails to agree with the plural "characteristics."

52. (H) (p. 372) ***English/Conventions of Standard English/Sentence Structure/Problems of Coordination and Subordination.*** The difficulty with the original is that the initial word grouping (ending with the comma) has no clear logical connection to the rest of the sentence. The phrase is not a complete thought, so it cannot stand on its own; it must be connected to something in the independent clause. (H) accomplishes the connection by turning the grouping into a prepositional phrase that modifies "diminished." (The advances explain how or why the constraints . . . diminished.) (G) and (J) seem to try this strategy but fail. "Advancing," (G), would create a participial phrase, but the phrase would be an adjective that would have to modify a noun, and there is no suitable noun in the independent clause. Similarly, "by advancing," (J), would seem to modify "constraints," but the constraints did not advance the situation.

53. (B) (p. 372) ***English/Conventions of Standard English/Sentence Structure/Fragments.*** The original version is not a complete sentence, just a fragment of a sentence, because the word grouping does not have a main verb. In the original, "casting" seems to be an adjective modifying "Equitable Building." So it should be the main verb, "cast," (B). The other two choices make an attempt to provide a main verb, but the tenses are inconsistent with the rest of the paragraph.

54. (G) (p. 372) ***English/Knowledge of Language/Style/Tone.*** The original is slang. "Anti" is a prefix meaning opposed to or against, not a noun. The meanings of "resistant," (H), and "averse," (J), are not exactly what the writer intends for this context.

55. (A) (p. 373) ***English/Conventions of Standard English/Sentence Structure/Unintended Meanings.*** What is the most logical placement for "only"? The word is intended to be part of the adverbial phrase that modifies "rise," stating how high a structure could be built. The current placement makes it clear that the rise was limited to just 100 feet. Putting "only" before "a building," (B), creates the impression that the only thing that New York permitted to rise to 100 feet was a building, which is not the intended meaning of the writer. Placing "only" after "rise," (C), implies that the building had to go upward from the sidewalk in a vertical fashion, obvious and therefore silly. And putting "only" after "directly," (D), suggest that buildings were built upon sidewalks.

56. **(H) (p. 373) *English/Production of Writing/Organization/Sentence-Level Structure.*** You can think of a question like this as a jigsaw puzzle—there's only one correct way to fit all the pieces together. And just as you would with a jigsaw puzzle, start with the edges. The last sentence of the preceding paragraph mentions the zoning plan, so it is likely that the first piece of this puzzle will be connected to that idea, and (2) should be the opening sentence. The next piece should fit snugly against the idea of the zoning law, so (4) should come next. Then, the topic of New York would suggest that (1) come next. And finally, the note about Chicago would be the last sentence of the paragraph.

57. **(A) (p. 373) *English/Production of Writing/Strategy/Effective Opening Sentence.*** The original version provides a good introduction to the paragraph since the author supplied a history of the "tallest building competition" that spans over a hundred years. The other choices do not fit the later development of the paragraph.

58. **(H) (p. 373) *English/Conventions of Standard English/Grammar and Usage/Nouns and Noun Clauses.*** This item tests the rule for creating a possessive noun. The general procedure is to add an 's, though there are a few exceptions. Here the original "countries" is the plural of the noun "country" and cannot be used to modify "building." (H) solves the problem. (G) is the possessive of the plural of the noun, but the context makes it clear that the writer is referring to just one country. (J) is not an acceptable form for any purpose.

59. **(B) (p. 374) *English/Production of Writing/Strategy/Appropriate Supporting Material.*** The first sentence of the last paragraph states that the two cities have been in a kind of competition for "tallest building" for a long time. The sentence in question gives specific examples of buildings that were at one time the "tallest" but gave up that distinction when another, taller structure was completed.

60. **(J) (p. 374) *English/Production of Writing/Strategy/Appropriate Supporting Material.*** The sentence provides information that gives an authoritative opinion on the issue raised by the question asked in the paragraph, so it would be relevant. And the reader is likely to find the information helpful or at least interesting.

61. **(C) (p. 375) *English/Conventions of Standard English/Grammar and Usage/Pronoun Usage and Sentence Structure/Fragments.*** The original version contains an ambiguous pronoun. "That" is a demonstrative pronoun in context and seems to refer to a noun or pronoun in the previous sentence. But it lacks an antecedent (referent). If "that" is read as a relative pronoun, then the original is a sentence fragment. (C) resolves the ambiguity and corrects the sentence. In the new version, "that" introduces a relative clause to modify "duel." As for (B), "what" should not be used to introduce a relative clause. And (D) inserts a gratuitous comma between the subject of the new relative clause and the verb.

62. **(J) (p. 375) *English/Conventions of Standard English/Sentence Structure/Problems of Coordination and Subordination.*** The problem with the original is that "by" needs a noun (or pronoun) object, but what follows has a subject and verb. (J) takes advantage of this by creating a dependent clause introduced by the subordinate conjunction "because" and modifying "boiled over" (stating why). (G) is no improvement since "of" also looks for an object. Finally, (H) is incorrect because "for the reason that" is not idiomatic.

63. **(D) (p. 375) *English/Production of Writing/Strategy/Appropriate Supporting Material.*** This item asks you to select a word that will extend the metaphor started in the preceding sentence. At the heart of the idea of "simmer" and "boil" is the notion of turning up the heat, (D).

64. **(J) (p. 375) *English/Conventions of Standard English/Punctuation/Commas.*** This item is a matter of proper punctuation. The original incorrectly uses the colon. A colon is used to introduce material that clarifies or adds detail to what has come earlier. A dash, (G), is inappropriate because the material to follow is not an aside. And using a period, (H), creates a fragment.

65. **(B) (p. 375) *English/Conventions of Standard English/Sentence Structure/Problems of Coordination and Subordination.*** The "which" in the original seems to introduce a relative clause modifying "challenge," but that job is already taken by "that." Also, "who" rather than "which" is the relative pronoun used to refer to people. (C) takes care of "who" but leaves the sentence with no clear logical structure, just as the original does. Finally, (D) completely blows up the logic of the sentence.

66. (F) (p. 375) ***English/Conventions of Standard English/No Change.*** "Accepted" and "excepted" are sometimes confused; the original makes the right choice. (C) and (D) don't have meanings that would work in this context.

67. (A) (p. 376) ***English/Production of Writing/Strategy/Appropriate Supporting Material.*** The essay is a historical narrative of the Hamilton-Burr duel fought at a certain time in a particular place. What happened during the next half century in other states is not relevant.

68. (G) (p. 376) ***English/Production of Writing/Strategy/Effective Transitional Sentence.*** This item asks for the appropriate word to show the temporal relationship between the death of Philip and the day of the Hamilton-Burr duel. "Earlier" makes the right connection. The other choices are related to the idea of time, but none of them has a meaning that shows that the son had died three years before the duel was fought.

69. (D) (p. 376) ***English/Production of Writing/Strategy/Effective Transitional Sentence.*** The purpose of the introductory phrase to provide a transition between the two paragraphs, and the writer means to signal that the new paragraph continues the description begun in the preceding paragraph. The phrase "at the time," (D), makes the continuity clear to the reader.

70. (F) (p. 376) ***English/Conventions of Standard English/No Change.*** This item raises a very subtle point of grammar. "Firing" in this context is a gerund and therefore a noun. But "party" is also a noun. So what is the logical connection between the nouns? The possessive form makes the connection one of ownership, that is, the firing belongs to the party—at least in the sense that the party controls the firing. Without the apostrophe, you'd have two nouns, "party" and "firing," but no way of showing that connection. (G) is wrong because "both" would need the plural "parties'." (H) is wrong because "parties" should be singular, as it is in the original. And (J) just does not make a logical statement.

71. (D) (p. 377) ***English/Conventions of Standard English/Sentence Structure/Run-On Sentences.*** The original is a run-on sentence: two independent clauses jammed together with no punctuation or conjunction separating them. (D) solves the problem by using a comma and the conjunction "but." (B) is a comma splice. It cements the same two clauses together with a comma but does not separate them with a conjunction. And (C) uses "so," which implies a causal or logical connection that the writer does not intend.

72. (G) (p. 377) ***English/Conventions of Standard English/Grammar and Usage/Adjectives versus Adverbs.*** The problem with the original is that "common" is an adjective and cannot be used to modify another adjective, in this case "accepted." An adverb (-ly) is needed. "Ordinary," (H), and "usual," (J), are both adjectives.

73. (D) (p. 377) ***English/Production of Writing/Strategy/Appropriate Supporting Material.*** This item asks for a work that achieves a particular goal. If the writer wants the reader to understand that Hamilton fired before he meant to, "prematurely," (D), is a good adverb.

74. (J) (p. 377) ***English/Conventions of Standard English/Sentence Structure/Unintended Meanings.*** Here is a pretty good example of the notorious dangling modifier. The participle used to introduce the sentence, "regaining," needs to be attached to a noun, so a reader will naturally associate the phrase with the first important noun after the initial comma, "physician." But the physician is not the one who was shot. The ambiguity can be resolved by moving "Hamilton" closer to "regaining," the strategy used by (J).

75. (A) (p. 377) ***English/Production of Writing/Strategy/Main Idea.*** The essay is a pretty interesting description of the Hamilton-Burr duel. The writer provides background, context, narrative, and enough detail about dueling to appreciate the story, but the essay is not a technical treatment of dueling. Therefore, (A) is the best choice.

Section 2: Mathematics

1. (C) (p. 378) ***Mathematics/Number and Quantity/Basic Arithmetic Manipulations.*** Two numbers that add up to zero are additive inverses: $a + (-a) = 0$. The additive inverse is the opposite of the original value: $\frac{2}{3}$ is the additive inverse of $-\frac{2}{3}$.

2. **(J) (p. 378) *Mathematics/Geometry/Lines and Angles and Circles.*** A central angle is equal to its intercepted arc, so $\overset{\frown}{AC} = \angle AOC = 70°$. An inscribed angle is equal to one-half the measure of its intercepted arc. Therefore, the measure of $\angle ABC$ is $\frac{\overset{\frown}{AC}}{2} = \frac{70°}{2} = 35°$.

3. **(D) (p. 378) *Mathematics/Algebra and Functions/Solving Quadratic Equations and Relations.*** Factor the quadratic equation:

$$x^2 + 6x + 8 = 0$$
$$(x+4)(x+2) = 0$$
$$x+4 = 0 \text{ or } x+2 = 0$$

Therefore, $x = -4$ or -2.

4. **(F) (p. 379) *Mathematics/Geometry/Lines and Angles.*** Fill in the given information and label the remaining angles:

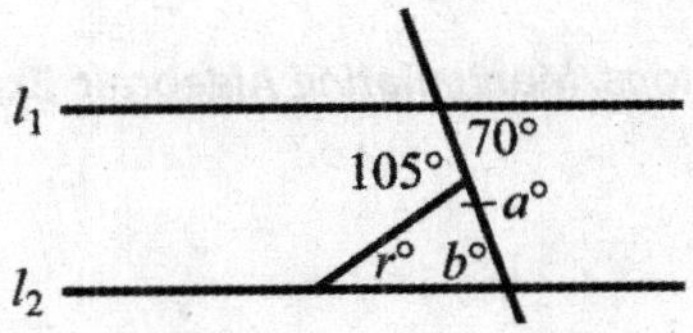

Since $b°$ is an alternate interior angle with $x°$, $b = 70$. And $a = 75$ because it is the supplement of $y°$. The three angles form a triangle: $r + a + b = 180$. Thus:

$$r + 75 + 70 = 180$$
$$r = 35$$

5. **(A) (p. 379) *Mathematics/Algebra and Functions/Manipulating Algebraic Expressions/Evaluating Expressions.*** Substitute the given values for *A* and *r* and solve for *g*:

$$A = \frac{2gr}{g+r}$$
$$4 = \frac{2g(1)}{g+1}$$
$$4(g+1) = 2g$$
$$4g + 4 = 2g$$
$$2g = -4$$
$$g = -2$$

6. **(H) (p. 379) *Mathematics/Algebra and Functions/Coordinate Geometry/Graphs of Linear Equations.*** V-shaped graphs usually indicate absolute value functions. Substitute the given coordinates $(2, 2)$, $(0, 0)$, and $(-3, 3)$ into the answer choices: only $y = |x|$ satisfies all the ordered pairs.

7. **(D) (p. 379) *Mathematics/Algebra and Functions/Manipulating Algebraic Expressions/Basic Algebraic Manipulations.*** The distributive property indicates multiplication over addition $[a(b+c) = ab + ac]$ and multiplication over subtraction $[a(b-c) = ab - ac]$. Thus, $x(x+2) = x^2 + 2x$.

8. **(K) (p. 380) *Mathematics/Number and Quantity/Percentages.*** The sales tax is 7% of \$600: $0.07(600) = \$42$. Thus, the total cost is $\$600 + \$42 = \$642$.

9. **(D) (p. 380) *Mathematics/Algebra and Functions/Evaluating, Interpreting, and Creating Algebraic Functions/Function Notation*.** Substitute -1 for x and evaluate:

$$\begin{aligned} -x^2-2x^3 &= -(-1)^2-2(-1)^3 \\ &= -1-2(-1) \\ &= -1+2 \\ &= 1 \end{aligned}$$

10. **(G) (p. 380) *Mathematics/Statistics and Probability/Measures of Center*.** The average is the sum of the numbers divided by the number of elements:

$$\begin{aligned} \text{average} &= \frac{(n+3)+(2n-1)+(3n+4)}{3} \\ &= \frac{6n+6}{3} \\ &= 2n+2 \end{aligned}$$

11. **(D) (p. 380) *Mathematics/Algebra and Functions/Manipulating Algebraic Expressions/Evaluating Expressions*.** Substitute 9 for x and evaluate:

$$\begin{aligned} x^0+x^{\frac{1}{2}}+x^{-2} &= 9^0+9^{\frac{1}{2}}+9^{-2} \\ &= 1+\sqrt{9}+\frac{1}{9^2} \\ &= 1+3+\frac{1}{81} \\ &= 4\frac{1}{81} \end{aligned}$$

12. **(G) (p. 380) *Mathematics/Number and Quantity/Basic Arithmetic Manipulations*.** To add radicals, rewrite the radicands (the numbers under the radical symbol) in terms of the same number, then combine the coefficients of the terms with the same radicands:

$$\begin{aligned} 4\sqrt{3}+3\sqrt{27} &= 4\sqrt{3}+3(3\sqrt{3}) \\ &= 4\sqrt{3}+9\sqrt{3} \\ &= 13\sqrt{3} \end{aligned}$$

13. **(D) (p. 381) *Mathematics/Statistics and Probability/Measures of Center*.** The average is the sum of the test scores divided by the number of tests:

$$\begin{aligned} \text{average} = 90 &= \frac{87+93+86+x}{4} \\ 4(90) &= 87+93+86+x \\ 360 &= 266+x \\ x &= 94 \end{aligned}$$

14. **(J) (p. 381) *Mathematics/Number and Quantity/Rates and Proportions*.** Each dime is 10 cents. Thus, $4x$ dimes would be $4x\ \cancel{\text{dimes}} \cdot \frac{10\text{ cents}}{\cancel{\text{dime}}} = 40x$ cents.

15. (E) (p. 381) ***Mathematics/Number and Quantity/Basic Arithmetic Manipulations.*** The shaded circle at -5 indicates either $\geq$ or $\leq$, and the unshaded circle at 3 indicates either $>$ or $<$, without the equal sign (the $<$ symbol indicates "less than," and the $>$ symbol indicates "greater than"). The graph indicates $x \leq -5$ or $x > 3$. The answers are connected by "or," meaning the union of those two sets of numbers. Therefore, the answer is $x \leq -5$ or $x > 3$. Note that $x \leq -5$ can be rewritten as $-5 \geq x$.

16. (H) (p. 381) ***Mathematics/Number and Quantity/Basic Arithmetic Manipulations.*** First, convert the mixed numbers to improper fractions:

$$2\frac{2}{5} - 1\frac{7}{8} = \frac{12}{5} - \frac{15}{8}$$

Since the lowest common denominator is 40, we have:

$$\frac{12}{5} - \frac{15}{8} = \frac{96}{40} - \frac{75}{40} = \frac{21}{40}$$

17. (D) (p. 382) ***Mathematics/Geometry/Circles.*** Use the equation for circumference of a circle:

$$\begin{aligned} C_{\text{circle}} &= 2\pi r \\ &= 2\pi(6) \\ &= 12\pi \end{aligned}$$

Therefore, 3π is $\frac{3\pi}{12\pi} = \frac{1}{4}$ of the circumference, which, in degrees, is $\frac{1}{4}(360°) = 90°$.

18. (J) (p. 382) ***Mathematics/Algebra and Functions/Solving Algebraic Equations or Inequalities with One Variable/ Equations Involving Rational Expressions and Equations Involving Radical Expressions.*** Solve the equation for x:

$$\begin{aligned} \frac{2x}{3\sqrt{2}} &= \frac{3\sqrt{2}}{x} \\ 2x(x) &= (3\sqrt{2})(3\sqrt{2}) \\ 2x^2 &= 9(2) = 18 \\ x^2 &= 9 \\ x &= \pm 3 \end{aligned}$$

Therefore, the positive value of x is 3.

19. (B) (p. 382) ***Mathematics/Algebra and Functions/Expressing and Evaluating Algebraic Functions/Function Notation.*** To determine the value of $g(f(2))$, first substitute 2 for x in $f(x)$ and evaluate:

$$\begin{aligned} f(x) &= 2x - x^2 \\ f(2) &= 2(2) - (2)^2 = 4 - 4 = 0 \end{aligned}$$

Now, substitute this value for x in $g(x)$ and evaluate:

$$\begin{aligned} g(x) &= x - 4 \\ g(0) &= 0 - 4 = -4 \end{aligned}$$

20. (F) (p. 382) ***Mathematics/Algebra and Functions/Solving Algebraic Equations or Inequalities with One Variable/ Equations Involving Absolute Value.*** Since $|5-2x| = 7$, we know that $5 - 2x = 7$ or $-(5-2x) = 7$. Solve each for possible values of x:

$$\begin{aligned} 5 - 2x &= 7 \\ -2x &= 2 \\ x &= -1 \end{aligned}$$

And:

$$
\begin{aligned}
-(5-2x) &= 7\\
-5+2x &= 7\\
2x &= 12\\
x &= 6
\end{aligned}
$$

Double-check each possible value for x in the original equation:

$$
\begin{aligned}
|5-2x| &= 7\\
|5-2(-1)| &= 7\\
|5+2| &= 7\\
|7| &= 7 \checkmark
\end{aligned}
$$

And:

$$
\begin{aligned}
|5-2x| &= 7\\
|5-2(6)| &= 7\\
|5-12| &= 7\\
|-7| &= 7 \checkmark
\end{aligned}
$$

Therefore, the solution set is $\{-1, 6\}$.

Alternatively, check the answer choice values by plugging them into the equation, starting with (F).

21. (D) (p. 382) ***Mathematics/Algebra and Functions/Manipulating Algebraic Expressions/Basic Algebraic Manipulations.*** To combine the fractions in the numerator, rewrite them using the lowest common denominator, which is x:

$$
\begin{aligned}
\frac{3-\frac{3}{x}}{x(x-1)} &= \frac{\frac{x}{x}\left(\frac{3}{1}\right)-\left(\frac{3}{x}\right)}{x(x-1)}\\
&= \frac{\frac{3x}{x}-\frac{3}{x}}{x(x-1)}\\
&= \frac{\frac{3(x-1)}{x}}{x(x-1)}\\
&= \frac{3\cancel{(x-1)}}{x}\cdot\frac{1}{x\cancel{(x-1)}} = \frac{3}{x^2}
\end{aligned}
$$

22. (K) (p. 383) ***Mathematics/Algebra and Functions/Coordinate Geometry/Slope of a Line.*** Use the equation for finding the slope of a line, where m is the slope and (x_1, y_1) and (x_2, y_2) are the two given points:

$$
\begin{aligned}
m &= \frac{y_2-y_1}{x_2-x_1}\\
&= \frac{7-5}{4-(-3)}\\
&= \frac{2}{7}
\end{aligned}
$$

23. (E) (p. 383) ***Mathematics/Geometry/Circles* and *Triangles/Pythagorean Theorem.***

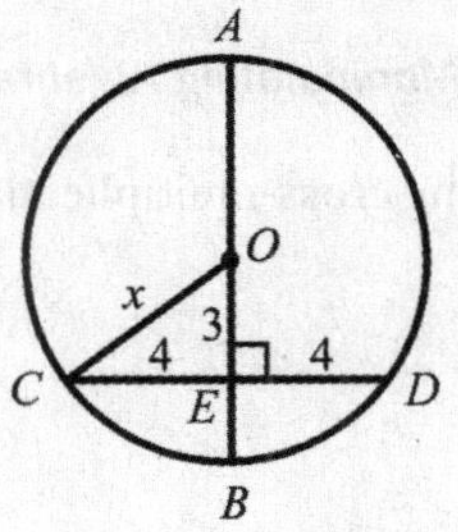

A diameter drawn perpendicular to the chord bisects the chord. Therefore, $\overline{AB}$ bisects $\overline{CD}$. A constructed radius $\overline{OC}$ forms right triangle OEC with $\overline{OC}$ as the hypotenuse. Since $\overline{OE} = 3$ inches and $\overline{CE} = 4$ inches, use the Pythagorean theorem ($a^2 + b^2 = c^2$):

$$(\text{Hypotenuse})^2 = (\text{Leg}_1)^2 + (\text{Leg}_2)^2$$
$$(\overline{OC})^2 = (\overline{OE})^2 + (\overline{CE})^2$$
$$x^2 = 3^2 + 4^2$$
$$x^2 = 25$$
$$x = \pm 5$$

Since length must be positive, the radius is 5.

24. (F) (p. 383) ***Mathematics/Geometry/Lines and Angles.*** The diagonals of a parallelogram bisect each other. Therefore:

$$\overline{DB} = 2(\overline{DE})$$
$$4x + 2 = 2(x + 4)$$
$$4x + 2 = 2x + 8$$
$$2x = 6$$
$$x = 3$$

25. (E) (p. 384) ***Mathematics/Geometry/Lines and Angles* and *Circles* and *Number and Quantity/Rates and Proportions.*** Since a figure isn't provided, draw one:

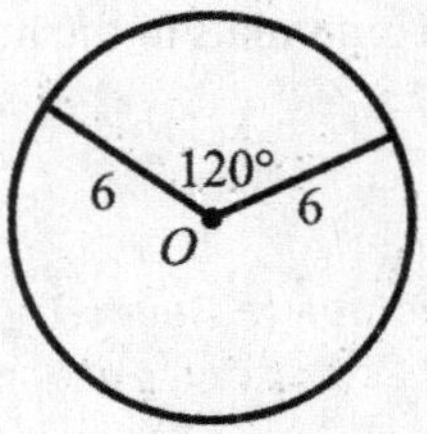

$$x = \text{area of sector}$$
$$\pi r^2 = \text{area of circle}$$

$$\frac{\text{area of sector}}{\text{area of circle}} = \frac{\text{central angle}}{360°}$$
$$\frac{x}{\pi r^2} = \frac{120°}{360°}$$
$$\frac{x}{36\pi} = \frac{1}{3}$$
$$3x = 36\pi$$
$$x = 12\pi$$

26. **(F) (p. 384)** ***Mathematics/Statistics and Probability/Sets.*** For all conditional statements, the original statement and its contrapositive are equivalent, "if *p*, then *q*" is equivalent to "if not *q*, then not *p*."

27. **(B) (p. 384)** ***Mathematics/Algebra and Functions/Manipulating Algebraic Expressions/Basic Algebraic Manipulations.***

Compare all the answer choices to the original using cross-multiplication. The original is $\frac{a}{b}=\frac{r}{t} \Rightarrow at=br$.

A. $\frac{a}{r}=\frac{b}{t}$

$at=br$ ✓

B. $\frac{a}{t}=\frac{b}{r}$

$ar=bt$ ✗

C. $\frac{a+b}{b}=\frac{r+t}{t}$

$t(a+b)=b(r+t)$

$at+bt=br+bt$

$at=br$ ✓

D. $\frac{b}{a}=\frac{t}{r}$

$at=br$ ✓

E. $at=br$ ✓

28. **(K) (p. 384)** ***Mathematics/Algebra and Functions/Solving Algebraic Equations or Inequalities with One Variable/ Simple Equations.*** Simply solve the given equation for *x*:

$$
\begin{aligned}
-2x+5 &= 2-(5-2x) \\
&= 2-5+2x \\
&= -3+2x \\
5 &= -3+4x \\
8 &= 4x \\
x &= 2
\end{aligned}
$$

29. **(E) (p. 385)** ***Mathematics/Geometry/Trigonometry/Trigonometric Relationships.*** Use the trigonometric relationships to evaluate the given expression. First, multiply the binomials in the numerator and in the denominator using the FOIL (First, Inner, Outer, Last) method:

$$
\begin{aligned}
\frac{(1+\sin x)(1-\sin x)}{(1+\cos x)(1-\cos x)} &= \frac{1-\sin x+\sin x-\sin^2 x}{1-\cos x+\cos x-\cos^2 x} \\
&= \frac{1-\sin^2 x}{1-\cos^2 x}
\end{aligned}
$$

Using the identity $\sin^2 x+\cos^2 x=1$, we have:

$$
\begin{aligned}
\sin^2 x+\cos^2 x &= 1 \\
\cos^2 x &= 1-\sin^2 x \\
\sin^2 x &= 1-\cos^2 x
\end{aligned}
$$

Therefore, by substitution:

$$\frac{1-\sin^2 x}{1-\cos^2 x}=\frac{\cos^2 x}{\sin^2 x}=\cot^2 x$$

30. (H) (p. 385) ***Mathematics/Geometry/Triangles/Properties of Triangles.*** The median to the hypotenuse of a right triangle is equal in length to half the hypotenuse ($\overline{BE} = \overline{AE} = \overline{CE}$):

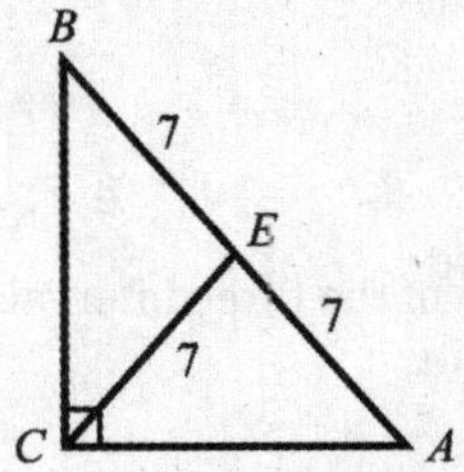

31. (E) (p. 385) ***Mathematics/Number and Quantity/Rates and Proportions.*** Since y varies directly as x, $\frac{y_1}{x_1} = \frac{y_2}{x_2}$. Therefore:

$$\frac{10}{\frac{1}{5}} = \frac{y}{\frac{1}{2}}$$
$$10(5) = y(2)$$
$$50 = 2y$$
$$y = 25$$

32. (G) (p. 385) ***Mathematics/Number and Quantity/Basic Arithmetic Manipulations.*** Cancel like terms in the numerator and denominator until the given expression is simplified:

$$\frac{(-1)(\cancel{2})(-\cancel{3})(\cancel{4})(-\cancel{5})}{(\cancel{5})(-\cancel{4})(\cancel{3})(-\cancel{2})(1)} = \frac{(-1)(\cancel{-1})(\cancel{-1})}{(\cancel{-1})(\cancel{-1})} = -1$$

33. (B) (p. 386) ***Mathematics/Number and Quantity/Properties of Numbers.*** The factors of 36 are: 1 and 36, 2 and 18, 3 and 12, 4 and 9, 6 and 6. Of those factors, only 2 and 3 are prime numbers. Therefore, 36 has only two positive prime factors.

34. (H) (p. 386) ***Mathematics/Geometry/Triangles/Properties of Triangles and Lines and Angles.*** An isosceles triangle has two equal sides and two equal base angles:

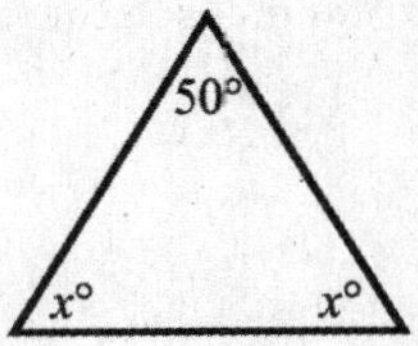

$$50 + x + x = 180$$
$$50 + 2x = 180$$
$$2x = 130$$
$$x = 65$$

35. (B) (p. 386) ***Mathematics/Statistics and Probability/Measures of Center.*** The median is the "middle" data element when the data are arranged in numerical order. There are 15 total terms, so the median is the 8th term. Since the highest score in the table is 50 and there are 7 scores of 50, the next lowest score will be the 8th term (counting terms from greatest to least) and the median: 30.

36. **(F) (p. 386)** ***Mathematics/Algebra and Functions/Solving Quadratic Equations and Relations.*** First, rewrite the inequality as an equation, factor, and solve:

$$x^2 - 2x - 3 = 0$$
$$(x-3)(x+1) = 0$$
$$x = 3 \text{ or } x = -1$$

Next, plot –1 and 3 on a number line and test each of the three intervals. Select any value from each of the three intervals, and determine if the inequality holds true.

From the first interval, $x < -1$, test $x = -5$ in the original inequality: $(-5)^2 - 2(-5) - 3 > 0 \Rightarrow 32 > 0$, which is true. This means we can eliminate (H) and (J).

Test the values $x = 3$ and $x = -1$ to determine whether (F), (G), or (K) is correct: each results in the original inequality being $0 > 0$, which is false, so they are not included in the solution set. Note that "not included" in the solution is indicated by an open circle above a value on the number line.

37. **(D) (p. 387)** ***Mathematics/Geometry/Trigonometry/Trigonometric Relationships.*** To simplify this expression, a common denominator is required. The lowest common denominator is sin *x*:

$$\frac{\sin x}{1}\left(\frac{\sin x}{\sin x}\right) + \frac{\cos^2 x}{\sin x} = \frac{\sin^2 x}{\sin x} + \frac{\cos^2 x}{\sin x}$$
$$= \frac{\sin^2 x + \cos^2 x}{\sin x}$$

Since $\sin^2 x + \cos^2 x = 1$, the expression reduces to $\frac{1}{\sin x}$.

38. **(K) (p. 387)** ***Mathematics/Number and Quantity/Basic Arithmetic Manipulations.*** Perform the indicated operations. When in doubt, write it out:

$$(2.5 \times 10^5)^2 = (2.5 \times 10^5)(2.5 \times 10^5)$$
$$= (2.5)^2 (10^5)^2$$
$$= (2.5)(2.5)(10^{5+5})$$
$$= 6.25 \times 10^{10}$$

39. **(E) (p. 387)** ***Mathematics/Algebra and Functions/Evaluating, Interpreting, and Creating Algebraic Functions/Function Notation.*** Substitute 2 for *x* in $f(x)$ and evaluate:

$$f(x) = \frac{-2x - x}{-x}$$
$$f(2) = \frac{(-2)(2) - 2}{-2}$$
$$= \frac{-4-2}{-2}$$
$$= \frac{-6}{-2}$$
$$= 3$$

40. **(F) (p. 387)** ***Mathematics/Algebra and Functions/Solving Quadratic Equations and Relations.*** Substitute the root for x in the equation and evaluate:

$$\begin{aligned} x^2 + kx - 12 &= 0 \\ (4)^2 + k(4) - 12 &= 0 \\ 16 + 4k - 12 &= 0 \\ 4k + 4 &= 0 \\ 4k &= -4 \\ k &= -1 \end{aligned}$$

41. **(E) (p. 388)** ***Mathematics/Geometry/Triangles/Properties of Triangles*** **and** ***Number and Quantity/Rates and Proportions.*** If $\overline{AB} = 10$ and $\overline{DB} = 4$, then $\overline{AD} = 6$; if $\overline{BC} = 20$ and $\overline{EC} = x$, then $\overline{BE} = 20 - x$.

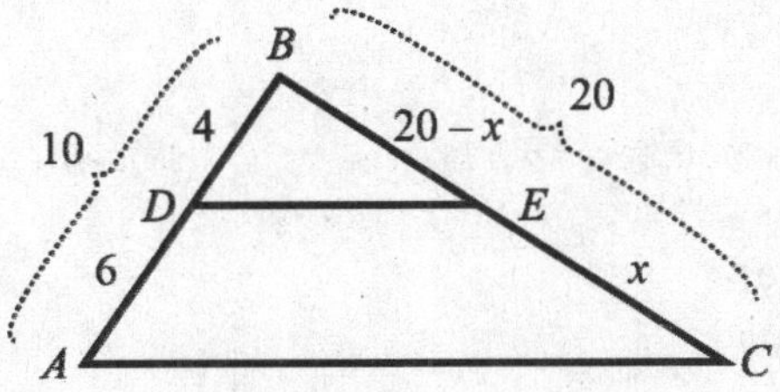

Since ΔABC and ΔDBE are similar triangles, create a proportion between the sides of the two triangles:

$$\begin{aligned} \frac{\overline{AD}}{\overline{AB}} &= \frac{\overline{CE}}{\overline{BC}} \\ \frac{6}{10} &= \frac{x}{20} \\ 10x &= 120 \\ x &= 12 \end{aligned}$$

42. **(H) (p. 388)** ***Mathematics/Algebra and Functions/Manipulating Algebraic Expressions/Basic Algebraic Manipulations.*** Expand each of the binomials in the expression by distribution according to the FOIL method (First, Outer, Inner, Last):

$$\begin{aligned} (x+2)(x-4) &= x^2 - 4x + 2x - 8 \\ &= x^2 - 2x - 8 \end{aligned}$$

And:

$$\begin{aligned} (x+4)(x-2) &= x^2 - 2x + 4x - 8 \\ &= x^2 + 2x - 8 \end{aligned}$$

Now, subtract the second expression from the first expression:

$$x^2 - 2x - 8 - (x^2 + 2x - 8) = -2x - 2x = -4x$$

43. **(B) (p. 388)** ***Mathematics/Geometry/Lines and Angles.*** The sum of the measures of the exterior angles of a polygon is 360° for all polygons. The sum of the measures of the interior angles of a polygon can be expressed as $180°(n-2)$, where n is the number of sides. Therefore:

$$\begin{aligned} 180(n-2) &= 360 \\ n - 2 &= 2 \\ n &= 4 \end{aligned}$$

44. (G) (p. 388) ***Mathematics/Geometry/Triangles/Properties of Triangles.*** If the perimeter is 12, then each side of the triangle is $\frac{12}{3} = 4$. The area of a triangle is $\frac{bh}{2}$, where b is the base and h is the height. So, draw a figure:

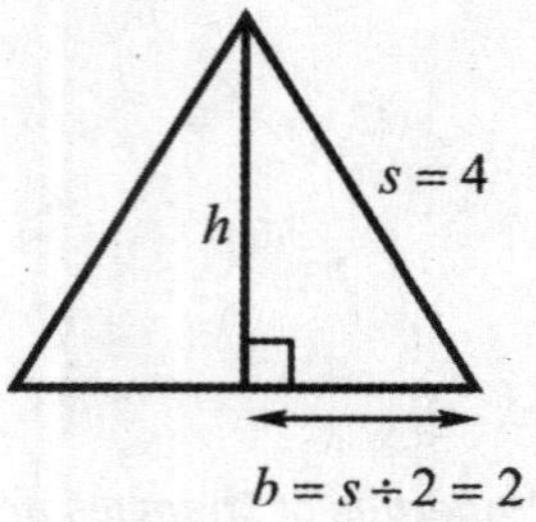

Use the Pythagorean theorem to solve for h:

$$\begin{aligned} 2^2 + h^2 &= 4^2 \\ h^2 &= 16 - 4 \\ &= 12 \\ h &= \pm\sqrt{12} = 2\sqrt{3} \text{ (length is positive)} \end{aligned}$$

Therefore:

$$\begin{aligned} \text{Area}_{\text{triangle}} &= \frac{sh}{2} \\ &= \frac{4(2\sqrt{3})}{2} \\ &= 4\sqrt{3} \end{aligned}$$

Alternatively, if you remember the formula for the area of an equilateral triangle, you can use that:

$$\begin{aligned} \text{Area}_{\text{equilateral triangle}} &= \frac{s^2\sqrt{3}}{4} \\ &= \frac{4^2\sqrt{3}}{4} \\ &= \frac{16\sqrt{3}}{4} \\ &= 4\sqrt{3} \end{aligned}$$

45. (A) (p. 389) ***Mathematics/Geometry/Lines and Angles.*** Let $8x$ equal one angle and x equal the other angle. Since complementary angles add to 90°, we have:

$$\begin{aligned} 8x + x &= 90° \\ 9x &= 90° \\ x &= 10° \end{aligned}$$

46. (H) (p. 389) ***Mathematics/Statistics and Probability/Probability.*** A square has four right angles; a rectangle has four right angles; a trapezoid does not have four right angles; a circle has no angles. Thus, the probability of four right angles is:

$$\frac{\text{\# of successes}}{\text{\# of possibilities}} = \frac{2}{4} = \frac{1}{2}$$

47. (C) (p. 389) *Mathematics/Number and Quantity/Rates and Proportions.* Set up a direct proportion:

$$\frac{320 \text{ miles}}{x \text{ miles}} = \frac{8 \text{ hours}}{2 \text{ hours}}$$

$$x \text{ miles} = \frac{320 \text{ miles} \cdot 2 \cancel{\text{hours}}}{8 \cancel{\text{hours}}}$$

$$= 80 \text{ miles}$$

Or, calculate the rate:

$$r \text{ miles per hour}(t \text{ hours}) = d \text{ miles}$$
$$r \text{ miles per hour}(8 \text{ hours}) = 320 \text{ miles}$$
$$r = 40 \text{ miles per hour}$$

So, traveling at a rate of 40 mph for 2 hours equals $\left(\frac{40 \text{ miles}}{\cancel{\text{hour}}}\right)\left(\frac{2 \cancel{\text{hours}}}{2}\right) = 80$ miles.

48. (H) (p. 389) *Mathematics/Geometry/Trigonometry/Trigonometric Relationships.* Use the common denominator, $(\sin x)(\cos x)$, to simplify the expression and apply the Pythagorean trigonometric identity $(\sin x^2 + \cos x^2 = 1)$:

$$\frac{\sin x}{\cos x}\left(\frac{\sin x}{\sin x}\right) + \frac{\cos x}{\sin x}\left(\frac{\cos x}{\cos x}\right)$$

$$= \frac{\sin^2 x}{(\sin x)(\cos x)} + \frac{\cos^2 x}{(\sin x)(\cos x)}$$

$$= \frac{\sin^2 x + \cos^2 x}{(\sin x)(\cos x)}$$

$$= \frac{1}{(\sin x)(\cos x)}$$

49. (E) (p. 390) *Mathematics/Statistics and Probability/Measures of Center.* The mode is the data element with the greatest frequency: 91° F.

50. (F) (p. 390) *Mathematics/Number and Quantity/Percentages.* Simplify the stem: "9 is what percent of 30?" Set up the "is-over-of" equation and solve for the missing value:

$$\frac{\text{is}}{\text{of}} = \frac{\%}{100}$$

$$\frac{9}{30} = \frac{x}{100}$$

$$x = \frac{9(100)}{30}$$

$$= 30\%$$

51. (B) (p. 390) *Mathematics/Algebra and Functions/Manipulating Algebraic Expressions/Factoring Expressions.* Rearrange the expression and then factor:

$$-7t + 6t^2 - 3 = 6t^2 - 7t - 3$$
$$= (3t+1)(2t-3)$$

52. (G) (p. 390) *Mathematics/Algebra and Functions/Solving Algebraic Equations or Inequalities with One Variable/ Equations Involving Integer and Rational Exponents.* If $2^{x^2+2x} = 2^{-1}$, then $x^2 + 2x = -1$. Thus: $x^2 + 2x + 1 = (x+1)(x+1) = 0$. This equation holds true only if $x = -1$.

53. (E) (p. 390) *Mathematics/Algebra and Functions/Evaluating, Interpreting, and Creating Algebraic Functions/Functions as Models.* If Joshua is *x* years old now and Jessica is 3 years younger, then Jessica is now $x - 3$ years old. Four years ago she was $(x-3) - 4 = x - 7$ years old.

54. (F) (p. 391) *Mathematics/Algebra and Functions/Evaluating, Interpreting, and Creating Algebraic Functions/Functions as Models.* The amount collected is equal to the number of students multiplied by the amount that each student contributed. Therefore:

$$x \cancel{\text{students}} \cdot \frac{y \text{ dollars}}{\cancel{\text{student}}} = \$18$$

$$xy = 18$$

And adding three more students, but with all paying one dollar less, changes the equation to $(x+3)(y-1) = 18$.

55. (A) (p. 391) *Mathematics/Number and Quantity/Basic Arithmetic Manipulations.* First, simplify each radical in the expression:

$$\frac{1}{2}\sqrt{112} = \frac{1}{2}(\sqrt{16})(\sqrt{7}) = \frac{1}{2}(4)(\sqrt{7}) = 2\sqrt{7}$$

$$\sqrt{28} = \sqrt{4}\sqrt{7} = 2\sqrt{7}$$

$$2\sqrt{63} = 2(\sqrt{9})(\sqrt{7}) = 2(3)(\sqrt{7}) = 6\sqrt{7}$$

Now, combine the parts as indicated in the stem:

$$\frac{1}{2}\sqrt{112} - \sqrt{28} + 2\sqrt{63} = 2\sqrt{7} - 2\sqrt{7} + 6\sqrt{7} = 6\sqrt{7}$$

56. (G) (p. 391) *Mathematics/Algebra and Functions/Solving Simultaneous Equations.* The stem asks for the value of *x*, so add the two equations to eliminate the *y* variable:

$$\begin{array}{rl} & \frac{1}{x} + \frac{1}{y} = \frac{1}{4} \\ + & \frac{1}{x} - \frac{1}{y} = \frac{3}{4} \\ \hline & \frac{2}{x} = 1 \Rightarrow x = 2 \end{array}$$

57. (D) (p. 391) *Mathematics/Geometry/Triangles/Properties of Triangles.* The sum of the lengths of any two sides of a triangle must be greater than the length of the third side. Check each of the answer choices:

A. $1 + 3 > 6$ ✗
B. $2 + 4 > 7$ ✗
C. $2 + 10 > 12$ ✗
D. $4 + 6 > 8$ ✓
   $4 + 8 > 6$ ✓
   $6 + 8 > 4$ ✓
E. $4 + 4 > 10$ ✗

58. (H) (p. 392) *Mathematics/Algebra and Functions/Solving Simultaneous Equations.* To eliminate the variable *y*, multiply the first equation by -1 and add the equations:

$$\begin{aligned} -ax - y &= -b \\ +\ 2ax + y &= 2b \\ \hline ax &= b \\ x &= \frac{b}{a} \end{aligned}$$

Substitute $\frac{b}{a}$ for *x* in the first equation and solve for *y*:

$$\begin{aligned} a\left(\frac{b}{a}\right) + y &= b \\ b + y &= b \\ y &= 0 \end{aligned}$$

The solution set $\{x, y\}$ is $\left\{\frac{b}{a}, 0\right\}$.

59. (A) (p. 392) *Mathematics/Geometry/Trigonometry/Determining Trigonometric Values and Triangles/Pythagorean Theorem.* Since $\sin\theta = \frac{\text{side opposite } \theta}{\text{hypotenuse}}$, we have:

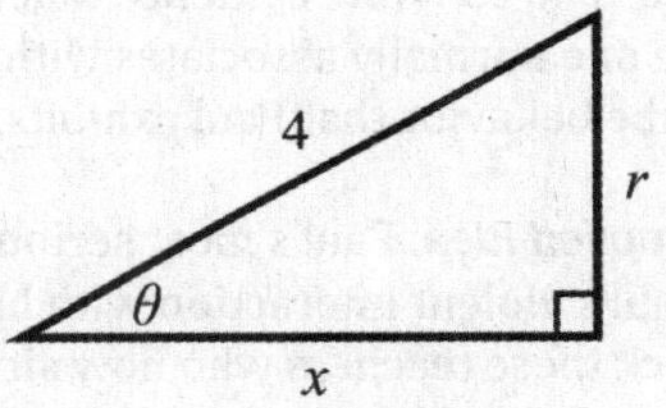

The third side of the triangle, *x*, is found using the Pythagorean theorem:

$$\begin{aligned} x^2 + r^2 &= 4^2 \\ &= 16 \\ x^2 &= 16 - r^2 \\ x &= \pm\sqrt{16 - r^2} \\ &= \sqrt{16 - r^2} \text{ (length is positive)} \end{aligned}$$

Since $\cos\theta = \frac{\text{side adjacent to } \theta}{\text{hypotenuse}}$, $\cos\theta = \frac{\sqrt{16 - r^2}}{4}$.

60. (G) (p. 392) *Mathematics/Number and Quantity/Rates and Proportions.* The number of sheets is directly proportional to the number of machines, as well as directly proportional to the amount of time. Thus:

$$\left(\frac{\text{sheets}}{\text{\# of machines} \cdot \text{time}}\right)_1 = \left(\frac{\text{sheets}}{\text{\# of machines} \cdot \text{time}}\right)_2$$

$$\begin{aligned} \frac{300}{3(3)} &= \frac{600}{6(t)} \\ \frac{300}{9} &= \frac{600}{6t} \\ \frac{100}{3} &= \frac{100}{t} \\ 100t &= 300 \\ t &= 3 \end{aligned}$$

Section 3: Reading

1. **(A) (p. 395) *Reading/Craft and Structure/Main Idea.*** A person's temperament is their usual mood or attitude towards the world, and it is an outgrowth of a person's character. For this reason, (A) is the correct answer choice. Cather's general purpose is to dramatize and examine how a certain type of character, or a person of a certain mood or attitude, responds to the world around him. As for the other answer choices, (B) and (C) are incorrect because they are not broad enough to encompass Cather's general purpose; how a person reacts under pressure, (B), and how a person changes over time, (C), are aspects of temperament, but Cather is interested in more than just these single aspects. Finally, (D) is incorrect because it is too general; as explained above, Cather is interested in a topic much more specific than people in general and their settings.

2. **(J) (p. 395) *Reading/Key Ideas and Details/Implied Idea.*** These phrases, as well as several other details throughout the passage, show Paul in a very unsympathetic light. Paul is shown to be an unpleasant character, (III), and the unrelenting nature of the negative description reveals that the narrator finds Paul to be unpleasant as well, (II). These introductory phrases do not describe Paul's reactions to his peers, (I), though, so (J) is the correct answer choice.

3. **(B) (p. 395) *Reading/Key Ideas and Details/Explicit Detail.*** At the end of the first paragraph, Cather describes a red carnation that Paul wears in his buttonhole. She says "This latter adornment the faculty somehow felt was not properly significant of the contrite spirit befitting a boy under the ban of suspension" (lines 11–14). In other words, the faculty does not find Paul's way of dressing appropriate to the situation at hand. So, (B) is the correct answer choice. As for the other answer choices, (A) is incorrect because the faculty considers the red carnation to be an act of defiance. (C) and (D) are both incorrect because there is simply no evidence to support either idea.

4. **(H) (p. 395) *Reading/Craft and Structure/Vocabulary.*** Although the descriptions in lines 17 and 35 suggest that Paul is unable to control his odd mannerisms, there is no concrete evidence that he suffers from delirium, (F); raving, (G); or frothing, (J). These are all conditions which one normally associates with intense physical illness or psychosis, and these are diagnoses that seem too severe for the behavior that Paul exhibits. So, (H) is the correct answer choice.

5. **(D) (p. 395) *Reading/Key Ideas and Details/Implied Idea.*** Paul's most serious flaw is vividly described and analyzed in lines 38–53. In these lines, Cather shows Paul's violent interaction with his English teacher, his habit of ignoring teachers during class, and his tendency to mock these teachers who now sit in judgment of him. In short, it is Paul's inability to hide his contempt for others that has landed him in trouble. So, (D) is the correct answer choice. As for the other answer choices, they are all incorrect simply because there is no evidence to support these ideas.

6. **(G) (p. 395) *Reading/Key Ideas and Details/Explicit Detail.*** In lines 56–57, Cather compares the faculty to a pack of predators. Specifically, she writes that they "fell upon him without mercy, his English teacher leading the pack." So, (G) is the correct answer choice.

7. **(A) (p. 395) *Reading/Key Ideas and Details/Implied Idea.*** In lines 62–63, Cather writes that "Older boys than Paul had broken down and shed tears under that baptism of fire." The "baptism of fire" is the inquisition performed by the faculty into student misbehaviors. So, (A) is the correct answer choice. As Cather says, most students broke down during such inquisitions. However, Paul manages the entire experience without any visible show of emotion at all.

8. **(H) (p. 395) *Reading/Craft and Structure/Vocabulary.*** Cather writes that Paul was always smiling, and the faculty attributed his constant smiling to "insolence or 'smartness'" (line 73). "Insolence" means "disrespect" or "rudeness." So, it is logical that "smartness" has a negative connotation in this context. Therefore, (H) is the correct answer choice since "impudence" also means "rudeness" or "disrespect." As for the other answer choices, they are all incorrect because they do not have the negative connotations required here.

9. **(D) (p. 395) *Reading/Key Ideas and Details/Implied Idea.*** In lines 25–27, Cather focuses on Paul's tendency to lie. As she writes, "Paul was quite accustomed to lying" (line 26). A person who lies cannot be described as "candid" or honest, so (D) is the correct answer choice. As for the other answer choices, Paul is shown to be defiant, (A); proud, (B); and flippant, (C), throughout the passage.

10. **(F) (p. 395) *Reading/Integration of Knowledge and Ideas/Implied Idea.*** (D) In the final paragraph, the drawing-master raises the point of Paul's early life and theorizes that the death of his mother might have had an emotional effect on Paul. He uses this information to conclude that Paul's problem is not the usual insolence of teenagers but something different. Thus the drawing-master is suggesting that the incidents for which he has been called before the principal are not entirely his fault.

11. (B) (p. 397) *Reading/Key Ideas and Details/Explicit Detail.* The correct answer choice is (B). In lines 7–9, the author says Joseph Rainey was the first African American elected to the House. As for the other answer choices, (A) is incorrect because Hiram Revels was the first African American in the Senate. (C) is incorrect because Joseph Rainey was from South Carolina. (D) is incorrect because there is no evidence in the passage that Rainey was a former slave.

12. (F) (p. 397) *Reading/Key Ideas and Details/Explicit Detail.* The correct answer choice is (F). In the last sentence of the third paragraph, the author states that since "the 1930s, nearly all African American representatives have been Democrats."

13. (A) (p. 397) *Reading/Key Ideas and Details/Explicit Detail.* In lines 20–21, the author says African American leaders after the Civil War "nearly all adhered to the Republican Party." In lines 47–48, the author then says that "Since the 1930s, nearly all African American representatives have been Democrats." So, (A) is the correct answer choice. The other answer choices are all contradicted by the fourth paragraph where the author details the activities of African American members of Congress during both the nineteenth and the twentieth century.

14. (H) (p. 397) *Reading/Craft and Structure/Implied Idea.* In lines 58–61, the author writes that "In the mid-twentieth century, African American representatives turned to the needs of urban areas. They asked for improved housing and job training." Given the context of this sentence, it is clear that "turned to" means "concentrated" or "devoted themselves to." So, (H) is correct. (F) and (G) are incorrect because they are the exact opposite of what the author intends to say in the above sentence. (J) is incorrect because the African American representatives did more than just "refer" to these issues; they dedicated themselves and took action to achieve specific goals related to these issues.

15. (A) (p. 397) *Reading/Key Ideas and Details/Explicit Detail.* In lines 37–40, the author writes that an "African American migration to northern cities established the foundation for political organization in urban centers" after World War I and in the following decade. So, (A) is the correct answer choice. As for the other answer choices, (B) and (D) are both incorrect because there is no evidence in the passage to support these ideas. (C) is incorrect because lines 47–48 indicate African American representatives from all regions of America were nearly all Democrats.

16. (J) (p. 397) *Reading/Key Ideas and Details/Explicit Detail.* Voting rights, (F), are mentioned or implied in lines 27, 55, and 69. Educational opportunities, (G), are mentioned or implied in lines 57 and 70. Finally, employment, (H), is mentioned or implied in lines 61 and 70. Only the issue of protecting people of African descent in other countries is not mentioned in the passage. So, (J) is the correct answer choice.

17. (C) (p. 397) *Reading/Key Ideas and Details/Explicit Detail.* In lines 12–18 and lines 29–32, the author discusses the strength of African American political organizations in southern states during the nineteenth century. In lines 36–40, the author mentions the strength of African American political organizations in northern states during the twentieth century. So, (C) is correct. As for the other answer choices, (A) is incorrect because the civil rights movement did not occur until the second half of the twentieth century. (B) is incorrect because, while the Fifteenth Amendment is mentioned in lines 2–3, it is not cited as a reason why African Americans won congressional seats during these two time periods. Finally, (D) is incorrect since there is no evidence to support this idea.

18. (J) (p. 398) *Reading/Key Ideas and Details/Explicit Detail.* In lines 65–72, the author discusses the Congressional Black Caucus. Specifically, the author says that the caucus "offered a formal means of representing the combined interests of African Americans." So, (J) is the correct answer choice. As for the other answer choices, (F) is incorrect because it is contradicted by lines 71–72. (G) and (H) are incorrect because there is no evidence in the passage to support these ideas.

19. (B) (p. 398) *Reading/Key Ideas and Details/Main Idea.* In the last paragraph, the author specifically mentions the "biographies of African Americans who served in the House and Senate" (lines 92–93) as well as "their stories" (line 95). Based on these details, it is logical to assume that this passage could serve as the introduction to a collection of biographies of African American members of Congress. So, (B) is the correct answer choice. As for the other answer choices, they are all incorrect because there is no evidence in the final paragraph to support these ideas.

20. (G) (p. 398) *Reading/Key Ideas and Details/Implied Idea.* In lines 96–98, the author praises African American members of Congress for their "long struggle to extend the ideals of the founders to include all citizens of the United States." In other words, they are praised for their efforts to ensure the rights of all Americans. So, (G) is the correct answer choice. As for the other answer choices, (F) is incorrect because it is never mentioned in the passage. (H) and (J) are incorrect because they are contradicted by the above quotation.

21. **(B) (p. 399)** ***Reading/Craft and Structure/Implied Idea.*** Jupiter is asked to decide which of three goddesses is the fairest—Juno, Minerva, or Venus. Regardless of which goddess he selects, he will anger the other two because he did not choose them. It is a no-win proposition in that he is bound to offend someone. So, (B) is the correct answer choice. As for the other answer choices, they are all incorrect since there is no evidence to support these ideas.

22. **(F) (p. 400)** ***Reading/Craft and Structure/Vocabulary.*** The passage tells us that "Ulysses, who had married Penelope, and was very happy in his wife and child, had no disposition to embark in such a troublesome affair" (lines 38–40). Given the context, it is clear that "disposition" means "inclination." In other words, Ulysses had no inclination to embark on the adventure since he is happy at home with his family. So, (F) is the correct answer choice. As for the other answer choices, they are all incorrect because they cannot substitute for "disposition" and create a sentence with the same meaning as the original

23. **(C) (p. 400)** ***Reading/Craft and Structure/Voice.*** In lines 1–2, the author asserts that Minerva once did a foolish thing, (A). In lines 33–34, the author asserts that the poems of Homer and Virgil were great, (B), as well as that the greatest poems of antiquity were about the Trojan War, (D). Nowhere in the passage, though, does the author claim that Helen was the fairest of her sex. Instead, it is Venus who identifies Helen as "the fairest of her sex" (line 24) and destines her for a relationship with Paris. So, (C) is the correct answer choice.

24. **(F) (p. 400)** ***Reading/Key Ideas and Details/Implied Idea.*** In line 43, the author says "Ulysses pretended to be mad" in order to avoid going off to war. The author then says Ulysses attempted to prove his madness by hitching a mismatched pair of animals together ("an ass and an ox") and sowing into the ground something that could never grow—salt. So, (F) is the correct answer choice. As for the other answer choices, they are all incorrect since there is no evidence to support these ideas.

25. **(C) (p. 400)** ***Reading/Craft and Structure/Implied Idea.*** In lines 45–49, Palamades visits Ulysses to take him to war. Ulysses does not wish to go and pretends to be insane. Palamades is skeptical of Ulysses' act, though, and thinks up a way to test him. He puts Ulysses' child in the path of a sharp plow that Ulysses steers across a field. Ulysses steers the plow so his young child's life is spared, proving that he is indeed sane. (C) is the correct answer choice because Palamades tries Ulysses in this manner to test him. As for the other answer choices, they are all incorrect because there is no evidence to support these ideas.

26. **(J) (p. 400)** ***Reading/Craft and Structure/Implied Idea.*** In lines 54–57, the author explains how Thetis, "one of the immortals, a sea nymph" tried to prevent her son Achilles from going off to war because she knew "that her son was fated to perish before Troy if he went on the expedition." Instead of stating explicitly that Thetis could read the future, the author merely mentions her immortal status and expects the reader to understand that this means she can see into the future. So, (J) is the correct answer choice. As for the other answer choices, they are all incorrect because there is no evidence to support these ideas.

27. **(C) (p. 400)** ***Reading/Key Ideas and Details/Explicit Detail.*** Juno, Venus, and Minerva, (A), are the goddesses mentioned in the first paragraph. Paris, (B), is "the beautiful shepherd" (line 12) who is asked to decide which of the goddesses is fairest. Eris and Thetis, (D), are the goddess of Discord (line 6) and a sea-nymph (line 55) respectively. Finally, in lines 35–36, the author says "Menelaus called upon his brother chieftains of Greece to fulfill their pledge." The author then explains how Ulysses and Achilles were gathered for the impending war; in other words, they too are chieftains of Greece. So, (C) is the correct answer choice.

28. **(F) (p. 400)** ***Reading/Key Ideas and Details/Implied Idea.*** Readers are expected to understand Ulysses' clever ploy at King Lycomedes' court even though it is not entirely spelled out. In short, Ulysses visits the court because he knows Achilles is hiding there. Ulysses disguises himself as a merchant and pretends to sell "female ornaments" (lines 61–62) to the women at the court. Mixed into this collection of ornaments, though, are several weapons ("some arms"). Now Achilles, who has disguised himself as a woman so he won't be recognized, comes to look through the wares being offered by this new merchant. Achilles looks only at the weapons and ignores the "female ornaments" entirely. In this manner, Achilles betrays himself "to the keen eye of Ulysses" (lines 65–67) and is discovered. (F) is the correct answer choice because, as shown above, the purpose of Ulysses' clever ploy is to trick Achilles into revealing himself.

29. **(C) (p. 400)** ***Reading/Key Ideas and Details/Development.*** In lines 55–56, the passage foreshadows the death of Achilles by telling us that Thetis knows "her son was fated to perish before Troy if he went on the expedition." So, (I) is true. In lines 31–34, the author describes Helen's elopement with Paris to Troy, from "whence arose the famous Trojan War"; in addition, the second paragraph describes the gathering of chieftains in preparation for war. So, (II) is true. Nowhere in the passage, though, is the downfall of Paris mentioned. So, only (I) and (II) are true. Therefore, (C) is the correct answer choice.

30. **(G) (p. 400)** ***Reading/Key Ideas and Details/Main Idea.*** (G) The feature of the story that is most striking is the use of tricks to attain results: Eris's strategy with the golden apple, Ulysses's pretending to be mad, Peleus's trick to get Ulysses to show that he was not really mad, Ulysses's trick on Achilles, and, of course, the grand finale of the "Trojan Horse."

31. **(D) (p. 402)** ***Reading/Key Ideas and Details/Explicit Detail.*** Lines 53–54 state that X-rays are found at wavelengths shorter than 100 Å, which is the lower end of ultraviolet radiation. The correct answer choice is (D).

32. **(G) (p. 402)** ***Reading/Key Ideas and Details/Explicit Detail.*** Lines 59–61 explain that short wavelengths contain a high amount of energy, which makes them more dangerous than long wavelengths. So, the correct answer choice is (G).

33. **(D) (p. 402)** ***Reading/Key Ideas and Details/Explicit Detail.*** The definition appears in lines 75–76. In short, it is the wavelength at which an object emits the maximum amount of energy. So, (D) is the correct answer choice.

34. **(G) (p. 402)** ***Reading/Key Ideas and Details/Main Idea.*** Lines 31–34 state the main point of the paragraph, which is to define the concept of black body radiation. So, (G) is the correct answer choice.

35. **(B) (p. 402)** ***Reading/Key Ideas and Details/Explicit Detail.*** According to the fifth paragraph, ultraviolet radiation is the radiation with wavelengths from 4,000 Å down to 100 Å.

36. **(J) (p. 402)** ***Reading/Key Ideas and Details/Explicit Detail.*** In lines 55–58, the passage states that we cannot see the radiation from a heat lamp but do experience it as warmth. Radiation of wavelengths 7,000 Å to 1 mm is infrared radiation. So, (J) is the correct answer choice.

37. **(D) (p. 402)** ***Reading/Key Ideas and Details/Explicit Detail.*** In lines 77–88, the author discusses the temperature of stars. In lines 84–85, the author states that "a hot star looks blue." So, (D) is the correct answer choice.

38. **(J) (p. 402)** ***Reading/Key Ideas and Details/Explicit Detail.*** The seventh paragraph describes three types of collisions: gentle, violent, and moderate. Lines 66–68 state that most of the collisions are of moderate intensity and produce photons of intermediate wavelengths. There are fewer gentle, (F), and violent, (G) and (H), collisions.

39. **(A) (p. 402)** ***Reading/Key Ideas and Details/Implied Idea.*** The passage states that the incandescent light bulb is a heated object (lines 30–34). The light is emitted when electrons collide in the filament because the filament is heated (lines 62–68). Therefore, answer (A) is correct.

40. **(G) (p. 402)** ***Reading/Key Ideas and Details/Application.*** The infrared portion of the spectrum includes light of wavelengths longer than the red end of the visible spectrum. These are primarily heatwaves such as those emitted by the human body. Choices (F), (H), and (J) mention sources that emit visible light with wavelengths toward the short wavelength end of the visible spectrum. The cooling embers of a fire, however, would glow orange or red and be emitting radiation at and below the red end of the spectrum.

Section 4: Science

1. **(A) (p. 405)** ***Science/Interpretation of Data/Comprehension.*** The most sensitive curve will have the steepest slope, suggesting the greatest rate of change. The sharpest sloping curve is for potassium nitrate, KNO_3.

2. **(H) (p. 405)** ***Science/Evaluation of Models/Analysis.*** The sodium salts, NaCl and $NaNO_3$, have different solubilities, indicating that solubility depends on more than the nature of sodium. Thus, (F) and (G) must be incorrect. (J) is incorrect because it is not known whether the solubility curves for all sodium compounds have been given. Additionally, the solubility of NaCl is less than 40 grams per 100 grams of water for temperatures lower than 80°C. (H) is correct because it takes into account the differences in solubilities of different sodium salts, as indicated in the given graph.

3. **(D) (p. 405) *Science/Interpretation of Data/Comprehension.*** The graph gives data only for aqueous solutions, not alcoholic. Additionally, the question asks about the volume of the solvent while the table indicates the mass of the solvent.

4. **(J) (p. 405) *Science/Interpretation of Data/Comprehension.*** Since the solubility curves cross at approximately 68°C, the temperature or the mass of the solute needs to be known.

5. **(B) (p. 405) *Science/Evaluation of Models/Application.*** According to the graph, the solubilities of gases (NH_3, SO_2, and HCl) in aqueous solutions decrease with increasing temperature. This implies that (B) is true: soda loses fizz (carbonation) as gas (carbon dioxide) leaves the liquid; in other words, the warmer the soda, the faster it loses carbonation. (A) shows the effect of pressure, not temperature, on solubility. (C) shows the effect of temperature on the solubility of a solid (sugar), which has nothing to do with the solubility characteristics of a gas. (D) deals with relative densities of gases, not with solubilities.

6. **(G) (p. 407) *Science/Interpretation of Data/Comprehension.*** Mercury's period of revolution equals approximately $0.25(\text{period of Earth's revolution}) = 0.25(365.3 \text{ days}) \approx 90 \text{ days}$. Mercury's period of rotation equals approximately $60(\text{period of Earth's rotation}) = 60(1 \text{ day}) = 60 \text{ days}$. The ratio of Mercury's revolution to rotation is $\frac{90}{60} = \frac{3}{2}$.

7. **(A) (p. 407) *Science/Interpretation of Data/Comprehension.*** The first equation given following Table 2 defines the density as the ratio of mass to volume. Look for the planet in Table 2 that has a ratio of mass to volume equal to approximately 1 relative to Earth. Of the choices, only Mercury fits.

8. **(J) (p. 407) *Science/Interpretation of Data/Comprehension.*** According to the second equation given following Table 2, rate is distance divided by time. Divide the average distance to the sun by the period of revolution to get the relative rate. The smallest relative rate is the slowest. In this specific case, the planet with the greatest relative period of revolution orbits the sun at the slowest rate: Neptune.

9. **(B) (p. 407) *Science/Evaluation of Models/Analysis.*** Mercury and Mars have the same surface gravity, but not the same mass or radius, so eliminate (A) and (C). Eliminate (D) because proximity to the sun has no correlation to surface gravity (as surface gravity increases, proximity fluctuates). Therefore, (B) must be correct. Indeed, gravity depends on both the planet radius and on the mass of the planet. Compare Mars and Mercury to see the effect of volume. Mars is more massive, but the smaller size of Mercury gives it an equivalent surface gravity.

10. **(H) (p. 407) *Science/Interpretation of Data/Comprehension.*** Neptune's radius is 3.86 times that of Earth's radius. Therefore $\text{diameter}_{\text{Neptune}} = 2((3.86)(\text{radius}_{\text{Earth}})) = 7.72(\text{radius}_{\text{Earth}})$.

11. **(B) (p. 407) *Science/Interpretation of Data/Comprehension.*** Relative distances to the sun are as follows: 0.39 (Mercury) < 0.723 (Venus) < 1 (Earth) < 1.524 (Mars) < 5.204 (Jupiter) < 9.582 (Saturn) < 19.201 (Uranus) < 30.047 (Neptune). The largest difference is between Uranus and Neptune: 30 – 19 = 11 times Earth's average distance to the sun.

12. **(F) (p. 408) *Science/Evaluation of Models/Analysis.*** The prostate cancer diagnosis rate for a man with 200–239 mg/dL total blood cholesterol is 1.03, while that for a man with less than 160 mg/dL total blood cholesterol is 2.02. Thus, (F) is correct. (G) contradicts the data for colon cancer, (H) ignores the direct relationship between coronary diagnoses and cholesterol intake, and cardiac arrest is a more common diagnosis than cerebral clots for men with total blood cholesterol greater than 240 mg/dL.

13. **(D) (p. 408) *Science/Evaluation of Models/Analysis.*** The depression diagnosis rate for the second, third, and fourth groups is 0.30. This number is lower than for men with less than 160 mg/dL total blood cholesterol, so (A), (B), and (C) are wrong. According to the data, total blood cholesterol of 160–199 mg/dL is just as effective in combating depression as 240+ mg/dL, so (D) is correct.

14. **(J) (p. 408) *Science/Interpretation of Data/Comprehension.*** Although having a total blood cholesterol level of 240+ mg/dL increases coronary arrest to the highest absolute diagnosis rate, the percentage increase is less than 100 percent (from 6.00 to 11.00). The percentage increase for coronary thrombosis is greater than 100 percent (from 5.02 to 10.05).

15. **(C) (p. 408) *Science/Interpretation of Data/Comprehension.*** (C) is the only group in which total blood cholesterol of 160–199 mg/dL decreases the diagnosis rate for all three illnesses. A total blood cholesterol of 160–199 mg/dL raises the probability of diagnosis for lung and colon cancer only. This question is probably best answered by recognizing that fact and eliminating those choices that include either lung or colon cancer: eliminate (A), (B), and (D).

16. **(G) (p. 409) *Science/Scientific Investigation/Application.*** Standardizing the diagnosis rate involves correcting for variables inherent in the subject groups but not involved in the experiment. Age, weight, and genetic histories are just some of the variables that the scientist must consider. (F) does not correct for intrinsic variables; rather, it ignores results that might not conform to a "neat" result. This does not standardize the diagnosis rate so much as "fudge" it. (H) involves an arbitrary assumption that is in fact incorrect. Assuming a zero diagnosis rate in the male population distorts the result of this experiment and does not correct for variations within the subject groups. (J) is incorrect because this experiment does not consider women at all. It might be valid to compare results with a different experiment involving women, but the actual diagnosis rates for men and women for different diseases are not necessarily similar (e.g., the gender-related differences for breast cancer).

17. **(C) (p. 410) *Science/Interpretation of Data/Analysis.*** Since voltage is directly related to current, voltage increases by the same factor as current if other variables are held constant. The same applies for resistance; therefore, the only possible correct formula is (C).

18. **(F) (p. 410) *Science/Interpretation of Data/Application.*** The total resistance R_s of the series resistors is $R_1 + R_2 = 2 + 2 = 4$. This resistance is double that of the circuit where $R = 2$. If R doubles, then the voltage doubles as long as the current remains the same.

19. **(A) (p. 410) *Science/Interpretation of Data/Analysis.*** The passage states that the voltage is directly proportional to the both the resistance and the current ($V \propto IR$), so the circuit with the greater resistance would have the greater voltage. Since resistance is directly proportional to resistivity, the germanium circuit would have the greater resistance and voltage.

20. **(H) (p. 411) *Science/Interpretation of Data/Application.*** Use the given formula for resistors in parallel:

$$\begin{aligned}\frac{1}{R_p} &= \frac{1}{4} + \frac{1}{4} \\ &= \frac{2}{4} \\ &= \frac{1}{2} \\ R_p &= 2\end{aligned}$$

21. **(A) (p. 411) *Science/Interpretation of Data/Application.*** If R is constant, then P increases with I^2; this is the definition of exponential growth.

22. **(J) (p. 411) *Science/Interpretation of Data/Analysis.*** Based on the information given in the passage, we have:

$$V \propto IR$$
$$I \propto \frac{V}{R}$$

Therefore, to keep I constant if V increases, R must be increased.

23. **(D) (p. 412) *Science/Evaluation of Models/Analysis.*** Compare Trials 2 and 3 to see what changing the concentration of only one component has on rate. In this case, there is no change in rate with change in concentration of A, so rate is independent of concentration of A.

24. **(F) (p. 412) *Science/Evaluation of Models/Analysis.*** Compare Trials 1 and 3 or Trials 2 and 4 to see what changing the concentration of only one component has on rate. In this case, rate increases in direct proportion with increasing concentration of A.

25. (C) (p. 413) ***Science/Evaluation of Models/Analysis.*** Compare Trials 1 and 4 or Trials 2 and 3 to see what changing the concentration of only one component has on rate. In this case, rate increases by the square root of the concentration of A.

26. (H) (p. 413) ***Science/Evaluation of Models/Analysis.*** Averaging or intermediate mechanisms do not work because one mechanism (Experiment 1) has no dependence on concentration of A with regard to rate. The likeliest explanation that reconciles Experiment 3 with Experiments 1 and 2 is that a different mechanism causes the reaction.

27. (B) (p. 413) ***Science/Evaluation of Models/Analysis.*** This is a subtle question. (C) and (D) are incorrect because they over-generalize from a single case. It cannot be said that mechanisms can always be changed, (C), or that in every case the mechanism depends on solvent effects, (D). (A) is a special case of (D), where the claim is made that all reactions are solvent dependent. (B) alone allows for the possibility that solvents need not have an effect (note the word "may").

28. (G) (p. 414) ***Science/Interpretation of Data/Comprehension.*** Since every object starts at 0 ft/sec, compare the instantaneous velocity of each object at a given time ($\frac{\Delta v}{\Delta t}$). For example, at 2 seconds the instantaneous velocity of the ball was 7 ft/sec, the instantaneous velocity of the sled was 9.80 ft/sec, and the instantaneous velocity of the box was 1.32 ft/sec. The sled has the highest instantaneous velocity at 2 seconds, meaning that the $\frac{\Delta v}{\Delta t}$ is highest for the sled, and the sled has the greatest acceleration.

29. (A) (p. 414) ***Science/Evaluation of Models/Analysis.*** To know if friction is playing a major role, the acceleration in the oiled board experiment should be calculated. Acceleration can be calculated by using the equation $d = 0.5at^2$. Each object travels the length of the board, 10 feet. Therefore, for the sled:

$$d = \frac{1}{2}at^2$$

$$10 = \frac{1}{2}a(2.02)^2$$

$$10 \approx \frac{1}{2}(a)(4)$$

$$a = 5 \text{ ft/sec}^2$$

For the ball:

$$d = \frac{1}{2}at^2$$

$$10 = \frac{1}{2}a(2.39)^2$$

$$10 \approx \frac{1}{2}(a)(5.7)$$

$$a = 3.5 \text{ ft/sec}^2$$

The acceleration (look at the 1s acceleration in the non-oil experiments) is the same in the normal and the frictionless environments so friction is not a major factor in either case. The difference is the rolling of the ball.

30. (H) (p. 415) ***Science/Evaluation of Models/Analysis.*** Experiment 4 shows that friction affects the relative acceleration between the box and either the sled or ball. Calculate the acceleration for the box:

$$d = \frac{1}{2}at^2$$

$$10 = \frac{1}{2}a(5.00)^2$$

$$10 \approx \frac{1}{2}a(25)$$

$$a = 0.8 \text{ ft/sec}^2$$

Because the oiling in Experiment 4 caused a change in the box's acceleration, friction is a factor. Rolling must also be a factor as per the answer explanation to item #29.

31. (A) (p. 415) ***Science/Interpretation of Data/Comprehension.*** The acceleration of the ball is constant at 3.5 ft/sec^2 (either Experiment 1 or 4). The acceleration of the sled is constant at 4.9 ft/sec^2 (Experiment 2 or 4). Therefore, the ratio of the ball's acceleration to the sled's acceleration is $\frac{3.5}{4.9} = \frac{5}{7}$.

32. (H) (p. 415) ***Science/Interpretation of Data/Comprehension.*** Although the acceleration of the ball is relatively insensitive to the amount of friction, the acceleration of the box is very sensitive to friction. Therefore, in a ratio, the effect of changing the amount of friction will change the numerator (ball acceleration) only slightly, whereas the denominator (box acceleration) will change significantly depending on friction. Note that (J) is not correct because the acceleration remains constant within each experiment.

33. (B) (p. 416) ***Science/Evaluation of Models/Analysis.*** Scientist 2 concludes by saying that Neanderthals and early modern humans merged into a single species by interbreeding, so Scientist 2 assumes that the two groups were sufficiently similar to permit interbreeding of the members. (A) distorts the position of Scientist 2. Scientist 2 says that the picture we have of the Neanderthals is based upon one individual, an individual who was not entirely representative of his species. In other words, the one Neanderthal with arthritis was the exception, not the rule. (C) also misreads the passage. Scientist 2 says that populations were spread out geographically, not that the two groups were separated physically from one another. (Indeed, they must have lived pretty close to each other to permit the interbreeding that Scientist 2 believes occurred.) Finally, as for (D), though Scientist 2 says that Neanderthals were apparently more muscular than early modern humans, this does not automatically mean that they would win a fight. Speed, intelligence, weapons, and a lot of other factors might affect the outcome.

34. (H) (p. 416) ***Science/Evaluation of Models/Analysis.*** For early modern humans to completely replace Neanderthals, there could not have been a region containing Neanderthals that did not also contain early modern humans.

35. (D) (p. 416) ***Science/Evaluation of Models/Analysis.*** The discovery of evidence of an isolated community of Neanderthals would not necessarily weaken either hypothesis. When the two scientists talk about populations being dispersed, they are not saying that the individuals were perfectly distributed—like so many salt and chlorine atoms in a water solution. A pocket of Neanderthals here or a concentration of early modern humans there would not be inconsistent with the general distribution pattern described.

36. (J) (p. 416) ***Science/Evaluation of Models/Analysis.*** This information suggests that early modern humans killed Neanderthals, which supports Scientist 1.

37. (C) (p. 417) ***Science/Evaluation of Models/Application.*** This fact shows that even if two species can breed, they may not do so voluntarily. Scientist 1 can therefore use this case as an example of the fact that two genetically compatible but dissimilar-looking animals choose not to interbreed. (D) is not readily relevant because lions and tigers are brought together artificially. No one disputed the notion that animals can interbreed, so (A) does not enter the argument. (B) is incorrect because lions and tigers do not share the same niche (tigers are solitary forest hunters while lions are group-hunting plains dwellers), and their ranges rarely overlap.

38. (H) (p. 417) ***Science/Evaluation of Models/Comprehension.*** The mixing of traits is part of Scientist 1's objections to Scientist 2's hypothesis.

39. (A) (p. 417) *Science/Evaluation of Models/Analysis.* Both hypotheses attribute the disappearance of Neanderthals to early modern humans.

40. (G) (p. 417) *Science/Evaluation of Models/Application.* (F) is a perfectly logical argument but it does not strengthen the position of Scientist 2. (J) does not strengthen the position of Scientist 2 since there is no way to prove from the given information whether others also died violently (clubs may have been used, or spearpoints that were used may have been valuable and were taken by the victors). Even if (J) is acceptable, it does not strengthen the position of Scientist 2. It only casts doubt on the position of Scientist 1. (H) is true in general. The only possible answer that strengthens a scientist's argument is (G).

SAMPLE ESSAY RESPONSES AND ANALYSES

Section 5: *Writing (p. 418)*

Above Average Response

During each election cycle, billions of dollars are spent on campaigns, and the amount rises every year. Because of this exorbitant spending, there should be limits on how much individuals and corporations can donate to a campaign, and also on the total amount of money a politician can spend on a single campaign. Limits could potentially allow a wider range of candidates to run for office and would decrease donors' influence on campaign proceedings. Furthermore, limits could make the whole campaign process less of a circus and allow politicians to devote more time to their actual jobs.

The high cost of campaigning bars people who are not independently wealthy or well-connected from running for Congress. With expenses such as advertisements, travel, and campaign teams, campaigning is an expensive process, and the cost resembles an arms race, as politicians continue to outspend each other. Those who cannot keep up with their competitors will not be as visible to voters, with fewer ads and public appearances. These campaigns would have made it impossible for many of the people who shaped U.S. history to hold office today. Presidents like Abraham Lincoln would not have been able to rise to prominence from a modest and obscure background. It is true that even with a limit on campaign funding, one would still need to come from an elite background or have powerful, wealthy friends to run for office. However, limitations may open the door a little wider for candidates who are less wealthy.

In addition to restricting who can run for office, campaign spending allows wealthy donors to disproportionately represent politicians' campaigns. Voters, whether rich or poor, will logically support candidates who are the most favorable to their concerns. Therefore, candidates who cater to the wealthy are more likely to receive more campaign funding. This makes it more difficult for lower income voters to elect politicians who will address their concerns. Although one may say that limiting campaign donations is a violation of free speech, I would argue that money is not speech. The high cost of running a campaign may actually limit the range of ideas that can be heard, if people must pay a certain price to gain influence. I do not agree that campaigns should be funded solely by taxpayer money, since this could lead to higher taxes. However, limiting private donations would level the playing field and allow campaigns to be less money-driven.

Finally, limiting spending may force politicians to make their campaigns shorter and less demanding of their time. Politicians who are up for reelection would have more time and energy to focus on fulfilling the duties of their office instead of running for it. It has become a cliché in American politics that the next campaign begins as soon as the previous one ends. For members of Congress who can be reelected for an unlimited number of terms, this means that they are always campaigning or preparing to campaign. However, if politicians could only raise a limited amount of money, their teams would spend less time fundraising, and furthermore, this limited amount of money would force them to shorten their campaigns. Although upper class voters may protest their weakened influence on campaigns, having politicians more focused on their jobs is a change that voters from all social classes and political parties could appreciate.

Although limiting campaign funding would not eliminate the influence of wealth on elections, it would be a step in the right direction. More people could be financially capable of running for office, and wealthy donors would be less likely to have a disproportionate influence on campaigns. Finally, with less emphasis on campaigning, politicians could focus more on what voters elected them to do.

Ideas and Analysis: The writer clearly states his or her thesis in the introduction: limited campaign spending would make campaigns less influenced by money and make politicians less focused on campaigning. The writer argues for Perspective 2 (spending limits for donors) but adds that the total amount of campaign spending per candidate should also be limited.

This essay does not argue for a "compromise" position, except for briefly stating that campaigns should not be solely funded through taxes. The author thoroughly develops three main arguments against campaign spending. However, the author also acknowledges the opposing point of view in Perspective 1 and argues against it.

Development and Support:

- The introduction opens with an attention-grabbing hook (stating the high amount of campaign spending).
- The writer clearly states the thesis in the second sentence of the introduction and previews the three main arguments.
- The body paragraphs begin with topic sentences that state the main point or argument to be made in the paragraph.
- The body paragraphs include a mix of reasoning and examples to support the author's opinion.
    - Body paragraph 1: The writer uses the metaphor of the arms race to explain the increasingly high cost of campaign spending. This metaphor and the example of Abraham Lincoln also demonstrate the writer's historical knowledge.
    - Body paragraph 2: The writer develops lines of reasoning to explain the antidemocratic nature of unlimited campaign spending. Although the reasoning is logical, the paragraph would be stronger with concrete examples.
    - Body paragraph 3: The writer ends with an argument that could appeal to a variety of readers, despite their political opinions: if politicians campaigned less, they would be more focused on their jobs. The writer supports this argument with the concrete example of running for Congress.

Organization:

- The writer introduces each paragraph with a topic sentence.
- The writer uses transitions to connect ideas between and within paragraphs. For example, the first sentence of the second body paragraph ("In addition to restricting who can run for office ...") transitions the discussion from wealthy candidates to wealthy donors.
- At the end of the second body paragraph, the two sentences about taxes did not directly relate to the topic (the influence of wealthy donors). Although this part of the paragraph acknowledges Perspective 3, the writer should incorporate the different perspectives into his or her argument, rather than just mentioning them.

Language Use and Conventions: The essay contains at least three principal strengths in this area:

- The essay does not have any mechanics/usage errors. As a result, the reader's attention is not distracted from the substance of the essay.
- The essay does not have any informal language.
- Stylistically, the writer varies sentence structures throughout most of the essay. However, the writer begins two sentences in a row with the transition "although" in the third body paragraph and the conclusion.

Summary and Conclusions: This essay demonstrates writing skills that are well developed and provides several arguments for campaign spending limitations. The writer incorporates Perspectives 1 and 2 into the argument but could develop Perspective 3 more thoroughly. This essay would likely receive a score of 10.

Below Average Response

Campaign spending should be limited because when campaigns are so expensive, only people who are rich or have rich friends can afford to pay for the campaign. This makes government less democratic because it only represents the rich. Also, the expensive campaigns are wasteful. Think of everything else you could do with that money.

The main reason that campaign funding should be limited is that with the current system, you have to be very rich to run for office. If you're opponent can afford to spend millions of dollars on a campaign and you can't, you will be at a disadvantage because you won't be able to afford to promote you're campaign as much. Also, high campaign spending means that people can basically buy influence in government. The more you can pay, the better shot your candidate has at leading a bigger campaign and winning the election.

The money spent on elections is also wasteful imagine what else you could do with it. For example, the billions of dollars used on campaign spending could instead be spent on charities or government programs that the politician supports. This would be a much more constructive use of people's money.

Campaign spending leads to unfair elections where the rich have a lot more influence then the rest of the country. Furthermore, it's just a huge waste of money that could be spent better elsewhere.

Ideas and Analysis: It is clear that the writer is against unlimited campaign spending, but the writer does not use enough reasoning or examples to support his or her argument. The essay develops Perspective 2, but the writer makes no mention of Perspectives 1 and 3. The essay would be stronger if the writer recognized multiple points of view and explained more thoroughly why he or she is against unlimited campaign spending.

Development and Support:

- The introduction previews the writer's opinions, but the writer only presents two main arguments against campaign spending, and the second argument is not well developed. Furthermore, the writer does not specify how campaign spending should be limited.
- In the body paragraphs, the writer does not use concrete examples to support his or her arguments.
- In the first body paragraph, the writer argues how unlimited campaign spending favors the rich. Although the reasoning is logical, the paragraph would be stronger with concrete examples, rather than just the writer's opinions.
- In the second body paragraph, the writer has a valid point when he or she says that campaign spending is a waste of money. However, the argument is not plausible. One cannot assume that the money a corporation or individual donor would have spent on a campaign would be used "constructively."

Organization:

- The writer states his or her opinions in the introduction but does not combine these arguments into a clear thesis.
- The topic sentences should have transitions to introduce new ideas in the following paragraph.
- The first body paragraph should have a topic sentence that is more general. The topic sentence just mentions that you must be rich to run for office, but the paragraph discusses the advantages of being a rich politician and a rich donor. Another solution would be to write one paragraph about politicians' wealth and a separate paragraph about donors' wealth.

Language Use and Conventions: The essay contains several weaknesses in this area:

- The essay contains some usage and mechanics errors.
  - Body paragraph 1: "you're opponent" and "you're campaign" should be changed to "your opponent" and "your campaign."
- Conclusion: "a lot more influence then the rest of the country" should be changed to "than the rest of the country." The word "than" should be used for comparison.
- The use of informal language is one of the main problems in this essay. The writer expresses a few ideas that could be turned into strong arguments if they were worded more carefully. For example, in the introduction, the phrase "you have to be very rich to run for office" could be reworded as "you must be wealthy to run for office." It might help to read this essay and reword phrases with slang or informal language.

Summary and Conclusions: The writer's opinion is clear and consistent, but not all of the main arguments are well developed, and the second body paragraph does not use logical reasoning. Furthermore, the writer does not consider the opposing viewpoints. This essay would likely receive a score of 5.

ITEM INDEX

In the following index, all of the numeric references are designed as follows: **Page #**/Item #.

English

Victory Student Text and The Practice Book, English

Adjectives versus Adverbs

Time Trial: **20**/2; **21**/8
Lesson 1: **27**/22–27; **28**/28
Directed Study Quiz: **60**/25
Victory Practice Test: **364**/10; **369**/36; **377**/72

Practice Book Quiz II: **8**/7
Practice Book Test 2: **112**/29; **119**/75
Practice Book Test 3: **161**/3; **172**/62

Apostrophes

Lesson 3: **41**/32, 34
Review: **74**/23

Appropriate Supporting Material

Anatomy: **17**/2
Lesson 4: **43**/1; **45**/10
Directed Study Quiz: **57**/17
Timed Quiz: **66**/16–17; **68**/28
Review: **73**/16; **76**/38
Victory Practice Test: **364**/6; **367**/24; **368**/31; **374**/59–60; **375**/63; **376**/67; **377**/73

Practice Book Quiz I: **4**/15; **7**/31
Practice Book Test 1: **57**/45; **59**/60; **61**/72
Practice Book Test 2: **109**/15; **110**/16; **112**/33; **114**/45; **117**/60
Practice Book Test 3: **167**/33; **168**/37, 40

Audience

Directed Study Quiz: **57**/15; **63**/32
Lesson 4: **43**/4
Review: **72**/14

Practice Book Quiz I: **7**/30
Practice Book Test 1: **55**/30; **61**/73

Clarity of Meaning

Lesson 4: **46**/19
Directed Study Quiz: **62**/29

Practice Book Quiz II: **8**/8; **10**/17, 19–20

Victory Student Text and The Practice Book, English

Colons

Lesson 3: **40**/26–27
Review: **73**/18

Practice Book Test 1: **56**/40

Comma Splices

Lesson 2: **32**/3–4

Practice Book Test 3: **164**/18

Commas

Anatomy: **17**/1
Time Trial: **20**/3; **21**/6
Lesson 3: **36**/1; **37**/7–8; **37**/10–12; **38**/15–18; **39**/19–20
Lesson 5: **47**/1
Timed Quiz: **64**/3, 5; **67**/19
Review: **73**/17–18; **77**/42
Victory Practice Test: **369**/33; **375**/64

Practice Book Quiz I: **3**/7–8
Practice Book Test 1: **54**/22; **56**/41; **58**/48; **60**/62
Practice Book Test 2: **113**/35; **119**/73
Practice Book Test 3: **161**/3; **165**/26; **174**/73

Conciseness

Anatomy: **18**/5
Lesson 4: **46**/13–18
Lesson 5: **48**/8; **49**/9
Directed Study Quiz: **53**/3; **54**/7; **58**/18; **61**/27
Timed Quiz: **65**/7–8; **66**/15; **67**/24
Review: **71**/9; **73**/19; **74**/24; **75**/30
Victory Practice Test: **366**/20; **368**/29

Practice Book Quiz I: **5**/16
Practice Book Quiz II: **9**/9
Practice Book Test 1: **51**/1, 3; **53**/12; **55**/32; **59**/54, 56, 58; **60**/63, 70
Practice Book Test 2: **107**/4; **111**/26, 28; **113**/34, 38; **115**/49; **116**/53–54
Practice Book Test 3: **164**/20; **165**/24, 28; **167**/36; **170**/47, 50; **171**/57

Victory Student Text and The Practice Book, English

Conventions of Standard English

Anatomy: **17**/1; **18**/3–4
Time Trial: **20**/1–3; **21**/4–8
Lesson 1: **24–31**/1–56
Lesson 2: **32–35**/1–24
Lesson 3: **36–41**/1–34
Lesson 5: **47**/1–2; **48**/4–7; **49**/10
Directed Study Quiz: **52**/1; **53**/4; **54**/5–6, 8; **55**/9, 11; **56**/12; **58–60**/19–26; **61**/28; **62**/30
Timed Quiz: **64**/1, 3–5; **65**/9, 11–13; **66**/14; **67**/18–20, 22–24; **68**/25–27
Review: **70**/1, 4–5; **72**/10, 12; **73**/17–18, 20; **74**/23, 25–27, 29; **75**/31–32; **76**/35, 37, 39–40; **77**/42, 44–47
Victory Practice Test: **363**/2; **364**/4–5, 7, 10–11; **365**/12–13; **366**/17–19, 21–22; **367**/26–27; **369**/32–34, 36; **370**/38–43; **371**/47–49; **372**/51–53; **373**/55, 58; **374**/61; **375**/62, 64–66; **376**/70; **377**/71–72, 74

Practice Book Quiz I: **2**/1–2; **3**/5–8, 10–12; **5**/17–19; **5**/21–22; **6**/24–28
Practice Book Quiz II: **7**/1–2; **8**/3–7; **9**/10–14; **10**/15, 18
Practice Book Test 1: **51**/2; **52**/4, 6–7, 9–10; **53**/13, 16–17; **54**/19–26; **55**/27–28; **56**/33, 35–41; **57**/43, 46; **58**/48–50, 52; **59**/57, 59, 61; **60**/62, 64–67, 69
Practice Book Test 2: **107**/1–3; **108**/5–6, 9, 11; **109**/12–14; **110**/18; **111**/24–25, 27; **112**/29, 31–32; **113**/35–37, 39–40, 42; **114**/43–44; **115**/46–48, 51–52; **116**/58; **117**/61–62, 64; **117**/65; **118**/66–68, 70, 72; **119**/73–75
Practice Book Test 3: **161**/1, 3; **162**/4, 6, 8–9; **163**/11–13; **164**/17–19, 21–22; **165**/26–27; **166**/31; **167**/35; **168**/38–39; **169**/43–44, 46; **170**/48–49, 51–54; **171**/59; **172**/60, 62; **173**/64–66, 68, 70; **174**/71, 73, 75

Dashes

Lesson 3: **40**/29–30
Review: **77**/42

Victory Student Text and The Practice Book, English

Diction

Lesson 1: **31**/51–56
Directed Study Quiz: **55**/11; **60**/26
Timed Quiz: **65**/11; **68**/25, 27
Review: **76**/35, 37; **77**/44
Victory Practice Test: **364**/11

Practice Book Quiz I: **2**/2; **5**/22; **6**/26
Practice Book Quiz II: **8**/4
Practice Book Test 1: **51**/2; **52**/6, 10; **53**/17; **54**/26; **55**/27; **56**/33, 37; **58**/49; **59**/61
Practice Book Test 2: **107**/2; **108**/5; **111**/24, 27; **112**/32; **114**/43–44; **115**/47–48
Practice Book Test 3: **161**/1; **162**/6, 9; **163**/12–13; **166**/31; **169**/44; **170**/51

Double Negatives

Lesson 1: **28**/29–30

Effective Concluding Sentence

Lesson 4: **45**/11
Directed Study Quiz: **56**/13
Review: **73**/21
Victory Practice Test: **365**/14; **370**/44

Practice Book Test 1: **52**/8
Practice Book Test 3: **169**/45

Effective Opening Sentence

Lesson 4: **43**/2; **45**/7
Review: **76**/36
Victory Practice Test: **373**/57

Effective Transitional Sentence

Review: **70**/2; **74**/22
Victory Practice Test: **364**/8; **366**/16, 23; **371**/46; **376**/68–69

Practice Book Quiz I: **2**/3
Practice Book Test 1: **53**/18; **59**/55
Practice Book Test 2: **108**/8; **110**/19; **118**/69
Practice Book Test 3: **164**/23; **167**/34; **173**/69

End-Stop Punctuation

Lesson 3: **40**/28

Faulty or Illogical Comparisons

Lesson 1: **29**/34–38
Review: **75**/31
Victory Practice Test: **371**/50; **372**/51

Practice Book Quiz II: **9**/14
Practice Book Test 2: **107**/1; **116**/58

Victory Student Text and The Practice Book, English

Faulty Parallelism

Lesson 2: **34**/15–17
Review: **72**/10; **73**/20; **75**/32
Victory Practice Test: **365**/13; **366**/21; **369**/34; **370**/40; **371**/48

Practice Book Quiz I: **3**/10; **6**/28
Practice Book Quiz II: **7**/1; **8**/5
Practice Book Test 1: **55**/28; **60**/64
Practice Book Test 3: **164**/17; **172**/60; **174**/75

Fragments

Time Trial: **20**/1
Lesson 2: **33**/5–6
Lesson 5: **48**/7
Timed Quiz: **64**/4; **66**/14
Review: **71**/4
Victory Practice Test: **372**/53; **374**/61

Practice Book Quiz I: **3**/5; **5**/18
Practice Book Test 1: **53**/16; **54**/20; **57**/46; **58**/52
Practice Book Test 2: **113**/42; **119**/73–74
Practice Book Test 3: **168**/38; **169**/43; **173**/65

Grammar and Usage

Anatomy: **18**/3
Time Trial: **20**/2; **21**/4–5, 7–8
Lesson 1: **24–31**/1–56
Lesson 5: **48**/4
Directed Study Quiz: **54**/5, 8; **55**/11; **58**/19; **60**/24–26
Timed Quiz: **64**/1, 3; **65**/11, 13; **67**/20, 22–23; **68**/25, 27
Review: **70**/1; **74**/26, 29; **75**/31; **76**/35, 37; **77**/44, 47
Victory Practice Test: **363**/2; **364**/7, 10–11; **365**/12; **366**/18–19; **367**/27; **369**/36; **370**/38–39, 41–42; **371**/49; **372**/51; **373**/58; **374**/61; **377**/72

Practice Book Quiz I: **2**/1–2; **3**/11–12; **5**/17, 19, 22; **6**/24, 26
Practice Book Quiz II: **8**/4, 6–7; **9**/10, 14
Practice Book Test 1: **51**/2; **52**/6, 9–10; **53**/13, 17; **54**/22–23, 26; **55**/27; **56**/33, 36–37, 40; **58**/49; **59**/59, 61; **60**/64–65
Practice Book Test 2: **107**/1–3; **108**/5, 9, 11; **109**/13–14; **110**/18; **111**/24–25, 27; **112**/29, 31–32; **113**/36, 39–40; **114**/43–44; **115**/46–48; **116**/58; **117**/61–62; **118**/67, 70, 72; **119**/75
Practice Book Test 3: **161**/1, 3; **162**/4, 6, 8–9; **163**/12–13; **164**/22; **166**/31; **167**/35; **169**/44; **170**/48–49, 51, 54; **172**/62; **173**/66, 68; **174**/71

Victory Student Text and The Practice Book, English

Idiomatic Expression

Lesson 4: **46**/20
Review: **75**/34

Practice Book Quiz I: **3**/9
Practice Book Quiz II: **9**/10; **10**/19–20
Practice Book Test 2: **117**/59
Practice Book Test 3: **166**/32

Incomplete Split Constructions

Lesson 2: **34**/18–19

Practice Book Quiz II: **7**/2

Knowledge of Language

Anatomy: **18**/5
Directed Study Quiz: **53**/3; **54**/7; **58**/18; **62**/29
Lesson 4: **46**/13–20
Lesson 5: **48**/8; **49**/9
Timed Quiz: **64**/2; **65**/6–8, 10; **66**/15; **67**/24
Review: **71**/9; **73**/19; **74**/24; **75**/30, 34
Victory Practice Test: **363**/1; **363**/3; **364**/8–9; **366**/20; **367**/25; **368**/28; **372**/50, 54

Practice Book Quiz I: **3**/9; **5**/16
Practice Book Quiz II: **8**/8; **9**/9; **10**/17, 19–20
Practice Book Test 1: **51**/1, 3; **53**/12; **55**/32; **58**/47; **59**/54, 56, 58; **60**/63, 70
Practice Book Test 2: **107**/4; **111**/26, 28; **113**/34, 38; **115**/49; **116**/53–54; **117**/59, 63
Practice Book Test 3: **164**/20; **165**/24, 28; **166**/32; **167**/36; **170**/47, 50; **171**/57; **172**/61; **173**/67; **174**/74

Main Idea

Lesson 4: **43**/3; **45**/12
Victory Practice Test: **365**/15; **371**/45; **377**/75

Practice Book Quiz I: **4**/13
Practice Book Test 1: **53**/15; **61**/74

Misplaced Modifiers

Lesson 2: **35**/20–22
Lesson 5: **49**/10
Victory Practice Test: **364**/4

Practice Book Quiz II: **8**/3; **9**/11; **10**/18
Practice Book Test 1: **60**/65
Practice Book Test 3: **164**/19

Victory Student Text and The Practice Book, English

No Change

Lesson 3: **36**/2–4; **37**/5–6, 9; **38**/13–14; **39**/21–22; **41**/31, 33
Lesson 4: **45**/9
Lesson 5: **47**/2; **48**/5–6
Directed Study Quiz: **53**/2, 4; **54**/6; **55**/9; **59**/22–23
Timed Quiz: **64**/2; **65**/6, 9–10, 12; **67**/18, 21
Review: **71**/5–8; **72**/11–13; **74**/25, 27–28; **75**/33; **76**/39–41; **77**/45–46
Victory Practice Test: **364**/5; **366**/22; **369**/32; **370**/43; **371**/47; **375**/66; **376**/70

Practice Book Quiz I: **3**/4, 6; **5**/20–21, 23; **6**/25
Practice Book Quiz II: **9**/12; **10**/16
Practice Book Test 1: **52**/5, 7; **54**/19, 21; **55**/31; **56**/34–35; **57**/42–43; **58**/51, 53; **60**/66, 68; **61**/71
Practice Book Test 2: **108**/6–7, 10; **110**/17, 21; **111**/22–23; **113**/37, 41; **115**/50–52; **116**/55–57; **117**/64–65; **118**/66, 71
Practice Book Test 3: **161**/2; **162**/5, 7; **163**/10–11; **164**/16, 21; **165**/27, 29; **168**/39, 41; **169**/42, 46; **170**/53; **171**/55, 58; **172**/63; **173**/64, 70; **174**/72

Nouns and Noun Clauses

Lesson 1: **28**/31–33
Directed Study Quiz: **58**/19
Timed Quiz: **64**/3
Victory Practice Test: **366**/19; **373**/58

Organization

Lesson 4: **43**/5; **44**/6; **45**/8
Lesson 5: **48**/3
Directed Study Quiz: **55**/10; **57**/14, 16; **63**/31
Timed Quiz: **68**/29
Review: **71**/3; **72**/15; **77**/43, 48
Victory Practice Test: **368**/29; **368**/30; **369**/35, 37; **373**/56

Practice Book Quiz I: **4**/14; **6**/29
Practice Book Test 1: **52**/11; **53**/14; **55**/29; **57**/44; **61**/75
Practice Book Test 2: **110**/20; **112**/30
Practice Book Test 3: **163**/14–15; **165**/25; **166**/30; **171**/56

Paragraph-Level Structure

Lesson 4: **43**/5
Review: **71**/3; **77**/43
Victory Practice Test: **368**/29; **369**/37

Practice Book Test 1: **52**/11; **55**/29; **61**/75
Practice Book Test 2: **110**/20
Practice Book Test 3: **165**/25; **166**/30

Victory Student Text and The Practice Book, English

Passage-Level Structure

Lesson 4: **44**/6; **45**/8
Directed Study Quiz: **57**/14, 16; **63**/31
Timed Quiz: **68**/29
Review: **72**/15; **77**/48
Victory Practice Test: **368**/30

Practice Book Quiz I: **4**/14; **6**/29
Practice Book Test 1: **53**/14; **57**/44
Practice Book Test 2: **112**/30
Practice Book Test 3: **163**/14–15

Problems of Coordination and Subordination

Anatomy: **18**/4
Lesson 2: **33**/7–13; **34**/14
Directed Study Quiz: **59**/21; **61**/28
Timed Quiz: **67**/24
Victory Practice Test: **372**/52; **375**/62, 65

Practice Book Quiz II: **9**/13
Practice Book Test 1: **54**/25; **58**/50; **60**/67
Practice Book Test 2: **109**/12
Practice Book Test 3: **171**/59

Production of Writing

Anatomy: **17**/2
Lesson 4: **43–45**/1–12; **46**/18
Lesson 5: **48**/3
Directed Study Quiz: **53**/2; **55**/10; **56**/13; **57**/14–17; **61**/27; **63**/31–32
Timed Quiz: **66**/16–17; **67**/21; **68**/28–29
Review: **70**/2; **71**/3, 6–8; **72**/11, 13–15; **73**/16, 21; **74**/22, 28; **75**/33; **76**/36, 38, 41; **77**/43, 48
Victory Practice Test: **364**/6; **365**/14–15; **366**/16, 23; **367**/24; **368**/29–31; **369**/35, 37; **370**/44; **371**/45–46; **373**/56–57; **374**/59–60; **375**/63; **376**/67–69; **377**/73, 75

Practice Book Quiz I: **2**/3; **3**/4; **4**/13–15; **5**/20, 23; **6**/29; **7**/30–31
Practice Book Quiz II: **9**/10; **10**/16
Practice Book Test 1: **52**/5, 8, 11; **53**/14–15, 18; **55**/29–31; **56**/34; **57**/42, 44–45; **58**/51, 53; **59**/55, 60; **60**/68; **61**/71–75
Practice Book Test 2: **108**/7–8, 10; **109**/15; **110**/16–17, 19–21; **111**/22–23; **112**/30, 33; **113**/41; **114**/45; **115**/50; **116**/55–57; **117**/60; **118**/69, 71
Practice Book Test 3: **161**/2; **162**/5, 7; **163**/10, 14–15; **164**/16, 23; **165**/25, 29; **166**/30; **167**/33–34; **168**/37, 40, 41; **169**/42, 45; **171**/55–56, 58; **172**/63; **173**/69; **174**/72

Victory Student Text and The Practice Book, English

Pronoun Usage

Time Trial: **21**/7
Lesson 1: **26**/13–19; **27**/20–21
Directed Study Quiz: **54**/5, 8
Timed Quiz: **64**/1; **67**/20, 23
Review: **77**/47
Victory Practice Test: **364**/7; **374**/61

Practice Book Quiz I: **2**/1; **3**/12; **5**/19
Practice Book Test 1: **52**/9; **53**/13; **54**/22; **56**/40; **59**/59; **60**/64
Practice Book Test 2: **107**/3; **109**/13; **110**/18; **111**/25; **112**/32; **113**/39–40; **117**/61; **118**/70
Practice Book Test 3: **167**/35; **173**/68

Punctuation

Anatomy: **17**/1
Time Trial: **20**/3; **21**/6
Lesson 3: **36**/1; **37**/7–8, 10–12; **38**/15–18; **39**/19–20, 23–25; **40**/26–30; **41**/32, 34
Lesson 5: **47**/1
Directed Study Quiz: **61**/28
Timed Quiz: **64**/3, 5; **67**/19
Review: **73**/17–18; **74**/23; **77**/42
Victory Practice Test: **369**/33; **375**/64

Practice Book Quiz I: **3**/7–8
Practice Book Test 1: **54**/22; **56**/39, 41; **58**/48; **60**/62, 69
Practice Book Test 2: **108**/9; **113**/35; **118**/68; **119**/73
Practice Book Test 3: **161**/3; **165**/26; **174**/73

Quotation Marks

Practice Book Test 1: **60**/69

Run-On Sentences

Lesson 2: **32**/1–2
Directed Study Quiz: **56**/12
Timed Quiz: **68**/26
Victory Practice Test: **377**/71

Practice Book Quiz I: **6**/27
Practice Book Test 1: **52**/4, 9; **54**/24
Practice Book Test 3: **170**/52

Semicolons

Lesson 3: **39**/23–25
Directed Study Quiz: **61**/28

Practice Book Test 2: **108**/9; **118**/68

Victory Student Text and The Practice Book, English

Sentence Structure

Anatomy: **18**/4
Time Trial: **20**/1
Lesson 1: **32**/1
Lesson 2: **32**/2–3; **32–35**/4–24
Lesson 5: **48**/7; **49**/10
Directed Study Quiz: **52**/1; **56**/12; **58**/20; **59**/21; **61**/28; **62**/30
Timed Quiz: **64**/4; **66**/14; **67**/24; **68**/26
Review: **71**/4; **72**/10; **73**/20; **75**/32
Victory Practice Test: **364**/4; **365**/13; **366**/17, 21; **367**/26; **369**/34; **370**/40; **371**/48; **372**/52–53; **373**/55; **374**/61; **375**/62; **375**/65; **377**/71, 74

Practice Book Quiz I: **3**/5, 10; **5**/18; **6**/27–28
Practice Book Quiz II: **7**/1–2; **8**/3, 5, 7; **9**/11, 13; **10**/15, 18
Practice Book Test 1: **52**/4, 9; **53**/16; **54**/20, 24–25; **55**/28; **56**/38; **57**/46; **58**/50, 52; **59**/57; **60**/64–65, 67
Practice Book Test 2: **109**/12; **113**/42; **119**/73–74
Practice Book Test 3: **164**/17–19; **168**/38; **169**/43; **170**/52; **171**/59; **172**/60; **173**/65; **174**/75

Sentence-Level Structure

Lesson 5: **48**/3
Directed Study Quiz: **55**/10
Victory Practice Test: **369**/35; **373**/56

Practice Book Test 3: **171**/56

Sequence and Verb Tense

Lesson 1: **30**/47–48; **31**/49–50
Timed Quiz: **67**/22
Review: **74**/26
Victory Practice Test: **370**/42

Practice Book Quiz I: **3**/11; **5**/17
Practice Book Test 1: **56**/36; **59**/59; **60**/65
Practice Book Test 2: **108**/11; **109**/13; **112**/31; **118**/72
Practice Book Test 3: **162**/4; **163**/13; **170**/48, 54

Victory Student Text and The Practice Book, English

Strategy

Anatomy: **17**/2
Lesson 4: **43**/1–4; **45**/7, 10-12
Directed Study Quiz: **56**/13; **57**/15, 17; **63**/32
Timed Quiz: **66**/16–17; **68**/28
Review: **70**/2; **72**/14; **73**/16, 21; **74**/22; **76**/36, 38
Victory Practice Test: **365**/14; **365**/15; **366**/16, 23; **367**/24; **368**/31; **370**/44; **371**/45–46; **373**/57; **374**/59–60; **375**/63; **376**/67–69; **377**/73, 75

Practice Book Quiz I: **2**/3; **4**/13, 15; **7**/30–31
Practice Book Test 1: **52**/8; **53**/15, 18; **55**/30; **57**/45; **59**/55–60; **61**/72–74
Practice Book Test 2: **108**/8; **109**/15; **110**/1, 19; **112**/33; **114**/45; **117**/60; **118**/69
Practice Book Test 3: **164**/23; **167**/33–34; **168**/37, 40; **169**/45; **173**/69

Style

Lesson 5: **48**/8; **49**/9
Directed Study Quiz: **53**/3; **54**/7; **58**/18; **61**/27; **62**/29
Timed Quiz: **65**/7–8; **66**/15; **67**/24
Victory Practice Test: **363**/3; **364**/6, 8; **366**/20; **368**/28; **372**/54

Practice Book Quiz I: **3**/9; **5**/16
Practice Book Quiz II: **8**/8; **9**/9–10; **10**/17, 19–20
Practice Book Test 1: **51**/1, 3; **53**/12; **55**/32; **58**/47; **59**/54, 56, 58; **60**/63, 70
Practice Book Test 2: **107**/4; **111**/26, 28; **113**/34, 38; **115**/49; **116**/53–54; **117**/59, 63
Practice Book Test 3: **164**/20; **165**/24, 28; **166**/32; **167**/36; **170**/47, 50; **171**/57; **173**/67

Victory Student Text and The Practice Book, English

Subject-Verb Agreement

Anatomy: **18**/3
Time Trial: **21**/4
Lesson 1: **24**/1–4; **25**/5–12
Directed Study Quiz: **60**/24
Review: **70**/1; **74**/29
Victory Practice Test: **363**/2; **364**/7; **366**/18; **370**/38

Practice Book Quiz I: **5**/17
Practice Book Quiz II: **9**/10
Practice Book Test 1: **54**/22–23
Practice Book Test 2: **109**/14; **111**/24; **113**/36; **114**/44; **115**/46; **117**/62; **118**/70
Practice Book Test 3: **170**/49; **173**/66

Unintended Meanings

Lesson 2: **35**/23–24
Directed Study Quiz: **52**/1; **58**/20; **62**/30
Victory Practice Test: **373**/55; **377**/74

Practice Book Quiz II: **8**/7; **9**/13; **10**/15
Practice Book Test 1: **56**/38; **59**/57

Verb Tense

Time Trial: **21**/5
Lesson 1: **29**/39–40; **30**/41–46
Lesson 5: **48**/4
Timed Quiz: **65**/13
Victory Practice Test: **365**/12; **367**/27; **370**/39, 41

Practice Book Quiz I: **6**/24
Practice Book Quiz II: **8**/4, 6
Practice Book Test 2: **108**/9; **118**/67, 70
Practice Book Test 3: **162**/8; **164**/22; **174**/71

Reading

Victory Student Text and The Practice Book, Reading

Application

Lesson 1: **98**/12–13; **100**/20; **104**/38
Lesson 2: **106**/2; **108**/8; **109**/13; **110**/15
Lesson 3: **122**/35
Lesson 4: **130**/26; **131**/29; **134**/42, 45
Directed Study Quiz: **138**/5; **139**/7
Timed Quiz: **148**/16–17
Review: **152**/7; **153**/12; **155**/20; **157**/29; **159**/37
Victory Practice Test: **402**/40

Practice Book Quiz I: **14**/3, 8
Practice Book Quiz II: **22**/17; **26**/29
Practice Book Test 1: **84**/20; **86**/24
Practice Book Test 2: **139**/14; **141**/28; **143**/35–36, 39
Practice Book Test 3: **196**/9; **198**/12; **199**/18; **201**/25

Craft and Structure

Lesson 1: **97**/6; **98**/7–8; **99**/14–15, 17; **100**/18; **101**/22, 24; **103**/29–34; **104**/39
Lesson 2: **109**/11–12; **110**/14; **111**/18; **113**/20–21, 23, 26; **114**/27–28, 30–33
Lesson 3: **116**/1–2, 4–7; **117**/8; **118**/11–14, 16–17; **119**/19; **121**/30–31; **122**/34, 36; **123**/38; **124**/42, 44–45
Lesson 4: **126**/1–3, 5; **128**/15; **131**/27; **132**/33
Directed Study Quiz: **137**/1; **139**/6; **143**/14
Timed Quiz: **146**/6; **148**/14–15, 17
Review: **151**/1, 5; **152**/7–9; **153**/10, 12; **154**/16; **155**/23; **156**/25; **157**/31; **158**/33; **159**/38
Victory Practice Test: **395**/1, 4, 8; **397**/14; **399**/21; **400**/22–23, 25–26

Practice Book Quiz I: **13**/1–2; **14**/5; **16**/10, 12, 14–15, 17
Practice Book Quiz II: **19**/9; **21**/12; **23**/18–19; **26**/28
Practice Book Test 1: **83**/14, 16; **84**/18; **85**/21–22; **86**/25–27, 30
Practice Book Test 2: **139**/15, 18–19
Practice Book Test 3: **195**/1–2, 4–5, 7; **198**/14; **204**/33

Victory Student Text and The Practice Book, Reading

Development

Time Trial: **89**/2
Lesson 1: **98**/7–8; **100**/18; **103**/34–35
Lesson 2: **109**/11; **113**/22, 26; **114**/33
Lesson 3: **119**/19; **122**/33, 36; **124**/42, 46
Lesson 4: **131**/28
Timed Quiz: **148**/15
Review: **151**/5; **157**/31
Victory Practice Test: **400**/29

Practice Book Quiz I: **14**/5; **16**/17
Practice Book Quiz II: **21**/12; **26**/28
Practice Book Test 1: **83**/15–16; **85**/21
Practice Book Test 3: **195**/1–2, 5; **204**/33

Explicit Detail

Anatomy: **87**/2
Lesson 1: **97**/3–5; **100**/19; **103**/28
Lesson 2: **106**/3; **108**/7; **111**/17; **113**/24; **114**/29
Lesson 3: **117**/8; **119**/20–21; **120**/27; **122**/32; **124**/41, 43, 45
Lesson 4: **126**/2, 4–9; **127**/10; **128**/14, 16; **129**/21–22; **130**/23–24; **130**/25; **131**/30–32; **133**/36–38; **134**/41, 43–44
Directed Study Quiz: **138**/4; **142**/10; **143**/13; **144**/16–18
Timed Quiz: **146**/3–4, 6–7
Review: **153**/10–11, 13–14; **154**/17; **155**/22; **156**/26; **157**/28, 30; **158**/35; **159**/36, 39; **161**/41, 43–46
Victory Practice Test: **395**/3, 6; **397**/11–13, 15–17; **398**/18; **400**/27; **402**/31–33, 35–38

Practice Book Quiz I: **14**/4, 7; **16**/9, 11; **17**/18
Practice Book Quiz II: **18**/2–4; **21**/11; **22**/16; **24**/20–21; **26**/25
Practice Book Quiz II: **19**/8; **26**/26–27
Practice Book Test 1: **81**/2, 6; **83**/11; **84**/19; **86**/23, 28; **88**/31–34, 36, 39
Practice Book Test 2: **137**/5–6, 10; **138**/12; **139**/16, 20; **141**/21–25, 27, 30; **142**/31; **143**/34, 38, 40
Practice Book Test 3: **195**/6–7; **198**/14–17; **199**/19–20; **201**/22, 26; **203**/31; **204**/32, 36–37, 39

Victory Student Text and The Practice Book, Reading

Implied Idea

Anatomy: **87**/3
Time Trial: **90**/3
Lesson 1: **98**/9–11; **101**/22–23; **103**/36; **104**/37
Lesson 2: **107**/5; **109**/10; **113**/25; **114**/28, 31
Lesson 3: **116**/1–6; **117**/9–10; **118**/12–16, 18; **119**/23; **120**/25, 28; **121**/29; **122**/34; **123**/39
Lesson 4: **126**/1, 3; **127**/11–12; **129**/19–20; **132**/34; **133**/35
Directed Study Quiz: **137**/3; **142**/11; **143**/12; **144**/15
Timed Quiz: **146**/1–2, 8–10; **147**/12; **148**/13
Review: **151**/3–4, 6; **154**/18; **155**/19, 24; **156**/27; **159**/40
Victory Practice Test: **395**/2, 5, 7, 9–10; **397**/14; **398**/20; **399**/21; **400**/24–26, 28; **402**/39

Practice Book Quiz I: **16**/13
Practice Book Quiz II: **18**/5; **19**/6–7; **21**/13, 15; **23**/19; **24**/23; **26**/25
Practice Book Test 1: **81**/1, 3–5, 7–10; **83**/12; **86**/26–27, 29–30; **88**/37–38
Practice Book Test 2: **137**/1–4, 7–9; **139**/13, 17–18; **141**/26, 29; **143**/33, 37
Practice Book Test 3: **196**/8, 10; **198**/13; **201**/23–24; **202**/27–30; **204**/34–35, 40

Integration of Knowledge and Ideas

Time Trial: **89**/2
Lesson 1: **103**/35
Lesson 2: **106–108**/1–9; **109**/13; **110**/15; **111**/19
Victory Practice Test: **395**/10

Practice Book Test 1: **84**/19–20
Practice Book Test 3: **196**/9–10

Victory Student Text and The Practice Book, Reading

Key Ideas and Details

Anatomy: **87**/1–3; **88**/4
Time Trial: **89**/1; **90**/3
Lesson 1: **97**/1–5; **98**/9–13; **99**/16; **100**/19–20; **101**/21, 23; **102**/25–26; **103**/27–28, 36; **104**/37–38
Lesson 2: **109**/10; **111**/16–17; **113**/22, 24–25; **114**/29
Lesson 3: **116**/3; **117**/9–10; **118**/15, 18; **119–121**/20–29; **122**/32–33, 35, 37; **123**/39–40; **124**/41, 43, 46
Lesson 4: **126**/4, 6–9; **127**/10–12; **128**/13–14, 16–18; **129**/19–22; **130**/23–26; **131**/28–32; **132–134**/34–45
Directed Study Quiz: **137**/2–3; **138**/4–5; **139**/7; **140**/8; **142**/9–11; **143**/12–13; **144**/15–18
Timed Quiz: **146**/1–4; **146**/5, 7, 9–10; **147**/11–12; **148**/13, 16
Review: **151**/2–4, 6; **153**/11, 13–15; **154**/17–18; **155**/19–22, 24; **156**/26–27; **157**/28–30, 32; **158**/34–35; **159**/36–37, 39–40; **161**/41–46
Victory Practice Test: **395**/2–3; **395**/5–7, 9; **397**/11–13, 15–17; **398**/18–20; **400**/24, 27–30; **402**/31–40

Practice Book Quiz I: **14**/3–4, 6–8; **16**/9, 11, 13, 16; **17**/18
Practice Book Quiz II: **18**/1–5; **19**/6–8; **21**/10–11, 13–15; **22**/16–17; **24**/20–23; **26**/24–27, 29
Practice Book Test 1: **81**/1–10; **83**/11–13, 15, 17; **86**/23–24, 28–29; **88**/31–39; **89**/40
Practice Book Test 2: **137**/1–10; **138**/11–12; **139**/13–14, 16–17, 20; **141–143**/21–40
Practice Book Test 3: **195**/3, 6; **196**/8; **198**/11–13, 15–17; **199**/18–20; **201**/21–26; **202**/27–30; **203**/31; **204**/32, 34–40

Victory Student Text and The Practice Book, Reading

Main Idea

Anatomy: **87**/1
Time Trial: **89**/1
Lesson 1: **97**/1–2; **99**/16; **101**/21; **102**/25–26; **103**/27
Lesson 2: **106**/1; **107**/4, 6; **108**/9; **111**/16, 19
Lesson 3: **120**/26; **122**/37; **123**/40
Lesson 4: **128**/17–18; **133**/39
Directed Study Quiz: **137**/2; **140**/8; **142**/9
Timed Quiz: **146**/5; **147**/11
Review: **151**/2; **153**/15; **155**/21; **157**/32; **158**/34; **161**/42
Victory Practice Test: **395**/1; **398**/19; **400**/30; **402**/34

Practice Book Quiz I: **14**/6; **16**/10, 16
Practice Book Quiz II: **18**/1; **21**/10; **24**/22; **26**/24
Practice Book Test 1: **88**/35; **89**/40
Practice Book Test 2: **138**/11
Practice Book Test 3: **198**/11; **201**/21; **204**/38

Victory Student Text and The Practice Book, Reading

Vocabulary

Anatomy: **88**/4
Lesson 1: **97**/6; **99**/17; **103**/29–33
Lesson 2: **109**/12; **110**/14; **111**/18; **113**/20–21, 23; **114**/27, 32
Lesson 3: **116**/7; **118**/11, 17; **121**/31; **123**/38
Lesson 4: **128**/15; **131**/27; **132**/33
Directed Study Quiz: **137**/1
Timed Quiz: **148**/14
Review: **151**/1; **152**/9; **154**/16; **156**/25; **158**/33
Victory Practice Test: **395**/4, 8; **400**/22

Practice Book Quiz I: **13**/1–2; **16**/15
Practice Book Test 1: **83**/14; **84**/18; **85**/22
Practice Book Test 3: **195**/4

Voice

Lesson 1: **99**/14–15; **101**/24; **104**/39
Lesson 2: **114**/30
Lesson 3: **119**/22; **121**/30; **124**/44
Lesson 4: **128**/13; **133**/40
Directed Study Quiz: **139**/6; **143**/14
Review: **152**/8; **155**/23; **159**/38
Victory Practice Test: **400**/23

Practice Book Quiz I: **16**/12, 14
Practice Book Quiz II: **19**/9; **21**/14; **23**/18;
Practice Book Test 1: **83**/13, 17; **86**/25
Practice Book Test 2: **139**/19
Practice Book Test 3: **195**/3

Math

Victory Student Text and The Practice Book, Math

30-60-90 Triangles

Lesson 4: **237**/9; **239**/16; **240**/18; **241**/23; **243**/32; **244**/36
Lesson 5: **247**/9
Directed Study Quiz: **262**/11

Practice Book Quiz II: **38**/11
Practice Book Test 3: **193**/59

45-45-90 Triangles

Time Trial: **195**/4
Lesson 4: **237**/7–8; **241**/23
Lesson 5: **247**/8

Practice Book Quiz I: **35**/20
Practice Book Test 1: **68**/25
Practice Book Test 2: **127**/31
Practice Book Test 3: **186**/42

Algebra and Functions

Time Trial: **195**/2–3
Calculator Exercise: **199**/8
Lesson Preliminaries: **202**/2–3; **203**/4–7
Lesson 1: **209**/9
Lesson 2: **216–226**/1–77
Directed Study Quiz: **259**/4; **261**/9; **262**/12; **263**/14; **266**/19
Timed Quiz: **268**/3, 6; **269**/8, 10, 13; **270**/15–16, 19
Review: **273**/6; **274**/14, 17; **275**/19, 22, 24; **276**/26
Victory Practice Test: **378**/3; **379**/5–7; **380**/9, 11; **382**/18–21; **383**/22; **384**/27–28; **386**/36; **387**/39–40; **388**/42; **390**/51–53; **391**/54, 56; **392**/58

Practice Book Quiz I: **33**/9; **34**/12–14
Practice Book Quiz II: **36**/1, 3, 5; **37**/6, 9; **38**/14, 16–17; **39**/18–20, 23, 25
Practice Book Test 1: **62**/1–2; **64**/7–8; **65**/11, 14; **67**/20–21; **68**/23; **69**/26; **70**/29, 31; **71**/33-36; **72**/37; **73**/42–43; **76**/51–55; **77**/57
Practice Book Test 2: **120**/2; **123**/15; **124**/16, 19; **125**/20–21; **126**/24; **128**/35; **129**/37–38; **130**/40, 43; **132**/47, 49–50; **133**/51; **134**/54–56; **135**/59–60
Practice Book Test 3: **175**/2; **176**/3; **177**/8–9; **178**/12; **180**/19–21; **181**/25; **182**/29; **183**/33; **184**/35; **185**/38–39; **187**/44–45; **188**/47; **190**/53–54; **191**/55; **192**/56–58

Bar, Cumulative, and Line Graphs

Lesson Preliminaries: **204**/12
Lesson 6: **253**/21–22; **254**/23–25

Victory Student Text and The Practice Book, Math

Basic Algebraic Manipulations

Lesson 2: **216**/1–2
Review: **274**/14, 17
Victory Practice Test: **379**/7; **382**/21; **384**/27; **388**/42

Practice Book Test 1: **70**/31; **71**/34, 36; **72**/37
Practice Book Test 2: **125**/19; **126**/24, 26; **129**/38; **132**/50
Practice Book Test 3: **182**/29; **185**/38; **188**/47

Basic Arithmetic Manipulations

Time Trial: **195**/1
Calculator Exercise: **199**/4, 7
Lesson Preliminaries: **205**/21; **207**/28
Lesson 1: **208**/2–4, 6–7; **209**/8, 10–13; **215**/42–46
Directed Study Quiz: **259**/2
Timed Quiz: **269**/11
Victory Practice Test: **378**/1; **380**/12; **381**/15; **385**/32; **387**/38; **391**/55

Practice Book Quiz I: **33**/6
Practice Book Quiz II: **36**/1
Practice Book Test 1: **63**/6; **66**/16; **71**/35
Practice Book Test 2: **126**/25, 28; **129**/36; **130**/41; **131**/45; **134**/57; **135**/58
Practice Book Test 3: **180**/22; **182**/26; **183**/32; **186**/43

Circles

Lesson Preliminaries: **203**/8; **207**/31
Lesson 4: **239**/15–17; **240**/19–21; **241**/24
Directed Study Quiz: **267**/20
Timed Quiz: **269**/12
Victory Practice Test: **378**/2; **382**/17; **383**/23; **384**/25

Practice Book Quiz I: **33**/10; **34**/15
Practice Book Quiz II: **38**/12, 17
Practice Book Test 1: **67**/18; **74**/47; **75**/48
Practice Book Test 2: **125**/22; **132**/49
Practice Book Test 3: **178**/14; **181**/23; **186**/41–42; **189**/50

Victory Student Text and The Practice Book, Math

Complex Figures

Lesson Preliminaries: **203**/8
Lesson 4: **240**/20–22; **241**/23–25; **244**/35
Directed Study Quiz: **261**/10; **267**/20
Timed Quiz: **269**/12
Review: **274**/11, 15; **275**/18

Practice Book Quiz I: **34**/15; **35**/18
Practice Book Quiz II: **38**/11
Practice Book Test 1: **70**/32; **74**/45, 47; **75**/48
Practice Book Test 2: **125**/22; **127**/31
Practice Book Test 3: **178**/14; **181**/23; **186**/41, 42; **187**/46; **189**/50; **193**/59

Complex Numbers

Lesson 1: **211**/22–23
Timed Quiz: **269**/7

Practice Book Quiz II: **39**/21, 25
Practice Book Test 1: **75**/50

Concepts of Domain and Range

Lesson 2: **222**/48–51
Directed Study Quiz: **263**/15

Practice Book Test 1: **76**/52, 55
Practice Book Test 3: **190**/53; **191**/55; **192**/58

Coordinate Geometry

Lesson Preliminaries: **203**/7
Lesson 3: **227**/1–3; **228**/4–5; **229–235**/7–28
Timed Quiz: **269**/13; **270**/19
Review: **273**/6; **275**/19
Victory Practice Test: **379**/6; **383**/22

Practice Book Quiz I: **34**/13
Practice Book Quiz II: **38**/17; **39**/19
Practice Book Test 1: **64**/7; **69**/26
Practice Book Test 2: **130**/40; **132**/47–49; **133**/51; **134**/55–56; **135**/60
Practice Book Test 3: **181**/25; **185**/39; **187**/44–45; **191**/55; **192**/56

Counting Methods

Lesson Preliminaries: **206**/22
Lesson 6: **250**/8–9
Directed Study Quiz: **260**/7
Timed Quiz: **268**/4

Practice Book Test 1: **63**/6
Practice Book Test 3: **175**/1

Victory Student Text and The Practice Book, Math

Data Representation

Time Trial: **195**/2
Lesson Preliminaries: **204**/12
Lesson 6: **253–255**/21–29
Directed Study Quiz: **264**/16–17
Review: **276**/27

Practice Book Quiz I: **33**/5; **35**/17
Practice Book Quiz II: **36**/2
Practice Book Test 1: **63**/5; **67**/19
Practice Book Test 3: **183**/30

Definitions of the Six Trigonometric Functions

Time Trial: **195**/5
Lesson Preliminaries: **203**/10
Lesson 5: **245**/1–4; **246**/5; **247**/7–10
Directed Study Quiz: **262**/11; **265**/18
Timed Quiz: **270**/17
Review: **276**/28, 30; **277**/32

Practice Book Quiz I: **35**/20
Practice Book Quiz II: **39**/24
Practice Book Test 1: **78**/59–60
Practice Book Test 2: **133**/52
Practice Book Test 3: **189**/52; **193**/60

Determining Trigonometric Values

Victory Practice Test: **392**/59

Practice Book Test 2: **132**/48

Distance and Midpoint Formulas

Lesson 3: **231**/16–19
Review: **275**/19

Practice Book Quiz II: **39**/19
Practice Book Test 2: **130**/40; **134**/55

Equations Involving Absolute Value

Lesson Preliminaries: **203**/6
Lesson 2: **221**/35–36
Directed Study Quiz: **263**/14
Victory Practice Test: **382**/20

Practice Book Test 1: **64**/8
Practice Book Test 2: **134**/54

Equations Involving Integer and Rational Exponents

Lesson 2: **220**/29–32
Timed Quiz: **268**/3
Victory Practice Test: **390**/52

Equations Involving Logarithms

Lesson 2: **220**/33–34
Review: **275**/24

Practice Book Quiz II: **39**/23

Victory Student Text and The Practice Book, Math

Equations Involving Radical Expressions

Lesson 2: **220**/25–28
Timed Quiz: **270**/16
Victory Practice Test: **382**/18

Equations Involving Rational Expressions

Lesson Preliminaries: **202**/3
Lesson 3: **219**/21–23
Timed Quiz: **270**/15
Victory Practice Test: **382**/18

Practice Book Test 1: **62**/1

Evaluating Expressions

Time Trial: **195**/3
Lesson 2: **216**/3–7
Timed Quiz: **268**/6; **269**/8
Review: **276**/26
Victory Practice Test: **379**/5; **380**/11

Practice Book Quiz I: **33**/9
Practice Book Test 2: **125**/20
Practice Book Test 3: **176**/3

Evaluating Sequences

Time Trial: **195**/2
Lesson Preliminaries: **202**/2
Lesson 2: **218**/15–18
Directed Study Quiz: **262**/12

Evaluating, Interpreting, and Creating Algebraic Functions

Lesson Preliminaries: **203**/4–5
Lesson 2: **221–223**/40–54; **225**/66–71; **226**/72–77
Directed Study Quiz: **263**/15
Victory Practice Test: **380**/9; **382**/19; **387**/39; **390**/53; **391**/54

Practice Book Quiz I: **34**/12, 14
Practice Book Quiz II: **36**/3, 5; **37**/6; **38**/14, 16
Practice Book Test 1: **62**/2; **70**/29; **71**/35; **73**/43; **76**/52, 54–55; **77**/57
Practice Book Test 2: **125**/21; **129**/37
Practice Book Test 3: **175**/2; **177**/8; **180**/19, 21; **181**/25; **190**/53; **191**/55; **192**/58

Factoring Expressions

Lesson 2: **217**/10–12
Victory Practice Test: **390**/51

Practice Book Quiz II: **37**/9; **39**/20, 25
Practice Book Test 1: **67**/20
Practice Book Test 2: **120**/2
Practice Book Test 3: **177**/9; **178**/12; **180**/20

Victory Student Text and The Practice Book, Math

Function Notation

Lesson Preliminaries: **203**/5
Lesson 2: **221**/40–41; **222**/42–47
Victory Practice Test: **380**/9; **382**/19; **387**/39

Practice Book Quiz I: **34**/12
Practice Book Quiz II: **36**/3; **38**/16
Practice Book Test 1: **62**/2; **70**/29
Practice Book Test 3: **180**/19

Functions as Models

Lesson Preliminaries: **203**/4
Lesson 2: **222**/52; **223**/53, 54; **225**/68, 71; **226**/74, 76
Victory Practice Test: **390**/53; **391**/54

Practice Book Quiz I: **34**/14
Practice Book Test 2: **129**/37
Practice Book Test 3: **175**/2; **180**/21; **181**/25

Geometry

Time Trial: **195**/4–5
Calculator Exercise: **199**/6, 9
Lesson Preliminaries: **203**/8–10; **204**/13–14; **205**/15–16; **206**/27; **207**/31
Lesson 3: **228**/6
Lesson 4: **236–244**/1–36
Lesson 5: **245–248**/1–12
Directed Study Quiz: **258**/1; **259**/3; **261**/10; **262**/11; **265**/18; **267**/20
Timed Quiz: **268**/1–2, 5; **269**/12; **270**/17, 20
Review: **272**/2, 4–5; **273**/10; **274**/11, 15–16; **275**/18, 23; **276**/28–30; **277**/31–32
Victory Practice Test: **378**/2; **379**/4; **382**/17; **383**/23–24; **384**/25; **385**/29–30; **386**/34; **387**/37; **388**/41, 43–44; **389**/45, 48; **391**/57; **392**/59

Practice Book Quiz I: **32**/3; **33**/8, 10; **34**/15; **35**/18, 20
Practice Book Quiz II: **37**/8, 10; **38**/11–12, 17; **39**/22, 24
Practice Book Test 1: **64**/9; **66**/15; **67**/18; **68**/24–25; **69**/28; **70**/32; **71**/34; **72**/39; **74**/45–47; **75**/48; **77**/56, 58; **78**/59–60
Practice Book Test 2: **121**/7; **122**/8, 11; **123**/13; **124**/17–18; **125**/22; **127**/31–32; **128**/33–34; **129**/39; **131**/44, 46; **132**/48–49; **133**/52–53
Practice Book Test 3: **176**/4; **177**/7; **178**/14; **179**/17; **181**/23, 25; **182**/28; **183**/31; **184**/37; **185**/39; **186**/41, 42; **187**/46; **188**/48–49; **189**/50–52; **193**/59–60

Graphs of First-Degree Inequalities

Lesson 3: **233**/22

Victory Student Text and The Practice Book, Math

Graphs of Linear Equations

Lesson 3: **232**/20–21
Victory Practice Test: **379**/6

Practice Book Test 2: **135**/60
Practice Book Test 3: **192**/56

Graphs of Quadratic Equations and Relations

Lesson 3: **233**/23; **234**/24

Practice Book Quiz II: **39**/19
Practice Book Test 2: **132**/49; **133**/51
Practice Book Test 3: **187**/44; **191**/55

Graphs of Trigonometric Functions

Lesson 5: **248**/11–12
Review: **277**/31

Practice Book Test 1: **77**/56
Practice Book Test 3: **188**/49

Inequalities Involving Absolute Value

Lesson 2: **221**/37–39

Inequalities Involving Rational Expressions

Lesson 2: **219**/24

Lines and Angles

Lesson Preliminaries: **204**/13–14; **205**/15–16; **206**/27
Lesson 4: **236**/1–4; **237**/5; **243**/30, 33
Directed Study Quiz: **258**/1; **259**/3; **267**/20
Timed Quiz: **268**/2
Review: **275**/18
Victory Practice Test: **378**/2; **379**/4; **383**/24; **384**/25; **386**/34; **388**/43; **389**/45

Practice Book Quiz I: **33**/8; **35**/18
Practice Book Quiz II: **37**/8
Practice Book Test 1: **66**/15; **72**/39
Practice Book Test 2: **121**/7; **122**/8, 11; **125**/22; **127**/32; **133**/53
Practice Book Test 3: **176**/4; **182**/28; **183**/31; **186**/41; **188**/48

Logarithmic Expressions

Lesson 2: **217**/13–14
Review: **275**/22

Practice Book Test 1: **76**/51

Victory Student Text and The Practice Book, Math

Manipulating Algebraic Expressions

Time Trial: **195**/3
Lesson 1: **209**/9
Lesson 2: **216– 217**/1–14
Timed Quiz: **268**/6; **269**/8
Review: **274**/14, 17; **275**/22; **276**/26
Victory Practice Test: **379**/5, 7; **380**/11; **382**/21; **384**/27; **388**/42; **390**/51

Practice Book Quiz I: **33**/9
Practice Book Quiz II: **37**/9; **39**/20, 25
Practice Book Test 1: **67**/20; **68**/23; **70**/31; **71**/34, 36; **72**/37; **76**/51, 53
Practice Book Test 2: **120**/2; **124**/16; **124**/19; **125**/20; **126**/24; **126**/26; **129**/38; **132**/50
Practice Book Test 3: **176**/3; **177**/9; **178**/12; **180**/20; **182**/29; **185**/38; **188**/47

Manipulating Expressions Involving Exponents

Lesson 2: **217**/8–9

Practice Book Test 1: **68**/23; **76**/53
Practice Book Test 2: **124**/16

Matrices and Vectors

Lesson 1: **212**/24–26
Review: **273**/8

Practice Book Quiz II: **37**/7

Measures of Center

Calculator Exercise: **198**/1
Lesson Preliminaries: **204**/11
Lesson 6: **249**/1–4; **250**/5–7
Directed Study Quiz: **260**/8
Timed Quiz: **269**/9
Review: **273**/7
Victory Practice Test: **380**/10; **381**/13; **386**/35; **390**/49

Practice Book Quiz I: **32**/1; **33**/7
Practice Book Quiz II: **38**/14
Practice Book Test 1: **65**/12; **68**/22; **75**/49
Practice Book Test 2: **122**/10; **123**/14; **126**/26
Practice Book Test 3: **184**/34

Victory Student Text and The Practice Book, Math

Number and Quantity

Time Trial: **195**/1, 3
Calculator Exercise: **198**/2; **199**/3–5, 7, 10
Lesson Preliminaries: **202**/1; **205**/17–21; **206**/23–26; **207**/28–30
Lesson 1: **208–215**/1–46
Lesson 2: **226**/72, 75
Lesson 4: **239**/14
Directed Study Quiz: **259**/2; **260**/5, 6; **264**/16
Timed Quiz: **269**/7, 11, 14
Review: **272**/1–3; **272**/5; **273**/8–10; **274**/12–13; **275**/20–21; **276**/25, 27
Victory Practice Test: **378**/1; **380**/8, 12; **381**/14–16; **384**/25; **385**/31–32; **386**/33; **387**/38; **388**/41; **389**/47; **390**/50; **391**/55; **392**/60

Practice Book Quiz I: **32**/2; **33**/4, 6; **34**/11, 16; **35**/17
Practice Book Quiz II: **36**/1–2; **36**/4; **37**/7; **38**/13, 15; **39**/21, 25
Practice Book Test 1: **62**/3; **63**/4, 6; **64**/10; **65**/11, 13; **66**/16, 17; **67**/19; **69**/27; **70**/30; **71**/35; **72**/38, 40; **73**/41, 43–44; **75**/50
Practice Book Test 2: **120**/1, 3; **121**/4–6; **122**/9; **123**/12; **124**/19; **125**/23; **126**/25–28; **127**/29–30; **128**/33–34; **129**/36, 38; **130**/41, 42; **131**/45; **133**/53; **134**/57; **135**/58
Practice Book Test 3: **176**/5–6; **177**/8, 10; **178**/11, 13, 15; **179**/16, 18; **180**/22; **181**/24; **182**/26–27; **183**/30; **183**/32; **184**/36; **186**/43

Percentages

Calculator Exercise: **199**/10
Lesson Preliminaries: **206**/26; **207**/30
Lesson 1: **208**/1; **214**/35–40
Lesson 2: **226**/72
Lesson 4: **239**/14
Directed Study Quiz: **264**/16
Review: **272**/2–3, 5; **274**/13; **276**/27
Victory Practice Test: **380**/8; **390**/50

Practice Book Quiz II: **36**/2
Practice Book Test 1: **62**/3; **67**/19; **70**/30; **72**/38; **73**/41, 43
Practice Book Test 2: **121**/6; **124**/19; **125**/23; **127**/30
Practice Book Test 3: **178**/15; **179**/16

Pie Charts

Lesson 6: **254**/26; **255**/27

Practice Book Quiz I: **33**/5

Victory Student Text and The Practice Book, Math

Probability

Lesson 6: **252**/16–19; **253**/20
Timed Quiz: **270**/18
Victory Practice Test: **389**/46

Practice Book Quiz I: **35**/19
Practice Book Test 3: **185**/40

Properties of Numbers

Time Trial: **195**/3
Calculator Exercise: **198**/2; **199**/5
Lesson Preliminaries: **205**/19; **207**/29
Lesson 1: **208**/5; **210**/14–19
Timed Quiz: **269**/14
Review: **274**/12
Victory Practice Test: **385**/30; **386**/33

Practice Book Quiz I: **34**/11–16
Practice Book Quiz II: **36**/4; **38**/13, 15
Practice Book Test 1: **63**/4; **73**/44
Practice Book Test 2: **121**/4–5; **122**/9; **123**/12; **127**/29; **128**/34; **129**/38; **130**/42
Practice Book Test 3: **176**/5; **177**/10; **178**/11, 13; **181**/24; **184**/36

Properties of Tangent Lines

Lesson Preliminaries: **203**/9
Lesson 4: **239**/16–17; **240**/18–19

Practice Book Test 2: **132**/49

Properties of Triangles

Lesson 3: **228**/6
Lesson 4: **238**/10–11; **240**/18, 21–22; **241**/25; **243**/32
Directed Study Quiz: **261**/10
Timed Quiz: **268**/5; **269**/12
Review: **272**/4; **273**/10; **274**/11, 15; **275**/18
Victory Practice Test: **386**/34; **388**/41, 44; **391**/57

Practice Book Test 1: **66**/15; **67**/18; **68**/25; **69**/28; **70**/32; **75**/48
Practice Book Test 2: **128**/34; **129**/39
Practice Book Test 3: **179**/17; **185**/39; **186**/41; **187**/46; **188**/48

Pythagorean Theorem

Time Trial: **195**/4
Lesson Preliminaries: **203**/8
Lesson 4: **237**/6; **238**/13; **243**/34
Lesson 5: **246**/5; **247**/7, 10
Timed Quiz: **270**/17
Review: **277**/32
Victory Practice Test: **383**/23; **392**/59

Practice Book Quiz II: **37**/10; **39**/24
Practice Book Test 1: **74**/45, 47
Practice Book Test 3: **187**/46

Victory Student Text and The Practice Book, Math

Qualitative Behavior of Graphs of Functions

Lesson 3: **234**/25–26
Directed Study Quiz: **266**/19

Rates and Proportions

Calculator Exercise: **199**/3
Lesson Preliminaries: **202**/1; **205**/17–20; **206**/23–25
Lesson 1: **212**/27–28; **213**/29–34; **214**/41
Lesson 2: **226**/75
Directed Study Quiz: **260**/5–6
Review: **273**/9–10; **275**/20–21; **276**/25
Victory Practice Test: **381**/14; **384**/25; **385**/31; **388**/41; **389**/47; **392**/60

Practice Book Quiz I: **33**/4; **35**/17
Practice Book Test 1: **65**/11, 13; **66**/17; **69**/27; **72**/40
Practice Book Test 2: **120**/3; **126**/27; **128**/33; **133**/53
Practice Book Test 3: **176**/6; **177**/8; **179**/18; **182**/27; **183**/30

Rectangles and Squares

Calculator Exercise: **199**/6, 9
Lesson 4: **238**/12–13; **239**/14; **240**/19–20, 22; **241**/23–24; **244**/35
Lesson 5: **247**/8
Review: **272**/2; **274**/15; **275**/18

Practice Book Quiz I: **32**/3; **34**/15
Practice Book Test 1: **64**/9; **68**/24–25; **70**/32
Practice Book Test 2: **123**/13; **124**/17; **127**/31; **128**/33; **131**/44
Practice Book Test 3: **177**/7; **178**/14; **181**/23, 25; **184**/37; **187**/46; **189**/50; **193**/59

Scatterplots

Lesson 6: **255**/29

Scientific Notation

Lesson 1: **211**/20–21
Review: **272**/1

Practice Book Quiz I: **32**/2
Practice Book Test 1: **64**/10
Practice Book Test 2: **120**/1

Sets

Lesson 6: **251**/10–15
Directed Study Quiz: **263**/13
Victory Practice Test: **384**/26

Practice Book Quiz II: **36**/4

Victory Student Text and The Practice Book, Math

Simple Equations

Lesson 2: **219**/19; **225**/66–67, 70, 73, 77
Directed Study Quiz: **259**/4; **261**/9
Victory Practice Test: **384**/28

Practice Book Quiz II: **36**/1
Practice Book Test 1: **65**/14; **67**/21; **71**/33

Simple Inequalities

Lesson 3: **219**/20

Practice Book Quiz II: **36**/5

Slope of a Line

Lesson 3: **229**/7–10
Timed Quiz: **269**/13
Victory Practice Test: **383**/22

Practice Book Quiz I: **34**/13
Practice Book Test 2: **134**/56

Slope-Intercept Form of a Linear Equation

Lesson Preliminaries: **203**/7
Lesson 3: **230**/11–15
Timed Quiz: **270**/19

Practice Book Test 3: **187**/45; **192**/56

Solids

Lesson 4: **242**/26–29
Timed Quiz: **270**/20
Review: **272**/5; **274**/16; **275**/23

Practice Book Test 1: **74**/46
Practice Book Test 2: **124**/18

Solving Algebraic Equations or Inequalities with One Variable

Lesson Preliminaries: **202**/3, 6
Lesson 2: **219–221**/19–39; **225**/66–67, 70; **226**/73, 77
Directed Study Quiz: **259**/4; **261**/9
Timed Quiz: **268**/3; **270**/15–16
Review: **275**/24
Victory Practice Test: **382**/18, 20; **384**/28; **390**/52

Practice Book Quiz II: **36**/1, 5; **39**/23
Practice Book Test 1: **62**/1; **64**/8; **65**/14; **67**/21; **71**/33
Practice Book Test 2: **123**/15; **134**/54

Solving Quadratic Equations and Relations

Lesson 2: **224**/61–65
Victory Practice Test: **378**/3; **386**/36; **387**/40

Practice Book Quiz II: **39**/18, 25
Practice Book Test 2: **128**/35; **135**/59
Practice Book Test 3: **183**/33; **192**/57

Victory Student Text and The Practice Book, Math

Solving Simultaneous Equations

Calculator Exercise: **199**/8
Lesson 2: **223**/55–59; **224**/60
Timed Quiz: **269**/10
Victory Practice Test: **391**/56; **392**/58

Practice Book Quiz II: **37**/6
Practice Book Test 1: **65**/11; **73**/42
Practice Book Test 2: **130**/43
Practice Book Test 3: **177**/8; **184**/35; **190**/54

Statistics and Probability

Time Trial: **195**/2
Calculator Exercise: **198**/1
Lesson Preliminaries: **204**/11–12; **206**/22
Lesson 6: **249–255**/1–29
Directed Study Quiz: **260**/7–8; **263**/13; **264**/16–17
Timed Quiz: **268**/4; **269**/9; **270**/18
Review: **273**/7; **276**/27
Victory Practice Test: **380**/10; **381**/13; **384**/26; **386**/35; **389**/46; **390**/49

Practice Book Quiz I: **32**/1; **33**/5, 7; **35**/17, 19
Practice Book Quiz II: **36**/2, 4; **38**/14
Practice Book Test 1: **63**/5, 6; **65**/12; **67**/19; **68**/22; **75**/49
Practice Book Test 2: **122**/10; **123**/14; **126**/26
Practice Book Test 3: **175**/1; **183**/30; **184**/34; **185**/40

Tables

Time Trial: **195**/2
Lesson 6: **255**/28
Directed Study Quiz: **264**/16–17
Review: **276**/27

Practice Book Quiz I: **35**/17
Practice Book Quiz II: **36**/2
Practice Book Test 1: **63**/5; **67**/19
Practice Book Test 3: **183**/30

The Coordinate System

Lesson 3: **227**/1–3; **228**/4–5
Review: **273**/6

Practice Book Quiz II: **38**/17
Practice Book Test 1: **64**/7; **69**/26
Practice Book Test 2: **132**/47
Practice Book Test 3: **181**/25; **185**/39; **191**/55

Transformations and Their Effects on Graphs of Functions

Lesson 3: **235**/27–28

Victory Student Text and The Practice Book, Math

Triangles

Time Trial: **195**/4
Lesson Preliminaries: **203**/8
Lesson 3: **228**/6
Lesson 4: **237**/6–9; **238**/10–11, 13; **239**/16; **240**/18, 21–22; **241**/23, 25; **243**/31, 34; **244**/36
Lesson 5: **246**/5; **247**/7–10
Directed Study Quiz: **261**/10; **262**/11
Timed Quiz: **268**/5; **269**/12; **270**/17
Review: **272**/4; **273**/10; **274**/11, 15; **275**/18; **277**/32
Victory Practice Test: **383**/23; **385**/30; **386**/34; **388**/41, 44; **391**/57; **392**/59

Practice Book Quiz I: **35**/20
Practice Book Quiz II: **37**/10; **38**/11; **39**/24
Practice Book Test 1: **66**/15; **67**/18; **68**/25; **69**/28; **70**/32; **74**/45, 47; **75**/48
Practice Book Test 2: **127**/31; **128**/34; **129**/39
Practice Book Test 3: **179**/17; **185**/39; **186**/41–42; **187**/46; **188**/48

Trigonometric Relationships

Lesson 5: **246**/6
Review: **276**/29
Victory Practice Test: **385**/29; **387**/37; **389**/48

Practice Book Quiz II: **39**/22
Practice Book Test 1: **77**/58
Practice Book Test 2: **131**/46
Practice Book Test 3: **189**/51

Trigonometry

Time Trial: **195**/5
Lesson Preliminaries: **203**/10
Lesson 5: **245–248**/1–12
Directed Study Quiz: **262**/11; **265**/18
Timed Quiz: **270**/17
Review: **276**/28–30; **277**/31–32
Victory Practice Test: **385**/29; **387**/37; **389**/48; **392**/59

Practice Book Quiz I: **35**/20
Practice Book Quiz II: **39**/22, 24
Practice Book Test 1: **77**/56, 58; **78**/59–60
Practice Book Test 2: **131**/46; **132**/48; **133**/52
Practice Book Test 3: **188**/49; **189**/51–52; **193**/60

Science

Victory Student Text and The Practice Book, Science

Analysis

Anatomy: **286**/2; **287**/3
Time Trial: **290**/1, 3–4
Lesson 1: **295**/2; **296**/6, 8–9; **297**/11–13; **299**/17, 19–22; **302**/28–30; **303**/31–33; **305**/36–39
Lesson 2: **307**/3–5; **309**/7, 9; **311**/15–17; **314**/21–23; **316**/26–27; **317**/28; **318**/31; **319**/32–33
Lesson 3: **321**/4–5; **322**/8–10; **323**/11; **324**/13–17; **326**/20, 23; **327**/28
Directed Study Quiz: **331–333**/3–6; **334**/11; **335**/12–14; **336**/15–16
Timed Quiz: **337**/3; **338**/7; **339**/8–10; **340**/14, 16
Review: **343**/2–5; **344**/11; **346**/16, 18; **348**/28–30, 32–33; **349**/35–36; **351**/46–48; **352**/49–51; **353**/52–54; **355**/58–59; **357**/61; **358**/63–64
Victory Practice Test: **405**/2; **407**/9; **408**/12–13; **410**/17, 19; **411–413**/22–27; **414**/29; **415**/30; **416**/33–36; **417**/39–40

Practice Book Quiz I: **43**/1, 3; **44**/5, 7; **46**/11–12; **47**/13–15
Practice Book Test 1: **91**/2, 7; **93**/11; **94**/13; **96**/18–20; **97**/22; **98**/24; **99**/27; **100**/31–32; **101**/34; **102**/37–38; **103**/39–40
Practice Book Test 2: **145**/1, 5–6; **146**/9; **147**/11; **149**/13–16, 18; **150**/20, 23; **151**/24, 26; **152**/28–29; **153**/32; **155**/37–38; **156**/39
Practice Book Test 3: **205**/1; **206**/6, 8–9; **207**/10; **208**/13–14; **209**/17–18; **210**/20–23; **211**/24; **212**/29; **213**/32; **214**/35; **215**/38, 40

Application

Anatomy: **287**/4
Lesson 1: **295**/3; **297**/14; **300**/27; **303**/34; **305**/40
Lesson 2: **307**/6; **310**/10–11; **311**/14; **317**/29; **319**/34
Lesson 3: **321**/3; **324**/18; **327**/29
Timed Quiz: **337**/2; **338**/5
Review: **343**/6; **344**/12; **346**/17, 19; **349**/37–38; **350**/39–40, 41; **358**/65
Victory Practice Test: **405**/5; **409**/16; **410**/18; **411**/20–21

Practice Book Quiz I: **43**/4; **44**/6, 8; **45**/9–10; **47**/16
Practice Book Test 1: **91**/3–6; **94**/14; **97**/21; **98**/26
Practice Book Test 2: **146**/10; **147**/12; **151**/27; **153**/31; **154**/33
Practice Book Test 3: **215**/39

Victory Student Text and The Practice Book, Science

Comprehension

Anatomy: **286**/1
Time Trial: **290**/2, 5
Lesson 1: **294**/1; **295**/4–5; **296**/7; **297**/10; **298**/15–16; **299**/18; **300**/23–26; **304**/35
Lesson 2: **306**/1; **307**/2; **309**/8; **311**/12–13; **314**/18–20; **316**/24–25; **318**/30
Lesson 3: **321**/1–2; **322**/6–7; **323**/12; **326**/19, 21–22; **327**/24–27
Directed Study Quiz: **331**/1–2; **333**/7–9; **334**/10
Timed Quiz: **337**/1; **338**/4, 6; **340**/11–13, 15
Review: **342**/1; **344**/7–10; **345**/13–15; **347**/20–27; **348**/31; **349**/34; **350**/42–44; **351**/45; **355**/55–57; **357**/60; **358**/62
Victory Practice Test: **405**/1, 3–4; **407**/6–8, 10–11; **408**/14–15; **414**/28; **415**/31–32; **417**/38

Practice Book Quiz I: **43**/2
Practice Book Test 1: **91**/1; **93**/8–10, 12; **96**/15–17; **98**/23, 25; **100**/28–30; **101**/33; **102**/35–36
Practice Book Test 2: **145**/2–4; **146**/7–8; **149**/17; **150**/19, 21–22; **151**/25; **153**/30; **154**/34; **155**/35–36; **156**/40
Practice Book Test 3: **205**/2–5; **206**/7; **207**/11; **208**/12; **209**/15–16; **210**/19; **212**/25–28, 30; **213**/31, 33; **214**/34; **215**/36–37

Victory Student Text and The Practice Book, Science

Evaluation of Models

Anatomy: **287**/4
Lesson 1: **296**/9; **297**/11, 13; **298**/15; **299**/17; **300**/23, 25
Lesson 2: **307**/2–6; **310**/10; **311**/12–13; **314**/21; **316**/27
Lesson 3: **321–323**/2–11; **324**/13–18; **326**/19–21; **327**/25–29
Directed Study Quiz: **331**/2–3; **332**/5; **333**/8; **335**/12
Timed Quiz: **338**/5, 7; **339**/9–10; **340**/11–14, 16
Review: **343**/3; **344–346**/11–19; **348**/28–30; **349**/34–38; **350**/39–41, 43–44; **351**/45, 48; **353**/53; **357**/60; **358**/64
Victory Practice Test: **405**/2, 5; **407**/9; **408**/12–13; **412**/23–24; **413**/25–27; **414**/29; **415**/30; **416**/33–36; **417**/37–40
Practice Book Quiz I: **44**/7; **46**/12; **47**/13
Practice Book Test 1: **96**/20; **97**/22; **99**/27; **100**/28–29, 32; **101**/34; **103**/39–40
Practice Book Test 2: **146**/9; **149**/14–15; **151**/24–27; **152**/28; **153**/32; **154**/34; **155**/36–37; **156**/40
Practice Book Test 3: **206**/9; **207**/11; **208**/13–14; **209**/15, 17–18; **210**/20; **212**/26, 28, 30; **213**/32; **214**/34–35; **215**/39–40

Victory Student Text and The Practice Book, Science

Interpretation of Data

Anatomy: **286**/1–2; **287**/3
Time Trial: **290**/1–5
Lesson 1: **294**/1; **295**/2; **297**/10, 12; **298**/16; **299**/18–22; **300**/24–27; **302–305**/28–40
Lesson 2: **306**/1; **309**/7, 9; **314**/23; **316**/26; **319**/32–33
Lesson 3: **321**/1; **323**/12; **326**/22–23; **327**/24
Directed Study Quiz: **331**/1; **333**/6–7, 9; **334**/10; **335**/13–14
Timed Quiz: **337**/1–3; **338**/4, 6; **339**/8
Review: **342**/1; **343**/2, 4; **344**/7–9; **347**/20–27; **348**/31, 33; **350**/42; **352**/49, 51; **355**/55–59; **357**/61; **358**/62–63, 65
Victory Practice Test: **405**/1, 3–4; **407**/6–8, 10–11; **408**/14–15; **410**/17–19; **411**/20–22; **414**/28; **415**/31–32
Practice Book Quiz I: **43**/1–4; **44**/5, 8; **46**/11; **47**/14–15
Practice Book Test 1: **91**/1–7; **93**/8, 11–12; **94**/13; **96**/15, 19; **97**/21; **98**/23–25; **100**/30–31, 33; **102**/35–36
Practice Book Test 2: **145**/1–6; **146**/7–8, 10; **147**/11; **149**/17; **150**/19–22; **153**/30–31
Practice Book Test 3: **205**/1–5; **209**/16; **210**/19, 22–23; **212**/25, 27, 29; **213**/31, 33; **215**/36–38

Scientific Investigation

Lesson 1: **295**/3–5; **296**/6–8; **297**/14
Lesson 2: **309**/8; **310**/11; **311**/14–17; **314**/18–20, 22; **316**/24–25; **317**/28–29; **318**/30–31; **319**/34
Directed Study Quiz: **331**/4; **334**/11; **336**/15–16
Timed Quiz: **340**/15
Review: **343**/5–6; **344**/10; **348**/32; **351**/46–47; **352**/50; **353**/52, 54
Victory Practice Test: **409**/16
Practice Book Quiz I: **44**/6; **45**/9–10; **47**/16
Practice Book Test 1: **93**/9–10; **94**/14; **96**/16–18; **98**/26; **102**/37–38
Practice Book Test 2: **147**/12; **149**/13, 16, 18; **150**/23; **152**/29; **154**/33; **155**/35, 38; **156**/39
Practice Book Test 3: **206**/6–8; **207**/10; **208**/12; **210**/21; **211**/24

Cambridge *Victory for the ACT® Test, 15th Edition*
Error Correction and Suggestion Form

Name/Location: ____________ Day Phone: ____________ E-mail Address: ____________

Part of Materials:
- ☐ *Essential Skills Student Text*, Specify Subject: ____________ Page: ______ Item: ______
- ☐ *Essential Skills Teacher's Guide*, Specify Subject: ____________ Page: ______ Item: ______
- ☐ *Victory Student Text*, Specify Subject: ____________ Page: ______ Item: ______
- ☐ *Victory Teacher's Guide*, Specify Subject: ____________ Page: ______ Item: ______
- ☐ *The Practice Book*, Specify Subject: ____________ Page: ______ Item: ______

Error/Suggestion: ____________

Part of Materials:
- ☐ *Essential Skills Student Text*, Specify Subject: ____________ Page: ______ Item: ______
- ☐ *Essential Skills Teacher's Guide*, Specify Subject: ____________ Page: ______ Item: ______
- ☐ *Victory Student Text*, Specify Subject: ____________ Page: ______ Item: ______
- ☐ *Victory Teacher's Guide*, Specify Subject: ____________ Page: ______ Item: ______
- ☐ *The Practice Book*, Specify Subject: ____________ Page: ______ Item: ______

Error/Suggestion: ____________

Part of Materials:
- ☐ *Essential Skills Student Text*, Specify Subject: ____________ Page: ______ Item: ______
- ☐ *Essential Skills Teacher's Guide*, Specify Subject: ____________ Page: ______ Item: ______
- ☐ *Victory Student Text*, Specify Subject: ____________ Page: ______ Item: ______
- ☐ *Victory Teacher's Guide*, Specify Subject: ____________ Page: ______ Item: ______
- ☐ *The Practice Book*, Specify Subject: ____________ Page: ______ Item: ______

Error/Suggestion: ____________

Part of Materials:
- ☐ *Essential Skills Student Text*, Specify Subject: ____________ Page: ______ Item: ______
- ☐ *Essential Skills Teacher's Guide*, Specify Subject: ____________ Page: ______ Item: ______
- ☐ *Victory Student Text*, Specify Subject: ____________ Page: ______ Item: ______
- ☐ *Victory Teacher's Guide*, Specify Subject: ____________ Page: ______ Item: ______
- ☐ *The Practice Book*, Specify Subject: ____________ Page: ______ Item: ______

Error/Suggestion: ____________

Mail form to Cambridge Educational Services, Inc. or fax form to 1-847-299-2933. For teacher's assistance, call 1-847-299-2930 or e-mail solutions@CambridgeEd.com. Visit our website at www.CambridgeEd.com.